COLLECTED WORKS OF ERASMUS

VOLUME 40

Engraved frontispiece of Petrus Rabus' edition of the *Colloquia*
Rotterdam: Renier Leers 1693
Reproduced by courtesy of the Centre for Reformation and Renaissance Studies,
Victoria University, Toronto

COLLECTED WORKS OF
ERASMUS

COLLOQUIES

translated and annotated by

Craig R. Thompson

University of Toronto Press

Toronto / Buffalo / London

The research and publication costs of the
Collected Works of Erasmus are supported by
University of Toronto Press.

© University of Toronto Press 1997
Toronto / Buffalo / London
Printed in Canada

ISBN 0-8020-5819-1

Printed on acid-free paper

Canadian Cataloguing in Publication Data

Erasmus, Desiderius, d. 1536
[Works]
Collected works of Erasmus

Includes bibliographical references.
Partial contents: v. 39–40. Colloquies /
translated and annotated by Craig R. Thompson.
ISBN 0-8020-5819-1 (v. 39–40)

1. Erasmus, Desiderius, d. 1536. I. Title

PA8500 1974   876'.04   C74-006326-X rev

University of Toronto Press acknowledges with appreciation the permission
of The University of Chicago Press to publish a revised translation
of *The Colloquies of Erasmus* with annotation.
University of Toronto Press acknowledges the financial assistance to its
publishing program of the Canada Council and the Ontario Arts Council.

Collected Works of Erasmus

The aim of the Collected Works of Erasmus
is to make available an accurate, readable English text
of Erasmus' correspondence and his
other principal writings. The edition is planned
and directed by an Editorial Board, an Executive Committee,
and an Advisory Committee.

Contents

Illustrations

VOLUME 40

FAMILIAR COLLOQUIES

Familiaria colloquia

A PILGRIMAGE FOR RELIGION'S SAKE

Peregrinatio religionis ergo

First printed in the February 1526 edition.

Erasmus visited the shrine of Our Lady of Walsingham in the summer of 1512 with a Cambridge friend (see n78 below and Ep 262). The text alludes to a previous visit also, but of that nothing is known (n7). The date of his visit to Canterbury, on which he was accompanied by John Colet, Dean of St Paul's, is uncertain but must have been between 1512 and late June or early July of 1514, when he left England.

The date of composition of this colloquy is equally uncertain. The supposititious letter from Mary is dated 1 August 1524; on this see n41. Erasmus might have written the dialogue at any time between 1514 and 1526, but if before 1522 could not then have intended it for the *Colloquies*, for apparently he did not think of adding to that little book until 1522. An early date of composition, when his impressions of Walsingham and Canterbury were fresh, might account for the numerous details in his descriptions of buildings and much else. Inaccuracies occur in the text we have; but had he waited a decade or longer before writing what he remembered, it would be surprising if there were not more of these. If the dialogue existed by 1522, why was it not printed until 1526? Since answers to such questions are lacking, it may be best to assume that the colloquy was composed between 1523 and 1526, though parts or drafts of it may have been in hand earlier.

This famous colloquy, one of three exceptionally provocative dialogues on religion in the February 1526 edition, is not the author's only contribution to pilgrim literature, but is easily the best: wholly characteristic in its blending of travelogue with observations on spiritual, social, even financial aspects of the tourist industry that pilgrimages resembled; typically Erasmian too in satirical and ironical comment on what this sensitive traveller found deceptive or distasteful. It was published before ideas or reforms associated with the Reformation had received any approval in England, yet certain institutions and customs described here came to an end in England sooner than its author or his earliest readers could have foreseen. It anticipates some of the arguments used by English rulers and reformers to justify the suppression of monastic houses. As late as 1531 Thomas Bilney of Cambridge, who had preached against relics, images, and pilgrimages, was arrested for heresy. He recanted, but four years afterwards he resumed preaching, was seized as a relapsed heretic, and was burned. In 1531, again, Convocation acknowledged Henry VIII as 'supreme head' of the church in England 'as far as the law of

Christ allows.' This qualifying phrase was omitted in the Act of Supremacy of 1534. In the next three years Parliament and Convocation, under pressure by the crown, abolished the papal prerogatives in England. In 1536 the government began to suppress monasteries, destroy shrines, and confiscate their treasures. (Note Erasmus' prediction in 'The Godly Feast' 199:1–4.) Archbishop Cranmer attacked images, adoration of saints, and purgatory in sermons of February and March 1536. Another bishop, reformer, and future martyr, Hugh Latimer, in a sermon preached before the clergy 9 June 1536, the day before the opening of Parliament, used strong language about the 'intolerable abuses' of images, pilgrimages, and relics (*Selected Sermons* 23–5). The first royal Injunctions for the clergy, issued by Thomas Cromwell as the king's deputy for ecclesiastical affairs in August 1536, forbade them to 'set forth or extol any images, relics, or miracles for any superstition or lucre' or to 'allure the people by any enticements to the pilgrimage of any saint'; the second Injunctions, October 1538, required that 'feigned images' be removed (*Documents Illustrative of English Church History* ed Henry Gee and W.J. Hardy [London 1896; repr 1910] 271, 277). By 1538 most of the smaller monasteries had been suppressed and the days of the larger ones, including Walsingham and Canterbury, were numbered. The wealthiest and most popular shrine in England, St Thomas Becket's in Canterbury, was destroyed in September 1538. In November of that year a royal proclamation declared that because of his opposition to his king, Henry II, Becket was no longer to be called saint or martyr 'but rather esteemed to have been a rebel and traitor to his prince,' and henceforth ignored by Henry VIII's loving subjects (*Tudor Royal Proclamations* ed P.L. Hughes and J.F. Larkin, 3 vols [New Haven, Conn 1964–9] I 275–6).

In 1536 or near that date an anonymous English translation of Erasmus' colloquy appeared as *A Dialoge ... by the noble and famose clarke Desiderius Erasmus intituled ye Pylgremage of pure devotyon* (STC 10454 and Devereux 4.12; text in de Vocht *Earliest English Translations* 101–95; Spurgeon 3–97). Since it is most unlikely that a work so useful as propaganda would have been allowed to come out at this time without permission of the government, there is good reason to think Cromwell approved this translation, which has a harsh anticlerical and antipapal preface. It was not the only colloquy convenient for purposes of propaganda. Official or semi-official sponsorship of translations of his writings was but one of many ways in which the learning and ideas of Erasmus circulated in Tudor society. On this subject see the important study by James K. McConica, *English Humanists and Reformation Politics under Henry VIII and Edward VI* (Oxford 1965). A few additional notes are in my 'Erasmus and Tudor England' *Actes du congrès Erasme ... Rotterdam 27–29 octobre 1969* (Amsterdam and London 1971) 29–68.

Unlike the earlier and briefer 'Rash Vows', this colloquy is based on personal experiences, though undoubtedly these were recollected in tranquillity with the aid of artistic imagination. Some critics have complained that Erasmus must be an unreliable witness. He gets some of the facts wrong. A few misstatements may be due to the familiar willingness of glib officials to impress inquisitive tourists. To expect the dialogue to have the accuracy of a guidebook is to misunderstand the author's purposes. On images, invocation of saints, and relics he wrote much to which orthodoxy could not object, much too that gave offence – some pages in 'The Shipwreck,' for example. As so often happens, it was not merely the statements themselves but their insinuations or tone that pleased many readers and provoked many others. That images provided 'silent poetry,' he granted (*De concordia* LB V 501B–C; *Explanatio symboli* LB V 1187D), but he deplored abuses attached to the *cultus divorum*. See his defence of this colloquy in 'The Usefulness of the Colloquies' 1103:39–1104:9 and in Allen Ep 2037:26–9. Superstition prevails 'when everything is sought from saints as though Christ were dead, or when we beg the help of saints as though they were more compassionate than God' (Allen Ep 2443:220–2). So he writes in March 1531 to his friend Jacopo Sadoleto, bishop of Carpentras, replying to a suggestion that he tone down his criticism of abuses. He maintained consistently that while he did not condemn the invoking of saints, the practice is tolerable only if superstition is excluded.

A Spanish translation of this colloquy was made by Alonso Ruiz de Virués c 1529 (Bataillon *Erasme et l'Espagne* xxix, 321).

J.G. Nichols' translation and notes, *Pilgrimages to Saint Mary of Walsingham and Saint Thomas of Canterbury. By Desiderius Erasmus* (London 1849; 2nd ed 1875), C. Eveleigh Woodruff and W. Danks *Memorials of the Cathedral and Priory of Christ in Canterbury* (London 1912), and J.C. Dickinson *The Shrine of Our Lady of Walsingham* (Cambridge 1956) are valuable for modern students of the colloquy. Important bibliographical aids on Canterbury and Becket are mentioned in the notes to this translation. On Erasmus as pilgrim see L.-E. Halkin 'Erasme pèlerin' in *Scrinium Erasmianum* II 239–52. A shorter paper by Halkin, 'Le Thème du pèlerinage dans les Colloques d'Erasme,' is printed in *Actes du congrès Erasme* (620 above) 88–98. *Dix conférences sur Erasme* ed Claude Blum (Paris and Geneva 1988) includes a historical and textual analysis of the colloquy by André Godin and a critical essay by Eva Kushner, 'Les Colloques et l'inscription de l'autre dans le discours.'

MENEDEMUS, OGYGIUS[1]

Menedemus What marvel is this? Don't I see my neighbour Ogygius, whom nobody has laid eyes on for six whole months? I heard he was dead. It's 5 his very self, unless I'm losing my mind completely.[2] I'll go to him and say hello. – Greetings, Ogygius.

St James dressed as a pilgrim, wearing on his hat and purse
a cockle-shell badge from the shrine in Compostella, Spain
Miniature in the margin of a fourteenth-century English manuscript
(British Museum Add MS 42130 fol 32 recto)
Courtesy of the Trustees of the British Museum

Ogygius The same to you, Menedemus.

Menedemus Where in the world do you return from, safe and sound? A sad rumour spread here that you'd sailed in Stygian waters.[3]

Ogygius No, thank heaven; I've seldom enjoyed better health.

5 **Menedemus** I hope you'll always be able to refute silly rumours of that sort! But what's this fancy outfit? You're ringed with scallop shells, choked with tin and leaden images on every side, decked out with straw necklaces, and you've snake eggs on your arm.[4]

Ogygius I've been on a visit to St James of Compostella[5] and, on my way 10 back, to the famous Virgin by the Sea,[6] in England; or rather I revisited her, since I had gone there three years earlier.[7]

Menedemus Out of curiosity, I dare say.

Ogygius On the contrary, out of devotion.

Menedemus Greek letters, I suppose, taught you that devotion.[8]

15 **Ogygius** My wife's mother had bound herself by a vow that if her daughter gave birth to a boy and he lived, I would promptly pay my respects to St James and thank him in person.[9]

Menedemus Did you greet the saint only in your own name and your mother-in-law's?

20 **Ogygius** Oh, no, in the whole family's.

Menedemus Well, I imagine your family would have been no less safe even if you had left James ungreeted. But do please tell me: what answer did he make when you thanked him?

Ogygius None, but he seemed to smile as I offered my gift, nodded his 25 head slightly,[10] and at the same time held out the scallop shells.

Menedemus Why does he give those rather than something else?

Ogygius Because he has plenty of them; the sea nearby supplies them.

Menedemus Generous saint, who both attends those in labour and gives presents to callers! But what new kind of vowing is this, that some lazy 30 person lays the work on others? If you bound yourself by a vow that, should *your* affairs prosper, *I* would fast twice a week, do you think I'd do what you had vowed?

Ogygius No, I don't, even if you'd sworn in your own name. For you enjoy mocking[11] the saints. But she's my mother-in-law; she had to be humoured. 35 You're acquainted with women's whims, and besides, I had an interest in it too.

Menedemus If you hadn't kept her vow, what risk would there have been?

Ogygius The saint couldn't have sued me at law, I admit, but he could have been deaf thereafter to my prayers or secretly have brought some disaster upon my family. You know the ways of the mighty.

40 **Menedemus** Tell me, how is the excellent James?

Ogygius Much colder than usual.

Menedemus Why? Old age?

Ogygius Joker! You know saints don't grow old. But this newfangled notion that pervades the whole world results in his being greeted more seldom than usual. And if people do come, they merely greet him; they make no offering
5 at all, or only a very slight one, declaring it would be better to contribute that money to the poor.[12]

Menedemus A wicked notion!

Ogygius And thus so great an apostle, accustomed to shine from head to foot in gold and jewels, now stands a wooden figure with hardly a tallow
10 candle to his name.[13]

Menedemus If what I hear is true, there's danger that other saints may come to the same pass.

Ogygius More than that: a letter is going round which the Virgin Mary herself wrote on this very theme.[14]

15 **Menedemus** Which Mary?

Ogygius The one called Mary from the Rock.

Menedemus Near Basel,[15] unless I'm mistaken.

Ogygius Yes.

Menedemus Then[16] it's a stony saint you tell me of. But to whom did she
20 write?

Ogygius This letter itself tells the name.

Menedemus Who delivered the letter?

Ogygius Undoubtedly an angel, who placed it on the pulpit from which the recipient preaches. And to prevent suspicion of fraud, you shall see the very
25 autograph.[17]

Menedemus So you recognize the hand of the angel who is the Virgin's secretary?

Ogygius Why, of course.

Menedemus By what mark?

30 **Ogygius** I've read Bede's epitaph,[18] which was engraved by an angel. The shape of the letters agrees entirely. Also I've read the manuscript message to St[19] Giles. They agree. Aren't these facts proof enough?

Menedemus Is one allowed to see it?

Ogygius Yes, if you'll promise to keep your mouth shut about it.

35 **Menedemus** Oh, to tell me is to tell a stone.[20]

Ogygius But some stones are notorious for giving secrets away.[21]

Menedemus Then tell it to a mute if you don't trust a stone.

Ogygius On that condition I'll read it. Lend me your ears.[22]

Menedemus I've lent them.

40 **Ogygius** 'Mary, Mother of Jesus, to Glaucoplutus:[23] greetings. Know that I am deeply grateful to you, a follower of Luther,[24] for busily persuading

people that the invocation of saints is useless.[25] Up to this time I've been
all but exhausted by the shameless entreaties of mortals.[26] They demanded
everything from me alone, as if my Son were always a baby (because he is
carved and painted as such at my bosom), still needing his mother's consent
5 and not daring to deny a person's prayer; fearful, that is, that if he did deny
the petitioner something, I for my part would refuse him the breast when he
was thirsty. And sometimes they ask of a Virgin what a modest youth would
hardly dare ask of a bawd[27] – things I'm ashamed to put in writing. Sometimes
a merchant, off for Spain to make a fortune, commits to me the chastity of
10 his mistress. And a nun who has thrown off her veil and is preparing to
run away entrusts me with her reputation for virtue – which she herself
intends to sully. A profane soldier, hired to butcher people, cries upon me,
"Blessed Virgin, give me rich booty."[28] A gambler cries, "Help me, blessed
saint; I'll share my winnings with you!" And if they lose at dice, they abuse
15 me outrageously and curse me because I wouldn't favour their wickedness.
One[29] who abandons herself to a base trade cries, "Give me a fat income!" If
I refuse anything, they protest at once, "Then you're no mother of mercy."

'Other people's prayers are not so irreverent as absurd.[30] An unmarried
girl cries, "Mary, give me a rich and handsome bridegroom." A married one,
20 "Give me fine children." A pregnant woman, "Give me an easy delivery." An
old woman, "Give me a long life without a cough or a thirst." A doddering
old man, "Let me grow young again." A philosopher, "Give me power to
contrive insoluble problems." A priest, "Give me a rich benefice." A bishop,
"Preserve my church." A sailor, "Give me prosperous sailings." A governor,
25 "Show me thy Son before I die." A courtier, "Grant that at the point of death
I may confess sincerely." A countryman, "Send me rain at the right time." A
country woman, "Save the flock and herd from harm." If I deny anything,
straightway I'm cruel. If I refer to my Son, I hear, "He wills whatever you
will."[31] So am I alone, a woman and a virgin, to assist those who are sailing,[32]
30 fighting, trading, dicing, marrying, bearing children, to assist governors,
kings, and farmers?

'What I've described is very little in comparison with what I endure.
But nowadays I'm troubled less by these matters. For this reason I would give
you my heartiest thanks, did not this advantage bring a greater disadvantage
35 along with it. I have more peace but less honour and wealth. Formerly I was
hailed as "Queen of Heaven,[33] mistress of the world"; now I hear scarcely an
"Ave Maria" even from a few. Formerly I was clothed in gold and jewels;[34]
I had many changes of dress; I had golden and jewelled offerings made to
me. Now I have hardly half a cloak to wear, and that one is mouse-eaten.
40 My annual income is scarcely enough to keep the wretched sacristan who
lights the little lamp or tallow candle. And yet all these hardships I could

St Bartholomew
Albrecht Dürer, 1523
Staatliche Museen Preussischer Kulturbesitz, Kupferstichkabinett, Berlin

St George
Albrecht Altdorfer, 1511
Bruckmann München, Bildarchiv

have borne if you weren't said to be plotting even greater ones. Now you're trying, they say, to remove from the churches all traces of the saints. Do reconsider what you're doing. Other saints have means of avenging injuries. If Peter is ejected from a church, he can in turn shut the gate of heaven

5 against you.[35] Paul has a sword;[36] Bartholomew is armed with a knife;[37] under his monk's robe William is completely armed, nor does he lack a heavy lance.[38] And what could you do against George, with his horse and his coat of mail, his spear and his terrible sword?[39] Antony's not defenceless either: he has his sacred fire.[40] Others likewise have weapons or mischiefs

10 they direct against anybody they please. But me, however defenceless, you shall not eject unless at the same time you eject my Son, whom I hold in my arms. From him I will not be parted. Either you expel him along with me, or you leave us both here, unless you prefer to have a church without Christ. I wanted you to know this. Think carefully what to answer, for I am deeply

15 concerned about the matter.

'From our stony house, on the Calends of August,[41] in the year of my Son's passion 1524, I, the Virgin from the Rock,[42] have signed this with my own hand.'

Menedemus A dreadful, threatening letter indeed. Glaucoplutus will take

20 warning, I imagine.

Ogygius If he's wise.

Menedemus Why didn't the excellent James write to him on this same subject?

Ogygius I don't know, except that he's rather far away, and all letters are

25 intercepted nowadays.[43]

Menedemus But what fortune brought you back to England?

Ogygius An unexpectedly favourable breeze carried me there, and I had virtually promised the Virgin by the Sea that I would pay her another visit in two years.

30 **Menedemus** What were you going to ask of her?

Ogygius Nothing new, just the usual things: family safe and sound, a larger fortune, a long and happy life in this world, and eternal bliss in the next.

Menedemus Couldn't the Virgin Mother here at home see to those matters? At Antwerp she has a church much grander than the one by the sea.[44]

35 **Ogygius** I can't deny that, but different things are bestowed in different places, either because she prefers this or (since she is obliging) because she accommodates herself to our feelings in this respect.

Menedemus I've often heard about James, but I beg you to describe for me the domain of the Virgin by the Sea.

40 **Ogygius** Well, I'll do the best I can in brief. She has the greatest fame throughout England, and you would not readily find anyone in that island

who hoped for prosperity unless he greeted her annually with a small gift, according to his means.

Menedemus Where does she live?

Ogygius By the north-west coast of England, only about three miles from
5 the sea.[45] The village has scarcely any means of support apart from the tourist trade. There's a college of canons, to whom, however, the Latin title of regulars is added: an order midway between monks and the canons called secular.[46]

Menedemus You tell me of amphibians, such as the beaver.

10 **Ogygius** Yes, and the crocodile. But details aside, I'll try to satisfy you in a few words. In unfavourable matters, they're canons; in favourable ones, monks.[47]

Menedemus So far you're telling me a riddle.

Ogygius But I'll add a precise demonstration.[48] If the Roman pontiff assailed
15 all monks with a thunderbolt,[49] then they'd be canons, not monks. Yet if he permitted all monks to take wives, then they'd be monks.

Menedemus Strange favours! I wish they'd take mine, too.

Ogygius But to get to the point. This college depends almost entirely on the Virgin's generosity for its support.[50] The larger gifts are reserved, to be sure,
20 but any small change, anything of trifling value, goes towards feeding the community and their head, whom they call the prior.[51]

Menedemus Do they live holy lives?

Ogygius They're not without praise. They're richer in piety than income. The church[52] is fine and splendid, but the Virgin doesn't dwell there; in
25 honour of her Son she yields that to him. She has her own church,[53] that she may be on the right of her Son.

Menedemus The right? Which direction does the Son face, then?

Ogygius I'm glad you remind me. When he faces west he has his mother on his right; when he turns to the east she's on the left. However, she doesn't
30 dwell here, either, for the building is not yet finished,[54] and the place is quite airy – windows and doors open, and Ocean, father of the winds,[55] nearby.

Menedemus Too bad. So where does she live?

Ogygius In that church, which as I said is unfinished, is a small chapel built on a wooden platform.[56] Pilgrims are admitted through a narrow door on
35 each side. There's very little light: only what comes from tapers, which have a most pleasing scent.

Menedemus All this is appropriate to religion.

Ogygius Yes, and if you peered inside, Menedemus, you would say it was the abode of the saints, so dazzling is it with jewels, gold, and silver.

40 **Menedemus** You make me impatient to go there.

Ogygius You won't regret the journey.

Menedemus Is there no holy oil there?

Ogygius Silly! That oil exudes only from the tombs of saints, such as Andrew and Catherine.[57] Mary isn't buried.[58]

Menedemus My mistake, I admit. But finish your story.

5 **Ogygius** That the cult may spread more widely, different things are displayed in different places.

Menedemus And, perhaps, that the giving may be more generous; as it is said, 'Gain quickly comes when sought by many hands.'[59]

Ogygius And custodians[60] are always present.

10 **Menedemus** Some of the canons?

Ogygius No, they're not used, lest when serving religion they might stray from devoutness, and while honouring the Virgin pay too little regard to their own virginity.[61] Only in the interior chapel, which I said is the inner sanctum of the Holy Virgin, a canon stands by the altar.

15 **Menedemus** What for?

Ogygius To receive and keep the offering.

Menedemus Do people contribute whether they want to or not?[62]

Ogygius Not at all, but a certain pious embarrassment impels some to give when a person's standing by; they wouldn't give if no one were present

20 to watch them. Or they give somewhat more liberally than they would otherwise.

Menedemus That's human nature. I'm no stranger to it.

Ogygius Nay, there are some so devoted to the Most Holy Virgin that while they pretend to lay an offering on the altar, they steal, with astonishing

25 nimbleness, what somebody else had placed there.[63]

Menedemus Suppose there's no witness: would the Virgin strike them dead on the spot?

Ogygius Why would the Virgin do that, any more than does the heavenly Father himself, whom men aren't afraid to rob of treasures, even digging

30 through the church wall for the purpose?

Menedemus I can't tell which to be the more astonished at, their impious audacity or God's mildness.

Ogygius Then, on the north side – not of the church (don't mistake me) but of the wall enclosing the whole area adjacent to the church – is a certain

35 gateway. It has a tiny door,[64] the kind noblemen's gates have, so that whoever wants to enter must first expose his shins to danger and then stoop besides.

Menedemus Certainly it wouldn't be safe to go at an enemy through such a door.

Ogygius Right. The guide told me that once a knight on horseback escaped

40 through this door from the hands of an enemy who was on the point of overtaking him in his flight. Desperate, he commended himself then and there

to the Holy Virgin, who was close by. For he had determined to take refuge at her altar if the door was open. And mark this wonder: suddenly the knight was entirely within the churchyard and the other man outside, furious.[65]

Menedemus And was this wondrous tale of his believed?

5 **Ogygius** Of course.

Menedemus A rational fellow like you wouldn't accept it so easily.

Ogygius He showed me a copper plate nailed to the door, containing a likeness of the knight who was saved, dressed in the English fashion of that period as we see it in old pictures – and if pictures don't lie, barbers had a

10 hard time in those days, and so did weavers and dyers.

Menedemus How so?

Ogygius Because the knight was bearded like a goat,[66] and his clothing didn't have a single pleat and was so tight that it made the body itself thinner. There was another plate, too, showing the size and shape of the

15 shrine.

Menedemus You had no right to doubt after that.

Ogygius Beneath the little door was an iron grating, admitting you only on foot. It was not seemly that a horse should afterwards trample the spot the horseman had consecrated to the Virgin.

20 **Menedemus** And rightly.

Ogygius To the east is a small chapel,[67] filled with marvels. I betake myself to it. Another guide receives us. After we've prayed briefly, we're immediately shown the joint of a human finger (the largest of three). I kiss it and then ask whose relics these are. 'St Peter's,' he says.[68] 'Not the apostle Peter's?'

25 'Yes.' Then looking at the great size of the joint, which might have been a giant's, I said, 'Peter must have been an extremely big man.' At this one of my companions burst into a loud laugh, which annoyed me no end, for if he had been quiet the attendant would have kept none of the relics from our inspection. However, we appeased him as best we could with a tip.

30   In front of the little building was a structure that during the wintertime (he said), when everything was covered by snow, had been brought there suddenly from far away.[69] Under this were two wells, filled to the top. They say the spring is sacred to the Holy Virgin. It's a wonderfully cold fluid, good for headache and stomach troubles.

35 **Menedemus** If cold water cures headache and stomach troubles, oil will put out fire next.

Ogygius You're hearing about a miracle, my good friend – besides, what would be miraculous about cold water quenching thirst?

Menedemus Clearly this is only one part of the story.

40 **Ogygius** That stream of water, they declared, suddenly shot up from the ground at the command of the Most Holy Virgin. Inspecting everything

carefully I inquired how many years it was since the little house had been brought there. 'Some ages,' he replied. 'In any event,' I said, 'the walls don't look very old.' He didn't deny they had been placed there recently, and the fact was self-evident. 'Then,' I said, 'the roof and thatch of the house seem
5 rather recent.' He agreed, 'Not even these cross-beams, nor the very rafters supporting the roof, appear to have been placed here many years ago.' He nodded. 'But since no part of the building has survived, how is it known for certain,' I asked, 'that this is the cottage brought here from so far away?'

Menedemus How did the attendant get out of that tangle, if you please?

10 **Ogygius** Why, he hurriedly showed us an old, worn-out bearskin[70] fastened to posts and almost laughed at us for our dullness in being slow to see such a clear proof. So, being persuaded, and excusing our stupidity, we turned to the heavenly milk of the Blessed Virgin.

Menedemus O Mother most like her Son! He left us so much of his blood
15 on earth; she left so much of her milk that it's scarcely credible a woman with only one child could have so much, even if the child had drunk none of it.[71]

Ogygius The same thing is said about the Lord's cross, which is exhibited publicly and privately in so many places that if the fragments were joined
20 together they'd seem a full load for a freighter.[72] And yet the Lord carried his whole cross.

Menedemus Doesn't it seem amazing to you, too?

Ogygius Unusual, perhaps, but by no means amazing, since the Lord, who multiplies these things as he wills, is omnipotent.

25 **Menedemus** You explain it reverently, but for my part I'm afraid many such affairs are contrived for profit.

Ogygius I don't think God will stand for anybody mocking him in that way.

Menedemus On the contrary, though Mother and Son and Father and Spirit
30 are robbed by the sacrilegious, sometimes they don't even bestir themselves slightly enough to frighten off the criminals by a nod or a noise. So great is the mildness of divinity.

Ogygius That's true. But hear the rest. This milk is kept on the high altar, in the midst of which is Christ;[73] on the right, for the sake of honour, is his
35 Mother. For the milk represents his Mother.

Menedemus So it's in plain sight.

Ogygius Enclosed in crystal, that is.

Menedemus Therefore liquid.

Ogygius What do you mean, liquid, when it flowed fifteen hundred years
40 ago? It's hard: you'd say powdered chalk, tempered with white of egg.[74]

Menedemus Why don't they display it exposed?

Ogygius To save the virginal milk from being defiled by the kisses of men.

Menedemus Well said, for in my opinion there are those who would bring neither clean nor chaste mouths to it.

Ogygius When the guide saw us, he rushed up, donned a linen vestment,
5 threw a sacred stole around his neck, prostrated himself devoutly, and adored. Next he held out the sacred milk for us to kiss. We prostrated ourselves devoutly on the lowest step of the altar and, after first saluting Christ, addressed to the Virgin a short prayer I had prepared for this occasion:[75] 'Virgin Mother, who hast had the honour of suckling at thy
10 maidenly breast the Lord of heaven and earth, thy Son Jesus, we pray that, cleansed by his blood, we may gain that blessed infancy of dovelike simplicity[76] which, innocent of all malice, deceit, and guile, longs without ceasing for the milk of gospel doctrine until it attains to the perfect man, to the measure of the fullness of Christ, whose blessed company thou enjoyest
15 forever, with the Father and Holy Spirit. Amen.'

Menedemus Certainly a devout intercession. What response did she make?

Ogygius Mother and Son both seemed to nod approval, unless my eyes deceived me. For the sacred milk appeared to leap up, and the Eucharistic elements gleamed somewhat more brightly. Meanwhile the custodian
20 approached us, quite silent, but holding out a board[77] like those used in Germany by toll collectors on bridges.

Menedemus Yes, I've often cursed those greedy boards when travelling through Germany.

Ogygius We gave him some coins, which he offered to the Virgin.
25 Next, through an interpreter who understands the language well (a smooth-tongued young man named Robert Aldridge, I believe),[78] I inquired as civilly as I could what proof he had that this was the Virgin's milk.[79] I wanted to know this clearly for the pious purpose of stopping the mouths of certain unbelievers who are accustomed to laugh at all these matters. At first
30 the guide frowned and said nothing. I told the interpreter to press him, but even more politely. He did so with the utmost grace, such that if with words of that sort he had entreated the Mother herself, recently out of childbed, she would not have taken offence. But the guide, as if possessed, gazed at us in astonishment, and as though horrified by such blasphemous speech, said,
35 'What need is there to inquire into that when you have an authentic record?' And it looked very much as if he would throw us out as heretics, except that we calmed the fellow's wrath with a bit of money.

Menedemus What did you do then?

Ogygius What do you suppose we did? As though beaten with a club, or
40 struck by a thunderbolt, we took ourselves out of there, humbly begging pardon (as one should in sacred matters) for such outrageous presumption.

Thence on to the little chapel, the dwelling-place of the Holy Virgin. At our approach a priest[80] turns up, one of the minor canons,[81] and gazes at us as though studying us; after we go a little farther a second one turns up, likewise staring at us; then a third.

5   **Menedemus** Perhaps they wanted to draw you.

Ogygius But I suspected something very different.

Menedemus What was that?

Ogygius That a sacrilegious person had filched something from the Holy Virgin's ornaments, and that their suspicion was directed against me. So

10 when I entered the chapel I greeted the Virgin Mother with a short prayer, like this: 'O thou alone of all womankind Mother and Virgin, Mother most blessed, purest of maidens, we who are unclean come now unto thee who art pure. We bless thee, we worship thee as best we can with our poor gifts. May thy Son grant us that, by emulating thy most blessed life, we too, through

15 the grace of the Holy Spirit, may be made worthy to conceive the Lord Jesus spiritually in our inmost hearts, and never lose him once conceived. Amen.' Kissing the altar at the same time, I laid some coins upon it and went away.

Menedemus What did the Virgin do at this? Didn't she indicate by the slightest nod that your short prayer was heard?

20 **Ogygius** As I told you, there was a dim religious light, and she stood in the shadows, to the right of the altar. Finally, the first custodian's harangue had so squelched me that I didn't dare lift my eyes.

Menedemus So this expedition didn't end very happily.

Ogygius On the contrary, quite happily.

25 **Menedemus** You've brought me back to life, for 'my heart had fallen to my knees,' as your Homer says.[82]

Ogygius After lunch we went back to the church.

Menedemus You dared to, when you were suspected of sacrilege?

Ogygius That may be, but I was not suspect in my own eyes. A good

30 conscience knows no fear.[83] I wanted to see the 'record' to which the guides had referred us. After searching for it a long time, we found it, but hung so high it could not be read by just any eyes. I'm no Lynceus so far as eyes are concerned,[84] nor am I totally blind, either.[85] So as Aldridge read, I followed along, not trusting him completely in so vital a matter.

35 **Menedemus** Were all your doubts cleared up?

Ogygius I was ashamed of having doubted, so clearly was the whole thing set forth before my eyes – the name, the place, the story, told in order.[86] In a word, nothing was omitted. There was said to be a certain William of Paris, a holy man, inasmuch as from time to time he was remarkably devoted to

40 searching the world over for saints' relics. After travelling through many lands, visiting monasteries and churches everywhere, he came at length to

Constantinople, where his brother was bishop. When William was preparing
to return, his brother confided to him that a certain nun had the milk of the
Virgin Mother and that he would be extremely blessed ever afterwards if by
prayer, purchase, or artifice he could get hold of a portion of it. All other
5   relics he had collected to date were as nothing compared with this sacred
milk. From that moment William could not rest until by his begging he won
half of this milk. With this treasure he thought himself richer than Croesus.[87]
Menedemus Why not? And beyond expectation, too.
Ogygius He headed straight home, but a fatal illness stopped him short.
10   **Menedemus** How brief and limited is human happiness!
Ogygius Aware of the danger, he summons a fellow pilgrim, a most
reliable Frenchman. Swearing him to secrecy, he entrusts the milk to him on
condition that if he reaches home safely he is to place this treasure on the
altar of the Holy Virgin who dwells in the great church in Paris overlooking
15   the Seine, which flows by on each side;[88] the river itself seems to give way
in honour of the Virgin's sanctity. To make a long story short, William is
buried; the other hurries on; and disease takes him, too. In despair of his life,
he gives the milk to an English companion but binds him by many oaths to
do what he himself had intended to do. He dies; the other takes the milk
20   and places it on the altar in the presence of the canons there (formerly called
regulars, as they are yet at St Genevieve's).[89] From them he begged half of
the milk. This he carried to England and finally brought to St Mary by the
Sea, summoned to this place by divine inspiration.
Menedemus Surely this story is very consistent.
25   **Ogygius** More than that: lest any uncertainty remain, there were inscribed,
above, the names of suffragan bishops who grant indulgences[90] as extensive
as their supply affords[91] to those who come to see the milk and don't neglect
to leave a small offering.
Menedemus How much do they grant?
30   **Ogygius** Forty days.
Menedemus Are there days even in the underworld?
Ogygius There's time, certainly.
Menedemus Once the whole supply's been granted, is there none left to
give out?
35   **Ogygius** On the contrary; what they grant is inexhaustible. And obviously
this is different from what happens to the jar of the Danaides, since that,
though continuously filled, is always empty;[92] but as for this, if you always
drain it, still the jar's no emptier.
Menedemus If forty days apiece are granted to a hundred thousand men,
40   each man has just the same?
Ogygius Yes.

Menedemus And if those who received forty days before lunch were to ask for the same number again at dinner-time it would be at hand to bestow?

Ogygius Oh, yes, even if they asked for it ten times an hour.[93]

Menedemus I wish I had such a money box at home! I'd ask merely for
5 three shillings if only they renewed themselves.

Ogygius Why don't you choose to turn into gold completely, since you can do the same again whenever you wish? But to return to the 'record.' The following point was added with pious simplicity: that although the Virgin's milk shown in a great many other places was of course to be reverenced,
10 nevertheless this was to be venerated more than that elsewhere, because that was scraped from rocks whereas this flowed from the Virgin's own breasts.

Menedemus How was this known?

Ogygius Oh, the nun of Constantinople, who gave the milk, said so.

Menedemus And perhaps St Bernard informed her?

15 **Ogygius** That's what I think.

Menedemus The one who in old age was privileged to taste milk from that same breast which the child Jesus sucked.[94] Hence I'm surprised he's called 'the mellifluous' instead of 'the lactifluous.'[95] But how can that be called the Virgin's milk which did not flow from her breasts?

20 **Ogygius** It did flow, but falling on the rock where she happened to be sitting when giving suck, it hardened and then, by God's will, so increased.

Menedemus Right. Continue.

Ogygius After this, while we're strolling about, looking at sights of interest before departing, the custodians turn up again, glance at us, point with the
25 finger, run up, go away, rush back, nod; they seemed to be on the point of accosting us if they could find courage enough.

Menedemus Weren't you at all scared then?

Ogygius Oh, no, I looked them straight in the eye, smiling and gazing at them as if inviting them to address me. At last one comes near and asks my
30 name. I give it. He asks if I was the man who two years earlier had put up a votive tablet in Hebrew.[96] I admit it.

Menedemus Do you write Hebrew?

Ogygius Of course not, but anything they don't understand they call Hebrew. Soon the protos-hysteros[97] of the college comes – having been sent
35 for, I imagine.

Menedemus What title is that? Haven't they an abbot?

Ogygius No.

Menedemus Why?

Ogygius Because they don't know Hebrew.[98]

40 **Menedemus** Nor a bishop?

Ogygius No.

Menedemus Why?

Ogygius Because the Virgin is still too hard up to buy an expensive staff and mitre.

Menedemus Haven't they at least a provost?

5 **Ogygius** Not even that.

Menedemus Why not?

Ogygius Because 'provost' is a title designating office, not sanctity.[99] And that's why colleges of canons reject the name of 'abbot,' while willingly accepting 'provost.'[100]

10 **Menedemus** But 'protos-hysteros' I never heard of before.

Ogygius Really, you're very ignorant of grammar.

Menedemus I do know 'hysteron proteron'[101] in figures of speech.

Ogygius Exactly. The man next to the prior is posterior-prior.

Menedemus You mean a *sub*prior.[102]

15 **Ogygius** This man greeted me quite courteously. He tells me how hard many persons toil to read those lines and how often they wipe their spectacles in vain. Whenever some aged DD or LLD came along he was marched off to the tablet. One would say the letters were Arabic; another, that they were fictitious characters. Finally one was found who could read the title. It was

20 written in Roman words and letters, but in capitals. The Greek lines were written in Greek capitals, which at first glance look like Latin capitals. Upon request, I gave the meaning of the verses in Latin, translating word for word. I firmly refused the small tip proffered for this bit of work, declaring there was nothing, however difficult, that I would not be very eager to do for the

25 sake of the Most Holy Virgin, even if she bade me carry a letter from there to Jerusalem.

Menedemus Why would she need you as postman when she has so many angels to wait on her hand and foot?

Ogygius He offered from his bag a piece of wood, cut from a beam on

30 which the Virgin Mother was seen to stand. A marvellous fragrance proved at once that the object was an extremely sacred one.[103] After kissing so remarkable a gift three of four times with the utmost devotion, while prone and bareheaded, I put it in my purse.

Menedemus May one see it?

35 **Ogygius** I'll let you see it. But if you aren't fasting, or if you had intercourse with your wife last night, I shouldn't advise you to look at it.[104]

Menedemus No danger. Show it to me.

Ogygius Here you are.

Menedemus How lucky you are to have this present!

40 **Ogygius** In case you don't know, I wouldn't exchange this tiny fragment for all the gold in Tagus.[105] I'll set it in gold, but so that it shines through crystal.

Women lighting candles before an image of the Virgin
Drawing by Hans Holbein the Younger in the margin of a copy
of the 1515 Froben edition of *Moriae encomium* (fol M verso)
Öffentliche Kunstsammlung Basel, Kupferstichkabinett

Then Hystero-protos, when he saw that I was so reverently delighted with this little gift and decided I was not undeserving of having greater matters entrusted to me as well, asked whether I had ever seen the secrets of the Virgin. This language startled me somewhat, but I didn't dare ask which

5   secrets of the Virgin he meant, since in subjects so sacred even a slip of the tongue can be dangerous. I say I haven't seen them but that I want to very much. I'm led on now as though divinely inspired. One or two wax tapers are lighted and a small image displayed, unimpressive in size, material, and workmanship but of surpassing power.

10   **Menedemus** Size has little to do with producing miracles. I've seen the Christopher at Paris, not merely a wagon-load or a colossus in size but fully as big as a mountain[106] – yet he was distinguished for no miracles that I ever heard of.

Ogygius At the Virgin's feet is a jewel, as yet unnamed by Latins or Greeks.

15   The French have named it from 'toad,' because it shows the figure of a toad in a way no art could achieve.[107] What's more wonderful, the stone is very small; the image of the toad does not stick out but shines through in the jewel itself, as if inlaid.

Menedemus Perhaps they imagine the toad's likeness, as we imagine an

20   eagle in a stalk of fern. And similarly, what don't children see in clouds: dragons breathing fire, mountains burning, armed men clashing.[108]

Ogygius For your information, no toad shows itself more obviously alive than that one did.

Menedemus So far I've put up with your stories. From now on, look for

25   someone else to convince with your toad yarn.

Ogygius No wonder you feel like that, Menedemus. Nobody could have persuaded me either, even if the whole faculty of theology had maintained it, unless I had seen it, inspected it, and made certain of it with these eyes – these very eyes, I tell you. But you do strike me as rather lacking in curiosity

30   about natural history.

Menedemus Why? Because I don't believe asses fly?

Ogygius Don't you see how Nature the artist enjoys expressing herself in the colours and forms of everything, but especially in jewels? Then, how marvellous the powers she put into those jewels: well-nigh incredible, did

35   not firsthand experience give us assurance of them. Tell me, would you have believed steel is pulled by a magnet without being touched, and repelled by it again without contact, unless you had seen it with your own eyes?

Menedemus No, never, even if ten Aristotles had sworn it to me.

Ogygius Then don't cry 'Incredible!' as soon as you hear about something not

40   yet known by experience.[109] In *ceraunia* we see the figure of a thunderbolt;[110] in *pyropus*, living fire;[111] in *chalazias*, the appearance and hardness of hail,

even if you throw it into the midst of the fire; in the emerald, deep, clear sea water.[112] *Carcinias* resembles a sea crab; adderstone, a viper; *scarites*, the fish called scarus; *hieracites*, a falcon. *Geranites* has a neck like the crane's; *aegophthalmus*, a goat's eye (one kind shows a pig's eye, another three human
5   eyes together); *lycophthalmus* paints the eye of a wolf in four colours: golden red, blood red, and in the middle black bordered by white. If you open *cyamea nigra*, you'll find a bean in the centre. *Dryites* looks like a tree trunk and burns like wood. *Cissites* and *narcissites* depict ivy; *astrapias* throws out flashes of lightning from its white or lapis-lazuli centre; *phlegontes* shows
10 inside the colour of flame, which does not die out; in the carbuncle stone[113] you see certain sparks darting; *crocias* has the colour of a crocus; *rhodites*, of a rose; *chalcites*, of brass. Eaglestone represents an eagle with a whitish tail;[114] *taos* has the image of a peacock; swallowstone,[115] that of an asp. *Myrmecites* contains the figure of a creeping ant; *cantharias* shows a complete beetle;[116]
15 *scorpites* illustrates a scorpion remarkably. But why pursue these examples, which are countless, since Nature has no part – in the elements, in living things, or in plants – that it does not illustrate, as if in sport, in precious stones. Do you wonder that a toad is imaged in this jewel?
     Menedemus I wonder that Nature has so much leisure to play thus at
20 imitating everything.
     Ogygius She wanted to arouse the curiosity of mankind, and so to shake us out of our idleness. And yet – as though we had no way of escaping boredom – we go crazy over jesters, dice, and jugglers' tricks.
     Menedemus Very true.
25 **Ogygius** Some sober people say that if stones of this kind are put in vinegar, the 'toads' will move their legs and swim.
     Menedemus Why is a toad set before the Virgin?[117]
     Ogygius Because she overcame, stamped out, extinguished all impurity, infection, pride, avarice, and whatever earthly passions there are.
30 **Menedemus** Woe to us who bear so great a toad in our breasts!
     Ogygius We shall be pure if we worship the Virgin zealously.
     Menedemus How does she like to be worshipped?
     Ogygius You will adore her most acceptably if you imitate her.[118]
     Menedemus Precisely[119] – but that's very hard to do.
35 **Ogygius** Yes, but most glorious.
     Menedemus Go on; continue what you began.
     Ogygius Next he shows us gold and silver statues.[120] 'This one,' says he, 'is all gold; the other one, silver gilded.' He adds the weight and worth of each, and the name of the donor. When, marvelling at every one, I was
40 congratulating the Virgin on such fortunate wealth,[121] the guide said: 'Since I notice you're a devout sightseer, I don't think it right to keep anything from

you: you shall see the Virgin's very greatest secrets.' At the same time he takes down from the altar itself a world of wonderful things. If I tried to enumerate them all, the day would not be long enough. Thus the pilgrimage ended very happily for me. I had my fill of sights, and I brought away with

5   me this priceless gift, a pledge from the Virgin herself.

Menedemus Didn't you test the power of your piece of wood?[122]

Ogygius I did. Before three days passed, I found at a certain inn a man who had gone mad; they were ready to chain him.[123] I slipped this wood under his pillow secretly. He fell into a long, deep sleep. In the morning he woke

10   up as sound as ever.

Menedemus Maybe it wasn't insanity but delirium tremens from drink. Sleep usually helps that malady.

Ogygius Joke as you please, Menedemus, but about something else. To make fun of the saints is neither reverent nor prudent. Why, the man himself

15   said that a woman of marvellous beauty had appeared to him in a dream and held out a cup to him.

Menedemus Hellebore, I dare say.[124]

Ogygius I don't know about that, but I do know the man's in his right mind.

Menedemus Did you overlook Thomas, archbishop of Canterbury?

20   **Ogygius** By no means. No pilgrimage is more devout.

Menedemus I long to hear about it, if that's not too much trouble.

Ogygius Oh, no, I want you to hear. There's a part of England called Kent, facing France and Flanders; its metropolis[125] is Canterbury. In it are two monasteries, almost adjacent, both of them Benedictine houses. That named

25   for St Augustine[126] is evidently older; the one now called after St Thomas appears[127] to have been the archbishop's see, where he used to live with a few chosen monks[128] – just as today, too, bishops have residences adjoining the churches but separate from the houses of other canons. (In old times both bishops and canons were usually monks;[129] evidence abounds to prove that.)

30   The church dedicated to St Thomas rises to the sky so majestically that it inspires devotion even in those who see it from afar. Thus by its splendour it now dims the glory of the neighbouring one and, so to speak, overshadows the spot that was anciently the most sacred. It has two huge towers,[130] as though greeting visitors a long way off and making the region ring far and

35   wide with the wonderful resonance of its bronze bells. At the south entrance of the church are stone statues of the three armed men who with sacrilegious hands murdered the blessed saint. Their surnames are added: Tusci, Fusci, Berri.[131]

Menedemus Why is so much honour paid to impious men?

40   **Ogygius** Obviously they have the same honour as Judas, Pilate, and Caiaphas, that band of accursed soldiers whom you see carefully carved on

gilded altars. The surnames are added lest anybody in the future speak well of them. Attention is called to them in order that hereafter no courtier lift a hand against bishops or church property. For those three conspirators went mad after committing their crime,[132] and would not have recovered had they
5   not begged help of the most holy Thomas.

Menedemus O the everlasting mercy of martyrs!

Ogygius When you enter,[133] the spacious grandeur of the building is disclosed. This part is open to the public.

Menedemus Is there nothing to see there?

10   **Ogygius** Nothing but the mass of the structure and some books – among them the Gospel of Nicodemus[134] – chained to pillars, and a tomb, I don't know whose.

Menedemus Then what?

Ogygius Iron screens prevent you from going further,[135] but they permit a
15   view of the space between the end of the building and the choir, as it is called. This is ascended by many steps, under which a certain vault gives access to the north side.[136] A wooden altar sacred to the Holy Virgin is shown there,[137] a very small one, not worth seeing except as a monument of antiquity, a rebuke to the luxury of our times. There the holy man is said to have spoken
20   his last farewell to the Virgin when death was at hand. On the altar is the point of the sword with which the crown of the good bishop's head was cut off, and his brain smashed, evidently to make death come more quickly.[138] Out of love for the martyr we reverently kissed the sacred rust of his sword.

    Leaving this place, we went down into the crypt.[139] It has its own
25   custodians. First is shown the martyr's skull, pierced through.[140] The top of the cranium is bared for kissing; the rest covered with silver. Along with this is displayed a leaden plate with 'Thomas of Acre'[141] carved on it. The hair shirt,[142] girdle, and drawers by which the bishop used to subdue his flesh hang in the gloom there – horrible even to look at and a reproach to our
30   softness and delicacy.

Menedemus Perhaps to the monks themselves, too.

Ogygius I can neither affirm nor deny that, nor is it any of my business.

Menedemus Very true.

Ogygius From here we return to the choir.[143] On the north side mysteries
35   are laid open. It is wonderful how many bones were brought forth – skulls, jaws, teeth, hands, fingers, whole arms,[144] all of which we adored and kissed. This would have gone on forever if my fellow pilgrim, an unobliging chap, had not cut short the enthusiasm of the guide.

Menedemus Who was this?

40   **Ogygius** An Englishman named Gratian Pullus,[145] a learned and upright man but less respectful towards this side of religion than I liked.

Menedemus Some Wycliffite, I suppose.

Ogygius I don't think so, although he had read his books.[146] Where he got hold of them isn't clear.

Menedemus Did he offend the custodian?

5 **Ogygius** An arm was brought forth, with the bloodstained flesh still on it. He shrank from kissing this, looking rather disgusted. The custodian soon put his things away. Next we viewed the altar table and ornaments;[147] then the objects that were kept under the altar[148] – all of them splendid; you'd say Midas and Croesus were beggars if you saw the quantity of gold and
10 silver.[149]

Menedemus No kisses here?

Ogygius No, but a different sort of desire came to my mind.

Menedemus What?

Ogygius I was sad because I had no such relics at home.[150]

15 **Menedemus** An unholy thought!

Ogygius Admitted, and I begged the saint's forgiveness before leaving the church. After this we were conducted to the sacristy.[151] Good Lord, what an array of silk vestments there, what an abundance of gold candelabra! There too we saw St Thomas' staff.[152] It looked like a cane plated with silver. It was
20 not at all heavy, had no ornamentation, and was no more than waist-high.

Menedemus No cross?

Ogygius None that I saw. We were shown a pallium,[153] silk to be sure, but coarse, without gold or jewels, and there was a face-cloth,[154] soiled by sweat from his neck and preserving obvious spots of blood. These memorials of
25 the plain living of olden times we gladly kissed.

Menedemus They're not shown to everyone?

Ogygius Certainly not, my good friend.

Menedemus How was it you were trusted so much that no secrets were kept from you?

30 **Ogygius** I had some acquaintance with the Reverend Father William Warham, the archbishop.[155] He gave me a note of recommendation.

Menedemus I hear from many persons that he is a man of remarkable kindness.

Ogygius More than that: you would call him kindness itself if you knew
35 him. His learning, integrity, and holiness of life are so great that you would find him lacking in no quality befitting an ideal prelate. – Next we were led up above, for behind the high altar you ascend as though into a new church. There in a small chapel is shown the entire countenance of the saint, gilded and ornamented with many jewels.[156] Here a certain unlooked-for accident
40 almost upset all our good luck.

Menedemus I'm waiting to hear what misfortune you mean.

Ogygius My friend Gratian was far from gracious on this occasion.[157] After a short prayer he asked the keeper, 'I say, good father, is it true, as I've heard, that in his lifetime Thomas was most generous to the poor?' 'Very true,' the man replied, and began to rehearse the saint's many acts of kindness
5 to them. Then Gratian: 'I don't suppose his disposition changed in this matter, unless perhaps for the better.' The custodian agreed. Gratian again: 'Since, then, the saint was so liberal towards the needy, though he was still poor himself and lacked money to provide for the necessities of life, don't you think he'd gladly consent, now that he's so rich and needs nothing, if
10 some poor wretched woman with hungry children at home, or daughters in danger of losing their virtue because they have no money for dowries, or a husband sick in bed and penniless – if, after begging the saint's forgiveness, she carried off a bit of all this wealth to rescue her family, as though taking from one who wanted her to have it, either as a gift or a loan?' When the
15 keeper in charge of the gilded head made no reply to this, Gratian, who's impulsive, said, 'For my part, I'm convinced the saint would rejoice that in death, too, he could relieve the wants of the poor by his riches.'[158] At this the custodian frowned and pursed his lips, looking at us with Gorgon eyes,[159] and I don't doubt he would have driven us from the church with
20 insults and reproaches had he not been aware that we were recommended by the archbishop. I managed to placate the fellow somehow by smooth talk, affirming that Gratian hadn't spoken seriously but liked to joke; and at the same time I gave him some coins.

Menedemus I quite approve of your sense of duty. But seriously, I wonder
25 sometimes what possible excuse there could be for those who spend so much money on building, decorating, and enriching churches that there's simply no limit to it. Granted that the sacred vestments and vessels of the church must have a dignity appropriate to their liturgical use; and I want the building to have grandeur. But what's the use of so many
30 baptistries, candelabra, gold statues?[160] What's the good of the vastly expensive organs, as they call them? (We're not content with a single set, either.) What's the good of that costly musical neighing when meanwhile our brothers and sisters, Christ's living temples, waste away from neglect and starvation?[161]
35 **Ogygius** Every decent, sensible man favours moderation in these matters, of course. But since the fault springs from excessive devotion, it merits applause; especially when one thinks of the opposite vice in those who rob churches of their wealth. These gifts are generally given by kings and potentates and would be worse spent on gambling and war. And if you try
40 to rid the churches of any of these things, that, in the first place, is regarded as sacrilege; next, those who are regular contributors stop their giving;

above all, men are incited to robbery. Hence churchmen are custodians of
these things rather than owners of them. In short, I'd rather see a church
abounding in sacred furnishings than bare and dirty,[162] as some are, and
more like stables than churches.

5   **Menedemus** Yet we read that in former times bishops were praised for
selling the sacred vessels and using the money to relieve the poor.[163]

Ogygius They're praised today, too, but only praised. In my judgment, they
neither can, nor want to, imitate them.

Menedemus I'm holding up your story. Let's have the *dénouement*.[164]

10   **Ogygius** Hear it, then; I'll be brief. While this was going on, the chief official
came forward.

Menedemus Who? The abbot of the place?

Ogygius He has a mitre and abbatial revenue; he lacks only the name of abbot
and is called prior,[165] because the archbishop serves instead of an abbot.[166]

15   In ancient times whoever was archbishop of this diocese was also a monk.

Menedemus Well, I wouldn't mind being called camel if I had an abbot's
income.

Ogygius He seemed to me a good, sensible man; something of a Scotist
theologian, too.[167] He opened for us the chest in which the rest of the holy

20   man's body is said to lie.

Menedemus You saw the bones?

Ogygius No, that's not permitted, nor would it be possible without the use
of ladders. But the wooden chest conceals a golden chest; when this is drawn
up by ropes, it reveals inestimable treasure.[168]

25   **Menedemus** What do I hear?

Ogygius The cheapest part was gold. Everything shone and dazzled with
rare and surpassingly large jewels, some bigger than a goose egg.[169] Some
monks stood about reverently. When the cover was removed, we all adored.
The prior pointed out each jewel by touching it with a white rod, adding its

30   French name, its worth, and the name of the donor. The principal ones were
gifts from kings.

Menedemus He must have a remarkable memory.

Ogygius Your guess is correct, though practice helps too, for he often does
this. From here he leads the way back to the crypt. There the Virgin Mother

35   has a residence, but a somewhat dark one, twice enclosed by iron screens.

Menedemus What's she afraid of?

Ogygius Only robbers, I suppose, for I've never seen anything more loaded
with riches.

Menedemus You tell me of dark riches.

40   **Ogygius** When the lanterns were brought closer, we saw a more than regal
sight.

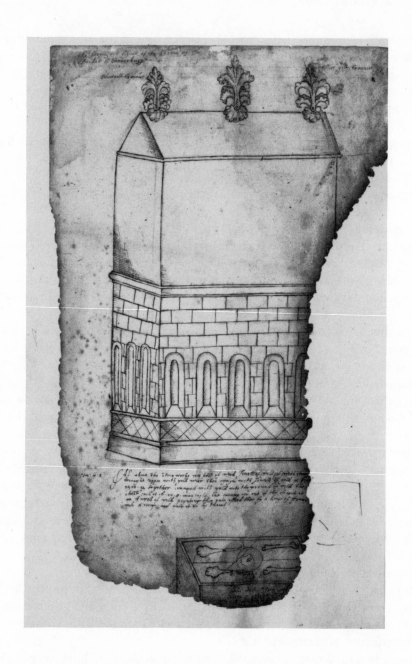

An antiquary's drawing, date unknown, of the shrine of Archbishop Thomas Becket
The lower part, of stone, contained the treasures. Beneath them was a box
containing Becket's bones. When the shrine was destroyed in 1538, the treasures
were seized by the government, and it was said the bones were burned.
Courtesy of the Trustees of the British Museum

Menedemus More wealth than that of St Mary by the Sea?

Ogygius It looks like much more. She alone knows her secret wealth. It isn't shown to any but persons of the highest importance or to special friends. At last we were led back to the sacristy. There a chest with a black leather cover

5 was brought out, placed on the table, and opened. Immediately everyone worshipped on bended knee.

Menedemus What was inside?

Ogygius Some linen rags, many of them still showing traces of snivel.[170] With these, they say, the holy man wiped the sweat from his face or neck,

10 the dirt from his nose, or whatever other kinds of filth human bodies have. At this point my friend Gratian again displayed something less than graciousness.[171] To him, since he was English and a well-known person of considerable standing, the prior kindly offered one of the rags as a gift, thinking he was making him a present that would please him very much.

15 But Gratian was hardly grateful for it. He touched the piece with his fingers, not without a sign of disgust, and put it back scornfully, puckering his lips as though whistling. (This is what he ordinarily did if he came across anything he thought contemptible.) Shame and alarm together embarrassed me dreadfully. But the prior, no fool, pretended not to notice this incident,

20 and after offering us a glass of wine dismissed us kindly, for we were returning to London.

Menedemus Why did you have to do that when you were already fairly close to your own shore?

Ogygius Yes, I was, but I willingly avoided that shore as much as possible.

25 It's more notorious for frauds and robberies than any Malean rocks are for shipwrecks.[172] I'll tell you what I saw on my last crossing.[173] Many of us were ferried in a boat from the Calais shore to a larger vessel. Among the passengers was a poor ragged French youth. He was charged sixpence;[174] so large a sum do they wring from each passenger for the very short ride. He

30 pleaded poverty. To amuse themselves they search him, and when they pull off his shoes they find ten or twelve shillings between the soles. These they take, laughing in his face and jeering at the damned Frenchman.

Menedemus What did the young fellow do?

Ogygius Mourned his loss. What else could he do?

35 **Menedemus** They had no right to do such things, had they?

Ogygius Exactly the same right they have to rob passengers' luggage and to snatch purses whenever they get a chance.

Menedemus It's extraordinary that they should dare to commit such a serious crime in the presence of so many witnesses.

40 **Ogygius** They're so used to doing it that they think it's quite all right. Many persons watched from the larger boat. In the small boat were some English

merchants, who protested in vain. Those fellows boasted about catching the
damned Frenchman as if it were a practical joke.

Menedemus I'd gladly crucify those pirates as a practical joke!

Ogygius But both shores are full of such men. Guess 'what masters could

5   do when knaves dare do such deeds.'[175] So from now on I prefer roundabout
routes to that short cut. In these respects, just as 'the descent to hell is
easy' but the return extremely difficult,[176] so entry by this shore is not
altogether easy, exit very hard. Some sailors from Antwerp were hanging
about London; I decided to take my sailing chances with them.

10   **Menedemus** Does that place have such conscientious sailors?

Ogygius As an ape is always an ape,[177] I confess, so a sailor's always a
sailor.[178] But if you compare them with professional thieves, they're angels.

Menedemus I'll remember that if ever I, too, get the urge to visit that island.
But go back to the road I took you away from.

15   **Ogygius** On the way to London, shortly after you leave Canterbury, you
find a very deep and narrow road; moreover, it has such steep banks on each
side that you can't get out of it. There's no other road you can take, either.
On the left side of this road is a little almshouse for some old beggars.[179] As
soon as they see a rider coming one of them runs up, sprinkles him with holy

20   water, and presently holds out the upper part of a shoe fastened to a brass
rim. In it is a glass that looks like a jewel.[180] People kiss it and make a small
contribution.

Menedemus On that sort of road I'd rather meet a house of old beggars
than a gang of able-bodied thieves.

25   **Ogygius** Gratian was riding on my left, closer to the almshouse. He was
sprinkled with water but he managed to put up with that. When the shoe
was thrust at him, he asked the man what he meant by this. He said it was
St Thomas' shoe. Gratian turned to me and said heatedly, 'What, do these
brutes want us to kiss all good men's shoes? Why not, in the same fashion,

30   hold out spittle and other excrements to be kissed?' I felt sorry for the old
man and cheered him up with a bit of money, poor fellow.[181]

Menedemus In my opinion, Gratian's anger was not entirely unreasonable.
If soles of shoes were kept as evidence of a simple life, I wouldn't object, but
I consider it shameless to push soles, shoes, and drawers at one to be kissed.

35   If one kissed them of his own accord, from some strong feeling of piety, I'd
think it pardonable.[182]

Ogygius I won't pretend it wouldn't be better to leave those things
undone, but from what can't be amended at a stroke I'm accustomed
to take whatever good there is. – Meantime, I was pleasing myself with

40   the reflection that a good man is like a sheep, a bad one like a beast
of prey. When an adder's dead, it can't sting, true, but its stench and

blood are injurious. A sheep, while alive, nourishes by its milk, provides clothing by its wool, enriches by its offspring; dead, it furnishes useful hide; and all of it can be eaten. So rapacious men, addicted to this world, are troublesome to everybody while alive; when dead, they're a nuisance to the living by reason of the tolling of bells, grandiose funerals,[183] and sometimes by the consecration of their successors – because that means new exactions. Good men, truly, are in every respect useful to everyone: as this saint, during his lifetime, encouraged people to godliness by his example, teaching, and exhortations, comforted the forsaken, and raised up the needy. In death his usefulness was almost greater. He built this very wealthy church;[184] he strengthened considerably the power of the priesthood throughout England.[185] Lastly, this piece of shoe supports a house of poor men.

Menedemus A noble thought indeed, but since you're of that mind I'm surprised you've never visited St Patrick's cave,[186] of which some marvellous tales are told. To me they're not entirely plausible.

Ogygius On the contrary, no story about it can be so marvellous that it is not surpassed by the fact itself.

Menedemus And have you been in it, then?

Ogygius I sailed in Stygian waters, to be sure; I went down into the jaws of Avernus;[187] I saw what goes on in hell.

Menedemus You'll do me a favour if you'll be kind enough to tell me about it.

Ogygius Let this serve as prologue to our conversation – and it's long enough, in my opinion. I'm on my way home to order dinner, for I've had no lunch.

Menedemus Why haven't you? Not because of religious observance.

Ogygius Oh, no, because of a grudge.

Menedemus A grudge against your belly?

Ogygius No, against greedy tavern keepers who, though they won't serve a decent meal, don't hesitate to charge their guests outrageous prices.[188] I get even with them in this way: if I expect a good dinner with an acquaintance, or at an innkeeper's who is a little less niggardly, my stomach won't stand much lunch, but if luck has provided the sort of lunch I like, I get a stomach-ache at dinner-time.

Menedemus Aren't you ashamed to seem so stingy and mean?

Ogygius Menedemus, those who take shame into account in such matters, believe me, are bad accountants. I've learned to keep my shame for other purposes.[189]

Menedemus I long to hear the rest of the tale, so expect me as a guest for dinner. You'll tell it more comfortably there.

Ogygius Well, thanks very much for inviting yourself, since so many who are pressed to come decline. But my thanks will be doubled if you'll dine at home today, for my time will be taken up with greeting my family. Besides, I have a plan more convenient for us both. Have lunch at *your* home tomorrow
5   for me and my wife. Then I'll talk until dinner – until you admit you're satisfied; and if you like, we won't desert you even at dinner. What are you scratching your head for? You get it ready; we'll be sure to come.
Menedemus I'd prefer stories I wouldn't have to pay for. All right: I'll furnish a light lunch; only it will be tasteless unless you season it with good stories.
10 **Ogygius** But look here: don't you itch to go on these pilgrimages?
Menedemus Maybe I'll itch after you've finished talking. As matters stand now, I have enough to do by going on my Roman stations.[190]
Ogygius Roman? You, who've never seen Rome?
Menedemus I'll tell you. Here's how I wander about at home. I go into the
15 living room and see that my daughters' chastity is safe. Coming out of there into my shop, I watch what my servants, male and female, are doing. Then to the kitchen, to see if any instruction is needed. From here to one place and another, observing what my children and my wife are doing, careful that everything be in order. These are my Roman stations.
20 **Ogygius** But St James[191] will look after these affairs for you.
Menedemus Sacred Scripture directs me to take care of them myself.[192] I've never read any commandment to hand them over to saints.

NOTES

1 Menedemus is 'stay-at-home.' The name Ogygius has the general sense 'primeval.' Ogygus was the legendary founder of Thebes. Proverbially 'Ogygian misfortunes' were ones of great antiquity or enormous injury. See *Adagia* II ix 50.
When defending what Ogygius says in one passage (648:30–1, 37–9), Erasmus expressly identifies himself with him (*Apologia adversus rhapsodias Alberti Pii* LB IX 1161E). Ostensibly Ogygius is the reporter or narrator of what was seen or heard in Walsingham and Canterbury. Some of his remarks are such as Erasmus or any other visitor to those places would share, but others – interpretations or opinions – draw from Menedemus critical or ironical replies we recognize as Erasmian. As author, Erasmus plays both roles; he is Ogygius in description and travelogue, Menedemus in satire and irony.
2 ... *nisi prorsus hallucinor*; cf 'Beggar Talk' 564:3–4 and n2. The opening lines are reminiscent of those in Lucian's *Menippus*. In the present colloquy, where wonders and credulity count for so much, there may be other echoes of Lucian too, for example of *Alexander*, which Erasmus had translated. More translated *Menippus* and *Philopseudes* (see the introduction to 'The Liar and the Man of Honour' 344).

3 Repeated at 649:20 below and in 'Charon' 821:27. In Greek mythology Styx is the river in the underworld.

4 Shells were associated especially with St James and with Compostella and were traditional symbols of the pilgrim's progress. The 'tin and leaden images' were badges or brooches worn on hats and coats; on them see Dickinson 116–20 and plates 8 and 9. 'Snakes' eggs' are beads, that is, a rosary worn on the arm.

5 Jerusalem was the ultimate goal of most devout pilgrims. In England Canterbury and Walsingham were the shrines most frequented, but on the continent the shrine of St James the Great, apostle, at Compostella in Galicia, was second only to Rome in popularity. Erasmus, like others, often mentions it in the same breath with Jerusalem and Rome (as in *Enchiridion* LB V 63E–F / CWE 66 124; Allen Epp 875:14–17, 1202:215–8 / CWE Epp 875:16–20, 1202:246–50; and see 'Rash Vows'). William Wey's *Itineraries* (for the Roxburghe Club [London 1857]) records his pilgrimage to Compostella in 1456 and includes a list of indulgences obtainable there (159–61). For another account a decade later see Leo of Rozmital *Travels* 116–7. Andrew Boorde says (1548) that the pilgrimage to Compostella by land – English pilgrims often went by sea – was a hard journey and that he would rather go to Rome five times than once to Compostella (*The fyrst boke of the Introduction of knowledge* ed F.J. Furnivall EETS extra series 10 [London 1870] 202–6). He was sceptical of the relics seen there. On the legend of St James in Spain consult T.D. Kendrick *St James in Spain* (London 1960). On the pilgrimage consult Georgianna Goddard King *The Way of St James* (New York and London 1920; repr New York 1980); Vera and Hellmut Hell *The Great Pilgrimage of the Middle Ages: The Road to Compostella* (London 1966); *Les chemins de saint-Jacques* ed R. Oursel (Paris 1970); Horton and M.-H. Davies *Holy Days and Holidays* (London and Toronto 1982).

6 The shrine of Our Lady of Walsingham, in the pilgrimage chapel of the priory of Walsingham in northern Norfolk, a few miles from the sea, dating from the twelfth century. By the fifteenth century the shrine had become a popular resort of Marian devotion in England. On its fame and the pilgrimage see Dickinson 3–47. Margery Kempe went there (*The Book of Margery Kempe* ed W. Butler-Bowdon [London 1936; Oxford 1954] 229–30; also ed S.B. Meech and H.E. Allen, EETS original series 212 [London and New York 1940; repr 1961]). Margaret Paston, writing to her ailing husband John, tells him that her mother promised to go (*Paston Letters* 28 September 1443; ed James Gairdner, 6 vols [London 1904] II 55 no 47); cf 'The Shipwreck' n27. Henry VI visited the shrine; Henry VII went at least three times. Henry VIII walked part of the way to Walsingham barefoot (the date is uncertain) and went again in 1511, after the queen was delivered of a boy, who died a few months later (Hall's *Chronicle* [1542; London 1809] 516–17). Queen Catherine of Aragon, who died in 1536, asked in her will that 'some personage go to our Lady of Walsingham in pilgrimage; and in going by the way to deal xx nobles' (Strype *Ecclesiastical Memorials* [Oxford 1822] I part 2 252).

7 In Ep 262 written from Cambridge 9 May 1512 to Andrea Ammonio, Erasmus announces that he is going to visit the Virgin of Walsingham and will hang up a Greek poem to her. On this poem see 636:30–637:26 below. Presumably he made his visit soon afterwards. Nothing is known of a previous visit. He was

not in England between June 1506 and July 1509, and no letters written by him between the end of 1508 and April 1511 survive.

8 Since there is no telling what odd ideas devotees of Greek may have. The suggestion here may be either respectful or, more likely, ironic. See 'The Abbot and the Learned Lady' n4.

9 Cf 'Rash Vows' 38:34–39:3.

Bishop Shaxton's injunctions for Salisbury diocese in 1538 warn midwives to avoid causing women, 'being in travail, to make any foolish vow to go in pilgrimage to this image or that image' after delivery (*Visitation Articles and Injunctions of the Period of the Reformation* ed W.H. Frere and W.M. Kennedy, 3 vols [London 1910] II 58–9).

10 Cf 'Military Affair' 58:15 and 'Alchemy 550:19; the same image is used at 632:31, 633:17, 634:19 below.

11 *os oblinere*; cf *Adagia* I v 48.

12 See n163 below.

13 Cf Allen Ep 2285:94.

14 When defending certain passages in *Enchiridion* and 'The Shipwreck' on Mary and on saints, Erasmus conceded that some readers may have thought the letter which follows here was actually written by the Virgin (*Apologia adversus rhapsodias Alberti Pii* [1531] LB IX 1162B–1167A). But it is a joke (*lusus*), he says, directed at those who publicly condemn the veneration of saints and have removed or destroyed images that had been in churches. Germans familiar with Greek understand, he adds, that by 'Glaucoplutus' Zwingli is meant (see n23 below). 'Nor do I introduce the very Mother of Christ but an image styled "from the rock" [*a lapide*]. Nor does she write from heaven but from her stony house' (LB IX 1166A–B). This may seem a lame, even disingenuous, explanation when we read later that the letter was delivered by an angel and its opening words name the writer as 'Mary Mother of Jesus'; cf also n42 below. But Erasmus replies in a similar vein in that same year to the Paris faculty of theology (*Declarationes ad censuras Lutetiae vulgatas* LB IX 948E–F).

As a piece of factitious cleverness this letter belongs in a large company of similar compositions. One such was the translation of a 'letter,' printed by Foxe, from Lucifer, prince of darkness, to all 'persecuting Prelates,' exhorting them to subvert the gospel by promising appropriate rewards (*Acts and Monuments* III 190–2). A few inventions of this kind may be true literary art; for example the *Epistolae obscurorum virorum* in Erasmus' time (and see 'The Exorcism' 540:34–541:9 and n39 above) and C.S. Lewis' *Screwtape Letters* in ours. In 1456 in Holland a confraternity of Our Lady generously provided a letter for a deceased member, recommending him to St Peter for admission through the heavenly gates (R.R. Post *Kerkgeschiedenis in de Middeleeuwen* 2 vols [Utrecht and Antwerp 1957] II 246n).

15 *apud Rauricos*; the Raurici were the tribe that anciently lived in the area. Their chief town was Augusta Raurica, the modern Augst. Maria a Lapide was the statue of the Virgin in the chapel at Mariastein, about seven miles south of Basel. The monastery, with a fine baroque church, is still a busy place of pilgrimage. Of the statues now placed above the two altars in the Gnadenkapelle, it is impossible to be certain which is the one to which Erasmus refers. The shrine is a chapel in the rock (hence the name), reached by descending a staircase. See Mauritius Fürst 'Erasmus und Mariastein' *Jahrbuch für Solothurnische*

Geschichte 47 (1974) 277–83; on the pilgrimage E.D. Baumann 'Die Wallfahrt von Mariastein' *Basler Jahrbuch* (1942) 110–39.

16 Then ... But] Added in the March 1533 edition

17 Greek in the original

18 In the monastic church at Durham. According to legend, *venerabilis* was added to the epitaph by the hand of an angel when a monk could not think of a suitable word to insert in the verse he had composed (Thomas Fuller *Church History of Britain* [1655] 2.3.17; in the edition by James Nichols, 3 vols [London 1842] I 150).

19 St] *divo.* Added in the September 1531 edition. When St Giles interceded with God for the remission of the king's sins, an angel appeared and placed on the altar a scroll announcing forgiveness. The story is in the *Golden Legend* (1 September).

20 *Adagia* I iv 89

21 Touchstones, which tell whether supposed gold is genuine (Pliny *Naturalis historia* 33.126; Erasmus *Adagia* I v 87)

22 *Adagia* III ii 56

23 'Owl-rich' in Greek, 'Eul-reich' in German, and thus a play on the first name of Huldrych Zwingli, the Swiss reformer

24 Although Zwingli agreed with Luther on many matters, his own program for reforms increasingly involved more radical departures from traditional sacramental theology and practice. As early as 1523 he had begun to make clear his disagreement with Luther on the Eucharist. On this question their differences became irreconcilable. See G.W. Locher 'Zwingli und Erasmus' in *Scrinium Erasmianum* II 325–50; translation in *Erasmus in English* 10 (1979–80) 2–11.

25 Efforts in Zürich, incited by Zwingli's sermons and writings, to correct what he considered gross errors in received doctrine and worship came to a head in 1523–4. The course of controversy can be followed in three disputations, the first in January 1523, the second in October of that year, the third in January 1524. Zwingli declared that the Bible was the sole guide to doctrine and worship and that the mass as a sacrifice must be rejected; he denounced fasting, intercession of saints, and clerical celibacy. Images of saints were called idols, and Zwingli urged their removal from churches and their destruction. After the third disputation, and despite the opposition of the bishop, the Zürich town council ordered organs, relics, and images to be removed from the minster (June and July 1524). Thus began the iconoclasm that was to be repeated in other neighbourhoods and cities. The organs in the Zürich minster were finally destroyed in 1527 (see n161 below). For convenient texts and translations of Zwingli and reform in German Switzerland see Kidd *Documents* 374–476 and *The Reformation in Its Own Words* ed and trans Hans J. Hillerbrand (London 1964) 104–69. For a recent review of Zwingli's teachings see W.P. Stephens *The Theology of Huldreich Zwingli* (Oxford 1987). Many of his theological writings not previously available in English are translated in Edward J. Furcha and H. Wayne Pipkin *Huldrych Zwingli: Writings* 2 vols (Allison Park, Pa 1984).

  Zwingli relates that it was his reading, as a young man, of a poem by Erasmus, *Expostulatio Iesu cum homine*, which first convinced him that Christ is the only mediator between God and man (Kidd *Documents* 378–9 no 160; see CWE 85–6 84–9, 497–501 no 43 / Reedijk *Poems of Erasmus* 291–6 no 85). Erasmus addressed the preface of *Spongia* (1523) to Zwingli (Ep 1378), but cordiality on both sides cooled as a consequence of Zwingli's teachings on the Eucharist – that it was not a sacrifice but only a commemoration of Christ's suffering – and his total hostility to images. Erasmus was later to witness the effects of Zwinglian ideas in Basel (see on this C. Augustijn 'Erasmus und die Reformation in der Schweiz' in *Basler Zeitschrift für Geschichte und Altertumskunde* 86 part 2 [1986] 27–42). Much as he himself deplored, and at times satirized, the superstitions connected with the use and abuse of images, he condemned the rash and violent actions of the iconoclasts. The difficulty about images, he wrote, was to treat them as reminders and symbols of truths without supposing, as the ignorant do, that these material objects and other things such as candles, pictures, and relics are efficacious in themselves or give access to God. True devotion to saints is the endeavour to emulate their virtues (see 'The Shipwreck' n38; 'The Well-to-do Beggars' n44). Erasmus' fellow pilgrim to Canterbury, John Colet, was once accused of preaching against images; see n146 below. See W.K. Jordan *Edward VI: The Young King* (Cambridge, Mass 1968) 182–5; John Phillips *The Reformation of Images: Destruction of Art in England, 1535–1660* (Berkeley 1973); and Eamon Duffy *The Stripping of the Altars* (New Haven and London 1992). The most comprehensive study of iconoclasm in England is Margaret Aston *England's Iconoclasts I: Laws against Images* (Oxford 1988).

26 Cf *Moriae encomium* LB IV 445C–446A / ASD IV-3 124:990–126:22 / CWE 27 115. Lucian makes similar observations about the pagan gods (as in *Icaromenippus* 25), as Erasmus knew well.

27 'Many seek from saints what they would not dare to ask of a good man' (*Modus orandi Deum* LB V 1119D, where Erasmus goes on to recall some of his experiences on his Canterbury pilgrimage; see also *Ecclesiastes* LB V 873C–D).

28 See 'Military Affairs,' especially 55:9, 56:37–40 and 'The Soldier and the Carthusian' 334:10–11.

29 One . . . Other people's] In the first edition the pronoun is masculine (*qui*); in the edition of March 1533 and other late ones consulted it is feminine (*quae*). With this reading the reference is to a bawd or prostitute. Similarly in line 18, *Aliorum* (masculine) is in the first edition; *Aliarum* (feminine) in the final authorized text of March 1533.

30 A comparable passage in a letter of March 1523 (Allen Ep 1347:77–93 / CWE Ep 1347:86–104), with petitions similar to those that follow here, is perhaps another indication that this colloquy was written near that time.

31 The status and popularity of Mary as mediatrix grew with the rise of Marian devotion and was very common in medieval religion. See Jaroslav Pelikan *The Christian Tradition: A History of the Development of Doctrine* 5 vols (Chicago 1971–89) III *The Growth of Medieval Theology (600–1300)* 160–74. Belief of the faithful in this Marian role was expressed in a variety of ways in early Christian literature, but the title of 'mediatrix' is first attested with certainty in the eastern church in the eighth century (see NCE IX 359a). In an *Obsecratio ad Virginem Matrem Mariam*, an unusually fervent and rhetorical supplication to the Virgin, written *in rebus adversis* and printed in his *Lucubratiunculae* in 1503 or 1504, Erasmus addresses her as 'the only hope in our calamities' and says it is unthinkable that she will not take pity, since 'the Son you bore is easily moved, and so loving of you, so compliant, so reverent, that he denies nothing to the suppliant' (LB V 1233E, 1235E). With this, contrast the tone and occasion

of Allen Ep 2178:13–22 (1529) and *Epistola contra pseudevangelicos* (1529 or 1530) LB X 1583C / ASD IX-1 301:506–7, where Erasmus declares that as a reaction to Lutheran excesses Catholic theologians have now produced extravagant claims of their own in many matters, among them that Mary has certain powers to rule the Son. On Erasmus and the cult of Mary see L.-E. Halkin 'La Mariologie d'Erasme' ARG 68 (1977) 32–54. Cf n75 below; 'The Shipwreck' n19; and the later colloquy 'The Sermon.'

32 For an example, see 'The Shipwreck' 355:28–31.

33 See 'The Shipwreck' n19 above.

34 On the wealth of the shrine at Walsingham see Dickinson 38–42, 59–61.

35 Since he had the keys (Matt 16:19; cf 'The Godly Feast' 177:3).

36 A common attribute of St Paul because, according to tradition, he was beheaded, or because he speaks of the sword of the Spirit (Eph 6:17) and of the word of God as a two-edged sword (Heb 4:12)

37 According to tradition Bartholomew, one of the twelve apostles, was martyred by being flayed alive. He is often portrayed holding a knife.

38 St William of Gellone, duke of Aquitaine (d c 812), who fought for Charlemagne against the Saracens. In 804 he founded a Benedictine monastery and afterwards became a monk. He was celebrated as the Carolingian model of warrior and monk.

39 Patron of soldiers. Like those of Barbara, Christopher, and some other popular saints, his name was removed from the liturgical calendar of the church in 1969, but he may still be venerated.

40 Fire and flames are associated with St Antony of Padua, but likewise with the Egyptian saint, signifying his fervour. It is sometimes said to be the bubonic plague, sometimes erysipelas or ergotism, against which his aid is sought (*Modus orandi Deum* LB V 1120C), or a symbol of the fire of hell, since St Antony suppressed the flames of sensuality that afflicted him. On Antony see also 'The Well-to-do Beggars' 475:6–9 and n43 and 'A Fish Diet' n328.

41 This date, 1 August 1524, is no certain clue to the date when the colloquy was written, but Allen has suggested that when Erasmus went from Basel on a visit to Burgundy in April of that year he may have journeyed via Mariastein (Ep 1440:4n). Whatever the date of composition, the date of the letter, 1 August 1524, is interesting in several respects. First, we have been told (624:13–14 above) that the letter has been in circulation for some time. Second, August 1524 was close to the date of iconoclastic activity in Zürich (June and July). Third, as Smith noted (*Key* 41), 1 August 1524 is the date of the letter (Ep 1476) dedicating the new edition (August–September 1524) of the *Colloquia* to Johann Erasmius Froben, son of the printer.

42 Virgin from the Rock] Editions before March 1533 have instead 'the blessed Virgin.' Cf n14 above.

43 Cf 'The Liar and the Man of Honour' 347:28–31.

44 The cathedral of Notre-Dame in Antwerp, admired particularly for its towering spire. See the frontispiece of Yale CWM 4, *Utopia*. More praises the building, and it was when he was coming from divine service there that he first met Raphael Hythloday (ibidem 48, 49).

45 A slip. Walsingham is in northern Norfolk (in the north-east) and about six miles from the sea.

46 'Regular' clergy lived according to a rule; secular priests did not. The Augustinian canons regular, who are meant here, lived by St Augustine's rule in a semi-monastic community. Erasmus belonged to this order. Secular canons took no vows. They were usually attached to a cathedral or collegiate church. Not all monks were priests but they lived by a rule and were claustrated; hence regular canons might be said to be 'midway' between monks and secular canons. Cf 'The Old Men's Chat' n59, 'The Well-to-do Beggars' n97, and 'Exorcism' n9.

47 The same jest occurs in Erasmus' letter to 'Grunnius'; Allen Ep 447:502–4 / CWE Ep 447:552–4.

48 *apodixin mathematicam*. See Gellius 17.5.5.

49 A bull of excommunication. See 'Faith' n3 above.

50 An error; half of its annual income came from endowments. See Dickinson 54.

51 William Lowthe, a character Erasmus must have remembered if he met him, and may have heard of even if he did not meet him. In August 1514, a month after the episcopal visitation, Prior Lowthe was removed from the office he had held since 1504. He had been an unworthy and even scandalous ruler, as the visitation records make abundantly clear (*Visitations of the Diocese of Norwich* ed A. Jessopp, Camden Society new series 43 [London 1888] 113–23, 146–8). He was accused by the brethren of keeping a fool whom he admitted to communion, of striking a field worker so hard that the man died, of concubinage, of misappropriation of jewellery, and of defiant refusal to reform. If Erasmus knew of Prior Lowthe, his memories of Walsingham, and therefore the account in this colloquy, may have been coloured by the recollection.

52 The conventual church

53 The Holy House with its little (about twenty-three by twelve feet) inner chapel, where the statue of the Virgin stood. See lines 33–4 below and Dickinson 95–105. Evidently the statue was the 'original attraction' of Walsingham and the reason for its subsequent fame. Records concerning the priory, shrine, and the excavations (map in Dickinson opposite 106 and photographs in appendix) have settled some but not all questions about the buildings; many uncertainties remain. H.M. Gillett *Walsingham and Its Shrine* (London 1934) is a briefer account of these topics and less satisfactory than Dickinson's, which I follow.

54 On this see Dickinson 101–2. Erasmus' visit may have coincided with the time when new windows were being provided for the building.

55 Perhaps an allusion to 'Oceanumque patrem rerum' in Virgil *Georgics* 4.382

56 'That church' refers to 'her own church,' mentioned a few lines earlier. The 'small chapel' (*sacellum angustum*) is the inner chapel (within the Holy House), containing the statue of the Virgin. See Dickinson 95–106; on the wooden platform 98–9. The Holy House was supposedly a copy of the Santa Casa at Loreto near Ancona in Italy. That house, believed by the devout to be the home in Nazareth where Mary received the Annunciation, was moved miraculously to Illyria and again to Italy, according to a late medieval legend, and became a favourite resort of pilgrims; on the legend see C.U.J. Chevalier *Notre Dame de Lorette* (Paris 1906). A ballad printed c 1496 says that the chapel of Our Lady at Walsingham was first intended for the site, near the east end of the conventual church, where the chapel of St Laurence later stood (Dickinson 83, 91–2, 95), but the timbers were removed by angels to its known site, that is, the one familiar in Erasmus' time (Dickinson 55, 95; he reprints the ballad 124–30).

In 1523 Erasmus had written a mass for Our Lady of Loreto at the request
of a friend. It was so pleasing to the bishop of Besançon that he granted
forty days' remission of penance to persons who used it. See CWE 85–6 361–3,
719–21 no 133 / Reedijk *Poems of Erasmus* 388–90 Appendix 1-6; Allen Ep 1391
introduction; Nati H. Krivatsy 'Erasmus and His Mass for the Virgin of Loreto'
Erasmus in English 4 (1972) 2. For the entire liturgy see LB V 1327A–1336B.
Erasmus does not refer there to the miraculous moving of the house.

57 Nothing is actually known of Andrew the apostle except what is written in the
Gospels, but many legends about him exist. His supposed remains, once in
Constantinople, were brought to Amalfi in the thirteenth century. Oil from the
sepulchre of St Andrew is mentioned in the *Golden Legend* (30 November).
St Catherine of Alexandria, martyr, was buried at Mt Sinai. On the oil at her
tomb see the *Golden Legend* (25 November).

58 An allusion to the doctrine, long held but not defined authoritatively until 1950,
of the Assumption of Mary: that upon completion of her earthly life, her soul
and body were received into heaven

59 Ovid *Amores* 1.8.92

60 *mystagogi*, guides who conduct visitors through sacred places

61 In More's *Dialogue Concerning Heresies* the Messenger says he heard a preacher
at St Paul's in London declare that 'our lady was a vyrgyn and yet at her
pylgrymages be made many a foule metynge' (Yale CWM 6 part 1 100).

62 The Articles of Inquiry relating to Walsingham asked whether the keepers
of the relics there put out tables for offerings as though a contribution was
required or to shame visitors into giving (Nichols *Pilgrimages* 210 article 6). It is
not impossible that this question, like others in the articles, was suggested by
Erasmus' colloquy.

63 Some of the canons accused Prior Lowthe of misappropriating offerings
and other conventual property (*Norwich Visitations* [n51 above] 114, 115, 117,
119).

64 Afterwards called the 'Knight's Door'; see Dickinson 57, 107. There is a drawing
of the gateway and door in Nichols *Pilgrimages* facing page 84.

65 The Articles of Inquiry mention the knight (Nichols *Pilgrimages* 211 article
14), and the story is related 'from an old manuscript' in Francis Blomefield's
History of Norfolk 5 vols (Fersfield and Norwich 1739–75) v 833–9; or see Nichols
Pilgrimages 82–4. Erasmus is quoted on the adventure of the knight and on the
sites of the Holy House and the statue (Blomefield v 838, 839).

66 *caprae*, feminine, but Pliny assures us that all goats have beards (*Naturalis
historia* 8.203–4).

67 This was the chapel of St Laurence, to the east of the church and close to two
wells that still exist (see Dickinson plates 2, 3b, 4b). The chapel of St Laurence
is thought to have been on the original site of the chapel of Our Lady. On the
wells see Dickinson 12, 83, 91–3; on the miraculous removal of the chapel of
Our Lady, n56 above.

68 One of the charges against Nicholas White of Rye, a suspected heretic, in 1529,
who was critical of pilgrimages, was that he spoke against the relic of St Peter's
finger. He abjured (Foxe *Acts and Monuments* v 28).

69 Some sort of shed over the wells, apparently, but Erasmus' remark that it had
been brought there suddenly from far away suggests confusion with the story
about the miraculous removal of the Holy House to its new position.

70 The bearskin was also known to the Articles of Inquiry (Nichols *Pilgrimages* 211 article 14).

71 Portions of the heavenly milk, the blood of Christ, and the cross on which he suffered were among the most precious and famous of all the many relics in Christendom, in England as in other lands, and legends about them have common characteristics. Erasmus' scepticism about the authenticity of relics and his satire of abuses of them are plain to see, especially in this colloquy. Cf 'The Shipwreck' 355:30–1; 'Faith' 427:14–15; 'The Exorcism' 540:2–4. When criticized by opponents for some of the passages on relics, including those in 'A Pilgrimage,' he defends himself on both literary and ethical grounds. That he convinced his critics is unlikely. On the milk see Dickinson 57.

The relic of the Blood of Hailes in Gloucester was undoubtedly known to Erasmus, though there is no evidence that he ever saw it. St Thomas Aquinas held that all the particles of the sacred blood shed by Christ in the passion were reassumed by him at his resurrection, and that the blood kept in some churches as relics must have flowed from some image (*Summa theologiae* III q 54 art 3 [2 in some editions]). Veneration of the relic at Hailes was evidently unaffected by such views. In 1538, however, the king's commissioners who examined the relic reported that it was spurious and not blood at all. Accordingly the bishop of Rochester, John Hilsey (successor to Fisher), showed the 'blood' in a sermon at Paul's Cross in November 1538, affirming that it was a false relic (Nichols *Pilgrimages* 89).

The Blood of Hailes was said to have been brought to England from Germany.

72 The same remark occurs in Erasmus' note on Matt 23:5 (LB VI 118E). Cf 'The Shipwreck' 355:30–1 above and an interesting passage in Calvin's *Traicté des reliques*, which may owe something to Erasmus' lines. He says if all the supposed pieces of the cross that exist were collected, 'il y en auroit la charge d'un bon grand bateau' (Editions Bossard [Paris 1921] 113). Reading and Bury St Edmund's were two other of the many places in England claiming to own relics of the cross.

The officials who investigated the monasteries reported that at Walsingham 'was seen much superstition in feigned relics and miracles' (LP X no 364 page 143). This may be so, but we must remember that Cromwell's agents were not disinterested civil servants and not likely to underestimate anything their employer could use against the monasteries. The records of episcopal visitations may be more reliable evidence of the internal condition of English monasteries.

73 The Blessed Sacrament

74 The relic of the Virgin's milk had been at Walsingham since at least 1300 (Dickinson 39–40). Purporting to come from a grotto in Bethlehem, where Friar Felix Fabri (*Friar Felix at Large* 148) and William Wey (*Itineraries* 52), among others, claimed to have seen it, the relic was widely distributed. Arnold von Harff saw it in three churches in Rome (pages 21, 30, and 33 of his account; on these three travellers see 'Rash Vows' n3). It seems to have been a standard item in large collections; for example the famous one of Frederick the Wise in the castle church at Wittenberg (*Ablass und Reliquienverehrung an der Schlosskirche zu Wittenberg* ed P. Kalkoff [1907] 61). Ogygius' remark that the relic at Walsingham looked like powdered chalk is probably reliable. According

to the *Chronicle* of Charles Wriothesley (d 1562) a relic of the milk in St Paul's, London, was found to be 'but a peece of chalke' (ed W.D. Hamilton, Camden Society new series 11 [London 1875] 31. The Articles of Inquiry concerning Walsingham asked whether the relic was liquid or whether water was added to it when it began to dry up (Nichols *Pilgrimages* 212 articles 18–19).

Some writers think Erasmus has 'put the worst interpretation on the facts' (Dickinson 56). Perhaps he did sometimes, but he was not alone in doing so, and with regard to many relics he was invincibly sceptical – not without reason. What would Jerome say if he saw the milk of Mary displayed here and there for gain and honoured almost as much as the Blessed Sacrament (*Annotationes in Novum Testamentum* LB VI 118E)? See also *De esu carnium* LB IX 1200C. Abuses and frauds were inevitable. The Fourth Lateran Council of 1215 had denounced deceptive relics (canon 62; Tanner I 263), but with little effect.

On his travels in western Europe in 1517–18, the Italian canonist Antonio de Beatis saw a vast number of relics in the numerous churches he visited. He cannot tell which relics are genuine and which are not, but he does not allow this fact to affect his belief in the articles of the faith. 'To believe is godly, and relics may be venerated, with due caution as to their authenticity.' Clergy have been remiss in investigating relics and permitting questionable ones to be displayed, he adds, but the abuse is so old that it must be tolerated, since there is so much vested interest – by cities, people, churches, sanctuaries – in them (*Travel Journal* 105, 121, 152, 153).

75 For other addresses to the Virgin in this colloquy see 634:11–16 and 636:30–1 and n96. Compositions by Erasmus, published elsewhere, in praise of the virgin are: 1/ *Paean divae Mariae* (CWE 85–6 276–99, 646–63 no 110 / Reedijk *Poems of Erasmus* 174–86 no 19 / LB VIII 572B–577E); 2/ *Paean Virgini Matri dicendus* written for his patroness Anne of Veere (LB V 1227E–1234C); 3/ an *Obsecratio ad Virginem Mariam in rebus adversis* (LB V 1233E–1240A); 4/ a mass for Our Lady of Loreto, with sermon added in the second edition (*Liturgia Virginis Matris* LB V 1327A–1330B; the sequence also in CWE 85–6 361–3, 719–21 no 133 / Reedijk *Poems of Erasmus* 388–90 Appendix 1-6); 5/ a prayer in *Precationes* (LB V 1200A–D); 6/ *Virginis et martyris comparatio*, written by request of nuns in Cologne (LB V 589A–600B; see Allen Ep 1346 introduction).

76 of dovelike simplicity] Added in the September 1531 edition in place of 'rational'

77 *tabellam*. In *Ecclesiastes* it means a collection plate or box in church (LB V 843C).

78 A Cambridge scholar who worked with Erasmus; later provost of Eton and bishop of Carlisle. He was a valued friend and correspondent. See Allen Ep 1656 introduction and CEBR.

79 As did the Articles of Inquiry: 'Item, what probacion or argument have they to shewe that the same are trewe reliques?' (Nichols *Pilgrimages* 210 article 5)

80 priest] *hierophanta*; in editions before September 1531 *mystagogus*

81 *illis minoribus*. A minor canon of a cathedral chapter was one who did not yet have a benefice (a share in the chapter's revenues), but Walsingham had no cathedral. None of the canons in the list printed by Dickinson 135–40 is termed 'minor.' The sixteenth-century texts of this passage that I have checked print *minoribus*, but two important seventeenth-century editions (Schrevelius 1693, first issued 1655, and Rabus 1693) capitalize the word: 'one of the

Minorites,' that is, Franciscans. There was a Franciscan friary on the outskirts of Walsingham, but the Augustinian canons of the priory church had charge of the shrine. It is inconceivable that they would have permitted a member of another order to serve there. Moreover Ogygius has said earlier that in the inner sanctum 'a canon stands by the altar' (630:13–14). Unless we evade the question and translate with Nichols (*Pilgrimages* 23) 'one of the inferior members of the convent,' we are left with either 'minor canons' or Minorites.' Clearly Erasmus means a canon.

82 *Iliad* 15.280; *Adagia* I viii 70

83 Cf 'The Epicurean' 1075:40–1076:2.

84 *Adagia* II i 54; see 'The Godly Feast' n22.

85 Erasmus had good eyesight and boasted in 1530 that he had never worn spectacles (Allen Ep 2275:25–8).

86 The source or sources of this account are unknown. Much of it may be Erasmus' invention, but it has some particulars found in other tales of saints or relics; for instance in traditions about how the Holy Blood came to Hailes.

87 King of Lydia, fabled for riches; *Adagia* I vi 74

88 Notre-Dame

89 This church of the patron saint of Paris was well known to Erasmus, who had lived nearby. In 1497 he wrote that he owed his recovery from a quartan fever to her intervention (Ep 50) and long afterwards wrote a poem of thanksgiving in her honour; it is also a eulogy of Paris. See CWE 85–6 168–77, 556–64 no 88 / Reedijk *Poems of Erasmus* 350–5 no 131). Ep 50 also describes briefly how the shrine of St Geneviève was carried in procession when the city invoked her aid during floods. See J.-C. Margolin 'Paris through a Gothic Window' in *Res publica litterarum: Studies in the Classical Tradition* (University of Kansas) 1 (1978) 207–8. On regular canons see n46 above.

90 See 'Rash Vows' n20.

91 *ex suo dimenso*, as in Terence *Phormio* 42

92 In Greek mythology the fifty daughters of Danaus who married the fifty sons of Aegyptus. All but one of the brides murdered their husbands on their wedding night. For this deed they were condemned to spend eternity in Hades filling a jar having holes in the bottom. See Aeschylus *Suppliants*.

93 Although the guilt of mortal sin and eternal punishment incurred thereby are remitted by divine grace when the sinner is truly repentant, he must still pay the temporal punishment for sin, in this life or in the place or state called purgatory, before being received into heaven. This doctrine, inferred from various biblical texts (the earliest are 1 Cor 3:11–15 and 2 Macc 12:39–45), was undefined and imprecise until Peter Lombard, then Thomas Aquinas and other scholastic theologians, refined it. A study by Jacques le Goff, *La Naissance du Purgatoire* (Paris 1981) trans A. Goldhammer *The Birth of Purgatory* (Chicago 1984) argues that the doctrine emerged not in the earlier years of the twelfth century, as is generally thought, but towards the end. However that may be, beliefs about purgatory became immensely influential on the religious attitudes and behaviour of Christians. Dante's *Purgatorio* remains the most imaginative expression of the punishments and promises of purgatory: promises, because however long and severe the necessary punishments there,

ultimate salvation is assured. Moving beyond Dante's vision, we meet the legalism and paradoxes and abuses of the penitential system, the scandals about indulgences and pardoners, and all the denunciations and defences of the system prominent in disputes during the Reformation era.

Temporal punishments due even for sins forgiven could be remitted to sincere penitents by partial (expressed in terms of time, so many days or years) or plenary (fully remitted, if God wills) indulgences. Many reformers before Luther had deplored scandalous abuses of indulgences; his protests in 1517 were merely the most dramatic. After a few years indulgences ceased to be a leading issue, but purgatory, because of its connection with indulgences and prayers for the dead, presented a difficulty for the more radical reformers. In England, for instance, Tyndale, Frith, and Latimer concluded that monasticism, indulgences, and purgatory were all corrupt and vain superstitions. More described purgatory with passionate and terrifying eloquence in his *Supplication of Souls* (1529); see for example Yale CWM 7 225. Erasmus satirized foolish confidence in indulgences when sincere repentance and amendment of life are urgently needed (see 'Rash Vows,' 'The Shipwreck,' and 'The Usefulness of the *Colloquies'* 1100:10–19).

The answer to Menedemus' question 'Are there days even in the underworld?' is yes, but the nature of the time granted by indulgences has never been defined. Theologians differed on the question. One explanation held that the days and years remitted by indulgences correspond to the length of time one would need to satisfy canonical penance. Scripture does not tell us about such matters. When it speaks of time and the Last Judgment, it accommodates the language to our capacities (*Explanatio symboli* LB V 1165E–F). In *Moriae encomium*, Folly scoffs at those who measure time in purgatory by centuries, years, months, days, hours as if from a mathematical table and without error (LB IV 444A / ASD IV-2 122:970–3 / CWE 27 114). That 'the grant is inexhaustible' is due to the church's 'treasury of merits,' the limitless store of the merits of Christ. The doctrine is stated in the bull *Unigenitus* of Clement VI (1343; text in Denzinger-Schönmetzer *Enchiridion symbolorum* 301 nos 1025–7).

When one is conscious that death is near, Erasmus advises, there is need of having appropriate texts of Scripture at hand, as Cornelius does in 'The Funeral' (776:30–2, 777:37–778:7, 779:2–6). With hope strengthened by these, purgatory will not terrify. Purchased pardons will not avail; prayers are more efficacious, and best of all is total submission to the divine mercy. These are the waters that cool the fires of purgatory (*De praeparatione ad mortem* LB V 1316E–1317A). Nowadays whoever doubts the pope's power over purgatory is burned for a heretic (*Apologia adversus monachos* LB IX 1057D). Erasmus implies doubt when he writes 'Would that [the pope] really could free souls from the punishments of purgatory!' (*Ratio verae theologiae* LB V 91A / Holborn 207:1–2; this remark was added in the 1522 edition). 'Would . . . could' (*Utinam . . . possit*) here conveys the same degree of dubiety as *Utinam . . . sit* in 'Faith,' where the reply to Aulus' 'What if God is in his vicar?' is 'I wish he may be' (422:10–11). The Council of Trent's decree concerning purgatory reaffirms the received doctrine but advises that the more difficult and subtle questions should be avoided in preaching to the uneducated (session 25 [1563]; Tanner II 774).

94 Bernard of Clairvaux (d 1153); see 'The Old Men's Chat' 67. See Murillo's
painting *The Vision of St Bernard* or *St Bernard Supplicating the Virgin* (c 1660). In
one of his visions he was thus rewarded for his writings and his devotion to Mary.
The painting is no 19 page 93 in *Bartolomé Murillo 1617–1682*, the catalogue of a
1982 Murillo exhibition in London issued by Weidenfeld and Nicolson. In T.F.
Crane's edition of *Liber de miraculis sanctae Dei genetricis Mariae* ('The Shipwreck'
n19) is a legend of a monk who, when thought to be dying, was revived by the
Virgin's milk (chapter 30 pages 36–8). See also *The 'Stella Maris' of John of Garland*
ed Evelyn Fay Wilson (Cambridge, Mass 1946) 155–6 / PL 156 1044B–1047A.

95 Flowing with honey instead of milk

96 Erasmus' votive offering was a poem of fourteen lines, in Greek, addressed to
the Virgin; it was first printed in the 1515 edition of his *Lucubrationes*. See CWE
85–6 120–3, 520–1 no 51 / Reedijk *Poems of Erasmus* 303 no 92.

97 The subprior (because he is posterior to the prior); as at 637:10, 'protos-hysteros'
is Greek in the original. For priors and subpriors of Walsingham see Dickinson
131–40.
Rabelais has a characteristic jest about 'prior' and 'posterior' in *Gargantua and
Pantagruel* 1.44 that he may have owed to this passage.

98 'Abbot' is from Syriac, which is here identified loosely with Hebrew.

99 *Papa, abbas, caritatis cognomina sunt, non potestatis* ' "Pope" and "abbot" are titles
that express charity, not power' (*Enchiridion* LB V 49B / Holborn 107:15–16 /
CWE 66 101).

100 Certain abbots were exempt from episcopal jurisdiction but had episcopal
insignia, including staff and mitre, and some had as well jurisdiction
comparable to that of bishops. Ogygius' remark implies either that the prior or
provost of Walsingham does not have sufficient sanctity to deserve the title of
abbot, or that the expense of obtaining the title and prerogatives of an abbey
would be too great. In the late fourteenth century a controversy resulted from
a Walsingham prior's attempt to become abbot (Dickinson 28–30). But Erasmus
could hardly have known of that.

101 Greek in the original. A figure denoting things said in reverse order: 'the tail
wags the dog,' 'the cart before the horse'; *Adagia* v i 30. If here synonymous with
'posterior prior,' it implies also that the subprior is a lackbrain or simpleton.

102 At the probable date of Erasmus' visit the subprior was Edmund Warham;
Norwich Visitations (n51 above) 114. Nothing is known of him except that he,
like other canons, complained about the prior, Lowthe, during the episcopal
visitation of July 1514. On Lowthe see the same note.

103 See 'The Apotheosis of Reuchlin' 250:13–14.

104 Abstention from sexual intercourse in the night before major feast days or
receiving holy communion was recommended, but whether it was obligatory is
uncertain. Cf CWE Ep 1301:129–34, citing St Gregory Ep 64 PL 77 1196, and for
other patristic and medieval opinions see Gratian *Decretum* part 2 c 33 q 4 c 7
(Friedberg I 1248–9). The relic Menedemus is allowed to see is so sacred that he
must be pure in every respect to be worthy of such a privilege.

105 River in Spain and Portugal, famous for its golden sands

106 At the entrance of the cathedral of Notre-Dame in Paris. See 'The Shipwreck'
n29. For 'wagon-load or colossus' see *Adagia* III ii 5 and III ii 69.

107 The crapaudine, toadstone, or bufonite

108 See 'The Exorcism' 535:26–536:6 and n6.

109 On magnets see *Adagia* I vii 56, where Erasmus cites Pliny *Naturalis historia* 36.126–30; otherwise, unless noted, the examples in this paragraph are borrowed from 37.187–91. For Erasmus' estimates and uses of Pliny, especially in *Adagia* and *Parabolae*, see Allen Ep 1544, Erasmus' preface to a 1525 Froben edition of the *Naturalis historia*. On Pliny in the Renaissance consult George Sarton *The Appreciation of Ancient and Medieval Science during the Renaissance* (Philadelphia 1955) 78–85 and Charles G. Nauert Jr 'Humanists, Scientists, and Pliny' in *American Historical Review* 84 (1979) 72–85. Theophrastus *De lapidibus*, Isidore *Etymologiae*, and the medieval *Liber de gemmis* by Marbodus (PL 171 1737–70) were other standard sources of inherited lore on stones. Useful studies include Joan Evans *Magical Jewels of the Middle Ages and Renaissance* (Oxford 1972); Thorndike *Magic and Experimental Science* VI 298–324; Guy de Tervarent *Attributs et symboles dans l'art profane 1459–1600: dictionnaire d'un langage perdu* (Geneva 1958; supplement and index 1964). Since identification of some stones in Erasmus' catalogue is uncertain, their classical names are printed and italicized here. Names of less doubtful stones are translated.

110 Thunderstone (Pliny *Naturalis historia* 37.132, 134). It deterred storms and aided voyagers, according to a sixteenth-century handbook for travellers (Thorndike *Magic and Experimental Science* VI 614). S.H. Ball in *Scientific Monthly* 47 (1938) says it is not known what *ceraunia* was.

111 Pliny *Naturalis historia* 34.94. Said to be composed of copper and gold; of fiery colour. Cf CWE 85–6 108, 513 no 50:21 / Reedijk *Poems of Erasmus* 229 no 34:21.

112 On the colour of emeralds from Cyprus, see Pliny *Naturalis historia* 37.66. Cf *Adagia* III iv 30. Some writers thought emeralds, if swallowed, were protection against poison (Thorndike *Magic and Experimental Science* VI 311, 315).

113 On anthracites see also Pliny *Naturalis historia* 37.99 and *Parabolae* LB I 598E / CWE 23 222:34–9.

114 *aetites*, thought to be useful in childbirth (Pliny *Naturalis historia* 36.151); *Adagia* III vii 1 LB II 881D, and see 'Patterns' n66.

115 *chelidonia*. The odd statement that this stone has the image of an asp appears to be due to a textual confusion. Pliny, followed by Erasmus, says 'taos has the image of a peacock,' adding immediately (in words omitted by Erasmus) 'and a stone which I find bearing the name "timictonia" similarly resembles an asp in colour' (*Naturalis historia* Loeb Classical Library 10 vols [London and Cambridge, Mass 1949–62] x tr D.E. Eichholz [1962] 317). Possibly Erasmus when writing 'swallowstone' then added 'asp' from Pliny's remark in 37.187. Pliny mentions swallowstones (*chelidoniae*) in 37.155 but does not refer there to an asp. The *Castigationes Plinianae* of Ermolao Barbaro (Rome 1493), after quoting Pliny's *aspidi quam vocari timictoniam invenio* (sig s2 verso) then says: *Legendum forte chelidoniam ex Galeno, qui unum genus aspidis ita nominat* 'Perhaps we should read "swallowstone" with Galen, who names this as one kind of asp.' The 1525 Froben Pliny prints *chelidoniam*. Modern editions have *timictoniam*. The only occurrence of this word known to the *Oxford Latin Dictionary* ed P.G.W. Clare (Oxford 1982) is in Pliny 37.187. It is some kind of gem, but what kind is unexplained.

116 On the cantharid beetle see *Parabolae* LB I 580F and 586E / CWE 23 182:30–3, 196:21–3. Cf 'The Poetic Feast' n16.

117 The toad was a symbol of evil but helpless before the purity of the Virgin. In legend the toad identifies or intensifies the ugliness of sin. A story in Bishop Lucas of Tuy's *De altera vita* 3.15 (thirteenth century) tells how some heretics in Burgundy were being burned at the stake. Suddenly a monstrous toad appeared and jumped into the flames. 'One of the heretics, who was reported to be their bishop, had fallen on his back in the fire. The toad took his place on this man's face and in the sight of all ate out the heretic's tongue. By the next day his whole body, except his bones, had been turned into disgusting toads, which could not be counted for their great number ... God omnipotent surely wished to show through the most unseemly and filthiest of animals, how foul and infamous are the teachings of heretics' (*Translations and Reprints from the Original Sources of European History* III no 6 [Philadelphia 1897] 6–7; reprinted in *Readings in European History* ed James Harvey Robinson, 2 vols [Boston 1904] I 365). For another anecdote about a toad see the colloquy 'Sympathy' 1041:10–22.

118 See The Well-to-do Beggars' n44

119 *numero dixisti; Adagia* III vii 58. On the comment and response see *Adagia* II i 12.

120 One of the gold and silver statues was that of Henry VII. It was given in his lifetime. His will left instructions for a similar statue to be placed in the shrine of St Thomas of Canterbury (Dickinson 42; Nichols *Pilgrimages* 108–9).

121 A decade after this colloquy was printed, and a year or two before publication of the English translation (introduction 620 above), the English government, through a commission reporting to Cromwell, began visiting the smaller monasteries to examine their condition and management and made an inventory of their revenues, the *Valor ecclesiasticus*. As a consequence the monasteries and convents were closed and the monks pensioned off. In 1538–9 it was the turn of the larger monasteries and priories, including Walsingham and Christ Church Canterbury. For texts of the Acts of Parliament on dissolution of the smaller monasteries (1536) and of the larger ones (1539), see Gee and Hardy (introduction 620 above) 257–68, 281–302.

The commissioners appointed by Cromwell, who was now vicar-general of ecclesiastical affairs, reported enough evidence of sloth, immorality, and corruption, and the *Valor ecclesiasticus* enough impressive evidence of the wealth of religious houses, to give the government excuse to seize the monastic properties, confiscate their wealth, and get rid of monasticism. The famous statue of the Virgin of Walsingham was taken to London and destroyed (1538). Of many accounts of these events the best introduction for the general reader is G.W.O. Woodward *The Dissolution of the Monasteries* (London 1966; New York 1967), but Knowles ROE III is the most comprehensive work on English religious houses of that era; part 3 (195–417) deals with the suppression. Philip Hughes *The Reformation in England* I (London 1950) and G. Baskerville *English Monks and the Suppression of the Monasteries* (London 1937) are readable narratives written from different points of view. On Walsingham alone see Dickinson 59–68. Woodward 59–67 prints selections from pertinent documents. For additional legal texts besides those in Gee and Hardy see J.R. Tanner *Tudor Constitutional Documents, A.D. 1485–1603, with an Historical Commentary* (Cambridge 1922); G.R. Elton *The Tudor Constitution: Documents and Commentary* (Cambridge

1960; 2nd ed Cambridge 1982); Hughes and Larkin *Tudor Royal Proclamations* (introduction 620 above). On the fate of the monks and friars and buildings see Woodward 139–50 and Knowles ROE III 383–417.

122 637:29–39 above

123 The common practice; cf *Romeo and Juliet* 1.2.56–8.

124 On hellebore see 'The Godly Feast' n63.

125 In ecclesiastical usage, an archbishop's see. Of many books on the history of Canterbury cathedral, two of the most useful older ones are A.P. Stanley *Historical Memorials of Canterbury* (London 1854; 11th ed 1912); and C. Eveleigh Woodruff and William Danks *Memorials of the Cathedral and Priory of Christ in Canterbury* (London 1912). For the architectural history of the cathedral see Robert Willis *The Architectural History of Canterbury Cathedral* (London 1845) and a recent work with the same title by Francis Woodman (London 1981).

126 Augustine of Canterbury, who arrived in England in 597 and founded this monastery a year or so later. It was dedicated to Sts Peter and Paul and nearly four centuries later rededicated to Peter and Paul and Augustine.

127 The second monastery was the priory of Christ Church, but Erasmus' statement that the church (cathedral, that is) was dedicated to St Thomas is ambiguous. It was dedicated to Christ. Its intimate association with St Thomas Becket led Erasmus into error here, unless he was thinking of the Trinity chapel (see n156 below) alone and not of the cathedral.

128 The archbishop's lodgings were near the west end of the cathedral. In later centuries the principal residence of archbishops of Canterbury was, and is, Lambeth Palace, London.

129 See 645:15 below.

130 There are three towers, two at the west end and the great central tower, the 'Bell Harry' tower as it was called, built between 1495 and 1503.

131 Erasmus' (or the compositor's) rather fanciful names for William de Tracy, Richard le Breton, and Reginald Fitzurse. The fourth knight, Hugh de Morville, he does not seem to have known of, for in his brief account in *Lingua* of Becket's murder (LB IV 709C / ASD IV-1A 111:795–803 / CWE 29 343) he refers to three murderers, just as here he speaks of three statues.

132 Many legends about the assassins were current; for example, that wherever they went they had wind and weather against them. The *Golden Legend* (29 December) describes some of their torments; and see Nichols *Pilgrimages* 113.

133 At the west end

134 Five editions of a translation into English of the apocryphal *Gospel of Nicodemus* or *Acta Pilati* were printed between 1507 and 1518 (see STC), but the chained copy seen by Erasmus may have been a bound codex rather than a printed book.

135 Gates and grille excluded lay people from the upper part of the choir (Woodruff and Danks [n125 above] 274).

136 Ogygius is being led to the scene of the martyrdom in the north-west transept.

137 Known as the 'altar of the sword point.' See next note.

138 The sensational murder of Becket in Canterbury cathedral, in the semi-darkness of late afternoon on 29 December 1170, was one of the most fully recorded events of medieval history. At least four of the early accounts come from eyewitnesses. On these and other important sources see David Knowles

'Archbishop Thomas Becket: A Character Study' *Proceedings of the British Academy* 35 (1949) 177–205, reprinted in his *The Historian and Character* (Cambridge 1963) 98–128. For a longer study of Becket's life and death at Canterbury see Stanley *Memorials* (n125 above). The most valuable biography is Frank Barlow *Thomas Becket* (Berkeley and Los Angeles 1986). Basic documents for Becket's career are collected in J.C. Robertson and J.B. Sheppard *Materials for the History of Thomas Becket* Public Record Office: Rolls Series 67, 7 vols (London 1875–85). Erasmus may have seen one or more of the narratives, for example John of Salisbury's. In *Lingua* he quotes or paraphrases Henry ii's wrathful outburst against the archbishop for daring to excommunicate some of his supporters, including two bishops (LB v 709C / ASD IV-1A 111:795–801 / CWE 29 343). This fit of rage prompted the four courtiers to hasten to Canterbury and confront Becket. Erasmus might easily have heard other stories about Becket's history from the reigning archbishop (his friend and patron Warham), Colet, and More. Some things he recalls and relates in the colloquy seem to derive from the kind of patter common to guides.

The spot (now known as the Martyrdom) in the north-west transept where Becket was killed is close to the Lady Chapel and to the stairway leading to the aisle of the north choir, where the monks were singing Vespers. The archbishop started to ascend the stairs but turned back when he heard or saw his pursuers. The altar to which Erasmus refers was not there in Becket's time, but the point of the sword that broke off after a tremendous stroke by one of the assailants, le Breton, which severed the crown of the archbishop's head, was found by the monks and preserved as a relic, enshrined in another altar placed in this area. This 'altar of the sword point,' as it was called, disappeared after the suppression of monasteries in 1538. That Becket's brain was 'smashed ... to make death come more quickly' is not Erasmus' invention but is in one of the early reports.

139 Some hours after the murder, during the night, the monks put the archbishop's corpse on a bier, which they then placed before the high altar. Within the next day or two they dressed the body in full archiepiscopal vestments and laid it in a marble sarcophagus (intended for some other burial), which they buried in the crypt of the Trinity chapel, at the east end of the cathedral.

140 The identification is doubtful. 'More probably the new relic of St Dunstan, which had recently been enclosed in a mitred bust of silver, since there is no other record of any part of St Thomas' head being kept in the crypt' (Woodruff and Danks [n125 above] 275; and see *Inventories of Christ Church Canterbury* ed J.W. Wickham Legg and W.H. St John Hope [Westminster 1902] 41, 123n). When St Dunstan's tomb was opened in 1508 the prior had a reliquary made, in the shape of a human head, for that saint's skull (Woodruff and Danks 213). The *Chronicle* of Charles Wriothesley (n74 above), recording the destruction of the shrine, removal of the treasures, and burning of the bones of St Thomas in September 1538, adds: 'They found his head hole with the bones, which had a wounde in the skull, for the monkes had closed another skull in silver richly, for people to offer to, which they sayd was St. Thomas skull, so that nowe the abuse was openly knowne that they had used many yeres afore' (86–7). Stow says it was in the shrine (see n168 below). John Gerard, the Elizabethan Jesuit, writes c 1594: 'About the same time, also, I was given a silver head of

St. Thomas of Canterbury, and his mitre studded with precious stones. The head is small and of no great value in itself, but it is quite a treasure because it contains a piece of the saint's skull. It is about the breadth of two gold crowns and it is thought to be the piece that was chipped off when he was so wickedly slain' (*John Gerard: The Autobiography of an Elizabethan* trans Philip Caraman [London 1951] 50).

141 Acre (Akka) is a town on the coast of Palestine. According to a medieval story, long circulated, Becket's mother was a Saracen.

142 It was seen by Leo of Rozmital in 1466 (*Travels* 44). Whether the relics shown to Erasmus three and a half centuries later were authentic is of course impossible to say. What is certain is that very soon after the murder, while Becket's body was lying where he fell, people from the neighbourhood were collecting his blood and pieces of his bloody clothing. The monks discovered, with surprise, that he wore many layers of clothing. His hair shirt and drawers were covered with lice and vermin. Long before Thomas Becket was officially canonized in 1173, relics of his blood were credited with miraculous power. On the cult of St Thomas, which became celebrated throughout Christendom, see Barlow *Becket* (n138 above) 264–72.

143 To the great treasury near the high altar. As one would expect, Canterbury possessed an amazing number of relics. They are listed in Wickham Legg and St John Hope *Inventories of Christ Church Canterbury* (n140 above) 41–97 and passim. Among them were Aaron's rod, a portion of the table used at the Last Supper, many pieces of the true cross, a piece of the stone on which Christ stood as he ascended to heaven, and some of the clay from which God made Adam.

144 Including part of an arm of St Jerome, which unfortunately Erasmus failed to see

145 That Pullus ('colt') is Colet cannot be doubted. See Allen Ep 1211:327n. In that letter Erasmus says he and Colet went on pilgrimage together, and in *Modus orandi Deum* (1524) that Colet was with him at Canterbury when they were invited to venerate some mean relics of St Thomas (LB V 1119F–1120A; see 647:8–21, 648:15–31 below). In an earlier colloquy, 'The Exorcism,' Erasmus puns on *pullus* when he apparently intends John Colt, More's father-in-law. With that identification there are some difficulties (see the introduction 531–2), but not with the one here.

146 'Gratian did not shrink from the teachings of Wyclif' Erasmus asserts when defending what he wrote in the present colloquy about relics (*Apologia adversus rhapsodias Alberti Pii* LB IX 1161D). Colet was not a follower of Wyclif or a Lollard, yet some of his convictions about the evils of pilgrimages and other ecclesiastical abuses, including clerical cupidity, were similar to Wyclif's. It is not surprising that some reputed heretics and Lollards thought well of Colet. See A.G. Dickens *The English Reformation* (London 1964) 26–8. Colet read heretical books, according to Erasmus, thinking he might learn something even from them (Allen Ep 1211:516–7 / CWE Ep 1211:561–2). He was once charged with heresy by the bishop of London, Fitzjames, but the charges were dismissed by intervention of Archbishop Warham. One of the accusations was that Colet had spoken against adoration of images (Allen Ep 1211:472–80, 538–44 / CWE Ep 1211:513–22, 585–91).

In the theological controversies of Erasmus' age the names of Wyclif and
Hus were commonly associated, not without reason. Hus was regarded as
a progenitor of Lutheran heresy. The flat statement of Ogygius (the voice
of Erasmus in this passage) in 1526 that Colet had read Wyclif would have
implied to some readers who detested Hus and Luther that Colet was not
beyond suspicion of unorthodoxy. Whether Erasmus intended any such
implication is quite a different question, but his 'I don't think so' is significantly
ambiguous.

Of Erasmus' own opinions of Wyclif's teachings we can only surmise that on
such subjects as relics, clerical corruption, and pilgrimages he concurred, but
he did not have to read Wyclif to learn about such matters. He declared in
1524 that he had never read either Wycliffite or Hussite books (*Apologiae contra
Stunicam* LB IX 383D), but he often couples Wyclif with Hus as heretics. Writing
to Adrian VI in 1523 on methods of suppressing Lutherans, he warns that
the use of force did not succeed in extinguishing the Wycliffites in England
(Allen Ep 1352:153–6 / CWE Ep 1352:173–77; similarly Allen Epp 1721:66–80,
from 1526, and 2136:154–72, from 1529). He was well aware of the abhorrence
of Wyclif and Wycliffites felt by More, Tunstall, and other English friends.
Tunstall denounces Wycliffites (Lollards) vigorously in a letter of June 1523
(Allen Ep 1367:62–84 / CWE Ep 1367:70–93). In his reply Erasmus comments
on Lutherans and Anabaptists but does not mention Wyclif or Wycliffites (Ep
1369).

On later Lollardy and English nonconformity see also Anne Hudson *The
Premature Reformation* (Oxford 1988); Margaret Aston *Lollards and Reformers*
(London 1985).

147 The high altar

148 In the vaulted chamber under the steps leading to the archbishop's throne

149 On Midas see *Adagia* I vi 24; on Croesus, I vi 74 (as at n87 above).

150 'Now shall the sight of such riches as are shewed at St Thomas's shrine, or at
Walsingham, move a man to love the commandments of God better, and to
desire to be loosed from his flesh and to be with God; or shall it not rather
make his poor heart sigh, because he hath no such at home, and to wish part of
it in another place?' (Tyndale *Prologue to the Book of Numbers* [1530] in Works I
[PS 42] 436).

151 Or vestry; perhaps the inner vestry where more treasures were kept (Woodruff
and Danks [n125 above] 277)

152 *pedum*, the ceremonial staff or crosier carried by archbishops and bishops;
usually surmounted by a cross. A fifteenth-century painting of Becket (Herbert
Norris *Church Vestments* [New York 1950] plate 16) shows him holding a crosier.
If his was only waist-high it was unusually short and must have 'looked like a
cane,' perhaps because only the top section survived.

153 Circular band of white wool worn on the shoulders by archbishops. It is
conferred on them by the pope. On St Thomas' see *Inventories of Christ Church
Canterbury* (n140 above) 42n.

154 Or napkin. In context, this was undoubtedly the archbishop's amice, worn
around the neck under the liturgical garments to protect them from sweat and
the wearer from chafing. It is not mentioned in the inventories. A relic of the

saint's blood was said to be still at Canterbury, but Archbishop Cranmer wrote to Cromwell in August 1538 that he believed this blood 'is but a feigned thing and made of some red ochre or of such like matter' (letter 237 in *The Works of Thomas Cranmer* ed J.E. Cox, PS 15–16, 2 vols [Cambridge 1844–6] II 378); also LP XIII part 2 no 126 page 45.

155 Archbishop of Canterbury 1504–32 and lord chancellor 1504–15. See Holbein's portrait of him (reproduced in CEBR III 428; drawing in CWE 4 74). One of Erasmus' earliest English patrons, Warham granted him pensions from two livings (Allen Ep 2159:26n). Erasmus' edition of Jerome (1516) was dedicated to him; see Ep 396. Erasmus praises him in the highest terms for his pure Christian character and modesty, and his encouragement of learning (*Annotationes in Novum Testamentum* LB VI 903E–905D). *Ecclesiastes* LB V 810E–812B and Allen Ep 2758:38–83 have interesting remarks on Warham's mode of life. Erasmus respected him as he respected very few other prelates.

156 In the chapel of the Holy Trinity, at the east end of the cathedral, the pilgrims see the 'entire countenance' (*tota facies*) of the saint. This, according to the usual explanation, was the mitred bust of St Thomas, enclosing what was called *corona* – 'Becket's crown' or (from its shape) his head (*Inventories of Christ Church Canterbury* [n140 above] 42–3, Woodruff and Danks [n125 above] 279). Nichols however (*Pilgrimages* 180) thinks what is meant is the whole figure or image rather than the head only. The term *corona* itself is confusing, because it was both an area (the Trinity chapel) and the relic kept there ('Becket's crown' or, as is sometimes intended, that part of his skull severed by the fatal blow). See Stanley *Memorials* (n125 above) 220–1.

157 The pun on 'Gratianus' may be additional evidence, if any is needed, that Gratian is Colet, for (as Lupton noted in his *Life of Colet* 210) Jerome interprets the name Ioannes as meaning one 'cui est gratia vel Domini gratia' (*Liber de nominibus Hebraicis* PL 23 [1883] 886).

158 See a comparable passage in 'The Godly Feast' 198:32–199:36, which makes specific reference to St Thomas' tomb.

159 Wrathfully; *Adagia* III iv 13

160 The Paris theologians carped at these questions. Erasmus retorted that these ornaments did nothing to reduce the sufferings of the poor; and anyway such wealth would be plundered sooner or later (*Declarationes ad censuras Lutetiae vulgatas* LB IX 948F–949B and *Apologia adversus rhapsodias Alberti Pii* LB IX 1157A–C).

161 The nature and place of music in churches in the time of Erasmus has not been neglected. This note is limited to Erasmus' criticism in these and comparable passages. Whether music is the gift of God and drives the devil away, as Luther thought (WA *Tischreden* 1 no 968, 4 no 4441, 6 no 7034), or whether, on the other hand, organs should be banned altogether, as they were by the Zwinglians (see Charles Garside Jr *Zwingli and the Arts* [New Haven and London 1966] 60–2), were attitudes obviously incompatible though perhaps not totally irreconcilable. In such matters Erasmus, in some moods at any rate, was nearer to the Calvinist and Zwinglian positions than to Luther's.
Erasmus knew music and thought about it seriously. He is said to have been a choirboy at Utrecht under the renowned composer Jacob Obrecht; whether he

was can be questioned, apparently (Allen I 56:9n). He praises the divine music of the Psalms (*Enarratio in psalmum* XXXVIII LB V 418A–428D). But congregational singing by men and women vexes him. How do the dissenting sects reconcile it with their professed adherence to apostolic teaching? For did not Paul say that women must keep silence in churches (*Epistola ad fratres Inferioris Germaniae* LB X 1595D)? Erasmus comments on chants and organs in his note on 1 Cor 14:18–19 (*Annotationes in Novum Testamentum* LB VI 731C–732C; cf Allen Ep 1573:4–11 / CWE Ep 1573:6–13). There is entirely too much singing, yet one can hear an edifying sermon scarcely once in six months. Choirs are too preoccupied with the music to pay much attention to the meaning of the words they sing, yet preaching is far more important and more profitable than this neighing and yelping (*hinnitus* and *gannitus*), as he unkindly terms it. Paul sensibly preferred to preach, not sing. Today, instead, congregations hear voices signifying nothing. What do people think of Christ who believe he is pleased by a din of this kind? Elaborate, theatrical music makes divine service noisier than Greek or Roman theatres. Organists (or organ-makers, *organorum opifices*, but they were often the same persons) are employed at high cost. Music is unobjectionable if kept within bounds, but in fact it is overemphasized, takes up too much time in divine service, and is seriously disturbing (*Ecclesiastes* LB V 942A–B). 'Which is more holy, to work with your hands to keep your children from starving or to spend the whole day listening to singing that is unintelligible and therefore useless?' (*Apologia adversus rhapsodias Alberti Pii* LB IX 1155D).

On Erasmus and music consult C.A. Miller 'Erasmus on Music' *Musical Quarterly* 52 (1966) 332–49 and J.-C. Margolin's monograph *Erasme et la musique* (Paris 1965). A more recent contribution is that of Helmut Fleinghaus, *Die Musikanschauung des Erasmus von Rotterdam* Kölner Beiträge zur Musikforschung 135 (Regensburg 1984). On Luther, R.H. Bainton's *Here I Stand: A Life of Martin Luther* (New York 1950) 140–7 summarizes the subject. For Calvin see H.P. Clive 'The Calvinist Attitude to Music, and Its Literary Aspects and Sources' BHR 19 (1957) 80–102; 20 (1958) 79–107; and Charles Garside Jr 'The Origins of Calvin's Theology of Music: 1536–1543' *Transactions of the American Philosophical Society* 69 no 4 (1979); for Zwingli, Garside *Zwingli and the Arts* (cited earlier in this note).

162 As, he assumes, Zwinglian churches were
163 He alludes to Ambrose and Paulinus of Nola. It was told of Ambrose that when he was chosen bishop of Milan he gave his wealth to the church and to the poor. After the defeat of the Roman army by Visigoths at Adrianople in 378, he ordered the vessels of his church to be melted and used to ransom the Christian captives. Paulinus (d 431) likewise, after conversion to Christianity, gave his fortune to the church and the poor. St Laurence (martyred 258) was not a bishop, but as one of the seven deacons of Rome was in charge of the church's treasures. When Pope Sixtus II was condemned to death during a persecution in Rome he instructed Laurence to distribute the wealth of the church to the needy. Laurence did so, and when commanded by the persecutors to produce the wealth pointed to the crowd of poor and sick: these, he said, were the treasures of the church. St Ambrose defends his own actions and St Laurence's in *De officiis ministrorum* 2.28 PL 16 139C–142A, a chapter Erasmus certainly had

in mind in this paragraph. From time to time he returns to this theme of using the wealth of the church to relieve human suffering instead of spending it on building. See n158 above. Earlier, in his letter to abbot Volz introducing the new edition of *Enchiridion*, he argues that it is better to relieve the poor than to spend or give money for building or for pilgrimages (Allen Ep 858:400–14 / cwe Ep 858:424–38). The language he uses may be compared with that of theses 43–6 of Luther's *Ninety-five Theses* (Clemen vi or Kidd *Documents* 23–4 no 11). More rejects such arguments in his *Dialogue Concerning Heresies* against Tyndale (Yale cwm 6 part 1 50:21–51:19).

164 The same phrase, *expecto catastrophen*, is in *Julius exclusus* (Ferguson *Erasmi opuscula* 99:631). On *catastrophe*, see *Adagia* i ii 26.

165 If a Benedictine monastery had an abbot, his authority was supreme and the prior was second in dignity. In some houses where the title of abbot was not used, the head of the monastery was styled prior. At the time of Erasmus' visit to Canterbury the prior was Thomas Goldstone ii, who held office from 1495 until 1517. He was responsible for the building of Christ Church gate and completion of the central tower.

166 *Ex officio*

167 Not intended as a compliment. Erasmus' comment on Fitzjames, the bishop of London who charged Colet with heresy in 1512, is typical of his dislike of Scotists: 'superstitious and invincible Scotist, and for that reason seemed half-divine to himself' (Allen Ep 1211:530–4 / cwe Ep 1211:576–80). On the Scotists and Erasmus' prejudices see above 'The Godly Feast' 192:19–26 and n190. Colet shared these opinions (Allen Ep 1211:425–7 / cwe Ep 1211:462–4).

168 This was the shrine of St Thomas, described succinctly by Erasmus as a chest within a chest; it was in the Trinity Chapel, behind the high altar. The lower part of the shrine was stone; above this was a wooden canopy, covered with plates of gold. When the canopy was drawn up by ropes the shrine was disclosed. See the detailed description in Stanley *Memorials* (n125 above) 181–251. Nichols *Pilgrimages* 188 quotes the description in Stow's *Annals*: 'This Shrine was builded about a man's height all of stone; then upward of timber, plaine; within the which was a chest of yron, conteyning the bones of Thomas Becket, scull and all, with the wounde of his death, and the peece cut out of his scull layde in the same wounde.' On the skull see n156 above. On the treasure, Stow writes: 'The spoile of which shrine, in golde and precious stones, filled two great chests, such as sixe or seaven strong men could doe no more then convey one of them at once out of the church' (ibidem 189). An account written in the earlier part of the sixteenth century says: '[The tomb] ... is entirely covered over with plates of pure gold; but the gold is scarcely visible from the variety of precious stones with which it is studded, such as sapphires, diamonds, rubies, balas-rubies, and emeralds; and on every side that the eye turns, something more beautiful than the other appears' (*A Relation of England* 30). Pope Pius ii (d 1464), who had seen the treasures, remarked that to offer any gift less precious than silver was considered sacrilegious (*Memoirs of a Renaissance Pope: The Commentaries of Pius II* trans Florence A. Gragg, ed Leona C. Gabel [New York 1959; repr 1962] 32).

169 Most famous was the 'Regale of France,' supposedly the gift of Louis vii of France. What kind of jewel this was is uncertain. The *Relation of England*

speaks of it as 'a ruby, not larger than a man's thumb-nail,' but surpassing all other gems there in beauty (30). Leo of Rozmital describes one stone seen at Canterbury as 'a carbuncle which shines at night and which is half the size of a hen's egg' but does not say this was the Regale of France (*Travels* 43–4, 50–1). After confiscation of Canterbury's treasures, Henry VIII is said to have had the Regale set in a ring which he wore on his thumb. On the Regale see Stanley *Memorials* (n125 above) 223–4, 291. In Holbein's portraits of the king he wears rings on his index fingers, as he does in a drawing by Metsys made a few years before Henry's death. Louis VII, accompanied by Henry II of England, went on pilgrimage to Canterbury in 1179. The story that the Regale was a gift from Louis seems traceable to the Icelandic saga about Becket, *Thomas Saga Erkibyskups*. See Amy Kelly *Eleanor of Aquitaine and the Four Kings* (New York 1957) 254.

170 Erasmus mentions these and other mean relics in writing to Warham a few years after his visit (Allen Ep 396:64–9 / CWE Ep 396:73–9) and later in *Modus orandi Deum* (1524) LB V 1119F–1120A.

171 Colet was amiable enough towards his friends, and Erasmus says elsewhere that he was *festivus* on this pilgrimage (Allen Ep 1211:327–8), but he was fastidious by temperament, *impatiens omnium sordium* 'impatient of everything slovenly' (Allen Ep 1211:329 / CWE Ep 1211:361), and did not suffer fools gladly. See an anecdote in Allen Ep 1347:31–58 / CWE Ep 1347:36–65.

172 *Adagia* II iv 46

173 With the story that follows compare Erasmus' own disaster when he was about to cross the channel in 1500. Customs officers seized eighteen of his twenty pounds. Although the seizure was legal, he never forgot or forgave it. See 'Patterns' n69. For complaint about another hazard in crossing, stolen luggage, see Allen Ep 295:4–18 / CWE Ep 295:6–21. The channel crossing, he warned a servant-pupil whom he was sending to England, was irksome and costly, but brief and therefore not notorious for shipwrecks (Allen Ep 1832:46–52). There might be other kinds of trouble, however, as his own experience had taught him.

174 *dimidium drachmae* is Erasmus' term. 'Sixpence' may seem a trifle, but in Erasmus' time it could have been a day's wages.

175 Virgil *Eclogues* 3.16

176 Virgil *Aeneid* 6.126–9

177 *Adagia* I vii 11

178 *Adagia* IV vii 92. 'I hate that horrible channel and those still more horrible sailors' (Allen Ep 756:34–5 / CWE Ep 756:35–6).

179 Herbaldown hospital as it was later called, at Harbledown ('Bobbe-up-and-doun' in *Manciple's Prologue* 2 in the *Canterbury Tales*), about two miles from Canterbury. This structure still existed in the middle of the nineteenth century (Nichols *Pilgrimages* 199–201).

180 According to Stanley *Memorials* (n125 above), one of the surviving relics from the medieval almshouse was 'an ancient maple bowl, bound with a brazen rim, which contains a piece of rock crystal, so exactly reminding us of that which Erasmus describes in the leather of St. Thomas's shoe, as to suggest the conjecture that when the shoe was lost, the crystal was thus preserved' (236). This so-called relic seems to have made a lasting impression

on Erasmus, who refers to it contemptuously in other writings: *Modus orandi Deum* LB V 1119F–1120A; *Annotationes in Novum Testamentum* LB VI 118E; Allen Ep 396:64–6 / CWE Ep 396:73–6; *Apologia adversus rhapsodias Alberti Pii* LB IX 1161B–1162B. In this last passage he reminds the reader that Gratian (Colet) 'did not shrink from the teachings of Wyclif' (see n146 above), but even so, he adds, Gratian's indignant reaction is sensible and justified.

181 Another relic surviving from the almshouse was 'a rude box, with a chain to be held by the hand, and a slit for money in the lid, at least as old as the sixteenth century. In that box we can hardly doubt, the coin of Erasmus was deposited' (Stanley *Memorials* [n125 above] 236).

182 Erasmus made a similar reply to the Paris theologians who had criticized these lines on relics (*Declarationes ad censuras Lutetiae vulgatas* LB IX 949C–D).

If one kissed ... pardonable.] This sentence was added in the March 1533 edition.

183 As in 'The Funeral' 772:27–773:26

184 The *Valor ecclesiasticus* and evidence collected in *Inventories of Christ Church Canterbury* (n140 above) confirm the wealth. A dozen years after this colloquy was printed all the wealth of Canterbury was confiscated by the government and Christ Church priory was dissolved.

185 The same assertion about what Becket achieved by his martyrdom is made in Erasmus' dedicatory letter to his Paraphrase on Mark, addressed to Francis I (Allen Ep 1400:243–64, particularly 261–3 / CWE Ep 1400:255–75, particularly 272–3). The entire passage was omitted in the English translation of the Paraphrases (1548; STC 2854). Archbishop Warham's agent in Rome reported in 1520 that he had told the pope 'theyr ways never a man that dyde schow more for [did more to advance] the lyberteys off the Churche than Syntt Thomas off Cantorbery' (*Christ Church Letters* ed J.B. Sheppard, Camden Society new series 19 [London 1877] 72).

Erasmus tells us nothing about St Thomas' miracles. In February 1173, less than three years after his murder, Thomas was canonized. Almost from the day of his death he was credited with miracles, and his shrine very quickly became one of the principal resorts of Christian pilgrims. The 'Miracles of Thomas Becket' comprise the largest collection of miracle stories connected with any medieval shrine. See R.W. Southern *The Making of the Middle Ages* (New Haven and London 1965) 254–5.

186 On an island in Lough Derg in county Donegal in the north-west corner of Ireland. It became a place of pilgrimage because St Patrick was said to have had a vision promising the devout who went to this cave a sight of the torments of sinners and joys of the redeemed in the next world. On the legend see Shane Leslie *Saint Patrick's Purgatory* (London 1932). *De praeparatione ad mortem* LB V 1312C alludes to the cave.

187 On Stygian waters see n3 above; on Avernus, Virgil *Aeneid* 6.126–9 as at 648:6–7 above. In *Adagia* I vii 77 Erasmus compares St Patrick's cave with the cave of Trophonius, on which see 'The Funeral' n2.

188 See 'Inns.'

189 Cf 'The Well-to-do Beggars' 471:5–13.

190 Processions to certain churches in Rome during Lent and at other special times. Indulgences were granted to participants.

191 Of Compostella
192 No single passage is meant but the precepts of both Old and New Testaments
    on responsibility for the proper care of wife and children. Allusion to Roman
    stations a moment earlier shows that Erasmus is thinking here, as in so many
    texts, of one's duty to stay at home and provide for one's family instead
    of roaming about the world on pilgrimages. Cf 'Rash Vows' n14 and 'The
    Shipwreck' n38.

A FISH DIET

Ἰχθυοφαγία

First printed in the February 1526 edition.

About the earlier history of this colloquy – when it was undertaken, or how long the writing took, or when it was completed and laid aside until Froben was ready to issue a new edition of the *Colloquia* – we know little or nothing. Sometimes internal evidence can give us clues. In the case of 'A Pilgrimage for Religion's Sake' and 'A Fish Diet' there is reason to think some lines were changes or additions dating from 1523 or 1524. Nor would that be surprising if we keep track of Erasmus' experiences, moods, and opinions during 1522–5. See further James D. Tracy 'On the Composition Dates of Seven of Erasmus' Writings' BHR 31 (1969) 362–4.

Necessarily the *terminus ad quem* of 'A Fish Diet' is January 1526, because the imagined speech of Charles v to his foe, Francis i, alludes to the French king's captivity after the battle of Pavia (24 February 1525). The emperor says 'I grant you life and liberty' (688:40), words which, to fit the meaning of the paragraph, would be applicable any time after Pavia. The royal prisoner was held in Spain. His release was not arranged until the Treaty of Madrid was made in January 1526, and he was not actually freed until two months later (see n79 below). Erasmus' memories of his visit to Johann von Botzheim's splendid home in Constance in September 1522 'nearly two years ago' were still fresh when he wrote the pages on his distracting illness there (714:13–33, and cf Allen Ep 1342:333–54 / CWE Ep 1342:369–90). So were his impressions of a more recent visit to another old friend, Udalricus Zasius, in Freiburg in March 1523; he writes of this to Zasius soon after the visit (Ep 1353, and see 713:18–714:8 and notes below). These passages and the vivid description of a band of drunken revellers near Basel in that same month (Allen Ep 1353:160–76 / CWE Ep 1353 179–99) suggest that at least some parts of the dialogue may have been written in 1523 or 1524. Another example is the close similarity between a cynical remark in the same letter of March 1523 (Allen Ep 1353:173–6 / CWE Ep 1353:195–9) and the butcher's comment in the colloquy that no one is shocked to see a Carthusian the worse for drink, but that if the monk has tasted meat he is deemed deserving of perpetual imprisonment (705:16–20 below). Again, what is said in the colloquy about punishment of contumacious and seditious conduct brings to mind Erasmus' interest in the lurid case of his Basel neighbour Steinschnider, who was executed in the spring of 1523 after horrible tortures (see n263 below).

The word ἰχθυοφαγία 'fish-eating' occurs in the commentary on Homer's *Iliad* by Eustathius of Thessalonica (twelfth century) 135:9 (ed G. Stallbaum, 4 vols [Leipzig 1827–30] I 111). Adjectival forms of the word are found in ancient authors, for example Herodotus 3.19, Strabo 720, 770, and Pausanias 1.33.4. Eustathius, whose commentaries on the *Iliad* and *Odyssey* are recommended to teachers in Erasmus' *De ratione studii* (LB I 527B / CWE 24 683:20–1) is cited forty-eight times in the *Adagia* (Phillips 'Adages' 397).

The complexity of the topics examined in this the longest of the colloquies, and the nuances of some questions and answers, require us to read deliberately before deciding which of the opinions expressed are Erasmus' own considered judgments and which are included to heighten the characterization or provide local colour. The structure of the work and the manner in which the talk shifts from raillery to seriousness, from jokes or stories to scriptural exegesis, casuistry, and moralizing permit the author to speak his mind freely on some persistent problems, yet without allowing his readers to forget who and what his characters are. The choice of low-life men to discuss some fundamental religious questions posed an aesthetic and ethical problem, that of decorum. Fishmongers and butchers have ever been regarded as men whose trades are among the most vulgar (Cicero *De officiis* 1.42.150); and as Erasmus says elsewhere, attempts by brash or uninformed laymen to argue about profound subjects can be ridiculous (*Supputatio* LB IX 636E). But these laymen are not offensively brash, and they are far from ignorant. Their social rank is mean, as they themselves remind us, yet they have native intelligence. One speaks of reading the Bible in a vernacular translation (681:18–19); the other says that he owes some of his ideas to acquaintance with the Dominicans to whom he sells fish (684:17–21). Both agree that their present conversation would seem presumptuous to many (720:32–5). This is informal dialogue, however, not formal debate; were it the latter it would seem intolerably pretentious. We soon begin to realize that these tradesmen are shrewd reasoners, and by the time a perceptive reader is well into the examination of 'Judaism' and subsequent questions he has no difficulty in recognizing the main ideas in the dialogue as typically Erasmian. They run through all of Erasmus' moral and religious treatises, commentaries on Scripture, and homilies. The fundamental topic here is Christian liberty – a favourite theme – as contrasted with 'Judaism': the contrast between Law and gospel, letter and spirit, a subject examined earlier in 'The Profane Feast' and 'The Godly Feast.' In the present colloquy it is introduced cleverly by banter on fasting, but this banter gives way to discussion, with enough learning added to make it profitable and with sufficient humour, personal allusion, and anecdote to keep it readable. See 'The Usefulness of the *Colloquies*' (1104:10–28) for a neat summary of purposes and methods in this dialogue.

Usually the fishmonger offers more conventional and conservative or official views than the butcher, but this is not always so. Erasmus is too careful an artist to give one speaker all the good lines and proper answers. We notice also that often assertions or judgments are qualified by 'so they say' (as at 685:16), 'it is not certain' (684:30), 'didn't you see' (686:25), 'does it seem right to you' (688:14), 'I'm inclined to doubt it' (689:39), 'I think' (712:7). We meet some teasing ambiguities. Neither speaker is always voicing Erasmus' opinions. Argument, anecdote, and repartee make the dialogue plausible, but Erasmus allows the reader (who after all is expected to know something about the subject) to follow the exchange of views intelligently, draw the right inferences, and reach the right or most probable conclusions.

The background of the major questions treated in the dialogue, their place in Erasmus' thought and writings, and the numerous allusions to earlier and contemporary persons and to subsidiary topics are elucidated in the notes.

BUTCHER, FISHMONGER

Butcher Tell me, you unsavoury seller of salt fish, haven't you bought a rope yet?

5 **Fishmonger** A rope, butcher?

Butcher Yes, a rope.

Fishmonger What for, in heaven's name?

Butcher What for? To hang yourself with – what else?[1]

Fishmonger Others may buy them. I'm not yet so bored with life.

10 **Butcher** But you soon will be.

Fishmonger I hope some god turns these prophecies against the prophet instead! But what's wrong?

Butcher If you don't know, I'll tell you. Plainly there's what they call a Saguntine famine[2] at hand for the likes of you, so the only thing to do will

15 be to hang yourselves straightway.

Fishmonger Please, butcher, please! Let *that* happen to our enemies. How is it you've changed suddenly from a butcher into a Pythian oracle,[3] to prophesy so dire a calamity?

Butcher Don't flatter yourself, it's no prophecy – this very thing is at your

20 door.

Fishmonger You slay me. Out with it, if you've anything to bring out.

Butcher I'll bring it out – and so much the worse for you. Rome has decreed that hereafter anybody is free to eat anything he wants. What's left for you and your set, then, except starvation among your rotten salt fish?

Fishmonger Whoever wishes may eat snails or nettles, for all I care. But no one is forbidden to eat fish, is he?

Butcher No, but permission is granted to eat whatever meat one likes.

Fishmonger If what you tell me is wrong, you're the one who deserves
5   hanging; if it's correct, you're the one who'll need a rope, not I. For I expect a bigger profit from now on.

Butcher Oh, you'll have a big increase – of hunger. You'll come to utter starvation. Or – if you'd like better news – you'll live more decently hereafter, and won't wipe your filthy, scabby nose on your sleeve as usual.[4]

10   **Fishmonger** Oh-ho, we have reached the limit: the blind man reproaches the one-eyed.[5] As if, forsooth, among butchers there were anything cleaner than that part of the body which is said to survive all efforts to wash it.[6] I wish your news were true, but I'm afraid you make me rejoice without reason.

15   **Butcher** My news is absolutely true. But why do you expect a larger profit?

Fishmonger Because I observe human nature to be such that if a thing's forbidden, it's the more irresistible to men.

Butcher What of it?

Fishmonger When they may eat anything they like, many men will abstain
20   from meat. As among the ancients, there will be no fine dinner without fish. And so I'm glad the eating of flesh is permitted. I only wish the eating of fish were forbidden. People would eat it the more eagerly.

Butcher A holy wish, so help me!

Fishmonger I'd hope and pray for it if, like you, I thought of nothing except
25   profits,[7] from love of which you've pledged your gross and carnivorous soul to devils.

Butcher You're quite a salty fellow even if your speech *is* unsavoury.

Fishmonger What reason persuaded Rome to relax the rule on meat-eating that had been observed for so many ages?

30   **Butcher** The plain fact of the matter has convinced them this long while. They realize, correctly, that the city is polluted and land, rivers, air, fire – and any other element there may be – corrupted by salt fish sellers; that human bodies are diseased, for eating fish fills the body with rotten humours, the source of fevers, consumption, gout, epilepsy, leprosy, and what not other
35   maladies.[8]

Fishmonger Tell me, then, Hippocrates,[9] why is it forbidden in well-governed cities to slaughter beef and hogs within the walls?[10] Public health would be guarded even better if cattle didn't have their throats cut. Why is a certain quarter assigned to butchers if not because they might
40   bring a plague on the whole city if they lived in various places? Or is any kind of filth more pestilential than the blood and gore of animals?

Butcher Sheer perfume if you compare it with the stench of fish.

Fishmonger Sheer perfume to you, I suppose, but it doesn't seem so to the magistrates who bar you from the city. People who hold their noses as they pass by show how sweet your butcher shops smell; those who prefer ten
5   pimps to one butcher as neighbours show it to all the world.

Butcher But neither lakes nor whole rivers suffice to wash the rotten stench of fish off you. As is truly said, you use water in vain. A fish always smells like a fish, though you smear it with sweet ointments. What wonder that dead fish smell so when many living ones smell as soon as they're caught?[11]
10   Meat pickled in brine keeps for many years; so far from rotting, it's even somewhat aromatic. Preserved in common salt, it lasts without spoiling. Smoked meat acquires a not unpleasant odour. If you treat fish in just the same way, it will still smell like nothing but fish. That no stench can be compared with the rottenness of fish, infer from the fact that salt itself –
15   which is given by Nature to protect things from spoiling, and by its own native power confines and cuts off decay while at the same time it excludes whatever could cause harm from outside, drying up the humours within where decay could have started – is rotted by fish. In fish alone is salt not salt. Some oversqueamish person may hold his nose as he walks by
20   our buildings, but nobody can endure sitting in a boat with your salt fish. Whenever travellers meet a cart filled with salt fish, what a scramble there is! What holding of noses! What spitting! What coughing! And if salt fish could somehow be brought fresh into town, as we carry slaughtered beef, the law would not overlook it.[12] What should one do, now, with those that
25   are rotten even when they're eaten? And yet how often do we see your wares condemned by the market-masters to be thrown into the river, and you fined! That would happen even more often, in fact, if the officials you bribed weren't looking out for their own private profit rather than for the public welfare. Nor is this the only way you injure the commonwealth, but
30   by a shameless plot you prevent the bringing into the city of fresher fish from somewhere else.[13]

Fishmonger As if no one ever saw a butcher fined for selling rotten pork, the hog's spotted tongue showing plainly it was diseased. Or a sheep drowned or choked in the mire; or maggoty shoulders of meat whose
35   rottenness the butcher covered up by washing and then smearing it with fresh blood.

Butcher But nothing from our side matches what came from you recently: that one eel pie killed nine guests at a dinner. That's the sort of sops *you* furnish for citizens' meals.

40   **Fishmonger** You mention an accident nobody could avoid if it's fated to happen. But with you it's an almost daily occurrence to sell fattened cats for

rabbits; you'd sell dogs for hares if the short ears and hairy feet allowed. And need I mention the meat pies made of human flesh?

Butcher You are holding me to account for accidents and human shortcomings – something you condemned me for. Those responsible
5   for such things should answer for them. I'm comparing trade with trade. Otherwise greengrocers would be blamed because sometimes they unsuspectingly sell hemlock or wolfsbane for cabbage;[14] and pharmacists because sometimes they hand out poisons instead of medicines. No profession is so blameless that accidents of this kind never occur. Though you
10   people may observe all the rules, what you peddle is poisonous. If you were to sell a torpedo,[15] sea serpent,[16] or sea hare[17] taken in with the catch, that would be an accident, not a crime; you would have no more responsibility than does a physician who sometimes kills a patient whom he is treating. This mischief could be borne if you displayed your rotten stuff only in winter;
15   sharp weather would allay the pestilence. But now you add rotten matter to the burning heat of summer; autumn, which is harmful enough by itself, you make worse. When the year is young and the hidden humours come forth again – not without danger to the body – you play the tyrant for two whole months[18] and corrupt the youth of the reborn year by bringing decline upon
20   it. And although this is Nature's plan, that bodies purged of unhealthful juices are reinvigorated by new ones, you load them with nothing but foul stenches and gore; and if bodies have any disease, you make it worse by adding ill to ill and especially by injuring the good juices of the body. This too could be borne if you injured only bodies. But since the mental organs are harmed by
25   changes in diet, the result is injury to the minds themselves. Generally men full of fish are themselves like fish: pale, stinking, stupid, silent.

Fishmonger A new Thales![19] How wise are people who live on beets? Why, as wise as beets themselves![20] How wise are those who devour steers and sheep and goats? Why, as wise as steers, sheep, and goats! You sell kids as
30   delicacies, and yet, since they're subject to epilepsy, they produce that same disease in those who are fond of meat. Wouldn't it be better to satisfy a hungry stomach with salt fish?

Butcher As if this were the only lie told by writers on natural history! And even if what they say were absolutely true, foods excellent in themselves are
35   often the worst for sick bodies. We sell kids for persons with intermittent fever and consumption, not with dizziness.

Fishmonger If eating fish is so very dangerous to mortal interests, why does the wisdom of prelates and princes permit us to sell our wares all the year round, when you must observe fasts a good part of the year?
40   **Butcher** What business of mine is that? Maybe this was arranged by rascally physicians, to make more money.

Fishmonger What rascally physicians are you talking about, when fish have no enemies so deadly as they?[21]

Butcher Lest you mistake, my good fellow, they don't do this because they care about you, or because they love fish, since no men avoid fish more
5   scrupulously; they're merely looking out for their own profit. The more people who cough or are exhausted and ill, the better their income.

Fishmonger I shan't defend physicians here; they'll get even if ever you fall into their clutches. For my argument, the holiness displayed by the ancients in their lives, the authority of those most esteemed, the sovereignty
10   of bishops, the common custom of Christian nations suffice. If you think all these are mad, I prefer to be mad with them than sane with butchers.

Butcher You decline to defend the physicians; for my part, I shouldn't want to accuse or criticize the ancients or general customs. My practice is to venerate them, not to revile them.[22]

15   **Fishmonger** In this at least you're a more wary than reverent butcher, or else I don't know you.

Butcher In my judgment, people are wise to avoid dealings with those who wield thunderbolts.[23] But what I understand from my Bible, which I read sometimes in a translation,[24] I shan't keep quiet about.

20   **Fishmonger** So now you turn from butcher into theologian.

Butcher I think that as soon as the first men came forth from the moist earth, they had strong, healthy bodies. Their longevity proves that. Next, paradise was by far the most comfortable spot, with the most healthful climate. In such a place such bodies could live without food by draughts of air and
25   by the fragrance of herbs, trees, and flowers everywhere, especially since the earth of itself brought forth everything in abundance without man's labour; there was neither death nor old age. Tending such a garden was really pleasure rather than toil.[25]

Fishmonger So far you're probably right.

30   **Butcher** From the varied yield of so extremely fertile a garden, nothing was forbidden save one tree.[26]

Fishmonger Absolutely true.

Butcher And that for no other reason than that through their obedience they might acknowledge their lord and creator.

35   **Fishmonger** Correct.

Butcher In fact, I believe everything produced by the earth when new was finer and of better flavour than the earth bears now, when it is growing old and almost feeble.[27]

Fishmonger Granted.

40   **Butcher** And especially in paradise.

Fishmonger Perfectly true.

Butcher So eating was a matter of pleasure there, not of necessity.

Fishmonger I've heard that.

Butcher And to refrain from slaughtering living creatures was humanity, not sanctity.

5 **Fishmonger** I don't know about that. I read that the eating of meat was permitted after the Flood;[28] that it was forbidden prior to the Flood, I don't read. What reason was there to allow it if it was already allowed?

Butcher Why don't we eat frogs? Not because they're forbidden but because we loathe them.[29] How do you know whether on that occasion God was 10 advising what food human frailty required, not what food he would allow?

Fishmonger I'm no soothsayer.[30]

Butcher But, we read, as soon as man was created: 'Have dominion over the fish of the sea, and over the fowl of the air, and over every living thing that moveth upon the earth.'[31] Of what use is dominion if it does not permit 15 eating?

Fishmonger Cruel master! So you eat your servants, maids, wife, and children? In the same fashion you even eat the chamber-pot you're owner of?

Butcher But hear me in turn, you unseasoned salt fish seller. Other creatures have their uses, and the name of master is not inappropriate. A horse carries 20 me on his back. A camel bears burdens. What can you do with a fish except eat it?

Fishmonger As though there aren't, in fact, countless medicines made from fish! In the next place, many things are created merely to please the sight of man and bring him to admire the creator. Perhaps you don't believe dolphins 25 carry men on their backs?[32] Then there are fish, such as the sea urchin, that foretell the approach of a storm.[33] Or wouldn't you like such a servant in your home?

Butcher Well, granting that before the Flood it was lawful to eat only the fruits of the earth,[34] it was no great matter to abstain from those foods which 30 the body did not need and which involved the cruelty of slaughtering. You'll admit that eating meat was first allowed on account of the weakness of human bodies. The Flood introduced cold, and today we see that in cold regions men naturally have larger appetites; also the Flood wiped out or corrupted the produce of the earth.

35 **Fishmonger** Agreed.

Butcher And yet after the Flood they lived to be over two hundred years old.

Fishmonger I believe that.

Butcher Why then did God permit those hardy people to eat anything 40 without exception and afterwards limit weaker and shorter-lived men to certain kinds of meat, as Moses commanded?[35]

Fishmonger As if it's up to me to give a reason for what God does! Still, I
think God did then what is usually done by masters who check their favour
towards servants when they see them abusing their lords' kindness. Thus
we take away beans and oats from an overspirited horse and feed him
5 little hay;[36] and we subdue him with sharper bit and spurs. The human
race had thrown off all reverence and plunged into great licentiousness, as
though there were no God at all. It was at this time that the barriers of laws,
limitations of ceremonies, and restraints of threats and commandments were
devised, to bring men to their senses.
10 **Butcher** Then why don't the restraints of that Law remain today?
Fishmonger Because the harshness of carnal servitude was removed after
we were adopted by means of the gospel as sons of God.[37] When more
abundant grace has touched us, commandments have less importance.
Butcher Since God calls his covenant eternal,[38] and Christ denied that
15 he destroyed the Law but declared that he fulfilled it,[39] how did later
generations have the presumption to abrogate a good deal of the Law?
Fishmonger That Law was not given to the gentiles,[40] and therefore
the apostles thought it wise not to burden them with the vexation of
circumcision,[41] lest they put their hope of salvation in bodily rites, like Jews
20 even today, rather than in faith and love of God.
Butcher I'm not talking about gentiles. What passage of Scripture openly
teaches that Jews converted to the gospel are freed from subjection to the
Mosaic law?[42]
Fishmonger That was foretold by the prophets, who promise a new covenant
25 and a new spirit;[43] and they present a God who abominates the feast days
of the Jews, turning away from their burnt offerings, despising their feasts,
rejecting their oblations, desiring a people circumcised in the heart.[44] The
Lord himself, who offers his body and blood to his disciples, calling it
the new covenant,[45] has confirmed their promises. If nothing of the old is
30 abolished, why is this called new? The Lord has abrogated the Jewish[46]
distinction of foods, not by his example, to be sure, but by his judgment,
when he denies that a man is defiled by foods taken into his stomach and
voided in private.[47] He teaches Peter the same thing in a vision;[48] in fact
Peter himself teaches it by eating with Paul and others the common foods
35 from which the Law had bidden them abstain. Paul teaches it everywhere in
his letters,[49] nor is there any doubt that what Christian people follow today
was handed down as though from the apostles and has finally reached us.
So the Jews were not so much emancipated as weaned from superstitious
reverence of the Law, as though from milk to which they were thoroughly
40 accustomed but which was now inappropriate.[50] And the Law was not
abrogated, but that part of it which was now superfluous was bidden

to yield. Foliage and blossoms are harbingers of fruit; when the tree is heavy with it, nobody misses the blossoms. Neither does anyone mourn his son's lost youth when the boy is grown up. Nor does anyone need lanterns and torches when the sun has risen. It is unnecessary to look

5   for a tutor when a son who is already grown up assumes his freedom and, in his turn, has authority over the tutor.[51] A pledge ceases to be a pledge when the promise is fulfilled. An engaged girl, before marriage, comforts herself with her fiancé's letters; she kisses the gifts that come from him; she embraces pictures of him. But when she possesses him in

10   person, out of love for him she sets aside the things she loved before. Now at first the Jews were wrenched with difficulty from their accustomed ways, as though a child used to milk should, when grown, bawl for the breast, scorning solid food. And so they were weaned almost by force from those allegories or shadows[52] or temporal consolations, that

15   they might now turn entirely to him whom that Law had promised and foreshadowed.

Butcher Who would have expected so much theology from a seller of salt fish?

Fishmonger Usually I supply fish to the Dominican house in our city, so it

20   happens that they often lunch with me, and I sometimes with them. I picked up these ideas from their disputations.

Butcher Indeed you deserve to become a seller of fresh fish instead of salt fish. Solve this one: if you were a Jew – and I'm not quite sure if you are or not – and were absolutely about to starve, would you eat pork[53] or would

25   you choose to die?

Fishmonger What I would do, I know; what I should do, I don't know – yet.

Butcher God forbade both: 'Thou shalt not kill' and 'Thou shalt not eat the flesh of swine.'[54] In such a circumstance, which commandment should yield to which?

30   **Fishmonger** In the first place, it is not certain that God forbade the eating of swine's flesh because he wants us to seek death rather than, by eating it, to preserve life. For the Lord himself excuses David, who broke the commandment by eating the sacred bread.[55] And in the Babylonian exile many things prescribed by the Law were not observed by the Jews. Therefore

35   I should think that that law which Nature herself also gave, and which is perpetual and inviolable, ought to be held more authoritative than one that did not always exist and was later to be abrogated.

Butcher Why then were the Maccabean brothers praised for preferring death under cruel torture to tasting swine's flesh?[56]

40   **Fishmonger** Because, I suppose, this eating commanded by the king involved renunciation of the whole law of the nation, just as circumcision,

which the Jews tried to force on gentiles, included adherence to the whole
Law, as a down payment binds one to fulfil the entire contract.

Butcher If, therefore, that grosser part of the Law was rightly removed after
the dawn of the gospel, why do we now see those same things, or more
5   burdensome ones, restored, particularly when the Lord calls his yoke easy
and Peter, in Acts, calls the Jewish law hard,[57] a law that neither the Jews nor
their fathers were able to bear? Circumcision was removed[58] but baptism
took its place[59] – almost a harder condition, I should say. Circumcision
was postponed until the eighth day,[60] and if in the interval some accident
10   carried off the child the pledge of circumcision was taken for the deed.
When children are scarcely out of their mothers' wombs, we plunge them
into cold water which has stood (I won't say stank) for a long time in a stone
font;[61] and if a child dies when one day old, or dies at birth, through no
fault of parents or attendants, the wretched creature is consigned to eternal
15   damnation.[62]

Fishmonger So they say.

Butcher The sabbath is removed, and yet not removed but transformed into
the Lord's day. What's the difference? The Mosaic law prescribed a few
days' fast; how many have we added to those! In the choice of food, how
20   much freer than we were the Jews, who could eat sheep, capons, partridges,
and kids the whole year long! No kind of clothing was prohibited to them
except that woven of wool and flax.[63] Nowadays, besides so many prescribed
and proscribed styles and colours of clothing,[64] are added various modes
of shaving the head, to say nothing meanwhile of the burden of confession
25   and the load of human regulations, complicated tithes, tighter restrictions
governing marriage, new laws of kinship through marriage, and many
others that make the Jewish law seem not a little easier in this respect than is
our lot.[65]

Fishmonger You're quite mistaken, butcher. Christ's yoke should not be
30   judged by the standard you suppose. A Christian is bound by many things,
by more difficult ones, and finally by heavier penalty; yet the greater power
of faith and love added to them renders easy what are by nature extremely
oppressive.

Butcher But since the Spirit once descended from heaven in the shape of
35   fiery tongues[66] and enriched the hearts of believers by the most plenteous
gift of faith and love, why is the weight of the Law lifted, as if from persons
weak and endangered under an unjust burden? Why does Peter, divinely
inspired, call the burden intolerable?[67]

Fishmonger It was taken away partly that Judaism[68] might not hinder the
40   glory of the gospel, as it had begun to do, and that gentiles might not be
alienated from Christ by hatred of the Law. Among the gentiles were many

weak persons, for whom there was a double danger: first, lest they believe no one could gain salvation without keeping the Law; second, lest they prefer to remain pagans rather than accept the yoke of the Mosaic law. It was necessary to entice the weak minds of these people as though by some

5 bait of freedom. Again, in order to relieve those who thought there was no hope of salvation by acceptance of the gospel without keeping the Law, circumcision, sabbaths, dietary rules, and other such matters, either they simply removed the regulations or they changed them to something else. Furthermore, Peter's protestation that he could not endure the burden of the

10 Law is not to be understood as referring to the kind of person he then was, since there was nothing he could not bear, but to the weak, dull-minded Jews, who chewed wearily the husk of barley, not yet having tasted the marrow of the Spirit.

Butcher In argument *you're* fairly dull-minded. – But today there are fully

15 as many reasons, it seems to me, why these corporal observances ought to be treated as matters of choice, not of obligation.

Fishmonger How so?

Butcher Recently I saw a painting, on a very large canvas, of the whole world. From it I learned how small a portion of the world wholeheartedly

20 and sincerely professes Christianity: part of western Europe, of course; then another part towards the north; a third stretching far away to the south; Poland seemed to be as far as the fourth part went, towards the east. The rest of the world contains either barbarians, not so very different from brutes, or schismatics or heretics, or both.

25 **Fishmonger** But didn't you see the whole southern shore and the scattered islands identified as Christian?[69]

Butcher I did, and I learned that plunder had been carried away from there; but I did not hear that Christianity had been brought in. Since, therefore, the harvest is so abundant,[70] it seems most urgent for the spreading of the

30 Christian religion that as the apostles removed the burden of the Mosaic law lest the gentiles backslide, so now, for attracting the weak, the rules about some things ought to be abolished. The world was saved without these in the beginning, and it could be saved now if only it had faith and gospel love. I hear and see that there are a great many who make places,

35 vestments, foods, fasts, gestures,[71] and chants the essence of religion and judge their neighbour by these, contrary to gospel commandment. Whence it happens that though everything is done in the name of faith and Christian love, both are destroyed by superstition about these matters. He who puts his trust in deeds of this kind is very far from the gospel faith; and far

40 is he from Christian love who, on account of food or drink that anybody can properly use, provokes his brother, for whose freedom Christ died.

What bitter quarrels do we witness among Christians, what hateful slanders, because a garment is girdled or dyed differently,[72] or because of seafood or land food! Had this evil infected only a few, it could be ignored. Nowadays we see the whole world shaken by reason of these deadly disputes. If these and ones like them were got rid of, we could live in greater peace, not bothering about ceremonies[73] but straining only after those things Christ taught, and other races would more readily embrace a religion joined with freedom.

Fishmonger Outside the habitation of the church there is no salvation.[74]

Butcher Granted.

Fishmonger Whoever does not recognize the Roman pontiff is outside the church.

Butcher No objection.[75]

Fishmonger But he who disregards his ordinances doesn't recognize him.

Butcher And for that very reason I hope that in the future this pope (Clement by name, most clement in spirit and holiness),[76] for the purpose of attracting all races into the fellowship of the church, may mitigate all conditions that have heretofore appeared to estrange some peoples from union with the Roman see; and that he may prefer the gain of the gospel to carrying out his own prerogative in everything. Every day I hear old complaints about annates,[77] pardons, dispensations,[78] and other taxes, about burdened churches; but I believe he'll so curtail all these that none but the shameless will venture to complain hereafter.

Fishmonger Would that all monarchs did the same! I have no doubt whatever that Christianity, now confined within narrow limits, would spread most fruitfully if the barbarous nations realized they were called not to human servitude, but to gospel freedom, and that they were sought out not for the purpose of plunder, but for the fellowship of happiness and holiness. When they have united with us and found in us truly Christian behaviour, they will contribute voluntarily more than any force could wring from them.

Butcher That will soon happen, I predict, if pestilential Strife, who has brought about a calamitous war between the two most powerful kings in the world,[79] takes her leave, damn her![80]

Fishmonger And I'm surprised this wasn't accomplished long ago, since nothing more humane than Francis can be imagined; and the emperor Charles, I believe, was indoctrinated by his tutors with the principle that the larger his empire grows by fortune, the more mercy and kindness he himself should add.[81] Besides, one of his age[82] usually has a special talent for affability and kindness.

Butcher You could find nothing lacking in either man.

Fishmonger Then what delays what the whole world longs for?

Butcher The lawyers are still arguing about boundaries;[83] besides, you know the uproars of comedies always end in marriage.[84] Princes conclude their tragedies in the same fashion. But in comedies the marriages occur quickly; here the business between great men is carried on with vast exertions. And
5   it's better for a wound to be healed somewhat more slowly than to break out soon again as an ulcer.

Fishmonger Do you think these matches are based on a strong bond of union?

Butcher I'd like to, certainly, but I notice that most wars usually originate in
10   these marriages; and if a war does break out among those who at the time are connected by marriage, the fire spreads more widely and is brought under control with more difficulty.[85]

Fishmonger I admit that and acknowledge what you say to be very true.

Butcher But does it seem right to you that because of the bickerings of
15   lawyers and delays over treaties,[86] the whole world should endure such woe? Truly nothing's ever safe now, and while there's neither war nor peace the worst men have a free hand.

Fishmonger It's not my place to talk about the policies of princes. But if someone made me emperor, I know what I'd do.

20   **Butcher** See, we make you emperor, and simultaneously Roman pontiff too, if you like. What do you do?

Fishmonger Make me emperor and king of France instead.

Butcher All right, be both.

Fishmonger Taking a vow of peace, I would at once proclaim a truce
25   throughout my entire realm and demobilize the army, threatening with capital punishment anyone who so much as touched another man's hen. Thus with my advantage, or (I should say) with the public's advantage, of a state of peace, I would negotiate a settlement about national boundaries or terms of marriage.

30   **Butcher** Have you no stronger bonds of agreement than marriage?

Fishmonger Yes, I think so.

Butcher Share them with me.

Fishmonger If I were emperor, I'd conclude an agreement without delay with the king of France in this manner:[87] 'Brother, some evil spirit[88] stirred
35   up this war between us, yet the struggle was not for survival but for power. You proved your worth as a brave and vigorous warrior. Fortune was on my side and of a king made you a captive.[89] What happened to you could have happened to me, and your disaster is a warning to us all of the human lot. We have learned how this kind of conflict is injurious to both sides. Come
40   now, let us contend in a different fashion. I grant you life and liberty; I accept you as an ally instead of an enemy. Let us forget all past misfortune.

Return free and unransomed to your people, keep your possessions, be a good neighbour, and hereafter let there be only this one rivalry between us, that each strive to outdo the other in good faith, duty, and generosity; let each of us try, not to rule a larger kingdom than the other one has, but to
5   govern his own dominion more righteously. In the earlier contest I was lucky enough to win. Whoever wins *this* one will gain a victory far more glorious. This reputation for mercy will surely bring me more true fame than if I had annexed all France to my rule. And appreciation of your gratitude will win you more renown than if you had driven me out of Italy entirely. Don't envy
10   me the praise I covet. In turn I will so promote your praise that you will gladly be indebted to this friend.'
Butcher Certainly France, nay the whole world, might thus be bound in friendship. For if this sore is covered up by bad terms rather than truly healed, I fear that when the wound is opened on some occasion soon
15   afterwards, the old poison may burst out with more harm than ever.[90]
Fishmonger How magnificent and laudable a glory would this humaneness give to Charles throughout the world! What nation would not willingly submit to a prince so humane and forbearing?
Butcher You've played emperor well enough; now play pope.
20   **Fishmonger** It would take a very long time to follow up every single topic. I'll summarize. I would so conduct myself that the whole world understood the ruler of the church was one who longed for nothing other than the glory of Christ and the salvation of all mankind. This would truly cure the prejudice against the papal name and bring real and lasting glory. – But
25   meanwhile we've fallen off the donkey, as the saying is.[91] We've strayed far away from our plan.
Butcher I'll quickly get you back to the road. You say, then, that papal laws are binding on all who are in the church?[92]
Fishmonger I say so.
30   **Butcher** On penalty of hell-fire?
Fishmonger They say so.
Butcher The laws of bishops, too?[93]
Fishmonger In each one's jurisdiction, I believe.
Butcher And of abbots?[94]
35   **Fishmonger** I hesitate to say, for they take up their rule on certain conditions, and they cannot burden their people with regulations unless authorized by the entire order.
Butcher What if a bishop receives his office on the same conditions?
Fishmonger I'm inclined to doubt it.
40   **Butcher** Has the pope power to rescind what a bishop has ordained?
Fishmonger I think he has.

Butcher Can nobody annul what the pope has decreed?

Fishmonger Nobody.

Butcher Then how is it we hear of papal judgments rescinded on the ground that popes were misinformed, and of regulations of earlier popes superseded by those of later ones because the former deviated from true piety?[95]

Fishmonger Those regulations were ones that crept in for a season, for ignorance about a person or fact can occur in a pope as a human being. But what proceeds from the authority of a universal council is a heavenly oracle and carries weight equal to that of the Gospels, or surely almost equal.[96]

Butcher Is it permissible to doubt concerning the Gospels?

Fishmonger Mind your language: surely not even to doubt councils solemnly convened and conducted, whose acts are proclaimed and received under the guidance of the Holy Spirit.

Butcher What if one should doubt whether these attributes belong to a council that is called in question, as I hear the Council of Basel is rejected by some and that of Constance is not accepted by everyone. I mean (omitting all mention of the last Lateran Council), doubt about those now considered orthodox?[97]

Fishmonger Let those who wish, doubt at their peril; I don't want to doubt.

Butcher Then Peter had authority to establish new laws?[98]

Fishmonger He had.

Butcher And Paul too, with the other apostles?

Fishmonger Each of them had in his churches appointed to him by Peter or Christ.

Butcher And is the power for Peter's successors equal to that of Peter himself?

Fishmonger Why not?

Butcher Then as much honour is due to a rescript of the Roman pontiff as to the Epistles of Peter? And as much to the regulations[99] of bishops as to Paul's Epistles?

Fishmonger Indeed I think even more is due if they prescribe and legislate with authority.

Butcher But is it lawful to doubt whether Peter and Paul wrote by the inspiration of the Holy Spirit?

Fishmonger Oh, no; whoever doubted it would be a heretic.

Butcher Do you think the same of the rescripts and regulations of popes and bishops?

Fishmonger Of a pope, I do think so; of bishops, I'm not sure, except that it's our duty to suspect no one falsely unless the matter plainly calls for suspicion.[100]

Butcher Why does the Spirit more readily allow a bishop to err than a pope?

Fishmonger Because it's more dangerous for the head to err.

Butcher If the regulations of prelates are worth so much,[101] what does the Lord mean in Deuteronomy by threatening so sternly against anyone's adding or taking away anything from the Law?[102]

5 **Fishmonger** One doesn't add to the Law by explaining more fully what was obscure and suggesting ways of keeping it. Nor does he take away who adjusts the Law to the capacity of his hearers, bringing out some aspects and concealing others, as the time requires.

Butcher The regulations of scribes and Pharisees weren't binding, were
10 they?

Fishmonger I think not.

Butcher Why?

Fishmonger Because they had authority to teach, not to make laws.

Butcher Which power seems greater, that of ordaining human laws or of
15 interpreting divine ones?

Fishmonger Ordaining human ones.

Butcher I disagree. For the judgment of one who has the right of interpreting carries the weight of divine law.

Fishmonger I don't quite follow.

20 **Butcher** I'll explain more clearly. Divine law commands us to help a parent. According to the Pharisees' interpretation, whatever is placed in the offering[103] is given to one's father, because God is the Father of all men. Doesn't divine law yield to this interpretation?

Fishmonger That is surely a false interpretation.

25 **Butcher** But after the authority of interpreting has once been handed over to them, how am I to tell whose interpretation is right, especially if the interpreters differ among themselves?[104]

Fishmonger If the meaning generally accepted hasn't satisfied you, follow the authority of prelates. That's the safest course.

30 **Butcher** Then the authority of scribes and Pharisees has descended upon theologians and preachers?

Fishmonger Yes.

Butcher But I hear no men insisting more often, 'Hear, I say unto you' than those who have no experience in theological debates.[105]

35 **Fishmonger** You should hear them all fairly but judiciously, provided they don't simply drivel; in that case the people ought to hiss them off, so they'll recognize their own folly. On the other hand, you should have confidence in anyone with a doctor's degree.

Butcher But among these I find some much more ignorant and absurd than
40 those who are completely uneducated. And I see extraordinary disagreement among the most learned men.

Fishmonger Select the best explanations and leave the unexplained matters to others, always adopting those views approved by the majority of lords and commons.

Butcher That's the safer course, I know. Are there unjust ordinances too,
5   then, as there are false interpretations?

Fishmonger Whether there are, let others decide. I think it's possible.

Butcher Did Annas and Caiaphas[106] have authority to ordain laws?

Fishmonger They did.

Butcher Their regulations about anything did not bind on pain of hell-fire,
10   did they?

Fishmonger I don't know.

Butcher Suppose Annas had ordained that no one home from the market-place should eat without washing: he who ate unwashed wouldn't be guilty of an offence deserving hell-fire?[107]

15   **Fishmonger** I don't think so, unless he made his offence worse by contempt of public authority.

Butcher Do all of God's commandments bind on pain of hell-fire?[108]

Fishmonger I suppose not, for God forbade all sin however venial, if we may believe theologians.

20   **Butcher** Perhaps 'venial' sin too would bring us to hell, did not God in his mercy help our helplessness.

Fishmonger Sounds sensible. I wouldn't venture to swear to it.

Butcher When the Israelites were exiled in Babylon,[109] the rite of circumcision, besides a great many others enjoined by the Law, was omitted
25   in many instances. Did all these men perish?

Fishmonger God knows.

Butcher If a Jew at point of starvation were secretly to eat pork, would he be guilty of a crime?

Fishmonger In my judgment, necessity would excuse the act, seeing that
30   David was defended by the voice of the Lord for eating, in violation of the Law, the sacred bread called the 'shewbread.' Not only did he eat of it but with it he fed also his fellow fugitives, who were heathen.[110]

Butcher If the same sort of necessity compelled one to choose between dying of hunger or committing a theft, which should he choose – death or
35   theft?

Fishmonger Perhaps in that event theft would not be theft.

Butcher Ho there, what do I hear? Isn't an egg an egg?[111]

Fishmonger Especially if one took something with the intention of restoring it and of gaining the owner's forgiveness as soon as possible.

40   **Butcher** What if a man were going to die unless he bore false witness against his neighbour? Which should he choose?

Fishmonger Death.

Butcher What if he could save his life by committing adultery?

Fishmonger Death will be preferable.

Butcher What if you could escape death by fornication?[112]

5 **Fishmonger** One should die, rather, so they say.

Butcher Why doesn't this egg cease to be an egg, particularly if no violence or injury results?

Fishmonger Injury to the girl's body results.

Butcher What if you could save your life by perjury?[113]

10 **Fishmonger** You ought to die instead.

Butcher What if you could save it by a harmless little white lie?[114]

Fishmonger They teach that death should be preferred. But I should have thought that in an emergency, or when some great public good is involved, a lie of this kind would either be no crime at all or else a very petty one, unless

15 it encouraged[115] the habit of dangerous falsehoods as well. Suppose that by a harmless lie he could save the bodies and souls of his whole nation: which would a good man choose? Would he shun the lie?

Butcher What others would do, I don't know. I myself would not shrink from telling fifteen Homeric lies[116] and I would soon wipe away that slight

20 stain with holy water.

Fishmonger I'd do the same.

Butcher So not just whatever is commanded or forbidden by God binds one on pain of hell-fire.

Fishmonger Apparently not.

25 **Butcher** The extent of obligation, therefore, depends not only on the author of the law but on the substance of it, since some laws yield to necessity and some don't.

Fishmonger So it seems.

Butcher What if a priest whose life were at stake could save himself by

30 marrying? Which should he choose?

Fishmonger Death.

Butcher Since divine law yields to necessity, why does this human law[117] play the part of Terminus,[118] yielding to none?

Fishmonger It's not a law but a vow that stands in the way.[119]

35 **Butcher** What if someone had vowed to visit Jerusalem[120] but could not do so except with certain loss of life: will he refrain from going[121] or will he die?

Fishmonger Die, unless released from the vow by the Roman pontiff.

Butcher Why is one vow remitted, another scarcely so?

40 **Fishmonger** Because one is a solemn vow, the other a private one.

Butcher What is a solemn one?

Fishmonger One that is commonly made.[122]

Butcher Then isn't the other kind, which is made every day, solemn too?

Fishmonger It's made, but privately.

Butcher Then if a monk privately makes a promise to an abbot, that would
5 not be a solemn vow?

Fishmonger You're joking. A private vow is remitted more easily because broken with less scandal, and he who makes it does so with the intention of changing his mind if it suits him to do this.

Butcher Then do those who privately pledge themselves to perpetual
10 chastity vow with this intention?

Fishmonger They should.

Butcher So perpetual is also not perpetual? What if a Carthusian monk were faced with the necessity of eating meat or dying: which should he choose?

Fishmonger Physicians teach that no meat is so efficacious but that *aurum*
15 *potabile*[123] and jewels might produce the same result.

Butcher Which is more useful, then: to rescue with gold and jewels a man in danger or by the price of these things to save many who are in peril of their lives and to give a sick man a chicken?[124]

Fishmonger I hesitate to say.

20 **Butcher** Yet the eating of fish or meat is not among those things they call essential.

Fishmonger Let's leave the Carthusians to their own judge.

Butcher Let's talk in general terms. Keeping the sabbath is stressed earnestly, frequently, and at length in the law of Moses.[125]

25 **Fishmonger** True.

Butcher Then should I save an endangered city by violating the sabbath or not?

Fishmonger But meantime do you take me for a Jew?

Butcher Yes, and a circumcised one, too.

30 **Fishmonger** The Lord himself solved this problem: the sabbath is made for man, not the contrary.[126]

Butcher Will that rule prevail, then, in all human regulations?[127]

Fishmonger It will unless something stands in the way.

Butcher What if the lawmaker should issue his law, not with the intention
35 of binding everyone on pain of hell-fire, no, or even on pain of any criminal guilt, but wanting his regulation to have no more force than that of an admonition?

Fishmonger My good friend, it is not the prerogative of the lawmaker to say how binding the law shall be.[128] He exercised his authority in making
40 the law, but to what degree it binds or does not bind one is in God's hands.

Butcher Why then do we hear our parish priests crying daily from the pulpit: 'Tomorrow you must fast on pain of eternal damnation,'[129] if we aren't certain how far a human law binds us?

Fishmonger They do that to frighten the obstinate more; for I think these
5 words apply to them.

Butcher But sometimes I'm uncertain whether they do frighten the obstinate by such pronouncements. Certainly they throw the weaker brethren into anxiety or danger.

Fishmonger It's hard to look out for both.

10 **Butcher** Do custom and law have the same force?

Fishmonger Sometimes custom is stronger.

Butcher Accordingly, then, even if those who introduce a custom don't intend to set a trap for anyone, the custom may nevertheless be binding whether they like it or not?[130]

15 **Fishmonger** I think so.

Butcher It can impose a burden but not remove it?

Fishmonger Of course.

Butcher So you see now, I expect, how dangerous it is for new laws to be imposed by men if no necessity compels or no great advantage invites.

20 **Fishmonger** I grant it.

Butcher When the Lord says, 'Swear not at all,'[131] he doesn't make any swearing whatever liable to hell-fire?

Fishmonger I don't think so. For that is a counsel, not a precept.[132]

Butcher But how can I be sure, when he forbade scarcely anything else more
25 explicitly or severely than swearing?

Fishmonger You'll learn from the Doctors.

Butcher And when Paul gives counsel, that is not binding on pain of hell-fire?

Fishmonger Not at all.

30 **Butcher** Why?

Fishmonger Because he doesn't want to set a snare for the weak.

Butcher Then it *is* in the lawmaker's power to bind under penalty of hell-fire or not to bind. And it *is* righteous to warn against ensnaring the weak with just any regulations.[133]

35 **Fishmonger** Yes.

Butcher And if Paul was guarded in this respect, much more ought priests, of whose inspiration we are uncertain, to be guarded.

Fishmonger Granted.

Butcher But a little while ago you were denying that the degree to which a
40 law binds us is in the power of the lawmaker.

Fishmonger Well, now I give it as counsel, not law.

Butcher Nothing is easier than to change the word. Is 'Thou shalt not steal'[134] a precept?

Fishmonger Yes.

Butcher 'Resist not evil'?[135]

5 **Fishmonger** It's a counsel.

Butcher But this latter one looks more like a precept than the former does. At least it is in the bishops' power whether they wish their ordinances to be precept or counsel?[136]

Fishmonger It is.

10 **Butcher** But you emphatically denied that a short time ago. In fact whoever does not intend his regulation to bind anyone on pain of criminal liability sincerely intends it to be a counsel, not a precept.

Fishmonger True, but it's not suitable for the common people to know this, lest they protest at once that whatever they don't want to observe is a

15 counsel.

Butcher But meantime what will you do, since so many weak consciences are so miserably confused by your silence? Come now, tell me: have the learned no marks by which they can discover whether a regulation has the force of a counsel or a precept?

20 **Fishmonger** They have, as I've heard.

Butcher May not one know the secret?

Fishmonger You may, unless you'd want to babble.

Butcher Oh, you'll tell it to a fish.[137]

Fishmonger When you hear nothing except 'We exhort,' 'We appoint,'

25 'We charge,' it's a counsel; when you hear 'We order,' 'We strictly enjoin,' especially if threats of excommunication are added, it's a precept.[138]

Butcher What if I'm in debt to my baker, and since I can't pay I prefer to run off rather than be thrown into jail: do I sin gravely?

Fishmonger I don't think so, unless the will to pay is lacking.

30 **Butcher** Then why am I excommunicated?[139]

Fishmonger That thunderbolt[140] terrifies the wicked; it does not burn the innocent. And you know that among the ancient Romans too there were dreadful, threatening laws made solely for this very purpose: such as that from the Twelve Tables about cutting into pieces the body of a

35 debtor – of which not a single example survives, because it was proclaimed not for use but for terrifying.[141] Now as a thunderbolt does not affect wax or flax but does affect brass,[142] so such excommunications don't affect poor, wretched creatures but obstinate ones. And yet – to speak frankly – to employ in trifles of this kind the thunderbolt received from

40 Christ seems almost, as the ancients used to say, wasting perfume on lentils.[143]

Butcher Hasn't the head of the household the same authority in his home that a bishop has in his diocese?

Fishmonger I think he has, relatively.

Butcher And his ordinances are binding in the same manner?

5 **Fishmonger** Why not?

Butcher I decree that no one should eat onions. Just how does he who does not obey risk God's displeasure?

Fishmonger Let him see to that.

Butcher Hereafter I won't say to my family, 'I order,' but 'I admonish.'

10 **Fishmonger** You'll be wise to do so.

Butcher But I observe that my next-door neighbour is in danger, and when I've got him alone I admonish him privately to quit the company of drunkards and gamblers. Scoffing at my warning, he begins to live a more abandoned life than before. My admonition doesn't bind him in this respect?

15 **Fishmonger** So it seems.

Butcher Then we escape the trap[144] neither by counselling nor by exhorting.

Fishmonger No, it's not the admonition but the subject of the admonition that makes the trap. For if a brother admonished to wear sandals neglected to do so, it would be no criminal offence.

20 **Butcher** I won't inquire here to what degree physicians' orders are binding. Does a vow bind on pain of hell-fire?

Fishmonger Most certainly.

Butcher Every vow?

Fishmonger Absolutely every one, provided it be licit, legitimate, and

25 voluntary.

Butcher What do you mean by 'voluntary'?

Fishmonger What no compulsion has wrung.

Butcher What is 'compulsion'?

Fishmonger Fear befalling a steadfast man.[145]

30 **Butcher** Even a Stoic, whom, 'if the world crashed, the ruins will strike unperturbed'?[146]

Fishmonger Show me the Stoic and I'll tell you.

Butcher But joking aside, fear of famine or infamy[147] doesn't befall a steadfast man, does it?

35 **Fishmonger** Certainly. Why not?

Butcher If a daughter not yet freed from parental authority marries secretly without her parents' knowledge, and without their consent if they do know, will her vow be lawful?[148]

Fishmonger It will.

40 **Butcher** Whether it be so, I know not. Surely if there are things which may be true, yet about which it is better to keep quiet because of the scandal to

weak natures, this is one of them. What if a girl who with parental consent has contracted a marriage[149] should secretly, and against her parents' wishes, dedicate herself by a vow to the order of St Clare:[150] will the vow be licit and legitimate?

5   **Fishmonger** If it's a solemn one.

Butcher What happens in the country, in an obscure little monastery,[151] isn't 'solemn,' is it?

Fishmonger It is so considered.

Butcher If the same girl, in the presence of a few witnesses at home, makes
10   a vow of perpetual chastity, it will not be legitimate?

Fishmonger No.

Butcher Why?

Fishmonger Because a holier vow stands in the way.[152]

Butcher If the same girl sells a piece of land, will the contract be valid?
15   **Fishmonger** I don't think so.[153]

Butcher And if she gives herself into another's power, will that be valid?

Fishmonger If she dedicates herself to God.[154]

Butcher Doesn't a private vow also dedicate a person to God? And doesn't he who receives the holy sacrament of matrimony dedicate himself to God?[155]
20   And do those whom God joins dedicate themselves to the devil? Only of married persons has the Lord said, 'Whom God hath joined together, let not man put asunder.'[156] Besides, when a youth scarcely grown up, or an innocent girl, by parental threats, cruelty of guardians, wicked instigation of monks, flattery, and hatred, is thrust into a monastery, that's not a free vow,
25   is it?[157]

Fishmonger If they're 'capable of wrong.'[158]

Butcher That age is especially 'capable of wrong' in that it can be imposed upon with the greatest of ease. What if I resolve to abstain from wine on Fridays: would the resolution have the force of a vow?
30   **Fishmonger** I don't believe it would.

Butcher Then what's the difference between a fixed resolution and a vow made by silent deliberation?

Fishmonger The intention of binding one's self.

Butcher Earlier you denied that intention prevails in this circumstance.[159] I
35   'resolve' if I'm able and I 'vow' whether able or not?

Fishmonger You have it.

Butcher I have clouds painted on a wall[160] – nothing, in other words! – And so, in a resolution, content need not be considered?

Fishmonger That's my opinion.
40   **Butcher** And as we should be careful in the one respect on account of the law, so in the other, on account of a vow?

Fishmonger Right.

Butcher If the Roman pontiff ordained that no one should marry within the seventh degree of consanguinity, would he who married a relation within the sixth degree be guilty of a crime?[161]

5 **Fishmonger** I suppose so; certainly he would risk it.

Butcher What if a bishop decreed to his people that no one should have intercourse with his wife except on Monday, Thursday, and Saturday: would one who had it secretly on other days be guilty of a crime?

Fishmonger I think he would.

10 **Butcher** What if he decreed that no one eat onions?

Fishmonger What has that to do with piety?

Butcher Onions are aphrodisiacs.[162] Suppose the same thing I say about onions to be said of cabbage.

Fishmonger I'm at a loss.

15 **Butcher** Why at a loss? Whence comes the power of human laws to bind?

Fishmonger From Paul's words: 'Obey them that have the rule over you.'[163]

Butcher Then it follows from this that every regulation of bishops and magistrates is binding?

Fishmonger Provided it's fair, just, and legitimately made.

20 **Butcher** But who will be judge of that?

Fishmonger He who established it. For it's the prerogative of the lawmaker to interpret the law.[164]

Butcher Therefore all regulations whatever, without distinction, must be obeyed?

25 **Fishmonger** In my opinion.

Butcher What if a foolish and unrighteous official[165] issues an unrighteous and unjust law? Will it have to stand because of his decision, and will the people – who have no legal right to decide on it – obey?

Fishmonger What's the good of dreaming of things that don't happen?

30 **Butcher** He who helps a parent, but wouldn't do so unless compelled by law, doesn't keep the law, does he?[166]

Fishmonger I don't think he does.

Butcher How so?

Fishmonger In the first place, he doesn't satisfy the intent of the lawmaker;

35 secondly, to a bad will he adds hypocrisy.

Butcher He who fasts, but wouldn't unless the church prescribed it, doesn't satisfy the law, does he?

Fishmonger You're changing both author and substance of the law.

Butcher Then compare the Jew, fasting on prescribed days in such fashion

40 that unless compelled by law he would not fast, with the Christian keeping a fast appointed by men – a Christian who won't keep it if you repeal the law.

Or, if you prefer, the Jew abstaining from pork and the Christian abstaining from meat and milky foods on Friday.[167]

Fishmonger Some failure to keep the law out of weakness is pardonable, I think, but deliberately opposing and murmuring against it is not.

5 **Butcher** But you admit that divine laws don't always bind on pain of hell-fire.

Fishmonger Why shouldn't I admit it?

Butcher You don't dare admit there's a human law which does not bind by that same penalty, but you leave mankind in doubt? Then you will seem to

10 attribute more to man's laws than to God's. Falsehood and slander are wrongs *per se* and forbidden by God; yet you admit there is some sort of falsehood and slander that does not make one liable to hell-fire, but you don't dare to free from hell-fire the man who in some manner or other eats meat on Friday.

Fishmonger It's not up to me to absolve or condemn anybody.

15 **Butcher** If divine and human laws are equally binding, then what's the difference between them?

Fishmonger Clearly that he who violates human law commits an offence *immediately* against man (if you permit me to use the fancy terms of the scholastics),[168] *mediately* against God; he who violates divine law does the

20 contrary.

Butcher What does it matter whether you mix vinegar or absinthe first, when I must drink both? Or what matter whether a stone glancing off me, after I'm hurt by it, strikes my friend or vice versa?

Fishmonger This is what I've learned.

25 **Butcher** And if the degree of obligation in both kinds of laws depends on their content and circumstances, what's the difference between God's authority and man's?

Fishmonger A wicked question!

Butcher Still, many people think there's a vast difference. God issued the

30 Law through Moses; it must not be violated. The same God proclaims laws through popes, or surely through a council. What's the difference between these laws and those? The law of Moses is given through a man; our laws through men. And what God proclaimed through one Moses appears to have less authority than what the Holy Spirit issues through a full council of

35 bishops and scholars.

Fishmonger It's not permissible to doubt concerning the inspiration of Moses.

Butcher Paul came in place of bishops. So what difference is there between Paul's precepts and those of any bishop?

40 **Fishmonger** That, beyond question, Paul wrote by the inspiration of the Spirit.

Butcher How far does this authority of writers extend?

Fishmonger Not beyond the apostles, I think, unless councils have inviolate authority.

Butcher Why isn't it permissible to doubt Paul's inspiration?

5 **Fishmonger** Because the consensus of the church forbids.

Butcher May one doubt concerning bishops?[169]

Fishmonger They should not be suspected rashly, unless the circumstances themselves point clearly to filthy lucre or unrighteousness.

Butcher What about councils?[170]

10 **Fishmonger** If they were duly convoked and conducted by the Holy Spirit, you may not doubt.

Butcher Is there any council, then, that lacks these qualifications?

Fishmonger Possibly. Otherwise theologians would not add this condition.

Butcher Then apparently it *is* possible to doubt concerning councils, too.

15 **Fishmonger** Not, I believe, after they have been accepted and approved by the judgment and consensus of Christian peoples.

Butcher Beyond the limits[171] set by God's will to the sacrosanct and inviolable authority of the Scriptures, there is in my opinion another distinction also between divine and human laws.

20 **Fishmonger** What?

Butcher Divine laws are immutable unless they are of the kind that seem given for the purpose of signifying or coercing at a particular time – the kind that the prophets predicted would cease, in the earthly sense, and that according to apostolic teaching should now be given up.[172] Furthermore,

25 among human laws there are sometimes wicked, foolish, and oppressive ones, on which account they are annulled either by higher authority or through general neglect by the public. Such is not the case with divine laws. Again, human law ceases of its own accord when the occasion for which it was made ends; as for example an ordinance requiring everyone to make

30 an annual contribution towards the building of a church: the force of the law ends when the church is completed. In addition, law made by man is not law unless it is acceptable to those who employ it. Divine law ought not to be judged, nor can it be abolished. Though even Moses took a vote before issuing a law, he didn't do this because he had to but in order to

35 render the people more obedient – since it is shameful to slight a law that you yourself voted for.[173] Finally, though human laws, which commonly prescribe corporal practices, are guides to godliness, they evidently come to an end when anyone has attained to such spiritual vigour as to need these restraints no longer[174] – provided he does his utmost to avoid shocking the

40 weak, not those who are overscrupulous out of malice. As if, for instance, a father should forbid a young daughter to drink wine, the better to protect

her virginity until marriage. When she's grown up and already given to a husband, she's no longer bound by her father's order. Many laws resemble drugs: indeed they're changed and yield to new circumstances with the approval of the physicians themselves, who would kill more people than they

5   cured if they always used the same remedies handed down by the ancients.

Fishmonger Well, you bring together many arguments, some of which I like, others I don't, and some I don't understand.

Butcher If a bishop's statute plainly savours of financial profit, that is, if in order to wring more money from them he requires every parish priest to

10 buy twice a year, for a gold ducat, the right of absolving in what are called reserved cases,[175] do you think it ought to be obeyed?

Fishmonger I do, but in the meantime there ought to be a protest – always short of rebellion – against the bad law. But how come you're my inquisitor, butcher? 'Let smiths mind their tools.'[176]

15 **Butcher** At dinners we're often troubled by such questions. Sometimes the argument becomes so heated it ends in blows and bloodshed.

Fishmonger Let those who want to fight do so. I myself believe the laws of our forefathers ought to be reverently received and dutifully obeyed, as though they came from God. It is neither safe nor right to conceive or sow

20 harmful suspicion concerning public authority. And if there is some tyranny, but not enough to force us to wrongdoing, better to endure it than to oppose it seditiously.[177]

Butcher I admit that will help those who hold powerful offices; and I feel as you do. I'm not jealous of them. But I'd like to hear how the liberty and

25 welfare of the people are to be provided for, too.

Fishmonger God will not desert his people.

Butcher But meanwhile where is that spiritual freedom[178] – which the apostles promise from the gospel, which Paul so often insists upon, proclaiming that 'the kingdom of God is not meat and drink,' and that we are

30 not children under a tutor, nor should we serve any longer the elements of this world;[179] and countless other things he says – if Christians are burdened with so many more regulations than Jews and if the laws of men bind more strictly than many of the precepts received from God?

Fishmonger I'll tell you, butcher. Christian freedom does not consist in

35 doing as one likes, unhampered by human regulations, but in fervour of spirit prepared for all things, doing readily and eagerly, as children rather than servants, what we are commanded to do.

Butcher A ready answer. But there were sons under the Mosaic law, too, and there are servants under the gospel – and that includes most men, I fear,

40 since those who do their duty because the law compels them are servants. So what's the difference between the New and the Old Law?

Fishmonger A great deal, in my opinion. What the Old Law taught under a veil,[180] the New Law placed before the eyes; what that foretold in riddles, this displayed more clearly; what that promised somewhat darkly, this for the most part displayed openly. That was handed down to one nation; this
5   teaches salvation to all men alike. That imparted extraordinary spiritual grace to a few prophets and distinguished men; this poured out generously every kind of gift – of tongues, healing, prophecies, miracles – unto people of all ages, sexes, and nations.

Butcher Then where are these miracles nowadays?[181]

10   **Fishmonger** They have ceased (but not perished utterly), either because there is no need for them now that Christ's teaching is widespread, or because most of us, Christians in name only, lack faith, which is the maker of miracles.

Butcher If miracles are needed on account of unbelievers and infidels, the
15   world is full of such men nowadays.

Fishmonger There is naïvely mistaken unbelief, such as that of the Jews who murmured against Peter for having received the family of Cornelius into the grace of the gospel;[182] such as that of the gentiles who regarded whatever religion they had inherited from their ancestors as conferring salvation,
20   and the teaching of the apostles as a foreign superstition. These men were converted by the miracles they beheld. Those who now are unbelievers in the gospel, when so great a light shines throughout the whole world, do not merely err but, blinded by sinful lusts, have 'left off to be wise, and to do good.'[183] No miracles would restore these men to a better mind. And now is
25   the time for correction; afterwards will be a time for punishment.

Butcher Though you've said many things quite convincingly, still I'm resolved not to trust a salt fish seller, but I'll go to some exceptionally learned theologian; whatever he decides about each matter will serve as an oracle from heaven.

30   **Fishmonger** Who's that? Pharetrius?[184]

Butcher A mere fool, and before his time, too – good for preaching to silly old women.

Fishmonger Bliteus?[185]

Butcher Am I to believe such a chattering sophist?

35   **Fishmonger** Amphicolus?[186]

Butcher I'll never trust him to answer questions. I trusted him – to my loss – with my meat. Could he solve problems honestly when he was not honest enough to pay his bill?

Fishmonger Lemantius?[187]

40   **Butcher** I don't use blind men as guides.

Fishmonger Who, then?

Butcher Cephalus,[188] if you want to know; a man splendidly learned in the three languages and all *belles lettres*, besides having studied the Bible and ancient theologians long and deeply.

Fishmonger I'll give you better advice. Go to hell; there you'll find Master[189]
5   Druin, who will remove all your difficulties with the double-edged Tenedian axe.[190]

Butcher You go ahead to prepare the way for me.

Fishmonger But joking aside, are you telling the truth – that permission has been granted to eat meat?[191]

10   **Butcher** I was joking, to torment you. And if the Roman pontiff should want to do it ever so much, the salt fish sellers as a class would rise in rebellion. In the next place, the world is full of pharisaical men who can prove their holiness only by such trivial observances.[192] They wouldn't stand for having that glory taken away from them now, nor would they allow their juniors to
15   have more liberty than they themselves had. It wouldn't even mean money in the butchers' pockets if the eating of anything whatever were permitted, for then our business would fluctuate; now our profit is more certain, with fewer risks and less work.

Fishmonger Very true, but the same inconvenience would come to us.

20   **Butcher** I'm glad we've finally found something a salt fish seller and a butcher can agree on. Now – to begin to speak seriously myself, too – just as I think it might be useful for Christian people to be bound by fewer minor regulations, especially if these contribute little or nothing to godliness (not to say hinder it), so am I unwilling to support those who reject all regulations
25   of all men and care not a straw for them.[193] More than that, they do many things just *because* they're forbidden to do them. – Still, I can't be astonished at the absurd judgments of men in a great many matters.

Fishmonger As for me, I can't marvel enough at them.

Butcher We turn the world upside down[194] if we suspect there's any danger
30   that the regulations and authority of the clergy may lose force, yet we pay no attention to the plainly evident danger of attributing so much to the authority of men that less is given to divine authority than is right. We steer so far wide of Scylla that we have no fear of Charybdis, a more deadly evil.[195] Who denies that honour is due to bishops, particularly if they do what their name
35   implies?[196] But it is impious to transfer to men the honour due to God alone, and, while we revere a man lavishly, revere God too little.[197] God is to be honoured in a fellow man, venerated in a fellow man; but all the same we must see to it that God is not defrauded, on this account, of the honour due him.

Fishmonger Similarly we see many persons trust so much in corporal rites
40   that, relying on these, they neglect what belongs to true godliness: arrogating to their own merits what comes of divine bounty, standing still where they

might have ascended to the more perfect, and slandering a neighbour on account of things neither good nor bad in themselves.[198]

Butcher Indeed, when in the same affair there are two choices, one of which is better than the other, we always prefer the worse. The body, and what is of the body, are everywhere more esteemed than the things of the spirit. To have killed a man is considered a very serious crime – as it is; but to have destroyed a man's mind with pestilential doctrine, with poisonous ideas, is sport. If a priest lets his hair grow long,[199] or wears a layman's garb,[200] he is thrown into jail and punished severely; if he boozes in a brothel, if he whores, if he dices, if he corrupts other men's wives,[201] if he never touches a Bible, he is none the less a pillar of the church. I don't excuse a change of costume, but I deprecate a preposterous judgment.

Fishmonger Nay, if he does not recite the Hours,[202] excommunication is at hand; if he lends money at interest[203] or practises simony,[204] he goes unpunished.[205]

Butcher If someone sees a Carthusian dressed in unorthodox fashion or eating meat, how he swears, how he shudders, how fearful is he lest the earth open wide and swallow both spectator and spectacle! Yet no one is similarly horrified to see the Carthusian drunk or ruining other people's reputations by telling lies about them or openly cheating a poor neighbour.[206]

Fishmonger It's as if one should see a Franciscan girded with an unknotted cord,[207] or an Augustinian girded with wool instead of leather,[208] or an ungirded Carmelite,[209] or a girded Rhodian.[210] Again, if one should see a Franciscan wearing shoes,[211] or a Crutched Friar half-shod,[212] wouldn't he stir up the Tyrian seas,[213] as the saying is?

Butcher What's more, in our part of town recently, one of two women – both of whom you would have credited with common sense – had a miscarriage[214] and the other a fainting fit because they spied some prefect of canons, in charge of nuns, walking about in the immediate neighbourhood, but still in public, without a linen habit covered with a black cloak.[215] But these same women had often seen birds of that sort revelling, singing, dancing – I won't say what else – and never felt upset at all.

Fishmonger Perhaps that should be overlooked on account of their sex. You know Polythrescus,[216] I dare say. He was dangerously ill – had consumption. The physicians tried long but in vain to get him to eat eggs and milky foods.[217] The bishop likewise urged him. Though not an uneducated man (he was a bachelor of divinity), Polythrescus seemed ready to die sooner than follow the advice of these doctors. So his physicians and friends decided to play a trick on him. They made a broth of eggs and goat's milk and said it was almond milk. He ate it willingly, and doing the same for several days began to improve a little, until some servant-girl gave the secret away.

Thereupon he started to vomit what he had eaten. Yet that same man who was so superstitious about milk felt no scruples about welshing on a debt he owed me;[218] he had secretly torn up a promissory note that was openly acknowledged. He took an oath; I yielded to him. He was so casual about it

5 that he seemed to wish to take such oaths every day. What could be more crooked than this course? He sinned against the judgment of the church in not obeying priest and physicians; and in a plain case of perjury he who was so delicate about milk had a good, strong conscience!

Butcher Here I'm reminded of a story told lately by a certain Dominican,

10 when preaching before a crowded congregation, to temper the sadness of his sermon – for this happened on the Day of Preparation and he was preaching about our Lord's death.[219] A young man had taken advantage of a nun; her swollen belly was proof of the deed. An assembly of nuns was convoked, the abbess presiding. The nun was accused. No ground for *status inficialis*;

15 the evidence was inescapable. She took refuge in the *status qualitatis* – or the *status translationis*, if you prefer. 'I was overcome by someone stronger.' 'But at least you could have screamed.' 'I would have done so,' says she, 'but there's a strict rule against making noise in the dorter.'[220] That's the story, anyway; only we must admit many things sillier that this are done.

20 Now I'll tell you something I saw with my own eyes; I won't give the name of the man and the place. I used to have a relative who was a prior, next in rank to an abbot,[221] in the Benedictine order, but he was one of those who don't eat meat except outside the place they call the great refectory.[222] He was thought to be learned and he himself wanted to be thought so. He was

25 about fifty years old. Drinking bouts and carousings were daily occurrences with him. Every twelfth day he would go to the public baths to clear his kidneys.[223]

Fishmonger How could he afford that?

Butcher He had an income of six hundred florins a year.

30 **Fishmonger** Enviable poverty!

Butcher From wine and lechery he became consumptive. When the doctors despaired of his life, the abbot ordered him to eat meat,[224] adding that terrifying phrase, 'on penalty of disobedience.'[225] On his deathbed he could scarcely be compelled to taste flesh – from which he had not shrunk for so

35 many years.

Fishmonger A prior worthy of such an abbot! But I can guess the ones you're talking about, for I remember hearing the same story from others.

Butcher Guess.

Fishmonger Isn't the abbot a large, fat man with a lisp, and the prior a

40 shorter man but straight and handsome?

Butcher You've guessed it.

Fishmonger Tit for tat:[226] you'll hear what I myself saw recently. I was
not only present but almost presided over it too. Two nuns were visiting
relatives. When they reached their destination, it turned out that their servant
had forgotten and left behind a prayer book according to the use of their
5   order and community. Good Lord, what an uproar! They didn't dare dine
unless Vespers were said,[227] and they couldn't bear to say them from any
other book than their own. Meanwhile the entire household went hungry.
To make a long story short, the servant went back on the gelding; late in
the evening he brings the missing book; prayers are said; and at ten o'clock
10   we've hardly had dinner.
Butcher So far I hear nothing very awful.
Fishmonger Well, you've heard only half the story. During dinner these
virgins began to feel jolly with wine,[228] and finally when laughter broke out
the party roared at jokes that were scarcely modest ones; nobody behaved
15   more loosely than those two who refused to eat dinner unless prayers were
said according to the use of their order. After dinner came games, dances,[229]
songs, and other things I don't dare mention; but I'm very much afraid
what was done that night was hardly virginal, unless the preliminaries, the
wanton games,[230] nods, and kisses, deceived me.
20   **Butcher** I don't so much blame the nuns for that waywardness as I do the
priests in charge of them.[231] But come; I'll match story with story. Nay, you
shall hear rather a tale of something I saw with my own eyes.[232] Recently
some persons were thrown into jail because they dared to bake bread on the
Lord's day, though they may have needed it.[233] Now I don't condemn the
25   arrest but I reject the sentence.[234] Some time later, on what is called Palm
Sunday,[235] it happened that I had to go to a neighbouring village. There,
about four in the afternoon, I'm confronted by a spectacle I wouldn't know
whether to call more pathetic or ridiculous; I do think no bacchanalian revels
were more shameful. Some people were staggering about drunk, as a ship
30   without a pilot is tossed by winds and waves. There were some who had
their arms around another to keep him from falling, but they themselves
were less than steady. Others fell down repeatedly and had a hard time
getting up. Some were crowned with oak leaves.
Fishmonger Vine leaves would have been more appropriate; and they
35   should have added the thyrsus.[236]
Butcher One old fellow, playing the part of Silenus,[237] was carried aloft on
their shoulders like a bundle, in the position corpses are sometimes borne –
feet first – except that he was carried head down to prevent his choking with
vomit, as would have happened had he had his head up. He was vomiting
40   wretchedly on the legs and heels of the hindmost carriers. There wasn't a
sober man among the bearers. Most were laughing, but in such a manner that

you'd say without hesitation they were crazy. The bacchic frenzy possessed them all.[238] And in this procession they entered the city – in broad daylight, too.

Fishmonger Where had they caught that madness?

5　**Butcher** In a neighbouring village wine was sold a little cheaper than in town, so some pot-companions had gone there to be mad more cheaply but more copiously – for there was no less money spent but more folly bought. Had these men tasted an egg, they would have been clapped into jail as if for confessed parricides,[239] though when (in addition to missing the sermon

10　and neglecting Vespers) so much licence was publicly tolerated on such a holy day,[240] no one punished them, no one denounced them.

Fishmonger But – to save you from being so surprised at that – in the middle of town, in taverns next door to the church, on any holy day whatever, there is drinking, singing, dancing, brawling with so much tumult and

15　shouting that the service can't be finished or the sermon heard. If those same folk had stitched a shoe at that time, or tasted pork on a Friday, they'd be accused of a capital crime. And yet the Lord's day was appointed especially to afford people leisure to hear the gospel, and therefore stitching shoes was forbidden in order that people might have time to mend souls. Isn't this a

20　wonderful twisting of values?[241]

Butcher Prodigious. Now, though in that very precept about fasting[242] there are two things, the one abstinence from food, the other selection of food,[243] nobody is unaware that the first is a divine precept, or almost a divine precept, certainly. The other surely is not only a human one but in

25　fact almost conflicts with apostolic doctrine, however we explain it away. Nevertheless, here too, by a perverse judgment, to sup brings no punishment as a rule; to have tasted food forbidden by man but permitted by God and likewise by the apostles[244] is a capital offence. Fasting, though we cannot establish beyond doubt that it was commanded by the apostles, is nonetheless

30　approved by their example and their letters. But that it is forbidden to eat the foods God created to be eaten thankfully[245] – how many arguments we should need in defending *that* case before Paul as judge! And yet nobody is offended by the sumptuous dinners that are served all over the world; if a sick man nibbles some chicken,[246] the Christian religion is in danger.

35　In England, during Lent, a regular supper is commonly prepared every other day.[247] No one is surprised by this. If a person with fever ventures to touch chicken broth, that is regarded as a crime worse than sacrilege. Those people in Lent – a fast which, as there is none more ancient, so is there none esteemed more sacred by Christians – dine freely, as I've said. If you try

40　the same thing on a Friday *not* in Lent, they won't put up with it. If you ask why, their excuse is 'the custom of the country.'[248] They detest the man who

The preacher
One of Hans Holbein the Younger's miniatures in his series of drawings for woodcuts published in The Dance of Death (Lyon 1538). As in all those woodcuts, Death lurks nearby. Except for the woman on the extreme left, who seems to be taking a nap, the listeners are attentive, though unaware of Death, who is mocking the preacher.

'Noise in church'
Woodcut illustrating Sebastian Brant's *Narrenschiff* (1494), section 44
From 'A Fish Diet' and many other Erasmian texts we learn that people who
attended divine service included the devout, the conforming, and the reluctant.
Some might brings their dogs or hawks along or chatter with friends,
others leave the sermon to go home and drink or to play ball.

disregards national custom, yet excuse themselves for disregarding the most ancient custom of the universal church.

Fishmonger He who without reason neglects the custom of the country in which he lives is censurable.

5 **Butcher** I bring no charge against those who divide Lent between God and their belly, but I do charge them with absurd judgment about these subjects.

Fishmonger Though the Lord's day is declared to be ordained principally to allow people to meet at the same time for the purpose of hearing the gospel preached, whoever does not hear mass is accursed; whoever skips the

10 sermon, preferring to play ball, is pure.[249]

Butcher How great an outrage they think is committed if someone takes communion with unwashed mouth![250] How undisturbed they are when they do the same with a heart unclean and soiled by wilful lusts!

Fishmonger How many priests there are who would rather die than sacrifice

15 with a chalice and paten not yet consecrated by the bishop, or in everyday vestments! But among those who feel thus, how many we see who do not shrink from approaching the sacred meal still fuddled from last night's drunkenness! What horror if they accidentally touch the Lord's body[251] with a part of the hand that was not touched by holy oil! But are we equally

20 scrupulous about not offending God by a profane heart?

Butcher The sacred vessels we touch not, and if this does happen by chance, we think expiation is in order. And meantime how lightly do we violate the living temples of the Holy Spirit![252]

Fishmonger Human ordinance forbids admission of a bastard, cripple,

25 or one-eyed man to holy orders.[253] How obstinate we are in this, and yet meanwhile we everywhere accept ignoramuses, dicers, drunkards, soldiers, and murderers. They say, 'Diseases of character are hidden from us.' I'm not talking about hidden ones; I'm talking about those that are more open than bodily defects.

30 **Butcher** There are bishops, too, who assume no duties beyond those connected with business matters and other mean affairs.[254] The office of preaching, which is the first duty of a bishop,[255] they leave to others, however despicable – as they wouldn't do unless they were taken in by fallacious judgment.

35 **Fishmonger** Whoever violates a feast day[256] ordained by a bishop is carried off to punishment. And yet some officials who boldly scorn as many regulations of popes and councils as they do excommunications, interfere with canonical elections, and destroy clerical immunities, not even sparing homes built by the charity of devout men for support of the aged, sick, and

40 needy, consider themselves fully Christian if they persecute those guilty of the slightest offences.

Butcher It's better to omit officials and talk about salt fish and meat.

Fishmonger All right, then, let's go back to fasting and fish.[257] Papal laws, I've heard, specifically exempt young, old, sick, weak, those who do heavy work, pregnant women, nursing mothers, and those who are extremely poor.

5   **Butcher** I've often heard the same myself.

Fishmonger Again, I've heard that a certain outstanding theologian – his name is Gerson, I think – adds that if any reason exists as important as those for which papal laws make specific exemption, the rule likewise ceases to apply.[258] Now there are special physical conditions that make fasting more

10 deadly than manifest disease, and there are some maladies or diseases that don't show themselves, though in fact they're the more dangerous. Hence one who knows his own condition has no need to consult a priest, just as little children don't consult a priest, because the law doesn't apply to them. And whoever forces youths, or very aged folk, or those who for any other

15 reason are weak, to fast or to eat fish sins twice: first, against brotherly love; second, against the intention of the popes, who don't want people to be bound by the law if obeying it endangers them. Whatever Christ ordained, he ordained for the health of body and mind. Nor does any pope arrogate so much power to himself that by his regulations he would force anyone

20 to risk his life; for example, if by evening fasting a man gets insomnia and the insomnia causes delirium,[259] he is a self-murderer, contrary both to the intention of the church and to the will of God.

Princes, as often as suits them, threaten capital punishment when promulgating a law. What they are permitted to do, I don't define. This I

25 will say: they would do better if they inflicted the death penalty only for the reasons set forth in the Bible.[260] In matters involving hatred the Lord calls upon us to stop far short of extremes, as from perjury, forbidding us to swear at all;[261] with respect to killing, forbidding us to be angry.[262] Because of a human ordinance we go to the extreme of killing; we term it

30 necessity! On the contrary, as often as a convincing reason appears, it is an act of charity to urge your neighbour on your own responsibility to do what his physical weakness demands. And if no reason appears, it is still an act of Christian charity to interpret kindly what may possibly be a sincere action, unless the person who eats shows himself openly scornful of the church.

35 A secular magistrate properly punishes those who eat contumaciously and seditiously; but what one eats at home for the sake of his health is the physicians' affair, not the magistrates'. And if the wickedness of some provokes public disturbance, let them be arrested for sedition,[263] not the one who has looked out for his health without violating any law, divine or

40 human. Certainly we have no right to excuse ourselves by appealing to the authority of popes, whose humanity is so great that when they recognize the

case is no unreasonable one they readily urge a person to do what health demands and protect him by briefs against the slanders of the wicked.

Finally, throughout the whole of Italy meat may be sold in certain butcher shops for the health of those whom the law does not restrict.[264]

5 What's more, I've even heard the somewhat less pharisaical divines say in sermons, 'Don't hesitate at mealtime to take a loaf and a measure[265] of wine or beer out of regard for bodily weakness.' If they assume so much authority as to permit the strong a light supper in place of a regular meal – and that contrary to the precept of the church, which decreed a fast, not a light

10 supper – why don't they allow a full meal to those whose infirmity requires it, since the popes, for reasons stated, have signified their consent? If some person disciplines his body too harshly, it may be called zeal, for everybody knows his own condition. But where is the piety, where the charity of those who, against the law of nature, against the law of God, against the sense of

15 pontifical law, drive a weak brother, lively in spirit but infirm in body, to death or to a disease more pitiless than death?

Butcher Your recital has reminded me of something I saw two years ago.[266] You know Eros,[267] now an old man in his sixties, of more than fragile health, and daily illnesses besides,[268] and so beset by the most troublesome and

20 toilsome studies that they could break even a Milo.[269] In addition, through some obscure quirk of nature, he has been from very boyhood so averse to eating fish and so incapable of fasting that he has never attempted it without danger to his life.[270] Eventually, he was amply protected from pharisaical tongues by papal briefs.[271] Recently, on invitation from friends, he had

25 visited the city of Eleutheropolis, a place not altogether corresponding to its name.[272] This was during Lent. One or two days were devoted to the whims of his friends. Meanwhile, in order to avoid giving offence to anybody, he was eating fish, although he had (if it were needed) a papal brief permitting him to eat whatever he liked. Already he felt his sickness coming upon

30 him – an old acquaintance, but more cruel than death.[273] He made ready to leave, and it was urgent to do so unless he wanted to take to his bed there. Suspecting he was leaving earlier because he couldn't bear eating fish,[274] certain persons arranged for Glaucoplutus,[275] a man of vast learning and of high authority in that community, to invite Eros to his house for breakfast.

35 Tired by now of the crowd he had been unable to avoid at an inn, Eros accepted, but on condition that nothing be provided except a couple of eggs; when he had eaten them, standing up, he would mount his horse and depart. This was promised. When he arrived, there was a chicken ready.[276] Annoyed, Eros touched nothing but the two eggs,[277] and breaking away from the party

40 took horse, accompanied by some scholarly friends. Somehow the smell of this chicken had reached the slanderers. By these a rumour was spread as

horrible as if ten men had been poisoned. Nor did only that city ring with the story, but almost simultaneously it flew to other cities three days distant. And as usual, report had added something to truth: that unless Eros had fled quickly, he would have been arrested and brought before a magistrate. As

5   this was completely false, so it was true that Glaucoplutus had to satisfy a magistrate who demanded an explanation.[278] Eros, as I've said, was already in such a condition that even if he ate meat in public, who would have reason to be offended? And yet in that same city all during Lent, but especially on holy days, there is drinking to the point of delirium, uproar, dancing,

10   brawling, dice-playing next door to the church, so that the sermon can't be heard[279] – and no one is upset in the least.

Fishmonger A wonderful perversity of judgment.

Butcher Here's a similar story.[280] Nearly two years ago that same Eros went on a visit to Ferventia for the sake of his health; I went along as his

15   companion. He stopped at the home of an old friend – a very important man and leading churchman – who had invited him by frequent letters. When it came to fish, Eros again began to be in serious trouble. A whole array of illnesses came upon him: fever, headache, vomiting, the stone. The host, though he saw his friend was in serious danger, nevertheless didn't

20   dare give him a bit of meat. Why not? He recognized that there were many reasons why it was permitted, he knew about the brief – but he feared men's tongues. And already the sickness had progressed to the point where giving meat would have been useless.

Fishmonger What did Eros do? I know the man's nature. He would die

25   sooner than bring his friend into any ill repute.

Butcher He shut himself up in his room and for three days ate as he usually did: his lunch was a single egg, his drink water boiled with sugar.[281] The moment his fever subsided he mounted his horse, taking his provisions with him.

30   **Fishmonger** What were they?

Butcher Almond milk in a bottle and raisins in his purse.[282] When he reached home, the stone made itself evident and he was in bed a whole month. And yet a cruel but groundless rumour of his eating meat followed this departure, too, and spread as far as Paris, often accompanied by glaring

35   lies. What do you consider an appropriate treatment for those who spread such scandal?

Fishmonger That everybody empty their chamber-pots on those creatures' heads, and if they happen to meet them, hold their noses while passing, so they'll recognize their own folly.

40   **Butcher** Surely this pharisaical wickedness deserved to be severely punished by denunciations of divines. Now what do you think of that host?

Fishmonger He strikes me as a prudent man who knew what slight reasons people have sometimes for raising great commotions.

Butcher Let's grant that what he did was prudential and interpret the good man's timidity kindly. But how many there are who, though on such an
5   occasion they would permit a brother to perish, pretend their reason is the custom of the church and public scandal![283] Yet in their own openly scandalous life how they behave in feastings, in love affairs, in gluttony, in sloth, in supreme contempt for sacred studies, in thefts, simony, and frauds, not caring a rap for public scandal!

10   **Fishmonger** There are some just like that. What they call piety is terrible and wicked cruelty. But still more cruel, I think, are those – especially the ones acting without public authorization – who do not merely leave a man in danger at times but devise dangers, as though setting traps, and bring many into manifest peril of body and soul.

15   **Butcher** I'm waiting for you to continue.

Fishmonger Thirty years ago I lived in Paris[284] in a college named from vinegar.[285]

Butcher I hear a word of wisdom. What's that you say? A salt fish seller in a college so sour? No wonder, then, if he's so full of theological controversies.
20   For, as I hear, the very walls there lean towards theology.

Fishmonger It's as you say, yet so far as I'm concerned I carried nothing away from there except a body plagued by the worst humours, plus a most generous supply of lice.[286] – But to continue what I began. That college was then ruled by Jan Standonck,[287] a man whose intentions were beyond
25   reproach but whom you would have found entirely lacking in judgment. Because he remembered his own youth, which had been spent in bitter poverty, he took special account of impoverished students. For that he deserves much credit. And had he relieved the poverty of young men enough to provide a decent support for honest studies, while making sure
30   they did not have too soft a life, he would have merited praise. But this he tried to do by means of bedding so hard, diet so harsh and scanty, by sleepless nights and labours so burdensome, that within a year his initial effort had caused the deaths of many very capable, gifted, promising youths and brought others (some of whom I myself knew) to blindness, nervous
35   breakdowns, or leprosy. Not a single student in fact was out of danger.

Who would deny that this was cruelty to a fellow human? Not content with these measures, he added cloak and cowl; and he deprived them of meat entirely. And tender shoots of this sort he consigned to distant regions.[288] But if everyone were to give way to their enthusiasms to the extent he did,
40   creatures like these would fill the whole world, since from such beginnings came the monasteries, which are now a threat to popes and kings. To rejoice

in the gain of bringing a fellow man to godliness is right; to seek glory in clothing or food is pharisaical. To relieve our neighbours' need is a duty; to watch lest they take advantage of good people's generosity and become dissolute is a lesson learned. But to drive a brother to disease, to madness, to
5 death by these things is cruelty – parricide. The desire to murder is missing, perhaps, but the killing is there. What pardon do these men deserve, then? Surely that deserved by the doctor who by his extraordinary incompetence kills the patient.

Someone will say, 'Nobody forces them to follow this mode of life;
10 they come voluntarily, seek admission, and are free to leave if tired of it.' Scythian reply![289] And so they require young men to see more clearly what is best for them than a man advanced in learning, experience, and age can do? One might just as well make the same excuse to a starving wolf caught in a trap.[290] Or will a person who serves unwholesome or even deadly food to
15 one who is famished thus excuse himself to the dying man: 'Nobody forced you to eat; you gobbled up of your own free will what was set before you.' Wouldn't the other be justified in retorting, 'You gave me poison, not food'? Need is a powerful weapon,[291] hunger a great torment.[292] Away, then, with those fine words, 'You had free choice.' On the contrary, whoever uses such
20 torments brings heavy pressure to bear. Nor has this harshness killed only poor youths; it has destroyed not a few sons of rich men and utterly ruined superior talent. To restrain licentious youth by counsels of moderation is a paternal office. But in the cold of midwinter those who ask for food are given a bit of bread; they are told to drink from a well that is pestilential or is
25 dangerous, even if it has only the chill of the early morning.

I know many who even today can't shake off the illness contracted there. On the ground floor were cubicles with rotten plaster, near stinking latrines.[293] No one ever lived in these without either dying or getting a terrible disease. I omit for the present the astonishingly savage floggings,[294]
30 even of the innocent. Thus, they declare, is 'wildness' tamed – 'wildness' being their name for unusual talent, which they zealously destroy, to render men more fit for monasteries. How many rotten eggs used to be eaten there![295] How much bad wine drunk! Perhaps these conditions have been corrected; but too late, obviously, for those who have died or who carry a
35 diseased body about. Nor, I assure you, do I mention these matters because I wish that college any bad luck; but I've judged it worth while to warn against human cruelty corrupting inexperienced and tender youth under the guise of religion. How much politeness or true religion is learned there nowadays I don't, at the moment, inquire. But if I saw that everyone who put
40 on a cowl put off his sinfulness, I'd urge everybody to don a cowl. Nowadays the case is altered; consequently youthful spirits should not be broken to this

sort of life, but instead the heart should be trained to godliness. Scarcely
ever has it been my lot to visit a Carthusian monastery without running into
one or two there who were either plain silly or raving mad.[296] – But it's high
time for us to return to the subject after such a long digression.

5 **Butcher** Oh, no, we haven't lost time by digression. We've been discussing
the very same subject, unless perhaps something occurs to you that you
think should be added to what has been said about human regulations.

Fishmonger To me, at least, whoever neglects to carry out the lawgiver's
intention fails to fulfil a human ordinance.[297] For he who on holy days abstains
10 only from labour, and yet hasn't time to go to church or hear sermons,
violates the holy day by disregarding the purpose for which the day was
instituted. Worthy work was forbidden that there might be something better.
Now surely he who instead of doing his usual work devotes his leisure to
taverns, whores, drunkenness, brawls, and dice violates the holy day twice.[298]

15 **Butcher** I believe, too, that a fixed number of holy prayers is assigned to
monks and nuns in order that by this exercise they may grow accustomed to
lifting their hearts to God; yet whoever does not complete this number runs
a risk. Whoever merely murmurs the words with his mouth, not troubling
to concentrate on what he utters, nay, not even applying himself to learn
20 grammar – without which what he utters is unintelligible – is reputed a good
man and considers himself one, too.

Fishmonger I know many priests who think it an inexpiable sacrilege to
have omitted any part of the prayers or to have mistakenly named the
Blessed Virgin when they should have named St Paul.[299] But these same
25 priests would think nothing of dice, whoring, and drunkenness, which are
forbidden by divine and human laws alike.

Butcher I've found not a few who would rather have been killed than say
mass after accidentally tasting food or swallowing some drops of water
while rinsing their mouths. But these same priests would confess to holding
30 grudges against certain men whom they'd kill if they had the chance; and
they didn't shrink from approaching the Lord's table in this frame of mind.[300]

Fishmonger Yet to sacrifice fasting is man's precept; to lay aside wrath
before approaching the sacred table is God's precept.[301]

Butcher How absurdly, moreover, do we pass judgment on perjury![302]
35 One who has sworn he would discharge a debt is considered disgraced if
convicted of non-payment.[303] A priest who openly lives in sin, when he has
publicly professed chastity, is not charged with perjury.[304]

Fishmonger Why don't you sing that song to bishops' vicars,[305] who swear
before the altar that all whom they present for holy orders they have found
40 to be of suitable age, knowledge, and morals, when sometimes scarcely two
or three in the lot are passable, many hardly fit for a plough handle?[306]

Butcher Whoever swears falsely,[307] whatever the reason, is cited for punishment; yet those who perjure themselves in every third word go unpunished.

Fishmonger They don't swear seriously.

5   **Butcher** You could plead the same specious excuse[308] for the person who kills a man 'not seriously.' Perjury is permissible neither in jest nor in earnest. And killing a man as a joke would be a more terrible crime[309] than killing him in a burst of anger.

Fishmonger What if one weighed in these same scales the oaths of princes
10   when they take office?[310]

Butcher Though those may be very serious, they are nevertheless imposed by custom and hence are not considered perjuries. There's the same complaint concerning vows. The marriage vow is unquestionably of divine ordinance, and yet it is broken by taking monastic vows – a human invention.[311]

15   **Fishmonger** Though no vow is more sacred than that of baptism, yet he who changes his robe or place is sought, seized, bound as if he had poisoned his father, and sometimes is killed for the honour of the order.[312] But those whose whole life is completely contrary[313] to the vow of baptism,[314] since they are wholly given over to the service of mammon, their belly, and the
20   vanities of this world, are esteemed; they're not accused of the crime of breaking their vow, or condemned, or called apostates,[315] but are considered Christians.[316]

Butcher Popular opinion is much the same with regard to good and evil deeds and the pursuit of happiness. How much disgrace dogs a girl who
25   has fallen from virtue! But to have a lying and disparaging tongue, and a heart corrupted by hatred and envy, is a far more serious fault. Where is a theft, however slight, not punished more severely than adultery? No one willingly keeps company with a person once soiled by thievery; but it's a fine thing to be on good terms with one who's involved in
30   adultery.[317] No one would think it proper to bestow his daughter on the public executioner, who carries out the law for a salary, just as the judge himself does, and yet we do not abhor a marriage with a soldier, who so often – against his parents' wishes and sometimes against the law[318] – has taken himself off to a mercenary war and is defiled by many whorings,
35   robberies, sacrileges, murders, and other crimes commonly committed in the army or in marching to and from war.[319] Him we accept as a son-in-law; him, a man worse than a hangman anywhere, the maiden dotes on. And we even recognize aristocratic rank achieved through some wrongdoing. Whoever steals coin, hangs; those who rob ever so many by graft, monopolies,
40   usury, and a thousand tricks and frauds are esteemed among leading citizens.

Fishmonger Those who give poison to someone pay the penalty as poisoners; whoever injure the public with bad wine or spoiled butter get off without punishment.[320]

Butcher I know some monks so superstitious that they think themselves in
5 the devil's power if perchance they are without their sacred habit. Yet they don't fear the devil's claws if they lie, slander, get drunk, bear envy.[321]

Fishmonger You may see many simple souls of that sort among us, too. They don't believe the house is safe from the violence of an evil spirit unless they have holy water,[322] sacred chaplets,[323] and taper at hand, and yet aren't
10 afraid for their own temples,[324] in which God is daily mocked and the devil honoured in so many ways.

Butcher How many there are who put their trust in the Virgin Mother's protection, or Christopher's, rather than that of Christ himself! They worship the Mother with images, candles, and canticles; Christ they offend recklessly
15 by their wicked life. When a sailor's in danger, he calls on Christ's mother or Christopher or some other saint sooner than Christ himself.[325] And they think the Virgin will help them because at nightfall they sing a hymn they don't understand, *Salve regina*,[326] and they don't fear instead that she may deem herself mocked by such hymns when they spend the whole day and a
20 large part of the night in smutty talk, drinking, and doings unmentionable.

Fishmonger So a soldier in danger thinks of George or Barbara[327] rather than Christ. Moreover, though no veneration pleases the saints more than imitation of their deeds, by which they themselves pleased Christ, we boldly scorn this office. And we believe Antony will be extremely good to us if we keep some
25 sacred swine for him, and if we have him painted with his pig, fire, and little bell on the doors and sides of houses.[328] We don't fear what ought to be feared more – that he may wish ill to houses where flourish those same vices the holy man always hated. We count out short rosaries and Hail Marys to the Virgin; why don't we rather count for her sake a puffed-up mind brought
30 under subjection, lust curbed, injury forgiven? Christ's mother is pleased by hymns of this kind, and by these works you would deserve well of both.

Butcher In like manner one who is dangerously ill thinks of St Roche[329] or St Denis[330] rather than Christ, the sole salvation of mankind. Not only that, but those who expound Sacred Scripture from the pulpit, which nobody
35 can understand properly or teach profitably without the inspiration of the Spirit,[331] prefer to invoke the assistance of the Virgin Mother rather than Christ himself or the spirit of Christ. And he who dares to murmur against this practice, which they call praiseworthy, is himself called into suspicion of heresy. But far more praiseworthy was the custom of the ancients, kept by
40 Origen, Basil, Chrysostom, Cyprian, Ambrose, Jerome, Augustine,[332] who repeatedly invoke the spirit of Christ, never begging the Virgin's assistance.

Nor are they indignant with those who have dared to change a custom so sacred, one derived both from the teaching of Christ and the apostles and from the example of the holy Fathers.[333]

Fishmonger An error of the same kind is common to many monks, who
5   persuade themselves that Benedict is well disposed as long as they wear his cowl and cloak, though I don't think he had ever worn a garment so full of folds and so expensive. They don't fear his indignation because their manner of living has nothing in common with his.

Butcher He who does not abandon the ash-grey robe and hempen girdle is
10   brother to Francis. Compare their lives: nothing is more of a contrast (I speak of most, not all). And this remark can be applied to all forms of orders and professions. From false judgment comes an absurd assurance; and from the same source absurd scandals. Let a Franciscan go out girded with a leather belt, having accidentally lost his rope cord; or an Augustinian wearing a
15   woolen girdle; or one ungirded who is usually girded – what horror will there be! How great the danger that women may miscarry at the sight![334] And from suchlike trifles, how great a breach of brotherly love! What bitter hatred! What venomous slanders! Against these the Lord exclaims in the Gospel; no less forcefully the apostle Paul.[335] Against these same things
20   should theologians and preachers exclaim.

Fishmonger Of course they should; but among them are many who find it to their advantage for the common people, yes even kings and bishops, to be like that. Again, there are those who in these matters are no wiser than the people; or if they are, they hide the fact, mindful of their bellies rather
25   than of Jesus Christ. And so it happens that everywhere the people, misled by preposterous judgments, are confident when a clear and present danger exists, anxious when there is no danger; they relax when they ought to push on, advance when they ought to withdraw. If you attempt to remove any of these misconceptions, you hear 'treason!' – as though it were treason for a
30   man to try to cure by better medicines some disease long encouraged by an ignorant physician and made almost natural.

But we must stop complaining; there's no end to it. And if people learned of this conversation of ours, there'd be danger of their bringing out a new proverb about how a salt fish seller and a butcher meddle in these
35   matters.

Butcher I'll retaliate with an old proverb: 'Even a kitchen gardener often talks sense.'[336] When I was discussing these topics at dinner recently, a beggarly, lousy, sallow, shrivelled, dried-up, ghastly fellow was present, unluckily. He had scarcely three hairs on his head; whenever he spoke he
40   shut his eyes; they said he was a theologian.[337] He called me a disciple of Antichrist[338] and mumbled a good deal else.

Fishmonger And you? Did you keep quiet?

Butcher I wished him a bit of sense in such a withered brain – if he even had a brain.

Fishmonger I'd be happy to hear this story from beginning to end.

5 **Butcher** You'll hear it if you come to lunch on Thursday. You'll have veal, ground and baked in a pie, and so tender you could suck it.

Fishmonger I accept on condition that you'll have lunch with me on Friday. I'll try to convince you that salt fish sellers don't always eat rotten salt fish.

NOTES

1 Cf Plautus *Pseudolus* 86–9.

2 Catastrophic, fatal; recalling a famous disaster in Spain during the second Punic war. See Cicero *Philippics* 5.10.27 and *Adagia* i ix 67.

3 Of Pythia, priestess of the shrine of Apollo at Delphi; therefore authoritative though not always clear

4 Thus in *De copia* LB I 17D / CWE 24 332:22–3; *De civilitate* LB I 1034C / CWE 25 274; *Adagia* II iv 8. These texts single out dealers in salt fish and meat as the most common examples of such habits, but the fault was a mark of other persons of mean birth or breeding too. See *Rhetorica ad Herennium* 4.54.67 ed and trans Harry Caplan, Loeb Classical Library (London and Cambridge, Mass 1954) 402 note b.

5 An ironical reversal of the adage that 'among the blind the one-eyed man is king' (*Adagia* III iv 90)

6 *Adagia* I x 90

7 Salimbene says that once in Reggio fishmongers' prices were so high that the town council forbade them to sell fish during Lent. Another time the citizens threatened butchers with the same treatment (*Chronicle* trans G.G. Coulton in *From St Francis to Dante* [rev ed London 1907; repr Philadelphia 1972] 224–5).

8 Writing in December 1524, perhaps close to the date when he wrote this colloquy, Erasmus recalls outbreaks of the sweating sickness in England and wonders if the fondness of the English for salt fish might have something to do with this. The English would be better off in any event if they ate more moderately (Ep 1532 passim). Salt fish could easily cause sickness if kept too long. River fish were less common as food (H. Brabant 'Erasme, ses maladies et ses médecins' in *Colloquia Erasmiana Turonensia* I 550).

9 Famous Greek physician (fifth–fourth centuries BC) and author of many works on medicine

10 Some towns and cities had ordinances forbidding shambles, where cattle were slaughtered, within the city walls. London, by an enactment of government in 1488–9, is one example. On London butchers in Erasmus' time and later see Philip E. Jones *The Butchers of London* (London 1983). More's Utopians had strict rules about such matters. No filthy or diseased meat, even if slaughtered outside the walls, could be brought in (Yale CWM 4 138, 139, 418).

11 Some fishmongers pretend that the fish they sell are fresh when in fact they have been dead for two days (*Adagia* IV i 74). The Collegium Trilingue in Louvain, in which Erasmus took so strong an interest, was near a fish market – a reason for some students in the university to disdain the new college, though Erasmus calls the site *honestus* (Ferguson *Erasmi opuscula* 194; Allen Ep 1221:18).

12 Literally 'would not sleep.' Cf Juvenal 2.37.

13 An ancient complaint; cf Athenaeus 6.225. For a contemporary one see *A Fifteenth Century School Book* ed William Nelson (Oxford 1956) 4 no 10, 8 no 30.

14 Both are poisonous. On hemlock see *Parabolae* LB I 565F / CWE 146:12; on wolfsbane 'The Godly Feast' 181:7–9. Both are mentioned in 'Sympathy' 1044:17–18, 27–8.

15 Electric ray fish, as at *Convivium religiosum* 'The Godly Feast' 181:41

16 *hydrum*. Erasmus tells an anecdote about it in *Adagia* III x 99.

17 *lepus marinum*, a fish fatal to him who tastes it; and to be touched by man is fatal to the fish. *Adagia* II i 15; *Parabolae* LB I 603B / CWE 23 231:33; 'Sympathy' 1040:38–9.

18 Spring, including Lent

19 *Adagia* III vii 26

20 See *Adagia* II iv 72 on *betizare* 'to behave stupidly.' In 'Patterns' (12:1–2) Erasmus makes fun of Noël Béda by punning on this name and *beta* 'beet.'

21 Cf 'The Profane Feast' n87.

22 In antiquity, says Erasmus in a passage added to the revised edition of his *Encomium medicinae*, laws fostered public health and physicians were responsible for carrying out measures to that end. Nowadays governments, to their shame, neglect this duty (LB I 542F–543A / ASD I-4 182:330–42 / CWE 29 46–7). As for venerating general customs, see 'The Profane Feast' n58.

23 Popes and bishops, who have authority to excommunicate

24 Since the fishmonger once lived in a college in Paris (715:16–17 below), he may be French; but whether French, Dutch, or German he could easily have read the Bible in his native language. Versions in those and some other native tongues were in print before 1500, but not in English, as a consequence of the prohibition of the Lollard Bible. The first printed New Testament in English, translated by William Tyndale, did not appear until 1525–6 (the 1525 Cologne printing was incomplete; the Worms 1526 was the first complete version). The fourteenth-century Wycliffite version, denounced and suppressed by authority, survived and circulated surreptitiously in manuscript copies. On vernacular Bibles in various languages see CHB II and Bruce M. Metzger *The Early Versions of the New Testament* (Oxford 1977). Erasmus' concern for the availability and use of Scripture in vernacular tongues by the laity is often recorded. The case for translation, especially of the New Testament, is made most eloquently in *Paraclesis*, his preface to his Greek New Testament of 1516 (LB VI *3 recto–4 verso / Holborn 139–49; translation in John C. Olin *Christian Humanism and the Reformation* rev ed [New York 1976] 92–106) and in the longer preface to the Paraphrase on Matthew (1522), addressed to the 'devout reader' (LB VII **2 verso–4 verso). See Craig R. Thompson 'Scripture for the Ploughboy and Some Others' in *Studies in the Continental Background of English Renaissance Literature* ed Dale B.J. Randall and George Walton Williams (Durham, NC 1977) 3–28 and 'Jerome and the Testimony of Erasmus in Disputes over the

Vernacular Bible' *Proceedings of the PMR Conference* (Augustinian Historical
Institute, Villanova University, Villanova, Pa) 6 (1981) 1–36.

25 This paragraph reflects classical as well as biblical tradition (Genesis). It brings
to mind Ovid's description of the Golden Age (*Metamorphoses* 1.89–112) and
Milton's *Paradise Lost*, especially book 4.

26 Genesis 2:8–9, 15–17

27 In the early church many Christians believed, on the basis of received preaching
of the gospel and inferences from recent events, that the Last Judgment was
near at hand. So the author of 1 John 2:18, for example, affirmed near the end
of the first century of our era. One of the best-known patristic expositions of
its nature is Augustine's *De civitate Dei* 20–1. The idea and even expectation of
it became fixed in the Christian consciousness. In Erasmus' time the famous
Nürnberg Chronicle concluded with a reference to the approaching end of the
world.
The butcher's comment was perfectly conventional and intelligible to Erasmus'
readers; cf a similar remark in *Antibarbari* (LB X 1696C–D / ASD I-1 48:17–20 /
CWE 23 26:15–18). Calvin observed that the present world is drawing to a
close even before completing its six thousandth year (ICR 1.14.1). Christian
theologians could not accept Aristotle's doctrine of the eternity of the world.
The notion of gradual decay in the physical universe, accompanied by moral
and social corruption in mankind, received due attention from sixteenth-
and seventeenth-century writers. Godfrey Goodman's *The fall of man* (1616;
STC 12023) and George Hakewille's *An apologie or declaration of the power and
providence of God* (1627; STC 12611) were representative statements; see Victor
Harris *All Coherence Gone* (Chicago 1949).

28 After the Flood 'every moving thing that liveth' could be eaten except 'with the
life thereof,' that is, its blood (Gen 9:3–4; cf Lev 11:9–12). This exception was
the consequence of Cain's murder of Abel (Gen 4:10–11). Blood, identified with
'life' or soul, was sacred (Deut 12:23). Hence the butcher is wrong in saying
that this prohibition was for the sake of humanity, not sanctity.

29 The butcher appears to be wrong here too. Of creatures living in water, 'all
that have fins and scales shall ye eat,' but those that do not are forbidden (Deut
14:9–10; Lev 11:11–12).

30 *ariolus*; Cf *Adagia* III v 25.

31 Gen 1:28

32 Alluding to the story of Arion. See 'Sympathy' 1038:22–3 and n22.

33 Cf *Parabolae* CWE 23 219:13–14, from Pliny *Naturalis historia* 18.361. On the
echinus see also 'The Profane Feast' n33.

34 Gen 1:29

35 See n28 above. The Mosaic legislation contained elaborate rules about 'clean'
and 'unclean' foods (Leviticus 11 and Deut 14:3–21).

36 Cf 'The Profane Feast' 143:34–6.

37 Cf Galatians 4, and see also 'Faith' 425:6–19.

38 Gen 9:15–16. The covenant with Noah was repeated to Abraham and successive
patriarchs and through them to all Israel.

39 Matt 5:17; see n42 below.

40 Cf John 1:17; Gal 3:24–5.

41 1 Cor 7:18; Acts 15:5–11

42 The Decalogue or Ten Commandments and the corpus of Hebrew laws revealed
to Moses and codified in Exodus, Leviticus, and Deuteronomy. These latter
regulations governing most practices and duties pertaining to religion, morals,
and equity are what Erasmus sums up as 'Judaism,' a fundamental theme
in the discussion that follows. The Ten Commandments were binding on all
Christians as well as Jews (Mark 12:29–31), but Jesus modified or reinterpreted
much of the Law, proclaiming that he had not come to abolish the Law and the
prophets but to fulfil them (Matt 5:17, 21–22, 27–8): 'Ye have heard it said ...
but I say unto you.' Chapters 5–7 of Matthew are the essence of the gospel,
and Erasmus' Paraphrases on them (LB VII) the key to his expositions of the
difference between Law and gospel. His paraphrase on Gal 5:2 leaves no
room for compromise: 'You must be clearly Jews and give up Christ or clearly
Christians and reject Judaism' (LB VII 961B / CWE 42 121).

43 For example Isa 42:1–4, 49:1–6, 50:4–9, 52:13–53:12; Jer 31:31–4 as these passages
were traditionally interpreted

44 Pss 40:6 (39:7 Vulg), 51:16 (50:18 Vulg); Hos 6:6; Jer 6:20; Isa 1:13–14; Deut 30:6

45 Matt 26:28; Mark 14:24; 1 Cor 11:25

46 Jewish] This word, omitted in earlier editions, was added in the March 1529
edition, but as Erasmus told his Paris critics, the meaning was clear anyway,
as fair-minded readers would have known (*Declarationes ad censuras Lutetiae
vulgatas* LB IX 950A–B).
The relation of Law to gospel with regard to distinction of foods is treated
in 'The Godly Feast' 188:8–41, 189:35–191:37. The law of Moses prescribed
right and defined wrong, but its accompanying requirements and burden
of ceremonies were superseded by the spirituality of the Gospels and the
doctrine of the Incarnation. Such at any rate was the absolute conviction
of Erasmus and his insistent message in his religious writings from first
to last, from *Enchiridion* to *Ecclesiastes*. Contrast between the letter and
spirit of the law, whether Mosaic or modern, secular or canonical, is
fundamental in his Christianity. See an emphatic passage on those differences
in *Ecclesiastes* LB V 790A–E, one of very numerous examples, and the paraphrase
on Galatians 5. Allusions to 'Judaism' as the Old Law occur in many
colloquies.

47 Matt 15:10–11

48 Peter's vision is described in Acts 10:9–29. On his later inconsistency and Paul's
rebuke see Gal 2:11–21.

49 Throughout Galatians and 1 Corinthians; Col 2:16–17; 1 Tim 4:3; Titus 1:15

50 1 Cor 3:2; Heb 5:12–14

51 Gal 3:23–9

52 Heb 10:1

53 Forbidden to Jews; Lev 11:7–8. See n35 above.

54 Exod 20:13; Lev 11:7

55 1 Sam 21:3–6, and cf Matt 12:3–4, Mark 2:25–6, Luke 6:3–4; for the sacred bread
Exod 29:32–3 and Lev 24:5–9

56 See in the Apocrypha 2 Maccabees 6:12–7:42 and 4 Maccabees chapters 5 to 16.
The book of 4 Maccabees was once attributed to Josephus. Erasmus contributed
a preface (Ep 842) and perhaps revision of a Latin translation of it (Cologne
1517 or 1518).

57 Matt 11:30; Acts 15:10. Erasmus' long note on Matt 11:30 in his *Annotationes in Novum Testamentum* uses many of the same arguments on Mosaic law versus Christian liberty found in this colloquy (LB VI 63B–65D).

58 Acts 15:1–35

59 *Ecclesiastes* LB V 830E–F. On the meaning of baptism see 'The Girl with No Interest in Marriage' nn27, 57; 'The Soldier and the Carthusian' n11. On the ceremony see 'The Godly Feast' 196:13–19 and the notes.

60 Gen 17:10–12; Lev 12:3; Luke 2:21

61 For methods of baptizing see 'The Godly Feast' n227.

62 The fishmonger and butcher know well enough that this doctrine was commonly held, but they do not discuss it, passing it by with 'So they say.' Their words allude to a famous theological deduction enunciated and emphasized by St Augustine. The doctrine was based on his interpretation of Rom 5:12. The Vulgate text of that verse reads: *Propterea sicut per unum hominem peccatum in hunc mundum intravit, et per peccatum mors; et ita in omnes homines mors pertransiit, in quo omnes peccaverunt* 'Wherefore, as by one man sin entered into the world, and death by sin; and so death passed upon all men, in whom all have sinned.' That was the sense of the text as Augustine understood it. He interpreted the phrase *in quo* (ἐφ᾽ ᾧ) to mean Adam. So does a commentary on Paul's Epistles ascribed to Ambrose but now credited to an unknown author labelled for convenience 'Ambrosiaster' (see 'The Godly Feast' n180): '*in quo*, id est in Adam' (PL 17 92C). The meaning of the text, according to Ambrosiaster, is that 'in Adam all have sinned as in a bulk' or lump (*massa*; on this word see Alexander Souter *A Glossary of Later Latin to 600 A.D.* [Oxford 1949]). Augustine reasons accordingly that every human being inherits the guilt of Adam's original sin, 'for we were all in that one man [Adam] when we were all that one man' (*De civitate Dei* 13.14). His great contemporary Chrysostom is less certain; see *In epistulam ad Romanos homiliae* 10.1 PG 60 474–5 and Erasmus *Annotationes in Novum Testamentum* LB VI 588B–D / CWE 56 146–7. Augustine held that if infants die unbaptized, without the 'laver of regeneration,' they are not saved but pass to eternal fire. Their sufferings there are much milder than those of actual and unrepentant sinners (*Enchiridion* 93 PL 40 275), but they are excluded from heaven (cf *De peccatorum meritis et remissione* 1.28.55 PL 44 140–1; *De Genesi ad litteram* 10.11.19 PL 34 415–16; *Sermones* 294.2–4 PL 38 1336–8; *Opus imperfectum contra Julianum* 3.199 PL 45 1332–3; *De correptione et gratia* 18 PL 44 926–7). All human beings are born corrupt; all need liberation by baptism, the sacrament that makes recipients members of the body of Christ, the church. For 'he that believeth and is baptized shall be saved' (Mark 16:16; cf John 3:5; Acts 2:37–42, 10:47–8; Gal 3:27).
Augustine was concerned to refute the Pelagians, who in his judgment attributed too much to man's will, too little to his dependence – did he but acknowledge it – on divine grace. Damnation of unbaptized infants was a common but not unchallenged corollary of Augustinian teachings on grace. Pelagians argued that unbaptized infants enter into the 'kingdom of God' but not into eternal life. Augustine held that the two were the same. Appalling though a doctrine of infant damnation may be, Augustine did not shrink from what his reading of Scripture seemed to require.
In the first edition of his New Testament, Erasmus suggested the change of *in quo* (ἐφ᾽ ᾧ) in Rom 5:12 to *quatenus*, thus changing the meaning from 'in

whom all have sinned' to 'inasmuch' [or 'since' or 'because'] all have sinned,'
and in subsequent editions he kept this changed translation; at the same time
expanding his brief note in the 1516 edition to one that runs to six folio columns
in the final (1535) edition and defending his translation on both grammatical
and doctrinal grounds (LB VI 584F–590B / CWE 56 137–61). The difference
between these two renderings is crucial, because – so Erasmus argues – the
Apostle did not mean that all persons since Adam are *guilty*. True, they all
inherit, as the human condition, the legacy or consequences of original sin; all
have a natural proclivity or tendency to do evil, *naturali quadam pronitate ad
peccandum*, but they do not inherit guilt. If they sin, they do so of their own
volition, not of necessity. Therefore he does not believe an unbaptized child
who 'dies when one day old, or dies at birth,' as the colloquy says, is 'consigned
to eternal damnation.'

Erasmus is credited with being the first to give the Greek phrase ἐφ' ᾧ a causal
sense. He had found a Latin manuscript containing thirteen commentaries on
the Pauline Epistles. The manuscript attributed these to Jerome, but Erasmus
judged that whoever the author was, he was certainly not Jerome – as all
scholars now agree. Nevertheless he published these texts, because of their
intrinsic value and antiquity, in the ninth volume of his edition of Jerome
(Basel 1516, 9 vols in 5), and later editors, including Migne in PL, did likewise.
The author was simply 'Pseudo-Jerome' to them. Erasmus noticed, as did some
other early readers of the commentaries, the presence of many characteristic
Pelagian ideas and teachings in this work. With some of these interpretations of
original sin and the will, including those in Rom 5:12–14, Erasmus agrees. What
he did not know, however, was that Pseudo-Jerome was Pelagius himself. This
identification was conjectured in the seventeenth century by Richard Simon
(1693) but never investigated thoroughly until Alexander Souter, in a series of
painstaking studies, proved that these expositions were the work of Pelagius.
See *Pelagius's Expositions of Thirteen Epistles of Paul* Texts and Studies 9, 3 vols
(Cambridge 1922–31): I *Introduction* (1922); II *Text and Critical Apparatus* (1926);
III *Pseudo-Jerome Interpolations* (1931).

Demonstration that these commentaries were by Pelagius would have pleased
some of Erasmus' critics who accused him of Pelagianism. He denied this
charge indignantly, but he can certainly be termed a 'semi-Pelagian.' Nor
is he alone, he adds, in his distrust of the Augustinian doctrine deduced
from Rom 5:12. Gerson too, he notes (*Institutio christiani matrimonii* LB V 622C),
questions it (*Oeuvres* v 350 no 232). So does More. Writing to a monk who
seemed to think the Fathers were never wrong, More brings up the name
of Augustine: 'He asserts that infants who died unbaptized suffer physical
torments in eternal punishment. How many now believe that?' (*Correspondence*
171:222–4). To differ with the Doctors about ambiguous texts is not, for
Erasmus, heresy (*Annotationes in Novum Testamentum* LB VI 589D–F / CWE 56
149–51; cf *Declarationes ad censuras Lutetiae vulgatas* LB IX 933A–B).

The passage in Pelagius' commentary on Rom 5:12 (II 45:10–23 in Souter's
edition) is quoted with approval in Erasmus' note (LB VI 586B–C / CWE 56 141–2;
see also his Paraphrase on Romans LB VII 793A–B and CWE 42 34 and 147 n12).
For studies of Erasmus as interpreter of Romans see John B. Payne in *Sixteenth
Century Essays and Studies* 2 ed Carl S. Meyer (St Louis 1971) 12–14; Albert Rabil Jr

Erasmus and the New Testament (San Antonio 1972) 115–39; Robert Coogan
'The Pharisee against the Hellenist: Edward Lee versus Erasmus' *Renaissance
Quarterly* 39 (1986) 476–506. On Augustine as exegete see CHB I 541–63.
Luther's lectures on the Vulgate text of Romans, written and delivered between
April 1515 and September 1516, followed the medieval glosses in identifying
in quo with Adam's original sin (WA 56 52 and n / LW 25 25–6). The first edition
of Erasmus' Greek New Testament with his notes was issued in the spring of
1516, probably too late for Luther to make use of it in his lectures. Not long
afterwards, at any rate, he told Georgius Spalatinus in a letter of 19 October
1516 (WA *Briefwechsel* 1 or Clemen 6 Ep 27) that he was troubled because
Erasmus did not take Augustine into account sufficiently when dealing with
Romans 5; Erasmus should be advised to read Augustine against the Pelagians
to improve his understanding. This message was brought to Erasmus' attention
tactfully in a letter from Spalatinus of 11 December 1516 (Allen Ep 501:47–83 /
CWE Ep 501:49–86), who does not name Luther but refers to him as a good
friend. This was Erasmus' introduction to Martin Luther (see my *Inquisitio
de fide* 6–7). A few years later Luther's translation of Rom 5:12 renders *in quo*
by *dieweil* 'since,' 'because' – equivalent to Erasmus' *quatenus* (WA *Deutsche
Bibel* 7 45). Tyndale in turn renders ἐφ' ᾧ by 'insomuch' ('insomuch that all
men sinned'), which is close to Erasmus' Latin and Luther's German. Tyndale
was familiar with both but probably consulted the Greek text directly, as
was his custom. Of subsequent English versions in the sixteenth century, the
Coverdale of 1535, Great Bible of 1539–41, Geneva of 1560, Bishops' of 1568
keep Tyndale's 'insomuch.' The Roman Catholic version of 1582 has 'in which';
the Authorized Version of 1611 'for that' with a marginal gloss 'Or, in whom.'
Thus a typical Erasmian investigation of a grammatical distinction led to
significant clarification and reinterpretation of a major theological text.

63 Lev 19:19; Deut 22:11

64 Sumptuary laws regulated such matters for the laity (see 'The Council of
Women' 909:22–910:5), but the allusions here are mainly to ecclesiastical dress.
Cf 705:16, 21–4, 28–30 below and 'The Well-to-do Beggars' 476:2–482:4; also
'The Seraphic Funeral.'

65 On confession see 'Youth' 96:31–97:35; on tithes 'The New Mother' 592:28–9;
on laws of marriage and affinity *Institutio christiani matrimonii* LB V 630–56
(633A–642A describes seventeen impediments, of various kinds, to marriage)
and, in the *Colloquies*, 'Courtship' nn48 and 84. Regulations controlling
marriage were legacies from Roman law, native custom, and religion. Elaborate
tables of consanguinity and affinity had become fixed in canon law. See
the *arbor consanguinitatis* and *arbor affinitatis* in Friedberg I 1425–6, 1431–2.
The second table is reproduced also in Steven Ozment *When Fathers Ruled*
(Cambridge, Mass 1983). Such tables sometimes presented almost insuperable
obstacles to matches.

66 Acts 2:1–4, describing the first occurrence of 'speaking in tongues'

67 Acts 15:10. The entire chapter helps to explain this allusion to Peter.

68 Often a deprecatory as well as descriptive term in Erasmus' commentaries on
biblical texts and writings on Christian life and morals. 'By Judaism I mean the
differentiating of foods and corporal things of this kind which by nature are
neither good nor bad' (*Supputatio* LB IX 473A).

69 The 'scattered islands' may be the Caribbean islands and whatever coastal regions of Central and South America had been explored or discovered by the time this colloquy was written. Allusions to the New World, the Americas, in Erasmus' pages are discussed at 'The Soldier and the Carthusian' n7 and 'The Well-to-do Beggars' n82. Columbus' letter of 14 March 1493 announcing his discovery was printed several times. Erasmus may have seen it, but whether he did so or not he had opportunities to read other accounts of the new lands – Vespucci's for example – and to hear of such matters in courts and councils. As humanist, moralist, and Christian he was in a sense compelled to take an interest in the New World, but it was no specialty of his.

The present passage is a sobering observation on an aspect of that new world that was of interest to Erasmus: is it really Christian, as the fishmonger's question implies? Of course 'wholeheartedly and sincerely professes Christianity' begs the question, but even nominal Christendom was a fairly small portion of the globe. 'How small a corner of the world is left to us!' (*Adagia* IV i 1 LB II 967F). Islam had conquered everything to the east. Christian efforts to win the Holy Land had ended in failure, and the so-called Christian realms now had to defend themselves against attacks by the Turks (see 'The New Mother' n19). No use to argue, then, about whether the recently discovered islands are Christian; first we had better make sure the Christianity we hope to export is the right kind. Other allusions by Erasmus to the constriction of Christendom occur in *De bello Turcico* LB V 357E–358A; *Ecclesiastes* LB V 813B–814A; *Explanatio symboli* LB V 1175A; *Epistola ad fratres Inferioris Germaniae* LB X 1623E–F / ASD IX-1 408:755–9; Allen Ep 1183:12–16 / CWE Ep 1183:14–18; *Vita Hieronymi* (Ferguson *Erasmi opuscula* 179:1198–1201 / CWE 61 52). Sebastian Brant's popular *Narrenschiff* (1494; issued a dozen times by 1521) has a long and melancholy section (99) on the decline of Christianity (trans E.H. Zeydel [New York 1944; repr 1962] 315–22). Erasmus, who had met Brant and thought well of him (Allen Ep 305:165–9, 255–6 / CWE Ep 305:170–4, 265), may have read the poem either in German or, more likely, in Latin translation.

70 An echo of Matt 9:37. The reflection in the lines that follow on the kind of Christianity that would be most persuasive – a simpler one than the European mode and freed from Mosaic law and the burden of unnecessary human ordinances – is characteristic of Erasmus. He wrote little on foreign missions, but was one of the very few humanists or reformers who wrote anything at all on this subject. See Marcel Bataillon 'Evangélisme et millénarisme au nouveau monde' in *Courants religieux et humanisme à la fin du xve et au début du xvie siècle* (Paris 1959) 25–36; George H. Williams 'Erasmus and the Reformers on Non-Christian Religions and *Salus Extra Ecclesiam*' in *Action and Conviction in Early Modern Europe* ed Theodore K. Rabb and J.E. Seigel (Princeton 1969) 333, 356–7. A few Spanish theologians were quick to perceive that native Indians presented an opportunity to which European Christians, through missions, had a duty to respond. See Lewis Hanke 'The Theological Significance of the Discovery of America' in *First Images of America* ed Fredi Chiapelli, 2 vols (Berkeley, Los Angeles, London 1976) I 363–89. An article on Erasmus and missions by C.J. Huygens in *Het Missiewerk* 17 (1936) 198–213 I have not seen. Consult Margolin *Bibliographie érasmienne (1936–1949)* 59 no 139, 126 no 363, 263 no 801.

71 Such as genuflections and making the sign of the cross. Erasmus has much to say about preachers' gesticulations in *Ecclesiastes* LB V 964C–965C, 987A–B. He must have in mind Matt 6:5–7 on ostentatious prayer also.

72 See 705:16–32 below.

73 Cf 'The Godly Feast' 196:3–9 and the explanation that follows, especially n220.

74 *Nulla salus extra ecclesiam* was an influential dictum from Cyprian Ep 73:21 CSEL 3 part 2 795 (compare his *De unitate* 6 CSEL 3 part 1 214–15). See 'Faith' n108 on its relevance to that colloquy, to 'The Godly Feast,' and to other writings by Erasmus. His opponents in the theological faculty at Paris deplored the butcher's arguments as both pernicious and arrogant, worthy of Wyclif and Luther, for they thought him wrong about the burden of Mosaic law. Erasmus replies that the butcher's arguments are countered by the fishmonger's, but he then proceeds to restate the butcher's, obviously with approval. He protests that he does not advocate disobedience of ecclesiastical ordinances prescribed by authority, but that there is too much assertiveness about the divine origin of what are in fact human ordinances. To love God with our whole heart and our neighbours as ourselves is a divine precept; to fast is a human regulation. For the same reason certain apostolic ordinances can be questioned; for example, that women should not speak in church (*Declarationes ad censuras Lutetiae vulgatas* LB IX 950B–951F).

75 Perhaps ambiguous. The definition of the church in 'Faith' (429:4–8) says nothing about the papacy, but note the ironic remark at 422:10–11.

76 The same play on *clemens* and *Clement* occurs in Allen Ep 1414:73. Clement VII, pope 1423–34, was a member of the Medici family, like his cousin Leo X. He succeeded Erasmus' friend Adrian VI (1522–3). Erasmus dedicated his Paraphrase on Acts to Clement in 1524 and received a flattering acknowledgment and a gift of money (Allen Epp 1414 and 1466:3–6 / CWE Ep 1414 and 1466:4–7). Erasmus concludes Ep 1414 with a fervent hope, as in this paragraph of the colloquy, that Clement's pontificate will revive a languishing church. For other correspondence of Erasmus and this pope see Epp 1418, 1438, 1588, 1846, 1987.

77 Tax, consisting of the first year's revenue, owed to the papal curia by one appointed to a bishopric or the headship of a monastery. Cf *Ratio verae theologiae* LB V 89A–B.

78 Granted for many canonical irregularities, often those affecting marriages. They were conferred by popes, bishops, sometimes by parish priests. An example occurs in 'The Funeral' 771:20–1. As was true of many other privileges, payment of a fee was expected (see Kidd *Documents* 113 no 61), and not only for dispensations but for performance of ordinary duties such as baptism. See 'The Funeral' 771:38 and 'The Godly Feast' 196:18.

79 *pestilens Ate*, the spirit of discord (*Iliad* 9.504–12). See *Adagia* I vii 13 and *Antibarbari* CWE 23 27:28, 39:8. In the pages that follow Erasmus refers to recent events in the rivalry between the two most powerful monarchs in Europe; Charles I of Spain, who had become Holy Roman Emperor as Charles V in 1519, and Francis I, king of France from 1515. Erasmus was on good terms with both monarchs and dedicated important writings to them: his Paraphrase on Matthew to Charles (1522) and on Mark to Francis (1523 but issued 1524). He was appointed to Charles' privy council in 1515. His duties were nominal, but

he was entitled to a stipend, which was paid irregularly (Allen Ep 370:18n).
He flattered rulers, as decorum required, yet was frank on topics he thought
deserving of frankness, reminding king and emperor alike of their Christian
duty to seek peace and pursue it. His dedicatory letter to Francis (Ep 1400)
tactfully avoids unseemly partisanship but is stern about the unappeasable
ambitions of rulers and the ruthlessness of their incessant warring.

War between France and the empire had broken out afresh in 1521. Charles
drove the French from Milan. He was supported by Henry VIII and the pope in
this conflict. In 1524 the French reconquered Milan; then the pope had second
thoughts and joined the French side. At Pavia in February 1525 the French
suffered a crushing defeat. Francis was captured and taken to Madrid, where
he was kept as prisoner until the Treaty of Madrid was signed in January
1526. By the treaty he surrendered his claims to Burgundy (now a Hapsburg
possession) and to Italian territories. These agreements he had no intention of
keeping, repudiating them as soon as he was liberated, and he was again at war
with the empire in 1527. He formed an alliance with the pope, Milan, Venice,
and Florence against Charles V; England gave formal but little active support.
One consequence of the war was the famous sack of Rome by imperial soldiers
in May 1527. See the introduction to 'Charon.'

80 In the original a proverbial expression in Greek (literally 'to the crows!')
alluding to exposure of a corpse in a field for carrion birds to devour. To be left
unburied was a hideous disgrace among ancient Greeks. The phrase is not in
Adagia, but see *Dialogus bilinguium ac trilinguium* in Ferguson *Erasmi opuscula*
208:62.

81 The *Institutio principis christiani* dedicated to Charles by Erasmus (Ep 393) is a
'mirror for princes' applicable to all rulers, and naturally Erasmus hoped this
prince would ponder and follow its counsels. Whether Charles read it, or how
much of it, is not known, but in any event it is for modern readers the best
compendium of Erasmus' political thought and therefore useful to students of
sixteenth-century ideas. See the critical edition by O. Herding in ASD IV-1; there
are English translations by Lester K. Born (New York 1936) and by Neil M.
Cheshire and Michael J. Heath in CWE 27 199–288.

As emperor, Charles V respected Erasmus, and he or his officers consulted him
occasionally on ecclesiastical affairs. See Allen Epp 2335:19–26, 2634:13–21.
When Erasmus informed Charles in September 1527 of attacks by some of the
emperor's Spanish subjects who were displeased by publication of translations
into Spanish of some of Erasmus' colloquies, Charles wrote a letter expressing
his gratitude for Erasmus' services to religion, adding that his books contained
nothing dangerous; if any 'human failing' is found in them, the author very
willingly corrects or explains them in such a way that no offence remains
(Allen Epp 1873 and 1920). For other letters by the emperor to or about Erasmus
see Epp 1270, 1380, 1731, 2318, 2553.

82 Charles was born in 1500.

83 'We can see that it often turned out that in striving to extend their power they
[the ancients, to whom Erasmus compares his contemporaries] lost even what
they already had' *Institutio principis christiani* LB IV 606F / ASD IV-1 212:423–5,
and see 214:490–5 / Born 247, 250 / CWE 27 281, 283. On lawyers, see *Querela
pacis* LB IV 628B / ASD IV-2 66:122–7 / CWE 27 296.

84 Erasmus makes a similar jest about Luther's marriage: until lately Lutheranism looked like a tragedy; now, since it ends in a marriage, we know it is a comedy (Allen and CWE Ep 1655:1–5).

85 Erasmus thought dynastic marriages a risky custom at best. A prince would do better to marry within his own nation or with close neighbours (*Institutio principis christiani* LB IV 603D–606A / ASD IV-1 208:286–209:341 / Born 241–3 / CWE 27 277–9). See E.V. Telle 'Erasme et les mariages dynastiques' BHR 12 (1950) 7–13.

86 Another source of endless trouble between states, since princes too often fail to keep their word (*Institutio principis christiani* LB IV 603A–604C / ASD IV-1 206:225–84 / Born 238–40 / CWE 27 275–6). A notable passage in More's *Utopia* is invincibly sceptical of the worth of treaties (Yale CWM 4 87–9). The Utopians simply refuse to make treaties (197–9). See also *Adagia* IV i 1 LB II 965A–C and the notes to 'Charon.'

87 Erasmus' tract on the cost and futility of war, *Adagia* IV i 1: *Dulce bellum inexpertis*, has an interesting analogue to this speech: a proposal by a litigant to his adversary that they settle their differences out of court by agreement or arbitration, Erasmus' favourite remedy for war. The situation here as described by the emperor is, from Erasmus' point of view, much the same. See LB II 965A–966C; translation in Phillips 'Adages' 340–3.

88 *malus ... genius*; see *Adagia* I i 72 and 'Rash Vows' n22.

89 At Pavia, (see n79 above). The Treaty of Madrid (January 1526) ended his captivity, but he was not actually released until March of that year, a month after publication of this colloquy. The remark that 'fortune ... made you a captive' must therefore have been written between February 1525 and February 1526. The same evidence applies to the mention in 'The New Mother' 592:19–20 of Francis as a 'guest' of the Spaniards. Whether Erasmus wrote 'A Fish Diet' with his usual rapidity or worked on it from time to time is not known, but probably it is safe to assume that both dialogues were completed or in parts revised in 1525.

Three months after the return of Francis to Paris, Erasmus sent him a letter (Allen Ep 1722, 16 June 1526) expressing his and the public's joy that the war between the two mighty monarchs, a war 'like that between sun and moon' and hence a peril to mortals, was ended. Then he turns to his other purpose in writing this letter: to complain of the scandalous behaviour of his Parisian enemies Noël Béda and Pierre Cousturier, who have slandered him and Lefèvre d'Etaples and Louis de Berquin. June 1526 was a difficult time for Erasmus. The faculty of theology at Paris had just censured the *Colloquies*, an action that impelled Erasmus to add a defence of the book to the June 1526 edition. See the introduction to 'The Usefulness of the *Colloquies*' 1096–7.

90 As it soon did. See introduction and notes to 'Charon.'

91 Made fools of ourselves; *Adagia* I vii 30

92 These lines introduce an inquiry concerning the central problem that controls the remainder of the dialogue. For a collection of official definitions and pronouncements on popes and papacy see Denzinger-Schönmetzer *Enchiridion*, Index systematicus III a. In addition to works already cited in this book see, concerning Erasmus' relations with Rome, Karl Schätti *Erasmus von Rotterdam und die Römische Kurie* (Basel and Stuttgart 1954); Georg Gebhardt *Die Stellung*

des Erasmus von Rotterdam zur Römische Kirche (Marburg 1966), and on this topic Bainton's comment in his review in ARG 59 (1968) 249–50; C.D. McCullough 'The Concept of Law in the Thought of Erasmus' ERSY 1 (1981) 89–112.

93 For some comments of Erasmus on bishops see n254 below.

94 See 'A Pilgrimage' n100. On the 'conditions' see the Benedictine Rule chapters 1, 3, 46. In *De libero arbitrio* Erasmus says some extremists hold that even the regulations of mere priors (priorculorum) are binding on pain of hell-fire (LB IX 1247A).

95 See *Annotationes in Novum Testamentum* LB VI 696D–697C; *Enarratio in psalmum XXXVIII* LB V 435B–C. For example, after a general chapter in 1322 Franciscan Spirituals, relying on the preamble to a bull by Nicholas III, *Exiit qui seminat* (1279), maintained that this pope had defined the absolute poverty of Christ as an article of faith. But John XXII declared the teaching heretical (*Cum inter nonnullos* [1323]; Denzinger-Schönmetzer *Enchiridion* 288–9 nos 930–1). Very many (*plerique*) theologians, says Erasmus, assert that the pope can abrogate what was instituted by the apostles, even by Peter (*Annotationes in Novum Testamentum* LB VI 696A; *Supputatio* LB IX 641D).

96 A 'true,' general, ecumenical council, as contrasted with a regional one, was considered to represent the entire church. 'Just as the universal church cannot err in determining matters of faith and morals, so too a true council, in its official capacity, cannot err ... nor can the pope' (Silvester Prierias *Dialogus de potestate papae*; Kidd *Documents* 31 no 15). See E.F. Jacob 'The Conciliar Movement in Recent Study' *Bulletin of the John Rylands Library* 41 (1958) 26–53. As the colloquy shows, disputes about conciliar theory were still alive in Erasmus' lifetime. We might expect that a writer so deeply concerned with reforms as he was would be a conciliarist; but he cannot be counted as one. He saw clearly the advantages of papalism and of conciliarism but had reservations about both. For practical and historical reasons he accepted papal primacy but had his doubts about papal infallibility and absolute authority. Popes can err and have erred. His attitude towards papal primacy may be compared with that towards the sacrament of penance: he accepts it, but does not agree that in its present form it was instituted by Christ. He does not advocate a general council. A *Consilium* (1521) he wrote (or had a hand in writing) proposed as a remedy for the Lutheran troubles the appointment of a learned commission by Charles V, Henry VIII, and Louis II of Hungary. For text of the *Consilium* see Ferguson *Erasmi opuscula* 338–61.
On Erasmus and papal primacy see H.J. McSorley 'Erasmus and the Primacy of the Roman Pontiff: Between Conciliarism and Papalism' ARG 65 (1974) 35–54. On Erasmus and conciliarism see J.K. McConica 'Erasmus and the "Julius"' in *The Pursuit of Holiness* ed Charles Trinkaus and H.A. Oberman (Leiden 1974) 462–7, and his article 'Erasmus and the Grammar of Consent' in *Scrinium Erasmianum* II 77–99 on *concordia* and the *consensus fidelium*, two principles vital to the integrity of the church, since, for Erasmus, the church is the *consensus populi Christiani* (Allen Ep 1729:26–9). Councils were once useful, but now are compromised by the conduct of princes, prelates, and preachers (*Annotationes in Novum Testamentum* LB VI 64F–65D).
Texts of councils are printed in Johannes Mansi et al *Sacrorum conciliorum collectio* 1758–98 (facsimile ed Paris 1901–13, 47 vols in 50) and see Tanner. The

most extensive history is C.J. Hefele and K. Hergenröther *Conciliengeschichte* (Freiburg 1855–90; French translation and enlargement by H. Leclerq, 10 vols in 19 (Paris 1907–38). For a concise history see Hubert Jedin *Ecumenical Councils of the Catholic Church* trans E. Graf (New York 1960). Other studies in English: Brian Tierney *Foundations of Conciliar Theory* (Cambridge 1955); *Unity, Heresy, and Reform 1378–1460* ed C.M.D. Crowder (New York 1977); Anthony Black *Monarchy and Community* (Cambridge 1970) and *Council and Commune* (London 1979); F. Oakley 'Almain and Major: Conciliar Theory on the Eve of the Reformation' *American Historical Review* 70 (1964–5) 673–90 and 'Conciliarism in the Sixteenth Century: Jacques Almain Again' ARG 68 (1977) 111–32.

97 The Council of Constance (1414–18) declared that its authority came immediately from Christ and that all men, including the popes, were bound to obey its orders in matters concerning the faith (session 4; Tanner I 408) and decreed (*Frequens*) that councils should meet frequently (session 39; Tanner I 438–9). When the council convened there were three claimants to the papacy. Gregory XII resigned; the council deposed Benedict XIII and John XXIII and elected Martin V. It condemned the teachings of Wyclif and Jan Hus, the Bohemian reformer, and turned Hus over to the secular power. For the text and translation of the proceedings of the council see Tanner I 405–51.
The Council of Basel (continued in several cities, 1431–45) renewed the conflict with the papacy. The most extreme conciliarists affirmed the ecumenicity of the Council of Basel, but the majority of later theologians rejected most or all of it; text and translation in Tanner I 455–591. On Basel see Black *Council and Commune* (preceding note) and J.W. Stieber *Pope Eugenius IV, the Council of Basel and the Secular and Ecclesiastical Authorities in the Empire* (Leiden 1978).
Pius II in the bull *Execrabilis* (1460) forbade under pain of excommunication appeals from the pope to future councils (Denzinger-Schönmetzer *Enchiridion* 345 no 1375).
The only other council held in Erasmus' lifetime was the Fifth Lateran (1512–17). Before he was elected pope, Julius II promised to convene a council within two years. When he failed to do so, the emperor Maximilian I and Louis XII of France, with a group of cardinals, called a council at Pisa (1511). Julius excommunicated the cardinals, the so-called council languished, and a few months later the pope summoned a council to meet at the Lateran palace in Rome. Julius died in February 1513 and was succeeded by Leo X. This council's chances of success seemed promising at first, but hopes were disappointed. It advocated a crusade against the Turks and enacted desirable but ineffectual measures of reform pertaining to printing, preaching, pluralism, and much else, including the apparently invincible problem of sacerdotal celibacy; text and translation in Tanner I 595–655. On this council see F. Oakley 'Conciliarism at the Fifth Lateran Council' *Church History* 41 (1972) 452–63; R.J. Schoeck 'The Fifth Lateran Council' in *Reform and Authority in the Medieval and Reformation Church* ed Guy F. Lytle (Washington, DC 1981) 99–126; and Nelson H. Minnich *The Fifth Lateran Council (1512–17)* (Brookfield, Vt 1993). Although Erasmus allowed that this council may have done some good, he doubted that it was a true council, for it was not a universal, and therefore not an ecumenical, one; cf Allen Ep 1268:35–41 / CWE Ep 1268:38–44. For Erasmus' treatment of it in *Julius exclusus* see Ferguson *Erasmi opuscula* 94:515–102:702 / CWE 27 190–5 / *The*

'*Julius Exclusus*' *of Erasmus* trans Paul Pascal ed J. Kelley Sowards (Bloomington 1968) 64:516–71:701; see also McConica's article in *The Pursuit of Holiness* (cited in the preceding note). On Luther's hostile reaction to this Lateran council see John Headley 'Luther and the Fifth Lateran Council' ARG 64 (1973) 55–78).

98 On the primacy of Peter and the papacy's Petrine claims see Erasmus' note on Matt 16:18 (LB VI 88C–F) and compare his Paraphrase on Matthew (LB VII 92F–93A). The note in LB VI recognizes that some persons apply Matt 16:18 to the Roman pontiff as *princeps* of the Christian faith, but Erasmus does not endorse this title. Augustine says in one place that 'upon this rock' means the faith in Christ professed by Peter in Matt 16:16 (*In epistolam Joannis ad Parthos tractatus* X 10.1 PL 35 2054). In another place Augustine says 'Peter' signifies the church (*Sermones* 76.1 PL 38 479). Later, in *Retractationes* 1.20 (21) (PL 32 618), he invites readers to decide which of these opinions is more probable. Erasmus agrees that Peter may be taken as a 'type,' 'one speaking for all,' as Cyprian thought (*Annotationes in Novum Testamentum* LB VI 88E–F; he means Cyprian Ep 59.7 CSEL 3 part 2 674). See further C.A.L. Jarrott 'Erasmus' Biblical Humanism' *Studies in the Renaissance* 17 (1970) 135–40.
Erasmus had no trouble with the jurisdictional authority of the papacy. Whatever the source of that authority, a pontiff is needed, not only to settle disputes but to restrain the tyranny of other bishops. The pope should not be blamed for everything that happens in Rome. Even Peter, if he were there now, would have to tolerate things he did not really approve of (Allen Ep 1183:68–85 / CWE Ep 1183:75–94). But Erasmus had grave doubts about claims of papal infallibility. 'Apostle,' 'pastor,' 'bishop' are designations of office, not of sovereignty; 'pope' and 'abbot' are attributes of love (*caritas*), not power (*Enchiridion* LB V 49B / Holborn 107:14–16 / CWE 66 101; *De concordia* and *De esu carnium* passim). Pope and church together, not the pope alone, share the keys. Similarly councils, if universal, may have the authority of a heavenly oracle as the fishmonger has assured us. For other references to papal authority and infallibility see *Ratio verae theologiae* LB V 90F–91B; *Apologiae contra Stunicam* LB IX 364A–365D, 370D–371F, 385E, 386A–389A; *Apologia adversus monachos* LB IX 1067A–1068D; *Apologia adversus rhapsodias Alberti Pii* LB IX 1179B–1181D; *Spongia* LB X 1631–72 / ASD IX-1 117–210 passim. On different sixteenth-century Roman Catholic interpretations of Matt 16:18 see John E. Bigane III *Faith, Christ, or Peter* (Washington 1981).

99 *constitutionibus*. Constitutions are ordinances or regulations of popes, bishops, and sometimes heads of religious orders (as in *De esu carnium* LB IX 1206B). A papal rescript is a reply to a question or request, usually but not always limited to the person who submitted it.

100 Erasmus told the Louvain theologians (1522) that 'If any pontifical or episcopal constitution whatever exposes us to the penalty of hell-fire, the position of Christians is hard indeed. If some constitutions bind us and some do not, no one is in a better position to make his purpose clear than the pontiff himself' (Allen Ep 1301: 66–8 / CWE Ep 1301:121–4). If bishops' regulations are useful and fair, they should be obeyed, at least until a synod meets and decides about them (*De concordia* LB V 504F–505B; cf *Supputatio* LB IX 641D).

101 See *Apologia adversus rhapsodias Alberti Pii* (1531) LB IX 1181E–1183A for a defence of what Erasmus had written on human ordinances.

102 Deut 4:2, 12:32

103 *in corbanam.* Literally 'what is for corban'; see Matt 27:6; Mark 7:9–13. Jesus
accused the Pharisees of evading the duty of helping one's parents by a pretence
that money used for such a purpose was dedicated to God in the offering
(*corban*, a Greek borrowing from Aramaic) and therefore was unavailable for
secular use. Thus they disobeyed the commandment 'Honour thy father and
thy mother.' Cf *Ecclesiastes* LB V 1025F.

104 The conversation at dinner in 'The Godly Feast' assumes a variety of possible
interpretations of scriptual passages, and Eusebius mentions 'the various
conjectures of commentators'; those referred to are identified in n116.

105 *in palaestris theologicis.* See *Adagia* V ii 10.

106 Annas was the father-in-law of Caiaphas, the high priest who tried Jesus; John
18:13.

107 See 'The Godly Feast' 182:31–3 and n95.

108 This question brings us closer to the heart of the argument, summed up at
701:21–702:5.

109 After the destruction of the city and temple of Jerusalem in 586 BC

110 See n55 above.

111 Proverbial; *Adagia* I v 10

112 *simplici stupro* 'simple fornication,' a technical term in moral theology. Cf
n201 below; and see *Enchiridion* LB V 53C–D / Holborn 115:9–10 / CWE 66 108;
Annotationes in Novum Testamentum LB VI 678F–679C. Erasmus allows that in
some circumstances there is no simple answer to the question of the gravity of
this sin (*Ecclesiastes* LB V 879B–C).

113 See 717:34–718:8 below.

114 On kinds of lies and their effects see 'The Liar and the Man of Honour'; 'Things
and Names'; 'Sympathy' 1045:33–1046:7; *Apologia adversus rhapsodias Alberti
Pii* LB IX 1194A–1196A. The remark on 'a little white lie' echoes one in *Moriae
encomium* LB IV 465B / ASD IV-3 148:414–6 / CWE 27 127.

115 'Opened a window to'; *Adagia* I iv 3

116 Colossal, wondrous; cf 'Benefices' 45:21 and n5.

117 Canons forbidding clergy in major orders, such as priests, deacons, and monks,
to marry date from the First Lateran Council of 1123 (canon 21; Tanner I 194)
and the Second of 1139 (canons 6, 7; Tanner I 198).

118 'Boundary-mark' and in Roman religion the god and protector of such marks
or limits. Erasmus used a representation of Terminus on an antique ring, given
to him by a royal pupil (the Scottish prince Alexander Stewart), as his personal
emblem, and he had a seal engraved by Metsys bearing the motto *Cedo nulli* 'I
yield to none.' See J.K. McConica 'The Riddle of Terminus' *Erasmus in English* 2
(1971) 2–7, and Robert D. Sider 'Concedo Nulli: Erasmus' Motto and the Figure
of Paul in the Paraphrases' in the same newsletter 14 (1985–6) 7–10.

119 Vows are temporal or perpetual, conditional or absolute, public or private,
solemn or simple. A vow is public if accepted in the name of the church
by an authorized ecclesiastical officer; otherwise it is private. It is solemn if
recognized by the church as such; otherwise it is simple. See, for example, the
study of the vow in the Middle Ages by James A. Brundage, *Medieval Canon
Law and the Crusader* (Madison, Milwaukee, and London 1969) 30–114; NCE
XIV 756 (sv 'Vow, Canon Law of'). A solemn vow is regarded as absolute and
irrevocable when accepted by authority. Public vows are 'reserved' to the pope
and can be abrogated or dispensed only by papal permission. Private vows

of 'perfect and perpetual chastity,' and vows taken when entering a religious order (in which solemn vows are required), are also reserved to the Holy See. Erasmus reminded critics that these terms 'solemn' and 'simple' are the words of men, not of Scripture. He denied an opponent's assertion that a solemn vow is one taken with mature deliberation, whereas a simple vow is not. On the contrary a simple vow, Erasmus contends, is often taken with the same deliberation as a solemn one. It is not so public but is just as much a vow as a solemn one is (*Apologia adversus rhapsodias Alberti Pii* LB IX 1185A; *Institutio christiani matrimonii* LB V 636A; *Appendix de scriptis Jodoci Clithovei* LB IX 814A–B).

120 Cf 'Rash Vows' 37:5–38:20, 'The Old Men's Chat' 458:30–8, 'The Usefulness of the *Colloquies*' 1098:25–1100:4.

121 refrain from going] Reading *non ibit* for *ibit*, as in all editions but the first, February 1526

122 *Quod solet fieri*. The Fishmonger's reply may strike the reader as odd. The explanation lies in the ancient derivation of *solemnis* from *solet fieri* 'is accustomed to happen'; see Isidore *Etymologiae* 6.18.1 (the reading of manuscripts CTUV in the Oxford Classical Texts edition).

123 'Drinkable gold,' volatile oil containing minute particles of gold and drunk as a medicine or cordial. The double meaning provided a common jest, for example in a letter by Warham to Erasmus (Ep 286) and in the General Prologue to Chaucer's *Canterbury Tales* 443–4.

124 See the account of Erasmus' visit to Freiburg at 713:18–714:8.

125 Exod 16:23, 20:8, 23:12, 31:13–14, 34:21, 35:2; Lev 23:3; Num 15:32–7; Deut 5:12. Cf the examples at 707:22–708:20 below.

126 Mark 2:27. In *Supputatio* LB IX 646A–F Erasmus defends against Béda what he had written about the sabbath. For a later exposition of the meaning of sabbath see *Explanatio symboli* (1533) LB V 1190B–1191D.

127 'I call law human whenever man prescribes to man what is not set forth in those writings whose authority it is unrighteous for anyone to doubt. Whatever good men do willingly, it is likely that the Spirit is not far from them. But we are not required to believe that the Spirit by whose divine influence the apostles wrote is present in all men who make law' (*Apologia adversus rhapsodias Alberti Pii* LB IX 1145B–C).

128 Cf 695:32–696:41 below.

129 Writing in 1522 to Joost Lauwereyns, a leading member of Charles V's council, and complaining of attacks on 'heresy' in the earlier colloquies – meaning certain pages of 'The Profane Feast' in the March 1522 edition (see n76) – Erasmus questions whether the pope would wish to bind people to eating fish under penalty of eternal damnation (Allen Ep 1299:69–71 / CWE Ep 1299:77–9; cf Allen Epp 1300:32–5, 1301:66–74 / CWE Epp 1300:35–9, 1301:121–38; *De esu carnium* LB IX 1204C). Furthermore, what a pope's or bishop's threat of eternal damnation means is in doubt. See *Annotationes in Novum Testamentum* LB VI 64C; *De esu carnium* LB IX 1202A, 1205C–F, 1206D, 1208F–1209B. Cf what is said of 'thunderbolts' (excommunications) at 696:31–41 below.

130 On custom in general, see 'The Profane Feast' n58; on liturgical customs, see 'The Godly Feast' 196:3–39. Some examples of the conflict between law (Mosaic) and custom are presented in *Ratio verae theologiae* LB V 86F–88C / Holborn 198:34–201:33. In *De esu carnium* Erasmus writes on the custom of fasting,

'Surely it is probable that custom does not bind anyone more strictly than the authors of the custom intended' (LB IX 1204F; cf 1206C).

131 Matt 5:34. Lev 19:12 has: 'Ye shall not swear by my name falsely, neither shalt thou profane the name of thy God'; that is, by adding an oath (cf James 5:12 and Num 30:2). Christ goes further: 'Swear not at all, neither by heaven, for it is God's throne, nor by the earth, for it is his footstool ... But let your communication be, Yea, yea, Nay, nay; for whatsoever is more than these cometh of evil' (Matt 5:33–7). He wants his followers to be such that there is no need of swearing. Some theologians, Erasmus tells us, took 'for whatsoever is more than these cometh of evil' to mean 'from lack of trust' or faith, not the evil of swearing (*Annotationes in Novum Testamentum* LB VI 29E–F). Mere avoidance of perjury is not, as it was in the Old Law, enough. A Christian should not swear by anything, for everything is sacred to the creator. An affirmation or denial must be sincere; and if it is, no swearing is necessary. 'And so,' as Erasmus paraphrases Christ's words, 'when I totally prohibit swearing I do not abrogate the law which forbids perjury but fulfil it' (*Paraphrase on Matthew* LB VII 33A–D. See also *Lingua* LB IV 692D–693A / ASD IV-1A 84:914–85:948 / CWE 29 316–17).
St Paul disapproved of oaths but calls attention to their public use. He uses them himself (as in Rom 1:9; 2 Cor 1:23, 11:31; Gal 1:20; Phil 1:8), though he was justified in doing so because his testimony was inspired. Ordinary folk, on the other hand, ought to eschew oaths because swearing might lead them to perjury (*Declarationes ad censuras Lutetiae vulgatas* LB IX 837C–D). Experience with non-Christians and unavoidable dealings with civil courts and other political authorities forced the church to interpret Matt 5:37 less literally and to accommodate it to otherwise intractable situations, as Erasmus regretfully acknowledges. Nevertheless his notes and paraphrase on Matt 5:37 cost him some trouble. For his explanations see his reply to Edward Lee (LB IX 131D–132A); to Béda and other Paris critics (LB IX 462A–E, 493F–494A, 575B–576C, 834C–840D); to the Spanish monks (LB IX 1078A–C); and to Alberto Pio (LB IX 1193E–1194A). Swearing an oath may be necessary but is a sign of human weakness (Allen Ep 1581:728–30 / CWE Ep 1581:813–14).

132 Technical terms commonly used in defining or describing Christian law and rules of morality. Precepts are rules or commandments, some found in Scripture (the Decalogue, for instance) and others imposed by the church, that are obligatory for all Christians. Counsels are advice or recommendations by which to improve or 'grow in grace' and goodness in moral behaviour. 'Honour thy father and thy mother' is a precept. 'Would that all men were even as I myself' (that is, celibate; 1 Cor 7:7) is not a precept but what is called sometimes an 'evangelical counsel.' 'Swear not at all' is an imperative, uttered by Christ. Is it not therefore surely a precept? Yet the fishmonger suggests it is a counsel, and whether he knows or is guessing, tradition agreed that oaths are sometimes necessary. See Thomas Aquinas *Summa theologiae* II–II q 89 art 2–3.
Aquinas held that the difference between 'precept' and 'counsel' is that a precept implies obligation, whereas a counsel is left to the option of one who receives it. A Christian has no choice about precepts; they must be obeyed (*Summa theologiae* I–II q 108 art 4). Many counsels are given by Christ and the apostles, and the devout and prudent will, of course, follow them as best

they can. But counsels do not bind unconditionally. Such distinctions were common knowledge. One of the reasons for disagreement over the argument of *Moriae encomium*, Erasmus remarks, is that Folly herself does not understand the difference between precepts and counsels (*Apologia adversus rhapsodias Alberti Pii* LB IX 1140F).

133 This is the answer to the assertion at 694:38–41, and the fishmonger concedes the point. In writing against Pio, Erasmus recalls two passages in earlier colloquies relevant to this question of human ordinances, 'Youth' 97:18–21 and 'The Godly Feast' 185:34–8 (*Apologia adversus rhapsodias Alberti Pii* LB IX 1182B–C, D–E).

134 Exod 20:15; Deut 5:19; Matt 19:18

135 Matt 5:39

136 See n100 above.

137 *Adagia* I v 29

138 To the fishmonger these words sound much alike. But when dire threats of excommunication are added, a counsel becomes in effect a precept. The intention of the person who utters the words makes the difference, though the fishmonger suspects 'it's not suitable for the common people to know this.' This practice of commanding with the addition of threats of punishment, even hell-fire, was to Erasmus a scandal, demanding rational and charitable settlement. See *De esu carnium* LB IX 1204D–1208E.

139 Ecclesiastical intervention, by means of papal or episcopal excommunication, was sometimes used to compel recalcitrant debtors to pay what they owed, no matter what their social rank or status. If a debtor died while excommunicated, his survivors might be required to pay for him. See H.C. Lea *Studies in Church History* (Philadelphia 1869) 439–48. In England bishops had to invoke the aid of the secular arm to arrest a fugitive debtor. (Such requests identified or 'signified' the person wanted; hence the warning by Chaucer's Summoner to beware *Significavit*; see General Prologue to the *Canterbury Tales* 662). Many details are provided by F. Donald Logan *Excommunication and the Secular Arm in Medieval England* (Toronto 1968). Among the numerous types of lay persons excommunicated, fishmongers and butchers are named. Erasmus' butcher is not joking or imagining impossibilities when he speaks of being excommunicated if, as an insolvent debtor, he might 'prefer to run off' rather than go to prison. If his creditors then complained to the bishop, the bishop could excommunicate the fugitive and call upon the secular power to seek and seize him. Such procedures appear to have been fairly successful, both on the Continent and in England, but resort to them diminished by the sixteenth century, as secular governments were increasingly taking such matters into their own hands.

140 Excommunication. Popes, general councils, and bishops or their authorized deputies in their own dioceses had power to excommunicate; parish priests did not.

141 The fishmonger means the code of Roman law (c 450 BC), whose extreme punishments – for example that debtors should be cut in pieces – were not enforced (Gellius 20.1.19, 39–55; Quintilian 3.6.84); see *Adagia* I x 24 CWE 32 244, 374. Cf *De esu carnium* LB IX 1209A.

142 Pliny *Naturalis historia* 2.137

143 Making a futile gesture. Cf *Adagia* I vii 23; *De copia* 1.11 CWE 24 308:1–2.

144 *Adagia* IV v 32

145 An aphorism or quotation, source unknown. It appears, with 'most steadfast' for 'steadfast,' in the *Chronica maiora* of Matthew Paris (d 1259); see Rolls Series 57, 7 vols (London 1872–83) III 481. G.G. Coulton says it is 'a stock phrase of the law-courts for a man pleading that he had signed or acted under compelling force' (*Europe's Apprenticeship* [London 1940] 251n).

146 The words quoted are from Horace *Odes* 3.3.7. Cf *De taedio Iesu* LB V 1275D–E.

147 The word play is in the original: *famis aut infamiae*.

148 Even a secret marriage was then valid. See 'Courtship' nn48 and 84.

149 'Contracted a marriage' (*contraxit matrimonium*) can mean here 'has married' or 'has promised to marry.' Cf n119 above.

150 The Second Order of St Francis, the nuns

151 The same illustration is found in *Apologia adversus rhapsodias Alberti Pii* LB IX 1185B.

152 In this example she has not taken a solemn vow to enter a religious order but only a simple vow, in the presence of a few relatives 'at home.' As Erasmus remarks elsewhere, that is not the same thing as taking a solemn vow, with certain rites, in a church. But whether public or private (*absque ceremoniis*), uncertainties remained. Erasmus questions whether rigid distinctions between 'solemn' and 'simple' were realistic and just. These and other perplexities are treated at length in *Institutio christiani matrimonii* LB V 634B–637B, 647A–648B.

153 It would not. See 'The Girl with No Interest in Marriage' 291:26–7 and n44.

154 By a solemn vow accepted by the church. She could do so when she reached the age of sixteen. See 'The Girl with No Interest in Marriage' n8.

155 On these and related topics of Christian marriage and monasticism see the introductions and texts of 'Courtship,' 'The Girl with No Interest in Marriage,' 'The Repentant Girl,' 'Marriage.' The best exposition of Erasmus' views is *Institutio christiani matrimonii* LB V 615A–714B.

156 Matt 19:6

157 There are echoes here of Erasmus' accounts of his own entrance into a monastery. See 'The Girl with No Interest in Marriage' introduction 282–4 and the references given there.

158 A legal phrase, *doli capax* (*Digest* 43.4.1) meaning capable or suitable for fraud or deceit, hence sane enough to be responsible for wrongdoing. When the butcher repeats the phrase he makes it passive, applicable to one who is wronged, not one who does wrong.

159 At 693:29–694:11

160 *Adagia* II iv 38. The phrase comes from the prefatory letter to a poem on *Cupido cruciatus* by Ausonius and is used aptly by Erasmus in his tribute to Albrecht Dürer (*De pronuntiatione* LB I 928E / CWE 26 398–9). See E. Panofsky ' "Nebulae in Pariete": Notes on Erasmus' Eulogy on Dürer' *Journal of the Warburg and Courtauld Institutes* 14 (1965) 34–41.

161 On marriage within prohibited degrees of consanguinity and affinity see n65 above.

162 According to *Adagia* III iv 44

163 Heb 13:17; cf 1 Pet 2:13–14.

164 Under pressure of the butcher's questions the fishmonger has shifted his ground, for his assertion here that 'it's the prerogative of the lawmaker to interpret the law' contradicts what he had said at 694:38–9. See n133 above.

165 *praepositus*, 'provost' or 'prior' in ecclesiastical usage; here it can signify either a civil or ecclesiastical officer, depending on context.

166 Cf n103 above.

167 Dairy products such as butter and cheese, as well as meat and eggs, were forbidden on fast days in Lent. Both Fridays and Saturdays and special seasons during the church year were usually meatless days. By Erasmus' time a large part of the year was meatless – by some reckonings about 150 days (*De esu carnium* LB IX 1202D–E; see Lucien Febvre *Life in Renaissance France* trans Marian Rothstein [Cambridge, Mass and London 1977] 127).

168 Thomas Aquinas uses these two terms sometimes in comparisons or contrasts. For a few examples see *Summa theologiae* I q 36 art 3; I q 93 art 8; I–II q 96 art 3; II–II q 58 art 7; II–II q 82 art 2; II–II q 85 art 3; II–II q 123 art 3; II–II q 129 art 1.

169 They must be respected as they deserve. In administering the sacraments they have the same power the apostles had, but we are not obligated to give the same weight to their words that we give to the apostles' writings, which it is forbidden to doubt (*Apologia adversus monachos* LB IX 1090C; *Apologia adversus rhapsodias Alberti Pii* LB IX 1178F). See also n254 below.

170 See 690:7–19 and notes above.

171 *pomeria*; see *Adagia* III vi 46. On the literal meaning of *pomerium* see Gellius 13.14.1–7.

172 Cf Allen Ep 1744:17–25; some examples in *Declarationes ad censuras Lutetiae vulgatas* LB IX 951D. In principle the church has always insisted on the distinction between unalterable (divine) and changeable (human) law. For other examples see R.C. Mortimer *Western Canon Law* (Berkeley and Los Angeles 1953) chapter 5.

173 The 'vote' could not change anything but reminded the people of their obligations. After the Ten Commandments were received by Moses and the book of the covenant read to them, the Israelites promised to obey them, thus in a sense ratifying the law that both they and Moses knew would stand, since it was divinely ordained (Exod 24:7–8).

174 The Sorbonne criticized these lines ('Finally ... no longer') as confusing the church's ordinances with the old Mosaic law (*Declarationes ad censuras Lutetiae vulgatas* LB IX 952B–C). The general question here is whether time-honoured constitutions, even the Mosaic laws, though they may have the character of precepts, can or should ever give way to a higher ethic. Christ's implicit approval of David's eating the sacred bread and his pronouncement that the sabbath is made for man and not man for the sabbath (692:30–1, 694:30–1 above) provide the answer. See *Ratio verae theologiae* LB V 106F–107B.

175 Those in which absolution for certain sins must be granted by higher authority (pope, bishop, or head of an order) instead of by an ordinary confessor. The Council of Trent restated the established rules (session 14 [1551] Teaching concerning ... penance, chapter 7 and Canons concerning ... penance, canon 11; Tanner II 708 and 713, with the notes). Cf *Exomologesis* LB V 157F–158A.

176 Horace *Epistles* 2.1.116, quoted in *Adagia* I vi 15. The next adage, 'Let the cobbler stick to his last,' is a more common proverb with the same meaning.

177 These words are quoted with approval by Erasmus in 'The Usefulness of the Colloquies' 1108:21–5. What is said here is defended in *Declarationes ad censuras Lutetiae vulgatas* LB IX 952A–B. Cf Chomarat *Grammaire et rhétorique* II 908–10.

178 A main subject in the examination of scriptural texts in 'The Godly Feast' (see especially 185:31–186:7, 196:11–39) and earlier in *Enchiridion*. See also Ep 1202 and C.A.L. Jarrott on this theme in Erasmus' *Annotationes in Novum Testamentum*, 'Erasmus' Biblical Humanism' *Studies in the Renaissance* 17 (1970) 140–9.

179 Rom 14:17; Gal 3:23–6, 4:3–9; see Erasmus' note on Gal 4:7–8 in LB VI 817D–E. Erasmus' Paraphrases on Romans and Galatians as well as his Annotations should be consulted. These Paraphrases are translated in CWE 42, the Annotations on Romans in CWE 56. Erasmus translated Chrysostom's commentary on Galatians 3–5 (LB VIII 294–313). Chapters 7 and 8–10 of 1 Corinthians are also basic texts (see 'The Godly Feast' 189:37–191:41). On Erasmus as interpreter of Paul see John B. Payne 'Erasmus: Interpreter of Romans' in *Sixteenth Century Essays and Studies* ed Carl S. Meyer 2 (1971) 1–35 and 'Erasmus and Lefèvre d'Etaples as Interpreters of Paul' ARG 65 (1974) 54–82.

180 2 Cor 3:12–14

181 'The religion of Christians today does not depend on miracles,' but we should firmly believe those recorded in Scripture (Allen Ep 2037:85–9, written to bishop Longland in 1528). In *Ecclesiastes* (1535) Erasmus says faith has supplanted miracles, as Scripture supplanted the oracles (LB V 825B).

182 Cornelius the centurion, a devout man who 'prayed to God always,' was told in a vision to seek St Peter. He did so and consequently was converted, with his household, to Christianity (Acts 10).

183 Ps 36:3 (35:4 Vulg)

184 Guillaume Farel, who studied in Paris with Lefèvre d'Etaples and later joined the reformers; in 1523 he went to Basel, where he knew Erasmus. They did not get along well, and as Farel's views became more extreme his differences with Erasmus and his rash temperament led to an irreconcilable breach. Some years later he was a prominent preacher and agitator in Bern, then was active with Calvin in Geneva. When both were expelled from Geneva (1538), Farel went to Neuchâtel, where he died in 1565. He was a zealot who did not suffer fools – all who opposed him – gladly. Erasmus was content to see the last of him after the hostile encounter in 1524 (Ep 1510).

185 'Insipid,' 'stupid'; *Adagia* II iv 72. Since the noun *blitum* or *blitus* means 'beet,' identification of Bliteus with Béda (Bédier), Erasmus' relentless critic in Paris, is certain. On Béda see 'Patterns' n35; for his criticisms of Erasmus *Supputatio* LB IX 441–720.

186 Jacobus Latomus (Jacques Masson), d 1544; academic theologian at Louvain. Luther considered him the best of those who had written against him and thought him superior to Erasmus (WA *Tischreden* 2 no 1709). Latomus' *De trium linguarum et studii theologici ratione* (1519) attacked what he regarded as Erasmus' excessive emphasis on linguistic studies. Erasmus replied with an eloquent *Apologia contra Latomi dialogum* (LB IX 79B–106E). On Erasmus' differences with Latomus see additionally G. Chantraine 'L'Apologia ad Latomum' in *Scrinium Erasmianum* II 51–75. They were differences between a champion of grammar (in the comprehensive sense of that term) and a defender of dialectic. Both men had been at the Collège de Montaigu under Standonck (on whom see n287 below).

Latomus' nickname means 'lame in both feet.' His enemies said that he sprained both ankles when fleeing after being taken in adultery. This story is found in a contemporary *Dialogus bilinguium et trilinguium* by Konrad or Wilhelm Nesen (Ferguson *Erasmi opuscula* 220:354–221:356 / CWE 7 344). Erasmus was thought by some to have had a hand in writing or revising the dialogue. On the authorship see Allen Ep 1061:505n and the introductions to Ferguson's Latin text and to the English translation in CWE 7.

187 'Blear-eyed'; Nicolaas Baechem (Egmondanus), prior of the Carmelites at Louvain and another detractor of Erasmus' New Testament and the *Colloquies*. See 'Rash Vows' n14.

188 Wolfgang Capito (Köpfel), d 1541, who admired both Luther and Erasmus, was a leader of reform in Strasbourg at the time this colloquy was published. Erasmus had known him in Basel and praised him (Allen Ep 456:169–74 / CWE Ep 456:187–93) before Capito joined the reformers and moved to Strasbourg in 1523. They continued to correspond, but relations cooled after Capito's conversion to the 'new gospel' or 'new church' church, as Erasmus terms it (Allen Epp 1459:61, 1482:16 / CWE Epp 1477B:72, 1482:19). Although, in this colloquy, Capito is included with other misguided or hostile men, he is not dismissed as ignorant. On him and his work see James A. Kittelson *Wolfgang Capito: From Humanist to Reformer* (Leiden 1975), 'Capito and Erasmus' *Erasmus in English* 11 (1981–2) 12–19, and the article in CEBR.

189 *rabinum*. Like *magister*, this title often had sarcastic or contemptuous connotations; see 'Military Affaris' n17, and cf 'The Well-to-do Beggars' n69.

190 *Adagia* I ix 29; the phrase is 'appropriate either for those who sentence and punish very severely or those who settle disputes and doubtful controversies with great speed' (CWE 32 197–8). See also *Adagia* IV i 6 and IV i 7. Erasmus alludes aptly to this proverbial phrase when protesting the heavy-handedness of Béda and other critics (Allen Ep 1581:553–69).

191 See 677:22–3 above.

192 This sentence displeased the Paris critics (*Declarationes ad censuras Lutetiae vulgatas* LB IX 952B–D). Cf n174 above.

193 *Adagia* I viii 6

194 *Adagia* I iii 81

195 Scylla was a monster in the straits of Messina that seized and devoured sailors; Charybdis a whirlpool opposite. To be 'between Scylla and Charybdis' was to be in equal peril no matter which course one took (*Adagia* I v 4).

196 The name, Greek in origin, means 'overseer,' 'guardian'; metaphorically 'shepherd' in Christian usage.

197 Apparently this passage was misunderstood by one critic, Alberto Pio (*Apologia adversus rhapsodias Alberti Pii* LB IX 1178F).

198 Erasmus defends this paragraph in *Declarationes ad censuras Lutetiae vulgatas* LB IX 952E–F.

199 A violation of clerical decorum. Those who had long hair (*comam nutriunt*; 1 Cor 11:14 Vulg) were censured as early as 506 by canon 20 of the Council of Agde (Mansi [n96 above] 8 328). The bishop of Basel in 1503 rebuked clerics who 'have not been ashamed to let their hair grow too long' (J.M. Vincent *Switzerland at the Beginning of the Sixteenth Century* Johns Hopkins University Studies in History and Political Science 22 no 5 [Baltimore 1904] 56, and see next note).

The Fifth Lateran Council in 1514 forbade clerics in cardinals' households to cultivate long hair or beards ([Bull on reform of the curia] On cardinals; Tanner I 619).

200 Cf 'The Well-to-do Beggars' 477:21–3. Statutes of the Synod of Basel (1503) contain many specific regulations of clerical dress. Canons must not go to market in choir dress during divine service to buy eggs or cheese. Whether in church or out, they must wear clothing suitable to their profession: no silk, no swords or daggers, no extravagant collars, no rings, no long hair (text in *Quellenbuch zur Schweizersgeschichte* ed W. Oechsli [Zürich 1886–93] II 373ff; translation in Vincent *Switzerland* [see preceding note] 55–8).

201 Cf *Ecclesiastes* LB V 1025B. Adultery was a more heinous sin than 'simple' fornication (see n112 above) or concubinage, as it was a violation of the sacrament of marriage (as well as a personal sin), hence a sacrilege. On clerical concubinage see 'The Well-to-do Beggars' n6.

202 See 'The Abbot and the Learned Lady' n26.

203 Usury was forbidden to clergy as early as the First Council of Nicaea in 325 (canon 17; Tanner I 14).

204 Sale or purchase of ecclesiastical office; so called from the original culprit, Simon Magus; see Acts 8:9–24. Always denounced, this evil was widespread and apparently impossible to eliminate. 'What was a crime then is custom now' (*Enarratio in psalmum XXII* LB V 331B). Avarice and debauchery, the main vices of priests, begot simony, which is now, Erasmus charges, almost a joke (*Ecclesiastes* LB V 791D).

205 *Exomologesis* (1524) contains a similar passage (LB V 163F–164A). Cf Allen Ep 447:613–22 / CWE Ep 447 679–89, the letter to 'Grunnius.'

206 Cf Allen Ep 1353:173–6 / CWE Ep 1353:195–9: 'No one who sees a Carthusian the worse for drink thinks he has committed a crime. But if the same Carthusian tasted meat, he deserved perpetual imprisonment.' On the Carthusians, see the introduction to 'The Soldier and the Carthusian' 328–9.

207 The knotted cord of the Franciscans was customary long before the time of Erasmus, by Francis' example or desire. When describing Francis as the saint appeared to him in a dream, Erasmus was pleased to report that his cord was unknotted: another superstition exposed! (Allen Ep 1700:47–8). Franciscan dress receives attention in 'The Seraphic Funeral'; on Ep 1700 see n17 there.

208 Augustinian monks wore leather girdles. See Allen Ep 2088:91–8.

209 Carmelites wore belts.

210 One of the Knights of Rhodes or Knights Hospitallers or Knights of Malta, whose specialty was protection of pilgrims and crusaders. They fought against the Turks in the fifteenth and sixteenth centuries.

211 St Francis and the earliest Franciscans went barefoot; later ones wore sandals. The common term 'discalced' when used of Franciscans or Carmelites is ambiguous, since it does not indicate whether the persons to whom it is applied are barefoot or wear sandals; but it does mean they do not wear shoes. See also 'The Sermon' n14; 'The Seraphic Funeral' n76.

212 See 'The Old Men's Chat' n70.

213 Make an uproar; *Adagia* IV iv 73. With the phrase compare *De esu carnium* LB IX 1202B. The religious orders had firm and zealously defended traditions about their origins, rules, and dress, but as with many other sodalities, sacred or

secular, the known facts do not always support cherished beliefs about ancient origins. Erasmus is typically impatient with fastidiousness about costume; for instance in Allen Ep 447:497–521 / CWE Ep 447:546–74, written in 1516 but not printed until 1529. Another example occurs in *Moriae encomium* LB IV 471A–473B / ASD IV-3 158:524–160:556 / CWE 27 131. On Erasmus' own experiences with clerical dress see 'The Well-to-do Beggars' n97.

214 Cf 'Courtship' 258:16–17 and 720:16 below.

215 Cf the anecdote in a letter of c April 1524 (Allen Ep 1436:100–4 / CWE Ep 1436:110–13). It may be compared with his experience in Italy (Ep 447:470–96 / CWE Ep 447:514–45). See also 'The Well-to-do Beggars' n97.

216 Literally 'much-revering,' of one who observes religious restrictions conscientiously; *threscus* is a transliteration of a word in James 1:26. If Erasmus has a specific contemporary in mind here, we do not know who he was.

217 These too were banned during fasts; see n167 above. But because of gradual alleviations, exceptions, and local customs, it is sometimes difficult to be certain about fasting at a particular time and place.

218 Other examples of such conduct are found in 'The Liar and the Man of Honour' 346:28–347:41.

219 That is, on Friday, the day before Passover, on which Jesus was crucified. To Dominican and Franciscan friars, the most active preachers in the late medieval church, Lent afforded an unsurpassed opportunity to move their hearers by eloquence and, as here, by *exempla* that would win and hold their attention. On methods and techniques of preaching see A.J. Krailsheimer *Rabelais and the Franciscans* (Oxford 1963). The principal exposition of Erasmus' ideas on preaching is *Ecclesiastes* (1535), already cited many times in these pages; but see too 'Youth' n48, 'The Well-to-do Beggars' n46, and 'The Sermon.' He recalls some downright silly sermons, as any habitual auditor can do (*Ecclesiastes* LB V 1031F–1032B, 1041C–1043A), and – like Folly (LB IV 475A–479D / ASD IV-3 162:587–168:696 / CWE 27 133–5) – he knew all the tricks of the trade, but was pained by excesses and bad taste, just as he was constantly annoyed by church music (on this see 'A Pilgrimage' n161). Inordinately long sermons could be trying. He says he heard a Parisian divine extend a sermon on the prodigal son throughout Lent (*Ecclesiastes* LB V 1042C–D). 'Passion sermons eight hours long' were one of the Roman church's customs condemned by Luther as unnecessary (*Vermahnung an die Geistlichen ... zu Augsburg* [1530] WA 30 part 2 350 / LW 34 55). Oecolampadius, Erasmus' fellow theologian in Basel, wrote a tract *De risu paschali* (Basel 1518) on making Easter enjoyable; see Allen Ep 1111:58n.
In *Ecclesiastes* Erasmus writes interestingly on the preacher as actor and the contrasts between good preaching and foolish or extravagant discourse (LB V 845D–847A, 859E–861E). There is an analysis of sermons, a form of discourse to which Erasmus gave much attention, in Chomarat's *Grammaire et rhétorique* II 1053–1154. On Roberto Caracciolo's preaching and Erasmus' interest in him see Moorman 522 and E.V. Telle 'En marge de l'éloquence sacrée aux xvᵉ–xviᵉ siècles: Erasme et fra Roberto Caracciolo' BHR 43 (1981) 449–70.
When he was a boy, Erasmus tells us, he heard the story of the nun told in the vernacular by a Dominican to rouse a sleepy congregation (*Ecclesiastes* LB V 861B–C). Anecdotes of this type, similar in most essentials, were current, for example in Heinrich Bebel's *Facetiae* (Tübingen 1506; see the edition by

G. Bebermeyer [Leipzig 1931] 65 nos 57, 58) and More *Latin Epigrams* 71, 191–2 no 149; see also Johannes Pauli *Schimpf und Ernst* (1519) ed Johannes Bolte (Berlin 1924) II 412 no 716. The most notable version of the story is that by Rabelais (1546) in *Gargantua and Pantagruel* 3.19. It is longer than Erasmus' and has a different ending, for the nun, immediately after the episode, confesses herself to the friar. He enjoins her, *sub poena*, not to divulge what had happened, and so she could not. Whether Rabelais borrowed at least the main part of the tale from Erasmus or from another source is not known. On these and later versions see V.L. Saulnier 'Histoire d'un conte rabelaisien: la nonne surprise et le devoir de silence (Tiers livre, XIX)' BHR 24 (1962) 545–58.

220 The Latin terms in this passage refer to the 'bases' or 'positions' in forensic rhetoric. Quintilian's analysis of *status* is long and complex. In 3.6.44 he cites Cicero (*Orator* 14.45) on the fundamental questions to be asked in any case – Was the deed done? What was done? What was the nature of the deed? – and Cicero remains his authority when he reviews methods of defence (3.6.80–4). The defendant's first position (*status conjecturalis*) is to deny the charge. The second defence (*status definitivus*) is to say that the deed was not committed. The third line of defence (*status qualitatis*) is to maintain that the act was justifiable. The last resort is to try to evade the charge on a point of law, to claim for example that the charge is brought illegally; under this heading Quintilian places questions of competence (or [*status*] *translationis*). Erasmus' summary in *Ecclesiastes* LB V 892F lists the *status* in a slightly different order and gives alternative names for each: '... an sit factum quod objicitur, quale sit et quid sit. Primus ... dicitur conjecturalis, sive inficialis, secundus qualitatis, sive juridicalis, tertius finis, sive definitivus.' The nun in the story told here has no grounds for *status conjecturalis* or *inficialis*, since 'the evidence was inescapable.' She adopts the *status qualitatis* (which in Quintilian may be taken to include the *status translationis*) – 'I was overcome,' and 'I would have [screamed] ... but there's a strict rule against making noise in the dorter.' In Allen Ep 2164:1–4 Erasmus defines *status translativus* as 'acknowledging the deed – since it is undeniable – in such a way as to blame it on someone else.'

221 Cf 'A Pilgrimage' n165 above.

222 Since the Benedictine Rule (chapter 39) prohibited the eating of the flesh of quadrupeds, this is an ironic way of saying that when the prior was not in the abbey he did not keep the rules.

223 These visits may be a sign of his lechery also. See 'Inns' n20.

224 See n258 below.

225 A strong passage in *Ecclesiastes* argues that the requirement of obedience to human ordinances is sometimes carried to such length that it obscures the higher obedience owed to God (LB V 1023E–F). Cf Allen Ep 1353:138–59 / CWE Ep 1353:155–78.

226 *Adagia* I i 35

227 Vespers were recited in the afternoon, but during Lent in the morning.

228 Jerome, in a famous letter to Eustochium, who wished to become a nun, warns against the insidious evils of wine: 'The spouse of Christ should avoid wine as though poison' (Ep 22.8 PL 22 399).

229 Leo of Rozmital was once invited to a convent at Neuss near Düsseldorf as the guest of the mother superior, who 'gave a fine dance in the nunnery. The nuns

were very finely dressed and knew all the best dances' (*Travels* 23–4). We hear of two English nuns who spent an evening 'in dancing and playing the lute with friars' (A. Hamilton Thompson *The English Clergy and Their Organisation in the Later Middle Ages* [Oxford 1947] 172). Charitas Pirckheimer, a sister of Erasmus' friend Willibald Pirckheimer, played the dulcimer while nuns danced at the celebration of her jubilee as an abbess (Franz Binder *Charitas Pirckheimer* [Frieburg 1878] 187, 189; *Charitas Pirckheimer Quellensammlung* III: *Briefe* ed J. Pfanner [Landshut 1966] 241:29ff. On nuns and dancing in Italy see E. Rodocanachi *La femme italienne ... pendant la Renaissance* (Paris 1922) 208. Roger Ascham saw nuns dancing at a wedding during his journey to Augsburg in 1551 (*The Whole Works of Roger Ascham* ed J.A. Giles, 3 vols [1864–5; repr New York 1965] I part 2 249). We hear of priests dancing in Krailsheimer *Rabelais and the Franciscans* (n219 above) 57. In Basel dancing was forbidden even to the laity as late as 1519 (Vincent *Switzerland* [n199 above] 26) and in due time by Calvin in Geneva. See Kidd *Documents* 558 no 20 (22), 583 no 295 (14), 637 no 311, 640 no 312.

230 *lascivi lusus.* The same phrase is used in Allen Ep 1233:107, where Erasmus speaks of the perils to chastity in such games. Love of literature and of study, so notable in the More daughters, are safeguards. See 'The Abbot and the Learned Lady' n16.

231 Cf the account of the prior and his brethren in 'The Girl with No Interest in Marriage' and 'The Repentant Girl.'

232 This narrative follows fairly closely what Erasmus had written in a letter to Udalricus Zasius in March 1523 (Allen Ep 1353:160–76 / CWE Ep 1353:179–99), shortly after visiting him in Freiburg. It is the first of three passages in this dialogue containing precious autobiographical testimony – conveyed through fiction but authentic nonetheless – recalling experiences important to Erasmus.

233 Cf 694:23–31 above. The same example of the deleterious effects of feast days is used in Allen Ep 1039:180–6 / CWE Ep 1039:190–6 (written in 1519) and *De concordia* (1533) LB V 504D–E.

234 The distinction is characteristic. Erasmus deplored and often criticized unneeded and harmful human ordinances but did not advocate open disobedience. He hoped to persuade, not incite, and like most of his contemporaries had a horror of sedition.

235 Allen Ep 1353:160n says Passion Sunday, but since every Sunday was a 'day of obligation' this orgy was unusually disgraceful. Erasmus' account, dated Monday, 23 March 1523, says the affair occurred 'yesterday' (Allen Ep 1353:160 / CWE Ep 1353:179).

236 A staff, encircled by ivy and vine leaves, carried by Bacchus and his company

237 A satyr, elderly and usually drunken; companion of Dionysus (Bacchus). For one of the many contemporary representations in art see Dürer's *Bacchanal with Silenus*. The vivid description of the man 'playing the part of Silenus' and 'carried head down to prevent his choking with vomit' resembles a similar description in Clement of Alexandria *Paedagogus* 2.2; but Erasmus seems not to have known Clement. In 'The Epicurean' he is called 'comic Silenus' (1086:32–3).
On another level than art or mythology, however, the name 'Silenus' signified for Erasmus something very different and more profound than a satyr. Beneath the outward and visible appearances lies an ethical and Christian meaning,

if one has eyes to perceive it. So Erasmus writes in an essay on 'The Sileni of Alcibiades,' first published in the 1515 edition of the *Adagia* (III iii 1) and later printed separately. The title was a proverbial expression for something that seems at first absurd and contemptible but when scrutinized more closely proves to be worthy, beautiful, glorious.

238 *Adagia* I vi 45. Sermons with ribald stories to entertain rather than edify and shameful 'bacchanalian revels' on Palm Sunday (or during Lent; see 714:8–1 below) were aspects of carnival or folk culture (like the Feast of Fools and institution of Boy Bishop), enjoyed and defended by the commons though strongly opposed by many churchmen and reformers. Erasmus witnessed a mock bullfight in a carnival at Siena in 1509. He condemns the spectacle and the behaviour of the people as unchristian and pagan (*Supputatio* LB IX 516C–517A; *Enarratio in psalmum XXXVIII* LB V 458F), and he thought the same about the real bullfight he saw in that year in the courtyard of Julius II's palace (Allen Ep 3032:417–33). On the conflict between carnival and Lent see the chapter on 'The Triumph of Lent' in Peter Burke *Popular Culture in Early Modern Europe* (New York 1978) 207–43.

239 Also in *De esu carnium* LB IX 1202A–B, 1212A, 1213D; Allen Ep 2037:78–80

240 On the profanation of the Lord's day by debauchery see *Exomologesis* LB V 162F–163A; similarly Allen Ep 1353:153–5 / CWE Ep 1353:170–3. Nowadays too many Christians use holy days as occasions for drinking bouts and worse (*Adagia* II vi 12).

241 Similar assertions about the mending of shoes on Sunday being a 'capital crime' are made in *Moriae encomium* LB IV 465B / ASD IV-3 148:411–414 / CWE 27 127. The sabbath was made for man, yet those and other holy days are burdensome upon workers who ought and wish to work to support their families. Fish days do not help the poor, who can afford neither fish nor flesh. The difficulty about not working on Sunday and yet having to support one's family was not new. The master-general of the Dominican order in 1274 advised Pope Gregory X that men should not be compelled to keep new feast days 'beyond the authority of the Roman church; and that except on major feast days instituted by the church, men who needed to work to feed their families should be permitted to do so after divine service' (Mansi [n96 above] 24 130).

242 This next part of the dialogue conveys accurately Erasmus' convictions and prejudices about compulsory fasting. That his two speakers exaggerate now and then is true enough, for as literary creations with personalities of their own they do more than merely parrot Erasmus' opinions. But Erasmus often repeats and defends the substance of what is said here. The entire passage may be compared profitably with what he wrote earlier in 'The Profane Feast,' first printed in the March 1522 edition of the *Colloquia* (see 143:15–146:5), and 'The Godly Feast' (188:8–191:37). His own aversion to fish made meatless days unpleasant. For the failure of the church to be more moderate about fasting he blames the bishops rather than the popes (see *De esu carnium* LB IX 1204C–1209D). He takes pains to stress that his quarrel is not with *publicas ecclesiae constitutiones* but with those imposed by some bishops and their officers ('In epistolam . . . de delectu ciborum . . . scholia' no 8 in *Scrinium Erasmianum* II 603 / ASD IX-1 68:98–107; on the publication of the *scholia* see n263 below). To tell someone that relief from the rules could be obtained from pope or bishop is a waste of time, for ordinary people must deal with their parish priest, who

acts for the bishop, administers the sacraments, hears confessions, and grants absolution or imposes penalties (LB IX 1203D–F). But the people believe the pope alone can alleviate rules of fasting.

243 'Fasting' and 'abstinence' are distinct yet closely related terms. Both denote avoidance of food, but Erasmus emphasizes the difference between fasting as total abstention from all food on occasion or for a time and discrimination or 'selection of food.' Fasting was thought to have scriptural warrant as 'a divine precept, or almost a divine precept' (see Acts 13:2, 14:23). Yet, as Erasmus points out elsewhere, neither Christ nor Paul ordained fasting (Allen Ep 858:458–64 / CWE Ep 858:484–91). Selection of foods, eating some and avoiding others, for instance eating fish on Fridays, involves what Erasmus considers a presumptuous judgment, for decrees, enforcement, and penalties concerning such regulations are made by men, not required by Scripture. They are in fact counsels at best.

Very soon after Easter 1522 Erasmus wrote *De esu carnium*, which was printed in August (English translation c 1530; STC 10489). This essay, addressed to Christoph von Utenheim, bishop of Basel and a supporter of reform, is the best non-dramatic presentation of his views on fasting and the institution of meatless days, a reasoned indictment of the situation and a powerful plea for change. In part at least *De esu carnium* was prompted by a recent and notorious violation of fasting laws in Basel; on that affair see 'The Godly Feast' n157 and n263 below. He wanted to help the culprit, Steinschnider, if he could; the more so, apparently, because he himself was now looked upon with suspicion by some in Basel. He does not excuse ostentatious or contumacious disobedience of laws of fasting. Indeed fasting has positive values, moral and physical (*De esu carnium* LB IX 1197E–1198A). But to attach unreasonable and severe penalties to ordinances and to ignore the arguments for mitigating them is injurious and unjust. Allowances for individuals' circumstances ought to be made. He himself has eaten flesh in private on fast days, he concedes, but only because of extreme necessity of health and because he had a papal dispensation to do so (LB IX 1212B–1213E; and see n271 in this colloquy). Above all, Christian charity, in the spirit of Pauline liberty, ought to govern religious discipline. (Compare his response to criticism by Spanish monks and his opponents in Paris (*Apologia adversus monachos* LB IX 1089A–D; *Declarationes ad censuras Lutetiae vulgatas* LB IX 831E–834C). A reader who turns to 'A Fish Diet' after examining *De esu carnium* will see that the dialogue includes the same topics and many of the same arguments, even some of the same phrases and illustrations. Clearly Erasmus wrote the dialogue with *De esu carnium* (1522) before him or in mind. In an attack on Protestants in 1529 Erasmus says the net result of their efforts was that the Roman church became more restrictive than it had been. Formerly no one troubled much about somebody's eating flesh in private, whereas now whoever tastes an egg in Lent for the sake of his health is in danger of capital punishment (*Epistola contra pseudevangelicos* [1529 or 1530] LB X 1583C / ASD IX-1 301:508–10). His rhetoric here is overwrought, but the entire passage of which this is part (LB X 1582E–1587D / ASD IX-1 300:472–309:723) is a good example of his bitter disappointment with the more radical reformers. By going too far they had only made matters worse for Catholics.

244 Particularly Paul; see 'The Godly Feast' 189:35–191:37.

245 1 Tim 4:34

246 See the account of Eros' visit to Freiburg 713:18–714:8 below.

247 Foreigners comment on the English fondness for eating – and sometimes overeating – and the abundance of their food. So *A Relation of England* (c 1500) 21, 23. That the English ate a supper every other day in Lent is repeated in Erasmus' *scholia* on *De esu carnium* no 52 (*Scrinium Erasmianum* II 617 / ASD IX-1 86:604–5). The testimony of More confirms the English custom of taking a more lenient view of Lenten diet than was usual in other lands (*Apology* chapter 31; Yale CWM 9 106).

248 A topic to which Erasmus often adverts. See 'The Profane Feast' n58.

249 *pila* refers to more than one kind of game. On preaching see 'The Well-to-do Beggars' n46. For Christians, church attendance was not an option. From the fifth or at latest sixth century, attendance at the Sunday Eucharist was not only expected but became mandatory, as is clearly implied in canon 47 of the Council of Agde (506), which ruled that people at Sunday mass must stay until the benediction or suffer public rebuke by the bishop (Mansi [n96 above] 8 332). In the context of the council such a rule is intelligible only if there was an antecedent assumption that the faithful must attend mass on Sundays. This standard had the force of law in the religious life of those people, not only for Sunday but for other holy days of obligation. See Gratian *Decretum* part 3 *De cons* D 1 c 62, 64 (Friedberg I 1311–12 / PL 187 1727–8). As early as the Hispana Canons of the sixth–seventh centuries, Christians were forbidden to leave church during the sermon; and going to games instead of divine service could bring excommunication (R.C. Mortimer *Western Canon Law* [Berkeley and Los Angeles 1953] 21–2).

250 Erasmus tells of a priest who, fasting in the evening before he was to say mass, had tasted some sugar. Next day, when robed for mass, he happened to become aware of a sweet taste in his mouth. Horrified, he sought Erasmus and asked if he should sacrifice. 'I laughed at his silliness and told him to put his mind at rest and say mass' (*Exomologesis* LB V 158C–D). Some misguided religious prize 'sacred obedience' so highly that their immoral lives are of less concern to them than obedience to superiors (*Ecclesiastes* LB V 1023F–1024A).

251 The Eucharistic bread, or host

252 1 Cor 6:19. Cf *Exomologesis* 163F–164A; *Apologia qua respondet invectivis Lei* in Ferguson *Erasmi opuscula* 293:1436–1445; *Lingua* LB IV 740A–D / ASD IV-1A 159:411–160:437 / CWE 29 392–3. Passages similar to this exchange occur in Luther; see the fifth of his eight Wittenberg sermons (1522) WA 10 part 3 40:1–43:6 / LW 51 88–9; *Confitendi ratio* (1520) WA 6 164:35–165:26 / LW 39 38–9; *De capitivitate Babylonica ecclesiae* (1520) WA 6 517:16–21 / LW 36 43.

253 Defects of birth or body, technically 'irregularities,' were loosely defined, and papal dispensations could be sought to waive some of them, as was done from time to time in the early church. For instance, the so-called *Apostolic Constitutions* (fourth century), canons 77–8, allow one-eyed and maimed men to become bishops, but not deaf or blind men (William Whiston's translation rev by James Donaldson, Ante-Nicene Christian Library 17 part 2 [Edinburgh 1870] 267). On a puzzling passage in 2 Sam 5:6–8, 'the blind and the lame shall not come into the house,' see *Adagia* IV v 47. Legislation was indeed 'human,' but the stated prohibitions rested upon explicit Mosaic law. Men blind or

lame or bastard were barred from the Hebrew priesthood (Lev 21:16–23; Deut 23:2). Erasmus himself was illegitimate but was allowed by his superiors to be ordained to the priesthood (Allen Ep 517:7–12 / CWE Ep 517:8–14). See Epp 187A (in Allen III xxix–xxx) and 517 and the introductions to these documents in CWE. When writing of physical handicaps to ordination Erasmus may have been thinking also of the famous case of Origen who, taking Matt 19:12 literally, castrated himself. Referring to this event in his biographical sketch of Origen, Erasmus comments that while such physical mutilation makes ordination prohibitive, authorities ought to be more vigilant to prevent those who are morally and spiritually defective from being ordained (*Vita Origenis* LB VIII 428A–D). The source of the account of Origen's self-mutilation is Eusebius' *Ecclesiastical History* 6.8.1–5. In an ironical passage of *Julius exclusus* the pope says that among numerous and stringent reforms suggested – by others – for the Council of Pisa was the castration of criminous priests (*Erasmi opuscula* 100:654–5 / CWE 27 183).

In his *scholia* on Jerome's letters (in the revised edition of his Jerome [Basel: Froben 1524–6] III 65–6), Erasmus attributed the constitution forbidding men with bodily defects to be admitted to clerical orders to Pope Anastasius I (399–401), who feared that otherwise defective men would be dedicated to the church and the whole ones to secular life.

254 People do not exist for the sake of bishops but bishops for the sake of people (*De esu carnium* LB IX 1207F). Bishops are to be heard, Erasmus says, if they teach what is worthy of Christ and if their own lives so shine before men that they are lanterns leading to Christ. Even their wrongdoings must be borne – if they do not cause us to do wrong (*Apologiae contra Stunicam* LB IX 369A).

255 The urgency of preaching by bishops was often voiced; for instance by Jean Gerson, the chancellor of Paris named a few lines later by the fishmonger. He emphasized preaching in *De officio pastoris*, a sermon of 1408 to the synod of Rheims (*Oeuvres* V 123–33 no 215). The Fourth Lateran Council (1215) had ruled that bishops unable, for good reasons (other duties or physical infirmities) or bad (lack of learning), to preach must provide suitable men to do it for them (constitution 10, On appointing preachers; Tanner I 239–40). The Council of Trent found it still necessary to remind prelates that they were 'personally bound' to preach unless a legitimate impediment prevented (session 5 [1546] Decree on instruction and preaching, nos 9–10, session 24 [1563] Decree on reform, canon 4; Tanner II 669, 763). Erasmus touches upon these and related themes in many writings, including a long passage in *Ecclesiastes* LB V 801C–818D. See also 'Things and Names' 811:5–6 and n6.

256 Festivals were movable (Easter) or fixed (Christmas). All Sundays were feast days; see nn240 and 241 above. Latomus rebuked Erasmus for suggesting in *De concordia* (1533) that since bishops and popes have introduced so many unnecessary feast days – for example those celebrating the Immaculate Conception of Mary, her nativity, and her presentation in the temple – they could just as easily abolish them. It would be better to have no solemn feast days except those for which there is a clear basis in Scripture (*De concordia* LB V 504D–F). Granted, replies Latomus, Scripture says nothing about those events, but tradition, approval by theologians, and the disciplinary and spiritual profit they provide fully justify such feast days (*Opera* [Louvain 1550] 180–1). The

same reasons justify the church's rules about fasting and abstinence from the eating of flesh (*Opera* 181–2). Erasmus disagreed. 'I don't know why the bishops constantly add holy days to holy days,' when it would be more prudent to reduce the number. To true Christians every day is holy; to bad ones holy days are not holy but profane (*Adagia* II vi 12 LB II 587A–B; cf *Apologia adversus rhapsodias Alberti Pii* LB IX 1154C–1155A, 1199F; Allen Ep 1039:180–96 / CWE Ep 1039:190–209). The plethora of religious festivals and the prevalence of superstitious practices are named in almost the same breath as misfortunes; obviously they are related in his mind (Allen Ep 2037:82–9, written to bishop Longland in 1528).

A useful history of holidays, with evidence drawn from many sources, is Edith C. Rodgers' *Discussion of Holidays in the Later Middle Ages* (New York 1940).

257 What is said in the following lines about 'special physical conditions' and confidence that papal regulations were not meant to cause unbearable hardships for those who needed exemption is both tactful and sincere. The same arguments appear earlier (1522) in 'The Profane Feast' 144:26–40; *De esu carnium* (1522) LB IX 1204C; Allen Ep 1353:45–55 / CWE Ep 1353:53–63 (1523); later in *De concordia* (1533) LB V 504E–F.

258 In his *De non esu carnium* (1401) Gerson writes that custom or the constitution of the universal church forbidding the eating of flesh need not be observed in clear cases of extreme necessity. Nor could one escape blame for homicide if, by eating meat, he could save a life yet willingly allowed himself or another person to die by fasting. To Gerson as to Erasmus in the colloquy, the crucial question is whether the ordinance on fasting is a divine commandment or a 'purely human ordinance'; we know that 'thou shalt not kill' *is* a divine law (*Oeuvres* III 80–1 no 93). On Gerson see 'The Shipwreck' n43. Luther is reported to have claimed Gerson as a precursor – without knowing it – of the Reformation (WA *Tischreden* 5 no 5523).

259 *paraphronesi*, transliterated from a Greek word in the Septuagint text of Zech 12:4

260 Under the Mosaic laws the death penalty applied to many offences, including blasphemy, sorcery, adultery, incest, sedition, treason, murder, profanation of the sabbath. The intimate connection in Hebrew society between crimes against the state and violation of religious ordinances was reflected in medieval law, though torture was not allowed in Hebrew law. Erasmus hopes the severity of Old Testament law can be modified by New Testament doctrines of charity, but he takes contumacy and sedition very seriously, as lines 34–6 below show.

261 Matt 5:34; see 695:21 and n131 above.

262 Matt 5:21–2

263 Seditious acts and incitement of public disturbance (*tumultum*) were always serious and often capital offences in the sixteenth century. The case of Sigismund Steinschnider is a gruesome example. Reference was made earlier (n243 above; see also 'The Godly Feast' n157) to this neighbour and acquaintance of Erasmus in Basel. On Palm Sunday 1522 Steinschnider and some boon companions defiantly ate pork without troubling to conceal the fact. Steinschnider was a skilful surgeon but a headstrong individual – perhaps mad, Erasmus suggested later (Allen Ep 1353:183–5 / CWE Ep 1353:206–8 and *scholia* on *De esu carnium* [on which see below in this note] in *Scrinium Erasmianum* II 601 / ASD IX-1 66:30–2) – who was evidently his own worst enemy. When

Erasmus wrote *De esu carnium* (printed in August 1522), he tried to protect Steinschnider by saying that his action was 'not *per se* a capital offence,' though deplorable and worrisome – for what would happen next? (LB IX 1197A). What transpired was worse than Erasmus could have foreseen. In February or March 1523 Steinschnider made the fatal mistake, whether irrationally or from sheer bravado, of crossing the border into Alsace, which was imperial territory. There he was promptly seized, charged with both blasphemy and treason, and executed. His death is described by Erasmus, on the basis of presumably reliable reports, in his *scholia* on *De esu carnium*: 'After atrocious tortures the flesh was twice plucked from his back by red-hot tongs. His four extremities together with his hips and shoulder blades were slowly and excruciatingly amputated. His skull was perforated and the tongue pulled out through the incision. Then the central part of his body except the heart was burnt' (*Scrinium Erasmianum* II 601 / ASD IX-1 66:25–8 / trans R.H. Bainton 'Erasmus and the Persecuted' in *Scrinium Erasmianum* II 202).

These *scholia*, written some years after publication of the August 1522 edition of *De esu carnium*, were issued by Froben in 1532 with the second edition of *De esu carnium*, a reprint of Erasmus' *Declarationes ad censuras Lutetiae vulgatas*, *Dilutio* on Josse Clichtove's attack on *Encomium matrimonii*, and his reply to Alberto Pio's criticism. Neither the *scholia* on *De esu carnium* nor the *Dilutio* was reprinted in LB. Consequently they were long unknown or inaccessible to most readers of Erasmus. In his preface to the *scholia* Erasmus says that he was persuaded by the bishop of Basel to publish *De esu carnium* but agreed with reluctance because he was sure he would make enemies – 'and I was not mistaken in that.' The *scholia* repeat, defend, and sometimes elaborate or clarify the arguments presented in *De esu carnium*. They confirm that in 1532 Erasmus had not changed his opinions on fasting and related subjects. The text of the *scholia* is edited by J. Coppens 'In Epistolam Des. Erasmi Roterodami de delectu ciborum ad Christophorum episcopum Basiliensem, scholia eiusdem defensoria' in *Scrinium Erasmianum* II 599–620 and by C. Augustijn, with introduction, in ASD IX-1 51–89; see also Coppens' article, 'Les scolies d'Erasme sur l'"Epistola de interdicto esu carnium,"' in *Colloquia Erasmiana Turonensia* II 829–36. On Clichtove and the *Dilutio* see the introduction to 'The Girl with No Interest in Marriage' 281. On Steinschnider see Allen Ep 1274:14n and CEBR.

264 For Erasmus' experience with fasting in Italy during Lent see *De esu carnium* LB IX 1206F, 1212D, and Allen Ep 1353:71–3 / CWE Ep 1353:81–3, Allen Ep 1539:106–14.

265 *heminam*, equivalent to a pint

266 This paragraph describes Erasmus' visit to Udalricus Zasius in Freiburg in March 1523. Another account is provided in Allen Ep 1353:24–44 / CWE Ep 1353:30–52, but Erasmus did not publish that letter; it was first printed in 1574, though he wrote it very soon after the visit. In it Erasmus writes strongly about fasting (Allen lines 45–239 / CWE lines 53–248), a passage that includes the story of the drunken orgy described earlier in this colloquy at 707:25–708:11 and an allusion to the fate of Steinschnider, on which see n263 above.

267 Erasmus. 'Erasmus' (or 'Erasmius') and 'Desiderius' are Greek and Latin equivalents respectively of 'beloved.'

268 Not in all respects, but we learn more about his maladies than about his good health. He boasted in 1530 that he never wore spectacles (Allen Ep 2275:26–8), which is remarkable, considering how much he read and wrote, but no doubt he followed the sensible advice he gave to youth: avoid studying at night and take time to get some daily exercise (Allen Ep 56:55–9 / CWE Ep 56:64–9; *De conscribendis epistolis* LB I 447E / ASD I-2 495:8–12), and when writing, stand up (Allen Ep 820:6–7 / CWE Ep 820:7; paintings of him by Dürer, Holbein, and Metsys show him standing at a writing desk). He survived until seventy, longer than most men of his epoch, yet he was harried and sometimes tormented by illnesses. Much is known about these, thanks to his allusions and sometimes detailed descriptions in letters. Investigations by historians of medicine have contributed careful analyses of his health.

Erasmus had an alarming experience in October 1518 with what may have been bubonic plague (Allen Ep 867:148–247 / CWE Ep 867:156–265). He was a martyr to recurrent fevers, gout or arthritis, and kidney stones; his digestive troubles suggest gallstones too. His worst affliction was renal and vesical calculus, 'the stone,' a tyrant 'far more cruel than any Mezentius or Phalaris' (Allen Epp 1283:10, 1352:14–15 / CWE Epp 1283:10–11, 1352:17–18). An attack he suffered in July 1522 nearly killed him: 'Your friend Erasmus,' he tells a correspondent, 'is nothing but skin and bone' (Allen Ep 1302:34–42 / CWE Ep 1302:41–50). Another savage attack and the treatment for it in March 1525 are described in Allen Ep 1558:56–135 / CWE Ep 1558:64–146; others in Allen Epp 1735:1–18, 1759:1–78. Epp 1735 and 1759 are addressed to physicians, inviting advice but without much expectation that they can help. 'Would that there were only one death! ... There's no hope in doctors' (Allen Ep 2260:320–9). Yet soon afterwards he reports some improvement (Allen Ep 2275:29–31). At various times he attributes his calculus to his habit of standing to write, though he was still doing so in 1533 (Allen Epp 1759:50–67, 2880:34), or to bad wine and beer (Allen Ep 226:5–6 / CWE Ep 226:7–8, Allen Ep 2260:325–6). He dates his first encounter with this affliction from his Venetian days in 1508, when he was working hard on *Adagia* (Allen Ep 1349:2–4 / CWE Ep 1349:2–6; *Adagia* II i 1 LB II 405C). If his account in 'Penny-Pinching' of life in the household of Andrea Torresani, father-in-law of Aldo Manuzio, is even partially accurate, his surmise about the consequences of his Venetian diet may be correct. In any event 'calculus racked him' (Allen Epp 3049:94–101, 3141:30–8 [Bonifacius Amerbach's letter written after Erasmus' death]; cf Craig R. Thompson 'Erasmus Research in the United States' *Erasmus in English* 5 [1972] 5 n6). Of many available surveys of medicine in Erasmus' Europe and of studies of his own health, the most satisfactory are H. Brabant's *Médecins, malades et maladies de la Renaissance* (Brussels 1966) and his two articles in *Colloquia Erasmiana Turonensia* I: 'Epidémies et médecins au temps d'Erasme' 515–37 and 'Erasme, ses maladies et ses médecins' 539–68. Consult also H.N. Cole 'Erasmus and His Diseases' *Journal of the American Medical Association* 148 (1952) 529–31. J.-C. Margolin reviews the subject in 'Erasme et la médecine' *Res publica litterarum: Studies in the Classical Tradition* (University of Kansas) 2 (1979) 187–205. See also Evert Dirk Baumann *Medisch-historische Studiën over Des. Erasmus* Etudes médico-historiques sur Erasme (Arnhem 1953); Peter Krivatsy 'Erasmus' Medical Milieu' *Bulletin of the History of Medicine* 47 (1973) 113–54.

A notion that Erasmus had an endemic or non-venereal form of syphilis received publicity when what were said to be his bones were exhumed nearly four centuries after his death (A. Werthemann *Schädel und Gebeine des Erasmus von Rotterdam* [Basel 1930]). It is now known that the wrong grave was opened in 1928. In 1974 a different skeleton was found buried nearby. The Metsys medal with it almost certainly identified the burial as that of Erasmus. See Bruno Kaufmann 'Das Grab des Erasmus im Basler Münster' in *Erasmus von Rotterdam, Vorkämpfer für Frieden und Toleranz* Ausstellung zum 450. Todestag des Erasmus von Rotterdam veranstaltet vom Historischen Museum Basel (26. April bis 7. September 1986) 66–7.
On Erasmus' final illness and death see 'The Return to Basel' 1122–36.

269 Of Croton, an athlete (sixth century BC) renowned for strength and endurance. He won in wrestling seven times at Olympia. See *Adagia* I ii 51, II iii 10, and II iv 44.

270 Erasmus' aversions to fish and fasting and to the domination of human ordinances over Christian liberty have been made plain in 'The Profane Feast,' 'The Godly Feast,' and the present colloquy, where we meet vivid recollections of his experiences, two of them in fairly recent visits to Freiburg and Constance, one from his university days in Paris. His antipathy to fish, which he hated worse than snakes ('The Profane Feast' 143:21) and could not even smell without feeling sick (Allen Ep 447:406–7 / CWE Ep 447:444–5), was unconditional and incurable.

271 Dispensations permitting him to eat meat, eggs, and cheese on fast days. See Allen Epp 1079:5n, 1353:5, 56, 83–7, 1585:22–3 / CWE Epp 1079:7 and n1, 1353:7, 64–5, 94–9, 1585:26–7; *De esu carnium* LB IX 1212D. Ep 1542 is the official notice of dispensation.

272 'Free city,' Freiburg in the Breisgau, where Erasmus lived from May 1529 until May 1535. See Allen Ep 2192:119–21.

273 An attack of kidney stone

274 fish] 'flesh' (*carnium*) in the first edition; later corrected to *piscium*

275 'Owl-rich,' for Udalricus Zasius. The same name is used for Huldrych Zwingli in 'A Pilgrimage'; see 624:40 and n23. Zasius (1461–1535) was a prominent jurist, professor at the University of Freiburg, and imperial councillor. Erasmus had known him since 1514. About thirty of their letters survive. See CEBR and the epitaph on Zasius in CWE 85–6 176–9, 567 no 92 / Reedijk *Poems of Erasmus* 357 no 135.

276 Prepared 'secretly and without my knowledge' by Zasius, Erasmus reminds him (Allen Ep 1353:13–14 / CWE Ep 1353:17–18).

277 'I myself, however, as you know, did not partake' (Allen Ep 1353:16 / CWE Ep 1353:20–1).

278 A rumour to this effect has reached him, Erasmus adds, and he asks Zasius if it is true. He is sceptical about it (Allen Ep 1353:1–12 / CWE Ep 1353:2–15). In the colloquy the unqualified assertion that Zasius had to give an explanation to a magistrate makes a better story but is unsupported by the letter. Either Erasmus had a lapse of memory here or simply chose to enhance the anecdote.

279 So 708:12–15 above. That such frivolities should interfere with divine service is bad enough, but especially objectionable if they interfere with hearing the

sermon. That is one reason he protests against church music: it takes time from the sermon. See 'A Pilgrimage' n161.

280 The next half-dozen paragraphs relate events in Erasmus' visit of several weeks in September 1522 to another close friend, Johann von Botzheim, canon of Constance ('Ferventia'). He was delighted with Botzheim's house and hospitality, as he says in Allen Ep 1342:336–80 / CWE 1342:372–418. On Botzheim see CEBR and 'The Godly Feast' introduction 172–3. Botzheim, of a noble Alsatian family, was both scholar and churchman and a friend of scholars. For these reasons he was a favourite of Erasmus. They shared similar opinions about the Reformation.

281 Evidently his usual diet when ill; Allen Ep 1610:89–90

282 On dried fruit in the invalid's diet see Allen Ep 1452:28n.

283 Cf 1 Cor 8:9.

284 What follows is a precious bit of autobiography, coloured by unforgotten indignation at conditions of life and learning in the University of Paris. Erasmus could write flatteringly of that famous institution when doing so suited his rhetorical purposes (as in *Panegyricus* LB IV 515F–516A / ASD IV-1 40:451–8), but more often his experience prompted him to satire or irony. This disposition is noticeable in later years when he was provoked by censure from theologians there and had to defend himself against the conservatism and what he saw as the arrogant hostility of the Sorbonists. His memories of the Collège de Montaigu were depressing. He had entered in the autumn of 1495, a graduate student rather than undergraduate with respect to age, intending to work for a doctorate in theology. He remained in Paris most of the ensuing four years but how long in Montaigu is not clear; not more than a year, but too long to please him.

The fishmonger's remark that he too had lived in a college is amusing. Was he a college servant or possibly even a student? We are allowed to assume the latter. Lest we think it incredible that a Paris student should later have sunk to the status of a fishmonger, we might remember that in a group of former Paris students we have met in 'The Old Men's Chat,' one, Polygamus, who afterwards renounced all pretensions to learning, became a manual worker. Another, Pampirus, went into trade.

285 *ab aceto*; punning on *acetum* 'vinegar' and French *aigu* (in 'Montaigu') 'sharp,' 'pungent.' 'A word of wisdom' because *acetum* suggests not only something sour (*Adagia* II iii 52) but 'shrewdness,' 'sense,' 'wit.'

The Collège de Montaigu succeeded the Collège des Aicelins, which dated from 1314. Aicelins declined but was refounded in 1388 by Pierre Aicelin de Montaigu, a cardinal and bishop, and it was henceforth called Montaigu. It existed until 1580. For its site see Thorndike *University Records* facing 448 or the map in Bainton *Erasmus of Christendom* 33. On the university and the intellectual milieu of Paris during Erasmus' years there, Augustin Renaudet *Préréforme et humanisme* is essential. Other useful surveys of Erasmus' Paris are M.M. Phillips 'Autour du Paris d'Erasme' in *Mélanges offerts à M. Abel Lefranc* (Paris 1936) 113–29; M. Reulos 'Paris au temps d'Erasme' in *Colloquia Erasmiana Turonensia* I 79–86. Histories of European universities, Paris in particular, are plentiful, but none need be named here except Hastings Rashdall's classic work, *The Universities of Europe in the Middle Ages* (Oxford 1895), new edition by

F.M. Powicke and A.B. Emden (Oxford 1936), and Thorndike *University Records*, which is concerned mostly with Paris but includes many fifteenth-century documents of interest to readers of Erasmus. The principal history of Montaigu is Marcel Godet *La congrégation de Montaigu* (Paris 1912), but on matters pertinent to Erasmus one must go to Renaudet's book also.

286 As was said earlier in 'Patterns' 11:38. Rabelais (1.37) remembered this observation.

287 Montaigu had so undistinguished a history that when its principal died in 1483 the chapter of Notre-Dame decided to close the college. They were dissuaded by Jan Standonck, an MA they had appointed guardian of the chapel and library. He was named principal and immediately showed himself a determined reformer and rigorous disciplinarian. A native of Mechelen, he had been a pupil of the Brethren of the Common Life in Gouda, then a student in Louvain. After moving to Paris and the Sorbonne he became a power in the university, served as rector, and was influential in establishing colleges in Louvain, Mechelen, Hainault, and Cambrai. It is necessary to distinguish the old Collège de Montaigu that Standonck took over in 1483 from a new foundation of his own that became part of the college. This was the Domus pauperum (1490), an order of eighty-six students, most of them in the arts course and a few in theology. Montaigu provided their instruction, but they had to live an austere, semi-monastic life, beg part of their food daily, and have as little contact as possible with the rest of the university. Nevertheless the order flourished and in due time received papal approval. Standonck's program, continued by his successor Béda, served as a source of recruits for reformers of many religious houses in the Paris area (James K. Farge *Biographical Register of Paris Doctors of Theology, 1500–1536* [Toronto 1980] 31 no 34).

Whether Erasmus was a member of the older Collège de Montaigu or the Domus pauperum is uncertain. Allen (Ep 73:9n and *Age of Erasmus* 202), followed by Preserved Smith (*Erasmus: A Study of His Life, Ideals and Place in History* [New York and London 1923; repr New York 1962] 25) says he entered the Domus pauperum. Renaudet (*Préréforme et humanisme* 267) and Johan Huizinga (*Erasmus of Rotterdam* trans F. Hopman [New York and London 1924; repr *Erasmus and the Age of Reformation* New York 1957] 21) urge that since he was furnished with means of support by the bishop of Cambrai he was not in the Domus. His status as a priest and the fact that he was considerably older than the youths in the Domus makes his membership there unlikely, but he would still be familiar with the harsh discipline and meagre diet for which Montaigu was notorious.

If we accept the testimony of Erasmus, the college was a cruel stepmother rather than an alma mater. On this subject his testimony can be checked by that of other witnesses and by local tradition. Even after making allowances for his resentment, his natural fastidiousness, and exaggeration – for he would have found imperfections in any college – we may believe he had reason to be bitter about his life there. Everything we know about Standonck tends to confirm the impression of him produced by the account in 'A Fish Diet': a man who had experienced and survived direst poverty but could not forget it; devout but fanatical, a disciplinarian so severe that his rule at Montaigu was at times almost sadistic; in short, a pious extremist whose notions of education were precisely the kind Erasmus and kindred spirits would find oppressive. Even his portrait (reproduced in CEBR III 281) seems intimidating.

In 1499, when Standonck was banished from Paris for a year because he spoke against Louis XII's effort to divorce his wife, Noël Béda and a colleague, Jean Mair, both of whom Erasmus detested, took over the management of Montaigu. After Standonck's death in 1504, Béda succeeded him as principal.

On Standonck see, besides Renaudet *Préréforme et humanisme* and Godet's history (n285 above), Renaudet 'Jean Standonck: un réformateur catholique avant la Réforme' in his *Humanisme et Renaissance* (Geneva 1958) 114–61; A. Hyma *The Christian Renaissance* (Grand Rapids 1924) 236–52; and CEBR.

Besides Erasmus, two other names of first importance in sixteenth-century religion had a connection with Montaigu: Jean Calvin and Ignatius Loyola. Calvin was there from 1523 until 1528 and studied under Béda, who in those years was attacking the writings of Erasmus, including the *Colloquies*. Calvin shifted from theology to law while in Paris, then moved on to Orléans. Loyola entered Montaigu in February 1528, a man of thirty-seven taking a place among boys to learn Latin, but in October 1529 transferred from Montaigu to the Collège Sainte-Barbe, where he remained until he received an MA degree in 1534. Some historians who noticed similarities between Loyola's constitutions for the Jesuits and Standonck's for students of the Domus pauperum (1500) inferred that Standonck's had important influence on Loyola's. In a careful examination of this question, I. Rodriguez-Grahit argues, convincingly in my opinion, that although Loyola lived at Montaigu under the discipline which Standonck took (except for its harshness) from the Brethren of the Common Life, he was, at thirty-seven, not an impressionable young man. On the contrary he had already experienced comparable spiritual discipline in Spain before coming to Paris; Montaigu was a parallel but not a novel experience. Loyola's *Spiritual Exercises* and other directions for Jesuit piety may have owed something to Montaigu, but even so the debt was only partial, not major or decisive. See 'Ignace de Loyola et le collège de Montaigu' BHR 20 (1958) 388–401, especially 394–400.

288 An allusion to Standonck's zeal in recruiting young men for monasteries. Before his death more than three hundred of his pupils had entered religious orders (Rodriguez-Grahit [preceding note] 392).

289 Barbarous, cruel; *Adagia* II iii 35

290 Similarly Erasmus, when replying to the urgings of Servatius Rogerus, prior of Steyn, that he return to the monastery he had left in 1493 or 1494, imagines someone arguing that he, Erasmus, had had the usual year and a day of probation there and was of mature age to decide whether to stay. 'What nonsense!' is his answer. 'As if one could require a youth of sixteen, with a largely bookish upbringing, to know himself – a considerable accomplishment even for an old man – or to learn, in a single year, what many greybeards have not yet grasped!' (Allen Ep 296:34–7 / CWE Ep 296:35–8). He goes on to declare that he was utterly unsuited to monastic life.

291 *Adagia* II iii 40

292 *Adagia* III vi 43

293 Unsanitary conditions, we are told by one authority, were much worse than in the preceding century: 'Nothing is further from the truth than extending the austerity and filth deplored by Erasmus in the Collège of Montaigu in the

sixteenth century to the well-regulated institutions of the fourteenth century' (Astrik L. Gabriel *Student Life in Ave Maria College, Medieval Paris* [Notre Dame, Ind 1955] 225–6). On sanitation in medieval Paris see Lynn Thorndike 'Sanitation, Baths, and Street-Cleaning in the Middle Ages and Renaissance' *Speculum* 3 (1928) 192–203 and cf 'The Soldier and the Carthusian' n48.

294 Rashdall's assertion that 'in all the university records of the Middle Ages there is not a single hint or allusion to corporal punishment until the fifteenth century' (*Universities of Europe in the Middle Ages* [n285 above] III 359) is surprising but has not been refuted, so far as I know. Such punishment was common in grammar schools, where the birch rod was the symbol of the master's authority, as many surviving descriptions and pictures prove. See 'School' 114:3–6, 17–25. In universities corporal punishment was not unknown in the fifteenth century. One of the Paston women, inquiring about her son's progress in learning, says, 'And if he hathe nought do well, nor wyll nought amend, prey hym [Grenefeld] that he wyll trewly belassch hym, tyl he wyll amend; and so ded the last maystr, and the best that ever he had, att Caumbrege' (*Paston Letters* 28 January 1458; ed James Gairdner, 6 vols [London 1904] III 123 no 362). Erasmus denounces the floggings common in grammar schools. In *De pueris instituendis* a well-known anecdote of the cruel beatings inflicted by a pedagogue of his acquaintance tells of one occasion when a young pupil was flogged although he had done nothing to deserve punishment. The master admitted as much, but said that even though innocent the youth 'simply had to be humbled.' This master may have been Standonck. See LB I 505A–C / ASD I-2 56:19–57:12 / CWE 26 327. Standonck's successors as principal of Montaigu, Béda and then Pierre Tempeste, continued the practice of severe discipline. On Béda see the testimony of a former pupil in a letter to Erasmus (Allen Ep 1963:19–29). Rabelais quotes a line of a student song deriding Tempeste, who he says was 'a mighty flogger of youths at Montaigu' (*Gargantua and Pantagruel* 4.21); see Renaudet *Préréforme et humanisme* 690).

295 Noël Béda, who had no sense of humour, was evidently annoyed by Erasmus' pleasantry about rotten eggs: 'a grave reason for making such a fuss!' (Allen Ep 1723:41–5). Nor was he likely to have forgotten Erasmus' earlier gibe that 'a beet savours of wisdom' (see 'Patterns' 12:1–2).

296 With this comment compare 'The Old Men's Chat' 457:15–17. On Erasmus and Carthusians see 'The Soldier and the Carthusian' introduction 328–9.

297 The subject introduced at 694:38 above

298 On the obligation see 711:7–9 and n249 above; with the behaviour described, cf 707:25–708:20 and 714:8–11 above.

299 On anxiety about slips of the tongue in sermons or prayers, for example naming Mary instead of Christ or the Holy Spirit, or naming them in the wrong order, see Allen Ep 2178:20–2; Latimer *Selected Sermons* 183; J.W. Blench *Preaching in England in the Late Fifteenth and Sixteenth Centuries: A Study of English Sermons 1450–c 1600* (Oxford 1964) 276n.

300 Cf 705:8–32, 711:14–29 above, and see 'The Well-to-do Beggars' nn46–7; 'The Abbot and the Learned Lady' n7.

301 Matt 5:23–4. Cf *Ratio verae theologiae* LB V 119F–120A.

302 A pervasive vice. See *Lingua* LB IV 692D–693B / ASD IV-1A 83:914–85:948 / CWE 29 316–17.

303 'Things and Names' 813:21–3

304 If he has a concubine, he is still a priest; 'if he makes her his wife, to the fire with them!' (*Annotationes in Novum Testamentum* LB VI 100E). For a summary of Erasmus' own views on sacerdotal celibacy see 'The Well-to-do Beggars' n6 and *Supputatio* LB IX 485D, 488A–489A (replies to Béda).

305 Vicars-general, who arranged ordinations. To present a candidate for holy orders and vouch for his moral character had been an office performed by archdeacons also.

306 Cf 711:24–39 above. For ordination a man had to have reached the age of twenty-five (Third Lateran Council of 1179 [canon 3; Tanner I 212–13], reaffirmed by Trent [session 23 [1563] Decree on reform, canon 12; Tanner II 748]). Standards of intellectual and moral competence should be strict, but some preachers Erasmus heard of were so scatterbrained that the people laughed at them (*Ecclesiastes* LB V 782E), and candidates were ordained in spite of deficient education (see 'The Well-to-do Beggars' n49). This is the sort of thing bishops should not tolerate (*De esu carnium* LB IX 1201D–E). In *Utopia* priests are of extraordinary holiness 'and therefore very few' (Yale CWM 4 227, 229, 231). On this subject Erasmus and More were of one mind. Cf 'The Usefulness of the Colloquies' 1100:37–8.

307 In a trial or some other legal proceeding when he is under oath. On such as 'perjure themselves in every third word' see 'The Liar and the Man of Honour.'

308 *colore*, as in Juvenal 6.28. *Color* in rhetoric is an argument or suggestion intended to put an act in a favourable light (Quintilian 4.2.88, 12.2.1–14).

309 crime] *crimen* in all editions through March 1529, then *discrimen* to and including the edition of March 1533; *Opera omnia* 1538–40 and LB have *crimen*.

310 On these see *Institutio principis christiani* LB IV 603C / ASD IV-1 206:247–52 / Born 239 / CWE 27 276. Cf *Lingua* LB IV 692E; ASD IV-1A 84:922–9 / CWE 29 317.

311 See 698:1–8 above with the notes.

312 See 'The Seraphic Funeral' 1011:15–37.

313 *ex diametro*; *Adagia* I x 45

314 In this context, unworthy monks or priests

315 Apostasy is renunciation and desertion of Christianity, defecting to Satan. Nowadays, says Erasmus, those who leave religious orders are called apostates. But it is far worse to lead a wicked life, whether in or out of an order, than to abandon a particular mode of life (as a religious) yet remain a sincere Christian (*Ecclesiastes* LB V 1024C–1025F). Erasmus had incurred a charge of apostasy by leaving his monastery (Steyn) and not returning. See Allen Ep 447:433–47, 615–30 / CWE Ep 447:473–89, 682–98. His anxiety over this difficulty was finally relieved by a dispensation from Leo x in 1517. See the introduction to 'The Girl with No Interest in Marriage' 284.

316 This question of whether fidelity to monastic profession ought to be honoured more than the vows every Christian takes, or are taken for him, in baptism, was asked and answered in an earlier colloquy, 'The Girl with No Interest in Marriage' 290:19–292:35; and see especially nn27 and 57 there.

317 Erasmus comments from time to time on the complacent attitude towards adultery, compared with the degree of social disgrace and punishment for other offences. In ancient Israel adultery was punished by death (Lev 20:10), in classical societies similarly; yet today, he adds, it is too often treated as a

kind of joke (*De concordia* LB V 499A; see also *Exomologesis* LB V 153F; *Institutio christiani matrimonii* LB V 648B, 700B–701C; *Adagia* IV vi 25). The contrast with public attitudes towards theft occurs again in *Institutio principis christiani* LB IV 599A / ASD IV-1 200:11–16 / Born 228 / CWE 27 269.

318 Some Swiss cantons forbade citizens to fight as mercenaries for foreign governments, but this legislation had little effect. See Vincent *Switzerland* (n199 above) Appendix 1.

319 As we read in 'Military Affairs,' 'The Soldier and the Carthusian,' and 'Cyclops.'

320 Cf 'Inns' 374:7–13. The present colloquy opens with banter about bad fish and bad meat.

321 Cf 720:4–8 below and, on priests, 711:14–29 and n252 above.

322 Used in exorcisms, as in 'Exorcism' 537:1–2

323 'Wreaths,' but here denoting strings of beads used in counting prayers in the rosary or other devotions

324 Cf 1 Cor 6:19, as at 711:23 above.

325 Erasmus often rebukes those who put their trust in saints more than Christ (cf *Declarationes ad censuras Lutetiae vulgatas* LB IX 953A–B). This does not mean he wholly rejected the efficacy of invoking saints or that he himself never prayed to them. He prayed to St Geneviève more than once when he was ill (Allen Epp 50, 124:13–15 / CWE Epp 50, 124:15–17) and see CWE 85–6 168–77, 556–64 no 88 / Reedijk *Poems of Erasmus* 350 no 131. In 1514 when he injured his back while riding he made a vow to St Paul that he would complete a commentary on the Epistle to the Romans if relieved of his pain (Allen Ep 301:18–29 / CWE Ep 301: 20–37). He did improve within a few days but never completed the commentary, though some of that material doubtless found its way into his *Annotationes in Novum Testamentum* and Paraphrase on Romans published in 1516 and 1517 (LB VI and VII).

He denies that there is any deprecation of trust in saints in these lines. He is simply calling attention, he insists, to the deluded judgments of persons who call upon Mary and the saints before praying to Christ or invoking him directly. Cf 'The Shipwreck' nn19 and 38 and, for an example, 'A Pilgrimage' 624:40–628:18. On the proper veneration of the Virgin Mary and of the saints see 'The Well-to-do Beggars' 475:12–13, and for some other typical remarks on these themes *Enchiridion* LB V 26E–27D, 31C–D / CWE 66 63–5; *In psalmum quartum concio* LB V 264C–D; *Enarratio in psalmum XXXIII* LB V 385E–386A, 501A–B; Allen Ep 1347:69–103 / CWE Ep 1347:78–115, Allen Epp 1581:708–16, 2443:209–26. A long passage in *Modus orandi Deum* (LB V 1116A–1120A) confirms Erasmus' essentially orthodox position on the truly reverent veneration of saints as contrasted with practices of vulgar superstition and ignorance. On Christopher see 'The Shipwreck' n26; *Ratio verae theologiae* LB V 136D; *Adagia* III iii 1 LB II 776B–C.

326 As in 'The Shipwreck' 355:11–12, 356:15, and see *Apologia adversus rhapsodias Alberti Pii* LB IX 1165D–F.

327 On George see 'A Pilgrimage' n39 and *Adagia* III iii 1: *Sileni Alcibiadis* LB II 776B; on Barbara, 'Military Affairs' n21 and Allen Ep 1347:80–8 / CWE Ep 1347:89–99. George and Christopher or Barbara and other auxiliary saints are often named together by Erasmus.

328 St Antony of Egypt, eldest of the desert Fathers. On the pig see 'The Well-to-do Beggars' 475:6–9 and n43); on the fire, 'A Pilgrimage' n40. He carries a bell (cf Allen Ep 3002:858), perhaps as a warning to demons.

329 Often spelled Rock. He won fame by nursing the sick during an epidemic (fourteenth century) in northern Italy. He is mentioned (along with Christopher, Barbara, George, and others) in *Enchiridion* LB V 26E, 27B / CWE 66 63, 64; *Modus orandi Deum* LB V 1120C, 1124E; with Antony in *Precationes* LB V 1206B. Cf *Adagia* III ix 38. His tomb in Venice was known to pilgrims.

330 Bishop of Paris and martyr c 258; patron saint of France. Later legendary accounts identify him with Dionysius the Areopagite (see 'The New Mother' n51) and Dionysius bishop of Corinth (c 170).

331 A basic principle, though difficult to define precisely. 'No one can interpret Scripture rightly [*recte*] unless he is inspired by that same Spirit who is the author of Scripture' (*Responsio ad disputationem de divortio* LB IX 967D). Some questions about the inspiration received by preachers are asked and answered interestingly in *Antibarbari* LB X 1740F–1742D / ASD I-1 132:4–134:30 / CWE 23 115:31–118:22. See also *Ecclesiastes* LB V 772B–781F and passim.

332 All these Fathers were favourites of Erasmus. The greatest if not earliest of Christian Platonists, Origen (c 185–c 254) was regarded by many later theologians as heretical or at least unorthodox on such questions as the eternity of the world and the nature of souls after death. Erasmus did not agree with all the articles of his philosophy and theology (see 'Faith' n117) but valued him very highly, considering him the best interpreter of Scripture among the Greek Fathers, as Tertullian was among the Latin (Allen Ep 1844:16–20). He once avowed that he had learned more Christian wisdom from a single page of Origen than from ten pages of Augustine (Allen Ep 844:251–4 / CWE Ep 844:271–4). His interest in Origen dated from 1501, when he asked a Franciscan friend for the loan of a volume of Origen's homilies. In 1504 he wrote to Colet of having read Origen with much profit (Allen Ep 181:38–41 / CWE Ep 181:45–8). This admiration continued as long as he lived. He published a translation, with an introductory essay, of some chapters of Origen's commentary on Matthew in 1527 (LB VIII 425A–440A, 439E–484B). It seems appropriate that when dying he was still busy with an edition of Origen in Latin. This was brought out in 1536, a few months after his death. Erasmus was roundly criticized by Béda for being too fond of Origen (Epp 1579, 1581), but Origen played an important part in his thinking about Christian doctrine and in his biblical exegesis. On various aspects of Origen's importance for Erasmus and his contemporaries see D.P. Walker 'Origène en France au début du XVIe siècle' in *Courants religieux et humanisme* (Paris 1959) 101–19; A.H.T. Levi *Pagan Virtue and the Humanism of the Northern Renaissance* (London 1974); Max Schär *Das Nachleben des Origenes im Zeitalter des Humanismus* (Basel 1979); A. Godin 'Erasme et le modèle origénien de la prédication' in *Colloquia Erasmiana Turonensia* II 807–20, 'The Enchiridion Militis Christiani: The Modes of an Origenian Appropriation' ERSY 2 (1982) 47–79, and his elaborate treatise *Erasme: lecteur d'Origène* (Geneva 1982).
On Basil, Chrysostom, Cyprian, Jerome, and Augustine see 'The Soldier and the Carthusian' nn21–5; on Ambrose 'The Godly Feast' n180. On Jerome see

additionally 'Youth' 93:4–5 and n17. Erasmus' introductions to his editions or translations of these theologians are the best sources of his estimates of them.

333 'They' refers to those who 'prefer to invoke' and 'call [this practice] praiseworthy.'

334 Franciscans were distinguished by rope cords; Augustinians wore leather belts (see n208 above). With the 'absurd scandals' – and the danger of miscarriage – mentioned here compare 705:16–32 above.

335 If Erasmus has specific passages in mind they may be Matt 6:25–31 and 1 Tim 6:6–11, but probably he is thinking of Christ's and Paul's preaching in entire discourses, such as the Sermon on the Mount in Matthew 5–7 and Paul's emphasis on Christian liberty in 1 Corinthians 6, 8, 10. Cf 'The Godly Feast' 189:37–192:4.

336 So *Adagia* I vi 1 in the 1508 edition. Erasmus quotes a Greek proverb from Gellius 2.6.9. 'Kitchen gardener' (*olitor*) renders a Greek word (κηπωρός) found in all the manuscripts of Gellius that Erasmus had seen. His admired friend Paolo Bombace (Bombasius), an eminent Hellenist, had some doubts about the authenticity of the Greek term and conjectured μωρός 'foolish' person. Though inclined to agree, Erasmus decided he could not go against the consensus of the manuscripts. Later however he came across this word μωρός 'foolish' in the proverb as found in a line attributed to Aeschylus (LB II 220E–221D). When quoting the proverb at the end of *Moriae encomium* he adopted 'foolish' (LB IV 504C / ASD IV-3 194:271 / CWE 27 153) yet still later kept the other word (*olitor*) when quoting the proverb in this colloquy.

337 There is no clue as to the identity of this fellow, if indeed Erasmus had a particular individual in mind, but he seems a suitable colleague for those mentioned at 703:30–704:3.

338 In 1519 a Carmelite theologian denounced Erasmus' New Testament as a sign of the advent of Antichrist, but later admitted that he had neither read nor even seen the book (Allen Ep 948:136–44 / CWE Ep 948:141–9). On Antichrist cf 'The New Mother' n18.

THE FUNERAL

Funus

First printed in the February 1526 edition.

Erasmus' dialogue 'The Funeral,' dramatizing the dying of two men, is related loosely to the tradition of *ars moriendi*. Those discourses on how to die were an established type of Christian edification; for the history of this genre see Mary Catharine O'Connor *The Art of Dying Well* (New York 1942). A French treatise on the theme was translated into English by Caxton and published by him in 1490 and 1491 (STC 786, 789). Nancy L. Beaty *The Craft of Dying* (New Haven 1970) surveys the tradition of *ars moriendi* in England. Erasmus contributed to this literature more than once. His *Declamatio de morte* (LB IV 617A–624A), a rather superficial composition, was written in 1509 and printed in 1517; it was later inserted in *De conscribendis epistolis* (ASD I-2 441:12–455:27 / CWE 25 156–64). An English translation appeared in 1531 (STC 10510). In 1534, when he was an old man with death never far from his thoughts, he produced the more impressive *De praeparatione ad mortem* (LB V 1293B–1318D / ASD V-1 339–92); an anonymous English translation was printed in London in 1538 (STC 10505). He undertook this essay at the request of Thomas Boleyn, Earl of Wiltshire (Ep 2884), to whom he had dedicated *Explanatio symboli* in 1533. According to the imperial ambassador, Eustace Chapuys, Catherine of Aragon read *De praeparatione ad mortem* towards the end of her life and received consolation from it (Allen Ep 3090:29–53). The book written for Thomas Boleyn comforted the queen whom his daughter Anne had supplanted.

Another *ars moriendi* of 1534 was Thomas Lupset's *A compendious treatyse teachynge the waye of dyenge well* (STC 16934). Lupset was a favourite pupil of Colet's at St Paul's School and well known to Erasmus (see the introduction to 'The Whole Duty of Youth' 88); their correspondence is printed in Allen. For the text see J.A. Gee *Life and Works of Thomas Lupset* (New Haven 1928) 263–90. This is a good piece of Tudor prose and a sound presentation of arguments Colet and Erasmus would both endorse – that life is a preparation for death and that the best way to die is to have lived a good and pious life.

Between 'The Funeral' and *De praeparatione ad mortem* there are many interesting points of comparison. Both express the commonplaces of all *artes moriendi*, but the differences in structure and tone show once more how Erasmus could fit matter to whatever form and whatever occasion he chose. *De praeparatione ad mortem*, hortatory and at times eloquent, is cast in a conventional mode. In 'The Funeral' he creates scenes and characters and does not exhort but dramatizes. In each of its two main parts language and style are perfectly appropriate to purpose. In the account of George's elaborate dying, banter, satire, even boisterous farce are used. By contrast with all this, the calm, subdued description of Cornelius' last hours is brief, but this very brevity enforces the distinction between hypocritical ostentation and simple, sincere Christian piety. The final paragraphs will recall to many readers, as they were no doubt meant to recall, the equanimity of Socrates in *Phaedo*. But Cornelius' death is intended to illustrate Christian confidence, not pagan virtue, however sublime. As much as could be said for Socrates had been said in 'The Godly Feast' (194:34).

Like 'A Pilgrimage for Religion's Sake,' 'The Funeral' must have pleased Cromwell and those who approved of his policies. An anonymous English translation (London 1534, printed by Robert Copland for John Byddell) was probably the earliest printing of an Erasmian colloquy in that language, though an earlier date has been claimed for an English version of *Coniugium* which has not survived (see Devereux 4.8.1). A copy of the 1534 translation, lacking the first leaf, came to light in 1960; it was bound with translations of *De esu carnium* and *Julius exclusus*. The English translator gives no clue to his identity. Whoever he was, he did his work well. See the edition by Robert R. Allen *The dyaloge called Funus & A very pleasaunt & fruitful Dialoge called The Epicure* (Chicago 1969), whose introduction gives the essential information. Five other translations of *Funus* had appeared before 1534, two into Spanish and three into German (*The dyaloge* ed Allen 6–7). The translation into Low German has on the title-page a woodcut showing George lying on the floor, with many friars close by; one of them is covering him with a Franciscan cloak. Cornelius is sitting up, hands folded, his wife, son, daughter, and a priest with crucifix at his side.

MARCOLPHUS, PHAEDRUS

Marcolphus Where does our Phaedrus come from? Not from the cave of Trophonius, are you?[1]

5 **Phaedrus** Why do you ask that?

Marcolphus Because you're uncommonly sad, dishevelled, dirty, wild-looking:[2] in short, as unlike your name as possible.[3]

Phaedrus If those who spend their time in coppersmiths' shops are bound to get blackened, why are you surprised if I'm gloomier than usual when

10 I've spent so many days in the company of two sick, dying, and buried men, both of them very dear to me?

Marcolphus Whose burials are you talking about?

Woodcut on the title-page of an early German translation of *Funus*
(Magdeburg 1531)
Herzog August Bibliothek, Wolfenbüttel

Phaedrus You know George Balearicus?

Marcolphus Only by name, not by sight.

Phaedrus I know you're not acquainted with the other one, Cornelius Montius.[4] We were intimate friends for many years.

5 **Marcolphus** I've never had the experience of being present at a deathbed.[5]

Phaedrus I have – oftener than I would wish.

Marcolphus But is death as dreadful a thing as it's commonly asserted to be?[6]

Phaedrus The road leading up to it is harder than death itself. If a man
10 dismisses from his thought the horror and imagination of death, he will have rid himself of a great part of the evil. In brief, whatever the torment of sickness or death, it is rendered much more endurable if a person surrenders himself wholly to the divine will. For awareness of death, when the soul is already separated from the body,[7] is, I think, either non-existent or else an
15 extremely low-grade awareness, because before nature reaches this point it dulls and stuns all areas of sensation.

Marcolphus We're born without our being aware of it.

Phaedrus But not without a mother's being aware of it.

Marcolphus Why don't we die in the same way? Why did God mean death
20 to be such a torture?

Phaedrus He meant birth to be painful and dangerous for the mother in order that she might love her offspring more dearly. But death he meant to be dreadful for everyone, lest men far and wide commit suicide. And since, even today, we see so many do violence to themselves, what do you
25 suppose would happen if death weren't horrible? Whenever a servant or even a young son got a thrashing, whenever a wife fell out with her husband, whenever a man lost his money, or something else occurred that upset him, off they'd rush to noose, sword, river, cliff, poison. As matters now stand, the bitterness of death makes life more precious to us, especially since
30 physicians can't cure a man once he's dead. Though all men don't die in the same way, just as they're not all born in the same way. Some find release in a quick death; others sink into a slow death. Persons with sleeping sickness, likewise those stung by an adder, die unconscious, stupefied with sleep. I've noticed this: that no kind of death is so bitter but that it can be endured if
35 one has resolved to die with steadfast mind.

Marcolphus Which man's death seemed more Christian?

Phaedrus To me, George's seemed more crowned with honour.

Marcolphus Does even death have its vainglory?

Phaedrus Never have I seen two men die so differently. If you've time to
40 listen, I'll describe each one's end. You shall judge which death would be preferable for a Christian.

Marcolphus Oh, yes, do be good enough to tell me. There's nothing I'd rather hear.

Phaedrus First hear about George, then. The moment unmistakable signs of death appeared, the company of physicians who had long attended the
5 patient began to demand their fees, hiding their feeling of hopelessness about his life.

Marcolphus How many doctors were there?

Phaedrus Sometimes ten, sometimes twelve; never fewer than six.

Marcolphus Enough to kill even a healthy man![8]

10 **Phaedrus** When they had their money, they warned the relatives confidentially that death was not far off; that they should look to his spiritual welfare, for there was no hope of his physical safety. And the patient was warned courteously by his close friends to entrust his body to God's care, concerning himself only with what belonged to making a good end. When
15 he heard this, George glared at the physicians in wild surmise, as though incensed at being deserted by them. They retorted that they were physicians, not gods; that what their skill could do had been performed; but that no medicine could prevail against destiny.[9] After this, they went into the next bedroom.

20 **Marcolphus** What? They lingered even after they were paid?

Phaedrus They had disagreed completely over what sort of disease it was. One said dropsy; another, tympanites;[10] another, an intestinal abscess – each one named a different ailment. And during the whole time they were treating the patient they quarrelled violently about the nature of his malady.

25 **Marcolphus** Lucky patient meanwhile!

Phaedrus To settle their dispute once for all, they requested through his wife that they be permitted later to perform an autopsy on the body[11] – quite a compliment, that, and done customarily as a mark of respect in the case of eminent persons. Furthermore, it would help save many lives and would
30 increase George's accumulation of merits.[12] Last of all, they promised to buy a trental of masses at their own expense for the repose of his soul.[13] Their request met with opposition, to be sure, but was finally granted, thanks to their flattery of his wife and relations. Business disposed of, the medical congress adjourned, because it's not right, they say, for those whose job
35 is to save life to look on at death or to attend funerals. Next Bernardine was summoned, a holy man (as you know), warden of the Franciscans; he was to hear confession. Hardly was confession over when the four orders commonly called mendicants[14] caused a disturbance in the house.

Marcolphus So many vultures at one corpse?[15]

40 **Phaedrus** Then the parish priest was called in, to give the man extreme unction[16] and holy communion.

Marcolphus Devoutly done.

Phaedrus Thereupon a bloody battle between the priest and the monks very nearly broke out.[17]

Marcolphus At the sick man's bedside?

5 **Phaedrus** Yes, and with Christ watching.

Marcolphus What provoked such unexpected uproar?

Phaedrus When the priest learned that the patient had confessed to the Franciscan, he declared he would not administer the rite of extreme unction, the Eucharist, or burial unless he had heard the patient's confession with his

10 own ears. He was the parish priest; he would have to render an account of his flock to the Lord; this he could not do if he alone were unfamiliar with the secrets of the man's conscience.[18]

Marcolphus Didn't that seem fair enough?

Phaedrus Not to them, you may be sure. They all objected vigorously,

15 Bernardine and the Dominican Vincent in particular.

Marcolphus What was their contribution?

Phaedrus They fell upon the priest and abused him violently, repeatedly calling him ass and fit for a swineherd. 'I,' says Vincent, 'am a full-fledged bachelor of sacred theology, and soon to be licensed, and even to be

20 distinguished by the title of doctor.[19] You scarcely read the Gospel,[20] so far are you from being able to probe the secrets of conscience. But if you like to be meddlesome, find out what your wife and bastards[21] are doing at home,'[22] and many other remarks of this kind that I'm ashamed to mention.

Marcolphus What did he do? Did he keep quiet at this?

25 **Phaedrus** Quiet? On the contrary, you'd say he was a cicada caught by the wing.[23] 'I could make much better bachelors than you out of beanstalks,'[24] says he. 'Where did Dominic and Francis, the founders and heads of your orders, learn the Aristotelian philosophy, or the reasonings of Thomas, or the speculations of Scotus? Or where were they granted their bachelor's

30 degrees?[25] You crept into a world still credulous, but you were few,[26] humble, and some of you even learned and holy. You nested in fields and villages.[27] Soon you migrated to some of the wealthiest cities and to the best part of town.[28] You used to work in whatever fields could not support a shepherd; nowadays you're never anywhere but in rich men's houses.[29] You

35 boast of papal favour,[30] but your privileges are worthless unless a bishop, pastor, or his vicar is inactive. None of you will preach in *my* church so long as I'm in possession as pastor.[31] I'm not a bachelor;[32] neither was St Martin, and yet he served as bishop.[33] If I lack any learning, I won't seek it from you. Or do you believe the world is still so stupid that whenever it sees the

40 garb of Dominic or Francis it thinks their sanctity is present too? Is it any of your business what I do at my own home? What you do in your retreats, how

you behave with the nuns,[34] even the public knows. How far from good or decent are the homes of the wealthy that you frequent[35] "is known to every blear-eyed man and barber."'[36]

The rest I don't dare repeat, Marcolphus. Altogether he treated those
5 reverend fathers with very little reverence. And there would have been no end to this had not George indicated with his hand that he wished to say something. After much effort, the bickering was stilled for a while. Then the sick man said, 'Let there be peace among you. I'll confess anew to you, priest.[37] Next you shall have money paid out to you for the tolling of bells,
10 funeral dirges, monument, and burial before you leave this house. I'll see to it that you have no reason to complain of me in any respect.'
Marcolphus The priest didn't refuse so fair a bargain as that, did he?
Phaedrus No. Only he grumbled somewhat about the confession, which he remitted to the patient.[38] 'What need is there,' says he, 'for tiring both patient
15 and priest by repeating it? Had he confessed to me in time, perhaps he would have made his will in a more Christian spirit. But it's your responsibility now.' The sick man's fairness vexed the monks, who were indignant that a share of the booty should fall to the parish priest. But I interceded and managed to settle the quarrel. The priest anointed the sick man,[39] gave him
20 communion, and after his money was counted out he left.
Marcolphus So a calm followed that storm?
Phaedrus Oh, no, a more severe storm broke out at once.
Marcolphus What caused it, please?
Phaedrus You'll hear. The four orders of mendicants had poured into the
25 house. They were joined by a fifth, that of the Crutched Friars.[40] Against this order, as a spurious one, these four raised a loud clamour. They asked where the Crutched Friars had ever seen a five-wheeled wagon,[41] or how they had the impudence to maintain there were more mendicant orders than there were evangelists. 'In the same fashion,' they said, 'you might as well
30 bring hither all the beggars from bridges and crossroads.'
Marcolphus What did the Crutched Friars say to this?
Phaedrus They countered by asking how the wagon of the church had run when no order of mendicants existed; then, how it ran when there was one and later three. 'For the number of the evangelists,' they said, 'has no more
35 connection with our orders than with dice, which show four corners on every side.[42] Who elected the Augustinians to the order of mendicants? Or who the Carmelites? When did Augustine beg, or when Elijah?' (For these men they make the founders of their orders.)[43] This and much else they thundered boldly indeed, but, unable by themselves to withstand the onslaught[44] of the
40 four orders, they retreated, only with dire threats.
Marcolphus You enjoyed calm weather after that, surely?

Phaedrus Not at all. That alliance[45] against the fifth order turned into a gladiatorial combat. Franciscan and Dominican contended that neither Augustinians nor Carmelites were genuine mendicants but bastard and spurious. This argument raged so furiously that I was quite afraid it would
5   come to blows.

Marcolphus Did the patient put up with this?

Phaedrus It didn't take place at the bedside but in the hall next to the chamber. Nevertheless every word reached him, since they weren't whispering but playing the piece *fortissimo*. Even apart from this, as you
10 know, invalids have rather sensitive hearing.

Marcolphus How did the war end?

Phaedrus The patient asked them, through his wife, to quiet down a little and he would compose the quarrel. So he requested the Augustinians and Carmelites to leave at once; they would lose nothing by doing so. 'For,'
15 said he, 'as much food will be sent to them at their house as would be given if they remained here.' He directed all the orders, even the fifth one, to attend his funeral, and a sum of money to be divided equally among them. But to prevent disorder he forbade them to come to the wake.

20 **Marcolphus** Evidently he was a good manager, who even when dying knew how to still the waves.

Phaedrus Tush! He'd been a general in the army for many years. Disturbances of this kind in the ranks are an everyday occurrence there.

Marcolphus Was he rich?

25 **Phaedrus** Very.

Marcolphus But, as usually happens, with ill-gotten gains from robberies, sacrileges, and extortions.

Phaedrus That at least is the common practice with generals.[46] I wouldn't swear he was different from the rest in his ways. If I knew the man well,
30 however, he grew rich by his wits rather than by violence.

Marcolphus How so?

Phaedrus He was clever at accounting.

Marcolphus What of it?

Phaedrus What of it? He reported thirty thousand troops to his commander
35 when there were scarcely seven thousand. And to many soldiers he paid out nothing at all.

Marcolphus A rich accounting indeed![47]

Phaedrus Besides, he waged war scientifically. He used to contract for monthly payments at the same time by villages and towns of both friend
40 and foe: from the enemy, so fighting wouldn't break out; from friends, for allowing them to trade with the enemy.

Marcolphus I'm familiar with the common practice of military men. But finish your story.

Phaedrus So Bernardine and Vincent, with some fellow members of their orders, remained with the sick man. Provisions were sent to the others.

5 **Marcolphus** Did those who held the fort get along satisfactorily?

Phaedrus Not in every respect. They were muttering something or other about privileges granted by papal briefs, but they pretended not to, for fear their business wouldn't get finished. At this time the last will and testament was produced, and covenants were made in the presence of witnesses

10 concerning those matters they had already settled among themselves.

Marcolphus I can't wait to hear these.

Phaedrus I'll summarize them, because it's a long story. He was survived by a wife of thirty-eight, a good, sensible woman; two sons, one nineteen, the other fifteen; as many daughters, but both young and unmarried. The

15 will provided that since the wife could not be induced to become a nun she should put on a Beguine's cloak[48] – an order midway between nuns and laywomen – and the elder son, since he flatly refused to become a monk –

Marcolphus You don't catch an old fox with a noose![49]

Phaedrus – was to hurry to Rome without delay after his father's funeral.

20 There, after being made priest by a papal dispensation before reaching legal age,[50] he should say mass for his father's soul[51] every day for a whole year in the Vatican basilica and every Friday crawl on his knees up the sacred steps in the Lateran.[52]

Marcolphus Was he glad to undertake this?

25 **Phaedrus** To be blunt, he was as glad as asses are to bear heavy burdens.[53] The younger son was promised to St Francis, the older daughter to St Clare, the younger daughter to St Catherine of Siena.[54] Only this much could be achieved. George's intention was to have God further in his debt by putting his five survivors into five mendicant orders, and he tried very hard to do

30 so, but his wife's age and that of his elder son yielded neither to threats nor to flattery.

Marcolphus A way of disinheriting them.[55]

Phaedrus The entire estate was so divided that after money for funeral expenses was set aside, one share[56] was allotted to the wife: half of this

35 for her support, half to the house she would join. If she changed her mind and backed out of the agreement, all the money was to pass to that society. Another share would fall to the son. He, however, would have passage money paid to him at once, and enough to buy the dispensation and take care of a year's living expenses in Rome. If he changed his mind and refused

40 to take priestly orders, his share would be divided between the Franciscans and Dominicans. And I fear that may happen, so strongly did the boy seem

to detest a priestly career. Two shares would go to the monastery receiving the younger son; likewise two each to the nunneries receiving the daughters, but on condition that if these children baulked at entering the religious life, the monastery and nunneries could still keep all the money.[57] Furthermore,

5   one share would go presently to Bernardine; the same amount to Vincent; half a share to the Carthusians, for a portion of all good works done by the entire order.[58] The one and one half shares remaining were to be distributed to undisclosed beggars approved by Bernardine and Vincent.

Marcolphus You should have said, lawyer-fashion, 'those beggars male and

10   female.'

Phaedrus So when the will had been read, the covenants were made in the following terms: 'Do you, George Balearicus, being alive and of sound mind, approve this testament that you have made of recent date and in accordance with your wishes?' 'I approve.' 'And is this your final and irrevocable will?'

15   'It is.' 'And do you appoint me and the said Vincent, bachelor, executors of your last will?' 'I do.' He was ordered to sign it again.

Marcolphus How could a dying man do that?

Phaedrus Bernardine guided the invalid's hand.

Marcolphus What did he write down?

20   **Phaedrus** 'May he who attempts henceforth to change any of this incur the wrath of St Francis and St Dominic.'

Marcolphus But weren't they afraid of a suit on grounds of inofficious testament?[59]

Phaedrus That kind of suit doesn't apply to property promised to God, nor

25   does anyone readily sue God at law.[60] When these matters were finished, the wife and children gave their right hand to the patient and swore they would keep the obligations laid upon them. After this, the funeral procession came up for discussion[61] – but not without argument. Finally they agreed that from each of the five orders nine members should attend, in honour

30   of the five books of Moses and the nine choirs of angels:[62] each order to carry its own cross before it and sing funeral dirges. With these and the relatives should march thirty torchbearers dressed in black (thirty being the number of coins for which the Lord was sold),[63] and – to lend distinction – twelve mourners (the number sacred to the band of apostles, that is) should

35   accompany them.[64] The bier was to be followed by George's horse,[65] draped in black, with head tied down to his knees to suggest that he was looking along the ground for his master. The pall[66] was to display on each side George's coat of arms. Likewise each torch and mourning garb should have his arms. Now the corpse itself was to rest at the right of the high altar in a

40   marble tomb four feet high. On top of the tomb was to be George's effigy carved in Parian marble,[67] in full armour from head to foot.[68] His helmet

was to have his crest (a pelican's neck),[69] and his left arm a shield bearing as insignia three boars' heads[70] of gold in a field of silver.[71] Nor was his sword with the golden hilt to be missing from his side, nor his gold baldric adorned with jewelled studs, nor his gold spurs from his feet; for he was a gilded

5   knight.[72] At his feet he was to have a leopard.[73] The borders of the tomb were to have an inscription worthy of such a man. He wanted his heart to be buried separately in the chapel of St Francis. His entrails he bequeathed to the parish priest for honourable burial in a chapel sacred to the Virgin Mother.[74]

10 **Marcolphus** A splendid funeral, no doubt, but too costly. At Venice any cobbler would be accorded a more splendid one for a minimum of expense.[75] His guild gives a fine bier; and sometimes six hundred[76] monks, dressed in tunics or cloaks, accompany a single corpse.

Phaedrus I too have seen and laughed at this inappropriate ostentation of

15 the poor. Fullers and tanners march in front, cobblers in the rear, monks in the middle; you'd say they were chimeras.[77] Nor would you have seen any difference here. George stipulated also that Franciscan and Dominican were to settle by lot which of them should have first place in the procession; then the rest, too, were to draw lots, to prevent any disorder on this account. The

20 parish priest and his clerks were to have the lowest place – that is, at the front – for the monks[78] would consent to no other arrangement.[79]

Marcolphus He was skilled in drawing up not only battle lines but parades as well.

Phaedrus It was stipulated, too, that the funeral rites, conducted by the

25 parish priest, should be accompanied by the harmonious singing of the choir, in George's honour. During the negotiations over these and other matters, the patient shuddered and gave unmistakable signs that his last moment was near. The final act of the play was therefore prepared.

Marcolphus We're not at the end yet?

30 **Phaedrus** A papal brief was read, promising forgiveness of all sins and banishing fear of purgatory entirely.[80] In addition, all his goods were accounted rightful.

Marcolphus The 'goods' he got by robbery?

Phaedrus By the law of war and military custom, surely.[81] But Philip the

35 lawyer, his brother-in-law, chanced to be present. He noticed in the papal brief a passage that was out of order and raised the question of fraud.[82]

Marcolphus Not at that time! Even if there was something wrong, it should have been ignored, and the sick man would have been none the worse.

Phaedrus I agree. And he was so upset by this news that he was almost in

40 despair. At this juncture Vincent proved himself a man. He told George not to worry, that he himself had authority to correct and supplement any error

or omission in the brief. 'If,' says he, 'the brief fails you, I hereby substitute my own soul for yours, so that yours goes to heaven and mine is abandoned to hell.'[83]

Marcolphus Does God accept such exchanges of souls? And if so, did such
5   a pledge seem sufficient security for George? What if Vincent's soul was due for hell without any exchange?

Phaedrus I'm telling you what happened. Unquestionably Vincent did succeed in causing the sick man to take heart. Next, warranties were recited by which George was promised partnership in all the works done by the
10   four orders, and by the fifth, the Carthusians.[84]

Marcolphus I'd be afraid of sinking down to hell if I had to carry so great a load.

Phaedrus I mean *good* works. They no more burden the soul in its upward flight than feathers do a bird.

15   **Marcolphus** Then to whom do they bequeath their evil works?

Phaedrus To German mercenaries.[85]

Marcolphus By what warrant?

Phaedrus By Gospel warrant: 'Whosoever hath, to him shall be given.'[86] At the same time a number – an enormous number – of masses and psalms were
20   recited; these were to accompany the soul of the deceased. Then confession was repeated and the blessing given.

Marcolphus And so he breathed his last?

Phaedrus Not yet. A rush mat was spread on the floor and rolled up at one end to form a sort of pillow.

25   **Marcolphus** Now what's going to happen?

Phaedrus They scattered a few ashes on it,[87] and there they laid the sick man. A Franciscan tunic was spread over him,[88] but only after being blessed by short prayers and holy water. A cowl was placed at his head (for at that time it could not be put on) and along with that his brief and the
30   covenants.

Marcolphus A new kind of death.

Phaedrus But they swear the devil has no jurisdiction over those who die thus. So, they say, St Martin and St Francis, among others, died.

Marcolphus But their lives corresponded to this kind of death. What
35   happened after that, please?

Phaedrus A crucifix and wax taper were held out to the sick man.[89] To the crucifix extended to him he said, 'In war I was accustomed to rely on my shield; now will I face my foe with this shield.' And after he kissed it, he turned on his left side. To the taper he said, 'I used to excel with my spear in
40   war; now will I brandish this spear against the enemy of souls.'[90]

Marcolphus Spoken like a soldier!

Phaedrus These were his last words, for presently death stopped his tongue and at the same moment he began to expire. Bernardine on his right, Vincent on his left, hung over the dying man, both in fine voice. One displayed an image of St Francis, the other that of Dominic. Others, scattered through the
5   bedroom, murmured some psalms in a doleful tone. Bernardine assailed his right ear with great clamours, Vincent his left.

Marcolphus What were they screaming?

Phaedrus Bernardine something like this: 'George Balearicus, if now you approve what's been done between us, turn your head to the right.' He did
10   so. Vincent, on the other side: 'Be not afraid, George, you have Francis and Dominic as your champions. Rest easy: think how many merits you have, what a papal brief; finally, remember my soul is pledged for yours if there is any danger. If you understand and approve this, nod your head to the left.' He nodded. Again, with like clamour: 'If you understand this,' he says,
15   'press my hand.' Then George pressed his hand. So what with nodding to this side and that, and pressing of hands, nearly three hours were spent. Just as George began to gape, Bernardine, standing up straight, pronounced the absolution, but George was dead before he could finish it.[91] This occurred at midnight. In the morning the autopsy was performed.[92]
20   **Marcolphus** What disease did they find in his body?

Phaedrus I'm glad you brought that up, because it had slipped my mind. A piece of lead was lodged in his diaphragm.

Marcolphus Where did that come from?

Phaedrus His wife told us he had once been struck there by a bullet. Hence
25   the physicians conjectured that a fragment of the melted lead was left in his body. Soon the mangled body was clothed somehow or other in a Franciscan cloak. After lunch, burial was made, with the procession that had been arranged.

Marcolphus I've never heard of a more troublesome death nor of a
30   more pretentious funeral. But you wouldn't want this story to get out, I suppose.

Phaedrus Why not?

Marcolphus To avoid stirring up a hornets' nest.[93]

Phaedrus No danger. And, in fact, if what I relate is righteous, it concerns
35   these very men that the public should know it; if less than righteous, as many of them as are good will thank me for bringing it to light. Some, made ashamed of themselves, may stop doing things like this. Also, uneducated persons may take warning against making a similar mistake. For the sincere and genuinely religious men among them have often complained to me
40   that because of the superstition or dishonesty of a few, an entire order is rendered odious among respectable people.[94]

Marcolphus Well said, and boldly. But now I'm impatient to hear how Cornelius died.[95]

Phaedrus As he lived without being burdensome to anyone, so he died.[96] He had a fever that recurred regularly each year. And then, either because of
5 his old age – for he was past sixty[97] – or for some other reason, it oppressed him more than usual, and he himself seemed to sense that his last day was close at hand. So, four days before his death – it was Sunday – he went to church, confessed to his parish priest, heard sermon and mass, devoutly took communion, and returned home.[98]

10 **Marcolphus** He didn't use physicians?

Phaedrus He consulted only one,[99] but one who was fully as good a man as he was a physician: James Castrutius by name.[100]

Marcolphus I know him. No man is truer.

Phaedrus He promised to do whatever he could for his friend but said he
15 thought there was more help in God than in doctors.[101] Cornelius received this reply as cheerfully as if he had been given absolute assurance of life. And so, even though he had always been as liberal towards the poor as his means permitted, he then distributed among the destitute whatever he could spare from the needs of his wife and children; not to those pushing
20 beggars whom one meets everywhere,[102] but to worthy ones who struggled against their poverty by working as hard as they could. I implored him to go to bed and summon the priest rather than exhaust his feeble body. He replied that he had always tried to help his friends, if possible, rather than be under obligation to them, and that he did not want to be any different
25 at death.[103] He didn't even take to his bed except for the last day and part of the night on which he left this earth. Meanwhile he used a cane because of his physical weakness, or sat in an armchair. Now and then he lay down on a little bed, but with his clothes on and his head up. At this time he either gave instructions for relieving the poor, particularly those who were
30 acquaintances or neighbours,[104] or he read from the Bible passages exhorting man to trust God and setting forth God's love for us. If weakness prevented him from doing even this for himself, he listened while a friend read. Often, with wonderful feeling, he urged his family to mutual love and harmony and to zeal for true godliness; and he comforted them very affectionately,
35 grieved as they were about his dying. From time to time he reminded his family not to leave any of his debts unpaid.

Marcolphus Hadn't he made a will?

Phaedrus He had attended to that long before, when he was well and strong.[105] For he held that those made by the dying weren't wills but rather
40 ravings.

Marcolphus Didn't he bequeath anything to monasteries or to the needy?[106]

Phaedrus Not a farthing.[107] 'I have shared my modest fortune as I could afford,' he said. 'Now, as I am handing over possession of it to others, so I hand over the spending of it. And I am confident that my family will spend it better than I myself have done.'

Marcolphus Didn't he send for holy men, as George did?

Phaedrus Not even one. Except his family and two close friends, nobody was present.

Marcolphus I wonder why he felt like that.

Phaedrus He insisted he didn't want to be troublesome to more people when dying than he had been when he was born.[108]

Marcolphus I await the end of this story.

Phaedrus You'll soon hear it. Thursday came. Feeling extremely weak, he did not leave his couch. The parish priest was called, gave him extreme unction, and again administered communion, but without confession, for Cornelius said he had no lingering anxieties on his mind.[109] At that point the priest began to discuss the funeral – what sort of procession and where he was to be buried. 'Bury me as you would the humblest Christian,' he said. 'It makes no difference to me where you lay this poor body; it will be found on the Last Day just the same, wherever you've put it. The funeral procession I care nothing about.'[110] Presently the subjects of tolling the bells,[111] trentals[112] and anniversary masses, a papal brief, and purchase of a portion of merits[113] came up. Then he said, 'Pastor, I'll be none the worse off if no bell tolls; or if you deem me worthy of one burial service, that will be more than enough. Or if there is anything else that because of the church's public custom can scarcely be omitted without scandal to the weak, I leave that to your judgment. I do not desire to buy up someone's prayers or deprive anyone of his merits.[114] There is sufficient abundance of merits in Christ, and I have faith that the prayers and merits of the whole church will benefit me if only I am a living[115] member of it. In two "briefs" rests my entire hope. One is the fact that the Lord Jesus, the chief shepherd, took away my sins, nailing them to the cross; the other, that which he signed and sealed with his own sacred blood, by which he assured us of eternal salvation if we place our whole trust[116] in him. Far be it from me that, equipped with merits and briefs,[117] I should summon my Lord to enter into judgment with his servant, certain as I am that in his sight shall no man living be justified.[118] For my part, I appeal from his justice to his mercy, since it is boundless and inexpressible.' Whereupon the priest departed. Eager and joyous,[119] as though with strong hope of salvation, Cornelius ordered to be read to him certain biblical passages confirming the hope of resurrection and rewards of immortality: as that in Isaiah on the postponement of Hezekiah's death, along with his hymn;[120] then the fifteenth chapter of Paul's first letter to the Corinthians; the story of Lazarus' death from John;[121] but above all, the narrative of Christ's passion from the Gospels. How eagerly he concentrated on every one of these,[122] sighing at some, giving thanks with folded hands at others, at some rejoicing and exulting, at others uttering brief prayers! After

5   lunch, when he had taken a short nap, he had the twelfth chapter of John read, to the very end. When this was done, you would have said the man was completely transformed and breathed upon by a new spirit.

Day was already turning to evening. He called for his wife and children; then, straightening up as much as his weakness permitted, he

10   spoke to his family thus: 'My dearest wife, those whom earlier God had joined together, now likewise he puts asunder; but in body only, and that for a little while. The care, love, and devotion you have been accustomed to divide between me and our sweetest children, transfer wholly to them. Do not suppose you can deserve better by any means, either of God or of me,

15   than by so nurturing, cherishing, and instructing those whom God gave to us as the fruits of our marriage, that they may be found acceptable unto Christ. Double your devotion towards them, therefore, and consider my share made over to you. If you do that – as I am confident you will – there will be no reason they should seem orphans. But if you remarry'[123] – at this word his

20   wife broke into tears and began to swear she would never think of marrying again. Then Cornelius: 'My dearest sister in Christ, if the Lord Jesus shall deem best to grant you that resolution and strength of spirit, do not fail the heavenly gift, for this will be more comfortable for you and the children alike. But if weakness of the flesh shall call otherwise, know that my death

25   releases you from the marriage bond, but not from the obligation you have in my name, and in your own, of caring for our children. As for marrying, use the liberty the Lord has given you. This only do I ask and warn you of: that you choose a husband of such moral character, and bear yourself towards him in such a way, that, guided by his own kindness and prompted

30   by your gentleness, he may love his stepchildren. Be cautious, therefore, about binding yourself by any vow. Keep yourself free for God and for our children. So train them to every form of godliness that you may dissuade them from committing themselves to any career before age and experience demonstrate what mode of life they are suited for.'[124] Turning next to his

35   children, he exhorted them to the pursuit of righteousness, to obedience to their mother, and to mutual love and concord among themselves. Having spoken these words, he kissed his wife and children, and making the sign of the cross invoked the favour and mercy of Christ. Then, looking upon all who were present, he said, 'By dawn tomorrow the Lord who

40   rose from the dead at daybreak will of his mercy vouchsafe to call this poor soul from the tomb of this poor body, and from the shades of this

mortality into his heavenly light. I do not wish to tire tender youth with vain watching. Let the others, too, take turns sleeping. I need only one watcher, to read the sacred page.'[125]

5 When the night had passed – it was about four o'clock – and all were come, he ordered read the entire psalm spoken by the Lord when praying on the cross.[126] After it was ended, he bade them bring a taper and a crucifix. And taking the taper he said, 'The Lord is my light and my salvation: whom shall I fear?' Kissing the crucifix, he said, 'The Lord is the strength of my life: of whom shall I be afraid?'[127] Presently he folded his hands on his breast, in
10 the manner of one praying, and with his eyes turned to heaven said, 'Lord Jesus, receive my spirit.'[128] And straightway he closed his eyes as though he were going to sleep, and at that moment expired with a slight gasp. You would have said he had fallen asleep, not died.[129]

Marcolphus I've never heard of a death less troublesome.

15 **Phaedrus** He was like that all his life.[130] Each of these men was my friend. Perhaps I'm not a fair judge of which one died in a manner more becoming a Christian. You, being unprejudiced, will decide that better.

Marcolphus I'll do so, but at my leisure.

NOTES

1 These opening lines are nearly the same as those in 'A Marriage in Name Only' 844:3–4.

2 In Greek legend Trophonius was swallowed up by the earth. Thereafter he was consulted as an oracle, but those who visited him returned from his cave melancholy and discouraged. See *Adagia* I vii 77, where the cave is compared to St Patrick's cave, so-called, in Ireland; on this, 'A Pilgrimage' n186. Cf *Moriae encomium* LB IV 405C / ASD IV-3 71:13 / CWE 27 86.

3 Phaedrus means 'radiant,' 'cheerful'; see 'The Cheating Horse-Dealer' 558:3–8. The origin of the name Marcolphus is uncertain. It appears in one of the letters in *Epistolae obscurorum virorum* (2.69), a book known to Erasmus. He may also have seen the Latin text of the medieval *Salomon et Marcolphus*, in which Marcolphus is a glib and impertinent jester. See the edition by Walter Benary (Heidelberg 1914). English, French, and German versions exist, some verse and others prose; an English version was printed in 1492 at Antwerp.

4 The name Balearicus is adapted from Βελίαρ 'Satan,' 'Belial,' or 'Antichrist' (see 2 Cor 6:15), from a Hebrew word meaning 'uselessness,' 'corruption'; hence it is appropriate to George. The name Montius occurs once in Erasmus' correspondence (Ep 759). Neither George nor Cornelius can be identified with persons Erasmus knew, but he was certainly acquainted with men of both kinds. We meet a number of them in the *Colloquies* alone. George may remind us in some respects of the Johann Poppenruyter at whom *Enchiridion* is believed to have been directed. See O. Schottenloher 'Erasmus, Johann Poppenreuter und die Entstehung des *Enchiridion Militis Christiani*' ARG 45 (1954) 109–16.

5 Lines 5–35 are the only lines from Erasmus quoted in *The Oxford Book of Death*
  ed D.J. Enright (Oxford 1983) 46.
6 'Death is the most terrible of all things; for it is the end' (Aristotle *Nicomachean
  Ethics* 3.6 1115a26–7). Erasmus begins *De praeparatione ad mortem* with
  this quotation. Phaedrus, who voices Erasmus' opinions consistently in
  this colloquy, assures Marcolphus that expectation of death is worse than
  experience of it. For 'the sense of death is most in apprehension' (*Measure
  for Measure* 3.1.77). Bacon's famous essay on death contains a Latin sentence,
  'Pompa mortis magis terret quam mors ipsa,' that looks at first glance like a
  memory of Erasmus' line 9, 'Iter ad mortem durius quam ipse mors,' but see
  Quintilian 8.5.5; the dictum may be proverbial. Bacon attributed it to 'him that
  spake only as a philosopher and natural man.' It may be derived from Seneca
  Epistulae morales 24.14; Erasmus admired Seneca's essay *De brevitate vitae* (Allen
  Ep 2091:205–7).
  What Erasmus urges through Phaedrus in lines 9–13 is something more than
  Senecan Stoicism or the courage and moral integrity of Plato's Socrates in
  Phaedo. When he says one should dismiss from his thought the horror and
  imagination of death, he intends, as his subsequent words show, that this
  advice should be understood in Christian terms. 'All hope is in Christ alone,'
  Erasmus wrote to Beatus Rhenanus in 1518 concerning his own poor health. In
  his youth he used to shudder at the mention of death, but gradually overcame
  this dread and learned better than to measure human happiness by length of
  days. After all, he adds, he has passed his fiftieth year, an age attained by few,
  so he cannot complain (Allen Ep 867:258–72 / CWE Ep 867:278–92).
  For an introduction to the scope and power of death in the history of ideas
  and of sentiments in the late medieval and Renaissance eras, see T.S.R. Boase
  Death in the Middle Ages (London 1972, with many illustrations) and John
  Huizinga *The Waning of the Middle Ages* trans F. Hopman (London 1924). See
  also Holbein's series of woodcuts on this theme, and consult L.P. Kurtz *The
  Dance of Death and the Macabre Spirit in European Literature* (New York 1934);
  J.M. Clark *The Dance of Death in the Middle Ages and the Renaissance* (Glasgow
  1950). We infer with good reason that such disasters as the Black Death in the
  fourteenth century and recurrent plagues and epidemics took their toll morally
  and socially as well as physically. Allusions to these matters in the pages of
  Erasmus, as of others who wrote on contemporary life and manners, often
  reflect what a modern reader may think a strange preoccupation with death.
  Preoccupation it was, but unavoidably and properly, given the nature of their
  experience.
  Certain exceptions or apparent exceptions to these generalizations can be
  found. Petrarch, for example, writes at times like a pious, orthodox Christian
  (his attitudes towards death are compared with those of Erasmus by E.W. Kohls
  '*Meditatio mortis* chez Pétrarque et Erasme' in *Colloquia Erasmiana Turonensia* I
  303–11), but sometimes what he says on death differs from what we expect to
  find and usually do find in fourteenth-century texts. For a well-documented
  study of some other late medieval Italian considerations of death see G.W.
  McClure 'The Art of Mourning: Autobiographical Writings on The Loss of a
  Son in Italian Humanist Thought (1400–1461)' *Renaissance Quarterly* 39 (1986)
  440–75.

7 Cf *Enchiridion* LB V 4D / Holborn 26:25–7 / CWE 66 28. On permanent separation of soul and body as the definition of death see Plato *Phaedo* 64A–E, 67D; Cicero *Tusculan Disputations* 1.74–7; Augustine *De civitate Dei* 13.9 and 10. On the soul see 'The New Mother' 596:24–605:2 above.

8 So *De praeparatione ad mortem* warns against having too many doctors in attendance. They will only give conflicting advice, disagree with one another, and confuse or distress the invalid (LB V 1312A–B / ASD V-1 378:965–379:978). On their promptness in demanding fees cf *Adagia* IV viii 36 and *Apophthegmata* LB IV 132E; with 'enough to kill even a healthy man,' compare Martial 1.47 and *Adagia* II vii 7.

9 Proverbial; *Adagia* III ix 12, 53, 86; Cicero *Tusculan Disputations* 1.5.9. With the physicians' announcement that it is now time to turn to spiritual concerns, cf 'The Seraphic Funeral' 1000:28–34.

10 Bloating

11 A common procedure, even a public one, in the sixteenth and seventeenth centuries. See nn91 and 92 below.

12 Earned rewards deserved for one's good works, 'counted unto him for righteousness' (Rom 4:3) when done for God; in short, good deeds fulfilling divine commandments. Merits, as part of the penitential system, were repudiated by Protestant reformers – most clearly by Luther – on the ground that no human being had claim to a divine reward, however good his works, all of which are in fact tainted. He can only rely on the divine mercy. Cf Cornelius' words at 777:26–37.

13 A series of thirty daily requiem masses for the repose of a soul. The term is used again at 777:21.

14 The most prominent mendicant orders: Franciscan, Dominican, Carmelite, and the Augustinian Hermit Friars. Of these the *Colloquies* have most to say of Franciscans; see 'The Well-to-do Beggars,' 'The Sermon,' and 'The Seraphic Funeral'; on Dominicans 'Military Affairs' n24 and 'The Seraphic Funeral' n51; on Carmelites 'The Apotheosis of Reuchlin' n3; on Augustinians n43 below. Bernardine and Vincent are common names of Franciscans and Dominicans, in honour of St Bernardine of Siena (d 1444), a famous Franciscan preacher, and St Vincent Ferrer (d 1419), Dominican missionary and preacher. Alexander Müller or Molitor, warden of the Franciscans in Basel in 1526, has been suggested as the model for Erasmus' Bernardine in the colloquy (Smith *Key* 43), but Erasmus hardly needed a specific individual as model. Bernardine is cast as a type rather than an individual. With Vincent the case is altered because, as Allen (Ep 1196 introduction) and Smith both note, he can be convincingly identified with Vincentius Theoderici, formerly of the Dominican *studium* in Paris and later of Louvain. He was severely critical of Erasmus, who ridicules him in this colloquy and in a letter which speaks of him as 'an ignoramus, a natural booby' (Allen Ep 1144:24 / CWE Ep 1144:28). With help from others Theoderici wrote a tract against Erasmus' *Exomologesis* and *De esu carnium* but was forbidden to publish it (Allen Epp 1571:65n, 1582:1–2).

Another suggestion is that these lines 'would appear to have given Shakespeare the names of his murderer and his duke, Barnardine and Vincentio' in *Measure for Measure*; also that the idea of making Isabella in the play a votaress of St Clare may have come from this colloquy, in which George's elder daughter is promised

to St Clare (771:26); see Kenneth Muir in *Notes and Queries* 201 (1956) 424.
One of Erasmus' most irritating and detested critics, Nicolaas Baechem of
Louvain, was a Carmelite; on him see 'Rash Vows' n14.

15 A common term for *captatores testamenti*, sycophants who are constantly at the
deathbeds of the rich in hopes of a legacy. See *Adagia* I vii 14 and *Dialogus
bilinguium et trilinguium* in Ferguson *Erasmi opuscula* 208:82 / CWE 7 337.

16 On this rite see n109 below.

17 These contentious friars are a ludicrous contrast with the two Franciscans in
'The Well-to-do Beggars,' where the friars are clearly superior to the parish
priest in learning and morals.
The terms 'monk' and 'friar' were often used interchangeably. The
interchangeability and distinctions are discussed in chapter 5 of R.J. Schoeck
Erasmus of Europe: The Making of a Humanist 1467–1500 (Edinburgh 1990)
especially 114 and n9.

18 Friction between regular and secular clergy had long existed, both as a fact
and as a subject for satire and complaint, as these pages and others remind us.
Erasmus observes elsewhere that although the various orders of mendicants
quarrel among themselves, they present a united front against the seculars, as
they do in this scene (cf *Annotationes in Novum Testamentum* LB VI 125D; 'The
Well-to-do Beggars' n4). Such animosities are a well-worn topic in histories of
the orders, and were still a subject for attention at the Fifth Lateran Council,
which in 1516 decreed that neither Eucharist nor extreme unction could be
administered by regulars to a dying person whose confession they had heard
unless the parish priest had without legitimate reason refused to administer
them (session 11 [On religious and their privileges]; Tanner I 647). The priest
in 'The Funeral' shares the common clerical resentment at intrusion into his
territory. One of many charges was that the mendicants lured penitents away
from parish priests, who had the primary right to hear their confessions; see
Knowles ROE II 101–3. Erasmus disliked the tendency of Dominicans and
Franciscans to specialize in hearing confessions, though he allows that the
laziness or incompetence of priests, and the failure of bishops to correct the
situation, were often to blame. A strong passage in *Adagia* II viii 65 reproves
the aggressiveness of these mendicants. In 'The Usefulness of the *Colloquies*'
Erasmus strongly defends 'The Funeral' both as a reproach to the vanity of rich
men and as a condemnation of unctuous, grasping friars. He denies that he
defames the religious orders as such, insisting that he merely calls attention to
one of their notorious faults (1104:29–1105:11 below).

19 Vincent is *baccalaureus formatus*, literally 'formed bachelor,' a phrase used also
in Allen Ep 143:112–3 and *Adagia* II v 98 LB II 582F. This means that he is already
baccalaureus biblicus, has lectured on the Bible for a year and on another book
for a second year, has completed his studies of Peter Lombard's *Sentences* and
taken part in disputations, and now after half a dozen years of graduate study
at the University of Paris is about to become licentiate in theology. When he
does so he will be qualified to teach theology; with still further study he can
become a doctor of theology. See Farge *Orthodoxy and Reform* 16–28.

20 Because he is too ignorant of Latin

21 *mamzares*, from Hebrew *mamzer* (Deut 23:2). See Alexander Souter *A Glossary of
Later Latin to 600 A.D.* (Oxford 1949).

22 On concubinage and clerical incontinence, and Erasmus' opinions on these
   subjects, see the introduction to 'The Girl with No Interest in Marriage' 279–81
   and 'The Well-to-do Beggars' n6.
   'A priest,' Erasmus advised, 'should entertain himself with good authors
   instead of a concubine' ('The Usefulness of the *Colloquies*' 1100:22–3).
23 Proverbial; see *Adagia* i ix 28 (misnumbered 38 in LB II), an entertaining account
   in which Erasmus compares the shrillness and persistence of the cicada's noise
   to the outbursts of over-sensitive poets; on this allusion see Reedijk *Poems of
   Erasmus* 74–5. *Adagia* i ix 100 is also about the cicada.
24 Proverbial; not in *Adagia* in this form, but cf i x 41.
25 Francis and Dominic were renowned for sanctity but not for learning.
26 Nowadays, Erasmus and More and other like-minded men agreed, there were
   too many priests, monks, and mendicant friars. Fewer but better ones were
   needed. See 'The Usefulness of the *Colloquies*' 1100:37–8; Allen Epp 1747:105,
   1891:214–28, 2700:109–11; *Institutio christiani matrimonii* LB V 647E; *De concordia*
   LB V 498D. Cf More *Utopia* Yale CWM 4 130, 131. Knowles estimates that there
   were about 3,000 friars in England c 1500 (ROE III 52).
27 The same metaphor is used in describing the earliest Benedictines and friars in
   Allen Ep 858:525 / CWE Ep 858:567, the prefatory letter to the new edition of
   Enchiridion (1518), and again, at length, in *De concordia* (1533) LB V 484A–F.
28 Cf the verses on the orders quoted in the *Catholic Encyclopedia* XII (1911) 356:
   *Bernardus valles, montes Benedictus amabat, / Oppida Franciscus, celebres Dominicus
   urbes* 'Bernard loved the valleys, Benedict the mountains, / Francis the towns,
   Dominic the populous cities.'
29 Critics of the mendicants liked to point to this change as a serious ethical lapse
   with deplorable consequences. Note Erasmus' remark in Allen Ep 2700:94–7.
   As early as 1243 the chronicler Matthew Paris, a Benedictine, accused English
   Franciscans and Dominicans of haunting the bedsides of sick folk 'in order
   that they may gape after gain, extort confessions and hidden testaments,
   commending only themselves and their own Order' (*Chronica maiora* Rolls Series
   57, 7 vols [London 1872–83] IV 280; trans G.G. Coulton *Europe's Apprenticeship*
   [London 1940] 253). When Erasmus in 1511 ventured to ask Colet for financial
   aid to Richard Croke, then a young scholar of promise, later a teacher of Greek
   at Cambridge and a canon of Christ Church, Oxford, Colet refused: 'I do not
   stand by the bedsides of the dying ... I do not seek to become the confidant
   of rich men, or praise their vices and infirmities, or bid them compound their
   crimes by putting money at my disposal' (Allen Epp 227:24–8, 230:32–8 / CWE
   Epp 227:30–4, 230:38–44). Hostility to mendicants existed long before Wyclif
   and Hus lived, but their criticism was typical. Wyclif was at first friendly with
   the friars at Oxford but later, when they opposed his theology, turned against
   them, finally becoming almost fanatical in his denunciations. See Herbert B.
   Workman *John Wyclif: A Study of the English Medieval Church* 2 vols (Oxford
   1926) II 92–108. In England the line runs through Wyclif's followers, the
   Lollards, to the early sixteenth-century Protestants. Judgments of monks and
   friars similar to Wyclif's were often expressed in more subtle and ironic, but
   arguably more persuasive, language by Erasmus in the *Colloquies* and other
   writings. That language is said by an eminent modern historian, himself a
   monk, to have 'penetrated deep into the consciousness and memories of his age

... It was a more civilized treatment of the topic than Wyclif's, a more Fabian approach, but the end would have been no less inevitable' (Knowles ROE III 151). But for Wyclif Erasmus had no use. See 'A Pilgrimage' n146.

30 In 1482 the faculty of theology in Paris condemned a claim made in a Lenten sermon by a Franciscan that members of the order were authentic priests and curates and better than parish priests, because Franciscans held their power from the pope, parish priests only from a bishop (*Collectio judiciorum de novis erroribus* ... ed C. du Plessis d'Argentré, 3 vols [Paris 1728–36; repr Brussels 1966] I part 2 305).

31 In saying this the priest is within his rights. Preaching was one of the principal activities of mendicant friars (see 'A Fish Diet' n219). They were trained for the work and were often popular with those who heard them, but they incurred the suspicion and hostility of parish clergy. As a result their freedom to preach was curtailed severely by the bull *Super cathedram* of Boniface VIII in 1300, which forbade them to preach in any parish church without permission of the priest or bishop. This bull was annulled by Boniface's successor, Benedict XI in 1304, but reinstituted by the next pope, Clement V, in 1311 (the Council of Vienne decree [10]; Tanner I 365–9).

32 Of arts or divinity, probably the latter. The *Reformatio Sigismundi* (1438) stipulated that every parish priest should be at least *baccalaureus* (Strauss *Manifestations of Discontent* 120). This was a counsel of perfection.

33 St Martin of Tours (d 397), bishop of Tours and founder of the first monastery in France; a famous preacher and missionary. See *Adagia* III iii 1 LB II 772D.

34 Hints of this are found in 'A Fish Diet' 707:2–21; see also 'The Girl with No Interest in Marriage' n15 and 'The Well-to-do Beggars' n6.

35 Cf Allen Ep 2700:73–92.

36 The priest is not a bachelor, but he remembers a tag from Horace *Satires* 1.7.3.

37 Despite the restrictions on their preaching in parish churches, mendicant friars could still practise their other specialty, the hearing of confessions, if certain conditions were met. A Christian was required to confess all his sins to his own parish priest at least once a year. This was usually done at Easter. Confession could also be made to friars, but at least one confession annually must be made to the priest. See 'Youth' n64. The conflict between George's confessing to the Franciscan and the priest's insistence on his right to hear it is resolved by George's offer to confess anew to the priest. Having won his point, the priest now allows the earlier confession to stand, then administers extreme unction and communion, collects his fee, and departs.

38 That is, agreed to spare him the repeating of it

39 Gave him extreme unction. See n109 below.

40 See 'The Old Men's Chat' n70.

41 'The fifth wheel of a wagon' was a common phrase for something insignificant and unneeded, used for example in the thirteenth-century *Chronicle* of the Franciscan Salimbene, translated by G.G. Coulton in *From St Francis to Dante* (rev ed London 1907; repr Philadelphia 1972) 53, 92, 155, 326.

42 A double meaning is hinted, for dicing was a dissipation of which friars and monks were often accused.

43 'Augustinian,' referring to an order, identifies one of the societies professing to follow the teachings or rule of St Augustine. Here the allusion is to the Hermit Friars of St Augustine. Luther belonged to one of the fifteenth-century

German reformed congregations of this order. Despite the name 'friars,' his order was monastic; he was a monk and calls himself a monk; he was never a mendicant. The Augustinian canons regular, of whom Erasmus was one, were neither monks nor friars but, as he often notes, had characteristics of both: it was an 'amphibian' society as he likes to say, a distinctive order within the Augustinian family (cf 'A Pilgrimage' n46). Carmelites, who claimed descent from the prophet Elijah, boasted of being the most ancient of all the orders. Neither the Augustinian Hermit Friars nor the Carmelites were originally mendicants. Accordingly they were scorned by the Franciscans and Dominicans, as in the 'gladiatorial combat' that follows here. The Crutched Friars' attitude towards the other four orders present is 'a plague on [all] your houses,' an attitude illustrated likewise in verses quoted by Huizinga *Waning of the Middle Ages* (n6 above) 161 and the execration of mendicants by the dying poet Raminagrobis in Rabelais *Gargantua and Pantagruel* 3.21.

44 *impressionem.* Cf Cicero *Ad familiares* 5.2.8.

45 *syncretismus,* used of those who were formerly enemies but then joined forces in order to oppose a common foe. See *Adagia* I i 11 and *Querela pacis* LB IV 638B / ASD IV-2 685–7 / CWE 27 314. Franciscans and Dominicans were natural rivals; competition between them had existed early in their history and continued in more or less the same manner in later generations. But sometimes these older orders stood together, as they do in this scene, against other orders. On the Carmelites see also H.C. Lea *A History of Auricular Confession and Indulgences in the Latin Church* 3 vols (Philadelphia 1896) III 253–77. Other allusions to wrangling friars are met in Erasmus' writings; for example *Enchiridion* LB V 45D–F / Holborn 100:26–101:12 / CWE 66 15; *Querela pacis* LB IV 629B–C / ASD IV-2 67:178–68:202 / CWE 27 298; *Annotationes in Novum Testamentum* LB VI 125C–D. On Franciscan history in general consult Moorman or Raphael M. Huber *A Documented History of the Franciscan Order, 1182–1517* (Milwaukee and Washington 1944); and see the notes to 'The Seraphic Funeral.' For the Dominicans see William A. Hinnebusch *The History of the Dominican Order* 2 vols (New York 1966–73). Hinnebusch's *The Dominicans: A Short History* (New York 1975) has brief chapters on the fifteenth and sixteenth centuries.

46 *Querela pacis* LB IV 640A–B / ASD IV-2 94:794–7 / CWE 27 318; *De bello Turcico* LB V 359B; *Annotationes in Novum Testamentum* LB VI 241F. The barbarous conduct of common soldiers, which we hear of in 'Military Affairs,' 'The Soldier and the Carthusian,' 'Charon,' and 'Cyclops,' was more destructive, but it is to be remembered that generals get their training by sharing the deeds of such 'preliminary campaigning' (see n81 below).

47 He was clever at getting 'dead pays,' appropriating pay for soldiers dead or discharged or for some other reason not under his command. 'Dead pays' was once a common term; see John Smythe *Certain Discourses Military* (1590) ed J.R. Hale (Washington 1964) xxxix n59.

48 The Beguines were a religious society of women who lived in community but without vows and devoted themselves to good works. They could own private property and leave the order if they chose. They were mainly in the Netherlands, where today the Begijnhof in Amsterdam commemorates their houses, but were also found in Cologne, Paris, and other cities. Their chapel in Amsterdam (1419), rebuilt several times, became a Protestant church in the sixteenth century. A similar society for men, the Beghards, was established

in the fourteenth century. See R.W. Southern *Western Society and the Church in the Middle Ages* (London 1970) 319–30; Ernest W. McDonnell *The Beguines and Beghards in Medieval Culture* (New Brunswick, NJ 1954; repr New York 1969).

49 *Adagia* I x 17; cf I x 31, II v 22. The folly of forcing a son or daughter to enter the religious life, as George intends, without proper consideration of their wishes or welfare, is almost an obsession with Erasmus, who warns against it in the conclusion of *Institutio christiani matrimonii* LB V 722D–724B. Compare Cornelius' advice to his wife at 778:32–4 below. The opposite difficulty, of young persons having rash desires to enter monasteries or nunneries, is the theme of 'The Girl with No Interest in Marriage' and 'The Repentant Girl.'

50 Acceptable moral character and intelligence were requirements to which, canonically, no exceptions could be made. See 'A Fish Diet' n306. As for illegitimacy or age, a papal dispensation could be sought. Since the canonical age for ordination to the priesthood was fixed at twenty-five in 1179 (Third Lateran Council, canon 3; Tanner I 212–13), and the older son is only nineteen, the need for a dispensation is clear.

51 'Let those who think masses and rites for relatives are of no benefit to the departed, do for the living poor what most people command to be done after death. Do not interfere with those who are persuaded that the good works which, when living, they took care to do, are beneficial to the dead.' (Allen Ep 2853:17–20). So Erasmus writes in 1533 to an unidentified person or group who sought his opinions on ecclesiastical reforms – some quite radical – advocated or introduced.

52 The Scala Sancta, marble steps to the papal chapel in the Lateran palace; believed to have been brought to Rome by St Helena from Jerusalem, where they had been in Pilate's palace and thus trodden by the feet of Christ. They were resited nearby in the late sixteenth century. Pilgrims ascend them on their knees. Arnold von Harff says he was told in Rome that whoever climbed the steps on his knees released a soul from purgatory (ed Malcolm Letts, Hakluyt Society 2nd series 94 [London 1946] 19). Erasmus alludes to this belief in *De praeparatione ad mortem* LB 1312C / ASD V-1 380:988–9. Luther crawled up those steps, kissing each one, in 1510, but the experience ended with disturbing doubt rather than exultation. See R.H. Bainton *Here I Stand: A Life of Martin Luther* (New York 1950) 50–1.

53 Horace *Satires* 1.9.20–1

54 That is, the older to the Poor Clares, the Second Order of St Francis (named after St Clare of Assisi); and the younger to the Third Order of St Dominic, of which St Catherine was a member.

55 See 772:22–3 below. Those who bequeath so much wealth to religious that they leave their children impoverished are condemned in *Annotationes in Novum Testamentum* LB VI 258F, 280F.

56 *uncia* (English 'ounce'), literally 'a twelfth.' The entire estate is divided into twelve shares.

57 See a decree of Clement v forbidding friars to use devious means of arranging that legacies be left to them (Council of Vienne decree [31]; Tanner I 387).

58 Writing in 1532 to a young priest he knew well, Erasmus speaks of reports that Franciscans persuade rich and ignorant men that by being buried in Franciscan

dress and giving money they will participate in all good works of the order (Allen Ep 2700:73–8).

59 In Roman law a testament was invalid if it deprived heirs of estates to which they were legally entitled. See Cicero *In Verrem actio secunda* 1.42.107.

60 Cf Job 9:32.

61 Men who prescribe over-elaborate arrangements for their funerals are ridiculed in *Moriae encomium* (LB IV 446B–447A / ASD IV-3 126:23–8 and note / CWE 27 115–16). An eloquent passage on this folly in More's *Supplication of Souls* (1529) is reprinted by P.S. and H.M. Allen eds *Sir Thomas More: Selections* (Oxford 1924) 101. One of the new translations from Lucian by Erasmus, added to the second edition (Paris 1514) of the Latin versions made by him and More and first published in 1506 (Paris: Josse Bade) was *De luctu*, a clever and characteristic satire of the superstition and hypocrisy of funeral customs. Text of the translation in LB I 194A–196E / ASD I-1 394–8.

62 Cherubim, seraphim, thrones, dominations, virtues, powers, principalities, archangels, angels. Beliefs or traditions about them derive principally from the *Celestial Hierarchy* attributed to pseudo-Dionysius; on him see 'The New Mother' n51. Number was profoundly significant in religious symbolism, whether in language as in Dante or in pictorial art. Every instructed Christian in Erasmus' time knew – and accepted that it was worth knowing – that the Persons of the Trinity were three, the apostles twelve, the wounds of Christ and the books of Moses five, the angelic choirs nine, the sorrows of Mary seven, and so on. The symbolism of numbers in a pageant or a funeral as elaborate as George's is to be would not only have been intelligible to many of the spectators but a source of pleasure and of religious satisfaction.
Analysis of number symbolism is as ancient as Pythagoras. Vincent R. Hopper *Medieval Number Symbolism* (New York 1938) is an introduction to the subject, and see E.R. Curtius *European Literature and the Latin Middle Ages* trans Willard R. Trask (New York 1953) 501–14.

63 Matt 26:14–15

64 The former were hired for the occasion, according to custom. 'Dressed in black' was also customary; 'We mourn in black' (Shakespeare *1 Henry VI* 1.1.17), though there were exceptions; for burial of infants the priest could be vested in white. At the funeral of Charles VI of France, members of the Parlement of Paris wore red (Boase [n6 above] figs 99, 100). Aldermen in London who marched as mourners at the funeral of another alderman sometimes wore their violet gowns if they did not have black (*The Diary of Henry Machyn, Citizen and Merchant-Taylor of London from A.D. 1550 to A.D. 1563* ed J.G. Nichols, Camden Society 1st series 42 [London 1848; repr New York 1968] xxiv; the *Diary* mentions well over 200 funerals and describes many of them, and for information about funeral processions in London during the years it covers it is invaluable, as is the editor's introductory 'Note upon Funerals,' xx–xxxii).

65 Another standard feature of funeral processions honouring monarchs, statesmen, or warriors was their favourite charger, either riderless (as apparently George's is) or ridden by a page but symbolically riderless nonetheless. In the funeral procession for Sir Philip Sidney in 1586 his horse was 'led by a footman, a page riding, trailing a broken lance' (as is shown in Thomas Lant *Sequitur celebritas et pompa funeris* [of Sir Philip Sidney] ... with

many illustrations [London 1587; STC 15224] 3). For the riderless horse in Queen
Elizabeth's funeral procession in 1603 see the drawing in William Camden's
Funeral Procession of Queen Elizabeth in Roland M. Frye *The Renaissance Hamlet*
(Princeton 1984) 98, 99. The riderless, decorated horse of Charles v is shown in
a contemporary drawing reproduced in B.H. Kervyn de Lettenhove *La toison
d'or* 2nd ed (Brussels 1907) facing page 90.

66 The cloth or coverlet draped over the coffin

67 Paros, an island in the Aegean, was famous for its white marble.

68 Erasmus deplored the exhibition in churches of banners, arms, and other
memorials of eminent personages. Yes, you can be buried beside the high altar
if you pay enough (*Adagia* I ix 12 LB II 338E). Cf 'The Godly Feast' 199:18–23
and *Modus orandi Deum* LB V 1121B. The symbolism in the rest of this paragraph
would have been recognizable enough to many of Erasmus' readers, but the
irony of it depends on the context.

69 Pelicans were common, like other birds and beasts, on tombs (*Modus orandi
Deum* LB V 1121B). In Christian art the pelican was a symbol of Christ's sacrifice
on the cross, because it was thought that the pelican fed its offspring with blood
from its own breast, and was thus an antetype of the Eucharist. (Cf Ps 102:6
[101:7 Vulg]: 'I am like a pelican of the wilderness.') Sometimes it is shown
above the cross, as in Francesco Pesellino's painting *Crucifixion with St Jerome
and St Francis*; see plate IV in George Ferguson *Signs and Symbols in Christian
Art* (New York 1954). But to those who knew Pliny's *Naturalis historia* as well
as Erasmus did, there could be a very different reason for the appropriateness
of the pelican's neck as George's crest. Pliny says (10.131) that the pelican is
insatiably greedy, and Erasmus notes that it makes a noise like an ass's braying
(*scholia* on the revised edition of Jerome's letters [Basel 1524–6] II 1128).

70 The boar too is known to heraldry. King Richard III of England had a lion
and a boar as his crest. A boar is merely a wild pig, and a pig in Christian
art represents gluttony and sensuality (see 'The Well-to-do Beggars' n43). If
George's shield shows three boars, these may be intended to suggest his fierce
courage, yet it is just as likely that Erasmus intends them as signs of ruthless
rapacity.

71 The rules of heraldry disapproved of having metal on metal. If so, 'gold in a
field of silver' would be another example of ostentation.

72 *eques auratus*, a pun on *auratus* 'gilded'; *auratus* and 'knight' are synonymous
here. See *Paraphrasis in Elegantias Vallae* ASD I-4 250:173. Gilded knights were
so called 'from their gilt Spurres, which they were wont to have put on at
their Creation' (John Selden *Titles of Honor* 2nd ed [1631] 437). After More was
knighted in 1521, Erasmus' next letter to him is addressed *equiti aurato* (Allen
Ep 1220).

73 In Christian symbolism it signifies sin and the devil, but in heraldry the leopard
is a lion 'passant gardant,' walking with head facing the spectator (as in the
arms of England).

74 Burial of parts of the body in different places, or even in different countries,
was not unheard of. Henry I of England furnishes one example (Boase [n6
above] 113), Henry VIII another. His entrails and bowels were removed 'after
the corps was cold, and seen by the Lords of the Privy Council' and other
nobles, and then 'were honorably buried in the chappel within the said place

[the palace of Whitehall at Westminster], with all manner of ceremonies thereunto belonging' (Strype *Ecclesiastical Memorials* [Oxford 1822] II part 2 289). The corpse was then wrapped, embalmed, cased in lead and buried after many ceremonies and three days of procession, in the choir of St George's Chapel in Windsor.

75 Since Erasmus had lived in Venice for eight months in 1508, the allusions in these paragraphs are very likely memories of his own observations there (see the introduction to 'Penny-Pinching' 979–82). His business in Venice was to prepare an enlarged edition of the *Adagia*. For the meaning and the pomp and circumstance of such Venetian events see the impressive book by Edward Muir, *Civic Ritual in Renaissance Venice* (Princeton 1981).

Sir Richard Guildford comments on the great number of guilds in religious processions he saw in Venice in 1506; see *The Pylgrymage of Sir Richard Guylforde* ed Henry Ellis, Camden Society 51 (London 1851) 8–9. Compare Wey's description of a doge's funeral there in 1462 (*Itineraries* [Roxburghe Club, London 1857] 85); on Guildford and Wey see 'Rash Vows' n3. Coryat in 1608 saw in Venice 'a marvelous solemn procession' consisting of 'every order and fraternity of religious men in the whole city' (*Crudities* I 367).

76 Often used by Erasmus as a synonym for 'innumerable' or 'a great many.' It occurs in another passage critical of funeral processions (*Ecclesiastes* LB V 809B). Sometimes it is ironical. As the lexicons suggest, its use as a figure of speech may have arisen because the Roman cohort originally consisted of six hundred soldiers.

77 Because they carried torches or were accompanied by torchbearers. Chimeras were mythical monsters with heads of lions, bodies of goats, and tails of dragons. They were armed with flames.

78 Ie the friars; see n17 above.

79 Marching order is ruled by prevailing notions of hierarchy, history, privilege, and local custom. In this paragraph 'front,' 'rear,' 'first,' 'last' (or 'lowest') can refer either to status and dignity or to place in the procession, depending on the speaker's meaning. Since the Venetian procession honours a cobbler, it is logical that fellow members of his guild should be the chief mourners. Therefore they march last (*inferne*), in the most honourable position; fullers and tanners 'up front' (*superne*). But when priests and clerks march in 'first' place at the front of the procession (*primus*), they march in the 'lowest' or least honourable position. The addition of *hoc est primum* after 'lowest' (*infimum*) in the September 1531 and subsequent editions makes this clear. In *Moriae encomium* when Folly reminds her audience that Ecclesiastes (1:17) says 'I gave my heart to know wisdom and to know madness and folly' she is audaciously affirming that folly is superior and therefore is in last place (LB IV 490E / ASD IV-3 180:943–8 / CWE 27 143). In modern academic processions persons with lower degrees (or none at all as yet) march first, those with higher degrees after them. This is also the established rule in all liturgical processions. In Robert Goulet's *Compendium universitatis Parisiensis* (1517), the oldest printed history of the university, the order of precedence in university processions differs from what we find in the colloquy and the passage in *Moriae encomium*; see the translation by Robert B. Burke (Philadelphia and London 1928) 78–80. Franciscans, Augustinians, Carmelites, and Dominicans march ahead of masters of arts; then come other

religious orders; then bachelors, doctors, rector and other university officials. Bringing up the rear is the book trade – booksellers, binders, paper-merchants, illuminators, parchmenters, and scriveners. Were these an afterthought, an addition to fill up the ranks, or were they included because they were useful servitors of the university, though not members of it?

To infer then that the most important person or group in a formal procession was always last would be a serious error. Other considerations or *ad hoc* decisions could overrule precedents. George, for instance, pays no attention to established rules about whether Dominicans or Franciscans should march first – whether that means ahead of everybody else or merely ahead of other religious. He simply tells them to cast lots. A far more common and important factor, we can suppose, was the number and variety of persons in the procession and how elaborate the whole spectacle was to be. In the ordering of the funeral for Stephen Gardiner in 1555, friars and monks march first, followed by clerks and priests. The chief mourner comes next, then the lesser mourners; then nobles; finally servants (*Letters* 502–17). Similarly in the funeral processions of nobles and even kings and many other worthies, as described in Machyn's diary (n64 above), the chief mourner is never, or very seldom, first or last. He is somewhere near the middle. He seems in his official capacity to symbolize the apex or crest of grief, those ahead of him preparing the way, in some sense preparing the spectators for his appearance. Thereafter curiosity or emotion can subside gradually. The procession is not ended; there are still more marchers, banners, horsemen, decorated wagons, minor mourners to see. These deductions, at any rate, seem justified after examination of the evidence offered by accounts of many sixteenth-century funeral processions.

80 A plenary indulgence, remitting temporal punishment in purgatory. 'Some, by means of a purchased document, promise freedom from purgatorial fire, but I fear this is not done to relieve the sick man but is a shameless way of deceiving him when he is at the point of death' (*De praeparatione ad mortem* LB V 1316F / ASD V-1 388:227–9).

81 See the colloquies 'Military Affairs,' 'The Soldier and the Carthusian,' 'Charon,' and 'Cyclops,' and *Querela pacis* passim. 'War covers the dregs of every crime. A general is not considered competent nowadays unless trained for his present rank by such preliminary campaigning' ('The Knight without a Horse' 887:14–16).

82 In this case forgery, an offence with which religious orders, particularly the mendicant friars, were sometimes charged; for instance by Castiglione in *The Courtier* 3.20. The charge was easier to make than to prove.

83 Such foolish promises are of course useless (*In psalmum quartum concio* LB V 290F) – even, said Luther, if the pope himself pledged his soul for them (*Ninety-five Theses* [1517]; Kidd *Documents* 24 no 11 thesis 52). Erasmus' word for 'hell' here is 'Orcus,' who was god of death and the underworld.

84 One might have expected 'Crutched Friars' instead of 'Carthusians' here, since the former have been named as the fifth order, but all early editions agree on 'Carthusians.' The warranties (*cautiones*) or pledges to which allusion is made may be 'letters of fraternity,' by which a lay person, by promise of a gift of money to the order, could be buried in Franciscan habit and receive from the friars prayers which would help him after death. That such pledges were

made is repeated by Erasmus in 1532, who names the Franciscan order (Allen Ep 2700:73–8). Cf 'The Seraphic Funeral' 1007:25–1008:6 and passim; and see Moorman 120, 514–5.

85 On these see the introduction to 'Military Affairs.'

86 Matt 13:12; Luke 19:26

87 A symbol of penance and of mortality. For detailed instructions about monastic use see *Monastic Constitutions of Lanfranc* ed and trans David Knowles (London 1951) 122.

88 See n58 above and *De praeparatione ad mortem* LB V 1305E / ASD V-1 366:635–8. The custom of putting a Franciscan robe on a dying man is treated at length in 'The Seraphic Funeral.' John Bale in *The Image of Both Churches* (c 1548) associates this custom particularly with kings and warriors and other 'strong men,' citing 'The Funeral' (*Select Works* ed H. Christmas, PS 1 [Cambridge 1849] 1, 329).

89 For a dying person to have a crucifix and taper held near him, or given him to hold, was another ancient custom; cf 779:6 below. A picture in the Grimani breviary (c 1500) shows a dying man with crucifix and taper held at the bedside, notaries and physicians nearby, while an angel drives a devil away (Boase [n6 above] fig 105). Pictures of saints too may be shown to the dying, to fortify them against despair (*De praeparatione ad mortem* LB V 1314B / ASD V-1 384:84–90).

The Jacobean dramatist John Webster borrows directly from this scene in *The White Devil* 5.3.135–45, where the death of Brachiano, with two friars in attendance, is enacted on the inner stage. Latin sentences are lifted from 774:35–775:14 here. See A.W. Reed in the *Times Literary Supplement* 14 June 1947 page 295.

90 With the imagery compare Prov 30:5; Eph 6:11–17.

91 Not unusual, Erasmus implies in *Exomologesis* LB V 160A–B.

92 To establish the cause of death. Erasmus, after describing Colet's final illness, takes the trouble to add that the autopsy furnished no new information but indicated a disordered liver (Allen Ep 1211:382–3 / CWE Ep 1211:415–17). The physicians' assurance to George's wife that 'anatomies' were a procedure *honoris causa* may have been prudent under the circumstances, but hardly necessary: relatives sometimes requested them out of curiosity. At public anatomies, on the other hand, the bodies dissected were commonly those of criminals. The cadaver anatomized in Rembrandt's famous painting was that of a criminal who was hanged the day before. Public anatomies in seventeenth-century Amsterdam and elsewhere were festive events. See William S. Heckscher's brilliant book *Rembrandt's 'Anatomy of Dr. Nicolaas Tulp': An Iconological Study* (New York 1958).

93 Proverbial; *Adagia* I i 60

94 With this bold claim for the purity of his motives in criticizing the mendicant orders, compare 'The Usefulness of the *Colloquies*' 1104:38–1105:11 and Allen Ep 2037:235–8. Erasmus repeats assertions of this kind many times.

95 His name recalls the Cornelius of Acts 10:2, 'a devout man and one that feared God with all his house.' At this point in the colloquy, farce and satire, having done their work, give place to sober narrative and modulated language. The register changes completely as we turn from the clamorous scene at George's

deathbed to the quiet but confident, even cheerful, discourse in which Cornelius proclaims his faith and makes his farewells while calmly awaiting his end. By witnessing in these few pages how Cornelius meets death we may even learn more about Erasmian piety than from many pages of *De praeparatione ad mortem,* which is ten times as long. That homily contains many good things but lacks the eloquence of Cornelius' simple sincerity and the effectiveness of dialogue.

96 This is what Erasmus says of a devout Franciscan, Dietrich Kolde (d 1515) whom he admired (Allen Ep 1347:109–10 / CWE Ep 1347:121–2). It is instructive to compare Ep 1347 with what he wrote of Vitrier in Ep 1211.

97 If Erasmus was born in 1467 he was close to sixty when this colloquy was published. The exact year of his birth is not known, and the evidence of his own statements is conflicting. Until 1970 many and probably most scholars favoured 1469 as the birth year, others 1466 or 1465. A.C.F. Koch's *The Year of Erasmus' Birth* (Utrecht 1969) provided new and persuasive reasons for thinking the correct year was 1467; though see J.B. Gleason 'The Birth Dates of John Colet and Erasmus of Rotterdam: Fresh Documentary Evidence' *Renaissance Quarterly* 32 (1979) 73–6.

Sixty was old indeed. Luther, commenting on Ps 90:10 (89:10 Vulg) and the longevity of the patriarchs before the Flood, observes that afterwards the span of life diminished until today, he says, forty or fifty years is the average, adding that the number of those persons who reach sixty is very small (*Sendschreiben an die zu Frankfurt am Main* WA 30 part 3 562:22–5 / LW 13 122). Men die later than women (*De votis monasticis* WA 8 661 / LW 44 388). Erasmus speaks of a woman of 'middle age,' about thirty, as a suitable bride for a man who does not want a young wife (*Institutio christiani matrimonii* LB V 665F). For references to what he and some of his contemporaries meant by old age, see 'The Soldier and the Carthusian' n4 and a long passage on the age of modern scholars and other writers (Allen Ep 1347:208–309 / CWE Ep 1347:225–332). This is the second half of a letter, c March 1523, to Joost Vroye of Gavere (on whom see Allen Ep 719 introduction and CEBR) first printed with *Exomologesis* in 1524. Vroye is named in 'The Epithalamium' 525:32. The first half of Ep 1347 is devoted in part to the theme of sudden death, the best kind of death for a good man (Allen Ep 1347:69, 139–64, 182–8 / CWE Ep 1347:78–9, 154–81, 198–205).

98 'I have never dared or would dare to approach the table of Christ, or depart from this life, without confessing to a priest what weighed upon my conscience,' Erasmus wrote in 1529; see Allen Ep 2136:216–8. For his opinions on confession see 'Youth' 96:31–97:35 and *Exomologesis* LB V 145–70.

99 Erasmus thought it a duty to consult physicians but had no illusions about what they could do for him. See *De praeparatione ad mortem* LB V 1312A–B / ASD V-1 378:965–79:978.

100 The name has not been explained, but Erasmus might have borrowed it from the Castrutius to whom Jerome wrote his Ep 68, assuring this friend (who was blind) that his physical affliction was not due to any sin. Cornelius' friend Castrutius cannot cure him but tries to cheer him up.

101 'And so I sent the doctors away, putting my trust in the Lord' (Allen Ep 1735:9–13) is typical. The doctors he has in mind were practitioners in Basel, 'the ones we have here: worthy of these people, who prefer drinking to doctoring.'

102 Such as the cunning sort described in 'Beggar Talk'

103 Cornelius' careful attention to aiding the deserving poor, setting his domestic affairs in order, and declining many of the usual trappings of burial are characteristic marks of Erasmian piety.

104 Cf *De praeparatione ad mortem* LB V 1304A / ASD V-1 362:529–32.

105 All necessary arrangements should be made before it is too late and not left for survivors to determine (*De praeparatione ad mortem* LB V 1303E–1304A / ASD V-1 360:510–362:532).

106 'What is given to monasteries is said to be given to God. True enough, provided it is given with devout motive. But those people are mistaken who suppose that what is given to children, wives, needy relatives is not given to God. On the contrary, those who deprive sons and household, distributing their money to colleges and monasteries, commit a major sin (*peccatum enorme*), a sin denounced by Paul too. And the Lord in the Gospel rebukes those who cheat their parents by giving for corban' (*Ecclesiastes* LB V 1025F). On corban see 'A Fish Diet' n103. The reference to Paul is 1 Tim 5:8. Erasmus comments on this verse in *Annotationes in Novum Testamentum* LB VI 940D–E; see also his paraphrase LB VII 1050B–C.
That Marcolphus asks about the poor may seem surprising, because Cornelius' concern for them has been made plain, but the needy here are probably the mendicant friars.

107 *Adagia* I viii 9. Erasmus defends this paragraph in *Apologia adversus rhapsodias Alberti Pii* LB IX 1159F–1160A. 'Modest fortune' is *facultatulas*, a diminutive in Jerome Ep 108.10.

108 See 776:3 above.

109 Extreme unction is the anointing administered when a person's death is thought to be near at hand. Erasmus treats it as he does other sacraments, as something comforting to recipients, its efficacy depending on their disposition. For he who is touched in the heart by the power of the Holy Spirit is blessedly anointed (*De puritate tabernaculi* LB V 310F).
Confession and the Eucharist before death, however, are much more important. That is why Cornelius attended to these duties on the Sunday preceding his death and why Erasmus affirmed in 1529 that he would not dare to die without confession (n98 above). Yet, confession having been made and communion received, Cornelius does not feel the need of confession again. Erasmus took pains to emphasize both the urgency of confessing all mortal sins and of not treating minor offences as mortal sins. See 'Youth' 97:14–21; and John Payne *Erasmus: His Theology of the Sacraments* (Richmond 1970) 216–19.
A passage in *De praeparatione ad mortem* repeats approval of the sacrament of confession as providing consolation and strengthening faith. But if for some good reason – sudden death, for example – one cannot avail himself of this or other sacraments, he should not despair. See the quotation on this subject in n130 below. Confession three or four times a year will remove anxiety over confession on one's deathbed (LB V 1305F–1306B / ASD V-1 366:636–49).

110 Cornelius' instructions about his funeral can be matched with other records, historical and literary, of the Reformation era. Colet (d 1519) in his will left funeral arrangements to the discretion of his executors and bequeathed nothing for commemorative masses (text of the will in Samuel Knight *Life of Dr John*

Colet [London 1724]; see 465 there). Colet was no Lutheran, to be sure, but he took an interest in Lollardy and was once accused of heresy by the bishop of London; see 'A Pilgrimage' n146. Erasmus, in his first will (1527), forbids an expensive, vulgar (*sordido*) or ostentatious burial, but he wants a burial in accordance with ecclesiastical rites, 'so that nobody could complain' (Allen vi 506:119–20 Appendix 19).

111 By old custom church bells tolled to announce the death of a parishioner and during the funeral procession to the church.

112 See n13 above.

113 See n84 above; on merits, nn12, 58 above.

114 Both the Paris theologians and Alberto Pio found lines 22–7 erroneous and impious (*Declarationes ad censuras Lutetiae vulgatas* LB IX 953B–C; *Apologia adversus rhapsodias Alberti Pii* LB IX 1159D–E). For Erasmus' replies, LB IX 953E–954A, 1159D–1160A.

115 *vivum*, but here with additional meaning of 'true,' 'actual,' 'committed.' On membership in the church see 'Faith' 429:4–8; *De praeparatione ad mortem* LB v 1306D / ASD v-1 368:668–74.

116 *totam fiduciam*, as in 'Faith' 424:1, 429:6–7. To understand and accept this commitment is the sum of what Erasmus terms his 'Christian philosophy' (Allen Ep 1039:228–37 / CWE Ep 1039:245–54).

117 Note 12 above; on briefs 773:30–1 and n80. Entrance to the heavenly Jerusalem 'is not achieved through ceremonies or papal bulls but by a heart cleansed by faith, a good conscience, and deeds of charity which, done for a neighbour, Christ wishes to be imputed to him' (*De puritate tabernaculi* LB v 301B).

118 'Hear my prayer, O Lord, give ear to my supplications: in thy faithfulness answer me, and in thy righteousness. And enter not into judgment with thy servant; for in thy sight shall no man living be justified' (Ps 143:1–2 [142:1–2 Vulg]).

119 The Christian soul, like the Socratic, longs for liberation from the body: 'Bring my soul out of prison' (Ps 142:7 [141:8 Vulg]). See *De praeparatione ad mortem* LB v 1295F / ASD v-1 344:89–98 and the colloquy 'The New Mother' 600:6–21. A mark of the true theologian is his teaching that death should be welcomed by the devout (*Paraclesis* LB vi *3 verso / Holborn 143:10–15).

120 Isaiah 38; also 2 Kings 20

121 John 11:1–45

122 'Happy is that man whom death finds meditating on these writings,' the Scriptures (*Paraclesis* LB vi *4 verso / Holborn 148:28–9).

123 Common in Erasmus' society. See Allen *Age of Erasmus* 192–5; Ruth Kelso *Doctrine for the Lady of the Renaissance* (Urbana 1956) 121–33. Erasmus' views on the subject are Pauline and conventional. Consult 1 Tim 5:3–16 and 1 Cor 7:8–9; for Erasmus *De vidua christiana* (1529), dedicated to Queen Mary of Hungary (LB v 723D–766E / CWE 66 184–257). See also 'The Old Men's Chat' n32.

124 See 'Youth' n76.

125 Passages on the divine mercy are recommended in *De praeparatione ad mortem* LB v 1314B–C / ASD v-1 383:80–384:90. Pictures illustrating that mercy (for example, of Christ and the woman of Samaria in John 4:4–26) may also be helpful.

126 Ps 22 (21 Vulg)

127 Ps 27:1 (26:1 Vulg)

128 Last words of Stephen, the first martyr, as he was stoned to death (Acts 7:59).
These words are recommended by Erasmus as most fit for utterance by the
dying Christian. See *De praeparatione ad mortem* LB V 1317A / ASD V-1 390:242–3.

129 See Ps 4:8 (4:9–10 Vulg) and, on the similitude of sleep and death, Erasmus'
commentary on this psalm in LB V 290D–F; see also 'Early to Rise' n12.

130 'No one can die badly who has lived well' (Allen Ep 1347:95–6 / CWE Ep
1347:106–7).
On Erasmus' death see 'The Return to Basel' 1122–36.

Echo

First printed in the June 1526 edition.

Acoustic conceits such as these echo scenes, in which the final phrase, word, or syllables of a verse are echoed immediately in the reply, were in antiquity and the age of Erasmus a fairly common form of linguistic dexterity. A useful account of them is provided by F.L. Lucas in his note on Webster's *Duchess of Malfi* 5.3.19–51, where the dramatist uses this device effectively (*Complete Works of John Webster* ed F.L. Lucas 4 vols [London 1927] II 195–6). We know Webster was familiar with Erasmus' *Colloquies*; see 'The Funeral' n89. Lucas traces the echo form to fragments of Euripides' lost *Andromeda*, parodied in Aristophanes' *Thesmorphoriazusae* 1056–97; the ancient example best known is Ovid's tale of Narcissus and Echo in *Metamorphoses* 3.358–401. Lucas thinks Erasmus' colloquy 'the most ingenious and amusing' specimen, an opinion not shared by Addison, who treats this form as a variety of 'false wit' and remarks that 'the learned Erasmus, though a man of wit and genius, has composed a dialogue upon this silly kind of device, and made use of an Echo, who seems to have been a very extraordinary linguist' (*Spectator* no 59).

Addison likewise condemns puns, which are evident throughout 'Echo,' as a mode of false wit (*Spectator* no 61). If echoing is involuntary or pathological ('echolalia'), as punning is not, it quickly becomes intolerable. And of course puns as such are not the best or sole test of echo's effectiveness. But if situation, context, and character are treated with artistic power, simple repetition of a word may be enough to move a reader or spectator, as when Iago uses it: 'By heaven, he echoes me' (*Othello* 3.3.110). The use of echo as a literary device has amused or otherwise pleased many readers, if not Addison, and has earned at least a modest footnote in literary history. Technically the echo device was an application of what rhetoricians term metalepsis or transumption and is similar to catachresis, as Erasmus notices in *De copia*. He does not discuss echo directly, but it is related to the other figures just named, as well as to synecdoche (on these *De copia* 1.19, 21–4 CWE 24 336–41). He refers to the figure of Echo in *Moriae encomium* LB IV 480C–481A / ASD IV-3 170:717–27 / CWE 27 137. For other examples of lexical play see his acrostic epigram in CWE 85–6 346–7, 706–7 no 124 / Reedijk *Poems of Erasmus* 330–2 no 111 and two other colloquies, 'The Imposture' and 'Non-Sequiturs.' Echo can be used in prose or verse. The technical names given by ancient grammarians or rhetoricians are no barrier to reading these entertainments.

Sir Philip Sidney wrote an unusual echo poem, an eclogue introduced by a few lines explaining how it is to be understood. For the text see *The Countess of Pembroke's Arcadia (the Old Arcadia)* (1590) ed Jean Robertson (Oxford 1973) 159–62, 446. George Herbert's short echo poem *Heaven* (1633) is often reprinted. All but two of Echo's replies there are monosyllables. In Erasmus' text all replies but one consist of two syllables. Seventeen of the answers are in Greek instead of Latin. In the present translation these are at 797:8, 798:2, 14, 16, 41, 799:2, 4, 8, 10, 15, 23, 32, 37, 39, 41, 800:10, 18.

In compositions of this kind Greek and Latin have advantages denied to uninflected languages such as English. A translation of *Echo* can be accurate and intelligible enough to suggest the sort of thing accomplished by the original, but it is an inadequate substitute for Erasmus' clever feat.

Readers of Erasmus' Latin and Greek text are warned not to take the pronunciation of Greek words used there for Echo's punning replies as indicative of what he regarded as correct for all other purposes. His opinions on that subject are explained in *De pronuntiatione* LB I 913–68 / ASD I-4 1–104 / CWE 26 347–475.

On echo poems consult Elbridge Colby *The Echo-Device in Literature* (New York 1920). John Hollander *The Figure of Echo* (Berkeley, Los Angeles, London 1981) deals mainly with the seventeenth century and after. Joseph Loewenstein *Responsive Readings* (New Haven 1984) is concerned with versions of echo in pastoral, epic, and Jonsonian masque. For a provocative analysis of Erasmus' 'Echo,' see J.-C. Margolin 'Culture, rhétorique et satire dans l'*Echo* d'Erasme' in *Dix conférences sur Erasme* ed Claude Blum (Paris and Geneva 1988) 49–78. This is a model of close reading, intertextuality, and literary history.

YOUTH, ECHO

Youth I'd like a few words with you if there's time.
Echo There's time.
5 **Youth** And if a young chap like me is welcome.
Echo Well, come on.
Youth But can you foretell the future for me, Echo?
Echo Oh, yes.
Youth And you know Greek? What's new?
10 **Echo** News.

Youth Among the arts, which is your favourite study?

Echo Divinity.

Youth So you believe those authors who lead us to good learning should be read?

5   Echo Readily.

Youth Then what shall we call persons who traduce these disciplines by their discourse?

Echo Coarse.

Youth But would that devotees of these studies were zealous after virtue as

10 well!

Echo Well would it be!

Youth The villainy of some individuals nowadays has caused whole classes to be disliked.

Echo Likely enough.

15 Youth And with many men learning passes for a sin.

Echo Asinine men!

Youth Yet they're not commonly thought to be badly off.

Echo Offal!

Youth What do those do who spend their lives in quibbling only?

20 Echo Only spin.

Youth They spin cobwebs,[1] maybe.

Echo May be.

Youth And Penelope's web they weave and reweave.[2]

Echo Weavers they are.

25 Youth What sort of career do you advise me to embark on?

Echo Honest.

Youth Should I marry soon or late?

Echo Late.

Youth What if I have the same luck as those whose wives turn out to be

30 shameless and childless?

Echo Lessons to be learned.

Youth But life with such women would be a fatal mistake.

Echo Take no part in it.

Youth What, is Fortune lord of the soul?

35 Echo Sole lord.

Youth It might be better to prefer a monastic life to wedlock.

Echo Lock yourself in?

Youth What remedy is left when one can't extricate oneself?

Echo Self-pity.

40 Youth But it's wretched for men to live alone.

Echo Lonely they are.

Youth What's your opinion of most modern monks?

Echo Monkeys!

Youth Then what causes some people to think them so wonderful?

Echo Foolish fear.

5   **Youth** What is it that makes an ecclesiastical career so welcome?

Echo Comfort.

Youth A priest has nothing to boot?

Echo Booty.

Youth How do bishops and the good life agree?

10   **Echo** Grievously.

Youth But no men live more at ease.

Echo Easily proved!

Youth What can bring them to understand how great a duty they must fulfil?

15   **Echo** Philosophy.[3]

Youth Then the priesthood is a fine thing if one carries out its responsibilities as one should?

Echo Should be.

Youth If I try my luck at kings' courts, shall I prosper?

20   **Echo** Perdition![4]

Youth But I see not a few who constantly prophesy that their chances of fortune there are wonderful.[5]

Echo Fools![6]

Youth Yet when they go about dressed in silks they seem men of high

25   worth.

Echo Worthless!

Youth You say, then, that (if one looks closely) men are gold without and worthless as figs within?[7]

Echo In fact less than that.

30   **Youth** Then those clad in fine linen, whom we reverence as gods, aren't worth much after all?

Echo Almost nothing.

Youth And of soldiers you'll perhaps think even less?

Echo Less than nothing.

35   **Youth** Astrologers, who tell fortunes from the stars, promise much by their craft.[8]

Echo Crafty!

Youth But grammarians[9] live laborious days.

Echo Dazed, yes.

40   **Youth** I suppose you've little use for hungry, pettifogging lawyers.[10]

Echo Lawyers are jackals.

Youth What shall I be like if I turn workman?
Echo Mannerless.
Youth Then from the arts, good or bad, will nothing else remain?
Echo Maintenance.
5   **Youth** Shall I be happy if I persevere in study?
Echo Decidedly.
Youth But what will make me dutiful?
Echo Fullness of time.
Youth I've already ground away ten years at Cicero.
10   **Echo** O you ass![11]
Youth What makes you call me such?
Echo Such you are.
Youth Perhaps you mean I shouldn't pore over Cicero so much that I neglect all the rest.
15   **Echo** Rest assured I do.
Youth Then you don't approve of a man's tormenting himself all his life long for the sole purpose of becoming a Ciceronian?
Echo An idiot!
Youth What's left for men too old for such work?
20   **Echo** Working the soil.
Youth If I were farther away, you'd be more eloquent, no doubt.
Echo No doubt.
Youth Speech in two syllables I dislike.
Echo Like it or leave it.
25   **Youth** I was the first to begin; nothing will stop you from having the last word, I see.
Echo See that I have it.
Youth So now you think I'm sufficiently instructed to manage life's problems well?
30   **Echo** Well indeed.
Youth Then tell me if you want me to go.
Echo Go!

NOTES

1   Waste time in frivolous or fruitless activities; *Adagia* I iv 47. Another proverbial phrase suggested by this line is equally applicable to quibblers, who in this context are sophists and academic dialecticians: *de lana caprina* 'about goat's wool,' alluding to tiresome arguments over trivialities (*Adagia* I iii 53, from Horace *Epistles* 1.18.15).
2   An enterprise secretly managed in such a way that it will never come to an end. Penelope, the chaste wife of Ulysses, promised to make a decision

about marrying one of her importunate suitors when she finished weaving a winding-sheet for Laertes, her father-in-law. She deceived the suitors by unravelling at night what she had woven by day (*Adagia* I iv 42, from *Odyssey* 2.85–110).

3 Johann Maier of Eck, usually called Eck, an opponent of Erasmus as well as of Luther, suspected that theological errors lurked in the Greek terms used in 'Echo' (Allen Ep 2392:34–41). Particulars of his objections are not known.

4 Literally 'Ate,' goddess of discord and strife, therefore a synonym for 'strife.' See 'A Fish Diet' n79. On the hard life of courtiers see *Moriae encomium* LB IV 480C–481B / ASD IV-3 170:717–38 / CWE 27 136–7.

5 Soothsayers (*qui solent . . . ariolari*); *Adagia* III v 25

6 Λάροι, persons trapped by their own greed. See *Adagia* II ii 33.

7 *ficulnos*; like fig trees, weak and useless. Cf Horace *Satires* 1.8.1 and *Adagia* I vii 85.

8 For Erasmus' opinions of them see 'The Soldier and the Carthusian' n14.

9 Wonderfully described in *Moriae encomium* LB IV 457A–458B / ASD IV-3 138:238–140:418 / CWE 27 122–3.

10 *legulei homines. Moriae encomium* LB IV 435A / ASD IV-3 42:749 / CWE 27 107, and see Cicero *De oratore* 1.55.236; Quintilian 12.3.11.

11 These two lines are quoted by Bacon in his *Advancement of Learning* 1.4.2 (*Works* ed James Spedding, R.L. Ellis, and D.D. Heath, 7 vols [London 1857–9] VI 119–20). The gibes in the lines that follow at pedantic imitators of Ciceronian style foreshadow a quarrel that agitated the world of learning for many years and had serious consequences in sixteenth- and seventeenth-century literary criticism. Erasmus made a characteristic and important contribution to this controversy by his satirical *Ciceronianus* (1528) LB I 973A–1016C / ASD I-2 583–710. See also the introduction to 'Penny-Pinching' 979–82. For a translation of *Ciceronianus* see CWE 28.

A FEAST OF MANY COURSES

Πολυδαιτία, *Dispar convivium*

First printed in the 1527 edition. Apparently *Dispar convivium* 'unequal feast' was added to suggest that variety of guests and dishes, if carefully chosen, is essential to a good feast. This alternative title was omitted in some later editions.

The specific recommendations of Apicius for managing a dinner party, and the general soundness of his advice, are confirmed by scenes in other colloquies and in many anecdotes or observations scattered throughout the pages of Erasmus' various writings. In 'A Lesson in Manners,' 'The Profane Feast,' 'The Godly Feast,' and 'The Poetic Feast,' we hear or see what makes a dinner enjoyable; in 'Inns' and 'Penny-Pinching' entertainment of a different quality is described. Here and there in Erasmus' letters too we get a glimpse of his preferences in food and drink and his ways of dealing with bores and boors, of welcoming amenities and avoiding discomforts. He grumbled about large dinners and tiresome after-dinner conversation but, despite incessant work and delicate health, enjoyed temperate conviviality with old friends, and did not, when God sent a cheerful hour, refrain.

Since prevalent notions of food and drink and entertainment – if such matters are taken seriously – furnish clues to standards of taste and decorum in a society, we can learn something about sixteenth-century life and manners even from such brief dialogues as this one. In the main, Apicius' admonitions convey familiar wisdom, dictated by custom and common sense and still useful. The sixteenth century, like our own, had plenty of books on manners and domestic economy for those who wanted them. And in this as in so many other aspects of civilized life, educated men were aware, or were expected to be aware, not merely of local or regional customs but of precepts bearing the stamp of classical authority. It is no surprise then that injunctions in these and other pages of Erasmus resemble those in Athenaeus' *Deipnosophistae*, Gellius' *Noctes Atticae*, and the *Quaestiones convivales* in Plutarch's *Moralia*. The standard sixteenth-century repository of lore about ancient dining is J.G. Stuck's *Antiquitatum convivialium libri tres* (Zürich 1582), in which evidence from 650 writers is collected.

SPUDUS, APICIUS[1]

Spudus Ho there, Apicius! Ho!
Apicius I don't hear you.

Spudus Ho there, Apicius, I say!

Apicius Who's this troublesome interrupter?

Spudus I want you – something important.

Apicius But I'm in a hurry to something important.

5 **Spudus** What?

Apicius Dinner.

Spudus The very subject I wanted to take up with you.

Apicius Too busy now to bother with lawyers, lest I lose time.[2]

Spudus You won't lose anything. I'll walk along with you to wherever
10 you're hurrying.

Apicius Well, tell me, but make it brief.

Spudus I'm hard at work planning a dinner party at which I want to please all the guests and displease none. Since you're a master of this art, I appeal to you as to an oracle.

15 **Apicius** Hear my answer – and in accordance with ancient custom it's in verse:

> If you daren't displease one,
> Then it's best to have none.

20

Spudus But this is a particularly important dinner; I must have many guests.

Apicius The more you invite, the more you must displease.[3] What play was ever so well written or acted that it pleased the entire audience?

25 **Spudus** But come on, Apicius, you favourite of Comus,[4] help me with your advice; I'll look upon you hereafter as godlike.

Apicius Then the first piece of advice is this: don't attempt the impossible.

Spudus What's that?

Apicius To be a host who pleases everyone. There's such a variety of tastes.

30 **Spudus** But I want to displease as few as possible at any rate.

Apicius Invite few.

Spudus I can't do that.

Apicius Then invite equals who have similar tastes.

Spudus I'm not free even to do that. I can't avoid inviting a large number,
35 people of different sorts, and in fact those who don't even speak the same language or come from the same country.

Apicius Well, what you describe is really not a collation but a commotion, where you're likely to have the kind of farce the Hebrews say occurred in the building of Babel: when someone asks for a cold dish, somebody else
40 hands him a hot one.

Spudus Come to my rescue, I beg you. You'll find me grateful, and I won't forget it.

Apicius All right, since you've no choice I'll give you some good advice in this difficulty. The gaiety of a dinner party depends to no small degree on where each person sits.[5]

Spudus Very true.

5 **Apicius** To solve this problem, let the seating be decided by lot.

Spudus Good advice.

Apicius Next, don't let the dishes move so slowly from the head to the foot of the table that they resemble the letter S or a snake, or go back and forth as the myrtle crown used to be exchanged at ancient feasts.[6]

10 **Spudus** What should be done, then?

Apicius Set a group of three dishes in front of each quartet of guests, with a fourth dish in the middle, as boys lay a fourth nut on top of three others.[7] Have different foods in each dish, so that each person may choose what he likes.

Spudus Very good. But how often shall I change dishes?

15 **Apicius** How many parts has a formal speech?

Spudus Five, if I'm not mistaken.[8]

Apicius How many acts to a play?

Spudus I've read in Horace that it should be no longer than five acts.[9]

Apicius Change dishes that often, so that you have something with a sauce

20 for prologue and a conclusion or epilogue of various desserts.[10]

Spudus What order of dishes do you recommend?

Apicius The same order Pyrrhus used in battle.[11]

Spudus What do you mean?

Apicius As in a speech, so at a dinner, the prologue should not be elaborate.

25 Furthermore the epilogue should be approved for its variety rather than lavishness. Accordingly, Pyrrhus' system is to be followed in the three courses: by having something choice at each end and the more commonplace fare in the centre. By this means you won't seem stingy and won't embarrass your guests with a disgusting abundance.

30 **Spudus** Good enough, so far as food is concerned. You've still to instruct me about the drinking.[12]

Apicius Don't *you* serve a cup to a single one but leave that to the servants, so that when they're asked for wine they'll learn what kind each guest prefers and when he beckons will serve him promptly what he likes. This

35 method has a double advantage: the drinking is more moderate as well as more pleasant, not only because one is freshly supplied at frequent intervals but also because nobody drinks unless thirsty.

Spudus Excellent advice. But how is it to be arranged that they all have a good time?

40 **Apicius** That depends partly on you.

Spudus How so, pray?

Apicius You remember the tag about 'A cheerful countenance is the best welcome.'[13]

Spudus What's the point?

Apicius That you should receive your guests cordially and greet them with
5   a smile, suiting your speech to each one's age, humour, and habits.

Spudus I'll come closer, in order that you may tell me better.

Apicius You know their language?

Spudus Nearly all.

Apicius To talk to every one in his own tongue from time to time and make
10   the dinner merry with entertaining stories, introduce a variety of subjects everyone likes to recall and no one hears with displeasure.[14]

Spudus What kinds of subjects?

Apicius There are peculiarities of temperament you'll observe better yourself. I'll generalize on some. Old men are fond of recalling what most
15   people have forgotten. They praise the good old days when they were in their prime. To wives it's sweet to revive memories of the time when they had suitors. Sailors, who have visited strange and distant parts of the world, talk readily about things which, because nobody has seen them, everybody marvels at. Also, as the proverb says, recollection of dangers past is pleasant
20   if they're such as are not joined with vice – if for example they're about war, travel, and shipwreck.[15] Last of all, everybody enjoys conversation about his own specialty and about what he's expert at.

     These are generalities. I can't describe idiosyncrasies one by one but – for example – one man is especially eager for praise, another wishes to
25   be thought learned, another is happy if thought rich. This man is somewhat garrulous, that laconic; some you'll find irritable, others genial. There are some who hate to appear old even though they are old, and others who want to be regarded as older than they are, posing in order to be admired for carrying their years so well. There are women who are vain of their figures,
30   others who are affected. When these dispositions are recognized, it's not hard to carry on conversations acceptable to anyone and to avoid topics that spread gloom.

Spudus Truly you're expert in the art of being a host.

Apicius Pooh! If I had spent as much time and labour on either branch of
35   the law, on medicine and theology, as I have on this art, I'd have won LLD, MD, and DD degrees and been at the head of my profession long ago.

Spudus I believe it.

Apicius But look here: to avoid mistakes, take care that the talk isn't spun out too long or doesn't lead to drunkenness. As nothing is more enjoyable
40   than wine if taken in moderation, on the other hand nothing is more troublesome if you drink too much. It's the same with talk.

Spudus You're right, but what remedy can you offer for this inconvenience?

Apicius When you notice that non-alcoholic intoxication[16] begins to appear, take the opportunity to interrupt the talk and introduce a different topic. No

5   need, I suppose, to remind you not to let an old wound be reopened at a dinner party, despite Plato's opinion that feasts are the occasion for curing certain faults, that wine banishes sorrow and wipes out the remembrance of a wrong.[17] But you should be warned not to greet your guests too often, though I do approve of your walking around from time to time and speaking

10   cordially now to these, now to those; a good host should play an active role. But nothing is more boorish than to call attention to what kind of food you have, how it's cooked, how much it cost.[18] The same goes for the wine. In fact you ought to apologize modestly for what is served. However, overemphatic disparagement of the fare is a form of boasting. Enough to say two or at most

15   three times, 'I hope you will be kind! If the fare's not grand, at least your welcome's very grand.' Season the talk with jokes now and then, but avoid ones that might offend. And it will help if you say a few words to a person in his own tongue from time to time. – I should have said at the start what has just come into my mind.

20   **Spudus** What?

Apicius If you don't like to choose places by lot, take the trouble to choose from all those present three persons who are naturally good-humoured and talkative. Put one at the head of the table, another at the foot, the third in the middle, to dispel the silence and moroseness of others. But if you notice that

25   the banquet's too glum with silence or unruly with shouting or likely to end in quarrels –

Spudus This often happens to me. What should I do then?

Apicius Try a remedy I've found very helpful.

Spudus I'm waiting to hear it.

30   **Apicius** Bring in a pair of mimes or buffoons to put on some comic pantomime.

Spudus Why no dialogue?

Apicius To afford everyone equal pleasure, they should say nothing or else speak in a tongue equally unknown to all. The language of gesture will be

35   intelligible to all alike.

Spudus I'm not clear about the kind of act you mean.

Apicius There are countless ones: for example a woman arguing with her husband over who's boss, or something similar from everyday life. The more ridiculous the posturing, the more fun it will be for everyone. The mimes

40   should be only partial fools; otherwise those who are complete simpletons sometimes blurt out things that hurt people's feelings.[19]

Spudus I beg you always to be as kind a Comus as you've been in giving me this good advice.

Apicius I'll add a conclusion or rather repeat what I said at the beginning: in this as in all of life, don't try too hard to please everybody. Then you may
5   sooner please them all. The best rule of life is: 'Nothing to excess.'[20]

NOTES

1 The name Apicius, the Roman expert on cookery, is still synonymous with 'gourmet.' See 'The Profane Feast' n5. Spudus ('earnest,' 'serious') is also the name of a speaker in 'The Epicurean' (it is there spelled 'Spudaeus').

2 The Latin here plays with several meanings of *actus* and *ago*. When Apicius speaks of losing time (*ne actum agam*) he uses legal jargon signifying that he cannot reopen a case already decided. See *Adagia* I iv 70.

3 The proper number of guests was three to nine, but exceptions to the rule were common. See 'The Profane Feast' n102. Avoid having too many guests (Plutarch *Moralia* 615D *Quaestiones convivales* 1.2). Sometimes unexpected and uninvited guests, 'shadows,' were brought along by invited ones; see 'Additional *formulae*' n24.

4 God of revels, as in *Moriae encomium* LB IV 411A / ASD IV-3 78:133 / CWE 27 89

5 On this question see Plutarch *Moralia* 615C–619A *Quaestiones convivales* 1.2.

6 The host must see to it that food and wine are placed and served properly. If some guests cannot sing a song when the lute is passed around, they must do something else instead, the best they can under the circumstances; they must, as a proverb says, 'sing to the myrtle' or laurel garland if not to the lute. For *canere ad myrtum* see *Adagia* II vi 21 and Plutarch *Moralia* 615B; *Questiones convivales* cf Allen Ep 363:1.

7 See 'Hunting' n6.

8 As the art and practice of classical rhetoric has five main parts governing eloquence in discourse (*inventio, dispositio, elocutio, memoria, actio*), so a speech or formal argument has five or six ways of dividing and arranging relevant material (*exordium, narratio, divisio, confirmatio* and *refutatio, peroratio*). Of theory and practice Quintilian and Cicero were, for Erasmus, the great masters.

9 *Ars poetica* 189–90

10 The number of courses and the variety of desserts vary in the *convivia* in the *Colloquies*. In all of them, conversation is more important than food; cf 'Additional *formulae*' 128:27–129:7 and 'The Profane Feast' 146:26–7. Linguistic variation no doubt influenced the menu at 'The Profane Feast'; guests are served a variety of roasts as a main course (capon, beef, mutton, venison, hare, rabbits, goose, partridges, pigeons – and pork is mentioned), *paté de fois gras*, and fruit and chestnuts for dessert (135:22–3, 139:35–143:15, 147:35–41). 'The Godly Feast' comes closest to the five-part menu recommended here: after an 'ovation' of eggs and greens, which is followed by a boiled capon (183:27, 186:11–14, 186:41–187:3), the host says that a roast, dessert, and 'the catastrophe' will follow (187:3–4); there are in fact several roasts (189:13–14). Dessert is probably fruit (198:3–5, 202:32–3), and the 'catastrophe' is not described. 'The

Poetic Feast' opens with melons, banter about beet greens substituted for lettuce, and figs (391:12–27, 393:4–7); next there are eggs , sliced cucumber with a sauce, a hen from the coop, and fruit for dessert (396:35–6, 397:7, 398:23–6, 404:25–6). Guests at 'The Fabulous Feast' and 'The Sober Feast' dine on stories; no food is mentioned at the first, and nothing is offered at the second but lettuce (without salt, vinegar, and oil) and water from the well (926:8–9).

11 Explained in Apicius' next comment. Pyrrhus, king of Epirus (d 272BC), was a masterly tactician and was remembered for defining a 'Pyrrhic victory' as one so costly as to be very nearly ruinous. Cf *Apophthegmata* LB IV 241A–B. Plutarch's *Lives* has an account of Pyrrhus.

12 If there is plenty of wine, give each guest as much as he wants; if not, give an equal portion to everyone (Plutarch *Moralia* 208B–C *Apophthegmata Laconica*). Cf 'The Fabulous Feast' 575:4–23.

13 Ovid *Metamorphoses* 8.677–8

14 Gellius 13.11.3–5, derived from Varro, gives what Erasmus considered the correct doctrine about table talk: that it must be interesting, agreeable, and shared by all.

15 *Adagia* II iii 43; cf 'The Shipwreck' n2.

16 Greek in the original, from Plutarch *Moralia* 716A *Quaestiones convivales*; used by Erasmus in *Adagia* I iii 3

17 The passage Erasmus seems to have in mind is *Laws* 671C–673D, where it is argued that if properly regulated – and not otherwise – conviviality will foster friendship and not breed quarrels; and therefore men will be the better for using wine. So Ecclus (Sirach) 31:30–2.

18 For an example see Horace *Satires* 2.8.

19 Erasmus sometimes found the noise and chatter of entertainers intolerable. See the protest in 'Inns' 374:33–41.

20 *Adagia* I vi 96; often found in Erasmus

THINGS AND NAMES

De rebus ac vocabulis

First printed in the 1527 edition.

'Things and names' is a deceptively simple phrase. A reader encounters a slight variant of it (*res et verba*) in the opening lines of *De ratione studii*, where he is informed that things and words – objects of thought or experience and language – comprise the whole of knowledge (CWE 24 666). Upon examination, however, the phrase soon begins to seem not simple but complex; and in fact it was a technical phrase with which learned men found many difficulties. Consideration of it led them to the mysteries of universals, of the reality of genera and species – topics pondered by philosophers since Plato, and since Abelard requiring discussion by logicians and metaphysicians in universities.

Erasmus, more moralist than metaphysician, employs 'things and names' to fix attention on whether ethical terms and their contraries (truth and lie, honesty and dishonesty, and so on) when used in daily life as criteria of behaviour have inherent, intrinsic meanings. Is there an *essential* bond between word and thing, or are the ordinary and usual connections merely conventions of linguistic and social custom? The answer makes a difference, for personal and public relationships depend in large measure on agreement over words.

This brief colloquy enforces some contrasts between appearance and reality, shadow and substance. As usual in these dialogues, Erasmus makes his points informally and agreeably, with illustrations from familiar situations – the only sensible method of presenting philosophy to young readers, as he says elsewhere ('The Usefulness of the *Colloquies*' 1097:10–1098:16). Some of the examples of trickery related here are surely taken from Erasmus' own experiences with double-dealers, especially with Franz Birckmann, whom he had attacked earlier in 'The Liar and the Man of Honour.' The sardonic passage on a false knight in the final lines of 'Things and Names' furnished material for a colloquy of 1529 which is aimed at another of the author's enemies, Heinrich Eppendorf, 'The Knight without a Horse.' It is more than coincidence that the men who tried, without much success, to arbitrate the quarrel between Erasmus and Eppendorf were Beatus Rhenanus and Bonifacius Amerbach, whose names are borne by the speakers in this colloquy.

Certain of the larger issues of Erasmus' subject are illuminated by J.-C. Margolin 'Erasme et la vérité' in his *Recherches érasmiennes* (Geneva 1969) 45–69 and by J. Chomarat *Grammaire et rhétorique* 86–90, 923–30, 1107–28.

A Spanish translation appeared in 1528 and was reprinted in a collection in 1530 (Bataillon *Érasme et l'Espagne* xxix nos 262, 268); an Italian one by Pietro Lauro in 1545 and 1549 (see BE 2nd series *Colloquia* III 271); and an English one at Canterbury c 1550 by Edmund Becke, who published with it his translation of *Cyclops* (Devereux 4.2.1; reprinted by De Vocht *Earliest English Translations* 31–51 and by Spurgeon 223–44).

BEATUS, BONIFACE[1]

Beatus Greetings to Boniface.

Boniface Greetings and more greetings to Beatus. But I wish we were each
5   what we're called – you rich and I handsome.[2]

Beatus So you think it's unimportant to have a splendid name?

Boniface Very unimportant indeed unless the substance be added.

Beatus But many mortals feel otherwise.

Boniface They may be mortals, but I don't think they're men.

10   **Beatus** Yes, they're men, my good friend – unless you suppose camels and
asses even now walk about in human form.

Boniface I'd sooner believe this than that those who value the name more
than the actual thing are men.

Beatus In certain respects most men prefer things to names, I grant; in many
15   they don't.

Boniface I don't quite follow.

Beatus But we ourselves furnish examples. You're called Boniface, and you
have what you're called; but if you were to be deprived of one or the other,
would you prefer to have an ugly face or be named Cornelius instead of
20   Boniface?

Boniface Certainly I'd rather be called Thersites[3] than have an awful face.
Whether I've a handsome one, I don't know.

Beatus Likewise if I were rich and had to give up either the thing or the
name, I'd rather be called Irus[4] than lose my wealth.

25   **Boniface** You're right; I agree.

Beatus It will turn out the same, I think, with those who have good health
or are endowed with other physical advantages.

Boniface Probably.

Beatus But how many we see who prefer the reputation of a learned and
30   godly man to being learned and godly!

Boniface I know a great many of that sort.

Beatus In our society, isn't reputation more important than reality?

Boniface So it seems.

Beatus Now if we had a logician at hand, to give us a clear definition of a king, a bishop, a magistrate, and a philosopher, perhaps we should find here too men who prefer reputation to reality.

Boniface So we should, if a king is one who by law and justice looks out
5   for the welfare of his people, not of himself;[5] if a bishop is one who devotes himself entirely to watching over his master's flock;[6] if a magistrate is one who wholeheartedly serves the public good;[7] and if a philosopher is one who, disregarding fortune's gifts, strives only to attain a good conscience.[8]

Beatus You see here how many examples of this kind I could gather.

10 **Boniface** Very many, clearly.

Beatus Will you deny all these are men?

Boniface I fear we ourselves would sooner lose the name of man.

Beatus But if man is a rational animal, how extremely unreasonable it is that in physical advantages (a more accurate name than 'goods') and in external
15 things granted and snatched away by the whim of fortune, we should prefer the substance to the name; in the true goods of the mind, should make more of the name than of the reality.[9]

Boniface A ridiculous choice, by Hercules, if you consider it.

Beatus But the same reasoning applies to the opposite circumstances.

20 **Boniface** Go on; I'm listening.

Beatus We ought to judge the names of things to be avoided in the same way we judged names of things to be sought.

Boniface Apparently.

Beatus For a man ought to shrink more from being a tyrant than from the
25 name of tyrant; and if a wicked bishop is, as the Gospel teaches, a thief and a robber,[10] we ought to hate not so much these names as the fact itself.

Boniface I'm with you.

Beatus Consider other cases in the same fashion.

Boniface I understand exactly.

30 **Beatus** Don't all men loathe the name of fool?

Boniface Absolutely.

Beatus Wouldn't one be a fool if he fished with a golden hook,[11] preferred glass to jewels, loved horses more than wife and children?

Boniface He'd be sillier than a Coroebus.[12]

35 **Beatus** Aren't men fools who rush off and enlist in the army in the hope of booty – not very much booty at that – at risk to body and soul?[13] Who toil to amass wealth when they have a soul in need of every good? Who wear fancy clothes and live in fine houses when their souls lie sloven and neglected? Who watch their physical health anxiously and ignore a spirit suffering from
40 so many fatal maladies? Who, finally, with the fleeting pleasures of this life earn everlasting torments?

Boniface Reason itself compels us to confess they're more than fools.

Beatus And though you see these fools everywhere, you'd find scarcely any who would put up with the *name* of fool, yet they don't object so much to *being* fools.

5 **Boniface** That's true.

Beatus Come now: you know how everyone resents the names of liar and thief.

Boniface Most hateful words, and rightly so.

Beatus Granted. But though seducing another man's wife is worse than
10 theft, still some men even take pride in the name of adulterer.[14] Call them thief and out come their swords in an instant.

Boniface There are many of that kind.

Beatus So, though many debauch themselves with whores and drink, freely and publicly, they resent the name of rake.

15 **Boniface** Yes, they boast of the thing but are horrified if it's called by its right name.

Beatus But hardly any name is more intolerable to our ears than that of liar.

Boniface I know of men who have avenged this taunt with bloodshed.

Beatus But would they were equally horrified by the thing itself! Have you
20 never had the experience of finding that someone who had promised to repay a loan by a certain day failed to keep his bargain?

Boniface Often, even when he'd sworn he'd pay – not once but over and over.

Beatus Unable to pay, perhaps.

25 **Boniface** Oh, they were able, all right, but they thought it more to their advantage not to repay the debt.

Beatus Isn't that lying?[15]

Boniface Quite obviously.

Beatus Would you dare reproach a 'creditor'[16] of that sort with 'Why do
30 you lie to me so often?'

Boniface Not unless I were ready for a fight.

Beatus Don't stonecutters, carpenters, goldsmiths, and clothiers make daily commitments of the same sort, promising something by a certain day but not keeping their word even if the matter's important to you?

35 **Boniface** They have an astonishing cheek. Add to these the lawyers with their promises of getting something done.

Beatus You can add six hundred[17] names, yet none of these persons will stand for 'liar.'

Boniface The world abounds with liars of this kind.

40 **Beatus** Likewise no one tolerates the name of thief, though they don't all shrink equally from theft.

Boniface I'm waiting for you to say it more clearly.

Beatus What's the difference between one who steals your money from a desk and one who denies something deposited with him?

Boniface None, except that one who robs the person who trusted him is the more villainous.

Beatus But how few are there who restore what's entrusted to them. Or if they do, they don't restore it intact.

Boniface Very few, I dare say.

Beatus Yet no one would endure the word 'thief,' though they don't mind the deed.

Boniface True enough.

Beatus Now consider what usually happens in administering the property of minors and in wills and legacies: how much sticks to the fingers of the executors?

Boniface Often the whole of it.

Beatus They love theft; the word they detest.

Boniface Of course.

Beatus The conduct of those who handle public funds, who debase the coinage, who now by inflating the value of money, now by deflating it, cause private citizens to lose their property, we are perhaps not free to discuss; of what we experience every day we may speak. A man who borrows money or goes into debt with no intention of ever repaying if he can help it – how little does he differ from a thief!

Boniface He's more careful, you might say, but he's no better.

Beatus Yet numerous as these are everywhere, still not one of them tolerates the name of thief.[18]

Boniface Their conscience is known only to God. Hence they're commonly said by men to be 'overdrawn,' not thieves.

Beatus It makes very little difference what they're called by men if they're thieves in God's sight. Surely each one knows his own conscience. And what about the man who, even though in debt, shamelessly squanders whatever money comes his way; who after going bankrupt in one city fools his creditors and flees to another, looking for strangers he can cheat – and does this repeatedly? Doesn't he proclaim clearly enough what sort of conscience he has?

Boniface Enough and to spare. Nevertheless they're used to covering up their doings with a smokescreen.

Beatus How?

Boniface Owing a lot of money to people puts them in the same class, they say, as leading citizens and even kings.[19] Therefore men endowed with this talent commonly try to pass themselves off as nobility.

Beatus For what purpose?

Boniface It's wonderful how much people will let a knight get away with.[20]

Beatus By what right? What laws?

Boniface The same as those by which governors of maritime districts claim
5 for themselves whatever is cast up by a shipwreck, even if the owner
survives; by which others want to keep as their own whatever they seize
from a thief or a pirate.

Beatus Thieves themselves could make laws of that sort!

Boniface Would, too, if they could enforce them. And they'd have an excuse
10 if they declared war before thieving.

Beatus Who granted this right to a cavalier rather than an infantryman?

Boniface Favour of the military. How to plunder the enemy is included in
their training for war.[21]

Beatus That's how Pyrrhus trained his soldiers for war, I believe.

15 **Boniface** No, it was the Lacedaemonians.[22]

Beatus Damn their training. But where does the title of so great a privilege
come from?

Boniface Some inherit it from ancestors; others buy it; some simply
appropriate it.

20 **Beatus** May anybody appropriate it?

Boniface If his behaviour corresponds.

Beatus What sort of behaviour is that?

Boniface If he never does a good deed, if he dresses like a dandy, wears
rings on his fingers, whores bravely, dices constantly, plays cards,[23] spends
25 his life in drinking and having a good time, never speaks of anything
commonplace but chatters solely of forts, battles, and wars, plays Thraso[24]
in everything. These fellows assume the right to declare war on anyone they
please, even if they don't own enough land to stand on.

Beatus Knights fit for a hobbyhorse, you mean. But Gelderland[25] has more
30 than a few such knights.

NOTES

1 The names of two of Erasmus' closest friends, Beatus Rhenanus and Bonifacius
Amerbach. Beatus Rhenanus (1485–1547) was associated with Erasmus from
1514, when Erasmus moved to Basel, by their common interests as scholars
and by Beatus' work as an editor and corrector for Johann Froben, Erasmus'
publisher. Beatus is connected too with the *Colloquia*, for he wrote the preface to
the first (unauthorized) edition, issued in November 1518. Later he performed
many other services for Erasmus, finally writing the earliest printed memoirs
of him; see Allen I 52–71. After 1526 he lived mainly in Sélestat but kept in

touch with the Froben press and with Erasmus. He was an important and prolific scholar.

Bonifacius Amerbach (1496–1562) was the youngest son of Johann Amerbach, Basel printer and publisher in the generation just preceding the arrival of Erasmus. Bonifacius, lawyer as well as scholar, was Erasmus' legal adviser and the principal executor of his will. He was deeply involved in religious, civic, and academic affairs in Basel. *Erasmi epistolae* contains more correspondence with him than with anyone else. His own family's correspondence, *Die Amerbachkorrespondenz* ed A. Hartmann and B.R. Jenny (Basel 1942–   ), is, like *Erasmi epistolae*, a treasury for students of the period, and the excellence of the editing matches that of Allen. On Bonifacius Amerbach see the essay in Myron Gilmore *Humanists and Jurists: Six Studies in the Renaissance* (Cambridge, Mass 1963) 146–77.

2 Beatus means 'blessed,' 'fortunate,' 'prosperous.' Bonifacius means 'handsome,' 'of a fair countenance.'

3 See *Adagia* IV iii 80 and 'Courtship' n37.

4 A surly beggar to whom the disguised Ulysses gave a beating after his return to Ithaca. See *Odyssey* 18:1–111. The name was proverbial for a beggar; *Adagia* I vi 76. A speaker in 'Beggar Talk' is named Irides 'son of Irus.'

5 A good king obeys the laws of his own free will. He is to the state what soul is to body ('The Fabulous Feast' 579:4–5 and n40). He is not above the law, and he must be careful 'not to be taken in by the false application of fine words ... the source from which practically all the world's evils arise' (*Institutio principis christiani* 3 LB IV 592D / ASD IV-1 188:691–2 / Born 212 / CWE 27 258–9). 'The Godly Feast' 184:4–186:35 is pertinent to this theme, as are 'Charon' and *Querela pacis*.

6 The emphatic word here is 'entirely.' On many occasions Erasmus took the episcopate to task for neglect of their primary duty, inherited from the primitive church, of instructing Christian people by preaching and teaching. Since they are in the very centre of spiritual authority, this negligence is the more lamentable. Too many bishops are now busy administrators. They are too worldly, too wealthy, too close to courts and kings, and therefore too often absent from their sees to be effective spiritual leaders. St John Chrysostom thought most bishops would not be saved (*In Acta apostolorum homiliae* 3 PG 60 39 / NPNF 1st series XI 23). This question appears from time to time in later centuries. Salimbene, the Franciscan chronicler (d 1288), tells of a prior of Clairvaux who was chosen bishop of Tournai but despite all efforts of the pope and of St Bernard refused the office. After his death he revealed to a monk in a vision that the Holy Trinity informed him that had he become a bishop he would have been among the damned (*Monumenta Germaniae Historica, Scriptores* XXXII 142–3; translation in G.G. Coulton *From St Francis to Dante* [rev ed London 1907; repr Philadelphia 1972] 95). Without troubling himself about such questions, Erasmus thought it a scandal, as other reformers did, for bishops to dodge their duty of preaching. See *Ecclesiastes* LB V 801C–818D and for other relevant texts 'A Fish Diet' nn169, 254, 255.

7 He must be mature (between fifty and seventy, Plato says in *Laws* 6.755), strict, impartial, and incorruptible. For a summary of his qualities and functions see *Institutio principis christiani* 7 (LB IV 601C–602F / ASD IV-1 204–6 / Born 235–7 / CWE 27 273–5).

8 By this short description a philosopher would seem to be a moderate Academic or Stoic, but what Erasmus more likely intends is a thoughtful Christian gentleman, sufficiently educated but not pedantic; a dutiful, pious, exemplary citizen. We meet his like in 'The Godly Feast.' On Erasmus' objections to the abstractness and terminology of formal philosophy, the kind prevalent in the universities, see 'The Godly Feast' n190. He was acquainted with that philosophy, to be sure, but unsympathetic and impatient with it. Moral wisdom, not metaphysics, came first with him. See Allen Ep 2533:109–15.

9 On the calculus of goods see 'The Epicurean.'

10 John 10:1

11 Foolish, because doing so risked something precious for the sake of a minor gain; *Adagia* II ii 60. But 'to fish with a golden hook' in Rome had another meaning: that it is foolish to go there seeking for a benefice unless one is well supplied with money. See 'In Pursuit of Benefices' 47:29–31 and n13.

12 Who tried to number the waves of the sea although he could count only to five; *Adagia* II ix 64

13 So 'Military Affairs'; 'The Soldier and the Carthusian' 333:18–24

14 In *Adagia* IV vi 25 Erasmus contrasts the severity of punishments for adultery in ancient societies with the comparative but disgraceful tolerance of this sin by Christians. He even writes ironically that 'nowadays to violate a nun is *pietas*' (LB II 1082A).

15 Like Montaigne, Erasmus could swear his soul shrank from a lie, and like Montaigne's essay 'Liars,' his colloquies show his deep abhorrence of lying – a part of his nature, he says ('Sympathy' 1045:33–1046:7; see 'The Liar and the Man of Honour,' in which a master of the art of lying demonstrates how easy it is). Other expressions or intimations of this interest in the 'art' occur in many colloquies; and see *Lingua* also. Nevertheless he is well aware, as are all moralists and casuists, of the innumerable distinctions made by philosophers, dialecticians, orators, and poets, and practised if not analysed by men of the world. Erasmus proposes distinctions of veracity and mendacity in *Apologia adversus rhapsodias Alberti Pii* (LB IX 1194A–1195D), but the analysis there is more laboured than eloquent. He is more effective when, in dialogue, he shows virtue and vice, truth and lies, in action.

16 Erasmus' word is *creditorem*, the opposite of what we might have expected, since Beatus refers to a debtor. In medieval Latin *creditor* was in some contexts equivalent to medieval French *créancier*, *débiteur*; it denoted one who stood surety for a debt. The conjuncture between *creditor* and *debtor* in the meaning of these lines is so close that 'creditor' is printed thus to indicate this nuance. See C. DuCange *Glossarium ad scriptores mediae et infimae Latinitatis* 6 vols (Paris 1733–6) sv *creditor*; F.E. Godefroy *Dictionnaire de l'ancienne langue française* 10 vols (Paris 1881–1902) II sv *créancier*, and a quotation from 1523 in the *Oxford English Dictionary* sv 'creditor' 3.

17 A great many; see 'The Funeral' n76.

18 Pseudocheus explains his 'professional skill' in such transactions in 'The Liar and the Man of Honour.'

19 In a money economy, and with wars or the likelihood of wars a constant peril, princes required ever more financing to pay troops, and after the war ended to repay loans. A strict distinction between a nation's 'public debt' and a

sovereign's personal debts did not exist. Some rulers were more fortunate or more penurious than others; Henry VII of England, for instance, left a large fortune to his successor. Francis I, Maximilian I, and Charles V were plagued by debts. Kings could and did borrow vast sums in the money markets of Genoa, Antwerp, and elsewhere but had to pay for loans by additional taxes upon their subjects, forced loans by their nobles, and even alienation of crown lands or other economic concessions to the lenders. Of the bankers the greatest was the Fugger house of Augsburg, said to be the wealthiest family in Europe. More than once it was the means, probably the sole means, of keeping Charles V financially alive. If Francis I, after his defeat and capture at Pavia in February 1525, agreed to pay two million crowns as part of his ransom, and if his conqueror at Pavia, Charles V, needed six hundred thousand ducats to pay his mercenaries in Italy after that campaign (Francis Hackett *Francis the First* [New York 1937] 305, 309), Erasmus' 'even kings' is anything but exaggeration. Princes of the church too sometimes had to resort to bankers to pay annates or other 'costs of doing business' with the papacy.

20 Cf 'The Knight without a Horse' 885:20–1, 887:38. The derogatory description in lines 23–8 below is expanded in that colloquy.

21 Cf 'The Funeral' n46 on military training as a school for plundering.

22 So Xenophon *Instituta Laconica* 2.7–9 and *Anabasis* 4.6.14–15; Plato *Laws* 1.633B; and see *Apophthegmata* LB IV 144D–F.

23 Commonly associated with gamblers. On the cards themselves see an interesting account by Laura A. Smoller 'Playing Cards and Popular Culture in Sixteenth-Century Nuremburg' *The Sixteenth Century Journal* 17 no 2 (1986) 183–214.

24 The braggart soldier in Terence *Eunuchus*

25 Province in east and central Netherlands where Birckmann, another person Erasmus detested, came from. See the introduction to 'The Liar and the Man of Honour' and CEBR.

CHARON

Charon

First published as one of the *Colloquia* in the March 1529 edition. The last edition of the *Colloquia* published by Johann Froben came out in 1527. After his death in the autumn of that year the business was carried on by his son Hieronymus and Johann Herwagen, whom his widow married; in 1529 they were joined by her son-in-law, Nicolaus Episcopius. Herwagen left the firm in 1530.

'Charon' had an unusual history, for it was issued six years before appearing in the *Colloquia*. It was printed in the same volume with the *Catalogus omnium Erasmi Roterodami lucubrationum* prepared by Erasmus and issued by Froben in April 1523. The *Catalogus* was then enlarged and corrected and published in September 1524. The *Catalogus* is the first text (a1–c3) in that April 1523 volume (the enlarged text of September 1524 is now in CWE 9 291–364 as Ep 1341A). It is followed by Erasmus' letter (Ep 1342) to Marcus Laurinus; the longer version of Ep 1301 addressed to Louvain theologians; a *Libellus* (1522) by Jacob Ziegler against Zúñiga's attacks on Erasmus, accompanied by copious examples of Zúñiga's invectives (on these see Allen Ep 1260:203n); then the colloquy 'Charon'; and a colophon April 1523, not the new date of September 1524. 'Charon' is named in Allen I 40:17 / CWE 24 695:37 / CWE Ep 1341A:1568. Early 1523 may be therefore the most likely date of composition. At least a few copies of 'Charon' alone were printed as single booklets also (Franz Bierlaire *Erasme et ses Colloques: le livre d'une vie* [Paris 1977] 97). ASD I-3 575–84 prints both the April 1523 and the March 1529 texts of the dialogue. The 1529 text has a few differences from the earlier version; these are recorded in notes to the present translation.

BE 2nd series *Colloquia* I 199 states that the first edition of the *Colloquia* to contain 'Charon' and the eight dialogues that follow it in this volume ('A Meeting of the Philological Society,' 'A Marriage in Name Only,' 'The Imposture,' 'Cyclops,' 'Non-Sequiturs,' 'The Knight without a Horse,' 'Knucklebones,' and 'The Council of Women') was one published by Eucharius Cervicornus (Cologne 1528; no month date). Smith initially accepted this assertion (*Key* 44) but later rejected it. Elsbeth Gutmann repeated the claim in 1968 (*Die Colloquia familiaria des Erasmus von Rotterdam* [Basel and Stuttgart 1968] 94–6). That Erasmus would have given these nine dialogues, eight of them unprinted before, to Cervicornus, with whom he had only slight connections, for a new and enlarged edition of the *Colloquia*, instead of publishing them through the Froben firm, is inherently improbable. Henry de Vocht solved the problem. In his introduction to *The Earliest English Translations of Erasmus' Colloquia* (Louvain 1928) he demonstrated that for both biographical and bibliographical reasons it is untenable to take the presence of these nine dialogues in a Cervicornus book dated simply '1528' as proof of their first appearance (xi–xii, with the notes). After their publication in the March 1529 Froben edition, they were quickly inserted as an *auctarium* in printed but unbound sheets of Cervicornus' book. The leaves are unsigned, whereas everything preceding and following the nine colloquies has signatures in regular order; nor are titles of the nine colloquies entered in the alphabetical index. How Cervicornus got hold of these dialogues is not known, but see Bierlaire 'Erasme, les imprimeurs et les *Colloques' Gutenberg-Jahrbuch* (1978) 108–9.

In theme and manner 'Charon' is clearly inspired by Lucian. A 1528 reprint of Erasmus' and More's Latin translations of Lucian (Lyons: Gryphius) 521–6 even includes Erasmus' dialogue, identifying it as his, perhaps to show how Lucianic a modern writer could be. Some of Lucian's *Dialogues of the Dead* (12, 13, 14) satirize monarchs who would conquer the world. In others (4, 10, 22) Charon and Hermes compare notes. In 4 Charon complains that he is unable to pay Hermes for repairs to his ferry until wars or plagues bring him more business; in 22 he quarrels with a passenger who will not pay the fare. Lucian, in his dialogue called 'Charon,' has Hermes take Charon on a tour of the upper world, which the visitor finds depressingly full of vanity and folly: 'How absurd are the affairs of unhappy mortals!' This dialogue, like the others mentioned here, was often translated and imitated in the fifteenth and sixteenth centuries.

Erasmus in his 'Charon' alludes to a favourite subject, the 'complaint of peace' in a world of wars. He does not mention such dramatic events as the capture and imprisonment of Francis I and the sack of Rome, both of which occurred after the 1523 text was published, but his readers in 1529 knew about them even if Charon does not. Francis had been captured at the battle of Pavia in February 1525 and held as hostage in Spain; see 'A Fish Diet' n79. When released in 1526, after the signing of the Treaty of Madrid, he joined with Milan, Florence, Venice, and the papacy in a league against Charles v. England supported the league. In the Italian campaigns that followed, the imperial forces were usually victorious. The fighting culminated in the famous sack of Rome by imperial soldiers in May 1527 (on this see Allen Epp 1831:16–22, 1839:110–12, 2059:1–9 – very brief comments on such a momentous disaster). A new Italian conflict broke out, but after six months the pope began efforts to make peace. Charles rejected the terms and the war continued until August 1529 (Peace of Cambrai), a few months after this colloquy was printed. By this date the empire had won control of Italy and Francis again renounced his Italian claims.

In 1522–3 Erasmus had dedicated his Paraphrases on the Gospels to Charles v, Francis i, Henry viii, and Archduke Ferdinand of Austria, and in prefatory letters called upon them to seek and preserve peace (Epp 1255, 1400, 1381, 1333). Similarly he had hoped that the pontificates of Leo x, Adrian vi, and now Clement vii would prove as calm as that of Julius ii was stormy. By the mid-1520s the wars between Charles and Francis, incursions of the Turks, Lutheran 'tumults,' and the Peasants' Revolt made Erasmus' prediction in 1517 of a coming 'age of gold' (Allen Ep 566:31–40 / cwe Ep 566:35–45, addressed to Leo x) a sad miscalculation.

In some colloquies ('The Soldier and the Carthusian,' 'Military Affairs,' 'Cyclops') he ridicules mercenary soldiers. In 'The Funeral' he satirizes a general. In 'A Fish Diet' and 'Charon' the folly and cupidity of rulers themselves are attacked. 'Charon' likewise shows his detestation of compliant churchmen, whether prelates who by flattering princes incite them to war or priests and friars who assure the populace that 'God is on our side.' Erasmus had intuitions of a body of international law capable of arbitrating disputes and keeping peace among governments, but he never worked these ideas out; that task was to be resumed a century later by his countryman, Hugo Grotius. His writings had little or no direct political effect. Nevertheless as a propagandist for peace he produced some of the best and most widely read arguments on war and peace, and they are still worth reading.

Alfonso de Valdés, one of Charles v's secretaries, a correspondent of Erasmus and like his brother Juan a member of a remarkable group of Spanish Erasmians, wrote two dialogues (both c 1529), Lactancio and Mercurio y Carón, in which he denounced the perfidy of Francis i in that king's dealings with the emperor, placing the blame for the sack of Rome in 1527 on the policies of Clement vii and his incompetent advisers and exonerating the emperor from responsibility. Mercurio y Carón is indebted both to Lucian and to Erasmus' 'Charon.' On this dialogue see Bataillon Erasme et l'Espagne 419–38; K.L. Selig 'Zu Valdes' Erasmisches Diálogo de "Mercurio y Caron"' bhr 20 (1958) 17–24. Lactancio is translated with an introduction by John E. Longhurst (Albuquerque 1950).

John R. Hale's Renaissance War Studies (London 1983) and War and Society in Renaissance Europe 1450–1620 (New York 1985; repr Baltimore 1986) should not be missed by readers of this and other colloquies on war.

CHARON,[1] the spirit ALASTOR[2]

Charon Why the hustle and bustle, Alastor?

Alastor Well met, Charon. I was speeding to you.

5   **Charon** What's new?

Alastor I bring news that will delight you and Proserpina.[3]

Charon Out with it, then. Unload it.

Alastor The Furies[4] have done their work zealously as well as successfully. Not a corner of the earth have they left unravaged by hellish disasters,

10   dissensions, wars, robberies, plagues: so much so that now, with their snakes let loose, they're completely bald. Drained of poisons, they roam about looking for whatever vipers and asps they can find, since they're as smooth-headed as an egg – not a hair on their crowns nor a drop of good poison in their breasts. So have your boat and oars ready, for there'll soon

15   be such a crowd of shades coming that I fear you can't ferry them all.

Charon No news to me.

Alastor Where did you learn it?

Charon Ossa[5] brought it two days ago.

Alastor Can't get ahead of that goddess! But why are you loitering here

20   without your boat, then?

Charon Business trip: I came here to get a good, strong trireme ready. My galley's so rotten with age and so worthless that it won't do for this job if what Ossa told me is true. Though[6] what need was there of Ossa? The plain fact of the matter demands it: I've had a shipwreck.

25   **Alastor** You *are* dripping wet, undoubtedly. I thought you were coming back from a bath.

Charon Oh, no, I've been swimming out of the Stygian swamp.

Alastor Where have you left the shades?

Charon Swimming with the frogs.

30   **Alastor** But what did Ossa report?

Charon That the three rulers of the world,[7] in deadly hatred, clash to their mutual destruction. Nor is any part of Christendom safe from the ravages of war, for those three have dragged all the rest into alliance. They're all in such a mood that none of them is willing to yield to another. Neither

35   Dane[8] nor Pole[9] nor Scot[10] nor Turk,[11] in fact, is at peace; catastrophes are building up; the plague rages everywhere, in Spain, Britain, Italy, France.[12] In addition there's a new epidemic, born of difference of opinion.[13] It has so corrupted everybody's mind that sincere friendship exists nowhere, but brother distrusts brother and husband and wife disagree. I've hopes of a

40   splendid slaughter one day, too, if the war of tongues and pens comes to actual blows.

Alastor Ossa reported everything quite correctly, for as the constant attendant and assistant of the Furies (who have never shown themselves more deserving of their name) I've seen more than this with my own eyes.

Charon But there's danger that some devil may turn up and preach peace
5 all of a sudden – and mortal minds are fickle. I hear there's a certain Polygraphus[14] up there who's incessantly attacking war with his pen and urging men to peace.

Alastor He's sung to deaf ears[15] this long while. He once wrote a 'Complaint of Peace O'erthrown';[16] now he's written the epitaph of peace dead and
10 buried. On the other hand, there are some as helpful to our cause as the Furies themselves.

Charon Who are those?

Alastor Certain creatures in black and white cloaks and ash-gray tunics, adorned with plumage of various kinds. They never leave the courts of
15 princes. They instil into their ears a love of war; they incite rulers and populace alike; they proclaim in their evangelical sermons that war is just, holy, and right.[17] And – to make you marvel more at their audacity – they proclaim the very same thing on both sides.[18] To the French they preach that God is on the French side: he who has God to protect him cannot be
20 conquered. To the English and Spanish they declare this war is not the emperor's but God's: only let them show themselves valiant men and victory is certain. But if anyone is killed, he doesn't perish utterly but flies straight up to heaven,[19] armed just as he was.

Charon And people believe these fellows?

25 **Alastor** What can a pretence of religion not achieve? Youth, inexperience, thirst for glory, anger, and natural human inclination swallow this whole. Thus people are easily imposed upon. And it's not hard to upset a cart that's already on the verge of collapse.

Charon I'll be glad to reward these creatures![20]

30 **Alastor** Give them a fine dinner. They like nothing better.

Charon A dinner of mallows, lupins, and leeks.[21] That's the only fare we have, as you know.

Alastor Oh, no, it must be partridges, capons, and pheasants if you wish to be an acceptable host.

35 **Charon** But what makes them such warmongers? Or what advantage do they gain from this?

Alastor They make more profit from the dying than from the living. There are wills, masses for kinsmen, bulls, and many other sources of revenue not to be despised. In short, they prefer to buzz in camp rather than in their
40 own hives. War spawns many bishops who in peacetime weren't worth a farthing.[22]

Death and the Lansquenet
Albrecht Dürer, 1510
A powerful pictorial expression of a theme often met in Erasmus' writings
on war, the inevitability of death, and the soldier of fortune's
characteristic unreadiness for it
Germanisches Nationalmuseum Nürnberg

Charon A canny lot.

Alastor But why do you need a trireme?

Charon I don't – so long as I am willing to be shipwrecked in the middle of the swamp again.

5   **Alastor** Because of the crowd?

Charon Of course.

Alastor But you haul shades, not bodies. Now how light are shades?

Charon They may be water skippers,[23] but enough water skippers could sink a boat. Then[24] too, you know, the boat is unsubstantial.

10 **Alastor** But sometimes, I remember, when there was a crowd so large the boat couldn't hold them all, I saw three thousand shades hanging from your rudder and you didn't feel any weight.

Charon Granted there are such souls, which departed little by little from bodies worn away by consumption or hectic fever. But those plucked on the

15 sudden from heavy bodies bring a good deal of corporeal substance along with them. Apoplexy, quinsy, plague, but especially war, send this kind.

Alastor Frenchmen or Spaniards don't weigh much, I suppose.

Charon Much less than others, though even their souls are not exactly featherweight. But from well-fed Britons and Germans[25] such shades come

20 at times that lately I've hardly dared to ferry even ten, and unless I'd thrown them overboard I'd have gone down along with boat, rowers, and passage money.

Alastor A terrible risk!

Charon Meanwhile what do you think will happen when heavy lords,

25 Thrasos,[26] and swashbucklers[27] come along?

Alastor None of those who die in a just war come to you, I believe. For these, they say, fly straight to heaven.[28]

Charon Where they may fly to, I don't know. I do know one thing: that whenever a war's on, so many come to me wounded and cut up that I'd be

30 surprised if any had been left on earth. They come loaded not only with debauchery and gluttony but even with bulls, benefices, and many other things.

Alastor But they don't bring these along with them. The souls come to you naked.

35 **Charon** True, but newcomers bring along dreams of such things.

Alastor So dreams are heavy?

Charon They weigh down my boat. Weigh down,[29] did I say? They've already sunk it. Finally, do you imagine so many obols weigh nothing?

Alastor Well, I suppose they are heavy if they're copper ones.

40 **Charon** So I've decided to look out for a vessel strong enough for the load.

Alastor Lucky you!

Charon How so?

Alastor Because you'll soon grow rich.

Charon From a lot of shades?

Alastor Of course.

5 **Charon** If only they'd bring their riches with them! As it is, those in the boat who lament the kingdoms, prelacies, abbacies, and countless talents of gold they left up there bring me nothing but an obol. And so everything I've scraped together in three thousand years has to be laid out for one trireme.

Alastor If you want to make money you have to spend money.

10 **Charon** Yet mortals, as I hear, do business better: with Mercury's help[30] they grow rich within three years.

Alastor But sometimes those same mortals go broke. Your profit is less but it's more certain.

Charon How certain I can't tell. If some god should turn up now and settle 15 the affairs of princes, I'd be utterly ruined.

Alastor I'll see to it. Leave it to me and you can sleep sound on either ear.[31] You've no reason to fear a peace within ten whole years.[32] Only the Roman pontiff is zealous in urging peace,[33] but he washes a brick.[34] Cities, too, weary of their troubles, complain bitterly. People – I don't know who they 20 are – mutter that it's outrageous for human affairs to be turned topsy-turvy[35] on account of the personal grudges or ambitions of two or three men. But the Furies, believe me, will defeat counsel, no matter how good it is. – Yet what need was there for you to go above for this purpose? Haven't we workmen of our own? We've Vulcan[36] surely.

25 **Charon** Fine – if I wanted a bronze ship.

Alastor Labour's cheap.

Charon Yes, but we're short of timber.

Alastor What, aren't there any forests here?

Charon Even the groves in the Elysian fields have been used up.

30 **Alastor** What for?

Charon For burning shades of heretics.[37] So that we've been forced of late to mine coal from the bowels of the earth.

Alastor What, can't those shades be punished at less expense?

Charon This was the decision of Rhadamanthus.[38]

35 **Alastor** When you've bought your trireme, where will you get rowers?

Charon My job is to hold the tiller;[39] the shades must row if they want passage.

Alastor But some haven't learned how to handle an oar.

Charon No distinction of persons with me: monarchs row and cardinals 40 row, each in their turn, no less than common folk, whether they've learned or not.

Alastor Good luck[40] in getting a trireme at a bargain! I won't hold you up any longer. I'll take the good news to Orcus.[41] But say, Charon –

Charon What?

Alastor Hurry back, so the crowd won't quickly overwhelm you.

5 **Charon** Oh, you'll meet over two hundred thousand on the bank already, besides[42] those swimming in the swamp. But I'll hurry as much as I can. Tell 'em I'll be there right away.

NOTES

1 Ferryman of souls across the river Styx to Hades. Cf 'Inns' n34.

2 In Greek mythology a destructive, avenging spirit; a *genius malus*. See *Adagia* I i 72.

3 Consort of Hades. She spent six months each year on earth and six in the underworld. Alastor implies that she will be pleased to hear about wars and plagues, which provide many newcomers in Hades.

4 Spirits of punishment. They had poisonous serpents for hair; these they sent to torment the consciences of the wicked. They inflicted many kinds of torture, including wars, on sinful mortals. See Virgil *Aeneid* 7.323–571; *Adagia* IV i 1 LB II 953E–F; *Moriae encomium* LB IV 439B–440A, 484D / ASD IV-3 116:873–7, 117:814–8 / CWE 27 111, 139.

5 The goddess Rumour or *Fama*; *Adagia* I vi 25

6 Though ... frogs.] Added in the March 1529 edition

7 The emperor Charles V, Francis I of France, and Henry VIII of England. For a summary of their alliances, enmities, and wars in the 1520s see 'A Fish Diet' 687:24–689:18 with the notes, especially nn79, 89, and the introduction to this colloquy 819–20 above. With the gloomy state of the world presented in this paragraph compare 'The New Mother' 592:17–35.

8 The reference may be due to Erasmus' acquaintance with the former king, Christian II (brother-in-law of Charles V), who went into exile in 1523. See *Puerpera* 'The New Mother' n6. His successor, Frederick I, was now actively supporting the Lutheran cause in Denmark.

9 nor Pole] Added in the March 1529 edition. See Ep 1819, a letter from Erasmus to King Sigismund I of Poland, commenting on Poland's difficulties with the Muscovites, Prussians, Tartars, and Turks and the question of a successor to the throne of Hungary, a matter of much concern to Poland.

10 Erasmus had very few contacts with Scots or Scotland after the death of Alexander Stewart, who had been a pupil of his in Italy in 1508–9. A natural son of King James IV of Scotland, Stewart became an archbishop and chancellor of Scotland. Father and son both perished in the battle of Flodden Field, September 1513. See Allen Ep 604:2n and 'A Fish Diet' n118. To say that the Scots were not 'at peace' at this time was a vague but safe affirmation; internally the kingdom was seldom at peace.

11 See 'The New Mother' n19.

12 Since typhus, bubonic plague, and other pestilences, including syphilis, were recurrent in Erasmus' time we cannot tell whether he refers here to a specific

epidemic. Probably not, but if he does the allusion may be to the plague which is said to have killed more than half of the French forces who were besieging Naples in the summer of 1528.

13 Lutheranism; an interesting remark on its effects at this date

14 Polygraphus] 'Erasmus' in the 1523 edition. 'Polygraphus' here is a semi-facetious term for an incessant scribbler. Erasmus uses it of Luther (Allen Epp 1173:87–8, 1236:76–7) and of himself in *Ciceronianus* (LB I 1013D / ASD I-2 681:3).

15 *Adagia* I iv 87

16 Erasmus' eloquent *Querela pacis undique gentium eiectae profligataeque* (1517). Text in LB IV 625A–642D and ASD IV-2 61–100; other critical editions by Holborn and by Y. Rémy and R. Dunil-Marquebreucq (Brussels 1953). It was widely read both in Latin and in translations. Thomas Paynell's English version (1559) is well known; see now the translation by Betty Radice in CWE 27 293–322. On its classical and Christian sources see R.H. Bainton 'The *Querela Pacis* of Erasmus' ARG 42 (1951) 32–48.

Querela pacis was preceded by two memorable essays in the *Adagia*: *Scarabeus aquilam quaerit* on kings (III vii 1) and *Dulce bellum inexpertis* on war (IV i 1), both from 1515. The second and longer was expanded from a few lines in the 1508 *Adagia*. Both essays were printed separately in 1517. In addition there was the important treatise of 1516, *Institutio principis christiani*. These four writings from 1515–17 climaxed but by no means concluded Erasmus' efforts in behalf of international peace; efforts which continued until the end of his life. His *De bello Turcico* came out in 1530. 'Now he's written the epitaph' does not refer to another composition but is a figurative way of saying that the chances of peace are even dimmer than they were earlier; melancholy news except to Charon.

17 Regulars: monks, friars, abbots. A similar passage in *Querela pacis* mentions Dominicans and Franciscans by name (LB IV 634F–635A / ASD IV-2 82:504–13 / CWE 27 308). That they 'never leave the courts of princes' echoes a remark in *Adagia* II viii 65 (LB II 654F).

'Whoever brings tidings of Christ brings tidings of peace. Whoever preaches war preaches one who is the very opposite of Christ' (*Querela pacis* LB IV 630B / ASD IV-2 70:237–8 / CWE 27 300). Condemnation of clerics whom he thought too complacent in endorsing their rulers' wars is found in all Erasmus' major writings on government and the Christian in society. A good brief example is a passage in *Adagia* IV i 1 (LB II 956E–957B), a long one in *Annotationes in Novum Testamentum* (LB VI 317C–321F). The clergy have, and must have, a special obligation to denounce war and preach peace. For some of Julius II's war-making Erasmus blamed the instigations of prelates (*Querela pacis* LB IV 635A / ASD IV-2 82:509–12 / CWE 27 308). He was convinced that such clerical aggressiveness was more prevalent among 'modern' churchmen than among earlier ones (*Adagia* IV i 1 LB II 964C–E).

18 Contrast the behaviour of priests in More's *Utopia*. On the battlefield they pray first of all for peace, next for victory, but victory with a minimum of bloodshed. If their own side wins they try to restrain the troops from pursuing and slaughtering the enemy (Yale CWM 4 230–1).

19 An idea with a long history, possibly an inference from early beliefs about Christian martyrs, of whom Tertullian writes that they alone go straight to

heaven (*De anima* 55 CSEL 20 388–9; *De resurrectione carnis* 43 CSEL 47 89). Whatever its origins, the assumption or promise of heaven immediately to soldiers killed in battle, whether in crusades or the more common wars fought by European states, recurs in Erasmus' time. In *Julius exclusus* the pope refers to his promise, 'in mighty bulls, that all who fought under Julius' banners should fly straight up to heaven, no matter what sort of life they had led before' (Ferguson *Erasmi opuscula* 78:252–7 / CWE 27 174).

20 In 'Patterns' 15:30–2 it is suggested that they should be put in the front lines.

21 Cf 'Courtship' 258:27–31 and 'Penny Pinching' 982:6.

22 Erasmus assures us that he had known some men whose praise of wars made them bishops (*Annotationes in Novum Testamentum* LB VI 27). 'Bishops are not ashamed to frequent the camp; the cross is there, the body of Christ is there, the heavenly sacraments become mixed up in this worse than hellish business, and the symbols of perfect charity are brought into these bloody conflicts. Still more absurd, Christ is present in both camps, as if fighting against himself' (*Institutio principis christiani* LB IV 610C / ASD IV-1 218:601–4 / CWE 27 286 / Born 255).

23 Plautus *Persa* 244

24 Then . . . unsubstantial.] Added in the March 1529 edition

25 Germans] 'Swabians' instead of 'Germans' in 1523 edition
An Italian visitor to England in 1497 observed that people there 'eat very frequently, at times more than is suitable' (*Two Italian Accounts of Tudor England* ed and trans C.V. Malfatti [Barcelona 1953] 37). *A Relation of England* (c 1500) confirms this report. See 'A Fish Diet' n247. Britons take pride in their hearty meals, says Folly (LB IV 448B / ASD IV-3 128:61 / CWE 27 117). When the French spy a man with a big belly they say 'he's as full as an Englishman, just as they ascribe heavy drinking to us' (that is, to Germans; *Adagia* II ii 68). Germans, Luther concedes, were notorious for gluttony and drinking, 'as though it were our special vice' (*An den christlichen Adel deutscher Nation* WA 6 467:7–10 / LW 44 214).

26 Thraso is a braggart soldier in Terence *Eunuchus*.

27 swashbuckler] Pyrgopolinices in editions from March 1529 to September 1531; Polymachaeroplacidae in the March 1533 edition. Pyrgopolinices ('tower-town taker') is the braggart captain in Plautus *Miles gloriosus*. Polymachaeroplagides ('son of many sabre strokes') is a character in Plautus *Pseudolus*; the spelling of the name varies slightly in early editions. In English 'swashbuckler' fits both names in this context.

28 On the concept of 'just war' see the introduction to 'Military Affairs' 54 and 'The New Mother' n19. 'They speak of a just war when princes play a match of which the outcome is to exhaust and oppress the commonwealth; they speak of peace when that is the very object against which they conspire among themselves' (*Adagia* III iii 1 LB II 775D–E / CWE 34 270–1). A truly Christian teacher never approves of war; and if ever he does seem to allow it, he does so with the greatest reluctance and sadness (*Adagia* IV i 1 LB II 964B). If just wars exist, they are those fought in self-defence when one's country is invaded by a barbarous foe bent on conquest. But wars fought between one Christian society and another are intolerable scandals and disasters (see *Querela pacis* LB IV 637F–638B / ASD IV-2 90:671–87 / CWE 27 314).

A Christian concept of just war is usually traced to Augustine Epp 138.12–15 and especially 189.4–6. Erasmus did not dissent from the Augustinian judgment but had to deal with states and societies officially Christian and with an ecclesiastical establishment containing clerics of many kinds. However widely read his writings on peace, the behaviour of heads of states and their advisers did not change in the fashion he was pleased to imagine in the scene between Charles and Francis in 'A Fish Diet' 688:18–689:18. In 'Charon' and other dialogues his powers of satire and irony present his opinions less argumentatively but more vividly, at least for some readers. Finally it must be added that even pagan or otherwise non-Christian princes who protect public peace by means of just wars and by just laws are serving Christ (preface to the 1518 edition of *Enchiridion*; Allen Ep 858:230–9 / CWE Ep 858:242–52 / CWE 66 13–14). But at times Erasmus tended to agree with the Ciceronian dictum that the most unjust peace is preferable to the most just war (*Ad familiares* 6.6.6), an opinion Colet dared to voice when preaching before Henry VIII in 1512. Colet found himself in some trouble afterwards when opponents tried to embarrass him. Erasmus tells the story (Allen Ep 1211:557–616 / CWE Ep 1211:606–73; there is a longer account in Lupton *Life of Colet* 189–93). In addition to the studies of Erasmus' pacifism and his opinions on just war mentioned in earlier pages consult those by R. Liechtenhan 'Die politische Hoffnung des Erasmus und ihr Zusammenbruch' in *Gedenkschrift* 144–65; O. Schottenloher 'Lex naturae und Lex Christi bei Erasmus' in *Scrinium Erasmianum* II 293–8; P. Brachin 'Vox clamantis in deserto: réflexions sur le pacifisme d'Erasme' in *Colloquia Erasmiana Turonensia* II 247–75; José A. Fernandez 'Erasmus on the Just War' in *Journal of the History of Ideas* 34 (1973) 209–25; John C. Olin *Six Essays on Erasmus* (New York 1979) 17–31.

29 Weigh down, did I say . . . copper ones.] Added in the March 1529 edition
30 *favente Mercurio*. Cf *Adagia* I i 72 and 'Patterns' n59; cf also *Adagia* IV vii 2: *Mercurio dextro*. Mercury was the god of trade and the patron of merchants.
31 Proverbial. *Adagia* I viii 19; Terence *Heautontimorumenos* 342
32 This sentence in the 1523 edition was left unchanged in the March 1529 text. The war ended in the summer of 1529.
33 When the 1523 edition appeared the pope was Adrian VI. He died in September of that year and was succeeded by Clement VII. 'What has become of papal authority?' asks Peace in *Querela pacis* (LB IV 636C–D / ASD IV-2 86:585 / CWE 27 311). The same question is asked in Allen Ep 1238:65–6 / CWE Ep 1238:73.
34 Wastes time in useless activity; *Adagia* I iv 48
35 *Adagia* I iii 85
36 We've Vulcan . . . labour's cheap.] Omitted in the 1523 edition. Vulcan was identified by the Romans with the Greek Hephaestus, god of fire and smithy.
37 For a few fairly recent instances between 1523 and 1527 see Allen Epp 1384:2n, 1388:7n, 1401:15n, 1540:20n. Burnings in England are very seldom, if ever, noted in Erasmus' correspondence; for these one must turn to Foxe. In the month after the publication of 'Charon' in the *Colloquia* of March 1529, Louis de Berquin was burned as a relapsed heretic in Paris. One reason for persecution of him by the Sorbonne was his tendentious French translations of Erasmus' *Querela pacis*, *Modus orandi Deum*, *Encomium matrimonii*, and nearly all of *Inquisitio de fide* (see the introduction to 'The Girl with No Interest in Marriage'

281). Erasmus lamented his terrible fate but thought him reckless and obstinate. See Allen Epp 2158:91–120, 2188:250–75. Berquin's translations of *Querela pacis* and *Inquisitio de fide* (both 1525) are reproduced in facsimile and provided with extensive introductions and notes by Emile V. Telle (Geneva 1978, 1979).
The grim joke in 'Charon' about the scarcity and cost of firewood because of the burning of heretics occurs earlier in Erasmus' letters; see Allen Epp 239:37–8, 240:38–9 / CWE Epp 239:41–3, 240:42–4.

38 Just and incorruptible judge of the dead; *Adagia* II ix 30, 31
39 *Adagia* III i 28
40 *dextro Mercurio*; *Adagia* IV vii 2. See n30 above.
41 God of the underworld, often identified with Pluto and Dis; also a synonym for the underworld, as in 'The Funeral' 774:3
42 besides . . . swamp] Added in the March 1529 edition

A MEETING OF THE PHILOLOGICAL SOCIETY

Synodus grammaticorum

First printed in the *Colloquia* in the edition of March 1529. On this date see introduction to 'Charon' 818–19.

In this colloquy Erasmus takes a holiday from more serious labours to settle a few scores by a brief and amusing satire of three old enemies, Paris theologians. Attacks on his edition and translation of the New Testament, his Annotations and Paraphrases, *Colloquia*, and other writings cost him time and trouble; they fill nearly five hundred columns in LB IX. In the age of print, opportunities for long and frequent exchanges, friendly or hostile, between scholars were plentiful. In Erasmus' fields of biblical, theological, and literary scholarship the record of controversies is a voluminous and at times melancholy testimony to the vigour and persistence of polemical activity. When aided by imagination and wit, controversies, like satire, could produce literary art. 'A Meeting of the Philological Society' is satire but cannot compare with *Moriae encomium* or *Ciceronianus* as literature; yet it achieves its purpose, which is ridicule.

This dialogue is a belated thrust at opponents in Paris whom Erasmus held responsible for instigating the faculty of theology's censure of the *Colloquia* in May 1526 and denunciation of the work as irreverent and dangerous to youth. Erasmus added to the June 1526 edition a spirited defence, 'The Usefulness of the *Colloquies*.' In 1525, 1526, and 1527 he wrote against two of his most persistent Paris critics, Noël Béda and Pierre Cousturier. In March 1529 he published this colloquy and in the next edition (September 1529) inserted additions to 'The Usefulness of the *Colloquies*' to bring it up to date. Still later, in 1532, he published a long reply to his Parisian detractors, *Declarationes ad censuras Lutetiae vulgatas* (LB IX 813E–954E).

On Béda, 'swimming beet' as he is called on 834:2, see 'Patterns' n35, Allen Ep 1571 introduction, and CEBR. An indefatigable academic defender of conservative causes affecting religion, he succeeded Jan Standonck as master of the Collège de Montaigu (see 'A Fish Diet' n287). Another adversary mentioned in the dialogue was Guillaume Duchesne (n18 below). Of these heresy-hunting theologians, one of Erasmus' principal targets here was Pierre Cousturier (see CEBR), a Carthusian (once of the Sorbonne) whose published *Apologeticum in novos anticomaritas* denounced those who held what he considered unacceptable notions about the Virgin Mary. Erasmus caricatures these divines as obscurantist and pedantic and laughs at them in a manner both philological and scurrilous, a manner that may have reminded his readers, with good reason, of the *Epistolae obscurorum virorum*.

Apparently the idea for this composition came from a letter to Erasmus by a Carthusian friend, Levinus Ammonius, dated 31 July 1528. As an earnest scholar with Erasmian sympathies, Ammonius had a strong dislike of Cousturier. His letter of July 1528 comments on Cousturier's book against the *anticomaritae*, mocks him for this ludicrous solecism (on which see n3 below) and makes remarks about a certain plant, called *comaron*, adopted by Erasmus in the colloquy (n29 below). See Allen Ep 2016:45–64. When the colloquy was published, Ammonius relished its gibes at his fellow monk (Allen Ep 2197:79–85).

On Sutor and Erasmus see further Heinz Holeczek *Humanistische Bibelphilologie als Reformproblem bei Erasmus von Rotterdam, Thomas More und William Tyndale* (Leiden 1975) 186–223.

ALBINUS, BERTULF, CANTHELUS, DIPHYLUS, EUMENIUS, FABULLUS, GADITANUS[1]

Albinus Anyone in this group good at arithmetic?

5 **Bertulf** What on earth for?

Albinus To determine how many of us grammarians are assembled here.

Bertulf No need for a counting-board, surely; our fingers can tell us. I count you on my thumb, myself on my index finger, Canthelus on the middle finger, Diphylus on the ring finger, Eumenius on the little finger. Now

10 switching to the left hand, I count Fabullus on my thumb, Gaditanus on my index finger. So unless I'm mistaken, we are seven. But what's the good of knowing this?

Albinus Because I hear the number seven constitutes a quorum at a meeting.

Bertulf What meeting do you mean?

15 **Albinus** There's a serious matter that has tormented me for a long time, and not me alone but many, including men by no means unlearned. I'll lay it before you, to have the question settled once for all by the authority of this congress.

Canthelus Must be something extraordinary if you don't have the answer,

20 Albinus, and if it has long tormented a mind as penetrating as yours. Hence we want to know for ourselves what this thing is – for I reply on behalf of us all.

Albinus Attend, then, all of you; lend me your ears and minds. Many eyes are better than one.[2] Can any of you explain the meaning of the word

25 *anticomarita*?[3]

Miseratur9.i.mīam impēsur9.a mi
seroŗ ratis.Inuitat·me.p.Uberem
me.coŗ.i.abūdam.vber·bŗis·ois
ge.ffastidiosi pauŗŗū·q nõ p̄t vi
dere uel audire pauŗes.cū genitiuo
Dierico·vltima acuta.Cameli·me.
p.mas.ge.i.aīalis gibbosi.Pŗestri-
cti.i.ante tacti ul stricti.a pstringo
gis qd est valde uel ante tangē uel
stringere.Impŗobis·me.coŗ.i.non
pbis.Perseuerat·pe.p.Uberioŗem
i.abundantioŗem.

Sup declaratione regu-
le fratrum minoŗum.

Atur9.i.semiatur9.a sero-
tis·seui·satū.Gnatos.i.do
ctos.Desides.i.pigros.de-
ses·sidis·cois ge. Colon9.i.inhabita-
toŗ.Delectu.i.differētia uel discre-
tiõe.mas.ge.7 q̄tte decli. a delego-
gis·legi: Curia vtis lo noīe sine·c.
Almū.i.scm.Insitū·me.coŗ.i.imis-
sum.ab inseroŗ retis·insitus sū·ad
modū surculi q arboŗi iseris.Emu-
latoŗes.i.iuidos psecutoŗes.Discri
minosa.i.piculosa.Agentibus.i.cõ
uersantibș.Eadē·me.coŗ.Allisit.i.
submersit.Degentiū.i.viuētium.
Cõsternauit.i.deiecit.Sterno·nas
tn coīter ē deponēs.Amftactibus.i
toŗtuosis excusatiõibș. amftactus.
mas.ge.7 q̄tte decli. via quā tenet
lepus ī fugiēdo. Differere.i.expli-
care.Sup ipsa regula.i.de.Edidim9
i.opŗuim9.Seriosi9.i.studiosius.
a serio.Tum.i.partim.Insultus.i.
aggressuras uel impes9.Emergen-
tiū.i.ctingētiū.Scrupulū.i.remoŗ

siū ppe lapill9 ē.mas.ge.Nihilomi-
nus·pe.coŗ.i.nõ min9. Subnectit
i.iūgit.Succinctoŗie.i.bŗeuis. In-
dicat·me.p.i.ipŗonat.Eatenus·pe.
coŗ.i.intātū.Cõdecet·me.coŗ.Quo
i.inquātū.Abdicationē.i.reŗū ex-
clusionē.Alueos.i.riuulos. Locu-
los.i.bursas. Condecens·me.coŗ.
Conricis.i.ostendit uel pbatur.cõ-
cio icis·cõricioŗ·ceris.Quinimo.i.
potius.Abdicet·me.coŗ.i.separet.
Quõlibet·pe.coŗ.i.aliq mõ. Quo
min9.i.ut nõ.oue ptes.Subŗogan
oā.i.substituēdā. Ingruēti.i.imi-
nēti siue instāti.Tractū.i.spatium
mas.ge.7 q̄tte decli. Innexū.i.ad-
iūctū.Pŗesto.i.i pritia.Serie.i.scri
ptura.Pŗefad.i.pdict.Superit·pe.
coŗ. Coaptēt.i.ad cõgruas expēsas
pte emēda se restringāt.Seriosa.i
studiosa 7 delibata. Icibș.i.pcus-
siõibș.mas.ge.7 q̄tte decli. Astruit
i.affirmat siue pbat.Aduertētes.i.
csiderātes.Passim.i.coīter uel in-
differēt.Fulciat.i.moueāt 7 astrin
gāt. Dacten9.i.hucusqȝ.Cenobijs
i.monasterijs.neu·ge. Adijciēs.i.
addēs.Quõlibet·pe.coŗ.i.aliq mõ
Vit9.i.venenū.neu.ge. p tres cas9
s.noīatiuū·accusatiuū 7 vocatiuū
Ausu.i.audacia.mas.ge.7 q̄tte decli.

Expliciūt expositiões 7 correctões
vocabuloŗ libŗi q appellat Mamo
trect9 tā biblie q̄ alioŗ plurimoŗū
libŗoŗ.Impŗesse Uenetijs p Fran-
ciscū de Hailbŗun 7 Nicholaum de
ffranckfoŗdia socios.
MCCCCLXXVI
Laus deo.

Mammetrectus, a glossary of the Bible and other religious works
by Johannes Marchesinus of Reggio, a Franciscan, was first printed
in Mainz in 1470. Erasmus deplored and denounced it.
This is the final page and colophon of the Venice 1476 edition.
From the Marjorie Walter Goodhart Medieval Library, Bryn Mawr College

Bertulf Nothing simpler. It means a kind of beet called by the ancients 'swimming beet,'[4] with a twisted and knotty stalk and remarkably insipid; it has a foul stench if you come in contact with it – as bad as stinking bean-trefoil.[5]

Canthelus 'Swimming beet,' eh? Nasty beast, rather.[6] Who ever heard or
5 read of the name 'swimming beet' before?

Bertulf On the contrary, this is clearly taught by *Mammetrectus*, as it's commonly but mistakenly called, since the right name is *Mammothreptus*, 'grandma's darling,' as you might say.[7]

Albinus What sort of title is this?

10 **Bertulf** You're to understand that the book contains nothing but sheer delights, because grandmas are generally fonder of grandsons than mothers are of their own children.

Albinus Certainly the work you describe is most enjoyable, for when I came across the volume recently I nearly died laughing.[8]

15 **Canthelus** Where did you find the book? It's very seldom met with.

Bertulf The abbot of St Bavo's, Livinus by name,[9] took me after lunch at Bruges into his private library, which the old gentleman, in his desire to leave some memorial of himself to posterity, was furnishing at no little expense. Not a book there that wasn't manuscript, and on parchment, too; none that was not
20 adorned with various pictures and bound in velvet and gold. Indeed, the very size of that collection of books had a certain indescribable grandeur about it.

Albinus What books were they?

Bertulf Oh, all the famous ones: *Catholicon*,[10] *Brachylogus*,[11] Ovid allegorized,[12] and countless others. Among them I found also the very
25 charming *Mammothreptus*. With these delights I came upon 'swimming beet.'

Albinus Why do they call it 'swimming?'

Bertulf I'll tell you what I read – let the author vouch for it. Because, says he, it grows in damp and rotten places, and never better than in filth or dung – saving your presence.[13]

30 **Albinus** So it has a disagreeable smell?

Bertulf A smell no excrement could beat.

Albinus Isn't this vegetable good for anything?

Bertulf Oh, yes, it's highly prized.

Albinus By hogs or asses or Cyprian oxen,[14] perhaps.

35 **Bertulf** No, by men; and fussy men at that. There's a race, the Pelini, who have long-drawn-out parties. The last round of drinks they call in their tongue the 'resumptive'[15] – dessert or sweetmeats,[16] as we should say.

Albinus What fine dessert!

Bertulf The rule of this drinking party is that the host is free to serve
40 whatever he pleases. The guests are forbidden to refuse it but must try to take it in good part.

Albinus What if he served hemlock or warmed-over cabbage?[17]

Bertulf Whatever's served must be eaten in silence then and there. At home, however, they're at liberty to vomit up whatever they've eaten. For this purpose they usually serve swimming beet or anticomarita (it's the same

5   thing, whichever name you use). They mix some oak bark[18] and a lot of garlic with it – that's how they make a salad.[19]

Albinus Who has persuaded them to accept so barbarous a rule?

Bertulf Custom, more powerful than any tyrant.[20]

Albinus It's a sad finale you describe if the result's so unpleasant.

10   **Bertulf** I've had my say, without prejudice to anyone who might have something more correct to add.

Canthelus But I've discovered that the ancients had a fish they called anticomarita.

Bertulf Name the author.

15   **Canthelus** I can show you the book; I can't tell you the name of the author. It's written in French but according to Hebrew forms.

Bertulf What does an anticomarita fish look like?

Canthelus It has black scales all over except for a white belly.

Bertulf I think you'll make the fish into a Cynic in a long cloak.[21] What does

20   it taste like?

Canthelus Nothing's more disagreeable. Why, it's a plague. It breeds in stinking pools and sometimes in privies; it's sluggish and muddy. The mere taste of it causes a thick phlegm you can hardly rid yourself of by vomiting. It's common in the land called Celtithrace[22] – considered a delicacy there,

25   where eating meat is more hateful than murder.

Albinus Damned country with its anticomarita!

Canthelus[23] That's as much as I have to say about it; I wouldn't want to prejudice anyone by my opinion.

Diphylus What need to look for an explanation of this word from

30   *Mammothreptus* or Hebrew writings when the etymology of the term is self-evident? Girls who are ill-mated are said to be *anticomaritae*,[24] inasmuch as they have feeble old men for husbands. It's not surprising that the scribes have turned *quo* into *co*, since the letters *c*, *q*, and *k* are cognates.

Eumenius There would be something in what Diphylus said if the

35   expression were Latin. To me it seems Greek, made up of three parts: ἀντί, that is, 'against'; κώμη, 'village'; and ὀαρίζειν, that is, 'to prattle,' as women do. Hence, with omicron elided by synaloepha,[25] you have *anticomarita*, 'one who annoys everybody with boorish chatter.'

Fabullus My friend Eumenius has spoken to the point,[26] to be sure. But in

40   my opinion the expression is made from as many words as it has syllables. For ἀν means ἄνους; τι, τίλλων; κω, κώδια; μα, μάλα; ρυ, ρυπαρά; (to spell it

with an iota is wrong); τα, τάλας. From these you get 'mad and miserable, plucking the hairs of dirty hides.'

Albinus The swimming beet Bertulf mentioned just now is fit nourishment for such work.

5   **Bertulf** Anticomarita for an anticomarita, no doubt.

Gaditanus You've all spoken to the point, but I think a disobedient wife is called *anticomarita* by syncope[27] (of *antidicomarita*), because she always opposes her husband.

Albinus If we accept such figures of speech, market-places [*fora*] will be
10   derived from dysentery [*foria*] and rabbit [*cuniculus*] will turn into cuckoo [*cuculus*].

Bertulf But Albinus, who is the consul in this senate, has not yet given his opinion.

Albinus I've nothing of my own to offer, but I won't hesitate to submit what
15   I learned recently from my host, a chatterbox of a fellow who when talking would change his story oftener than a nightingale his song.[28] He swore the word was Chaldean, composed of three parts. Of these, he said, *anti* means 'stubborn and hare-brained'; *comar*, 'rock';[29] *ita*, 'of a cobbler.'[30]

Bertulf Who ever credited a rock with brains?

20   **Albinus** Nothing absurd about that, if only you change the gender.[31]

Gaditanus The common saying 'As many opinions as there are men'[32] is illustrated perfectly in this assembly. What's the decision, then? The opinions can be counted but not so divided that the majority defeats the minority.

Albinus Then let the better part defeat the worse.

25   **Gaditanus** But for that another assembly would be needed, for every man thinks his own bride the fairest.[33]

Albinus If that were true, we'd have fewer adulteries. But I've an easy solution. Let's draw lots with beans.[34] Whoever wins shall decide for us all.

Canthelus But the lot falls on you. Wasn't I right?

30   **Albinus** I like best the first and last explanations.

Canthelus If I may speak for the company, we all accept that.

Albinus Come, let this be one of those matters it is not lawful to question.

Canthelus Of course.

Albinus If anyone differs, what shall be his punishment?

35   **Canthelus** He shall be labelled in capital letters:[35] 'HERETIC IN GRAMMAR.'

Albinus I'll add – luckily,[36] I hope – what I believe should not be omitted. I'll inform my friends of what I learned from one Syrus, a doctor.

Bertulf What's that?

Albinus If you crush swimming beet, oak gall, and leather-blacking[37] in a
40   mortar, then sprinkle six ounces of dung on it and make it into a poultice, it's an instant remedy for dog mange and hog itch.

Bertulf But look, Albinus, you who bring this business of anticomarita upon us all, in just what author is the word found?

Albinus I'll tell you, but in your ear and yours alone.

Bertulf Agreed, but on condition that I alone may whisper it in turn to just
5 one person.

Albinus But units multiplied finally become thousands.

Bertulf You're right. When once you've made a dyad from a monad, the flow of the dyad is no longer in your control.

Albinus What's known to few can be concealed; what many share, cannot. –
10 Triad, however, refers to a multiplicity.[38]

Bertulf Of course. Whoever had three wives at the same time would be said to have many, but would a man who had three hairs on his head or three teeth in his mouth be said to have many or few?

Albinus Sophist, lend me your ear.

15 **Bertulf** What do I hear? This is no less absurd than if the Greeks were unable to name the city they launched so many ships against, calling it Sutri[39] instead of Troy.

Albinus But this sage has lately come down from the clouds.[40] Unless the heavenly power had come in person to the rescue of human affairs, we'd
20 have been searching this long while for true men, piety, philosophy, letters.

Bertulf Really, this fellow belongs in the front rank of Folly's favourites. He deserved to be called Arch-Fool hereafter, along with his Anticomaritans.

NOTES

1 Of the seven speakers in the dialogue, the only one identifiable as an acquaintance of the author is Hilarius Bertholf, a secretary and messenger of Erasmus in 1522–24. On him see CEBR. He appears in three other colloquies; see 'Inns' n1. Other speakers in the present dialogue are merely labelled: Albinus 'whitewasher,' Canthelus 'ass,' Eumenius 'gracious,' Fabullus 'talkative,' Gaditanus 'Spaniard,' we would say; Athenaeus 2.50e–51a uses the name Diphylus in a passage following one that alludes to the arbutus or wild strawberry, a plant contributing to one of the jokes in the dialogue (see n29 below).

2 Proverbial. It is quoted in Richard Hooker *Of the Laws of Ecclesiastical Politie* 7.14.4. I do not find it in *Adagia*, but see Tilley E268.

3 Pierre Cousturier, to Erasmus' mind the most stupid and detestable of his critics, had published a book against those he regarded as detractors of the Virgin Mary, *Apologeticum in novos anticomaritas* (Paris: Jean Petit 1526). This title contained a blunder that Erasmus seized upon with pleasure. For *maritae* means 'wives' if a noun, 'wedded' if an adjective; Cousturier ought to have written *antimariani* or *antidicomariani* (as Erasmus says in 'The Usefulness of the *Colloquies*' 1105:19–20), since his subject was Mary. A charitable reader might have assumed that the

error was the compositor's, not the author's, but Erasmus welcomed it as an opportunity to expose Cousturier's culpable ignorance. The harshness in this colloquy is intentional, for its aim is ridicule, and the best way to ridicule is to humilitate a pretender to learning by showing him to be an ignorant, conceited fool. See also n10 below on the article 'Antidicomaritae' in *Catholicon*.

The ancient Antidicomarians or Antidicomarianites, members of the Ebionite sect of Jewish Christians in Palestine, denied the perpetual virginity of Mary. The name was applied by Epiphanius, bishop of Salamis (a contemporary of Augustine and Jerome), who writes on them in chapter 78 of his *Panarion* (text in *Epiphanii episcopi Constantiae opera* ed W. Dindorf 5 vols in 3 [Leipzig 1859–62] III part 1 494–527 and in PG 42 833–86). The *editio princeps* of his major writings did not appear until 1544. Erasmus had read the very brief reference to the Antidicomarians in Augustine *De haeresibus* 56 (PL 42 40 and 46) and in Jerome's defence of the doctrine of the Virgin Birth and of Mary's perpetual virginity (*Adversus Helvidium* PL 23 [1883] 193–216 / NPNF 2nd series VI 334–46). Erasmus believed in the perpetual virginity but denied that it could be proved from Scripture. See 'Faith' n42, *Annotationes in Novum Testamentum* LB VI 5C–10E, and 'The Sermon,' which like the present colloquy was pertinent to current discussions and controversies about Mary.

Thomas More was the first to use *antidicomariani* 'Mary's adversaries' in English (*Confutation of Tyndale's Answer* [1532] book 3 [Yale CWM 8 part 1 315]).

4 The adjective is *natatilem*, a pun on 'Natalis,' the Latin form of Noël Béda's name.

5 Anagyris. Pliny says it has a strong smell (*Naturalis historia* 27.30). See *Adagia* I i 65.

6 *Natatilem betam ... cacatilem bestiam*. The last word may be indebted to 1 Cor 15:32, which Erasmus had quoted when commenting on Cousturier in 1526 (Allen Ep 1678:23–6), and to Titus 1:12.

7 *Mammotrectus, Mammotrepton, Mammothreptos, Mammaethreptus* are variant titles of this medieval dictionary of the Bible and other religious subjects. It is attributed to Johannes Marchesinus of Reggio, a Franciscan, and was first printed in 1470. By calling it 'Grandma's darling' (cf *Ecclesiastes* LB V 977D–E) Erasmus hints at the book's character as pap for beginners, in this case clerics who must preach. In addition to brief interpretations and commentary on Scripture it provides aid to priests by sections on orthography, accents in pronunciation of names and words in the Bible, information on hymns, saints' lives, and so on: elementary stuff, but in an age when seminaries for the training of clergy did not exist, many priests needed all the help they could get. Like *Catholicon* and *Brachylogus* it is mentioned contemptuously by Erasmus when he wishes to belittle the learning, or lack of learning, in earlier times, for example in *Antibarbari* CWE 23 34, 36, 67 and Allen Epp 337:317, 535:29–30 / CWE Epp 337:330, 535:33; see Allen *Age of Erasmus* chapter 2, especially 53–5; Chomarat *Grammaire et rhétorique* I 202–4.

8 Seneca *Epistulae morales* 113.26; *Adagia* IV i 86

9 The abbot of St Bavo's in Ghent at this time was Lieven Hugenoys; see CEBR. He was well known to Erasmus, who treats him and his library with a certain condescension here, though a decade earlier he was indebted to him for

permission to examine a manuscript of the Latin Gospels there (Allen Ep 373 introduction). In his first will (1527) Erasmus names this abbot as one of the persons who was to receive a copy of his collected works. His final will (1536) made no provision for such an edition. See 'The Return to Basel' 1124.

10 A large grammar and dictionary, in some respects an encyclopaedia, of the Latin Bible (thirteenth century) by Giovanni Balbus of Genoa, a Dominican; printed in Mainz in 1460 (photographic reprint London 1971), with an eloquent colophon possibly by Gutenberg. It deals with syntax, prosody, rhetoric, biblical names, and a variety of other subjects. It was reissued as late as 1506 by one of Erasmus' publishers, the humanist printer Josse Bade of Paris. Erasmus had a very poor opinion of it; see for example *Annotationes in Novum Testamentum* LB VI 1017E. The early pages of *Antibarbari* record his strong feelings about *Catholicon, Mammotrectus*, and other grammars and dictionaries he despised. Yet the *Catholicon* was obviously found useful and was a valued possession of some clerics; we hear of copies left in wills in the first half of the sixteenth century (Peter Heath *The English Parish Clergy on the Eve of the Reformation* [London and Toronto 1969] 85). See Allen *Age of Erasmus* 43–50 and Chomarat *Grammaire et rhétorique* I 199–201.

If Cousturier consulted *Catholicon* before writing his *Apologeticum in novos anticomaritas*, he would have found there a short article (fol 78 verso of the Mainz 1460 edition) on 'Antidicomaritae.' That might have been the source of his own erroneous title.

11 Probably intended for *Breviloquus* or *Breviloquium*. Medieval lexicons with such titles were ascribed to Johannes de Mera (Allen Ep 35:86n) and others including, very improbably, Erasmus' contemporary Reuchlin (*Epistolae obscurorum virorum* 6:68n). Whoever the compiler was, the disappearance of such works as the three named here was a heartening sign, wrote Erasmus in 1522, that sound learning does advance (*De conscribendis epistolis* LB I 370B–C / ASD I-2 285:11–14 / CWE 25 54–5).

12 In the Middle Ages the poetry of Ovid, particularly his *Metamorphoses*, was highly esteemed as moral and even religious and allegorical as well as narrative art. Nor is this surprising; all of Homer's and Virgil's poetry, Erasmus tells us, can be taken allegorically (*Enchiridion* LB V 7F / CWE 66 33) – a notion Rabelais scoffs at (*Gargantua and Pantagruel* book 1, prologue). *Ovide moralisé*, a long versified translation (fourteenth century) of the *Metamorphoses* with additions from other works, affords interesting examples. In each book the author comments on the allegories, identifying pagan persons and events in Ovid with biblical ones. Who this author was is disputed. Text ed C. de Boer (Amsterdam 1915–38; repr Wiesbaden 1966–7). Consult E.K. Rand *Ovid and His Influence* (Boston 1925) 134–7; L.K. Born 'Ovid and Allegory' *Speculum* 9 (1934) 362–79.

13 Cf Quintus Curtius 5.1.38; same phrase (*honos sit auribus*) in Cicero *Ad familiares* 9.22.4.

14 So stupid that they fed on human excrement (*Adagia* I x 95); hence a proverb appropriate to one who 'talks filthily among the filthy, ignorantly among the ignorant' (*Adagia* I x 96, and cf II x 3)

15 *resumptam*. 'Resumptive' is an obsolete medieval term for 'restorative' (*Oxford English Dictionary*). It occurs in a disparaging allusion of 1528 to Béda, where it

appears to mean an academic discourse (perhaps resumé) or ceremony (Allen Ep 2077:37–40). The 'Pelini,' then, must be Erasmus' opponents at the Sorbonne. As the ASD editors point out, a Greek adjective transliterated *pelini* means 'of clay' or 'of mud.' The name may be used here to identify the Pelini with the pedants in Paris (see 'The Seraphic Funeral' n6), who were 'muddled' in more ways than one. See 'The Profane Feast' n99.

16 *bellaria aut tragemata;* the terms are borrowed from Gellius 13.11.6–7 (cf Macrobius 2.8.3).

17 Both fatal. On hemlock, see 'Sympathy' 1044:17–18 and n87; on cabbage, *Adagia* I v 38.

18 A gibe at Quercus (de Quercu), Guillaume Duchesne, an active opponent of Erasmus in proceedings of the Sorbonne. An earlier allusion to him occurs in 'Patterns' (n35). See Allen Ep 1188:29n and CEBR.

19 *moretum,* a country dish of garlic, oil, and other ingredients; Ovid *Fasti* 4.367

20 On custom see 'The Profane Feast' n58.

21 Their usual dress. Cf Lucian *Cynicus* 1. This was one of the dialogues translated by More.

22 In this context Paris, the abode of the Sorbonists

23 Canthelus] 'Bertulphus' until the March 1533 edition

24 See n3 above.

25 Synaloepha is the reduction of two syllables to one, especially where a vowel at the end of one word is lost or merged with a vowel at the beginning of the following word. In this fantastic example two vowels eta and omicron are lost and only the alpha remains.

26 to the point] Earlier editions have 'better than he did,' meaning Diphylus.

27 By omission of *-di-* (meaning 'apart,' 'asunder')

28 *Adagia* III vi 77

29 Albinus' informant (actually Levinus Ammonius; see Allen Ep 2016:45–64) invented a connection between *anticomarita* and *comaron,* the European arbutus or wild strawberry tree, which Pliny says is also called *unedo* ('I eat one'), because nobody would want to eat more than one (*Naturalis historia* 15.98–9). It is hard to digest and injurious to the stomach (23.151); Athenaeus adds that it causes headaches (2.50e).

30 'Cobbler' is *sutor,* here alluding to Cousturier (Petrus Sutor).

31 *petra* 'rock' is feminine. The masculine *Petrus* 'Peter' would refer, more appropriately, to Cousturier, who is both stubborn and hare-brained.

32 *Adagia* I iii 7; a Terentian tag from *Phormio* 454

33 *Adagia* I ii 15

34 Athenians chose their magistrates by lot, using beans for this purpose; Lucian *Vitarum auctio* 6, and cf *Adagia* v i 36.

35 Béda's name is printed in capital letters in *Supputatio calumniarum Natalis Bedae* (1527) LB IX 518A to emphasize Erasmus' scorn of his role in the Sorbonne's censure (1526) of the *Colloquies* and other writings.

36 *bonis avibus; Adagia* I i 75, common in Erasmus

37 Béda, Duchesne, and Cousturier respectively

38 Metaphysical jargon, familiar to university students and professors of philosophy. These terms had a place in speculations about the holy Triad; that is, the Trinity in Christian theology.

39 A town in ancient Etruria. 'As if they're off to Sutri' was a proverbial expression
   referring to going somewhere at someone else's bidding but paying your own
   expenses, or being invited to dinner but told to bring your own food (*Adagia* IV
   iv 52). Although the pertinence of 'Sutri' in this passage is a whispered secret,
   it must mean Paris, the home of these learned men.
40 *Adagia* I viii 86

A MARRIAGE IN NAME ONLY,
OR
THE UNEQUAL MATCH

Ἄγαμος γάμος, sive Coniugium impar

First printed in the *Colloquia* in the March 1529 edition. On the date see the introduction to 'Charon' 818–19.

The Greek title is recollected from Sophocles *Oedipus tyrannus* 1214 or Euripides *Helen* 690. An 'unequal marriage,' *coniugium impar*, is one in which there is disparity of class, health, religion, or some other serious impediment to harmony between husband and wife (*Annotationes in Novum Testamentum* LB VI 875F). Erasmus argues with unmistakable earnestness that marriage, a forced marriage at that, between a healthy and a diseased person is outrageous in fact if not in law. The young bride, Iphigenia, is well named because she is deliberately 'sacrificed' by her parents in a grotesque marriage.

Many of Erasmus' colloquies, including some of the best ('Courtship' and 'Marriage') voice pungent, provocative opinions on topics relating to women and marriage. 'A Marriage in Name Only' is valuable both because of its connection with other colloquies and because of its frank comments on one of the social evils of the day. It expresses in dialogue, with considerable elaboration, what Erasmus had already written in his treatise *Institutio christiani matrimonii* (1526) LB V 667A–668D on the importance of sound health and compatibility in bride and groom and of wise parental guidance. All the major points and many of the minor ones made in this colloquy can be found in the earlier treatise, including the remark about victims of venereal disease taking pleasure in infecting other persons with it (852:7–9; cf LB V 667E). After reading Erasmus' unsparing denunciation of parents who allow a diseased man to marry their daughter (LB V 668B), we can appreciate better the passage in More's *Utopia* (1516) assuring us that in Utopia an affianced pair are shown to each other naked to prevent ignorance or deception about the health of the future spouse (Yale CWM 4 188, 189).

Whether syphilis had existed previously in Europe or arrived suddenly with Columbus' voyagers in 1493 is a disputed question. The certainty is that the disease spread rapidly and with devastating consequences. This colloquy by Erasmus is one of many comments, and a memorable one. His description of the pox, which is confirmed in distressing detail in many other texts, allows or compels us to compare its reported consequences with those of our contemporary AIDS: the same sense of helplessness, horror, and incredulity; the same anxiety about who will be the next victim of this pestilence; the same hopes of finding a sure remedy or a cure; and, *mutatis mutandis*, comparable psychological, social, and political effects.

The situation described in this colloquy is a painful contrast with that of 'The Girl with No Interest in Marriage,' where sensible parents try to dissuade their stubborn daughter from entering a convent. Here selfish parents are blind to reason, and their daughter, the bartered bride, passive or resigned to her cruel fate. But parents are usually selfish; that is only to be expected (Allen Ep 3104:34–42).

By 1529, when this dialogue appeared in the *Colloquia*, the prevalence and treatment of venereal disease had been discussed in many books and tracts. Girolamo Fracastoro's popular Latin poem *Syphilis* (Verona 1530) reprinted five times before 1600, gave the worst form of treponematosis its name, syphilis, after the shepherd who, because he had offended the sun-god, Apollo, was stricken with this malady. With regard to subject, therefore, Erasmus' colloquy was no novelty. Its interest lies rather in the author's outrage and dismay, his sympathy with the young bride, and his observations on the marriage bond. If he had an actual marriage in mind when he wrote the colloquy, we do not know whose or where it was; nor does this uncertainty make any difference to our response to the argument.

In his *De institutione feminae christianae* 2.4, Juan Luis Vives has an anecdote that illustrates the kind of situation described by Erasmus but teaches a different lesson. Vives names a woman of Bruges, Clara Valdaura (his mother-in-law), who had married a much older man and then discovered he had the pox. The point of the story is her perfect wifely devotion, for she nursed him for the rest of his life, though he lived for many years with the most loathsome disease (*Opera omnia* IV 196–8).

For references to early writings on syphilis see n12 below. Fracastoro's *Syphilis* has been edited and translated by H. Wynne-Finch (London 1935) and by Geoffrey Eatough (Liverpool 1984). On this poem and the theme in art see Erwin Panofsky in *Nederlands Kunsthistorisch Jaarboek* 12 (1961) 1–33, an essential article. Fracastoro, a physician, also published a treatise *De contagione et contagiosis morbis* in 1546 (trans Wilmer Cave Wright [New York and London 1930]). To the world of learning this was his most important work. H. Brabant *Médecins, malades, et maladies de la Renaissance* (Brussels 1966) surveys many aspects of medicine; chapter 1 deals with the pox. The same author's articles on epidemics and Erasmus' illnesses ('Epidémies et médecins au temps d'Erasme,' 'Erasme, ses maladies et ses médecins' in *Colloquia Erasmiana Turonensia* I 515–38, 539–68) are recommended.

PETRONIUS, GABRIEL

Petronius Where from, friend Gabriel, with such a dismal look? Not come out of Trophonius' cave, are you?[1]

5 **Gabriel** Oh, no – from a marriage.

Petronius A less marriageable face I've never seen. Wedding guests generally look happier and merrier for six whole days afterwards; greybeards grow ten years younger. So what wedding are you talking about? That between Death and Destruction,[2] I suppose?

10 **Gabriel** No, between a young nobleman and a girl of sixteen in whom you'd find no lack of beauty, manners, family, or fortune – in short, fit to be the wife of Jove.

Petronius Huh! So young a girl for such an old fellow?[3]

Gabriel Kings don't age.[4]

15 **Petronius** Then why so glum? Maybe you're jealous of the groom who forestalled you and carried off the captured spoils?

Gabriel Pooh! Not at all.

Petronius It wasn't the sort of thing they say occurred at the feast of Lapiths?[5]

20 **Gabriel** By no means.

Petronius What? Did you run out of wine?

Gabriel On the contrary, there was more than enough.

Petronius No flute players on hand?

Gabriel Yes, fiddlers, harpers, flutists, and bagpipers.

25 **Petronius** What, then? Wasn't Hymen[6] present?

Gabriel He was summoned in vain by ever so many voices.

Petronius Nor the Graces?[7]

Gabriel Not the slightest sign[8] of one. Nor Juno, who presides over marriages; nor golden Aphrodite; nor Jove, the marriage-god.[9]

30 **Petronius** Really, you describe a wedding simply unlucky and without benefit of clergy;[10] or rather a marriage without marriage.

Gabriel Had you seen it, you'd go further than that.

Petronius No dancing, then?

Gabriel No, it was a wretchedly lame affair.[11]

35 **Petronius** So no favouring deity was there to gladden the nuptials?

Gabriel No divinity at all, save one goddess the Greeks call Pox.[12]

Petronius You tell of a scabby wedding, I think.

Gabriel An ulcerous and festering one, rather.

Petronius But why, my dear Gabriel, does this mention of it bring tears to
40 your eyes?

Gabriel Petronius, this affair could draw tears from flint.

Petronius I believe it could – if flint had seen it. But please do tell me, what is this awful misfortune? Don't conceal it and don't keep me in suspense any longer.

Gabriel You know Lempridius Eubulus?[13]

5 **Petronius** There's no man better – or better off – in this city.

Gabriel Well, you know his daughter, Iphigenia?[14]

Petronius You've named the flower of the age.

Gabriel So she is. But do you know whom she's married?

Petronius I'll know if you tell me.

10 **Gabriel** She's married Pompilius Blenus.[15]

Petronius What? Not that Thraso,[16] who's in the habit of boring everyone to death with his boastful yarns?

Gabriel The very one.

Petronius But he's long been notorious in this city for two things: lies, and

15 the pox that doesn't yet have an exclusive name, since it goes by such a variety of them.[17]

Gabriel It's a most presumptuous pox. In a showdown, it wouldn't yield to leprosy, elephantiasis,[18] ringworm, gout, or sycosis.[19]

Petronius So the medical tribe proclaim.

20 **Gabriel** Why should I now describe, Petronius, a girl already known to you? Though her attire added a great deal of charm to her natural beauty. My dear Petronius, you'd have said she was some goddess: altogether lovely. Meanwhile, enter our handsome groom: nose broken, one foot dragging after the other (but less gracefully than the Swiss fashion would be),[20] scurvy

25 hands, a breath that would knock you over, lifeless eyes, head bound up, bloody matter exuding from nose and ears. Other men have rings on their fingers; this one even wears rings on his thigh.

Petronius What possessed the parents to trust their daughter to such a monster?

30 **Gabriel** I don't know, except that a great many people seem to have lost their minds these days.

Petronius Perhaps he's very rich.

Gabriel He's rich, all right – in debts.

Petronius If the girl had poisoned her grandparents on both sides, what

35 worse punishment could have been inflicted on her?

Gabriel Had she defiled her ancestors' ashes,[21] it would have been punishment enough to have to kiss such a monster.

Petronius I agree.

Gabriel To my way of thinking, this treatment is more cruel than flinging

40 her naked to bears or lions or crocodiles. Wild beasts would have spared one so beautiful, or a quick death would have ended her torment.

Petronius What you say is true. In my opinion, this deed is worthy of Mezentius, who (according to Virgil) tied dead bodies to living ones, fastening hands to hands and mouth to mouth.[22] Though, unless I'm mistaken, not even Mezentius was so savage that he would yoke so lovely a

5 girl to a corpse. And there's no corpse you wouldn't rather be bound to than such a stinking one, for his breath is sheer poison,[23] his speech a plague, his touch death.

Gabriel Just imagine, Petronius, what pleasure she'll take in his kisses, his embraces, his lovemaking and caresses.

10 **Petronius** I've sometimes heard theologians discussing marriage between unequals. Surely this could be called with perfect justice a marriage of unequals – as though you set a jewel in lead. But I marvel at the young woman's recklessness. Usually such girls are scared almost to death at the sight of a ghost[24] or a spectre. Will this one dare to embrace such a corpse at

15 night?

Gabriel The girl has excuses: the authority of her parents, the entreaty of friends, and the innocence that goes with her age. For my part, I can't sufficiently marvel at the parents' madness. Who has a daughter so homely that he'd be willing to give her in marriage to a leper?

20 **Petronius** In my judgment, no one with the slightest tinge of sanity. If I had a one-eyed daughter who was lame in the bargain and as deformed as Homer's Thersites,[25] and dowerless to boot, I'd refuse a son-in-law of that sort.

Gabriel Yet this plague is both more hideous and more harmful than every kind of leprosy, for it progresses quickly, recurs over and over again, and

25 often kills, while leprosy sometimes allows a man to live to a ripe old age.

Petronius Perhaps her parents were unaware of the groom's disease.

Gabriel Not at all; they knew about it perfectly well.

Petronius If they hated their daughter so, why didn't they tie her in a sack and throw her into the Scheldt?[26]

30 **Gabriel** That would have been a milder form of insanity, to be sure.

Petronius What quality recommended the groom so highly to them? Does he excel in any profession?

Gabriel Many of them: he's an indefatigable gambler, an invincible boozer, a reprobate whoremonger, a past master of cheating and lying, a ready thief,

35 a total bankrupt, an abandoned rake. Why elaborate? Universities teach only the seven liberal arts, but this fellow has more than ten illiberal ones.

Petronius Still, there must have been something to recommend him to her parents.

Gabriel Only his glorious title of knight.[27]

40 **Petronius** What sort of knight is one whose pox scarcely allows him to sit in the saddle? But perhaps he owns splendid estates.

The syphilitic
An early illustration by Dürer (c 1496) of the effects of the 'new' disease
The sphere above recalls an ominous conjunction of planets in Scorpio (1484),
which some astrologers later regarded as prophetic of the Spanish invasion of Italy
and the appearance of syphilis.
Staatliche Museen Preussischer Kulturbesitz, Berlin

Gabriel He did have middling ones, but thanks to his extravagance[28] nothing's left except one little tower, from which he sallies forth at regular intervals in search of prey, a tower so nobly furnished you wouldn't want to keep your hogs there. Yet all the while he prattles about castles, fiefs, and
5   other fine-sounding names, and hangs up his coat of arms everywhere.

Petronius What insignia does his shield bear?

Gabriel Three golden elephants in a field of scarlet.

Petronius Elephant for the elephant – that's appropriate, surely.[29] Must be a bloodthirsty fellow.

10   **Gabriel** No, a wine-thirsty one, for he's wonderfully fond of red wine. That's your man of blood.

Petronius Then that snout of his would be useful for drinking.

Gabriel Indeed it would.

Petronius Thus his insignia proclaim a great and confirmed fool and wine-
15   guzzler. For his colour isn't that of blood but of unmixed wine, and the golden elephant indicates that whatever gold he gets his hands on goes for wine.

Gabriel That's true.

Petronius What dowry will this Thraso[30] bring to his bride, then?

Gabriel What? A very great –

20   **Petronius** How could a bankrupt give a very great one?

Gabriel Give me a chance to tell you: a very great, I say, and very bad pox.

Petronius Damned if I wouldn't rather have my daughter married to a horse than to such a horseman![31]

Gabriel But I'd rather have mine married to a monk. No, this isn't marrying
25   a man but a man's corpse. If you had seen this sight – tell me, would you have held back the tears?

Petronius How could I when I can hardly hear about it without tears? Were her parents so lacking in all natural affection that they would hand over their only daughter, a girl so beautiful, so talented, with such winning manners,
30   to be slave to such a monster simply on account of a lying shield?

Gabriel But this outrage – than which you could find nothing more barbarous, more cruel, more wicked – is even a laughing matter[32] with the governing class nowadays, despite the fact that those born to rule ought to have as robust health as possible.[33] And in fact, the condition of the body
35   has its effect on mental power. Undeniably this disease usually depletes whatever brains a man has. So it comes about that rulers of states may be men who are healthy neither in body nor in mind.

Petronius Men who preside over affairs of state need not only sound minds and robust health but superior bearing and dignified presence as well.
40   Though the first excellence of princes is wisdom and honour, nevertheless a ruler's physical appearance does make a difference.[34] If he's wild-looking,

his ugliness draws much ill will to him; but if he's honourable and dutiful, 'More pleasing valour when with beauty joined.'[35]

Gabriel Rightly so.

Petronius Don't people pity the wretchedness of women whose husbands develop leprosy or epilepsy after marriage?

Gabriel Yes, and they should.

Petronius Then what madness it is willingly to hand over a daughter to one who's worse than leprous!

Gabriel More than madness. If a lord undertook to breed dogs, would he couple a scabby, spiritless dog with a full-blooded bitch?

Petronius No, he'd be very careful to match her with one purebred in every respect, so the litter wouldn't be mongrels.

Gabriel And if a general wanted to strengthen his cavalry, he wouldn't couple a diseased or broken-down horse with a prize mare, would he?

Petronius He wouldn't even admit a diseased horse into a common stable, lest infection spread to the other horses.

Gabriel But they think it doesn't matter whom they couple with a daughter and from what sort of stock come the children who will not only inherit all the wealth but even govern the commonwealth.

Petronius A farmer wouldn't mate just any bull and heifer, or just any horse and mare, or just any hog and sow, since bullock is bred for plow, horse for carriage, and pig for kitchen.

Gabriel Note how consistent men's judgments are: if some commoner dares to kiss a girl of noble birth, people think this insult must be avenged by war.

Petronius A most ferocious war, too.

Gabriel And yet these very people, having free choice, well aware of what they're doing, experienced in the ways of the world, give away their dearest possession to a repulsive monster. As private individuals, they're disloyal to their family; as citizens, to the state.

Petronius If a bridegroom otherwise normal has a slight limp, how the marriage is dreaded! Whereas this terrible evil is no impediment to betrothals.

Gabriel If someone has farmed out his daughter to a Franciscan,[36] how great the horror, how loud the lamentation over the maiden foully placed! Yet remove the habit and she has a man of sound physique. But this bride passes her whole life with a corpse that is only half alive. If a girl marries a priest, people joke about an 'anointed' man, but this girl married a man who's worse than smeared with ointment.

Petronius Enemies scarcely do this to girls captured in war, pirates to those they kidnap; and yet parents do it to an only daughter, and a magistrate doesn't put them under a guardian?

Monk and maiden
Leonhard Beck, 1523
Staatliche Museen Preussischer Kulturbesitz, Kupferstichkabinett, Berlin
A contemporary illustration of an allusion in 'A Marriage in Name Only' to
renting or selling a daughter to a friar. Here a confident monk offers a large coin
to the blustering father, who, although he has sword in hand, is obviously about to
take the money. His daughter's eyes are on the monk. The mother utters sorrowful
words, but her smirking countenance betrays her acceptance of the situation.
An older monk (left) regrets this barter but says he is powerless to intervene.
Everyone present understands that the daughter will go with the monk.

Gabriel How will a physician cure a lunatic if he himself is mad?

Petronius But it's amazing that princes, whose duty it is to look out for the commonwealth, at least in matters pertaining to the person – and in this regard nothing is more important than sound health – don't devise some

5 remedy for this situation.[37] So huge a plague has filled a large part of the globe – and yet they go on snoring as if it made no difference at all.

Gabriel One must speak guardedly of princes, Petronius. But bend your ear; I'll whisper a few words into it.

Petronius Alas! If only you were mistaken in what you say!

10 **Gabriel** How many types of disease do you suppose are caused by wine spoiled and decayed in a thousand ways?[38]

Petronius Countless ones, if you believe the doctors.

Gabriel Aren't inspectors on the watch for this?

Petronius Certainly they're on the watch – to collect excise taxes.

15 **Gabriel** The girl who knowingly marries a diseased man perhaps deserves the trouble she's brought upon herself, though if I were head of the government I'd run them both out of town. But if she married this baneful pest when he misrepresented himself as sound – if I were pope I'd annul this marriage even if it had been made with a thousand marriage contracts.[39]

20 **Petronius** On what pretext,[40] since a marriage lawfully contracted cannot be annulled by mortal man?[41]

Gabriel What? Do you think one made by a wicked fraud is contracted lawfully? The contract isn't valid if the girl is deceived into marrying a slave she thought a free man. Here the husband is slave to a loathsome mistress,

25 Pox, and this slavery is the more wretched because she sets none free; no hope of release can mitigate the misery of the bondage.[42]

Petronius You've discovered a pretext, clearly.

Gabriel Besides, marriage exists only between the living. Here the girl is married to a dead man.[43]

30 **Petronius** That's another pretext. But I suppose you'd permit scabby to marry scabby, in accordance with the old saw, 'like to like.'[44]

Gabriel Were I permitted to do what would benefit the commonwealth, I'd let them marry, all right – but once they were married I'd burn them.

Petronius Then you'd be acting the part of a Phalaris,[45] not a prince.

35 **Gabriel** Does the physician who amputates some fingers or cauterizes a part of the body, lest the whole body perish, seem a Phalaris to you? I regard it as mercy, not cruelty. Would it had been done when this mischief first began to appear! Then the welfare of the whole earth would have been promoted by the destruction of a few. And we find a precedent for this in French

40 history.[46]

Petronius But it would have been more merciful to castrate or deport them.

Gabriel What would you do with the women, then?

Petronius Put chastity belts on them.

Gabriel That would protect you against getting bad eggs from bad hens.[47]
But I'll admit this is the more merciful method if you'll admit the other is
5 safer. For even eunuchs experience lust. Besides, the disease is transmitted
not by one means alone but spread to other persons by a kiss, by conversation,
by touch, by having a little drink together.[48] And we observe that this disease
is accompanied by a mortal hatred, so that whoever is in its clutches takes
pleasure in infecting as many others as possible,[49] even though doing so is
10 no help to him. If deported, they may possibly escape; they can fool others
at night or take advantage of persons who don't know them. From the dead
there's no danger, surely.

Petronius It's safer, I grant, but I don't know whether it suits Christian
compassion.

15 **Gabriel** Come, tell me: which are the worse menace, mere thieves or these
creatures?

Petronius Money's much cheaper than good health, I admit.

Gabriel And yet we Christians crucify thieves, and that isn't called cruelty
but justice. And it's a duty, if you consider the public welfare.

20 **Petronius** In that instance, however, the penalty is paid by the one who
committed the crime.

Gabriel *These* fellows confer a favour, of course! But let's grant that many
people get this disease through no fault of their own (though all the same
you'd find few victims who hadn't invited it by their own misconduct).
25 Jurists hold that there are times when it is right for innocent persons to
be put to death if this is essential to the public safety, just as the Greeks
slew Astyanax, son of Hector, after the destruction of Troy lest the war be
renewed through his efforts.[50] And it is not thought wrong, after a tyrant is
killed, to butcher his innocent children also.[51] What about the fact that we
30 Christians are constantly at war despite our realization that most of the evils
in war befall those who haven't deserved to suffer? The same thing occurs in
what are called 'reprisals': the one who did the injury is safe, and the trader,
who so far from being responsible for the deed never even heard of it, is
robbed.[52] Now if we use such remedies in cases of minor importance, what
35 do you think should be done in the cruelest case of all?

Petronius I yield. It's true.

Gabriel Then consider this. In Italy, buildings are locked up at the first
sign of pestilence; those who attend the sufferer are quarantined. Some call
this inhumanity, though actually it's the highest humanity, for because of
40 this precaution the plague is checked with few fatalities. How great the

humanity of protecting the lives of so many thousands! Some people accuse the Italians of inhospitality because, if pestilence is reported, they banish a stranger at evening and make him spend the night in the open air; but it is morally right to inconvenience a few for the sake of the public good.[53] Some
5   fancy themselves very brave and dutiful because they dare to visit a sufferer from pestilence even if they haven't any business there. But when, on their return, they infect wives, children, and the entire family, what is more foolish than that 'courage,' what more undutiful than that 'duty' of greeting somebody else to bring your nearest and dearest into imminent danger of
10 their lives? Yet how much less is the peril from plague than from this pox! Rarely does the plague affect close relatives; as a rule it spares the aged; and those it does attack it either releases quickly or restores to health stronger than ever. *This* disease is simply slow but sure death, or rather burial. Victims are wrapped like corpses in cloths and unguents.[54]
15 **Petronius** Very true. At least so deadly a disease as this should have been treated with the same care as leprosy.[55] But if this is too much to ask, no one should let his beard be cut, or he should be his own barber.[56]
    Gabriel What if everyone kept his mouth shut?
    Petronius They'd spread the disease through the nose.
20 **Gabriel** There's a remedy for that trouble, too.
    Petronius What?
    Gabriel Let them imitate the alchemists: wear a mask that admits light through little glass windows and allows you to breathe through mouth and nose by means of a tube extending from the mask over your shoulders and
25 down your back.[57]
    Petronius Fine, if there were nothing to fear from contact with fingers, sheets, combs, and scissors.
    Gabriel Then it would be best to let your beard grow to your knees.
    Petronius Evidently. In the next place, make a law that the same men may
30 not be both barber and surgeon.
    Gabriel You'd reduce the barbers to starvation.
    Petronius Let them cut costs and raise prices a little.
    Gabriel Passed.
    Petronius Then make a law to prohibit the common drinking cup.
35 **Gabriel** England would hardly stand for that![58]
    Petronius And don't let two share the same bed unless they're husband and wife.
    Gabriel Accepted.
    Petronius Furthermore, don't permit a guest at an inn to sleep in sheets
40 anyone else has slept in.[59]

Gabriel What will you do with the Germans, who wash theirs barely twice a year?

Petronius Let them get after the washerwomen. Moreover, abolish the custom, no matter how ancient, of greeting with a kiss.

5 **Gabriel** Not even in church?[60]

Petronius Let everyone put his hand against the board.[61]

Gabriel What about conversation?

Petronius Avoid the Homeric advice to 'bend the head near,'[62] and let the listener in turn close his lips tight.

10 **Gabriel** The Twelve Tables[63] would scarcely suffice for these laws.

Petronius But meanwhile what advice have you for the unhappy girl?

Gabriel Only that by being cheerful in her misery, she lessen her misery by that much; that she cover her mouth with her hand when her husband kisses her; and sleep with him armed.

15 **Petronius** Where do you hurry off to now?

Gabriel Straight to my study.

Petronius To do what?

Gabriel To compose an epitaph instead of the wedding song they ask for!

NOTES

1 The opening lines of 'The Funeral' are very similar. On 'Trophonius' cave see *Adagia* I vii 77 and 'The Funeral' n2.

2 The alliteration is in the Latin: *mortis . . . cum Marte.*

3 'Old fellow' seems a jocular reference to 'Jove' in the preceding line. A man as notorious as this groom, Pompilius Blenus, must be older than the bride of sixteen. A man of the world, he is 'old in sin,' seeming prematurely aged because of his debauchery and his disease, like the soldier in 'The Soldier and the Carthusian.'

4 Not in *Adagia* or Tilley; perhaps a variant of the legal maxim 'the king never dies.' Webster in *The White Devil* has 'The Gods never wax old, no more doe princes' (4.2.39).

5 See 'The Godly Feast' n310.

6 God of weddings

7 For a happy marriage attended by the Graces, Muses, and the heavenly Venus see 'The Epithalamium.'

8 Proverbial; *Adagia* II i 84

9 Cf 'The Epithalamium' 524:22–5. The marriage-god is Jupiter Gamelius, as in *Institutio christiani matrimonii* LB V 619B. 'Having care of marriages' was one of his titles. The word, transliterated from Greek, occurs in Jerome *Adversus Jovinianum* 1.48.

10 Literally 'godless'; Greek in the original

11 Both literally and figuratively. Syphilis is crippling; cf 'The Soldier and the Carthusian' 334:36–335:2.

12 Psora, scabies. 'Pox' was a catch-all term for syphilis, leprosy, scabies, mange, and other maladies causing painful or repulsive disfiguration. See 845:17–19 below.

On the origins of venereal syphilis see Francisco Guerra, 'The Problem of Syphilis' in *First Images of America* ed Fredi Chiapelli, 2 vols (Berkeley, Los Angeles, London 1976) II 845–51. This new and horrible affliction first came to public attention as a consequence of the French invasion of Italy in 1494–5, particularly of the French occupation of Naples in February–May 1495. It quickly began to receive comment from medical men, then from others. See *The Earliest Printed Literature on Syphilis, Being Ten Tractates from the Years 1495–1498*, facsimile texts ed Karl Sudhoff and Charles Singer (Florence 1925). These texts were printed in Italy and Germany.

Niccolò Leoniceno's *Libellus de epidemia* (Venice 1497) a iii says Italians called the new malady the French disease; the French called it the Neapolitan disease (Sudhoff and Singer 123); and it was often known, as we read in Erasmus, as the Spanish disease. It became a familiar topic in writings by laymen as well as physicians; for instance by Ulrich von Hutten, who wrote from firsthand experience with it in his treatise *De morbo Gallico* (1519; text in Hutten *Opera* v 399–497). When Hutten was in Basel in December 1522 Erasmus excused himself from receiving 'this swashbuckler ... pox and all' in his house (Allen Epp 1496:6–11, 1331:57–8 and note / CWE Epp 1496:8–14, 1331:63 and n24). Hutten died of syphilis in August 1523. Allusions to the pox are commonplace, in England as on the Continent, in the first half of the century. Colet exhorts men to 'Call to remembrance the meruailous and horryble punysshment of the abhominable great pockes, dayly apperynge to our sightes' (*A right fruitfull monicion*, reprinted in Lupton *Life of Colet* 307 Appendix D from the rare edition of 1534; date of composition unknown). Fisher, in a sermon printed in 1509, paints a dark picture of men 'vexed with the frensshe pockes, poore, and nedy, lyenge by the hye wayes stynkynge and almoost roten above the grounde, havyinge intollerable ache in theyr bones' (*English Works* ed J.E.B. Mayor, EETS extra series 27 [London 1876; repr 1975] 240). One of the allegations against Cardinal Wolsey, Tyndale writes, was that he 'breathed ... in the king's face, when he [Wolsey] had the French pox' (*Practice of Prelates* [1530; STC 24465] k2 verso; in *Works* II [PS 43] 335). But the sexual origin of syphilis, though suspected, was not understood at first.

13 'Good counsellor,' the name of reasonable and respectable men in 'The Girl with No Interest in Marriage' and 'The Poetic Feast' but wholly inappropriate for this bride's father, who is blind to his daughter's welfare.

14 In Greek mythology the daughter of Agamemnon and Clytemnestra. Told by the seer Calchas that the goddess Artemis demanded the sacrifice of their daughter, Agamemnon prepared to carry out the sentence, but Artemis relented at the last moment and saved Iphigenia by spiriting her away and substituting a hind in her place. This is the version presented in Euripides' *Iphigenia in Aulide*. Erasmus translated this play in 1506.

15 A fictional character so far as we know. The name suggests *blennus* 'blockhead,' 'dolt' as in Plautus *Bacchides* 1086. French *blennorragie* means 'gonorrhoea.'

As Smith emphasized (*Key* 47–8), the language about him in these pages would be applicable to two of Erasmus' former friends and later enemies, Heinrich Eppendorf and Ulrich von Hutten. Erasmus had many difficulties with Eppendorf; see 'The Cheating Horse-Dealer' and 'The Knight without a Horse,' which mocks Eppendorf's pretensions to knightly rank. Hutten, a far better known person, was an assertive patriot, a Lutheran, and an important writer who came to a bad end (see n12 above). Eppendorf and Hutten were acquainted in Basel for a few years in the early 1520s. When Erasmus and Hutten fell out, Erasmus accused Eppendorf of inciting Hutten to write against him (Epp 1383, 1437). Erasmus' relations with Eppendorf went from bad to worse, even after this March 1529 colloquy was printed, and continued to trouble him for several years longer. On Eppendorf and Hutten see CEBR and notes to 'The Knight without a Horse.'

On Hutten and Erasmus the fullest account is W. Kaegi 'Hutten und Erasmus: Ihre Freundschaft und ihr Streit' *Historische Vierteljahrsschrift* 22 (1924–5) 200–78, 461–514. For Erasmus' *Spongia* (1523), a reply to Hutten's *Expostulatio* against him, see LB X 1631A–1672F; English translations of *Expostulatio* and *Spongia* in Randolph J. Klawiter *The Polemics of Erasmus of Rotterdam and Ulrich von Hutten* (Notre Dame, Ind 1977).

16 The braggart soldier in Terence *Eunuchus*

17 See n12 above; cf Allen Ep 1593:88–9; *Institutio christiani matrimonii* LB V 667A.

18 In August 1525 Erasmus refers to an incursion of this skin disease into Italy. He does not give a date but says that the epidemic soon disappeared (Allen Ep 1593:75–6). Possibly he knew of it when he lived in Italy in 1506–9.

19 *Sycosis barbae*, chronic folliculitis

20 See 'Military Affairs' n3.

21 *Adagia* II viii 23. See 'Penny-Pinching' n43.

22 The allusion to the cruel tyrant Mezentius' practice is in Virgil *Aeneid* 8.485–6. This striking image of uniting the living to the dead became fairly common in discussions of syphilitics who married (as in *Institutio christiani matrimonii* LB V 667C). An excellent example is Alciato's *Emblemata* no 198: *Nupta contagioso* (Padua 1621; repr New York 1976); Fracastoro (introduction 843 above) tells those who have or fear the pox, 'Shun Venus' (*Syphilis* 2.113).

23 See 853:18–25 below and *Ecclesiastes* LB V 773C.

24 ghost] 'Mouse' (*muris*) in the first and second editions; changed (*lemuris*) in the edition of September 1531

25 See *Adagia* IV iii 80 and 'Courtship' n37

26 Said to have been a punishment for Roman parricides. 'Worthy of the sack' was proverbial; *Adagia* IV ix 18. The Scheldt flows past Antwerp, and Erasmus may have known or heard of a marriage there resembling the one he describes here.

27 'O the madness of parents who think it better for a daughter to marry a knight than a good farmer or skilled craftsman!' (*Institutio christiani matrimonii* LB V 668F).

28 *protervia*, a word used proverbially in describing a sacrifice in which everything offered must be consumed; hence reckless waste. Explained in *Adagia* I ix 44, where Erasmus uses it as a text for denouncing the vices of German Junkers, which he does more elaborately in 'The Knight without a Horse.' This adage was an addition to the 1528 edition (Phillips '*Adages*' 129–30), and there is no

doubt that Erasmus had Eppendorf in mind, as Smith (*Erasmus: A Study of His Life, Ideals and Place in History*. [New York and London 1923; repr New York 1962] 386) was the first to notice.

29 *Adagia* II ix 90: 'There's no difference between you and an elephant' alludes to being 'thick-skinned'; in this context that means thickheaded and stupid as well. Equally pertinent is a remark in *Adagia* I ix 44 about German knights who 'get a shield painted on which is a hand brandishing a sword and cutting up an elephant.'

30 See n16 above.

31 *equo . . . equiti* (here 'knight')

32 See *De bello Turcico* LB V 346C; cf Allen Ep 2260:51–2.

33 In the opening lines of *Institutio principis christiani* Erasmus merely says of a young prince that 'some thought should also perhaps be given to his state of health' (LB IV 561B / ASD IV-1 136:12–13 / Born 139 / CWE 27 206).

34 Virgil *Aeneid* 5.344. See *Oratio de virtute amplectenda* (1503) LB V 67D–524A / CWE 29 5–6. Very similar is a passage in *Panegyricus ad Philippum* (1504) LB IV 523E–524A / CWE 27 33–4.

35 Virgil *Aeneid* 5:344

36 See illustration 850.

37 In antiquity physicians accepted this duty, but today kings ignore it (*Encomium medicinae* LB I 542F–543A / ASD I-4 182:330–41 / CWE 29 46–7). Cf *Institutio christiani matrimonii* LB V 667D–E.

38 Cf *Encomium medicinae* LB I 543A / ASD I-4 182:327–42 / CWE 29 47.

39 Literally, 'six hundred,' see 'The Funeral' n76.

40 *color*, a rhetorical term; see 'A Fish Diet' n308.

41 The essence of marriage was *consensus*, consent between the parties; see 'Courtship' n48. Divorce was impossible; see 'Marriage' n16.

42 If the man had the pox and concealed this fact from his fiancée and her parents at the time of betrothal or marriage, then, in Erasmus' opinion, the engagement ought to be cancelled or the marriage annulled (*Ratio verae theologiae* in Holborn 207:27–36; *Institutio christiani matrimonii* LB V 649A–B, 667A–668D).

43 See 846:1–7 above, and cf 853:13–14 below.

44 Greek in the original; cf *Adagia* I ii 20, I ii 21, and I i 35. Cf also *Institutio christiani matrimonii* LB V 658D–E, 660A.

45 Tyrant of Agrigentum in Sicily, sixth century BC. When one of his subjects devised a brazen bull in which to roast the tyrant's victims, Phalaris chose him as the first (Lucian *Phalaris 1*). See *Adagia* I x 86 and *Parabolae* CWE 23 228:30.

46 Possibly an allusion to drastic steps taken during a plague, but identification has eluded all editors.

47 The English form of a proverb (cf Tilley B376) that in *Adagia* has 'crows' instead of 'hens' (I ix 25)

48 Erasmus is sure that syphilis is contagious ('transmitted by a kiss') and spread by unhygienic practices, yet at the same time emphasizes sexual promiscuity as a cause. But because the sexual origins of venereal disease were not sufficiently or generally understood, and no clear distinction between acquired and congenital syphilis was known, the disease could be regarded as a misfortune rather than a consequence of personal behaviour – or misbehaviour. Erasmus however blames personal irresponsibility or carelessness more than bad luck

for the persistence of the pox. See 'The Epicurean' 1080:23–1081:12 on the 'stimulus of unlawful pleasure.'

49 So *Institutio christiani matrimonii* LB V 667E

50 He was hurled from the walls of Troy by the victorious Greeks. See Euripides *Troades* 719–89. In Seneca *Troades* 1068–1103 he jumps from the walls.

51 In Lucian's *Tyrannicida* the tyrannicide kills the tyrant's son when he fails to find the tyrant. When, later, the tyrant discovers his son's body he commits suicide.

52 *represalibus*, medieval Latin; permission or right to do unto others as they have done unto you, specifically the right to regain seized or stolen property by seizing or stealing the property of others

53 Erasmus' residence in Italy in 1506–9 gave him unpleasant firsthand experience of reactions to pestilence there, as he relates in Epp 296:175–89, 447:470–96 / CWE Epp 296:185–200, 447:514–45. Coryat, a century later, says that cities in eastern Lombardy forbade strangers to enter unless they had a clean bill of health from the last city visited (*Crudities* I 214). In the sixteenth century hospitals for incurables, including syphilitics, were established in Italy by societies, partly lay, partly clerical. See H.O. Evenett *The Spirit of the Counter-Reformation* (Cambridge 1968) 26–7.

54 In H. Brabant *Médecins, malades, et maladies de la Renaissance* (introduction 843 above) figure 2 shows a syphilitic wearing a sort of bib, required by the effects of treatment with mercury, which was commonly administered to victims of the disease. Cf Fracastoro *Syphilis* (843 above) 2.445–8. The other supposed cure, praised by Fracastoro, was gum guaiacum, lignum vitae.

55 Erasmus was no pioneer in epidemiology, but as a careful observer with long experience he made shrewd inferences about infectious and contagious diseases in these lines and elsewhere; see for example 'Inns' 372:16–32, where the guests are described as laughing about such dangers. Men of the world joke about the pox; he who does not have it is considered a mere yokel (Allen Ep 2260:51–2; *De bello Turcico* LB V 346C–D; 'The Knight without a Horse' 884:22–5). The contagiousness of the pox and the severity of its effects caused enlightened men to protest, as Erasmus does here and in other places, against customs that spread the disease. Thus Gilbert Cousin (on whom see introduction to 'The Master's Bidding' 64–5) in Οἰκέτης *sive de officiis famulorum* condemns masters who foolishly ignore a servant's loose living until he brings the pox into the household (Chaloner's translation [1543] B5–6). Erasmus insisted that any servant of his be above suspicion in this matter (Allen Ep 2963:3–8).

56 See the illustration (1520) of the barber-surgeon in *Colloquia Erasmiana Turonensia* I 521.

57 An early writer on syphilis, Hans Widmann, advises men to avoid the breath of those who have *morbus Gallicus* (*De pustulis et morbo* [1497]; see Sudhoff and Singer [n12 above] 238). This had long been advice with respect to leprosy.

58 *A Relation of England* 219 makes the same observation. Erasmus noticed the custom in England (Allen and CWE Ep 999:67–8, and cf 'The Lover of Glory' 970:36–7), but in one of the later editions of *Adagia* says that 'with us it is now less common because of fear of the new pox' (IV vii 70). Montaigne confesses to fastidiousness in avoiding a common drinking cup (*Essays* 3.13

'Of Experience'; Frame 831). In Ep 1532 Erasmus suggests ways of improving hygienic arrangements in English houses.

59 In 'Inns' 375:22 Erasmus' traveller complains of dirty sheets; so did Montaigne (*Travel Journal*; Frame 879). For more favourable reports on German inns see 'Inns' n8.

60 'In England men kiss women by way of greeting, even in church' ('The Lover of Glory' 970:34–5). See 'Inns' n7; Allen Ep 103:17–24 / CWE Ep 103:19–29.

61 That is, instead of kissing it. The board (*tabellum*) is the pax-board, a small tablet or disc kissed by the celebrant at mass and then by each worshipper in turn. Some pax-boards were made of ivory or silver; which is why Bardolph in Shakespeare's *Henry v* stole one (3.6.42–7).

62 *Odyssey* 1.157, 4.70, 17.592. Erasmus quotes the Greek.

63 See 'A Fish Diet' n141.

THE IMPOSTURE

Impostura

First printed in the *Colloquia* in the March 1529 edition. On the date see introduction to 'Charon' 818–19.

Like 'Echo' and 'Non-Sequiturs,' this is a Lucianic *jeu d'esprit*. In the Greek writer's *Pseudosophista* (cleverly translated by H.W. and F.G. Fowler *The Works of Lucian of Samosata* [Oxford 1905] IV 181–90), a man who prides himself on the correctness of his grammar and idiom fails to detect the intentional blunders made by a friend, though challenged to do so. The comparable trick in *Impostura* of disguising verse as prose is one that Erasmus says he himself had played on an English friend, the eminent scholar Thomas Linacre (not More, as Smith *Key* 48 has; see *De conscribendis epistolis* LB I 347F / ASD I-2 217:20–218:7 / CWE 25 16). Cf Allen Ep 2241:21–2.

Ingenious exercises of this kind, however frivolous or pedantic they may seem, appealed strongly to sixteenth-century readers and writers, whose schooling was predominantly linguistic and rhetorical. Examples of verbal preciosity, metrical experimentation, and elaborate *schemata* occur so often in Renaissance literature, both Latin and vernacular, that we are constantly reminded of the degree to which appreciation depended on a good ear, not merely visual attentiveness. In 'The Imposture' Philip's self-confidence is the more culpable because he ought to have *heard* the scansion of the verses. For silent reading, a practice gradually made universal by printing, was not yet so completely 'natural' in Erasmus' time, or even in Shakespeare's, that people had ceased to 'hear' the words of a text even when reading them.

The speakers in this dialogue were most likely named after Lieven Algoet and Philippus Montanus, two of Erasmus' servant-pupils and messengers; on both see CEBR. Algoet, a native of Ghent, lived with Erasmus for six or seven years c 1519–25 and was in touch with him for half a dozen more. He appears in several colloquies; see 'Patterns' n33. Montanus was in Erasmus' service briefly in 1528. Afterwards, as a Parisian scholar, he edited patristic texts and became finally rector of a college in Douai. Erasmus left him 150 gold crowns in his final will (Allen XI 364:17–18 Appendix 25). See Allen Ep 2065 introduction. Montanus was first identified with the Philip of this colloquy by Smith (*Key* 48).

LIVINUS, PHILIP

Philip How do you do, Livinus.

Livinus I'll do well enough, if you please.

5   [1] But now I warn you, please beware, be on your guard,
         For I intend to play a trick unless you're sharp.[1]

Philip An enemy who announces his intentions isn't much to be feared. But come on; trick me if you can.

Livinus [2] Tricked already have you been, without your knowing; mind

10   once more.

Philip I suppose I'm dealing with a magician, for I don't perceive any deception.

Livinus [3] Watch again, be on guard; you've been fooled here by me
         More than once; now I mean further tricks to display.

15 **Philip** I'm ready; begin.

Livinus [4] What you've asked of me I've performed already.

Philip What's been done, or what performed? I don't see any trick.

Livinus [5] Lend me your ears; often I've warned; still you don't heed; try
                                                            now again.

20 **Philip** A new kind of magic! I'm fooled, you say, yet I'm not aware of any trick, though I've watched your eyes and hands and tongue. But come on, start again.

Livinus [6] Now again and again I've begun with my trick,
         And as soon as I do you fall in to the trap.

25 **Philip** By what means do you trap me?

Livinus [7] This my tongue plays tricks that you hear not, see not;
         Once more harken; try now to open ears and
         Pay strict heed; then see if you're clever this time.

Philip I can't open them any more than I've done already, even if my life

30 depended on it. But trick me again.

Livinus [8] Once more are you fooled yet you don't see how skill can fool you.

Philip You're killing me! Tell me, I beg you, what sort of illusion is this?

Livinus [9] All this while in verse I've spoken and in verse I'm speaking
                                                            still.

35 **Philip** Nothing further from my thoughts than that!

Livinus First I answered you in two iambic trimeters [1]. Next in a trochaic tetrameter catalectic [2]. Presently I spoke in straight cretics [3]. After that in Phalaecean[2] hendecasyllable [4]. Next wholly in choriambics [5]. In addition to this, wholly in anapaests [6]. Again, in three sapphics [7]. Then in

40 Sotadean[3] verse [8]. Last of all, in trochaic tetrameter [9].

Philip [10] Immortal God! I never dreamt I'd fall for tricks of that sort.
If I live long enough, I shall pay you back some day.

Livinus Go ahead if you can.

Philip [11] Here I go, paid you twice, tit for tat;[4] yet you don't see the trick.

5   **Livinus** What! So soon?

Philip I threatened you in an iambic tetrameter catalectic [10] followed by
five cretics [11].

Livinus So it turns out, I see, according to the proverb, 'Cretan meets
Cretan.'[5]

10   **Philip** Yes, but I hope no more harmful deception may ever befall either
of us!

NOTES

1 Similarly in 'The Liar and the Man of Honour' a trickster warns an acquaintance
that he is going to lie to him without being detected, and does so.

2 After Phalaecus, an early Greek poet

3 The Greek poet Sotades (third century BC) is believed to have invented this
metre: hendecasyllable with an anapaest inserted in the second foot.

4 *par pari; Adagia* I i 35

5 When the tables are turned on a cheater; *Adagia* I ii 26 and 29. See 'The Cheating
Horse-Dealer' n8.

CYCLOPS, OR THE GOSPEL-BEARER

Cyclops, sive Evangeliophorus

'Cyclops' was one of nine new colloquies in the March 1529 edition. But another colloquy in that edition, 'Charon,' had already appeared in 1523; on that circumstance see the introduction to 'Charon,' 818–19 above. It was his study of 'Cyclops' that prompted Henry de Vocht to examine and reject the assertions in BE 2nd series *Colloquia* I 199 concerning the presence of this dialogue and eight others in an edition brought out by Eucharius Cervicornus of Cologne in 1528. De Vocht showed by bibliographical evidence that these nine colloquies were later insertions, an *auctarium*, in the Cologne edition, where they lack signatures. They were first printed in the Froben edition of March 1529.

In addition to convincing bibliographical objections, there are serious biographical obstacles to the supposition that 'Cyclops' was first printed by Cervicornus in 1528. First, although it is certain that Polyphemus is Felix Rex, there is no proof that he was in Erasmus' service earlier than October of that year (Allen Epp 2068:1, 2121:4n, 2130 introduction). Second, a quarrel between Polyphemus and Ludovicus Carinus, mentioned in Allen Ep 2112:30–43 (March 1529), occurred in February 1529 (on Carinus see 'The Poetic Feast' n1). Third, for the allusion in this colloquy to preachers warning of the end of the world (869:32–3), taken as a reference to an Anabaptist's recent visit to Basel – and this seems the only plausible interpretation – no date earlier than 1529 is possible, since Erasmus' account of the incident as a recent event was written in April of that year (Allen Ep 2149:4–50). See De Vocht *Earliest English Translations* xi–xii, with the notes.

The interlocutors are two of Erasmus' *famuli* who served him as amanuenses and messengers. Both, he says, had expressed a desire to appear in the *Colloquies* (Allen Ep 2147:11–20). Whether they were pleased with his presentation of them we do not know. Nicolaas Kan (Cannius) of Amsterdam was a member of Erasmus' household from the spring of 1527 until July of 1530, when he returned to Holland and entered the church; when this colloquy came out he was twenty-four years old. Polyphemus is Felix Rex of Ghent, who was in Erasmus' service for about a year, 1528–9. His nickname of 'Polyphemus' ('many-voiced') may have testified to his knowledge of languages, or his chattering, but also recalls the boorish Cyclops of the *Odyssey*. Erasmus had his troubles with Polyphemus, a reckless, quarrelsome fellow and given to drink. He drifted about for a few years after Erasmus got rid of him and finally became librarian to Duke Albert of Prussia in 1534. He died c 1549.

According to Erasmus, Polyphemus 'used to carry with him a beautifully decorated volume of the Gospels, though nothing could be more soiled
than his own life' (Allen Ep 2147:18–20). In the colloquy Polyphemus – who
talked of enlisting against the Turks when he left Erasmus' service (Allen
Ep 2230:1–4) – already has a share of the swaggering insolence and impiety
found in soldiers portrayed in Erasmus' writings, Thrasymachus in 'Military
Affairs,' for instance. Few encounters between ignorance and effrontery are
more amusing than that in which Polyphemus 'absolves' a friar by whacking
him on the head with Erasmus' translation of the New Testament.

Another passage in this dialogue was thought by some to be a libel on a
leading citizen of Basel, Johannes Oecolampadius. Erasmus was troubled by
the report and changed the offending words in the next edition. This tempest
in a teapot injured no one but is of some interest as a sign of tensions in Basel
at a time when controversies over the Reformation were coming to a climax
there and Erasmus, as a consequence, was preparing to move to Freiburg.

Nicolas Mercier, who produced an expurgated edition of the *Colloquies*
(Paris 1656), says in his dedication that Kan had once been engaged in a
similar labour but his work 'perished long ago' (a2 verso in the Paris 1673/4
edition). The source of this assertion is unknown. See Franz Bierlaire *Les
Colloques d'Erasme* 144 n6.

German and Italian versions of *Cyclops* (1545) are reported, and an
English version by Edmund Becke was issued at Canterbury c 1549. The
volume contained also a translation of *De rebus ac vocabulis*. There is a text of
the translation of *Cyclops* in De Vocht's *Earliest English Translations* 7–31 and
in Spurgeon 193–223.

POLYPHEMUS,[1] CANNIUS[2]

Cannius What's Polyphemus hunting here?
Polyphemus What could I be hunting without dog or spear? Is that your
5 question?
Cannius Some wood nymph, perhaps.[3]
Polyphemus A good guess. Look, here's my hunting net.
Cannius What a sight! Bacchus in a lion's skin[4] – Polyphemus with a book[5]
– a cat in a saffron gown![6]
10 **Polyphemus** I've painted this little book not only in saffron but bright red
and blue, too.
Cannius I'm not talking about saffron; I said something in Greek.[7] – Seems
to be a soldierly book, for it's protected by bosses, plates, and brass clasps.
Polyphemus Take a good look at it.

Cannius I'm looking. Very fine, but you haven't yet decorated it enough.

Polyphemus What's lacking?

Cannius You should have added your coat of arms.

Polyphemus What coat of arms?

5 **Cannius** The head of Silenus peering out of a wine jug.[8] But what's the book about? The art of drinking?[9]

Polyphemus Be careful you don't blurt out blasphemy.

Cannius What, you don't mean it's something sacred?

Polyphemus The most sacred of all, the Gospels.

10 **Cannius** By Hercules![10] What has Polyphemus to do with the Gospels?

Polyphemus You might as well ask what a Christian has to do with Christ.

Cannius I'm not sure a halberd isn't more fitting for the likes of you.[11] If I were at sea and met a stranger who looked like this, I'd take him for a pirate; if I met him in a wood, for a bandit.

15 **Polyphemus** Yet this very book of Gospels teaches us not to judge by appearances.[12] Just as a haughty spirit often lurks under an ash-coloured cowl, so a cropped head, curled beard, stern brow, wild eyes, plumed cap, military cloak, and slashed breeches sometimes cover a true Christian heart.[13]

20 **Cannius** Of course. Sometimes a sheep lurks in wolf's clothing, too. And, if you trust fables, an ass in a lion's skin.[14]

Polyphemus What's more, I know a man who has a sheep's head and a fox's heart. I could wish him friends as fair as his eyes are dark and that he be as truly golden as the sallow gold of his complexion.[15]

25 **Cannius** If a man with a sheepskin cap has a sheep's head, what a load you carry, with both a sheep and an ostrich on your head! And isn't it rather ridiculous to have a bird on your head and an ass in your heart?

Polyphemus That hurt!

Cannius But it would be well if, as you've decorated the Gospels with 30 various ornaments, the Gospels in turn adorned you. You've decorated them with colours; I wish they might embellish you with good morals.

Polyphemus I'll see to that.

Cannius After your fashion, yes.

Polyphemus But insults aside, you don't condemn those who carry a volume 35 of the Gospels about, do you?

Cannius The last person in the world to do that.[16]

Polyphemus What? I seem to you the least person in the world, when I'm taller than you by an ass's head?

Cannius I don't believe you'd be that much taller even if the ass pricked up 40 its ears.[17]

Polyphemus Certainly by a buffalo's.

Cannius I like the comparison. But I said 'last'; I wasn't calling you 'least.'
Polyphemus What's the difference between an egg and an egg?[18]
Cannius What's the difference between middle finger and little finger?
Polyphemus The middle one's longer.

5   **Cannius** Very good. What's the difference between ass ears and wolf ears?
Polyphemus Wolf ears are shorter.
Cannius That's right.
Polyphemus But I'm in the habit of measuring long and short by span and ell, not by ears.

10   **Cannius** Well, the man who carried Christ was called Christopher.[19] You, who carry the Gospels, ought to be called Gospel-bearer[20] instead of Polyphemus.
Polyphemus Don't you think it's holy to carry the Gospels?
Cannius No – unless you'd agree that asses are mighty holy.

15   **Polyphemus** How so?
Cannius Because one of them can carry three thousand books of this kind. I should think you'd be equal to that load if fitted with the right pack-saddle.
Polyphemus There's nothing far-fetched in thus crediting an ass with

20   holiness because he carried Christ.[21]
Cannius I don't envy you that holiness. And if you like, I'll give you relics of the ass that carried Christ, so you can kiss them.
Polyphemus A gift I'll be glad to get. For by touching the body of Christ that ass was consecrated.

25   **Cannius** Obviously those who smote Christ touched him, too.[22]
Polyphemus But tell me seriously, isn't carrying the Gospels about a reverent thing to do?[23]
Cannius Reverent if done sincerely, without hypocrisy.
Polyphemus Hypocrisy's for monks. What has a soldier to do with

30   hypocrisy?
Cannius But first tell me what hypocrisy is.[24]
Polyphemus Professing something other than what you really mean.
Cannius But what does carrying a copy of the Gospels profess? A gospel life, doesn't it?

35   **Polyphemus** I suppose so.
Cannius Therefore, when the life doesn't correspond to the book, isn't that hypocrisy?
Polyphemus Apparently. But what is it truly to bear the gospel?
Cannius Some bear it in their hands, as the Franciscans do their Rule.[25]

40   Parisian porters, and asses and geldings, can do the same. There are those who bear it in their mouths, harping on nothing but Christ and the gospel.

That's pharisaical. Some bear it in their hearts. The true gospel-bearer, then, is one who carries it in hands and mouth *and* heart.

Polyphemus Where are these?

Cannius In churches – the deacons, who bear the book, read it to the
5   congregation, and have it by heart.[26]

Polyphemus Though not all who bear the gospel in their hearts are devout.

Cannius Don't quibble. A man doesn't bear it in his heart unless he loves it through and through. Nobody loves it wholeheartedly unless he emulates the gospel in his manner of living.

10 **Polyphemus** I don't follow these subtleties.

Cannius But I'll tell you more bluntly.[27] If you carry a jar of Beaune wine[28] on your shoulder, it's just a burden, isn't it?

Polyphemus That's all.

Cannius But if you hold the wine in your throat, and presently spit it out?

15 **Polyphemus** Useless – though really, I'm not accustomed to doing that.

Cannius But if – as you *are* accustomed – you take a long drink?

Polyphemus Nothing more heavenly.

Cannius Your whole body glows; your face turns rosy; your expression grows merry.

20 **Polyphemus** Exactly.

Cannius The gospel has the same effect when it penetrates the heart. It makes a new man of you.

Polyphemus So I don't seem to you to live according to the gospel?

Cannius You can best decide that question yourself.

25 **Polyphemus** If it could be decided with a battle-axe[29] –

Cannius If someone called you a liar or a rake to your face, what would you do?

Polyphemus What would I do? He'd feel my fists.

Cannius What if someone hit you hard?

30 **Polyphemus** I'd break his neck for that.

Cannius But your book teaches you to repay insults with a soft answer,[30] and 'whoever shall smite thee on thy right cheek, turn to him the other also.'[31]

Polyphemus I've read that, but it slipped my mind.

35 **Cannius** You pray frequently, I dare say.

Polyphemus That's pharisaical.

Cannius Long-winded but insincere praying is pharisaical.[32] But your book teaches us to pray without ceasing, yet sincerely.[33]

Polyphemus Still, I do pray sometimes.

40 **Cannius** When?

Polyphemus Whenever I think of it – once or twice a week.

Cannius What do you pray?

Polyphemus The Lord's Prayer.

Cannius How often?

Polyphemus Once. For the Gospel forbids vain repetition as 'much
5   speaking.'³⁴

Cannius Can you concentrate on the Paternoster while repeating it?

Polyphemus Never tried. Isn't it enough to say the words?

Cannius I don't know, except that God hears only the utterance of the heart.
Do you fast often?

10 **Polyphemus** Never.

Cannius But your book recommends prayer and fasting.

Polyphemus I'd recommend them too if my belly did not demand something
else.

Cannius But Paul says those who serve their bellies aren't serving Jesus
15 Christ.³⁵ Do you eat meat on any day whatever?

Polyphemus Any day it's offered.

Cannius Yet a man as tough as you are could live on hay or the bark of
trees.

Polyphemus But Christ said that a man is not defiled by what he eats.³⁶

20 **Cannius** True, if it's eaten in moderation, without giving offence. But Paul,
the disciple of Christ, prefers starvation to offending a weak brother by his
food;³⁷ and he calls upon us to follow his example, in order that we may
please men in all things.

Polyphemus Paul's Paul, and I'm me.

25 **Cannius** But Egon's job is to feed she-goats.³⁸

Polyphemus I'd prefer to eat one.

Cannius A fine wish! You'll be a billy-goat rather than a she-goat.

Polyphemus I said *eat* one, not *be* one.³⁹

Cannius Very prettily said. – Are you generous to the poor?

30 **Polyphemus** I've nothing to give.

Cannius But you would have if you lived soberly and worked hard.

Polyphemus I'm fond of loafing.

Cannius Do you keep God's commandments?

Polyphemus That's tiresome.

35 **Cannius** Do you do penance for your sins?

Polyphemus Christ has paid for us.⁴⁰

Cannius Then why do you insist you love the gospel?

Polyphemus I'll tell you. A certain Franciscan in our neighbourhood kept
babbling from the pulpit against Erasmus' New Testament.⁴¹ I met the man
40 privately, grabbed him by the hair with my left hand, and punched him with
my right. I gave him a hell of a beating; made his whole face swell. What do

you say to that? Isn't that promoting the gospel? Next I gave him absolution by banging him on the head three times with this very same book, raising three lumps, in the name of Father, Son, and Holy Ghost.

Cannius The evangelical spirit, all right! This is certainly defending the
5   gospel with the Gospel.

Polyphemus I ran across another member of the same order who never stopped raving against Erasmus. Fired with evangelical zeal, I threatened the fellow so much he begged pardon on both knees and admitted the devil had put him up to saying what he said. If he hadn't done this, my halberd
10   would have bounced against his head. I looked as fierce as Mars in battle. This took place before witnesses.

Cannius I'm surprised the man didn't drop dead on the spot. But let's go on. Do you live chastely?

Polyphemus I may – when I'm old. But shall I confess the truth to you,
15   Cannius?

Cannius I'm no priest. If you want to confess, find somebody else.

Polyphemus Usually I confess to God,[42] but to you I admit I'm not yet a perfect follower of the gospel; just an ordinary chap. My kind have four gospels. Four things above all we gospellers seek: full bellies; plenty of
20   work for the organs below the belly; a livelihood from somewhere or other; finally, freedom to do as we like.[43] If we get these, we shout in our cups, '*Io triumphe*;[44] *Io, Paean!*[45] The gospel flourishes! Christ reigns!'

Cannius That's an Epicurean life,[46] surely, not an evangelical one.

Polyphemus I don't deny it, but you know Christ is omnipotent and can
25   turn us into other men in the twinkling of an eye.

Cannius Into swine, too, which I think is more likely than into good men.

Polyphemus I wish there were no worse creatures in the world than swine, oxen, asses, and camels. You can meet many men who are fiercer than lions, greedier than wolves, more lecherous than sparrows, more snappish than
30   dogs, more venomous than vipers.[47]

Cannius But now it's time for you to begin changing from brute to man.

Polyphemus You do well to warn me, for prophets these days declare the end of the world is at hand.[48]

Cannius All the more reason to hurry.
35   **Polyphemus** I await the hand of Christ.

Cannius See that you are pliant material for his hand. But where do they get the notion that the end of the world is near?

Polyphemus They say it's because men behave now just as they did before the Flood overwhelmed them. They feast, drink, stuff themselves, marry
40   and are given in marriage, whore, buy, sell, pay and charge interest, build buildings.[49] Kings make war, priests are zealous to increase their

wealth, theologians invent syllogisms, monks roam through the world,[50] the commons riot, Erasmus writes colloquies.[51] In short, no calamity is lacking: hunger, thirst, robbery, war, plague, sedition, poverty. Doesn't this prove human affairs are at an end?

5 **Cannius** In this mass of woes, what worries you most?

Polyphemus Guess.

Cannius That your purse is full of cobwebs.[52]

Polyphemus Damned if you haven't hit it![53] – Just now I'm on my way back from a drinking party. Some other time, when I'm sober, I'll argue with you

10 about the gospel, if you like.

Cannius When shall I see you sober?

Polyphemus When I'm sober.

Cannius When will you be so?

Polyphemus When you see me so.[54] Meantime, my dear Cannius, good

15 luck.[55]

Cannius I hope you, in turn, become what you're called.[56]

Polyphemus To prevent you from outdoing me in courtesy, I pray that Cannius, as the name implies, may never lack a can![57]

NOTES

1 For further biographical details of Felix Rex see Alphonse Roersch *L'humanisme belge* (Brussels 1910) 83–100; Allen Ep 2130 introduction; and CEBR. J. Hoyoux thought Polyphemus was not to be identified with Felix Rex but with the one-eyed scribe Pieter Meghen ('Les moyens d'existence d'Erasme' BHR 5 [1944] 56–7). Erasmus, who knew Meghen well, calls him 'Cyclops' in Allen Epp 477:22, 787:15, but usually refers to him as *cocles* or *unoculus* 'one-eyed.' The classical Cyclops, Polyphemus in the *Odyssey*, was *unoculus*, to be sure, but the fact that Erasmus and his friends may have dubbed Meghen 'Cyclops' does not diminish the far greater probability that Felix Rex was the original of the Cyclops in this colloquy. We know he wanted to be in the book (Allen Ep 2147:13–20). His established nickname of 'Polyphemus' is of course a synonym of 'Cyclops.'
On Pieter Meghen, the scribe famous as a copyist of manuscripts in England, see J.B. Trapp in CEBR and 'Pieter Meghen 1466/7–1540: Scribe and Courier' *Erasmus in English* 11 (1981–2) 28–35, the same article, but with illustrations and extra references. An important article by Andrew J. Brown, 'The Date of Erasmus' Latin Translation of the New Testament' *Transactions of the Cambridge Bibliographical Society* 8 (1984) 351–80 corrects previous assumptions about the date of Erasmus' Latin translation of the New Testament in relation to the date of copies of biblical texts made by Meghen; see 'The Young Man and the Harlot' n19.
Polyphemus was impulsive, adventurous, not without learning, but brash. Erasmus was often exasperated by his conduct, especially his drinking. See for example Allen Ep 2288:24 and 870:8–14 of the colloquy. Bonifacius Amerbach,

writing from Basel in May 1532, remarks that if his behaviour continued he would be known as Polypotus ('boozer') instead of Polyphemus (Allen Ep 2649:26–7). Erasmus was glad to see the last of him. 'I am so fond of him that I wish he were in the Indies' (Allen Ep 2415:14).

2 On Nicolaas Kan see *Literae virorum eruditorum ad Franciscum Craneveldium 1522–1528* ed H. de Vocht (Louvain 1928) 617–19 and CEBR. The only surviving letter by Erasmus to him contains advice on proper behaviour when visiting foreign countries, including England (Allen Ep 1832:24–32, 55–64). De Vocht implies that Kan was in Erasmus' service as early as 1524 (*Literae ad Craneveldium* 618), but the earliest date we can be certain of appears to be 1527.

For various reasons relations between them cooled after publication of this colloquy. In a letter of November 1529 Erasmus refers to him as 'intolerabilis' (Allen Ep 2236:14). In April 1531 he mentions a letter from Kan, who by that time had become a priest (Allen Ep 2484:6–8). By this date the bad feeling between them had subsided somewhat, but they were never on very cordial terms again.

3 *hamadryadem*; Virgil *Eclogues* 10.62; Ovid *Metamorphoses* 1.690

4 For the origins of the story see *Adagia* I iii 66. In the seventh of the *Homeric Hymns* (not mentioned by Erasmus) the usually effeminate Bacchus (Dionysus), after being captured by pirates and taken aboard ship, turns into a lion. The sailors, terrified, escape by jumping overboard. Cf Ovid *Metamorphoses* 3.582–691.

5 A marvel; borrowed, with the name changed, from the opening of Lucian's *Lexiphanes*. His *Adversum indoctum* too may have been in Erasmus' mind here.

6 Greek in the original: γαλῆ κροκωτόν (*Adagia* I ii 72). The proverb means something totally incongruous or ludicrous, as formal dress would be for an uncouth and undeserving person or, in this instance, a book in the hands of Polyphemus; for another example see *Ciceronianus* LB I 991C / ASD I-2 634:17–23 / CWE 28 380. The adage can be translated in various ways: 'a party-frock for the cat' in CWE 31 211; cf the familiar 'Puss in boots,' the English title of Charles Perrault's famous tale 'Le chat botté' (1697) in his *Contes*. Erasmus was fond of this proverb. He applied it to himself when referring ironically to rumours that he would be offered a cardinalate (see 'Inns' n13).

7 Polyphemus had caught κροτωτόν but missed γαλῆ.

8 On Silenus see 'A Fish Diet' n237.

9 'Polyphemus bibit ... fortiter' (Allen Ep 2288:24). He was then (March 1530) in Bohemia.

10 Greek in the original

11 On Polyphemus' desire for military service see his amusing letter of March 1529, in which he says he has been promised a place in Archduke Ferdinand's army (Allen Ep 2130:60–78). The promise was not kept, nor is it easy to believe his sponsors were serious in making it.

12 A recollection of John 7:24; aptly quoted, for it shows that Polyphemus does know something of what is inside the book he carries. The description that follows includes features recognizable in many pictures of soldiers in the time of Erasmus. See notes to 'Military Affairs' and 'The Soldier and the Carthusian.' Robert Greene remembered this paragraph in *A Notable Discovery of Cozenage* (1591) where he speaks of 'a terrible fellow with a side hair and a fearful beard,

as though he were of Polyphemus' cut' (*Elizabethan Prose Fiction* ed Merritt Lawlis [New York 1967] 421). The soldiers in the two colloquies named above in this note wore beards; that Polyphemus too was bearded is attested by Erasmus (Allen Ep 2112:32). On 'military cloak' (*sagum*) see *Adagia* IV viii 10; on 'slashed breeches' (*caligae intersectae*), 'The Soldier and the Carthusian' n1. Erasmus speaks disparagingly of such fashions, which are foolish affectations (*De civilitate* LB I 1037B / CWE 25 279). In 1530 the city of Bern decreed that wearers of slashed breeches be punished (J.M. Vincent *Costume and Conduct in the Laws of Basel, Bern, and Zurich 1370–1800* [Baltimore 1935] 47). Calvin opposed such breeches for the Geneva militia, considering them evidence of intolerable pride (Eugène Choisy *La théocratie à Genève au temps de Calvin* 90, cited by J.H. Hexter 'Utopia and Geneva' in *Action and Conviction in Early Modern Europe* ed Theodore K. Rabb and J.E. Seigel [Princeton 1969] 79). *Caligae*, 'soldiers' boots' in classical usage ('sandals' in Acts 12:8 Vulg; cf *Annotationes in Novum Testamentum* LB VI 481F), also meant 'greaves,' then 'hose,' in late medieval and Renaissance Latin. 'Hose' or 'drawers' covered waist and legs; see 'Knucklebones' 892:7–8, where 'the sort of hose' that covers the body from waist to toe is *caligarum genus*.

13 A similar remark occurs in *De concordia* LB V 483B–C.

14 *Adagia* I iii 66, I vii 12

15 What's more ... complexion.] In the first edition of this colloquy, published in March 1529, shortly before Erasmus moved from Basel to Freiburg, the second sentence was followed (after 'complexion') by 'briefly, by a heart as big as his nose.' (On big noses see 'Benefices' introduction and n9.) These words were deleted when the second edition was printed in September 1529. Polyphemus' remark and Cannius' reply caused Erasmus embarrassment because the passage was immediately taken as ridicule of Johannes Oecolampadius, the eminent Basel scholar and divine. He and Erasmus had long been friends (see Ernst Staehelin 'Erasmus und Ökolampad in ihrem Ringen um die Kirche Jesu Christi' in *Gedenkschrift* 166–82), and Oecolampadius had helped Erasmus with Hebrew in his biblical studies, but estrangement developed after Oecolampadius became a sacramentarian and a leader of the Zwinglians in Basel. Erasmus may have intended for some time to write something against him and his change of theological views; De Vocht thinks for nearly two years (*Earliest English Translations* xii), though this is not certain. What does seem certain is that Erasmus was annoyed by Oecolampadius and that consequently he can hardly be taken at his word when he assures Oecolampadius that the offensive passage was aimed at Nicolaas Kan, who had a prominent nose, that both Kan and Felix Rex wanted to be in a colloquy (Allen Ep 2147:13–20), and furthermore that he had not known Kan wore a sheepskin cap similar to Oecolampadius'.

In a letter to Oecolampadius c 10 April 1529, Erasmus blandly denies malevolence in the colloquy and passes the affair off as an unfortunate misunderstanding. He repeats this assertion a few months later (Allen Ep 2196:81–6). He does not say plainly that Oecolampadius himself resented the passage in question but that certain clerics in Basel did so. At any rate he found it prudent to explain away the offending words and to reassure Oecolampadius, who seems to have accepted the explanation with good grace after a talk with Erasmus (Allen Ep 2196:87–93) and was generous enough to express regret at Erasmus' decision to emigrate to Freiburg (Allen

Ep 2149 introduction). Whether or not Erasmus had intended a thrust at Oecolampadius, his prompt and tactful retreat is understandable though perhaps less than wholly sincere. He had had enough trouble of late in Basel and did not want more.

For a sketch of Oecolampadius' career see Gordon Rupp *Patterns of Reformation* (London 1969) 3–46; on the religious situation in Basel during Erasmus' final months there in 1529, Bainton *Erasmus of Christendom* 217–23.

16 *minime gentium*; taken by Polyphemus as derogatory, but Cannius assures him (866:1) that he meant not 'least' but 'not *in* the least' or 'not for anything in the world.' The word-play is possible because *minime* can be either an adjective in the vocative case ('O least of men') or an adverb ('least in the world,' ie 'not for anything'). Cf Terence *Phormio* 1033, *Eunuchus* 625.

17 Also Terentian (*Andria* 934); *Adagia* III ii 56

18 *Adagia* I v 10

19 On this saint see 'The Shipwreck' n26; on the name, Allen Ep 3086:1–10.

20 That is, Evangeliophorus

21 This witticism is older than the *Colloquies*. Poggio, in his *Facetiae*, tells of a priest insistently asking his congregation who could have been more fortunate than St Christopher, who carried his Saviour on his back. 'The ass,' replied one of his auditors, 'who bore both the Son and his Mother,' alluding to the flight into Egypt (Matthew 2:14) and Christ's entrance into Jerusalem (Matthew 21:5). See Poggio *Opera omnia* (Basel 1538; repr 4 vols Turin 1964–9) I 473. Luther, in more serious vein, says in a sermon, 'If a great good work would accomplish anything' towards salvation, 'asses and horses would also earn the kingdom of heaven' (see Harold J. Grimm 'The Human Element in Luther's Sermons' ARG 49 [1958] 56).

22 Matt 27:26; Mark 14:65, 15:15, 19; John 18:22, 19:1, 3

23 A student in Wittenberg testified in 1520 that there were practically no students who did not go round with the Bible in hand (Ernest G. Schwiebert 'New Groups and Ideas at the University of Wittenberg' ARG 49 [1958] 71). In the letter dedicating his Paraphrase on John's Gospel to Archduke Ferdinand (1523), Erasmus emphasizes as he does here the difference between bearing the Gospel on one's person and in one's heart. Some people carried verses of John's Gospel around their necks to ward off sickness or accidents (Allen Ep 1333:250–7 / CWE Ep 1333:266–73).

24 For a description see *Annotationes in Novum Testamentum* LB VI 34E–F on Matt 6:2; cf *Lingua* LB IV 691C / ASD IV-1A 82:853–62 / CWE 29 315. A hypocrite acts according to whether he thinks God is watching (*Ecclesiastes* LB V 781A).

25 Franciscans do not feel safe unless they have a copy of the Rule with them (*Paraclesis* LB V 142F).

26 They read or chanted the Gospel at mass.

27 *crassiore Minerva*, a favourite proverb; *Adagia* I i 37, 38

28 On Erasmus' preference for Beaune see 'The Profane Feast' n16. Alessandro Benedetti, in his *Diaria de bello Carolino* 1496 (ed and trans Dorothy M. Schullian [New York 1967] 134) says that to German mercenaries wine was more important than gold or silver.

29 *bipenni*, a double-edged axe

30 Prov 15:1

31 Matt 5:39; Luke 6:29

32 Matt 6:5–7

33 1 Thess 5:17. On prayer see 'Youth' n36.

34 *battologiam*. The word, used in Matt 6:7, is adapted from a rare Greek verb meaning 'stammer,' 'babble,' 'chatter,' and hence glossed as 'much speaking.' Its origin is obscure, despite Erasmus' elucidations in *Adagia* III vii 76, but see his note on Matt 6:7 in *Annotationes in Novum Testamentum* LB VI 35E–36D. Its presence in the Gospel has made it familiar. In Erasmus it is synonymous with *multiloquium*. *Modus orandi Deum* has a careful distinction between *battologia* or *multiloquium* and authentic fervour in prayer (LB V 1112B–F); for a defence of his opinions see *Declarationes ad censuras Lutetiae vulgatas* LB IX 895C–896C.

35 Rom 16:18; but the verse is not about gluttons, though Cannius implies it is.

36 Matt 15:11. For Erasmus' translation of Origen's comment on this passage see LB VIII 466A–467A.

37 Rom 14:15; 1 Cor 6:12–13, 8:13, 9:19–22, 10:31–3. See the exegesis of 1 Cor 6:12 in 'The Godly Feast' 189:37–191:37 and the discussion of law versus Christian liberty in 'A Fish Diet.'

38 Shepherd in Virgil *Eclogues* 3.2. Cannius pretends to have misunderstood Polyphemus' 'ego sum ego' for 'ego sum Egon.'

39 'Esse dixi pro edere.' The pun is possible because *esse* is a form of the infinitive of *edo* 'eat' and also the infinitive of *sum* 'be.'

40 Erasmus notes in *De libero arbitrio* (LB IX 1247A) the Lutheran emphasis that 'there is no need of any satisfaction' (part of the sacrament of penance, along with contrition and confession), 'since Christ has paid the penalties for the sins of all' who truly repent. See Luther *De captivitate Babylonica ecclesiae* WA 6 544, 548 / LW 36 83–4, 89.

41 Identified as Frans Titelmans of Hasselt (Smith *Key* 48), formerly of Antwerp but now of Louvain. He was one of the traditionalists who opposed Erasmus on points of New Testament interpretation in 1528–9 and was therefore an appropriate candidate for attention in this colloquy. Erasmus had admonished him in a letter as early as May 1527 (Allen Ep 1823) and ridiculed him again in a letter of January 1530 (Allen Ep 2261:71–7). For other anecdotes of Franciscans hostile to Erasmus' New Testament see 'The Young Man and the Harlot' 384:35–385:19 and 'The Sermon.'
The New Testament carried about by Polyphemus was probably a copy of an edition of Erasmus' Latin translation, first issued separately in September 1519.

42 Erasmus approves both of the customary sacramental confession to a priest and of confessing in secret to God. He compares the two modes of confessing in *Exomologesis* LB V 145A–170D. See also the counsel in 'Youth' 96:31–97:35.

43 Erasmus made the same remark about the evangelicals just a year earlier, March 1528 (Allen Ep 1977:43; repeated in 1529 in *Epistola contra pseudevangelicos* LB X 1579D, 1580A).

44 Horace *Odes* 4.2.49–50

45 On this phrase see *Adagia* II iv 28.

46 In the usual sense of prizing pleasure. Contrast the use of the word in the colloquy 'The Epicurean.'

47 Cf the passage beginning 'Reflect that whatever variation there is in kinds or classes of animals, or in individual ones, all this exists in mankind' in 'The Lover of Glory' 970:12–41 and the observations in 'Sympathy.' The

presence of beastly characteristics in men, and the representation of human passions or traits by animal terms, have always been commonplace in moral and symbolic writings, both sacred and secular. See Burton *Anatomy of Melancholy* 'Democritus Junior to the Reader' (1 65–66); William M. Carroll *Animal Conventions in English Renaissance Non-Religious Prose* (New York 1954); Elizabeth C. Evans 'Physiognomics in the Ancient World' *Transactions of the American Philosophical Society* new series 59 (1969) part 5 1–101.

48 Cf Erasmus' observation concerning Anabaptists in a passage inserted into the text of Ep 1369 (1523) when it was published in the *Opus Epistolarum* of 1529: 'They wish to be taken for prophets, but everyone laughs at them' (Allen Ep 1369:45 / CWE Ep 1369:49–50; Allen failed to date the passage in question correctly). Zürich and Basel had been troubled by Anabaptists from time to time and took severe measures against them. On the expectations of some Anabaptists concerning the end of the world see G.H. Williams *The Radical Reformation* (Philadelphia 1962) 45, 163, 164, 174, 176, 178, 189, 226, 277, and passim. When reporting in April 1529 the visit to Basel of an itinerant evangelical, evidently Anabaptist, who preached 'Repent, repent, repent: the hand of the Lord is imminent' and had gone to the cathedral to denounce the corrupt lives of the clergy, Erasmus remarks that the reader must decide for himself whether the incident was more in keeping with Democritus or Heraclitus, with laughter or tears (Allen Ep 2149:4–13). Although fully aware of the Anabaptists' eccentricities and excesses, he commends, on another occasion, what he has heard of their sincerity and morality (Allen Ep 2134:212–15). Despite the aversion of the orthodox, and the fright or hatred of the public and of governments, whose memories of the Peasants' Revolt of 1524–6 caused them to regard all so called Anabaptists as suspect (see 'The New Mother' n11 and Allen Epp 2149:37–50, 2241:15–18) – attitudes confirmed some years later as a result of the behaviour of Jan of Leiden and his followers in Münster in 1534–6 – Erasmus, who feared and hated violence from whatever source, nevertheless acknowledged the moral qualities of peaceable Anabaptists. On Jan of Leiden see Williams *The Radical Reformation* 368–75 and CEBR.

49 A standard comparison, based on Matt 24:38–9 and Luke 17:26–8 (cf also Eccles 2:4, 'I builded me houses' – the work of vanity). It appears in a letter from Jan van Fevijn to Craneveldt in 1524 (*Literae ad Craneveldium* [n2 above] 230 Ep 89:29), and cf Allen Ep 2260:56–61 (January 1530, to Pieter Gillis). Erasmus exclaims, after a gloomy passage on the evils of the day in another letter, 'What remains except the final calamity, the Flood?' (Allen Ep 2149:48–9; similar pessimism is expressed in Allen Ep 2236:28–30). A conjunction of planets in the sign of Pisces in February 1524 led some astrologers to predict a universal flood (Thorndike *Magic and Experimental Science* v 178–233).

50 Instead of remaining in their monastic houses as they should. *Stabilitas loci* was explicitly required by the Benedictine Rule (chapter 58) and in principle by other monastic orders. The comment could also refer to the mendicant friars; see 'The Funeral' n17.

51 With the whole description of the evils of the time compare, in the *Colloquies*, 'The New Mother' 592:17–35 and, on the wars, 'A Fish Diet' 688:14–689:18 and 'Charon.' The ironic climax to the list of disasters, though characteristic, is the only pleasantry of the kind in the *Colloquies*.

52 Echoing Catullus 13.7–8

53 *rem acu tetigisti; Adagia* II iv 93, from Plautus *Rudens* 1306

54 With this exchange, cf 'Patterns' 12:3–6. On Polyphemus' drinking see n1 and 865:4–6 above.

55 *Sis felix*, 'be happy,' with a pun on the speaker's own name, Felix, as though Polyphemus is saying '*You* be Felix.'

56 That is, 'Gospel-bearer' (*Evangeliophorus*), though Polyphemus 'famous,' 'much talked of,' may also be meant

57 Of liquor; a pun on Cannius' name (*Kan* 'mug' or 'cup')

NON-SEQUITURS

Ἀπροσδιόνυσα, sive Absurda

First printed in the *Colloquia* in the March 1529 edition. On the date see the introduction to 'Charon' 818–19.

Some of the younger readers for whom the early colloquies were written may have been puzzled at first by this dialogue, a pleasantry that illustrates talking at cross-purposes. The Greek title, Ἀπροσδιόνυσα 'not pertaining to Dionysus,' was in classical antiquity applied to something irrelevant to the subject at hand (see Lucian *Dionysius* 5). According to one explanation in *Adagia* II iv 57: *Nihil ad Bacchum* 'What has this to do with Bacchus?' (Οὐδὲν πρὸς Διόνυσον) the saying arose when Greek poets began to write plays dealing with material other than the myth of Dionysus (Bacchus), which by tradition was their original and proper subject, with the result that the spectators shouted 'What has this to do with Bacchus?' (LB II 542A / CWE 33 220). The phrase became proverbial as a reminder or admonition that one should stop digressing and get back to the point. *Adagia* II iv 57 presents various ancient texts and quotations about the proverb but leaves the question of its origin undecided. The present dialogue is Lucianic in manner, and Lucian quotes the phrase in his *Bacchus* 5 and 6, but there is no direct model in Lucian for Erasmus' colloquy. Cf also *Adagia* II ii 49.

ANNIUS, LEUCIUS[1]

Annius I hear you attended the wedding of Pancratius and Albina.

Leucius Never did I have an unluckier voyage than I had that time.

5 **Annius** What's that you say? Was there such a crowd?

Leucius And never were my chances of survival slimmer than on that occasion.

Annius See what wealth can do! Few would come to *my* wedding, and poor ones at that.

10 **Leucius** Scarcely had we put to sea when a gale came up.

Annius You describe an assembly of gods. So many princes attended? So many noblewomen?

Leucius The north wind ripped the sail to pieces and blew it away.

Annius The bride I know: the loveliest thing imaginable.

15 **Leucius** Presently the waves smashed the rudder.

Annius So everyone supposes. And the bridegroom is not altogether inferior to her in good looks, as they say.

Leucius How do you imagine we felt then?

Annius It's rare enough nowadays for brides to be virgins.

5 **Leucius** We had to row for it.

Annius You tell of an incredible dowry.

Leucius Then – presto! Another danger.

Annius Why did they entrust an innocent to such a brute?

Leucius A pirate ship came into view.

10 **Annius** That's the way it goes: in many a man villainy makes up for age.

Leucius There we had a double fight on our hands: one with the sea, the other with the pirates.

Annius Whew! So many presents? while nobody gives a penny to the poor.

15 **Leucius** What, were we to surrender? Quite the contrary: mortal danger only made us more resolute.

Annius If what you say is true, I fear the marriage will be barren.

Leucius Not at all: we threw in our grappling hooks.

Annius Oh-ho, something new – pregnant before marriage?

20 **Leucius** Had you witnessed that struggle, you'd allow I'm no weakling.

Annius As I hear, this marriage was not only a mating but a consummating too.

Leucius We boarded the pirate ship.

25 **Annius** But I'm surprised that you, who aren't related, were invited when I was passed over. I'm connected with the bride's father in the third degree of kinship.

Leucius We hurled them headlong into the sea.

Annius You're right; a man who's down on his luck has no relatives.

30 **Leucius** The booty we divided among ourselves.

Annius I'll protest to the girl the first time I see her, too.

Leucius Soon came an unexpected calm; halcyon weather,[2] you'd have called it.

Annius If she has wealth, I have will. I care nothing for her generosity.

35 **Leucius** So instead of one ship we brought two into port.

Annius Let him who keeps her be angry!

Leucius Where am I going, you ask? To church, to dedicate a piece of the sail to St Nicholas.[3]

Annius I'm not free today, for I'm expecting guests at home. Another time I

40 won't refuse.

NOTES

1 The speakers' names are borrowed from Greek. Annius means 'grieved' or 'gloomy'; Leucius means 'happy.' They do not appear in other colloquies, but for speculation about Annius see ASD I-3 610:2n.

2 Calm, serene days when halcyons (kingfishers), according to ancient belief, charmed the sea in order that they might breed in their floating nests and at the same time do something for the general good, if we may believe Pliny (*Naturalis historia* 10.89–90). See *Parabolae* CWE 23 227, 257–8.

3 A bishop of Lycia (fourth century). Nearly everything else about his life is uncertain, but what is beyond doubt is his widespread and enduring popularity in art and legend as the patron saint of sailors, children, merchants, many churches, and Russia. His name is no longer in the liturgical calendar of the Roman church.

THE KNIGHT WITHOUT A HORSE,
OR FAKED NOBILITY

Ἱππεὺς ἄνιππος, sive Ementita nobilitas

First printed in the *Colloquia* in the March 1529 edition. On the date see the introduction to 'Charon' 818–19.

Erasmus had strict opinions about nobility; an eloquent exposition of them can be found in *Institutio christiani matrimonii* (LB V 668D–670A). His equally strong convictions about false or degenerate nobility are expressed in many places, including the *Colloquies*. In 'The Knight without a Horse' his depiction of Harpalus is both a personal attack and a satire of a type of pretender for whom he had only contempt. This self-styled knight was recognized by some of Erasmus' readers as Heinrich Eppendorf, a native of Saxony, whose name is connected with an earlier colloquy, 'The Cheating Horse-Dealer.' Eppendorf, whose claims to noble birth are derided by Erasmus, became acquainted with him in Louvain in 1520 and in 1522 knew him well in Basel. When Erasmus quarrelled with Ulrich von Hutten over Luther, Eppendorf sided with Hutten, then became estranged from Erasmus and later actively hostile. He caused Erasmus serious annoyance for some years, and Erasmus for his part was unrelenting.

Eppendorf came to Basel again in January 1528 and had an interview with Erasmus. It was not a success. Both spoke at one time or another of going to law, but were persuaded to allow Erasmus' close friends Beatus Rhenanus and Bonifacius Amerbach to arbitrate their dispute. Eppendorf was to abandon his intention of publishing a book against Erasmus, who in turn was to dedicate a book to Eppendorf. The attempted reconciliation proved to be only a truce at best, and the quarrel continued for several years. Not only did Erasmus evade his reluctant promise to dedicate something to Eppendorf, but in March 1529 he printed this colloquy, in which Eppendorf is exposed as merely a foolish pretender to nobility. In the September 1528 edition of his *Adagia* Erasmus had inserted a short but scornful passage (*Adagia* I ix 44 / LB II 349E–350E / CWE 32 204–5) on German Junkers, young wastrels who insolently boast of noble birth, to which they have no claim. The description closely resembles many lines in the present colloquy. 'Suppose one of them is born in a village – let us say his name is Ornithoplutus and his village called Isocômus – he never signs himself an Isocomian; any plebeian could do that. He is Ornithoplutus *von* Isocômum.' Since this fictitious name is an approximate translation of 'Heinrich von Eppendorf' into its Greek equivalent, we can be certain that Erasmus is taunting Eppendorf in this passage.

In late 1530 Erasmus published *Admonitio adversus mendacium*, justifying his conduct in the long quarrel (LB X 1683C–1692B). Eppendorf replied with *Iusta querela* (text in Hutten *Opera* II 447–54). Like many controversies among the learned, this one was embittered by personal antipathies as well as self-righteous indignation. The course of it is summarized most conveniently by the article on Eppendorf in CEBR, but see also Allen introductions to Epp 1122 and 1934 and Allen IV 615–19 Appendix 14. On Hutten see references in 'A Marriage in Name Only' nn12 and 15 and CEBR. For many modern readers details of the quarrel are likely to be of less interest than the colloquy's satirical picture of a swaggering knight, or so-called knight, a literary descendant of the *miles gloriosus* of ancient comedy and a popular figure in Renaissance as well as classical fiction and drama. Nestor's ironic advice on how to be a fashionable young man about town on nothing a year – an inversion of the doctrines of the courtesy books – is another popular motif in Renaissance fiction.

HARPALUS, NESTOR[1]

Harpalus You can help me by your advice. You'll find I'm neither a forgetful nor an ungrateful fellow.

Nestor I'll come to the rescue so that you can be what you'd like.

5 **Harpalus** But it's not in our power to be born nobles.

Nestor If you're not so by birth, strive by your good deeds to establish a noble line.

Harpalus A long, drawn-out business!

Nestor The emperor will sell you a title for a trifling sum.

10 **Harpalus** Nobility got by purchase is commonly an object of ridicule.

Nestor Since nothing is more absurd than faked nobility, why do you covet the title of knight so badly?[2]

Harpalus I've reasons – no slight ones, either – that I won't mind telling to you if you'll show me how to pass myself off on the public as a nobleman.

15 **Nestor** The name without the reality?[3]

Harpalus Reputation is the best substitute for reality. But come on, Nestor, let's have your advice.[4] When you hear my reasons, you'll admit they're worth the trouble.

Nestor Since that's the way you want it, I'll tell you. First of all, go far away
20 from home.

Harpalus I'm minding.

Nestor Force your way into the company of young blades who are genuinely high society.

Harpalus I understand.

Nestor From this time on you'll immediately be taken for the same sort as
5   those you associate with.

Harpalus Right you are.

Nestor See that there's nothing low-class about you.[5]

Harpalus What do you mean?

Nestor Your dress.[6] Don't wear wool but either silk or, if you can't afford
10   that, fustian.[7] Better plain canvas than patches.

Harpalus Correct.

Nestor See that nothing's whole but slash your cap, doublet, hose, shoes, nails if you can.[8] Avoid mention of anything mean. If a stranger from Spain turns up, ask him how the emperor gets along with the pope, what your
15   kinsman the count of Nassau is doing,[9] and what your other cronies are up to.

Harpalus I'll see to it.

Nestor Wear a small jewelled signet ring on your finger.

Harpalus If my purse will stand it.

20   **Nestor** A small brass ring gilded, with a fake jewel, costs little. But add a shield with insignia.

Harpalus What do you advise me to choose?

Nestor Two milking-pails, if you like, and a tankard of beer.

Harpalus You're joking. Come on, tell me seriously.

25   **Nestor** Ever been in battle?

Harpalus Never even saw one.

Nestor But you've cut the throats of farmers' geese and capons now and then, I dare say.

Harpalus Many times – and quite gallantly, too.

30   **Nestor** Put a butcher-knife of silver and gilt heads of three geese on it.

Harpalus On what sort of field?

Nestor Why, gules, what else? – a memorial of blood bravely spilled.

Harpalus Yes, why not? Goose blood's as red as men's. But please go on.

Nestor Then be sure to have this shield hung up at the gates of every inn
35   you happen to stop at.[10]

Harpalus What sort of helmet shall I add?

Nestor You do well to remind me. Have one with a slit for the mouth.

Harpalus What for?

Nestor To allow you to breathe; secondly, to match your dress.[11] – What's to
40   crown it?

Harpalus I'm waiting.

Nestor The head of a dog with drooping ears.

Harpalus That's commonplace.

Nestor Add two horns; *that's* not common.[12]

Harpalus Good enough. But what beasts will support the shield?

5   **Nestor** Princes have a corner on stags, hounds, dragons, and griffins. Put two harpies on yours.[13]

Harpalus Excellent advice.

Nestor There's still the matter of a family name.[14] In this connection you must be careful, first of all, not to let yourself be called, in vulgar fashion,

10   Harpalus Comensis but Harpalus von Como,[15] for that's the aristocratic style;[16] the other's fit for beggarly divines.

Harpalus So I remember.

Nestor Have you anything you could call your own?

Harpalus Not even a pigpen.

15   **Nestor** Were you born in a famous city?

Harpalus In an obscure village. You daren't lie to a person whose help you're after.

Nestor That's right. But is there no mountain in the neighbourhood of the village?

20   **Harpalus** Yes, there is.

Nestor And has it a rock somewhere or other?

Harpalus A very steep one.

Nestor Then you should be Harpalus, Knight of the Golden Rock.

Harpalus But the custom of nobles is for each one to have his own motto,

25   as Maximilian[17] used to have 'Observe the mean'; Philip,[18] 'He who wills'; Charles,[19] 'Farther still'; others likewise, each to his taste.

Nestor Do you inscribe: 'Cast all the dice.'[20]

Harpalus An excellent suggestion, really.

Nestor Now to strengthen the popular impression, make up letters from

30   eminent personages in which you're constantly addressed as 'most illustrious knight' and reference is made to great affairs, fiefs, castles, huge sums of money, offices, a wealthy marriage. See to it that letters of this kind fall into other people's hands as though dropped or inadvertently left behind.

Harpalus That will be easy for me, for I'm good at writing and I've practised

35   this skill a great deal; I can easily imitate anybody's hand.

Nestor Stick the letters inside your clothes sometimes or leave them in your purse, so the tailors will find them there when you have your clothes mended. They'll be sure to blab; and as soon as you learn of it, put on an indignant, injured look, as if the mischance offended you.

40   **Harpalus** This too I've long studied, so that I can change my countenance as easily as a mask.

LB I 835B / ASD I-3 613

Nestor Do it in such a way that the trick won't be found out and a convincing story is spread.

Harpalus I'll take good care to do that.

Nestor Next you should get hold of some accomplices, or even servants,
5   who'll bow and scrape before you and address you in public as 'Herr Junker.'[21] Don't be afraid of the expense of this. There are plenty of young chaps who like to play this part for nothing. What's more, this neighbourhood abounds in young fellows with a smattering of learning who have a marvellous passion, not to say an itch, for writing.[22] And there's no
10   lack of starving printers who'll stop at nothing if a profit's in prospect.[23] Bribe some of them to proclaim you in their pamphlets 'a nobleman of his country' and to reprint it frequently in capital letters. In this way they'll celebrate 'a nobleman of his country' even in Bohemia, for pamphlets circulate faster and farther than word of mouth or even chattering servants.

15   **Harpalus** Not a bad idea. But servants must be supported.

Nestor Yes, but you won't keep servants who are without hands and therefore helpless.[24] Let them be sent hither and yon; they'll turn up something. There are various opportunities for such things, you know.

Harpalus Enough; I understand perfectly.

20   **Nestor** And there are professions, too.

Harpalus I'm eager to hear about them.

Nestor Unless you're a good dicer, a skilful card player, an infamous whoremonger, a heavy drinker, a reckless spendthrift, a wastrel and heavily in debt, decorated with the French pox besides, hardly anyone will believe
25   you're a knight.[25]

Harpalus I'm an old hand at these matters. But how's the expense to be met?

Nestor Just a moment – I was coming to that. Have you an inheritance?

Harpalus A mere pittance.

Nestor After your reputation for nobility has been widely accepted, you'll
30   easily find fools to trust you. Some will be scared of you and afraid to refuse you credit. Now there are a thousand ways to cheat your creditors.[26]

Harpalus Indeed I'm not unfamiliar with them. But creditors will press me at last when they find out that all I possess is mere talk.

Nestor On the contrary, there's no easier path to a kingdom than to be in
35   debt to as many people as possible.[27]

Harpalus How so?

Nestor In the first place, the creditor treats you with respect, as if obliged for some great favour; and he's fearful of providing an occasion[28] that may cause him to lose his money. No servants so fawning as a debtor's creditors.
40   If you pay them something once in a while, they're more pleased than if you gave them a present.

Harpalus I've noticed that.

Nestor But see that you shun poor men, for they make a tremendous fuss over a trifling sum. People who are better off are easier to get along with. Shame checks them, hope dupes them, fear deters them – they know what

5 knights are capable of! Last of all, when you're simply head over heels in debt, find an excuse to move to some other town, and then another, and so on. There's nothing in this to embarrass you. No men are more deeply in debt than great princes.[29] If some country fellow should press you for payment, pretend to be insulted by his impudence. Give him something now

10 and then, but don't pay in full and don't pay everybody. Wherever you are, make sure no one suspects your pockets are absolutely empty. Always show off.

Harpalus Show what – when you're broke?

Nestor If a friend has left anything in your keeping, display it as your own,

15 but do so cleverly – mere coincidence, you know! For this purpose borrow money occasionally and repay it promptly. From a purse bulging with brass coins, bring out the two gold pieces you keep there – guess the rest for yourself.

Harpalus I understand. But in the end I'm sure to be ruined by debt.

20 **Nestor** You know how much knights are indulged in our society.

Harpalus A great deal, and they get away with it, too.

Nestor And then keep servants who aren't slow off the mark or close relations who in any event have to be supported. A trader will turn up whom they can waylay and rob.[30] They'll find something unguarded in inns

25 or dwellings or ships. Get it? Let them remember man wasn't given fingers for nothing.

Harpalus Provided it could be done safely –

Nestor See that they're decked out handsomely in livery. Entrust them with faked letters to eminent people. If your servants steal something on the sly,

30 nobody will dare to accuse them even if suspicious, for fear of the knight their master. But if they win any loot by force, it will be called the spoils of war. These are training exercises for war.[31]

Harpalus Good advice.

Nestor Now the fundamental principle of knighthood must always be

35 maintained: that for a knight to relieve a common traveller of his money is just and right. What's more outrageous than for a vulgar trader to be rich while a knight hasn't enough to spend on whores and dice? Always attach yourself to the most important people; or rather, force yourself upon them. Stop at nothing. Put on a bold front,[32] especially with strangers, and to that

40 end you will be wise to spend your time in some well-known spot, say the baths or the most popular inns.

Harpalus I've already thought of that.

Nestor In this respect, fortune often throws a prize in your way.

Harpalus How so, I beg you?

Nestor Suppose so and so has left his purse or absent-mindedly left behind
5   the key to his storeroom. You know the rest.

Harpalus But –

Nestor What are you afraid of? Who will dare suspect one of your bearing,
one of such haughty speech, the Knight of the Golden Rock? And if anyone
so shameless does turn up, who will have the nerve to accuse you? Suspicion
10 will be diverted meanwhile to some guest who left the day before. Have
your retinue of servants start a row with the innkeeper. Play your role
calmly. If a modest, good-hearted man is robbed, he'll keep quiet about it
for fear of incurring disgrace as well as financial loss by his carelessness in
guarding his property.

15 **Harpalus** What you say makes sense. – You know the Count of the White
Vulture, I imagine?

Nestor Of course.

Harpalus As I heard the story, he entertained a certain Spaniard, a
gentleman in dress and livery, who stole six hundred florins; and the count
20 never dared to complain, so high and mighty was the fellow.

Nestor There's an example for you! From time to time send one of your
servants off to war, of course. By robbing whatever churches and monasteries
he comes to, he'll return loaded down with the spoils of war.[33]

Harpalus Yes, that's perfectly safe.

25 **Nestor** And there's another way of getting money, too.

Harpalus Tell me, please.

Nestor Drum up some excuses for quarrelling with those who are well off,
especially with monks or priests, who nowadays have almost everybody's
ill will. One of them scorned your coat of arms or spat on it;[34] another spoke
30 insultingly of you; another scribbled something that could be represented as
an insult. Through your ambassador declare irreconcilable war[35] on them.
Scatter dire threats of execution, destruction, total war.[36] Terrified, they'll sue
for peace. At this juncture, put a high price on your dignity; that is, ask an
unconscionable indemnity, in order to win a reasonable one. If you demand
35 three thousand guilders, the other side will be ashamed to offer less than
two hundred.

Harpalus The rest I'll threaten with law suits.

Nestor That comes a bit close to slander. Still, it does help here somewhat.
But look, Harpalus, I almost forgot what I should have mentioned at the
40 outset: you must lure some well-dowered girl into the snare of matrimony.
You've a love charm: you're a young, fair, engaging, good-humoured

good-for-nothing with a winning smile. Spread the word that you've been
received with large promises at the emperor's court. Girls love to marry
bigwigs.

Harpalus I know men for whom this worked well. But what if the bubble
5   finally bursts and creditors spring at me from all sides? I'll be laughed at for
posing as a knight, a crime worse than robbing a church – in the opinion of
that set.

Nestor Here's where you must remember to put on a bold face.[37] Above all,
bear in mind that insolence has never passed more readily for wisdom than it
10   does today. You must devise something you can put forward as an excuse. And
there'll be no lack of innocents to believe your story. Some of the more polite
will pretend they don't know it's a dodge. Finally, if nothing else will do, you
must run off to a war somewhere, into the roar of battle. As 'the sea washes
away all the sins of mankind,'[38] so war covers over the dregs of every crime.
15   A general isn't considered competent nowadays unless trained for his present
rank by such preliminary campaigning.[39] This will be the final resort if all else
fails. But you should leave no stone unturned[40] before matters come to this
pass. Don't let your guard down. Steer clear of little towns where you can't
even break wind without people's knowing it. In large and crowded cities
20   (unless it's one like Marseilles)[41] there's more freedom. Find out on the sly
what's being said about you. When you learn that remarks of this kind grow
common: 'What's he doing? Why does he hang around here so many years?
Why doesn't he go back to his own country? Why does he neglect his castles?
What's his family tree? Where does he get the money from for such lavish
25   spending?' – when, I say, remarks of this sort begin to spread, then you must
think of moving out promptly.[42] But go out like a lion, not a hare.[43] Pretend
you're summoned to the emperor's court on urgent business, that you'll soon
be with the army. Those who have anything to lose won't dare mutter against
you in your absence. But above all I advise you to beware of that irritable
30   and ill-humoured breed of men, the poets. They spill their malice on paper,
and whatever they put down is quickly scattered throughout the world.[44]

Harpalus Damned if your advice doesn't please me tremendously. I'll give
you to understand you've met with an apt pupil and a young man who's far
from ungrateful. The first good horse I find at pasture I'll send to you with
35   my compliments.

Nestor Now it's your turn to carry out your promise. What is it that attracts
you so very much to a spurious reputation for knighthood?

Harpalus Simply that knights do as they please and get away with it.[45] Or
does this seem a trivial matter to you?

40   **Nestor** Should the worst happen, you owe Nature one death, even if you've
lived in the Chartreuse.[46] And men who die on the wheel have an easier

death than those killed by the stone, gout, or paralysis. For the soldierly creed is that nothing survives a man but his corpse.

Harpalus My view exactly!

NOTES

1 Harpalus in Greek means 'greedy' or 'eagerly,' as in *Odyssey* 6.250. Nestor is the wise counsellor of the Greeks in the *Iliad*.
2 The word-play in the Latin – *emptitia ... ementita* 'by purchase ... faked' – cannot be reproduced in English. Spurious nobility was a 'plague' in Germany, according to Erasmus *Adagia* i ix 44.
3 The theme of 'Things and Names'
4 In *De conscribendis epistolis* (1522) Erasmus proffers ironical advice on how to succeed as a courtier (LB I 448E–450A or III 1887E–1889A / ASD I-2 449–502 / CWE 25 195–7). Much is said there about cultivating the good will of the prince and how to look out for one's own advantage; but although shrewd – Samuel Pepys thought this 'letter' to be 'most true and good' (see CWE 26 195 n6 page 544) – the discourse is less lively and entertaining than this colloquy.
5 To impress the world as a Junker he must act and talk like a soldier and a gallant (*Adagia* i ix 44).
6 For 'clothes make the man,' a trite saying, but endorsed by Quintilian (8 prooemium 20) who, Erasmus surmises, had in mind some lines in the Nausicaa episode in the *Odyssey* (6.25–30, 242–3). See *Adagia* III i 60.
7 Thick twilled cotton cloth
8 For other examples of slashed doublet and hose, see 'The Soldier and the Carthusian' 330:1–2 and n1 and 'Cyclops' 865:18; cf also 'The Well-to-do Beggars' 480:3–15. 'Slash' here is *disseca*, which fits cap, doublet, and hose, but Erasmus allows it to apply to nails too. 'Cut your nails,' he means, 'don't go around with untrimmed nails.'
9 One line of the house of Nassau settled in the Netherlands in the fifteenth century. From it descended William the Silent, founder of the Dutch republic. The title of the 1516 edition of Erasmus' *Panegyricus* (1504), as printed in LB IV 507, mentions the count of Nassau; other allusions to him occur in Allen Epp 829:12 (1518) and 1192:79 (1521) / CWE Epp 829:14–15 and 1192:90–1, when Henry count of Nassau was governor of Holland and Zeeland.
10 Cf 'Inns' 374:13–15
11 Since cap, doublet, and breeches are slashed, the helmet should be like them in this respect.
12 Proverbial (*Adagia* IV vi 99). Drooping ears may be commonplace, unsuitable for energetic creatures such as Harpalus, but he is mistaken in supposing that two horns would be better. For 'before this, I thought you had horns' was said of those formerly considered brave but when tested were found to be cowards (*Adagia* III iii 12).
13 Mythical monsters, half bird and half woman. See 'The Apotheosis of Reuchlin' n21. A pun on 'Harpalus' may also be intended.
14 The lines that follow, on assuming an aristocratic name and concealing low birth in an obscure village, are adapted from *Adagia* i ix 44; see the introduction

above. In this and other passages Erasmus makes derisory comments on Eppendorf's other affectations: his helmet with its 'windows,' his shield (decorated with a sword across it), which he hangs up in the courtyard of the inn where he stays. These particulars are found again in a letter of February 1528 where Erasmus complains that Eppendorf had talked incessantly about his paternal estates and that his servants always addressed him as a noble (Allen Ep 1934:102–3, 130–5). Boasting and loud assertiveness were characteristic of Thraso. Erasmus often refers to Eppendorf as a Thraso or as thrasonical (six times in Ep 1934).

15 Suggestive of κώμη 'village.' Cf *Adagia* IV i 2 LB II 970F; *Moriae encomium* LB IV 410A / ASD IV-3 78:112–15 / CWE 27 89. Eppendorf signs himself 'Equ' (*eques* 'knight'); *Adagia* I ix 44 and Allen Ep 1934:100–2.

16 But Eppendorf's name, Erasmus conjectures, came from a tavern kept by his forebears (Allen Ep 1934:102–11; 360–3).

17 King of Germany and from 1493 to 1519 Holy Roman Emperor. See 'The Fabulous Feast' n51.

18 Philip the Handsome (d 1506), duke of Burgundy and archduke of Austria, son of Maximilian and father of Charles

19 The emperor Charles V. These three monarchs are named together in 'The Epithalamium' 523:7.

20 *Adagia* I iv 32; leave everything to chance or fortune. The motto is a variation of the words uttered by Julius Caesar when he finally began to cross the river Rubicon and invade Italy in 49 BC to oppose Pompey and the Roman senate (Suetonius *Julius* 32). Erasmus is taking an opportunity to call attention to Eppendorf's addiction to dicing, which he refers to also in *Adagia* I ix 44 and Allen Ep 1437:14 / CWE Ep 1437:16.

21 *Adagia* I ix 44; Allen Ep 1934:130–1

22 *scribendi . . . scabie*; cf Juvenal's *scribendi cacoethes* (7.52).

23 'Printers . . . have lost all sense of shame' (Allen Ep 1284:19–20 / CWE Ep 1284:20–1). See *Adagia* II i 1 LB II 404D.

24 Greek in the original and a pun. See ASD I-3 615:109.

25 Cf 'Things and Names' 814:23–7, another example of Erasmus' obsession with Eppendorf in the March 1529 edition of the *Colloquies*. All these marks of a Junker are named in *Adagia* I ix 44 except the 'French pox.' Erasmus does not say plainly that Eppendorf had the pox (syphilis), but that it was common in men of Eppendorf's kind was made sufficiently clear in 'A Marriage in Name Only.' In 1524 he writes that when in Freiburg (1520–2) Eppendorf spent his money on 'whores, wine, and dice,' adding that he ran up so many debts he does not dare to return (Allen Ep 1437:8–15).

26 For some examples see 'The Liar and the Man of Honour.'

27 The first part of Panurge's discourse on debtors and creditors in Rabelais *Gargantua and Pantagruel* 3.3 develops the ideas in the next few lines in a fine display of rhetoric.

28 Proverbial; *Adagia* I iv 4

29 See 'Things and Names' 813:39–41.

30 As a frequent traveller Erasmus was familiar with this peril and often alludes to it. Writing to Beatus Rhenanus from Louvain in March 1518, for example, he says he will go to Basel to work on the New Testament 'provided it is safe

to enter Germany, which with all these robberies is in a worse state than hell itself, for you can neither enter nor leave' (Allen Ep 796:14–17 / CWE 796:15–18). He blames the prevalence of robberies in Germany partly on the numerous political entities, partly on the cunning and covetousness of the robbers. Other lands, such as Switzerland, have the problem under better control (Allen Ep 1039:24–40 / CWE Ep 1039:24–42). He praises Henry VIII for suppressing robberies in England, 'from which no part of England was safe hitherto' (Allen Ep 964:51–2 / CWE Ep 964:56–8).

31 Cf 'Things and Names' 814:12–13. After these they stop at nothing (*Adagia* I ix 44, and see n39 below).

32 *perfricanda frons est*; proverbial (*Adagia* I viii 47)

33 Cf 'Military Affairs' 56:29–34.

34 Eppendorf is said by Erasmus to have been extremely sensitive to doubts or denials of his claims to nobility (Allen Ep 1934:94–105 and passim).

35 Greek in the original; *Adagia* III iii 84

36 Greek in the original; *Adagia* I x 27

37 *Adagia* I viii 47, as at n32 above.

38 Quoted in Greek in the original, from Euripides *Iphigenia in Tauris* 1193; *Adagia* III iv 9

39 See n31 above, and cf 'The Funeral' n46. The Germans, Erasmus had written in 1519, trained for war by engaging in robbery, and vice versa: when the war ended, they then used what they learned there. That is why fraud, theft, and double-dealing abound: they are profitable (Allen Ep 1039:24–32 / CWE Ep 1039:24–34).

40 Proverbial; *Adagia* I iv 30

41 Cf *Adagia* II iii 98. Athenaeus 12.523 says that the inhabitants were effeminate, but an allusion to the city in Plautus *Casina* 963 is interpreted by Erasmus as implying the opposite – that Marseilles was a place of strict morals and manners (and so in *Spongia* LB X 1667F). This interpretation fits the context here. Erasmus points out, however, that more than one ancient place was confused with the French Marseilles (Massilia).

42 Cf Allen Ep 1934:435–47, 1992:43–9.

43 *leonina, non leporina*. Again, the word-play is impossible to reproduce in English.

44 There are several echoes of Horace in these lines. See Ep 2.2.102 (also quoted in *Adagia* I ix 28), *Satires* 1.14.36–8, 85, 91.

45 Cf 885:20–1 above and 'Things and Names' 814:2.

46 That is, in austerity. For Erasmus' opinions of the Carthusians see the introduction to 'The Soldier and the Carthusian' 328–9.

KNUCKLEBONES, OR THE GAME OF TALI

Ἀστραγαλισμός, sive Talorum lusus

First printed in the *Colloquia* in the March 1529 edition. On the date see the introduction to 'Charon' 818–19.

Erasmus' attention to sports and recreations, evident in the *Colloquies* as in other writings (see 'Sport' and Ep 55), was a natural consequence of his concern with youth, education, history, and classical scholarship. The game he describes here with such ample learning – antiquarianism of a kind popular and respected in books for the 'general reader' of his day – was one of several varieties of games of chance used by the ancients. Eros and Ganymede played with golden knucklebones on Olympus (Apollonius of Rhodes *Argonautica* 3.111–30). Patroclus killed a youth in an argument over knucklebones (*Iliad* 23.87–8). A picture from the first century of the Christian era shows women playing this game (reproduced in André Malraux *Voices of Silence* trans Stuart Gilbert [New York 1953] 40). In Pieter Brueghel's well-known painting *Children's Games*, this is one of the recreations shown (lower left-hand corner), and of course it is included in Rabelais' catalogue of games in *Gargantua and Pantagruel* 1.22.

Knucklebones (ἀστράγαλοι, also known as hucklebones), though often made of ivory, were originally the tarsal joints of certain animals, corresponding to the *tali* or ankle joints of man in form or structure. In the game described here each side of the *talus* was assigned a different value, 1, 3, 4, and 6. The highest number won by a throw of a single *talus* was therefore six, but in the game of knucklebones the highest score when four *tali* (as customary) were cast was made when each of the four sides showed a different number, as the dialogue explains.

Mere description of a game is not enough for Erasmus. The colloquy opens with a semantic query, which in turn leads to etymologies, quotations of classical texts, and a demonstration of the game, all presented in the author's usual informal but instructive fashion. As the text makes clear, his exposition is based on Aristotle's *Historia animalium* and *De partibus animalium*, but he knew all the other relevant passages in classical literature as well as some more recent ones, such as those by Theodorus Gaza (1400–c 1476), an erudite Greek who became professor at Ferrara and taught later at Rome and Naples. And Erasmus could not have overlooked a still more recent account of *tali* by Niccolò Leonico Tomeo (Leonicus Thomaeus), a highly regarded humanist scholar of Padua and Venice, where Erasmus may have met him. On his esteem for Leonico see Allen Epp 2347:1–2, 2443:387–9, 2526:18–21. In *De ludo talari*, one of his *Dialogi* (Venice 1524), Leonico describes the same features of *tali* that we read of in Erasmus' colloquy. What is more, he cites or quotes the same passages from Aristotle's treatises, Persius, Martial, Suetonius, Lucian, Julius Pollux, and Theodorus Gaza as those found in Erasmus' dialogue. Once these similarities are brought to our attention (as they were very briefly, by E. Garin 'Noterella Erasmiana' *La Rinascita* 5 [1942] 332–4), there can be no doubt of Erasmus' indebtedness. His library contained a copy of Leonico's *Dialogi* (Husner in *Gedenkschrift* 243 no 366). On Leonico see CEBR.

CHARLES,[1] QUIRINUS[2]

Quirinus 'Learn,' says Cato, 'but from the learned.'[3] So, my dear Uutenhove, I wish to learn from you, a master, why bishops of the ancient church
5 ordained that clerics should wear 'talarian,' that is ankle-length, gowns.[4]
Charles For two reasons, I think. First, for the sake of decency, lest any nakedness be exposed to view. In early days the sort of hose that now covers the body from waist to toetips hadn't been invented, nor were breeches or drawers commonly worn.[5] Likewise is it shameful for women to wear
10 clothes shorter than becomes the modesty of their sex. The second reason was that in dress as well as in conduct clerics should differ from laity, amongst whom the most ungodly delight to wear the shortest gowns.
Quirinus What you say is not improbable. But from Aristotle and Pliny I've learned that human beings don't have knucklebones [*tali*]. Only quadrupeds
15 have them; not all quadrupeds, however, but very many of the cloven-hoofed ones, though only in their hind legs.[6] How then can a garment worn by men be called 'talarian' unless men were once quadrupeds – as in the tale told by Aristophanes?[7]
Charles Oh, if we believe Oedipus, four-footed and three-footed as well as
20 two-footed men are found.[8] Often they come back from the wars with one foot, sometimes with none. But as for the word knucklebone [*talus*], you'll have more reason to be surprised if you read Horace, who credited even plays with knucklebones. For so he writes in the *Art of Poetry*, I believe: 'Heedless whether the play falls or stands straight on its feet [*talo*].'[9]
25 **Quirinus** Poets are privileged to talk as they please. According to them Tmolus has ears,[10] ships speak,[11] and oak trees dance.[12]
Charles Why, your Aristotle could have taught you that there are hemi-astragals, which he calls ἡμιαστράγαλοι; the lynx has this type, he informs us.[13] Lions, he adds, have something in place of a *talus*, only crooked,
30 which he terms 'labyrinthine'; Pliny renders it 'twisted.'[14] In fact, wherever

bones are joined together to make bending easy, concave ones fit convex; these are protected on each side by a slippery cartilage and have their parts coated, so to speak, to prevent injury from friction, as Aristotle likewise teaches.[15] In these joints there is usually something similar to a knucklebone
5   in form and function; as for example at the bottom of the shinbone, next to the heel, where the whole foot bends, something like a *talus* protrudes – the Greeks call it σφυρόν [ankle].[16] Again, in the bending of the knee, which if I mistake not they call ἰσχίον and some call *vertebrum*.[17] We see something similar in hipbones and shoulderbones; last of all in the joints
10 of fingers and toes. Lest this surprise you, the Greeks relate that the word ἀστράγαλος is applied by approved authors even to the bones to which the spine is attached, especially in the neck. And they cite this verse: 'My neck was severed from the spine [ἀστραγάλων].'[18]
     Now Aristotle tells us that an animal's forelegs are given to it for
15 speed and for that reason have no *tali*; the hind ones for balance, because the weight of the body inclines to that part, and likewise for strength in those beasts that fight by kicking.[19] Horace, when he wants to signify that a play was not hissed off the stage but played through to the end, says it stood up firm on its feet [*talo*];[20] attributing anklebones to a play in precisely the same
20 manner that we credit a book with a 'heel' [*calx*][21] and a scroll with a 'navel' [*umbilicus*].[22]
     Quirinus Really, you do very well as a grammarian.
     Charles But to be even more convincing: – Greek philologists would derive ἀστράγαλος from στρέφω [bend] and alpha privative,[23] because the
25 knucklebone [ἀστράγαλος] scarcely bends at all but is stationary instead. Others, however, prefer the view that ἀστράγαλος is used for ἀστάγαλος [not standing], ρ being an interpolation; because the knucklebone, owing to its slippery roundness, can't stand up.[24]
     Quirinus You could make a lot of guesses in that fashion. It would be
30 simpler to say 'I don't know.'
     Charles The conjecture won't seem so unreasonable if you reflect on the obscurity of word origins.[25] And then there's no inconsistency in the matter, as will be evident if you examine it more closely. The knucklebone does turn round, but in such a way that it steadies the part to which it is attached.[26] In
35 the second place, bone joins bone, to prevent easy dislocation.
     Quirinus Seems to me you'd make a good sophist if you liked.
     Charles But there's no reason why the etymology of the word should bother us, Talesius. For what the Greeks today call ἀστράγαλος the ancients – Callimachus, for instance[27] – spoke of as ἄστριον; his hemistich has: 'And
40 ten dice [ἄστρια] took as ransom.' From this it appears that they used to say ἀστρίζειν[28] as well as ἀστραγαλίζειν for 'to play knucklebones.'

Quirinus Then what sort of thing is the *talus*, properly speaking?[29]
Charles A girls' game nowadays;[30] once a boys' game, like cob-nuts.[31] The Greeks have a saying about it, 'upset over knucklebones,' when they mean angry for a trivial reason.[32] Again, Horace in the *Odes*: 'Nor shall you dice
5   for lordship of the feast.' Likewise in his *Satires*: 'Dice and nuts, Aulus,' etc.[33] Finally, there's that aphorism of the Lacedaemonian, I believe, about tricking boys by knucklebones, men by oaths.[34]

This *talus*, they say, is not found in any animal that is solid-hoofed, except the single-horned rhinoceros,[35] or that has the foot split into many
10   toes or claws.[36] The lion, panther, dog, ape, man, birds, and many other creatures belong to this class. Most of the truly δίχηλα or cloven-hoofed have the *talus*, and, as you correctly remarked, on the hind legs.[37] Man is unique in having a double reason for being without the *talus*: first, because he is a biped, secondly because he has feet split by five toes.

15   **Quirinus** I've often heard about that. But I'd like very much a description of the shape and location of the *talus*. For this sort of game is scorned even by girls today; they take up dice, cards, and other masculine amusements instead.

Charles No wonder, since they take up theology, too.[38] But even if I were
20   a mathematician or painter or sculptor, I couldn't show you the shape of a *talus* better than by a *talus* itself, unless you prefer that I describe it in words, as is generally done.

Quirinus Have you a *talus*?
Charles Here you are: a sheep's bone from the right leg. Only four sides,[39]
25   you see, though a cube and a die have six: four on the sides, two on top and bottom.

Quirinus That's right.
Charles On a *talus*, since top and bottom are rounded, there are only four sides, one of which, you notice, has a sort of hump.

30   **Quirinus** I see.
Charles The side directly opposite is concave. Aristotle calls the former 'prone,' the latter 'supine';[40] as in sexual intercourse between husband and wife for the purpose of begetting children the woman is supine, the man prone; and if the palm of the hand faces the ground, it's prone; if reversed,
35   supine. (Poets and orators sometimes misuse these terms, but that doesn't concern us just now.)

Quirinus You've given a fine demonstration indeed. What's the difference between the two remaining sides?

Charles One is somewhat concave, in order to fit the bone to which it's
40   joined. The other is hardly concave at all and is less protected by a coating of cartilage; it's covered only by tendon and skin.

Children's Games, detail: girls playing knucklebones
Pieter Brueghel the Elder, 1560
Kunsthistorisches Museum, Vienna

Quirinus I see.

Charles The prone side has no tendons, but a tendon sticks to the hollow of the supine side, as to the top of the right side and the bottom of the left.

Quirinus Very good, but how am I to tell right from left?

5 **Charles** You do well to remind me, for I've taught you badly if you don't understand that this *talus* comes from the right leg. I'll explain it better, then, and at the same time point out its location, as you wish. The *talus* is actually in the hock of the leg, below the hipbone.

Quirinus Many people think it's next to the foot.

10 **Charles** They're mistaken. What is properly called the *talus* is in the hocks, which the Greeks name καμπαί [bendings],[41] but of the hind legs, as I've said. Between your foot and knee is the shin.

Quirinus So I believe.

Charles Behind the knee is the καμπή.

15 **Quirinus** I agree.

Charles The bending that a man has in his arms, quadrupeds have in the hind legs. (I except the ape, a half-man.) Thus elbow is to arms what knee is to legs.[42]

Quirinus I see.

20 **Charles** So bending corresponds to bending.

Quirinus And this applies, you say, to the front and hind legs.

Charles Correct. In the hock, therefore, corresponding to the one behind the knee, the *talus* stands straight up when the animal stands.[43] Top and bottom curve slightly, though not exactly in the same way, for the upper is bent

25 back into horns that Aristotle calls κεραῖαι[44] (Theodorus renders *antennae*); the prone side lies under these where they are joined to it. The bottom has nothing of this kind.

Quirinus I quite understand.

Charles Hence the side facing the forelegs Aristotle calls supine; the one

30 opposite this, prone. Also there are two sides, one of which faces inward, that is, it faces the hind legs – either right or left, let's say; the other faces outward. The one facing inward Aristotle calls κῶλον; the one facing outward, ἰσχίον.

Quirinus I see the thing exactly with my eyes. Now it remains for you

35 to describe the old method of playing knucklebones; for the game of our recollection doesn't agree with what we find in ancient writers on this kind of play.[45]

Charles But surely it's possible that just as we use cards and dice for various sorts of play nowadays, the ancients had different ways of playing

40 knucklebones.

Quirinus That's probable.

supine   prone   Chian   Coan

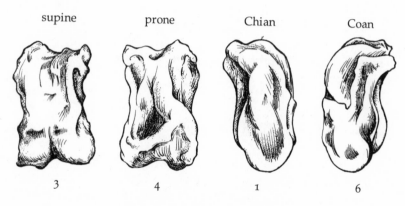

3   4   1   6

The four sides of the knucklebone

Charles Theodorus Gaza (or, as others prefer to call him, Theodorus of Thessalonika),[46] in his translation of book 2 of Aristotle's *History of Animals*, says the side of the *talus* turned outward is called the 'dog'; the side turned inward, towards the other shank, 'Venus.' But the fact is he adds this on
5   his own authority, for Aristotle says only: '. . . the prone side faces out, the supine side faces in, and the sides called κῶλα turned in towards one another, those called ἰσχία outside, and the "horns" on top.'[47] But since it's certain from other authors that the throw is called 'Venus' whenever no two of the four *tali* show the same number, I wonder what source Theodorus followed
10 in calling one side 'Venus.' Our common friend Erasmus – no expert on such subjects, to be sure – gives in his *Adagia* some information from ancient authors about the game of knucklebones. For instance, in the proverb 'Not Chius but Cous' he tells us that *Cous* and *senio* are the same thing the Greeks call ἑξίτης [sice]. Likewise in the proverb 'Chius to Cous,' where he adds that
15 Chius is the same as 'dog' and that the throw of 'Cous' was lucky, of 'dog' unlucky;[48] as Persius testifies:

> My sole question was to know
> What the lucky sice would bring, how much
20 > The unlucky 'dog' would strip me of.[49]

Similarly Propertius:

> Always the ruinous 'dogs' leaped up.[50]
25

Ovid too, in book 2 of *Tristia*, called them 'ruinous dogs.'[51] Erasmus adds from Martial that sice by itself was lucky, but unlucky if accompanied by 'dog.' For Martial says:

Nor sice with ace shakes my ivory box.[52]

Martial indicates in his *Apophoreta* that the throw of 'Venus' was rare but was the luckiest:[53]

5

When no one *talus* stands with the same face as another,
You'll say I've given you generous gifts.[54]

As many knucklebones were used in play as each *talus* has sides; in dicing, no
10 more than three as a rule. But the method of play is made more clear by what
Suetonius writes in *Octavius Augustus*, quoting the following from a letter
of Augustus to Tiberius: 'At dinner, both yesterday and today, we gambled
like old men.[55] For when the *tali* were thrown, whoever cast "dog" or sice
paid a denarius for each *talus*; whoever threw "Venus" won them all.'[56]
15 **Quirinus** You've explained that the throw is luckiest when all four *tali* show
different sides, just as in dicing the one called 'Midas' is luckiest;[57] but why
this throw is called 'Venus' you haven't explained yet.
Charles Lucian will solve that difficulty for you. In his *Amores* he says: '...
and with luck at play, especially if he made the lucky throw of the goddess,
20 when no two sides of the knucklebones show the same number, he gave
thanks, in expectation of soon attaining his desire.' Now here he's speaking
of 'Venus.'[58]
Quirinus If Theodorus is wrong, only two sides have names of their own.
Charles He may have followed some source that eludes us. The literary
25 evidence I've presented. Some writers mention a number, 'Stesichorian,'[59]
which they think is an eight in knucklebones; also 'Euripidean,'[60] which
amounted to forty.
Quirinus It remains for you to lay down the rules of the game.[61]
Charles I don't think boys used those same rules that Octavius writes he
30 used. And it's unlikely that the sort of playing he mentions was popular.
Had it been so, he needed to say merely 'At dinner we played knucklebones.'
But he seems to me to suggest they had found a new mode of playing – one
suitable for old men, as it were, and with very few of the exacting intellectual
demands that make so many games more laborious than studies these days.
35 **Quirinus** Bring out the rest of the knucklebones, please, so we can try them.
Charles But we've no dice-box for rolling the *tali*,[62] and no board either.
Quirinus This table will serve for giving some sort of demonstration. A
glass or a cap will do for a dice-box.
Charles Even enclosing them in the hollow of your hands will do. The throw
40 turns up the supine side more often than the prone and the prone more often
than sice or 'dog.'

Quirinus Evidently.

Charles If one 'dog' turns up among four knucklebones, put down a coin; if two, two coins; if three, three; if four, four.[63] And every time you throw sice, take up one of the coins.

5 **Quirinus** What if I throw sice and 'dog?'

Charles If you like, each player will add a coin; neither will take anything. Whoever is the first to get 'Venus' will win the stakes.

Quirinus What if the *talus* shows the prone or supine side?

Charles That throw won't count, and either you'll have to throw again or it 10 will be my turn.

Quirinus I agree to its being your turn.

Charles Now lay down your stake.

Quirinus Let's try without a penalty.

Charles You want to learn so great an art for nothing?

15 **Quirinus** Still, it's not fair to match a novice with an expert.

Charles But hope of winning and fear of losing will make you try all the harder.

Quirinus How much shall we play for?

Charles If you want to get rich in a hurry, a hundred ducats.

20 **Quirinus** I only wish I had them to put down! It's safer to grow rich by degrees. Here's a whole farthing.

Charles Come, we'll add little to little, as Hesiod advises, and thus accumulate a large sum.[64] Roll them and throw. A good start! You have a 'dog.' Lay down a coin, and hereafter recognize the unlucky side. Give me 25 the *tali*.

Quirinus A better start! You've three 'dogs.' Lay down the coins.

Charles Fortune has something in store for you. Throw; but be sure to shake them first, my good friend. – Work's wasted: you've the prone and supine sides. My turn; hand me the *tali*.

30 **Quirinus** Oh, well done! I see three 'dogs' again.

Charles Don't crow too soon.[65] Fortune does beckon to you, I say. But look: this was the way I was taught the game, but I think Octavius played it differently.

Quirinus How?

35 **Charles** Whoever had thrown 'dog' laid down a denarius, as we said; whoever threw sice won nothing, but the other player laid down.

Quirinus What if many sices turned up?

Charles The other player added as many coins. The first throw of 'Venus' won the rather sizable stakes. And you may add that the player who gets 40 neither sice nor 'dog' loses nothing but his turn at throwing.

Quirinus I don't decline.

Charles And it's nicer, I think, if the one with the *tali* has three throws and then gives the other his turns.

Quirinus All right, but how many throws of 'Venus' will end the game?

Charles Three, if that suits you; then you'll be free to start over again.
5 Though Venus' favours are few and far between. Let's play now and hope for good luck.

Quirinus Go ahead. But it's best to shut the doors, so our cook won't see us playing like children.

Charles Like dotards, rather. Have you such a blab of a cook?

10 **Quirinus** So loose-tongued that if there were no men to whom she could tell what happens at home, she'd spin a long yarn to the hens and cats.[66]

Charles Ho there, boy, shut and bolt the door, to keep some spectator from popping in without notice. Then we can play to our heart's content.

NOTES

1 Charles is undoubtedly named for Karel Uutenhove of Ghent, who lived with Erasmus in Basel for at least six months (July 1528 to January 1529) as a student. Erasmus dedicated to him an edition of some minor writings by Chrysostom in February 1529 (Allen Ep 2093).

2 Quirinus Talesius was in Erasmus' service for about seven years (1524–31). Afterwards he returned to his native Haarlem and became a leading citizen, serving as burgomaster ten times. He perished in the Spanish siege of the town in 1572 (see Allen Ep 1966 introduction). Erasmus thought well of him, for in the month this colloquy was published he gave Talesius a present of 150 crowns. His first will provided a bequest of 200 florins for him 'if he is alive at the time of my death' (Allen Ep 2113 introduction; Allen vi 506:124–5 Appendix 19). He is not to be confused with Quirinus Hagius, Erasmus' secretary a few years later (Allen Ep 2704 introduction). On both consult CEBR.

3 *Disticha Catonis* 4.23 (ed Marcus Boas [Amsterdam 1952] 219); and see *Adagia* iv viii 37. On the *Disticha* ascribed to Cato see 'Patterns' n2.

4 A convenient pun on Quirinus' nickname, Talesius ('spinner,' 'clothmaker,' his father's trade). The Fifth Lateran Council in 1514 affirmed the ancient rule that priests' garments (the black cassock) should be ankle length ([Bull on the reform of the curia] On cardinals; Tanner i 619).

5 On the terms for these garments see 'Cyclops' n12.

6 Aristotle *De partibus animalium* 4.10 690a4–27; *Historia animalium* 2.1 499b6–27; Pliny *Naturalis historia* 11.255

7 See Plato *Symposium* 189–90.

8 A reference to the riddle of the Sphinx; see 'The Profane Feast' n71.

9 Not in the *Ars poetica* but in his *Epistles* 2.1.176

10 Mountain in Lydia and god of the mountain, who 'shook his ears free from the trees' when about to judge a musical contest between Pan and Apollo (Ovid *Metamorphoses* 11.156–61)

11 In the *Argonautica* by Apollonius of Rhodes, the ship *Argo* urges the pilot
Tiphys and his comrades to set forth (1.524–5). In a more memorable
passage the ship speaks again with human voice, prophesying woe
(4.580–91).

12 They responded in this manner to the music of Orpheus' lyre (Horace *Odes*
1.12.11–12; Ovid *Metamorphoses* 10.86–105). Erasmus writes of an oak preaching
when he jokes about a critic, Duchesne (de Quercu; cf *quercus* 'oak'). See
'Patterns' n35.

13 Aristotle *Historia animalium* 2.1 499b24–5

14 Aristotle *Historia animalium* 2.1 499b25–6; Pliny *Naturalis historia* 11.255. On
'labyrinthine' see also *Adagia* II x 51.

15 Aristotle *De partibus animalium* 2.9 (654b20–7)

16 On σφυρόν and ἰσχίον see Aristotle *Historia animalium* 1.15 (494a4–10).

17 Erasmus is mistaken here; the ἰσχίον is the hip joint, not the kneebone. *Vertebrum*
is used in late medical writers for the hip joint, eg Caelius Aurelianus *Acutae
passiones* 1.10.71.

18 Greek in the original, from Homer *Odyssey* 10.599–60, 11.64–5; quoted in the
entry on ἀστράγαλος in *Etymologicon magnum* (on which see n24 below)

19 Aristotle *De partibus animalium* 4.10 (690a14–21)

20 See 892:22–4 and n9 above.

21 The *calx* or heel was the 'foot' of a page or conclusion of a book.

22 Rollers attached to the ends of ancient papyrus books had projecting knobs
(*umbilici*) as ornaments. See Martial 4.89: *pervenimus usque ad umbilicos* 'we've
come to the end.'

23 Alpha prefixed to a word beginning with a consonant may be used in Greek to
create a negative.

24 These lines undoubtedly recall what Erasmus had read in the *Etymologicon
magnum* (ed Thomas Gaisford [Oxford 1848] 159:40). On that work see 'The
New Mother' n97.

25 On Erasmus and etymology see Chomarat *Grammaire et rhétorique* I 252–9.

26 Cf *De partibus animalium* 4.10 690a4–21, where Aristotle calls it a 'connecting
rod.'

27 Greek poet and scholar (fourth–third centuries BC). The line of verse quoted
here is Greek in the original. Literally ἄστρια means 'little stars.' In writing
ἄστρια Erasmus probably followed Suidas, which treats this diminutive as
synonymous with ἀστράγαλος (ed A. Adler [Leipzig 1928–38; repr 1971] I
part 1 no 4255, citing Callimachus). The *Etymologicon magnum* (n24 above)
159:28 and modern editions of Callimachus read ἄστριας; see *Callimachus and
Lycophron* trans A.W. Mair, Loeb Classical Library (London and Cambridge,
Mass 1921) fragment 84/238 and *Callimachus* ed R. Pfeiffer, 2 vols (Oxford
1949–53) fragment 276.

28 So Julius Pollux *Onomasticon* 9.99. This lexicographer (second century AD) is
mentioned by Erasmus in Allen Ep 260:47–50 / CWE Ep 260:52–6 and *De ratione
studii* ASD I-2 123:2–5 / CWE 24 674:5–8.

29 *Astragali* or *tali* used in knucklebones are small bones, oblong in shape, with
two rounded ends and four more or less flat sides. Since they cannot rest on
the rounded ends, it is only the four sides which counted in the game. These
were numbered 1, 3, 4, 6. For further description see n40 below.

Allusions to the lore of dicing and *tali* are found in *Adagia*, for example I ii 13, II ii 9, II vii 68. For a contemporary description of knucklebones see the *Liber de ludo aleae* by the physician and mathematician Girolamo Cardano (1501–76) in *Cardano* ed Oysten Ore, with translation by S.H. Gould (Princeton 1953) 192–3, 237–9.

30 Known as 'jacks'
31 On this game see 'Hunting' n6.
32 Erasmus quotes the Greek from Homer *Iliad* 23.88.
33 *Odes* 1.4.18; *Satires* 2.3.171–2
34 *Adagia* III iii 43; from Plutarch *Moralia* 229B *Apophthegmata Laconica*
35 The 'Indian ass'; Aristotle *Historia animalium* 2.1 499b19–20
36 Aristotle *Historia animalium* 2.1 499b23–4; *De partibus animalium* 4.10 690a24–5
37 See 892:14–16 and n6 above.
38 See 'The Abbot and the Learned Lady' n36.
39 See n29 above.
40 Aristotle *Historia animalium* 2.1 499b. The illustration from sexual intercourse, however, is likely to be Erasmus' own, perhaps suggested by some words in Theodorus Gaza.
   The knucklebone sits in the hock of the animal. Its rounded top and bottom fit into sockets in the two bones which it joins. In these lines Erasmus is attempting the difficult task of explaining, in ordinary language, the precise position of the knucklebone in the leg. Aristotle had said that when the animal is standing, the astragal is upright; his account, however, implies that normally the astragal tilts slightly forward so that it is possible to speak of one side being 'on top' (prone) and the opposite side 'underneath' (supine). Of the other two sides one faces inwards (ie towards the other leg) and the other faces outwards. The prone side is described as 'humped.' It faces towards the back of the animal. Its value in the game was four. The opposite side (supine) is concave and faces towards the front legs of the animal. Its value is three. The side facing inward, known in the game as 'the Coan,' is slightly concave. It has the highest value, a six. The opposite side, which faces outwards, has the lowest value, namely, one. It was called 'the Chian' or the 'dog.' For further on these names see nn47, 48.
   The writer of this note would like to thank Brady's Belmont Butcher, in Queensland, Australia, and the much lamented Hecuba, a deer of Edenside, New Brunswick, for their contribution to the solution of several philological problems in Erasmus' description of knucklebones.
41 Aristotle *Historia animalium* 2.1 499b27; see next note.
42 Erasmus here lacks his usual clarity. He is explaining that the knucklebone is not in the ankle, but in the hock, which has similar 'bendings' to the elbow and the knee. He goes on to make the point that the human elbow bends in the same direction as the hind leg of a quadruped. The front and the back legs of a quadruped bend in opposite directions, thus: « ». In humans the elbow has the same angle as the back leg of an animal and the knee resembles an animal's front leg. There is much on this topic in Aristotle *De incessu animalium* 13 712a1–22. For the intermediate nature of the ape see Aristotle *De partibus animalium* 4.10 689b31–4.
43 Aristotle *Historia animalium* 2.1 499b26–7

44 Aristotle *Historia animalium* 2.1 499b29–30. Top and bottom of the knucklebone are rounded, but the top has two small projecting points or 'horns,' which stand over the 'prone' ('humped') side.

45 Here again we are reminded that later ways of scoring in knucklebones may differ from those used by the ancients. Cf Harold W. Johnston *The Private Life of the Romans* (Chicago 1932) 242–3.

46 See the introduction 891 above. His Greek grammar (Venice 1495) was considered by Erasmus and others to be the best. Erasmus translated books 1 and 2 of this (Louvain 1516, 1518; text in LB I 117–64); see Epp 428 and 771. Gaza's Latin versions of Aristotle *Historia animalium* and *De partibus animalium* were printed in 1476 (Venice).

47 Erasmus quotes the Greek from *Historia animalium* 2.1 499b27–30. When Aristotle says that the prone side faces out, he means that it faces back; similarly the supine side faces in, ie towards the front of the animal.
κῶλα and ἰσχία are mistaken manuscript readings which Erasmus found in his text of Aristotle and copied here; they were left unchanged in his final authorized edition of March 1533, as in the *Opera omnia* of 1538–40 and LB. Neither Greek word makes sense in the context. Gaza saw that the correct readings should be κῶα and χία, and Erasmus accepted these readings in the *Adagia*. See next note.

48 Two adages are referred to. The first (II ii 9) is given in the form 'Not Chius but Cius,' although Erasmus knew the correct variant Cous for Cius, which he cited from the ancient critic and scholar Aristarchus of Samothrace. In the second, 'Chius to Cous' (II vii 68), the two Greek terms are correctly explained as belonging to the game of knucklebones, where, as we have seen, 'Chius' stands for one and 'Cous' for sice or six. Sice was the luckiest number. But the luckiest throw (the 'Venus' throw) was when no two *tali* came up with the same number.

49 Persius 3.48.50

50 Propertius 4.8.46

51 *Tristia* 2.474, but see n60 below.

52 Martial 13.1.6

53 If you throw often enough, a proverb promises, you will sooner or later throw a 'Venus' (*Adagia* I ii 13; cf I iii 9).

54 Martial 14.14

55 Dotards sometimes revert to childishness, Erasmus observes (*Adagia* I v 36), but says that for them to indulge now and then in games of childhood is harmless and can be a sensible relaxation from serious affairs (Allen Ep 1402:13–17). Augustus is said to have played sometimes at cobnuts with children (*Augustus* 83). In Cicero *Ad Atticum* 1.16.3, *in ludo talari* refers to a gambling den; but the emperor's game of knucklebones with his guests was merely an amusing and innocent way of passing the time.

56 This passage from *Augustus* 71 is quoted in *Adagia* I ii 13. Erasmus' editions of Suetonius and of the *Historia Augusta* were printed together by Froben in 1518. The dedicatory letter to Dukes Frederick and George of Saxony (Ep 586) is an incisive essay on rulership.

57 On 'Midas' see *Adagia* II ix 87.

58 Lucian *Amores* 16. Erasmus quotes the Greek.
'he gave thanks . . . his desire'] Added in the September 1529 edition

59 When the total was eight; so called because the tomb of the ancient Greek poet Stesichorus was octagonal in shape (Julius Pollux *Onomasticon* 9.100)

60 Here a nickname given to the cast of forty in dicing; from one Euripides (not the dramatist) who held office with the Forty in Athens. See Athenaeus 6.247a and Julius Pollux *Onomasticon* 9.101. The Forty were Athenian justices who heard cases of minor claims (Aristotle *Constitution of Athens* 53.1).

61 They are summarized in C. Daremberg and E. Saglio *Dictionnaire des antiquités grecques et romaines* 5 vols in 9 (Paris 1877–1919) v 28–31, with illustrations.

62 Because of their irregular shapes *tali* could not easily be rolled or tossed from a box. We are told that boys would sometimes spin them like tops or spindles; these players enclose them in the hollow of their hands.

63 Four 'dogs' or aces would be the lowest score.

64 *Works and Days* 361–2; cf *Adagia* I viii 94.

65 Literally 'No triumph song before the victory!' a proverbial expression quoted here in Greek. See *Adagia* I vii 55.

66 Quirinus' reply recalls Erasmus' irrepressible servant Margarete Büsslin, whose namesake we met in 'The Poetic Feast.' See the introduction 390.

THE COUNCIL OF WOMEN

Senatulus, sive Γυναικοσυνέδριον

First printed in the *Colloquies* in the March 1529 edition. On the date of publication see the introduction to 'Charon' 818–19. A remark in 'The Usefulness of the *Colloquies*' (1105:31–4) seems to indicate that this colloquy was written earlier than 'The Knight without a Horse,' but in the printed versions 'The Knight without a Horse' comes first.

This diversion was inspired by remembrance of a passage in the life of the emperor Heliogabalus attributed to Aelius Lampridius and included in the *Historia Augusta (Heliogabalus* 4.3–4). It was mentioned by Erasmus in *Lingua* (1525; LB IV 731F / ASD IV-1A 146:979–87 / CWE 29 379). *Senatulus*, the 'little' or 'miniature' senate, a diminutive of Erasmus' devising, was obviously adapted from *senaculum*, a council-hall where matrons related to Roman emperors were formally honoured. Heliogabalus (or Elagabalus), who reigned from 218 until 222, established a women's 'senate' over which his mother Symi-amira presided. This assembly presumed or pretended to enact rules about deportment and etiquette for ladies: dress, precedence, even the question of who might kiss whom, a topic sometimes thought by readers of Erasmus to be a peculiarly English subject. In Erasmus' dialogue similar concerns are propounded by Cornelia, a no-nonsense woman dedicated to advancing the status of her sex and at the same time keeping commoners in their places.

To make fun of feminine foibles was long the assumed prerogative of every male satirist. By allowing women to legislate – a motif as old as the *Ecclesiazusae* of Aristophanes – Erasmus is having a gentleman's joke. Yet he does more than that. Cornelia's strictures on the impertinence of the lower orders, who put on airs and boldly imitate their betters in dress and bearing, invite attention to the perennial question of inequality. This dialogue is an entertainment, not a contribution to social philosophy. Nevertheless it contains the germ of an idea, engagingly treated, about social and therefore political status or privilege. Like 'Courtship,' 'Marriage,' and 'The Abbot and the Learned Lady,' it pleases by comedy but at the same time invites reflection on social institutions.

For Erasmus' ideas on dress in general see 'The Well-to-do Beggars.' He took an interest in the essay *De re vestiara* by Lazare de Baïf (Basel 1526), who discusses some of the matters noticed by Cornelia in the colloquy. Erasmus knew Baïf, thought well of him (Allen Ep 1479:1–18 / CWE Ep 1479:6–21, Allen Ep 1962:1–9; *Ciceronianus* LB I 1012A / ASD I-2 674:11–14 / CWE 28 421), owned his book (Husner in *Gedenkschrift* 238 no 73), and praised it: Baïf, he says, has done for ancient dress what Budé did for ancient coinage in *De asse* (mentioned in 'Benefices' 48:35). Baïf was French ambassador in Venice 1529–34. On him see Allen Ep 1962 introduction and CEBR.

Some source books dealing with Renaissance women are cited in the notes. Three studies of particular value may be named here. Ruth Kelso *Doctrine for the Lady of the Renaissance* (Urbana 1956), in addition to a skilful presentation of texts and doctrine, has a copious bibliography. An older work, E.P. Rodocanachi *La femme italienne avant, pendant, et après la Renaissance* (Paris 1922), is still very useful; it has many illustrations. Ian Maclean *The Renaissance Notion of Woman* (Cambridge 1980) is a concise survey of what contemporary learning and thought held about women and how all this contributed to the emergence of modern feminism.

'The Council of Women' is the only Erasmian colloquy, so far as I know, to have been translated into Irish. A seventeenth-century version, 'Párliament na mBan,' dedicated to the translator's young pupil, is described, with quotations from the text, by James Stewart in *Celtica* 7 (1967) 135–41.

CORNELIA, MARGARET, PEROTTA, JULIA, CATHARINE

Cornelia Your full and prompt attendance at this meeting today – happy and auspicious[1] event may it prove for this group and the entire commonwealth
5 of women! – gives me every hope that a gracious God may direct the mind of each one of you to what concerns the general welfare and the dignity of us all. You are all aware, I believe, of how much our interests have suffered from the fact that while men transact their business at daily assemblies, we neglect our cause by sitting at distaff and loom. Hence matters have come
10 to such a pass that we are entirely ignorant of political science; men treat us virtually as amusements and scarcely think us deserving of the name of human. If we go on like this, figure out for yourselves how it will end, for I'm afraid to utter such ominous words. Though we may neglect our social position, we should at least be concerned about our security. 'In the
15 multitude of counsellors there is safety,' wrote the wisest of kings.[2] Bishops have their synods, congregations of monks their chapters, soldiers their assigned stations, thieves their rendezvous. And, to make the list complete, even ants have their assemblies. Of all living creatures, only we women never have intercourse –
20 **Margaret** Oftener than we should!
Cornelia – It's not yet time to interrupt. Let me finish my speech; then each one will have a chance to talk. We're not introducing a novelty; we're

recalling precedent. Since, more that thirteen hundred years ago, if I'm not mistaken, that most revered emperor Heliogabalus –

Perotta 'Most revered?' How come, when we know he's the one who was dragged along by a hook and thrown into a sewer?[3]

5   **Cornelia** Interrupted again! If we approve or disapprove of a person on this basis, we shall call Christ bad because he was crucified, Domitian good because he died at home.[4] But the worst charge against Heliogabalus is that he hurled to the ground the sacred fire kept by the vestal virgins[5] and that in his domestic chapel he kept images of Moses and Christ,[6] whom they

10 disparagingly called 'Chrestus.'[7] Well, this Heliogabalus decreed that as the emperor had his senate with which to deliberate about public affairs, so also his mother Augusta should have a senate of her own for dealing with women's business.[8] Either as a joke, or else to distinguish it, men called this the 'petty senate.'

15   This precedent, abandoned for so many centuries, our situation has long warned us to restore. And let no one be upset because the apostle Paul forbids women to speak in the assembly he calls a church.[9] He refers to a meeting of men; this is a feminine meeting. Otherwise, if women always had to keep silence, why did nature give us, too, tongues as ready as men's

20 and voices just as loud – though men sound hoarser and more like donkeys than we do. But we must all take care to treat this business so seriously that men won't speak of the 'petty senate' again or maybe think up some nastier name, since they're accustomed to making fun of us whenever they please. Yet if *their* parliaments were described as they deserve, they might seem

25 worse than womanish. We see monarchs who have done nothing but make war for many a year now; theologians, priests, bishops, and people never agree together; there are as many opinions as there are men,[10] and among these men a more than feminine fickleness. There's no peace between state and state, neighbour and neighbour.[11] Unless I'm much mistaken, human

30 affairs would go better if the reins were handed over to us. Perhaps feminine modesty forbids me to accuse such leading citizens of stupidity, but I dare say one's allowed to repeat what Solomon wrote in the thirteenth chapter of Proverbs: 'Only by pride cometh contention: but with the well advised is wisdom.'[12]

35   But I must not allow this prologue to delay you any longer. That everything may be done decently and in order, without disturbance, let us consider first who should attend the council and who should be excluded. Too large a crowd means an uproar rather than a council; and a group limited to a few smacks of dictatorship. I'm of the opinion that no virgins should be

40 admitted, because many things will come up that are not proper for them to hear.

LB I 842C / ASD I-3 630

Julia But how could you identify the virgins? Will whoever have the reputation of virgins be regarded as such?

Cornelia No, but I think we should admit only married women.

Julia Even among married women some are virgins: the wives of eunuchs.

5 **Cornelia** But let this mark of respect be paid to marriage, that by 'women' we mean married women.

Julia In any event, if we exclude only virgins there will still be an enormous throng; it won't diminish much.

Cornelia Those married more than three times shall be excluded too.

10 **Julia** Why?

Cornelia Because they deserve retirement as *emeritae*. Likewise, I think, for those over seventy years of age. A wife should be forbidden to speak disrespectfully of her husband by name; husbands as a class may be discussed, but temperately: 'Nothing to excess.'[13]

15 **Catharine** Why may we speak less freely of husbands here than they talk everywhere about us? My Titius, if he wants to be the life of the party, tells what he did with me the night before and what I said;[14] and often he invents a good deal of it.

Cornelia If the truth must be told, our dignity depends on our husbands.[15]

20 If we slander them, what is that but dishonouring ourselves? Now though we have more than a few causes for just complaint, our position, on the whole, is stronger than theirs. In their pursuit of wealth they fly over land and sea,[16] not without risk to their lives; if war breaks out and the trumpet calls, they stand ironclad in the battle line[17] while we sit safe at home. If they

25 break laws, they're judged more seriously; we're let off lightly because of our sex.[18] After all, it is largely up to us how agreeable our husbands are.

It remains to draw up rules about the order of seating, so as to avoid what often happens to the ambassadors of kings, princes, and popes, who wrangle in councils for three whole months before they can get down to

30 business. Consequently I think there should be first an aristocracy in which those with four degrees of nobility shall have precedence; next, those with three; then those with two; after them, those with one; last, those with a half. And in each rank a place shall be decided by ancestry. Bastards shall have last place in their respective ranks. There shall be a second assembly of

35 commoners. In this the women who have borne the most children shall have first place. Among equals, age shall decide. A third assembly will consist of those who have not yet had children.

Catharine What will you do with widows?

Cornelia You're right to remind me. Their place shall be in the midst of the

40 matrons, provided they have or have had children; barren ones shall have last place.

Julia What place do you assign to the wives of priests and monks?

Cornelia We'll consider that in our next session.

Julia What about prostitutes?

Cornelia We won't let this senate be contaminated with the likes of them.

5 **Julia** What about concubines?

Cornelia There's not just a single class of these. We'll deliberate about them at our leisure. Also for the agenda is the question of how decisions should be recorded, whether by points or stones[19] or voice votes or show of hands or division.[20]

10 **Catharine** In stones there's trickery; and likewise in points. If we walk over to the side we favour, we'll stir up a lot of dust, since we wear long dresses. Therefore the best method is to show one's preference by a voice vote.

Cornelia But it's hard to count voices. Furthermore, we must be careful we don't have clamour instead of council.

15 **Catharine** Nothing is to be done without clerks, lest anything be forgotten.

Cornelia All very well for counting votes, but how will you avoid the clamour?

Catharine No one may speak unless asked and in her turn. Whoever violates the rule shall be ejected from the senate. And if anyone babbles about what 20 is transacted here, she shall be punished by three days' silence.

[**Cornelia**] So much for procedures.[21] Now hear what subjects we should debate. Our first concern should be our social standing. This depends most of all on dress, a matter so much neglected that nowadays you can hardly tell a noblewoman from a commoner, a married one from an unmarried girl 25 or widow, a housewife from a harlot. Decorum is so far gone that women of every class put on whatever airs they please.[22] You can see women worse than commoners, and from the lowest class, dressed up in silks, pleats, flowered patterns, stripes, fine linen, gold, silver, sables and marten furs[23] when all the time their husbands are at home stitching shoes. Their fingers 30 are heavy with emeralds and diamonds[24] – they turn up their noses at pearls these days! – to say nothing of their amber and coral and gilded sandals. It used to be enough for women of modest means to use silk girdles, out of respect for their sex, and to decorate the hems of their clothing with a silk fringe. Nowadays there's a double mischief: the family budget's strained, 35 and rank, the safeguard of dignity, is confounded. If commoners are borne in chariots and litters inlaid with ivory and covered with velvet,[25] what's left for the rich and powerful? And if the wife of a man who's scarcely a knight wears a train fifteen ells long,[26] what shall a duchess or countess do?

And this situation is the more intolerable because we constantly change 40 the fashions so recklessly.[27] Linen ribbons used to hang from 'horns' sticking out behind the head. By this adornment you could tell aristocratic women

from commoners. Noble women, to maintain the distinction, took to wearing caps with white fur on the outside varied by black spots. At once the rabble followed suit. When fashion changed again, they wore black linen veils.[28] The lower classes not only had the nerve to imitate this, but even added gilt
5   edging and finally jewellery. Formerly the upper classes gathered their hair on top of the head, plucking the hairs from the forehead and the temples. This didn't please them long – everybody else was soon doing the same thing. Finally they wore their hair across the forehead. Straightway the lower classes copied them.[29] Only ladies used to have escorts and pages to
10   walk before them, and one pretty fellow among them to give madame a hand when she was about to rise and support her left arm with his right when she walked. This honour was accorded only to those of good family. Nowadays, while wives far and wide follow custom, they permit anyone at all to perform this service, just as they let anyone carry their train.
15   Again, only noblewomen used to greet one another with a kiss;[30] and they wouldn't allow every Tom, Dick, or Harry to kiss them. What's more, they wouldn't even extend their right hand to just anyone. Now fellows reeking of leather claim a kiss from a woman of the very best family. Not even in marriages is class distinction kept up. Aristocrats marry commoners,
20   commoners aristocrats; as a result we breed a race of mongrels.[31] No woman is so baseborn that she hesitates to use all the cosmetics of fine ladies, though common women ought to be satisfied with froth of new beer[32] or fresh juice extracted from the bark of a tree, or anything else that's cheap. Rouge, white lead,[33] stibium,[34] and other choice shades they should leave to women
25   of distinction. At dinner parties and in public procession these days, what disregard of rank! Often a merchant's wife thinks it beneath her to give place to one who has noble blood on both sides.
          This particular situation, then, has long demanded that we legislate something definite on these subjects.[35] And they could have been settled
30   easily among ourselves, seeing that they concern only women. But in fact we find we have to deal with men too, who exclude us from every social rank and treat us almost as washerwomen and cooks. They think they know best about everything. We'll yield to them when it comes to political offices and the conduct of military affairs. But who could stand their habit of always
35   putting the wife's insignia on the left side of the scutcheon even if her nobility exceeds her husband's by three degrees? Furthermore, it's fair for the mother to have an equal voice in arranging marriages. And perhaps we'll also win the right to have our turn in holding public office; at least those offices which can be held within the city and without bearing arms.
40   This is a summary of the things I think it essential for us to debate. Regarding these, let each woman take thought in order that senatorial

decisions may be made about every single subject; and if anything else comes to anyone's mind, she should bring it up tomorrow. For we'll meet daily until adjournment. There should be four clerks to take down whatever's said, plus two presiding officers to grant or deny permission to speak. Let this be
5 an assembly and not a debate as to who should have the right to speak.[36]

NOTES

1 *felix faustumque*; see 'The Fabulous Feast' n6.
2 Solomon; Prov 11:14, 24:6
3 *Historia Augusta: Heliogabalus* 17.1–2
4 True, but Cornelia fails to add that the emperor Domitian was murdered there (96 AD). See Suetonius *Domitian* 16–17.
5 *Historia Augusta: Heliogabalus* 6.6–9; see *Scriptores Historiae Augustae* trans David Magie, Loeb Classical Library, 3 vols (London and Cambridge, Mass 1921–32) II 117–18, with the notes.
6 The emperor Severus Alexander (not Heliogabalus) is said to have kept statues of Christ and Abraham (not Moses) in the sanctuary of his Lares (*Historia Augusta: Severus Alexander* 29.2).
7 According to Suetonius, dissensions in the Jewish community at Rome (c 50 AD) had something to do with a certain 'Chrestus.' Subsequently the emperor Claudius banished the Jews from Rome (*Claudius* 25). Tacitus, describing the burning of Rome in the reign of Nero (64 AD), relates that Nero chose the Christians, as they were now called, as scapegoats and killed with dreadful tortures those who confessed to being Christians – so named, Tacitus tells us, after one Christ, who had been executed by Pontius Pilate in the reign of Tiberius (*Annals* 15.44). Christian tradition taught that St Peter and St Paul were also victims of the Neronian persecution.
Erasmus' remark about 'Chrestus' is somewhat misleading. The name means merely 'good' or 'kindly.' 'Christus' – Christ – was the disparaged name. Literally it means 'stained or smeared with oil,' but to Christians signified much more: 'anointed,' the word identifying the Messiah, Christ.
8 Her name was Symiamira (*Historia Augusta: Heliogabalus* 2.1). She was also known as Julia Soaemias and Julia Augusta. 'Augusta' was the title of an emperor's wife or mother – in modern idiom 'her Majesty.'
9 1 Cor 14:34–5; 1 Tim 2:12
10 Terence *Phormio* 454; *Adagia* I iii 7
11 With these comments compare 'The New Mother' 592:17–35 and 'Cyclops' 869:36–870:4.
12 Prov 13:10
13 Proverbial; *Adagia* I vi 96
14 'If it is disgraceful to make known what men say in their cups, how much more disgraceful is it to be unable to keep to oneself acts of which only the nuptial couch should be a witness!' (*Lingua* LB IV 686C–D / ASD IV-1A 75:591–3 / CWE 29 307).
15 A doctrine expounded in an earlier dialogue, 'Marriage'

16 Cf Horace *Epistles* 1.1.45–6; quoted in *Enchiridion* LB V 23E / Holborn 60:29 / CWE 66 58.

17 Not always, says the wife in 'The New Mother'; sometimes they run away (594:8–9, 17–19).

18 With this comment on lighter punishment for women compare 'The Well-to-do-Beggars' 479:34–7 and n87; on women's responsibility for their husbands' good temper, see also 'Marriage' 312:2, 318:2–3.

19 That is, by making a point or dot in a waxen tablet or by placing a white or black stone in an urn

20 Walking over to the side one favours. This method quickly showed whether a bill or proposal was about to be passed or rejected, unless the vote was so close that a head-count had to be taken. *Adagia* II vii 12; and see A.H.J. Greenidge *Roman Public Life* (London 1911) 271–2.

21 Cornelia ... the right to speak.] Both the first and final authorized editions of this colloquy (March 1529 and March 1533) assign this long speech to Catharine (abbreviated CA), as do early reprints by other printers (for example Paris: Yolanda Bonhomme 1533; Cologne: Gymnicus 1537; Lyons: Gryphius 1538 and 1542; Basel: Bryling 1540; Cologne: Agrippina 1559). In the *Opera omnia* of 1538–40 and LB, however, these lines are spoken by Cornelia (CO), a correction required by coherence and artistic unity, for Cornelia is convenor of this assembly of women and obviously the originator of its concerns.

22 Decent and appropriate dress is abandoned for vulgar, extravagant ostentation. Erasmus had written emphatically on this theme a few years before in *Institutio christiani matrimonii* (1526). See LB V 705A, 707A–708B, where he begins, as Christian moralists generally did, with Peter and Paul (1 Pet 3:1–6; 1 Tim 2:9–10); and see Paraphrase on Timothy LB VII 1042B–C. St Peter on 'adorning' was quoted in an earlier colloquy, 'Marriage' 310:11–15. That is the point of departure for Cornelia here.

After apostolic times female dress and adornment continued to be a topic of concern for Christian preachers and writers. Tertullian's *De cultu feminarum* is a patristic specimen. He criticizes the use of jewellery, of colour in clothing, of cosmetics, of dyeing the hair (1.6, 1.8, 2.5, 2.6; CSEL 70 66–7, 68–9, 78–80, 80–2), subjects of attention by moralists through the centuries. Jerome is a familiar example of ecclesiastical strictness on all such matters. A thousand years after Jerome lived we find many earnest preachers, especially the friars, dwelling on these same themes. Some of the affectations of current fashions in Erasmus' time receive admonitory attention from the popular Franciscan preacher Michel Menot (*Sermons choisis (1508–1518)* ed Joseph Nève [Paris 1924] 77–8, 132, 226, 227, 254). On Menot see Chomarat *Grammaire et rhétorique* II 1071–9.

Decorum in dress regulated what was considered proper attire for public appearance. What jewellery, and even what kinds of vehicles were suitable, are reported as aims of the *senaculum* established by Heliogabalus for his mother (*Historia Augusta: Heliogabalus* 4.3–4). Peasants now wear silk clothes and gold chains; burghers' wives dress better than countesses, Brant complains in his *Narrenschiff* (section 82; trans Zeydel 269–70).

23 *pellibus zebellinis, madauricis.* The adjectives are late Latin. Erasmus says of *pellibus madauricis* that they were commonly called *marders* (Allen VI 503:15–16 Appendix 19).

24 Some of the numerous pilgrims who stopped in Venice on their way to Jerusalem were impressed by the jewellery and luxury in dress of Venetian women. See for instance H.F.M. Prescott *Friar Felix at Large* (New Haven 1950) 83, 84. The *senaculum* led by Symiamira, mother of Heliogabalus, made rules about who might wear gold or jewels on their shoes. Erasmus notes in *Apophthegmata* (LB IV 285C) that Severus Alexander, who succeeded Heliogabalus as emperor, decreed that women of the royal household must be limited to one hairnet, one pair of earrings, one necklace, and one cloak decorated with gold (*Historia Augusta: Severus* 41.1–2). Von Harff (on whom see 'Rash Vows' n3) 65 comments on the high heels worn by Venetian women.

25 Chariots were *pilenta*, stately four-wheeled carriages used by Roman ladies, including vestals. Litters were what the seventeenth and eighteenth centuries called 'sedans' or 'sedan-chairs.' For 'inlaid with ivory' cf Plautus *Aulularia* 168.

26 Between five and six feet. Long trains offended moralists. They were denounced as the devil's carriage in the thirteenth century (*The Exempla of Jacques de Vitry* ed T.F. Crane, Folk-Lore Society Publications 26 [London 1890; repr 1967] 235 no 243); in the fifteenth century by the *Destructorium viciorum* of Alexander Carpenter (ed G.R. Owst [London 1952] 29); and in the sixteenth by Erasmus (*Ecclesiastes* LB V 891C). In Allen Ep 447:530–6 / CWE Ep 447:584–91 he compares fashionable trains with those of cardinals. In 'The Well-to-do Beggars' a friar mocks this affectation, which even certain cardinals are not ashamed to imitate (480:26–9); cf *De civilitate* LB I 1037A / CWE 27 279. A Bohemian visitor to England in 1466 reported that he had never seen such long trains as those worn by English women (Leo of Rozmital *Travels* 53).

27 In his lifetime, Erasmus remarks, he had seen many changes in fashion (Allen Ep 1479:16–18 / CWE Ep 1479:20–1). Those of sixty years ago would seem ridiculous today (*Ciceronianus* LB I 991D–E / ASD I-2 635:10–13 / CWE 28 381). He is not optimistic about the chances of getting English or Italian women to take seriously St Paul's admonitions about dress (*Annotationes in Novum Testamentum* LB VI 932E). They dress as they please. In a ruthlessly rational society like Utopia, the material and colour of men's and women's clothing never change (*Utopia* Yale CWM 4 126–7, 133–5).

28 *flammea*, usually flame-coloured bridal veils, but the ones meant here are black.

29 A similar complaint about hair styles is made in *Ciceronianus* (LB I 991E / ASD I-2 635:13–15 / CWE 28 381). The subject seems to have fascinated moralists and social critics since the time of St Paul, who was offended by braided hair (1 Tim 2:9).

30 Another subject of attention for the *senaculum* ruled by Heliogabalus' mother (*Historia Augusta: Heliogabalus* 4.4). Cornelia's criticism is dictated by her notions of decorum, which ought to govern and protect class distinctions. As we have learned from earlier colloquies, Erasmus denounced both promiscuous and customary kissing because of risks to health ('A Marriage in Name Only' 852:5–6, 854:3–4; see also 'Inns' n7). The lines in Allen Ep 103:17–24 / CWE Ep 103:19–29 on the casual plenty of kisses in England is a *locus classicus*. See also 'The Lover of Glory' 970:34–5 and n54. On the dangers of kissing in another context, see 'Courtship' 268:16–25 with the notes.

31 Suitable marriages (as we hear in 'Courtship' 263:39–264:19) are those between persons of comparable birth, health, age, and talents. Matches between rich and

poor, old and young, healthy and unhealthy, ignorant and educated, violate decorum and imperil social order. So Erasmus warns in *Institutio christiani matrimonii* LB V 685B–C. The principals in 'Courtship' are well matched; for a sad contrast see 'A Marriage in Name Only.'

32 'Flower of new ale,' as it was called in England. Roman women used beer as a cosmetic for the face, as Pliny says (*Naturalis historia* 22.164). Ovid's list of recipes for cosmetics, *De medicamine faciei* (100 lines) is usually printed with his *Ars amatoria*.

33 Worldly widows painted their faces with these, Jerome says (Ep 127.3; PL 22 1088).

34 Antimony, a whitish metallic element long used in the form of powder as a cosmetic. It is mentioned in the Bible (4 Kings 9:30 Vulg): Jezebel 'painted her eyes with stibium.'

35 The particular follies and excesses Cornelia has described are among those Erasmus tells us he had heard condemned by preachers. He himself censures them in *Institutio christiani matrimonii* LB V 707A–708B and *Ecclesiastes* LB V 891A–E. There is no end to study – and disapproval – of fashions in dress and of cosmetics. Hamlet's outburst 'God hath given you one face and you make yourselves another' (3.1.150) is one of innumerable examples in sermons, tracts, and literature. Illustrations of the fashions or fads named by Cornelia are available in many sixteenth-century books or are reproduced in modern works on Renaissance costume. Baïf's treatise has already been mentioned in the introduction to this colloquy. Heinrich Vogtherr *Libellus artificiosus* (Strasbourg 1539) includes several hundred woodcuts of head-dress, gloves, shoes, and much else. German fashions later in the sixteenth century are shown in the 122 woodcuts in Jost Amman's *Gynaeceum sive theatrum mulierum* (Frankfurt 1586). Even more comprehensive is Cesare Vecellio *Degli habiti antichi et moderni* (Venice 1590; repr New York 1977, 1979), containing 500 woodcuts (nearly half of them Italian costumes), including many of Asian and African dress.
The younger Holbein, who spent much of his early career in Basel, knew Erasmus well and painted splendid portraits of him. He illustrated *Moriae encomium* and made interesting drawings of styles favoured by the ladies of Basel. On these drawings see H. Knackfuss *Holbein* trans Campbell Dodgson (Bielefeld and Leipzig 1899) 54–8 and figures 42–4. A Dürer drawing shows a lady in Venetian costume contrasted with a German housewife (no 59 in Erwin Panofsky *Life and Art of Albrecht Dürer* 4th ed [Princeton 1955]). E. Rodocanachi *La femme italienne* (introduction 906 above) 89–106 has many excellent illustrations. For others see Frederic Stibbert *Civil and Military Clothing in Europe* (New York 1968); Wolfgang Bruhn and Max Tilke *A Pictorial History of Costume* (translation of *Das Kostümwerke*; New York 1973); Max Tilke *Costume Patterns and Designs* (London 1956); Michele Vocino *Storia del costume* (Rome 1952); François Boucher *History of Costume in the West* (London 1967); C.W. and P. Cunnington *Handbook of English Costume in the Sixteenth Century* (London 1970); Georgine de Courtais *Women's Headdress and Hairstyles in England from* AD *600 to the Present Day* (London 1973).
On English interest in these and related matters see Louis B. Wright *Middle-Class Culture in Elizabethan England* (1935; repr Ithaca 1965) chapter 13, and Carroll Camden *The Elizabethan Woman* (Houston 1952; repr Mamaroneck, NY 1975)

chapter 7. 'There is nothing in Englande, more constant, then the inconstancie of attire,' as John Lyly put it in *Euphues and His England* (ed Edward Arber [Westminster 1900] 437. The abundance of tracts and sermons in print tends to confirm our impression that women's dress and deportment were closely watched by critical observers, both lay and clerical. Not without reason was a sermon 'Against Excess of Apparel' added in 1563 to *The seconde tome of homelyes* (STC 13663), pulpit discourses to be read in church by Elizabethan clergy who were not licensed to preach sermons of their own making. Of course excess of attire in men as well as women was deplored, but not so forcefully when decorum or morals were at issue, since the apostolic admonitions (1 Tim 2:9–10; 1 Pet 3:1–6) were addressed to women.

Some of the extravagances described in Erasmus' colloquy, for instance outlandish headdress and expensive materials, were mentioned from time to time in sumptuary legislation. Enactments regulating excesses in food and drink and other aspects of daily life, not only dress, received attention from civil as well as ecclesiastical authorities. Sumptuary regulations promulgated by Henry VIII in 1517 specify how many dishes different classes may have at a meal and what game (text in Hughes and Larkin *Tudor Royal Proclamations* I 128–9): 'Item, partridge, plovers, woodcocks, and all other wildfowl of like greatness, but six in a dish for a cardinal only, and four in a dish for all other lords' (no 81). Such rules may not have been easy to enforce, but there can be little doubt of the seriousness with which they were written. For some other examples consult two volumes of Johns Hopkins University Studies in History and Political Science: 44 no 1, Frances Elizabeth Baldwin *Sumptuary Legislation and Personal Regulations in England* (1926) 120–91; 36 no 2, Kent R. Greenfield *Sumptuary Law in Nürnberg* (1918) 106–25; also John M. Vincent *Costume and Conduct in the Laws of Basel, Bern, and Zurich 1370–1800* (Baltimore 1935) 42–52; Rodocanachi *La femme italienne* 131–60.

36 The Latin for 'debate . . .' is *divinatio*, which, strictly speaking, refers to the Roman legal process to determine who is to be appointed prosecutor in a criminal case. The Romans had no public prosecutor. On *divinatio* see Gellius 2.4; Quintilian 3.10.3.

EARLY TO RISE

· Diluculum

First printed in the September 1529 edition.

Writing in March 1492 to his son Giovanni, who at the age of sixteen had just become a Roman cardinal, Lorenzo de' Medici, 'the Magnificent,' added to other practical advice this admonition: 'One rule above all others I recommend that you follow with utmost diligence, and that is to rise early in the morning, for besides being good for your health, this will enable you to think about and arrange all the business of the day.' The youthful cardinal was to become Pope Leo x in 1513. Erasmus – who had been ordained priest in April 1492, shortly after Giovanni de' Medici's elevation to the cardinalate – corresponded with this pope, dedicated to him his edition of the Greek New Testament (1516), and was indebted to him for some important favours. On those see in this volume the introduction to 'The Girl with No Interest in Marriage' 284.

Such counsel as Lorenzo de' Medici's on getting up betimes was both sincere and wise. From Solomon and Homer to the present day, poets, pedagogues, and other earnest reformers have repeated this advice. Some of them have found it easier to preach than to practise. 'I have, all my life long, been lying till noon,' Johnson confessed to Boswell. 'Yet I tell all young men, and tell them with great sincerity, that nobody who does not rise early will ever do any good' (*Journal of a Tour to the Hebrides* ed Frederick A. Pottle and Charles H. Bennett [New York 1936] 169).

Erasmus himself was a poor sleeper, thanks to a naturally delicate constitution, digestive troubles, and overwork. He could not fall asleep until late, and if once awakened could not go back to sleep for hours. He was compelled therefore to sleep during those golden hours of early morning when, by his own doctrine, he should have been up and, as this colloquy puts it, 'alive' (Allen Ep 447:398–406 / CWE Ep 447:436–44). 'No man practises as well so he writes,' Dr Johnson observed (ibidem). But the doctrine was sound and in the present dialogue persuasive. For other statements of the theme see, from 1497, Allen Ep 56:57 / CWE Ep 56:66–7; for one from 1535, *Ecclesiastes* LB V 788E–9A. His model schoolboy, Gaspar in 'The Whole Duty of Youth,' gets up at five or six o'clock (92:1–2); none too early, for many sixteenth-century schools began the day's activities at six in summer and seven in winter. The boys in 'Off to School' are hurrying to meet a five o'clock roll call (114:6–12). A labourer's day ran from five in the morning until seven or eight at night.

The working day in More's Utopia was only six hours – an utterly fantastic notion by contemporary standards. See Yale CWM 4 126:23–37; 404.

The Italian text of Lorenzo de' Medici's letter to his son will be found in appendix 66 of William Roscoe's *Life of Lorenzo de' Medici* (Liverpool 1795; many editions).

NEPHALIUS, PHILYPNUS[1]

Nephalius I was hoping to meet you today, Philypnus, but they swore you weren't at home.

5 **Philypnus** They didn't fib altogether: I wasn't at home to you, but to myself I was very much at home.

Nephalius What kind of riddle is this?

Philypnus You know the old proverb, 'I don't sleep for everybody.' And you're not unfamiliar with the joke about Nasica. When he wanted to see

10 his friend Ennius, the maid, on master's orders, said Ennius wasn't at home. Nasica understood and went away. But when Ennius in turn called at Nasica's house and asked the boy if he was in, Nasica shouted from an inner room, 'I'm not at home.' And when Ennius, recognizing his voice, said, 'You nervy fellow, don't I recognize your voice?' Nasica replied, 'You're even

15 worse: you refuse to believe me, when I believed your maid.'[2]

Nephalius Maybe you were too busy?

Philypnus Quite the contrary – I was pleasantly relaxed.

Nephalius Once again you torment me with a riddle.

Philypnus Then I'll explain; and I won't call a spade anything but a spade,

20 either.[3]

Nephalius Explain.

Philypnus I was sound asleep.

Nephalius What's that you say? But it was already past eight, though the sun rises before four this month.

25 **Philypnus** For all I care the sun is free to rise at midnight, provided I may sleep as late as I like.

Nephalius But was this an accident or is it your custom?

Philypnus Simply custom.

Nephalius But addiction to something bad is the worst kind of custom.

30 **Philypnus** No, there's no sleep sweeter than that after sunrise.

Nephalius At what hour do you usually get up?

Philypnus Between four and nine.

Nephalius Enough leeway! Queens are dressed in less time than that. But how did you fall into this habit?

Philypnus From the practice of keeping up our drinking parties, games, and fun until late at night. We make up for that loss by morning sleep.

Nephalius Hardly ever have I seen a man more ruinously wasteful than you.

5 **Philypnus** Seems to me more like thrift than extravagance. I don't burn candles all the while or wear out clothes.

Nephalius A ridiculous thrift – saving glass in order to lose jewels![4] The philosopher thought otherwise; when asked what was most precious, he answered, 'Time.'[5] Moreover, since early morning is certainly the best part

10 of the whole day, you cheerfully waste what is the most precious part of the most precious thing of all.

Philypnus Is what's granted to the frail body wasted?

Nephalius On the contrary, it's taken from the frail body, which is treated most kindly and is most invigorated when refreshed by seasonable and

15 moderate sleep and strengthened by morning alertness.

Philypnus But to sleep is delightful.

Nephalius What can be delightful when you're insensible?

Philypnus This very insensibility to trouble is delightful.

Nephalius Yet by that account they're happier who sleep underground,

20 never troubled by insomnia.

Philypnus They say the body is exceedingly nourished by sleep.

Nephalius That's the food of dormice,[6] not men. Animals intended for banquets are properly fattened. What's the good of a man's growing fat except to have a heavier load to walk about with? Tell me: if you had a

25 servant, would you prefer him fat or brisk and fit for all his duties?

Philypnus But I'm no servant.

Nephalius Enough for me that you'd prefer a competent worker to a fat one.

Philypnus Of course I'd prefer that.

30 **Nephalius** But Plato said a man's soul is the man, the body nothing but its dwelling or instrument. Surely you'll admit, I suppose, that soul is the principal part of man and body the servant of soul.[7]

Philypnus Granted, if you like.

Nephalius Since you wouldn't want your servant to be a slow belly[8] but

35 prefer him active and alert, why do you furnish your soul with a fat and lazy worker?

Philypnus I yield to the truth.

Nephalius Now consider another loss. As soul far excels body, so you'll admit the riches of the soul far surpass the goods of the body.

40 **Philypnus** Probably.

Nephalius But among the goods of the soul, wisdom is chief.

Philypnus Granted.

Nephalius For attaining wisdom no part of the day is more useful than dawn,[9] when the sun, rising anew, brings strength and vigour to everything and dispels the usual vapours that are produced by the stomach and becloud the habitation of the mind.

Philypnus I don't deny it.

Nephalius Now imagine how much learning you can acquire in those four hours you waste by sleeping at the wrong time.[10]

Philypnus A lot, surely.

Nephalius In studies, I've found, one morning hour is worth more than three afternoon ones, and that without any harm to the body.

Philypnus So I've heard.

Nephalius Then count how much the total will be if you add up the loss for each of those days.

Philypnus A huge one, to be sure.

Nephalius A person who squanders gold and jewels is regarded as a spendthrift and receives a guardian. Isn't one who wastes *these* goods, which are so much more precious, a far more shameful spendthrift?

Philypnus So it appears if we judge the matter rationally.

Nephalius Now consider what Plato wrote: 'Nothing is more fair, nothing lovelier, than wisdom, which, could it be viewed with physical eyes, would provoke unbelievable passion.'[11]

Philypnus But it can't be viewed.

Nephalius Not with physical eyes, I admit; but it is perceived with the eyes of the mind, which is the more powerful part of man. And where love is incredibly strong, there, necessarily, the highest pleasure exists whenever the mind joins with such a beloved.

Philypnus Sounds convincing.

Nephalius Go now and exchange sleep, the image of death,[12] for this pleasure, if you think proper.

Philypnus But meantime my nightly amusements are gone.

Nephalius The worse changed for better, dishonourable for honourable, most sordid for most precious – well do they come to an end. Well does he lose lead who turns it into gold. Nature has assigned night for sleep; the rising sun, though it summons living creatures of every kind, calls man above all to the duties of life. 'They that sleep,' says Paul, 'sleep in the night, and they that be drunken are drunken in the night.'[13] What is more disgraceful, then, than the fact that though all living creatures rise with the sun (some even greet him with song at his approach, before he yet appears), though the elephant worships the rising sun,[14] a man snores away long after sunrise? As often as that golden splendour brightens your bedroom, doesn't it seem to rebuke the sleeper? 'Fool, why are you glad to lose the best part of your life? I don't shine for you to sleep in secret but that you may busy yourself with good, honest work. Nobody lights a lamp to sleep by but to do some task; and by this the fairest of all lamps do you nothing but snore?'

5   **Philypnus** You declaim beautifully.

Nephalius Not beautifully but truly. Come, I don't doubt you've often heard that line of Hesiod, 'Thrift at the bottom of the chest is too late.'[15]

Philypnus Very often. The wine in the middle of the jug is best.[16]

Nephalius But in life the first part, namely youth, is best.

10 **Philypnus** So it is, undoubtedly.

Nephalius Yet dawn is to day what youth is to life. Aren't they fools, then, who waste their youth in trifles, their morning hours in sleep?

Philypnus Evidently.

Nephalius Or is there any possession comparable to human life?

15 **Philypnus** Not even the whole Persian treasury.[17]

Nephalius Wouldn't you hate vehemently a man who could – and would – shorten your life by several years through evil arts?

Philypnus For my part, I'd want to take *his* life.

Nephalius But worse, and more harmful, I think, are those who voluntarily

20 shorten their own lives.

Philypnus I agree – if such could be found.

Nephalius Could be found? Why, everyone who's like you does it.

Philypnus What an idea!

Nephalius The best there is. So ponder it. Don't you think Pliny was

25 perfectly right in saying 'Life is wakefulness, and the more time a man spends in study, the more hours he adds to life'?[18] For sleep is a kind of death,[19] and therefore it is feigned to come from the underworld and is said by Homer to be death's brother.[20] And so those filled with sleep should be considered neither among the living nor among the dead, yet more dead

30 than alive.

Philypnus So it seems, yes.

Nephalius Now calculate how much of life is forfeited by those who lose three or four hours in sleep every day.

Philypnus An enormous amount, I see.

35 **Nephalius** Wouldn't you regard as a god an alchemist who could add ten years to life and restore advanced age to the vigour of youth?

Philypnus Of course I would.

Nephalius But you can confer so divine a favour as this on yourself.

Philypnus How?

40 **Nephalius** Because morning is the youth of the day, it glows until noon; presently comes the season of mature vigour, succeeded by old age –

evening, so to speak. Sunset follows the evening, like the death of the day. 'Thrift is a large income,'[21] but nowhere larger than here. Or isn't it an enormous gain for a man to stop losing a large part of life – and that the best part, too?

5   **Philypnus** You're perfectly right.

Nephalius Quite shameful, then, seems the complaint of those who find fault with nature for making man's life so short when they themselves voluntarily cut off so much of what is granted to them. Man's life is long enough if spent frugally.[22] It's no small profit to do things at the right time.

10   After lunch, when the body, stuffed with food, oppresses the mind, we're hardly half-men, nor is it safe to summon to higher levels, from the stomach's workshop, the spirits that are doing the work of digestion; after supper, much less so. But in the morning a man is a whole man, while the body tends briskly to every function, while the mind thrives and is alert, while all

15   the mental organs are calm and serene, while (as the poet says) a particle of the divine spirit knows its source and is borne up to what is noble.[23]

Philypnus You preach elegantly indeed.

Nephalius Agamemnon in Homer is told, I believe, 'A counsellor should not sleep the whole night through.'[24] How much more disgraceful to lose so

20   much of the day in sleep!

Philypnus True – for a counsellor. I'm not commander of an army.

Nephalius If anything is dearer to you than yourself, never mind Homer's saying. A coppersmith rises before daybreak for the sake of a slight profit. Cannot the hope of wisdom rouse us at least to hear the sun summoning

25   us to countless wealth? Physicians don't as a rule give a drug except at dawn. They know the golden hours when they can help the body; do we not know them for the purpose of enriching and restoring the mind? If this consideration has little weight with you, hear what divine wisdom speaks through Solomon: 'Those that seek me early shall find me.'[25] In the mystical

30   psalms,[26] now, how great is the praise of morning![27] In the morning the prophet extols the mercy of the Lord; in the morning is his voice heard; in the morning his prayer comes before the Lord;[28] and in Luke the evangelist the people seeking health and instruction from the Lord throng to him in the morning.[29] – Why do you sigh, Philypnus?

35   **Philypnus** I can scarcely hold back the tears when I think how much of life I've thrown away.[30]

Nephalius Useless to torment yourself on account of what can't be recalled; yet it can be corrected by diligence hereafter. So set to work and don't lose the future also through vain regret over the past.

40   **Philypnus** You do well to admonish me, but a habit of long standing has claimed me for its own.

Nephalius Pooh! One nail drives out another:[31] habit is overcome by habit.

Philypnus But to give up what you're used to is hard.

Nephalius At the start, yes, but a different habit first relieves that distress and soon transforms it into the greatest delight, so you shouldn't mind a bit
5 of trouble.

Philypnus I fear it will continue.

Nephalius If you were in your seventies, I wouldn't pull you away from fixed habits. Now you're hardly over seventeen, I imagine. And what is there this age cannot overcome if only it makes up its mind to do so?

10 **Philypnus** Well, I'll try – try to become learned instead of lazy.[32]

Nephalius If you do that, my dear Philypnus, I'm sure that after a few days you'll both congratulate yourself sincerely and thank me for reproving you.

NOTES

1 Nephalius, also the name of a speaker in an earlier colloquy, 'The Godly Feast,' signifies 'sober,' 'temperate,' hence 'alert' or 'watchful'; Erasmus remembers the Greek of 2 Tim 4:5. Philypnus means 'fond of sleep.'

2 Two well-known anecdotes are conflated in these lines; see 'Patterns' nn82, 84.

3 In the original 'call a fig a fig,' a proverbial or semi-proverbial expression from Lucian, who has 'call a fig a fig and a spade a spade' in *Zeus tragoedus* 32. See *Adagia* II iii 5.

4 Not in *Adagia* in this form, but cf I ix 30.

5 Thales, a presocratic philosopher and one of the seven sages of ancient Greece. For the quotation see Diogenes Laertius 1.35. The observation was attributed to others too, Erasmus reminds us (*Apophthegmata* LB IV 348B). Thales said time is 'the wisest of things,' for it brings everything to light. His name became synonymous with speculative as well as practical wisdom; see *Adagia* III vii 26.

6 *Adagia* prolegomena 13 LB II 12F, from Martial 3.58.36, 13.59

7 Soul is the true man, the self; the body is its instrument and possession (Plato *Alcibiades* I 129C–31B; *Laws* 959A–B). Soul is also called the 'immortal principle,' accompanied by a mortal body (*Timaeus* 69C). The body is dwelling, garrison, prison (*Phaedo* 62B and passim) or (in *Cratylus* 399B) grave; cf 'The Godly Feast' 194:1–7. For a brief exposition of Aristotelian doctrines of the soul see 'The New Mother' 601:29–605:2.

8 Titus 1:12; cf Erasmus' note in *Annotationes in Novum Testamentum* LB VI 968D–E.

9 Early morning is congenial to the Muses, suitable for studies (Allen Ep 56:57 / CWE Ep 56:66–7), and that is the reason, Erasmus writes elsewhere, that Aristotle lectured on physics in the morning and on rhetoric in the afternoon (*Ecclesiastes* LB V 788E–789A).

10 A bad thing for young children, Erasmus warns in *Institutio christiani matrimonii* LB V 711A–B. As for adults, Plato declares that to spend the whole night in sleep is shameful. Master and mistress of the household should be early

risers (*Laws* 807E). An Italian proverb recommended 'five hours for the student, six for the merchant, seven for the people, eight for the sluggard' Thorndike *University Records* 390). Six hours of sleep are enough for students, a fourteenth-century physician tells his sons, and 'too much is a sin' (ibidem 157).

11 In *Phaedrus* 250D–251A Plato insists that wisdom cannot be seen with eyes; only beauty can. Cicero quotes the passage in *De officiis* 1.15 and *De finibus* 2.52.

12 So also *In psalmum quartum concio* IV LB V 286D. Of the dying Cornelius in 'The Funeral' we read: 'You would have said he had fallen asleep, not died' (779:12–13). Donne's 'rest and sleepe, which but thy pictures bee' (*Holy Sonnets* 10) is one of the more familiar Renaissance allusions to sleep as *imago* of death. Sleep as metaphor for death was common in primitive Christianity (1 Cor 15:6; 1 Thess 4:13; 2 Pet 3:4)

13 1 Thess 5:7

14 So Plutarch *Moralia* 972B–C *De sollertia animalium*. Pliny reports that elephants salute both sun and moon (*Naturalis historia* 8.1), as does Aelian (*De natura animalium* 4.10, 7.44).

15 *Works and Days* 368–9; see *Adagia* II ii 64. Cf 'Youth' 93:24–30.

16 Hesiod, as in preceding note

17 *gaza*, a Persian loan-word in Greek and Latin, as in Horace *Odes* 1.29.2, 2.16.9

18 Preface to *Naturalis historia* 18–19. The idea is a commonplace. Both sleep and excessive fatigue are detrimental to study (Plato *Republic* 537B). Cf 'Morning is when I am awake and there is a dawn in me. Moral reform is the effort to throw off sleep . . . To be awake is to be alive' (Henry David Thoreau *Walden* 2 'Where I Lived, and What I Lived for').

19 Note 12 above

20 *Iliad* 14.231, 16.672, 682; but see Cicero *Tusculan Disputations* 1.92.

21 Cicero *Paradoxa Stoicorum* 49

22 Seneca *De brevitate vitae* (in *Dialogi*) 1.3. For a religious reflection on this dictum see *De praeparatione ad mortem* LB V 1305A–B.

23 Cf Horace *Satires* 2.2.76–81. On the effects of overeating see 'The New Mother' n50.

24 *Iliad* 2.24; spoken by a dream sent by Zeus to Agamemnon who, as leader of the Greeks, is the 'counsellor' responsible for the host besieging Troy. The line became proverbial; see *Adagia* II vii 95.

25 Prov 6:17

26 'Mystical' here serves to distinguish psalms with strongly spiritual and devotional language from others concerned largely with historical events, Israel's woes, or hopes for deliverance from enemies.

27 Found in Pss 5:3 (5.4 Vulg), 30:5 (29:6 Vulg), 49:14 (48:15 Vulg), 55:17 (54:18 Vulg), 59:16 (58:17 Vulg), 65:8 (64:9 Vulg), 88:13 (87:14 Vulg), 92:2 (91:3 Vulg), 119:147 (118:148 Vulg), 130:6 (129:6 Vulg), 143:8 (142:8 Vulg). Erasmus' interpretations of the Psalms are of two kinds: those in extensive commentaries on eleven of them (LB V 171–556) and in notes or allusions throughout his writings on religion and religious texts. The eleven Psalms are 1, 2, 3, 4, 15 (14 Vulg), 23 (22 Vulg), 29 (28 Vulg), 34 (33 Vulg), 39 (38 Vulg), 84 (83 Vulg), 86 (85 Vulg). The commentary on Ps 15 (14 Vulg) was printed as *De puritate tabernaculi* (1536), that on Ps 84 (83 Vulg) as *De concordia* (1533), and that on

Ps 29 (28 Vulg) was hardly a commentary at all, since it became *De bello Turcico* (1530).

On Erasmus' attention to the Psalms consult G. Chantraine 'Erasme, lecteur des Psaumes' in *Colloquia Erasmiana Turonensia* II 691–712.

28 As in Isa 33:2, 50:4; Jer 21:12; Ezek 12:8, 24:18, 33:22; Hos 6:4; Amos 4:4; Zeph 3:5

29 Luke 6:13–17

30 *iacturam fecerim*, as in 'The Shipwreck' 353:20 (see n14); a common expression but apparently not proverbial

31 *Adagia* I ii 4

32 A pun: 'ex Philypno fiam Philologus'

THE SOBER FEAST

Νηφάλιον συμπόσιον

First printed in the September 1529 edition.

Νηφάλιον in the Greek title refers to ancient Athenian sacrifices at which libations were made without honey, only water mixed with wine being used. Hence a sober feast, like the one here, a social occasion instead of a religious rite, may have the same title if it is wineless and abstemious. So Erasmus tells us in *Adagia* II ix 96.

The opening lines of the dialogue recall the garden setting of some other colloquies, particularly 'The Godly Feast.' Although this convivium is much shorter, it meets the Erasmian requirements that at such gatherings the conversation, like the setting, should be both pleasant and instructive. Thanks to his prodigious knowledge of classical and patristic literature and his memory of texts, Erasmus had always at hand a store of anecdotes, aphorisms, and illustrations. Many of them in this and other colloquies can be found in *Adagia* or in *Apophthegmata* (1531; LB IV 93–380), a collection of maxims from ancient kings, philosophers, and other notable persons. Many of these sayings come from Plutarch's *Lives* and *Moralia*. Between 1514 and 1526 Erasmus published translations of eleven essays from the *Moralia*. One, on how to distinguish a friend from a flatterer, he dedicated to Henry VIII (Ep 272); another, on taking profit from one's enemies, to Wolsey (Ep 284). His versions of Plutarch are reprinted in LB IV 1–92 and ASD IV-2 117–322. No Greek writer is more sound than Plutarch on ethical subjects (Allen Ep 2431:89–91, and see 'The Godly Feast' n303). The sixteenth century shared Erasmus' conviction that essential lessons of history can be learned from the words as well as deeds of the ancients.

ALBERT, BARTHOLINUS, CHARLES, DENIS, AEMILIUS,
FRANCIS, GERARD, JEROME, JAMES, LAWRENCE[1]

Albert Have you ever seen anything more delightful than this garden?
Bartholinus The Fortunate Isles[2] have scarcely anything more pleasing, I
5   dare say.
Charles Indeed I seem to see the paradise for which God appointed Adam guardian and gardener.
Denis Nestor and Priam both could grow young again here.

Francis Nay, even the dead could revive.

Gerard I'd willingly add to your exaggeration if I could.

Jerome Everything, in fact, is wonderfully attractive.

James We ought to dedicate this garden with a few drinks.

5   **Lawrence** Our friend James is right.

Albert This place was consecrated by such rites a long time ago. But understand: I've nothing to offer you by way of lunch unless you like a dry drinking party.[3] I'll serve lettuce without salt, vinegar, and oil. There's not a drop to drink except what this well affords. I haven't even bread or a cup;

10   and this is the season of the year that feasts the eyes more than the belly.

Bartholinus But you have playing boards and balls.[4] We'll dedicate the garden with a game if it can't be done conveniently with a party.

Albert Since we're a gathering of such fine fellows, I've thought of something – call it both fun and feast if you like – that in my opinion would

15   be much more suitable for dedicating this garden.

Charles What?

Albert Let each one make a contribution of his own; we'll have no lack of feast, as agreeable as it is abundant.

Aemilius What shall we contribute who've come here empty-handed?

20   **Albert** Empty-handed – you who carry such riches in your mind?

Francis We await your pleasure.

Albert Let each offer to the company the best thing he's read this week.

Gerard A good idea. At parties of this kind nothing is more appropriate to you, the host, or to this place. We'll all follow you, the promoter of this

25   scheme.

Albert I won't decline, if it's agreeable to you. I was extremely delighted today with a most Christian saying by one who was not a Christian.[5] After Phocion, a man scarcely surpassed by any Athenian in probity and in devotion to public good, had been condemned, through envy, and was

30   about to drink the hemlock, he was asked by friends what were his final instructions for his sons. 'That they should never wish to remember this injury,' he said.[6]

Bartholinus You'd hardly find an example of such remarkable forbearance today among the Dominicans and Franciscans![7] So I'll relate a comparable

35   one, since I can't equal it. Aristides was very similar to Phocion; a man so incorruptible that the common people nicknamed him 'the Just.' Jealousy of this title led to ostracism of the man who best deserved the homage of his country: he was ordered to leave his native soil. After he had understood that the people were offended with him solely because of his nickname,

40   'the Just,' though otherwise they had always found that justice working to their advantage, he calmly obeyed. In exile he was asked by friends what

he would wish for his most ungrateful city. 'Nothing,' he said, 'except
prosperity so great that Aristides never comes into their heads.'[8]

Charles It's surprising that Christians aren't ashamed of themselves for
becoming incensed over an injury, however slight, and plotting revenge by
5   hook or by crook.[9] The entire life of Socrates, in my opinion, was simply an
example of moderation and long-suffering.

But in order not to hold back my contribution, I'll tell one story that
pleased me most. As Socrates was walking along the street, some villain
punched him. When Socrates bore this in silence, his friends urged him to
10   get even, but he said, 'What shall I do to the fellow who struck me?' 'Have
him arrested,' they replied. 'Nonsense,' said he. 'If a donkey had kicked me
should I have had the law on him, with you for witnesses?' Meaning that that
rascally lout was no better than a donkey, and that it's petty to be incapable of
putting up with abuse from a blockhead that you'd bear from a brute beast.[10]
15   **Denis** Examples of restraint are fewer and less remarkable in Roman annals,
nor do I suppose one would win high praise by his forbearance if he spared
the vanquished and overthrew the proud.[11] Still, I think it should not be
forgotten that the elder Cato, when a certain Lentulus foully spat in his face,
retorted only with 'Hereafter I'll have an answer for those who say you have
20   no cheek.' (The Latins said those who had no shame had no countenance, so
the joke depends on an ambiguity.)[12]

Aemilius Everyone to his taste. Among all the famous sayings of Diogenes
nothing delights me more than his reply to someone who had asked him how
he might best avenge himself on an enemy. 'By showing yourself as upright
25   and honourable a man as possible,' he said.[13] I wonder what deity inspired
such thoughts. But a dictum of Aristotle's too, seems strongly consistent
with Pauline teaching. Asked what his philosophy did for him, he answered,
'It causes me to do of my own accord what most men do by compulsion.'
For Paul teaches that those inspired by Christian charity are not subject to
30   the Law, because they perform voluntarily more than the Law could wring
from them through dread of punishment.[14]

Francis When the Jews muttered against Christ for eating freely even with
publicans and sinners, he replied that those who were whole had no need
of a physician, but those who were sick had.[15] Not inconsistent with this is
35   the saying of Phocion reported by Plutarch. When rebuked for defending
a worthless rascal in court, he said, no less wittily than kindly, 'Why not,
when no good man needs such defending?'[16]

Gerard This too is an example of Christian goodness, after the example
of the eternal Father who maketh his sun to shine not only on the just but
40   likewise on the unjust – to do as much kindness as we can, both to righteous
and unrighteous.[17]

But more surprising, perhaps, will be an example of moderation in a king. Demochares, nephew of Demosthenes, was Athenian ambassador to King Philip of Macedon. Upon dismissal by the king after gaining what he had sought, he was asked politely if there was anything else he wished.

5   'That you might hang yourself,' retorted Demochares. This outburst was an expression of hatred; the person thus insulted was a king – and a worthy one. Yet he didn't lose his temper, but turning to Demochares' colleagues said, 'See that you inform the people of Athens about this, in order that when they know the facts they may decide which of us they think the better: myself,

10 who heard it with forbearance, or the man who spoke it.'[18] Where now by comparison are the monarchs of the world, who think themselves equal to gods and because of a word uttered over the wine stir up dreadful wars?

Jerome The thirst for glory has tremendous power and is an emotion that leads many men astray.[19] One of these asked Socrates how he could find a

15 short cut to the most honourable reputation. 'By showing yourself to be what you long to be thought,' was the answer.[20]

James Indeed, I don't see what could be spoken more briefly and more perfectly. Fame is not to be sought after but accompanies virtue of its own accord, as disgrace accompanies vice.

20   You admire the men. A girl, a Lacedaemonian, took my fancy. When she was being offered for sale at auction a certain bidder went up to her, saying, 'Well, will you be good hereafter if I buy you?' 'Even if you don't buy me,' she replied; meaning that she did not practise virtue for the sake of some individual, but naturally, for its own sake; because virtue is its own

25 reward.[21]

Lawrence A manly saying from a girl, truly. But I consider it a remarkable example of constancy in the face of fortune, however smiling, that when Philip of Macedon received news of three extraordinary blessings on the same day – that he had won a victory in the Olympic Games, that his

30 commander Parmenion had vanquished the Dardanians, and that his wife Olympias had borne him a son – he prayed to heaven with uplifted hands that God would permit so great a prosperity to be atoned for by some slight misfortune.[22]

Albert Nowadays there's no prosperity so great that anyone need fear envy

35 of it; but if people have had a stroke of luck they boast all the same, as if Nemesis were dead or deaf.

If this luncheon pleases you, the little garden here, which you've dedicated by conversation as pleasant as it is profitable, will provide you with one whenever you like.

40 **Bartholinus** Surely Apicius[23] couldn't have served a more delightful dish. So expect us often; only do excuse us for bringing, on this occasion, not what

was worth your hearing but what was thought of on the spur of the moment.
When we've deliberated we'll provide richer fare.

Albert You'll be the more welcome for that.

NOTES

1 Albert, the host, has nine guests, the favourite number, as we have learned
  in other colloquies; see 'The Profane Feast' n102. Each guest has at least one
  opportunity to take part in the conversation. Smith conjectured (*Key* 51) that
  Bartholinus might be Riccardo Bartolini of Perugia, a scholarly canon and poet
  who spent much of his life and career in Germany. He corresponded with
  Erasmus, but whether they ever met is doubtful. See CEBR. Charles could be
  Karel Uutenhove, who lived with Erasmus for six months in Basel in 1528–9;
  he appears in 'Knucklebones.' Aemilius may be Emiglio de' Migli of Brescia,
  who translated Erasmus' *Enchiridion* into Italian (1531) and exchanged letters
  with him in May 1529, a few months before this colloquy was issued; see Allen
  Epp 2154, 2165. Gerard was the baptismal name of Gerardus Listrius, who
  wrote part of the commentary added to *Moriae encomium* in 1515; it was also
  the surname of Cornelis Gerard, an Augustinian canon and scholar who was a
  friend and correspondent on Erasmus in the 1490s; Allen Ep 17 introduction.
  These suggested identifications cannot be proved. Nor are there reliable clues
  to whether the other speakers here bear names of Erasmus' friends.
2 Described by Lucian in *Vera historia* 2.5–14. Cf 'Benefices' n3.
3 ἄοινος *compotatio*. Cf *Adagia* I iii 3, citing Plutarch *Moralia* 716A *Quaestiones
  convivales*.
4 Boards for dice games or knucklebones. Most of the games played in 'Sport'
  are ball games.
5 Another allusion to a subject Erasmus took seriously and sometimes introduced
  in memorable passages, for example in 'The Godly Feast' 192:5–194:36; see
  especially nn187 and 215 there.
6 Phocion was an Athenian statesman, orator, and soldier and an opponent of
  Demosthenes. He was charged with treason in 318 BC and executed by the
  Athenians. See Plutarch *Phocion* 36.3; *Moralia* 189A–B *Regum et imperatorum
  apophthegmata: Phocion* 19. Cf Erasmus *Apophthegmata* LB IV 221B; *Lingua* LB IV
  742F–743A / ASD IV-1A 164:558–60 / CWE 29 396.
7 For Erasmus' judgments of the mendicant friars in the *Colloquies* see particularly
  'The Well-to-do Beggars,' 'The Funeral,' 'The Sermon,' and 'The Seraphic
  Funeral.'
8 *Apophthegmata* LB IV 244E–F, 245E, from Plutarch *Aristides* 7. Like Phocion a
  virtuous statesman and soldier (he fought at Marathon and Salamis), Aristides
  served Athens well but through political intrigue was brought down. He was
  ostracized in 482 BC but recalled from exile in 468 BC. On ostracism see *Adagia*
  II i 51. Phocion and Aristides were models, for Erasmus and other writers, of
  men who acted justly and righteously in public life (*De concordia* LB V 485D).
9 *per fas nefasque*; Livy 6.14.10 and Horace *Epodes* 5.87. See 'Youth' n33.
10 *Apophthegmata* LB IV 157F–158A, and again in *Lingua* LB IV 743A / ASD IV-1A
  164:567–70 / CWE 29 396, from Diogenes Laertius 2.21; for the sequel see

Plutarch *Moralia* 10C *De liberis educandis*. The offender was mocked so much by witnesses of his boorish behaviour that he hanged himself. For other effects of anger, taken from Plutarch *Moralia* 452F–464D *De cohibenda ira*, see *Parabolae* LB I 587D–588E / CWE 23 198–200.

11 Virgil *Aeneid* 6.853. Other nations, says Virgil, will win fame for art and science; Rome's mission is to bring peace and civilization, to 'spare the vanquished and overthrow the proud' (*parcere subiectis et debellare superbos*).

12 Marcus Porcius Cato Senior, the Censor (234–149 BC), was famed for his stern moral and political principles, military career, and literary talents. 'Cheek' and 'countenance' are different connotations of the same word, *os* 'mouth,' 'face,' which can mean 'modest countenance' or its opposite, 'impudence' or 'effrontery.' This anecdote in *Apophthegmata* LB IV 263F–264A comes from Seneca *De ira* 3.38.2, where it accompanies a similar one about Diogenes. Other dicta by Cato are collected in *Apophthegmata* LB IV 260A–264B.

13 *Apophthegmata* LB IV 191A, from Plutarch *Moralia* 88B *De capienda ex inimicis utilitate* 4; other quotations from Diogenes in LB IV 172B–192C

14 *Apophthegmata* LB IV 339A, from Diogenes Laertius 5.20; quoted also in *Declarationes ad censuras Lutetiae vulgatas* LB IX 827F. There too it is followed by reference to St Paul on the superiority of voluntary compliance over compulsion. See 'The Godly Feast' 189:37–191:37 on 1 Cor 6 and 'A Fish Diet' 682:39–703:25. These two long dialogues contain the best expositions in the *Colloquies* on Pauline (and Erasmian) interpretations of liberty versus legalism or what Erasmus calls Christian freedom as contrasted with 'Judaism.' Aristotle's retort to the question of what philosophy did for him may be compared with that of Socrates who, when someone slandered him and angered his friends by doing so, told them, 'I would be everything he calls me had not philosophy taught me temperance' (*Apophthegmata* LB IV 163D; *De immensa Dei misericordia* LB V 566A). Erasmus does not name his sources, but those were undoubtedly Cicero *De fato* 5.10–11 and *Tusculan Disputations* 4.37.80. 'More justly,' Erasmus adds, 'did the worthy Francis attribute to the divine mercy what Socrates attributed to philosophy' (*De misericordia* ibidem). See 'The Seraphic Funeral' n32.

15 Matt 9:10–13. See 'The Godly Feast' 187:28–188:3.

16 Plutarch *Phocion* 10.2

17 Matt 5:43–5

18 *Apophthegmata* LB IV 196B–C, from Seneca *De ira* 3.23.2–3

19 The theme of 'The Lover of Glory'

20 *Apophthegmata* LB IV 156C. This is in Xenophon *Cyropaedia* 1.66.22 and *Memorabilia* 2.6.39. Cicero quotes it in *De officiis* 2.12.43.

21 This anecdote, one in a group illustrating the virtue and curt speech of Spartan women (*Apophthegmata* LB IV 148E–152A), is from Plutarch *Moralia* 242C: *Lacaenarum apophthegmata*. The same story is told of a young man in Erasmus' *Apophthegmata* LB IV 138C–D.

22 *Apophthegmata* LB IV 191E; Plutarch *Moralia* 105A–B *Consolatio ad Apollonium*

23 Roman gourmet. See 'The Profane Feast' n5.

THE ART OF LEARNING

Ars notoria

First printed in the September 1529 edition.

In this dialogue addressed to his godson, Johannes Erasmius Froben, but intended for all young students of language and literature, Erasmus voices strong doubts about certain fads and fallacies in education and lays down some hard truths about sound learning. Unfortunately his good counsel seems to have had no effect on Erasmius, though it may have been helpful to other schoolboys who read it in the *Colloquies*.

The familiar word *memorandum* refers to what is known and should be kept in mind, 'noted.' *Ars notoria* was a medieval term signifying the 'art' of acquiring knowledge and memorizing it with marvellous facility, an art ascribed to Solomon among others. It carried with it more than a hint of magic and was suspect because of earlier associations with alchemy, occult wisdom, and astrology – demonic arts. Other and less pretentious or esoteric techniques of memorizing also existed. These, principally Greek, were known to orators, philosophers, and authors in antiquity, and later to medieval scholars. For a survey of these various kinds of memory systems see Frances Yates *The Art of Memory* (London and Chicago 1966), which begins with Cicero (*De oratore* 2.86.350–2.88.360), Quintilian (11.2.1–51), and the *Rhetorica ad Herennium* (3.16.28–3.24.40).

Erasmus was scornful of factitious learning but, like any person of superior intellect and erudition, prized the proper recording and memorizing of texts. To us, note-taking seems a natural, obvious tactic; in fact it was an important innovation. Erasmus wrote careful directions about it (*De copia* LB I 100B–105F / ASD I-6 258:506–269:846 / CWE 24 635–48). A judicious combination of note-taking and memorizing could enable an interested person with a retentive mind to have many topics and passages at his command, available for use in any branch of composition. 'Judicious' is the key word here, because both note-taking and memorizing could easily be abused. Notes were to be taken, Erasmus warned, for preserving and classifying relevant information or ideas encountered in one's reading. But this material had to be organized in notebooks or 'commonplace books,' which henceforth would be the immediate sources of that *copia* or abundance of material so highly prized and effectively exploited by Renaissance writers and rhetoricians (see CWE 23 xxxviii). In like manner memorizing had to be controlled. If a specious system of memorizing promised a quick and easy path to learning, it was fraudulent and useless. 'The Renaissance,' as

R.R. Bolgar writes, 'was the age of memorising. Books were written outlining fantastic schemes for the use of scholars ... [The authors'] ingenuity was misplaced; but their works survive to show the significance which was attached to the learning by heart of isolated facts – facts which could be arranged in lists' (*The Classical Heritage and Its Beneficiaries* [Cambridge 1954] 274–5).

In *De ratione studii* (1512; revised edition 1514), Erasmus sketches a curriculum for liberal education (LB I 521A–530B / ASD I-2 83–109 / CWE 24 666–91; cf *De recta pronuntiatione* LB I 922E–923C / ASD I-4 30:556–31:586 / CWE 26 387–8). This training includes Greek, Latin, 'enough dialectic,' rhetoric, geography, and a smattering of arithmetic, music, and natural science – all by the age of eighteen. When asked whether this is to be accomplished by *ars notoria*, Erasmus' answer is an emphatic negative (*De recta pronuntiatione* LB I 923A / ASD I-4 31:572–3 / CWE 26 388). What is essential is the learning of fundamentals first, and so thoroughly that they will not have to be learned again and again. For such is the true art of learning. The short cut young Erasmius longs for does not exist. Although Erasmus as an educator was patient and humane, desirous of making studies attractive, he never allowed pupils to lose sight of the effort required. In September 1520, Johannes Brassicanus, who appears in an earlier colloquy ('The Apotheosis of Reuchlin'), asked him how to become learned. Erasmus' reply, which Brassicanus wrote down at once, was that one could become learned by associating with learned men, listening to them respectfully, reading their works strenuously, learning these thoroughly, and finally, by never thinking oneself learned (Allen Ep 1146 introduction) – the same advice he gives to Erasmius Froben nine years later.

In addition to studies mentioned in this introduction and in notes to the translation, see Thorndike *Magic and Experimental Science* II chapter 49; Margolin *Recherches érasmiennes* 70–84; *Jeux de mémoire: aspects de la mnémotechnie médiévale* ed Bruno Roy and Paul Zumthor (Montreal 1985).

DESIDERIUS, ERASMIUS[1]

Desiderius How do your studies progress, Erasmius?
Erasmius I'm not the Muses' darling, apparently. But studies would go
5   better if I could get something from you.
Desiderius Anything you ask, provided it be to your advantage. Just tell me what's the matter.
Erasmius I'm sure none of the abstruse arts has escaped you.

LB I 849C / ASD I-3 647

Desiderius I wish you were right!

Erasmius I hear there's a certain method that enables a fellow to learn all the liberal arts thoroughly with a minimum of trouble.

Desiderius How's that? Have you seen the book?[2]

5 **Erasmius** I've seen it, but only seen it, because I didn't have the resources of a teacher.

Desiderius What was in the book?

Erasmius Various figures of animals – dragons, lions, leopards – and various circles with words written in them,[3] partly Greek, partly Latin, partly

10 Hebrew, and others in barbarous tongues.

Desiderius The title promised a knowledge of the arts within how many days?

Erasmius Fourteen.[4]

Desiderius A splendid promise, surely, but do you know anybody who

15 emerged a learned man through this method of instruction?

Erasmius No indeed.

Desiderius Neither has anyone else ever seen one, or ever will, unless we first see someone made rich through alchemy.[5]

Erasmius Well, I wish there *were* a true method.

20 **Desiderius** Perhaps because you're reluctant to buy learning at the cost of so much labour.[6]

Erasmius Of course.

Desiderius But heaven has so decreed. Riches in the ordinary sense – gold, jewels, silver, palaces, a kingdom – it sometimes grants to the

25 slothful and worthless; but it has ordained that what are true riches, and peculiarly our own, must be won by toil.[7] The labour by which wealth so great is achieved should not seem grievous to us when we see many men struggle, through terrible dangers, through countless exertions, for wealth that is both temporary and quite ignoble if compared with

30 learning; they don't always get what they seek, either. And the drudgery of studies has a generous mixture of sweetness, too, if you advance a little in them. Now removing much of the irksomeness depends largely on you.

Erasmius How do I do it?

35 **Desiderius** First, by persuading yourself to love studies. Secondly, by admiring them.

Erasmius How shall this be done?

Desiderius Observe how many men learning has enriched, how many it has brought to the highest honour and power. Reflect at the same time how much

40 difference there is between man and beast.

Erasmius Good advice.

Desiderius Next you must discipline your character in order to win self-control and to find delight in things productive of utility rather than pleasure. For what are in themselves honourable, even if somewhat painful

5 at first, prove agreeable by becoming habitual. So it will come about that you will tire the tutor less and understand more easily by yourself; according to the saying of Isocrates, which should be painted in golden letters on the title-page of your book: 'If you are a lover of learning, you will learn much.'[8]

10 **Erasmius** I'm quick enough at learning, but what's learned soon slips away.

Desiderius A jar with holes in it, you mean.[9]

Erasmius You're not far from the mark.[10] But what's the remedy?

Desiderius The chink must be stopped up to prevent leaks.

Erasmius Stopped up with what?

15 **Desiderius** Not moss or plaster but industry. Whoever learns words without understanding the meaning soon forgets, for words, as Homer says, are 'winged'[11] and easily fly away unless held down by the weight of meaning. Make it your first task, therefore, to understand the matter thoroughly; next to review it and repeat it frequently to yourself; and in this respect your

20 mind (as I remarked) must be disciplined so that whenever necessary it may be able to apply itself to thought. If one's mind is so wild that it can't be tamed in this way, it's unfit for learning.[12]

Erasmius How hard this is I understand only too well.

Desiderius One who is so giddy-minded that he can't concentrate on an idea

25 is incapable of paying attention for long when somebody is speaking, or of fixing in memory what he's learned. A thing can be stamped on lead to stay; on water or quicksilver nothing can be stamped, since they are always fluid. But if you can subdue your nature in this respect, then, through constant association with learned men, whose daily conversation affords so much

30 that is worth knowing, you'll learn a great deal with a minimum of effort.[13]

Erasmius True enough.

Desiderius For besides the table talk, besides the daily conversations, immediately after lunch you hear half a dozen witty sayings, selected from the best authors; and as many after dinner. Now just reckon how large a sum

35 these amount to every month and year.

Erasmius Splendid – if I could remember them.

Desiderius In addition, since you hear nothing but good Latin spoken,[14] what's to prevent you from learning Latin within a few months, when uneducated boys learn French or Spanish in a very short time?[15]

40 **Erasmius** I'll follow your advice and see whether this nature can be broken to the yoke of the Muses.

Desiderius For my part, I know no other art of learning than hard work, devotion, and perseverance.

NOTES

1 Johannes Erasmius Froben, Johann Froben's younger son, to whom the *Colloquies* were dedicated in the March 1522 edition and again, with a new dedicatory letter, in the September 1524 edition; see 2–3. On confusion between 'Erasmus' and 'Erasmius,' which occurred in many editions of the *Colloquies*, see 1120–1.
Erasmius was thirteen when this dialogue was published.
2 Many books of this kind existed. If Erasmus had a particular example in mind, it might have been the well-known *Margarita philosophica* of Gregor Reisch (Strasbourg 1503), a summary of the liberal arts; reprinted a dozen times by 1517. It contains many drawings and diagrams. Chomarat proposes the more compact but dense *Logica memorativa: chartiludium logice sive totius dialectice memoria* by Thomas Murner (*Grammaire et rhétorique* I 516–17). The Strasbourg 1509 edition was reissued in photographic facsimile in 1967 (Nieuwkoop). If this book is typical of those condemned by Erasmus, his aversion to them is easy to understand. Plates and figures in Yates *Memory* show the ingenious and imaginative schemes produced by the *ars notoria*. These illustrations deserve close inspection.
A famous expert on artificial memory was the 'divine Camillo' (c 1480–1544), who devoted much of his life to devising a 'memory theatre.' Erasmus had met Guilio Camillo during his residence in Italy (1506–9; see Allen Ep 3032:221–2), long before Camillo built the celebrated memory theatre. Erasmus did not hear of this wonder until nearly three years after this colloquy was printed. It was then described to him by a friend in March and June 1532 (Allen Epp 2632:174–205, 2657:30–70). Camillo's theatre was a small wooden building filled with images and figures and 'little boxes' purporting to furnish the key to occult knowledge (see plan in Yates *Memory* 144–5). Since Camillo spent so much time on his theatre that he never had leisure to write a book about it, Erasmus' reaction, dependent on hearsay, can only be conjectured; but his sceptical attitude towards even scholastic memory systems indicates that he would not have been impressed by Camillo's project. On Camillo consult Yates *Memory* chapters 6–7.
3 Names, signs, or marks that furnish clues to aid one's recollection; a kind of shorthand
4 Roger Bacon, the thirteenth-century Franciscan philosopher, is said to have promised a sufficient reading knowledge of Greek and Hebrew within three days (Beryl Smalley *The Study of the Bible in the Middle Ages* 2nd ed [Notre Dame, Ind 1964] 333).
5 A recurrent illusion. See 'Alchemy.'
6 John of Salisbury charges his adversary Cornificius with boasting that he could make people eloquent and expert in philosophy without any work on their part (*Metalogicon* 1.3; trans D.D. McGarry [Berkeley and Los Angeles 1955] 14).

For other complaints about teachers and students looking for short cuts see Lynn Thorndike *University Records* 14–15, 16.

7 Erasmus tells a story about a Dutchman who went to Paris to learn French and after four days there complained that he had not yet learned to speak it (*Adagia* IV v 55; and see 'Patterns' n75).

8 *Ad Demonicum* 18, quoted in Greek here. It is used also in *De pueris instituendis* LB I 503F / ASD I-2 54:2–3 / CWE 26 324.

9 Or 'sieve,' *pertusum dolium*, the same phrase used by Conradus Goclenius to describe Erasmius Froben's lack of aptitude for studies: 'a mind like a sieve' (Allen Ep 2352:287). See Plautus *Pseudolus* 369 and *Adagia* I x 33.

10 Proverbial; *Adagia* I x 30

11 Erasmus quotes the Greek. 'Winged words' (ἔπεα πτερόεντα) is a favourite phrase in Homer; see for instance *Odyssey* 11.56, 209, 396.

12 These judgments are like others by Erasmus on memorizing. Memory is essential if one is to be a good or even merely competent speaker or writer, but he distrusts and discourages too much reliance on the old classical devices of *loci et imagines* 'places and images' (on which see Quintilian 11.2.17–31) and their later medieval forms, for these techniques burden the mind with anxiety over method and promise more than they can produce. The best training of the memory, he believes, is careful reading and rereading of texts until these are thoroughly understood (*De ratione studii* LB I 522C–D / CWE 24 671:5–25; on the teaching of texts see LB I 522E–530B / CWE 24 672–91). In *Ecclesiastes* (1535) he repeats that learning things by heart should not be thought an acceptable substitute for close reading. When preachers, for whom *Ecclesiastes* was written, must cite or quote many biblical passages, they will do better to read from notes than to depend on memory. Announcing the chapter or source of every scriptural text is unnecessary. Sometimes just say 'as Paul states in Romans' or 'as Matthew says.' The best aid to memory, not only for preachers but other speakers and writers, is strict sobriety of life and concentration on one's reading (*Ecclesiastes* LB V 955C–956B). In the world of printed books, as Erasmus recognized early and profitably, something more satisfactory than 'artificial memory' – the excess baggage of an old scholasticism – is needed. To stimulate memory, thought, and imagination, he recommends copies of paintings (not diagrams or astrological signs), quotations, maxims, and proverbs placed on the walls of a library or study (as in 'The Godly Feast' 205:23–206:25; the galleries of Eusebius' house are covered with pictures as well), or written on rings or cups. He enjoyed Johann von Botzheim's home in Constance, where 'all speaks in paintings that attract and retain the attention' (Allen Ep 1342:341–2 / CWE Ep 1342:377–8). In *De ratione studii* he writes on the value of such visual aids (LB I 522D–E / ASD I-2 118:8–119:5 / CWE 24 671:15–25). To be used successfully memory depends on one's understanding. Visual aids of the right kind give immediate pleasure while reminding a sensitive viewer of their lasting significance; see the introduction to 'The Godly Feast' 173. Erasmus' seal depicting Terminus is another example; see 'A Fish Diet' n118.

13 See the reference to Brassicanus in the introduction to this colloquy. Erasmius Froben had unusual opportunities for such converse because of the presence of learned men in his father's shop and the solicitude of Erasmus and Beatus Rhenanus for his welfare.

14 Whether good or bad, nothing but Latin was heard by Montaigne, by his father's orders, until he was six years old (*Essays* 1.26 'Of the Education of Children'; Frame 128–9).

15 Erasmus uses the same illustration in *De pueris instituendis* LB I 501E / ASD I-2 49:15–18 / CWE 26 320; and *De ratione studii* LB I 524A / ASD I-2 125:6–8 / CWE 24 675:18–20.

THE SERMON, OR MERDARDUS

Concio, sive Merdardus

First printed in the September 1531 edition.

The asperity of Erasmus' ridicule in this reply to an ignorant detractor of his edition and Latin translation of the Greek New Testament is more readily understood if we recall that his labours on the New Testament met with immediate hostility as well as praise. By the standards of modern scholarship, his edition of the Greek text had serious deficiencies, yet it was a landmark in the history of biblical studies. It provided something new and exciting, a fresh way of approaching and understanding the Bible. Issued by Froben early in 1516, it was the first printed edition of the Greek New Testament to be published; new editions followed in 1519, 1522, 1527, and 1535. The Greek New Testament volume of the vast Complutensian Polyglot Bible (Alcalá 1522) was printed by 1514 but not actually published until several years after Erasmus' edition had appeared. As the *editio princeps*, his edition of 1516 had a symbolic value that is easily perceived when we encounter contemporary reactions to it. The first edition of the whole Bible in Greek to be published, with the Septuagint version of the Old Testament and Erasmus' 1516 text (with a few changes) of the New Testament, came from the Venetian Aldine press in 1518–19. On the Complutensian Polyglot see CHB III 50–63.

The 1516 New Testament was accompanied by the Vulgate Latin text and Erasmus' annotations on both Greek and Vulgate. In the second (1519) and subsequent editions he replaced the Vulgate text with his own original translation. On Erasmus' research and preparation for this project see Erika Rummel *Erasmus' 'Annotations' on the New Testament* (Toronto 1986) 18–26.

In 'The Sermon' Erasmus rebukes the effrontery of a court preacher who had accused him of a perverse explanation of the Magnificat (Luke 1:46–55). Since the sixth century or earlier this canticle has been sung or recited at Vespers and on special occasions in the western church. What prompted the offensive sermon that aroused Erasmus was his interpretation of the word ταπείνωσις (Luke 1:48) in a brief note in the 1516 edition and later expanded (see *Annotationes in Novum Testamentum* LB VI 225F–227C; only the first six lines of this note were in the first edition). The Greek text of Luke 1:46–9 in Erasmus' edition is as follows:

Καὶ εἶπε Μαριάμ, Μεγαλύνει ἡ ψυχή μου τὸν Κύριον, καὶ ἠγαλλίασε τὸ πνεῦμα μου ἐπὶ τῷ Θεῷ τῷ σωτῆρί μου· ὅτι ἐπέβλεψεν ἐπὶ τὴν ταπείνωσιν τῆς δούλης αὐτοῦ·

ἰδοὺ γάρ, ἀπὸ τοῦ νῦν μακαριοῦσί με πᾶσαι αἱ γενεαί· ῞Οτι ἐποίησέ μοι μεγαλεῖα ὁ δυνατός· καὶ ἅγιον τὸ ὄνομα αὐτοῦ.

The Vulgate Latin is:

Et ait Maria: Magnificat anima mea Dominum, et exultavit spiritus meus in Deo salutari meo, quia respexit humilitatem ancillae suae: ecce enim ex hoc beatam me dicent omnes generationes: quia fecit mihi magna, qui potens est, et sanctum nomen eius.

Erasmus' own translation differs from the Vulgate in three places: he changed *salutari* to *servatore*; changed *magna* to *magnifica*; and added the preposition *ad* before *humilitatem* to make the meaning more precise, as he explains at length in the colloquy at 943:38–945:9.

The attack to which Erasmus replies in this colloquy was by no means the first on his 'daring to correct the Magnificat' (see n25 below). We hear of several in 1519 by monks or friars, another in 1528 (Allen Ep 948:94–117 / CWE Ep 948:99–121, Allen Ep 2045:42–54). What was his offence? That he interpreted the word ταπείνωσις in Luke 1:48 as *parvitas* 'humble condition' ('low estate' as the Authorized Version renders it), not 'humility,' which would be ταπεινοφροσύνη. In the fourth edition of his Greek New Testament (1527) he tells of a certain unnamed Paris theologian, 'in his own estimation the very Atlas of a tottering church' (*Annotationes in Novum Testamentum* LB VI 226C), who denounced this gloss, accusing Erasmus of irreverence and of Lutheran tendencies. His interpretation smacked of Lutheranism, his critics contended, because, by exalting Mary's humble condition, he was denying that by her virtue she *deserved* the unique blessing she had received – a typical Lutheran denigration of merits. Erasmus scornfully rebuts this charge in *Annotationes* LB VI 226C–227C, in *Supputatio* LB IX 490E–491A, and in the present colloquy. By insisting on the difference between 'humble condition' in life and humility as a moral virtue, he tries once again to convince an obstinate opponent that linguistic precision and contextual analysis are essential for understanding biblical discourse.

During the Diet of Augsburg in the summer of 1530, a Franciscan called Metardus or Medardus, in a sermon preached before King Ferdinand of Hungary, his sister Mary, and a large congregation, denounced Erasmus for his gloss of Luke 1:48. Of Medardus very little is known. According to Smith (*Key* 51) and Allen (Ep 2408:8n) his name was Medardus von (der) Kirchen. Erasmus learned of his diatribe from a friend who was angered by it, as were others who heard it (Ep 2408). This friend, Adriaan Wiele of Brussels, a secretary of Charles V, joked about the similarity between 'Medardus' and *moutarde* 'mustard.' Erasmus in his dialogue, besides mocking his critic's ignorance and arrogance, insults him by changing his name from Medardus to Merdardus 'dung.' See n21 below; on Wiele and Medardus see CEBR.

On other passages in the *Colloquies* concerning the Virgin Mary see 'The Shipwreck' n19; 'An Examination concerning the Faith' n42; 'A Pilgrimage for Religion's Sake' nn31 and 75; 'The Seraphic Funeral' n51. For a survey of Erasmus' writings and opinions on this subject see L.-E. Halkin 'La Mariologie d'Erasme' ARG 68 (1977) 32–55.

HILARY, LEVINUS[1]

Hilary Good God, what monsters the earth breeds and nourishes! So the seraphic gentlemen[2] stop at nothing, eh? I expect they think they're talking
5   to mushrooms, not men.[3]
Levinus What's Hilary muttering to himself? Making verses, I dare say.
Hilary How I'd like to stuff the babbler's dirty mouth with dung!
Levinus I'll accost the chap. – How are you, Hilary? Not very hilarious?
Hilary You turn up at just the right moment, Levinus. I can pour out[4] this
10   distress on you.
Levinus I'd prefer that you poured it into a basin rather than on me. But what's the trouble and where do you come from?
Hilary From a sermon.[5]
Levinus What has a poet to do with sermons?
15   **Hilary** I've no objection to sacred discourse, but I've encountered one 'sacred' in the sense that Virgil calls the thirst for gold 'sacred.' And such ravings are the reason I seldom listen to preachers.
Levinus Where was the sermon preached?
Hilary In the cathedral.[6]
20   **Levinus** After lunch? That's when people generally take a nap.
Hilary I wish they had all slept for that chatterbox. He's hardly fit to preach to geese.[7]
Levinus A goose is a cackling creature. They say, though, that the patriarch[8] Francis sometimes preached to his sisters the birds, who listened to him in
25   complete silence.[9] But come: is there a sermon even on Saturday?
Hilary One is given in honour of the Blessed Virgin Mother; on Sunday Christ is preached. It's fitting for the Mother to have priority.
Levinus What was the theme?
Hilary He expounded the Canticle of the Virgin.[10]
30   **Levinus** A commonplace topic.

Hilary Yes, and quite suitable to the preacher,[11] for I suspect he's worked up this one theme; as there are said to be priests who know no part of the liturgy except the Office for the Dead.[12]

Levinus Then let him be styled 'Preacher of the Magnificat,' or, if you like,
5 'Magnificatician.'[13] But what sort of bird was he, exactly, or adorned with what plumage?

Hilary Not unlike a vulture.

Levinus And from what coop?

Hilary The Franciscan.

10 **Levinus** What's that? From so holy a company? Perhaps from the degenerate sort known as Gaudentes, who wear dark dress, whole shoes, and white cord; who – I tremble to mention it – don't shrink from touching money with bare fingers.

Hilary Oh no, he's from the most select set – the ones who rejoice in the
15 name of Observants, have ash-grey dress, hempen cord, and sandals,[14] and who would sooner kill a man than touch money with bare nail.[15]

Levinus Not surprising for rose gardens to have briers. – But who brought such a player onto this stage?

Hilary You'd have even more reason to say that had you seen his tragic
20 mask. He was a huge fellow with red cheeks, big paunch, a fighter's frame; you'd have called him an athlete. And, unless I miss my guess, he'd drunk more than a pint at lunch.

Levinus Where does a fellow who won't touch money get so much wine?

Hilary He has a ration of four pints a day from King Ferdinand's
25 cellar.[16]

Levinus A badly misdirected bounty. Perhaps he was learned.

Hilary Aside from barefaced impudence and an unbridled tongue, he had nothing.

Levinus Then what was it that tricked Ferdinand into bringing a bull into
30 the wrestling ring?[17]

Hilary To be precise,[18] piety and princely liberality. The man was well spoken of, and he'd lean his head on his right shoulder.[19]

Levinus Thus Christ hung on the cross. – But was the sermon well attended?

Hilary How could it have been ill attended in Augsburg, in a very famous
35 church, and during a conference of so many monarchs whom the emperor Charles had assembled there from all Germany, Italy, Spain, and England? Not only that, but many men of learning were present at this sermon, especially from royal courts.[20]

Levinus I'm astonished if that swine could offer anything worthy of such
40 an audience.

Hilary But he uttered much that was worthy of himself.

Levinus Just what was it, if you please? But first I must ask you to tell me the man's name.

Hilary That's not advisable.

Levinus Why not, Hilary?

5 **Hilary** I don't like to do such creatures a favour.

Levinus What, do a slanderer a favour?

Hilary To take any notice whatever is to do them the utmost kindness.

Levinus Give me his name at least. I'll keep it quiet.

Hilary He's called Merdardus.[21]

10 **Levinus** I know that Merdardus very well. Why, he's the same man who at a dinner party recently called our Erasmus a devil.

Hilary You're right. But what he said at a dinner party, even though it didn't go altogether unrebuked, was attributed by the more courteous guests to his tipsiness – something to be written in wine.

15 **Levinus** But what excuse did he make when chided?

Hilary Said he hadn't spoken seriously.

Levinus How could he have spoken seriously when he'd neither brains nor heart?

Hilary But to me, and to all educated men, it seems intolerable that publicly,
20 in that spot, before such an audience, and – last of all – at so renowned an assembly of rulers, Merdardus should pour out his stinking filth.

Levinus I long to know what he said.

Hilary In a most stupid, raving fashion he denounced our friend Erasmus. This was the gist of it: 'In these times,' said he, 'a certain new Doctor Erasmus
25 – excuse me, I meant to say Doctor Ass[22] – has turned up'; and straightway he explained to the people what 'ass' would be in German.

Levinus That's an awfully funny story.

Hilary Funny? How so? Foolish, rather.

Levinus But doesn't it seem funny to you for such an ass to call anyone else
30 an ass, let alone Erasmus? One thing I do know: that if Erasmus himself had been present, he would have laughed in spite of himself.

Hilary Yes, the man's as asinine in his stupidity as in the colour of his dress.

Levinus In all Arcadia[23] I don't believe there's any ass better qualified by asininity to eat hay.

35 **Hilary** He's Apuleius reversed. Apuleius concealed his humanity under the guise of an ass;[24] this fellow hides his asininity under the guise of a man.

Levinus But nowadays we fatten such asses with cakes and ale, so it's no wonder if they bite and kick anyone they please.

Hilary 'This Doctor Ass,' he said, 'dares to correct the Magnificat,[25] though
40 this song was uttered by the Holy Spirit through the mouth of the most holy Virgin.'

Levinus I recognize the brotherly[26] saying!

Hilary And he went on to exaggerate it as if blasphemy in the highest degree had been committed.

Levinus Now my heart throbs with fear. What was the crime?

5 **Hilary** Erasmus, he told us, had altered what the church sings, 'For the Lord hath regarded the low estate [*humilitatem*] of his handmaiden,' to 'For he hath regarded the meanness [*vilitatem*] of his handmaiden';[27] and this word sounds more derogatory in German than in Latin.[28]

Levinus But who would deny that it is an accursed blasphemy to call Christ's

10 most holy Mother, a being exalted above the rank of angels, a mean [*vilem*] handmaiden?

Hilary Well, now, what if somebody called the apostles unprofitable servants?

Levinus I'd get the faggots ready for the blasphemer!

15 **Hilary** What if somebody called that glorious apostle Paul unworthy of the name of apostle?

Levinus I'd cry, 'To the fire!'

Hilary Yet Christ, the sole irrefutable teacher, taught his disciples to speak so: 'When ye shall have done all those things which are commanded you, say,

20 we are unprofitable servants.'[29] And Paul, not unmindful of this injunction, declares of himself, 'I am the least of all the apostles and not meet to be called an apostle.'[30]

Levinus But when holy men say such things about themselves, modesty is a virtue; no virtue is more pleasing to God. If somebody else said the same

25 thing of them, especially of those received into the fellowship of the saints, it would be grievous blasphemy.

Hilary You've cut the knot[31] neatly. If, then, Erasmus had called the Blessed Virgin 'the mean handmaiden of the Lord,' nobody would deny it was irreverently spoken. But since she speaks in the same fashion about herself,

30 she both yields to God's glory and shows us an edifying example of modesty; for inasmuch as whatever we are, we are by the bounty of God, the greater anyone is, the more humbly he should bear himself.

Levinus So far we agree, surely. But when these men[32] say 'correct,' they mean 'corrupt' or 'falsify.' We must see therefore whether the word

35 'meanness' [*vilitas*] corresponds to the Greek term that Luke wrote.

Hilary After the sermon I rushed to the book for this very purpose.

Levinus I wait to hear what you found.

Hilary The words that Luke, by the inspiration of the Spirit, set down with his own most sacred fingers, read as follows: ὅτι ἐπέβλεψεν ἐπὶ

40 τὴν ταπείνωσιν τῆς δούλης αὐτοῦ. Our Erasmus rendered them thus: 'Quia respexit ad humilitatem ancillae suae,' merely adding a preposition. It is not

lacking in Luke; good Latin style does not reject it; nor is it superfluous so far as meaning is concerned.[33] For thus Terence speaks in *Phormio*: 'Have regard *to* me' [*Respice ad me*].[34] In his Annotations, however, Erasmus reminds us that Luke said 'Look upon me' [*Aspice ad me*] rather than 'Have regard to me'
5   [*Respice ad me*].

Levinus What's the difference, then, between *respicere* and *aspicere*?

Hilary Not very much; but some, nevertheless. He 'has regard to' [*respicit*] who turns his head and observes what is behind him; he 'looks upon' [*aspicit*] who merely beholds, as in Terence, Phaedria 'sees' [*aspicit*] Thais coming
10 out of the house and says, 'I tremble all over, Parmeno, I've the shivers, when I've caught sight of [*aspexi*] her.'[35] But his brother Chaerea speaks thus: 'When I turn around and look towards [*respicio*] the girl'[36] – for he had faced the old man but turned towards the girl after the old man had finished talking.

15   Sometimes, however, *respicere* is used for 'be mindful of,' 'attend to,' either of something imminent or present. Thus the satirist: 'Bade him bear in mind [*respicere*] the end of life's long course.'[37] For death follows hard upon us, as though threatening from behind; whenever we think of it we 'turn our eyes' towards it. And Terence: 'Be mindful of [*respice*] your old age.'[38]
20 Hence one who neglects his children, giving his attention elsewhere, is said 'not to look after' [*non respicere*] them. Again, one who, after other matters have been discussed, turns his attention this way, is said correctly to 'attend to' [*respicere*] a thing. But God beholds [*contuetur*] in a single view all things past, present, and future; and yet in Scripture speaks with us in human
25 fashion. He is said to 'turn away from' [*aversari*] those whom he rejects, to 'be mindful of' [*respicere*] those he deems worthy of his favour, as though they had been neglected for a time.

        Luke, however, would have made this matter more clear had he said ἀπέβλεψεν;[39] we now read ἐπέβλεψεν. But whichever you read does not
30 affect the sense much.

Levinus Yet repeating the preposition seems superfluous.

Hilary Unquestionably the Latins too speak in the same fashion: 'He came *up to* me' [*ad me*], 'He directed his thoughts *to* writing' [*ad scribendum*]. Here the preposition does not seem superfluous to me, for one who happens to
35 glance behind him, gazing at nothing in particular, can look back [*respicere*]; but when you hear 'He was mindful *of* me' [*respexit ad me*], the special kindness of one who wishes to help this or that person is expressed. Likewise we sometimes 'see' [*aspicimus*] things we come across by accident – things we care nothing about, nay, that we should prefer not to see. But whoever 'looks
40 *at* someone' [*ad aliquem aspicit*] is especially attentive to what he beholds. Moreover we 'see,' but don't 'look at,' many things at the same time. Thus

the Holy Spirit, desirous of expressing to us the unique favour towards the most blessed maiden, spoke thus through her mouth: 'Because he hath had regard to [*respexit*] the low estate of his handmaiden.' God turns his eyes from those who are mighty in their own estimation and bends his gaze upon
5   her who was the least in her own sight. Unquestionably there were many learned, powerful, rich, high-born men who expected the Messiah would come from their own stock; but God, rejecting them, directed the gaze of his most merciful favour towards a maiden unknown to fame, poor, married to a carpenter, without even wealth of offspring.
10   **Levinus** I hear nothing yet about 'meanness' [*vilitate*].
     Hilary This was the slanderer's word, not Erasmus'.
     Levinus But perhaps he mentions 'meanness' in his Annotations.
     Hilary Not at all. On the word ταπείνωσις he simply notes, quite modestly: 'Take it as referring to humble condition, not to a moral virtue, and the sense
15   is, "And even if I am the lowliest servant, yet the Lord hath not turned away from me."'
     Levinus If these words are true and wholly reverent, what are the asses braying about?
     Hilary Their ignorance of Latin idiom produced these uproars. *Humilitas*,
20   when used by careful speakers among the ancients, does not signify the moral virtue opposed to arrogance and called modesty,[40] but an inferior worldly lot – the sense in which we say low-class, poverty-stricken 'outsiders,' and despised people are 'humble,' as though they crept along the ground. Hence, as we say to eminent personages, 'I beg your Highness to grant me
25   this favour,' so those who refer to themselves when seeking to advance their fortunes usually say, 'I beg you to raise my humble condition by your kindness.' Sometimes emphasis on personal pronouns has a touch of arrogance; for example, '*I* say so'; '*I'll* do it.' The most modest of maidens, then, did two things at once: she depreciated her own lot and
30   praised the Almighty's bounty to her: not content with calling herself 'handmaiden,'[41] she added, 'humble handmaiden and of low estate.' As, according to the proverb, 'Servant takes precedence over servant,'[42] so too among handmaidens one excels another in proportion to the dignity of their service: a hairdresser is more respectable than a laundress.
35   **Levinus** But I'm surprised Merdardus failed to recognize the form of speech, since I myself have often heard Franciscans talk like this: 'My poverty thanks you for the generous refreshment.'
     Hilary Some wouldn't be far wrong if they said 'my depravity'! But since the Greek word ταπεινοφροσύνη seems to have a broader meaning than
40   Latin *modestia*, Christians preferred to say 'humility' rather than 'modesty'; that is, they preferred to speak expressively rather than elegantly. For one

who appraises himself discreetly, crediting himself with nothing above his deserts, is called 'modest.' But praise for ταπεινοφροσύνη is not appropriate except to one who claims *less* merit than he possesses.

Levinus But in claiming modesty we run the risk of vanity.

5 **Hilary** How so?

Levinus If Paul spoke the truth, 'I am not meet to be called an apostle,' and if Mary was correct in saying she was a 'humble handmaiden,' that is, of very low estate, those who extol either one with magnificent praise run the risk of falsehood.[43]

10 **Hilary** No danger of that, my good friend. When we shower praise on devout men and women, we proclaim the grace of God in them; when they abase themselves, they have in mind what their strength and deserts would be if divine favour were withheld. And failure to claim what one does in fact possess is not mere lying. If one speaks sincerely, it can perhaps be called a

15 mistake; it cannot be called a lie. But God loves this mistake of ours.

Levinus Yet Paul, who denies that he is worthy of the name of apostle, boasts grandly in other passages when recalling his achievements. 'I have laboured more abundantly than all of them,' he says, and 'Those who seemed to be somewhat added nothing to me.'[44] The Blessed Virgin, however, is not

20 reported to have said any such thing.

Hilary But Paul calls those achievements his 'infirmities,' by means of which the power of God is made manifest, and he calls the mention of them 'foolishness' to which he was driven by the wickedness of false apostles.[45] Because of them he had to vindicate his apostolic authority – not because he

25 himself exulted in human glory but to further the gospel, whose care had been entrusted to him. The same consideration did not apply to the Virgin Mother, for the office of preaching the gospel was not assigned to her. Then too, her perfect modesty and shamefastness were appropriate to her sex, to the Virgin, and finally to the mother of Jesus.

30 I come now to the root of this error. Those who don't know Latin think *humilitas* signifies only an unusual modesty, whereas it sometimes refers to a state or condition, not a moral virtue; at other times it refers to the will in such a way as to suggest a fault.

Levinus Even in Sacred Scripture?

35 **Hilary** Certainly. Here's a passage in Paul for you, in the second chapter of Colossians: 'Let no man beguile you of your reward in a voluntary humility and worshipping of angels.'[46] The expression here is not ἐν ταπεινώσει, as in the Canticle of the Virgin, but ἐν ταπεινοφροσύνη. The passage is somewhat obscure, admittedly, but the authentic meaning in my opinion is

40 that advanced by scholars: 'Do not be so humble and abject in spirit that after you have dedicated yourselves to Christ, the sole author of salvation, you

let yourselves be talked into putting your hope of salvation in the angels
who some fancy have appeared. Lift up your hearts, so that even if an angel
really does come from heaven and proclaim to you a gospel other than the
one Christ gave, he may be cursed by you as a wicked angel and an enemy
5 of Christ. Much less does it become you to be so low in spirit that you let
yourselves be drawn away from Christ by imaginary apparitions of angels.
To put your hope of salvation in Christ alone is religion; to expect it from
angels or saints is superstition.' Paul means, therefore, that it is the mark of
a grovelling [humilis] and abject spirit to turn away from the heavenly Christ
10 to the pretended appearances of angels; the sign of a low nature to be blown
about by every wind of doctrine. Here, you see, ταπεινοφροσύνη is taken over
to denote a weakness.

Levinus Why shouldn't I see it?

Hilary Once more in the same chapter: 'After the commandments and
15 doctrines of men, which things have indeed a show of wisdom in will
worship, and humility.'[47] Here again ταπεινοφροσύνη denotes a fault.

Levinus Clearly.

Hilary Yet in 1 Peter 5 it is used for the virtue opposed to pride, τὴν
ταπεινοφροσύνην ἐγκομβώσασθε,[48] which we read as: 'Be clothed with
20 humility.' Again in Philippians 2: τῇ ταπεινοφροσύνῃ ἀλλήλους ἡγούμενοι
ὑπερέχοντας ἑαυτῶν,[49] that is, 'in lowliness of mind let each esteem other
better than themselves.'

Levinus You've demonstrated that ταπεινοφροσύνη has either meaning,
whereas in Latin modestia would not be used except as praise. But can you
25 show that ταπείνωσις is taken as 'modesty'?

Hilary There would be nothing odd about using it in that sense, since
nothing forbids our treating submissiveness or lowliness as modesty. But
whether you could find it so used in Sacred Scripture I don't know.

Levinus See if it's not taken in that sense in St James: 'Let the brother of low
30 degree rejoice in that he is exalted; but the rich, in that he is made low [in
humilitate sua].'[50]

Hilary Yes. This passage has ἐν ταπεινώσει, not ταπεινοφροσύνη. But if you
argue that here humility is taken for modesty, it follows that we should take
exaltation for pride and immediately a double absurdity results. For as one
35 who boasts and brags about his modesty isn't modest, so one who brags
about his pride is doubly arrogant.

Levinus What does the apostle mean, then?

Hilary He commends equality among Christians. The poor man is called
'low' because of his shabby lot; the rich man is called 'exalted,' certainly as
40 this world goes, because of the splendour of his fortune. Here the rich man
lowers himself to the condition of paupers and the pauper is elevated to

equality with the rich. Each has reason to rejoice: the one is happy that the wants of the poor are relieved by his wealth; the other glorifies Christ, who inspired that thought in the rich.

Levinus Nevertheless the rich man is praised for modesty.

5   **Hilary** Perhaps, but ταπείνωσις doesn't immediately signify 'modesty' on that account. There are some who, in their pursuit of men's praises, distribute large sums to the poor. Yet each is 'modest' provided true devotion is present: the rich man so long as he does not grumble at being reduced to the level of the pauper for Christ's sake; the pauper so long as he

10 does not grow vain over the honour received but gives the thanks to Christ and glories in him. Beyond question ταπείνωσις in the Bible is very often used for 'dejection' or 'abasement' due to suffering or the misery of one's lot. Thus Paul in Philippians 3: 'shall change our vile body,'[51] ταπεινώσεως. Likewise in Psalm 9: 'Consider my trouble [*humilitatem*]

15 which I suffer of them that hate me,' ταπείνωσιν.[52] Again, in Psalm 118: 'This is my comfort in my affliction [*humilitate*],' ἐν ταπεινώσει,[53] which is surely 'in affliction.' There are many passages of this kind which it would take a long time to cite here. As, therefore, ταπεινός 'one who is in low estate,' could figuratively be called ὁ ταπεινόφρων 'one who is

20 modest in disposition,' 'not in the least puffed up,' so there would be nothing extraordinary in one's calling 'lowliness' [ταπείνωσις] 'modesty' [ταπεινοφροσύνη] – in scriptural use, I mean. But those who argue that in the Canticle of Mary ταπείνωσις means modesty of spirit interpret in like fashion, no doubt, what we read in Genesis 29: 'The Lord hath looked upon

25 my affliction' (ταπείνωσιν).[54] Leah does not boast about her modesty but calls her husband's lack of interest in her (because of her plainness) an 'affliction.' In the same way Deuteronomy 26: 'and looked on our affliction, and our labour, and our oppression.'[55] Doesn't this passage call ταπείνωσις 'affliction'?

30 **Levinus** Then what prompts these men to interpret *humilitatem* in the Canticle 'modesty of spirit'?

  Hilary I see no reason except that many theologians have neglected the cultivation of languages and the study of Latin idiom, as well as the ancient Doctors of the church, who cannot be fully understood without these helps

35 – a condition very hard to rectify, moreover, once it is firmly fixed in one's mind. You can find some who pay such deference to scholastic opinions that they'd rather distort Scripture than correct human judgments by the rule of Scripture.[56]

  Levinus But this is sillier than the saying about the 'Lesbian rule.'[57]

40 **Hilary** Bede the monk, not a particularly safe guide when he strays from paths trodden by others, mentions 'pride' in connection with *humilitas*.[58] But

the Greek writer Theophylact, who usually followed the most approved Greek authors, denies that τaπeίνωσιs can be taken for a virtue.[59]

Levinus What need to prove it from authority when common sense itself rejects this interpretation?

5 **Hilary** Right. For though modesty is in some respects the summit[60] and safeguard of all virtues, to claim it is immodesty. We allow that in the Blessed Virgin this virtue was supreme and beyond comparison – Christ always excepted – but her modesty is the more admirable for this very reason: that she herself does not praise it but, acknowledging her low estate,

10 ascribes the greatness of the mystery to divine mercy. 'Mary,' they say, 'deserved by her modesty to become the Mother of God.' Let's grant that this is partially true, but just what sort of modesty is it for the maiden to assert this of herself?

Levinus Nay, the very tone of the Canticle indicates that she is speaking of

15 her own unworthiness; and therefore it begins thus: 'My soul doth magnify the Lord.'[61] But whoever says 'I deserved by my modesty to become the mother of God' magnifies herself, not the Lord. Presently Mary adds, 'For behold, from henceforth all generations shall call me blessed.'[62] 'Behold' signifies something sudden and unexpected. But one who deems herself

20 worthy of no honour does not expect the highest honour. Nor is it called blessedness if one gets what one deserved. Horace denies he should be called 'blessed' on the score of having been admitted by Maecenas to the list of his friends.[63]

Hilary Why?

25 **Levinus** Because he was accepted as the result of a deliberate judgment, not an unearned favour. Maecenas awarded him what he judged was due to Horace's virtues.

[Hilary][64] What follows is relevant, therefore: 'For he that is mighty hath done to me great things: and holy is his name.'[65] She did not say, 'hath done

30 to me great things because he judged me deserving' but because he is mighty and does whatever he wishes; he makes unworthy persons into ones worthy of his favour, and therefore is his name holy ('holy' expressed 'glorious'). As much as we claim to ourselves on our merits, so much do we detract from the glory of the divine name. For Paul says his 'strength is made perfect in

35 weakness.'[66]

Next, in the verse 'He hath put down the mighty from their seats and exalted them of low degree,'[67] the word is not ταπεινόφρονas but ταπεινούs, that is, 'the despicable by worldly standards,' as opposed to 'the mighty.' This verse is illustrated by the following one, in the manner of prophetic

40 eloquence: 'He hath filled the hungry with good things: and the rich he hath sent empty away.'[68] Those she had just now called 'of low degree' she here

calls 'hungry,' that is, poor; the ones she had just called 'mighty' she here calls 'rich.' In the next verse mention is made of the mercy poured out upon all peoples.[69] In the last verse she proclaims the assurance of God's promises: 'As he spake,' etc.[70] Glory, that is, the power, goodness, and truth of God, is
5 proclaimed by the entire canticle; there is no mention of merits.

Levinus But as pride accompanies wealth and power, so does poverty teach modesty.

Hilary I don't deny this sometimes happens, of course, but you can see plenty of poor people who are exceedingly arrogant. If you deny it, I'll
10 confront you with many Merdarduses! But, granting your point – though it's not always true – the question now is not what kind of person the Blessed Mother of Jesus was but what kinds of things she proclaimed about herself in this canticle.

Levinus I marvel at the obstinacy of those who don't come to their senses,
15 though repeatedly warned and even laughed at.

Hilary How often have they been warned that 'declamation' is the treatment of a *fictitious* theme, used for practising a branch of eloquence![71] And yet to them a declamation is no different from a sermon. How often has it been protested to them that a 'celibate' is one who has no wife even if he keeps
20 six hundred[72] concubines. And yet to them celibacy is no different from continence and chastity.[73] The same with respect to 'humility' and many other terms.

Levinus Where does so obstinate a stupidity come from?

Hilary As for the Merdarduses, my answer is that they haven't worked at
25 language and literature from childhood and haven't had enough teachers and books. And if any stipend for this purpose does come their way, they prefer to spend it on their bellies. They think their sacred garb quite sufficient to give them a reputation for piety and learning both. Finally, they think sanctity consists partly in knowing as little as Francis did about
30 speaking Latin.[74]

Levinus Indeed I know many who in this respect exemplify beautifully the founder of their order, who said *capero* [hood] for *galerus* [cap][75] and also, I believe, *vestimentibus* [vestments] for *vestibus* [clothing].[76] Yet Francis repeatedly refused the honour of presbyter, as did Benedict and Dominic
35 too, I think.[77] These fellows nowadays, with their own *vestimentibus*, don't shrink from a cardinal's hat.

Hilary What's that? Why, not even from the triple crown.[78] And these lowly sons of poor Francis offer their sandals for the mightiest monarchs in the world to kiss!
40 **Levinus** Now if 'meanness'[79] *had* been mentioned, what dreadful sin would that have been?

Hilary None at all, if by 'mean' you understand one who is slightly regarded by men or seems contemptible in his own eyes. But what need is there to defend what was not said?

Levinus Wasn't Merdardus ashamed to lie in this fashion, and in so famous
5   a church, so crowded an assembly of rulers, in the presence of so many learned men, most of whom had read Erasmus' studies?

Hilary Ashamed, you say? On the contrary, the rascal imagined he had scored a resounding triumph. This is the fourth vow of the tribe of Merdarduses,[80] a vow far more sacred than those others: to have no shame
10   whatever.

Levinus Yes, most of them are strict observants of that one!

Hilary There wasn't merely a single falsehood. In the first place, the Canticle of Mary, as written by Luke, remains intact. How can one be accused of 'correcting' when he changes nothing? Secondly, the word *humilitatem* isn't
15   changed, nor is there mention anywhere of 'meanness' [*vilitatis*]. Last of all, one who renders honestly what Luke wrote doesn't 'correct' the canticle but clarifies it.

Levinus I perceive a triple lie worthy of an impudent rascal.

Hilary Wait: you haven't heard the most shameless one of all.
20   **Levinus** Even worse?

Hilary 'That Doctor Ass,' he bellowed, 'was the head, chief, and leader of the entire insurrection by which Christendom is now shaken to its foundations.'

Levinus What's that you say?

Hilary 'It's his fault that the church is split into so many factions, that priests
25   are robbed of their tithes, that bishops are scorned, that the sovereignty of the sacred pontiff is widely flouted, that the peasants have copied the ancient example of the giants.'[81]

Levinus He said this in public?

Hilary With much sound and fury.
30   **Levinus** But those who look carefully into Erasmus' books think far otherwise. Many of them testify to having drawn the nourishment of true godliness from his writings. All this fire was started by the monks[82] and fanned to such a heat by them that even now their attempts to put it out have no more effect than pouring oil on the flames, as the saying is.[83]
35   **Hilary** The worst wild beast is the belly, you see.[84]

Levinus You've hit the nail on the head.[85] Obviously it suits this sort that there should be as much superstition and as little true devotion as possible among Christians. But what did the congregation do? Put up with the Cumaean ass[86] braying so violently from the pulpit?[87]
40   **Hilary** Some wondered what had happened to the man. The more indignant got up and left the church,[88] muttering, 'We came here to listen to praise of

the Blessed Virgin and this sot vomits mere slanders.' Among these persons were quite a few women.

Levinus But as a rule their sex is marvellously partial to this order.

Hilary You're right, but women too have begun to show sense. Most of the
5   learned men present fumed; some even hissed him.[89]

Levinus An ass isn't bothered by hissing. It would have taken rotten eggs or rubbish to drive such a brawler from the pulpit.

Hilary There were some who thought he deserved this, but respect for the place deterred them.

10   **Levinus** But the sanctity of the place should not save those who have profaned it by wrongdoing. As it's not right that those who murder a man within the precincts of a church should find asylum there, so likewise one who grossly abuses both the sanctity of the place and the people's patience in sermons is not entitled to protection by what he has profaned through his
15   own effrontery. The man who rejected as consul one who did not recognize him as senator was praised by the ancients;[90] nor is it right for the people to accept as preacher one who does not treat them as a congregation.

Hilary They're afraid of bishops' thunderbolts. 'If anyone, by instigation of the devil,' and so on: you know the law.[91]

20   **Levinus** But bishops ought to be the first to brandish the thunderbolt against such brawlers.

Hilary They too fear them.

Levinus Fear whom?

Hilary Those very brawlers.

25   **Levinus** For what reason?

Hilary Simply because they *are* brawlers.

Levinus The apostles did not fear the threats of kings and governors; and are these men afraid of a single mendicant?

Hilary But the very fact that they're mendicants makes them more
30   formidable. They've nothing you can seize; they do have means of injuring. Go to a wasps' or hornets' nest,[92] if you like, and touch any one of them with your finger. If this turns out well for you, come back and call the bishops cowards for refusing to provoke one mendicant. Don't the most powerful monarchs of Christendom reverence – and perhaps fear – the Roman pontiff?

35   **Levinus** No wonder, for he's the vicar of Christ.

Hilary But Alexander vi, a man neither fool nor dunce, used to say, according to report, that he would rather offend some of the mightiest rulers than a single ordinary mendicant friar.[93]

Levinus Leave pontiffs out of the discussion. When report of this outrage
40   reached the ears of the princes then at Augsburg,[94] wasn't the fellow punished?

Hilary They were all indignant, but especially King Ferdinand and his sister, Mary (the glory of womanhood in this age);[95] Cardinal Bernhard of Trent;[96] and Balthasar, bishop of Constance.[97] The preacher was sternly rebuked, but by none more sharply than Johannes Fabri, bishop of
5 Vienna.[98]

Levinus What good's a rebuke? An ass feels nothing but a cudgel.

Hilary Especially if you hit him in the belly! But what could the princes, preoccupied by far more serious problems, have done to that blockhead?

Levinus Surely they could have taken away his licence to preach and
10 withdrawn their favour from him.

Hilary But the artful dodger had postponed his poisonous slander until the very breaking up of the council, when they had to adjourn anyway.

Levinus Devils are said to depart in the same manner, leaving a terrible stench behind.[99]

15 **Hilary** And so he was dismissed by King Ferdinand, but well fed. Rebukes took not an inch off the fellow's waistline.

Levinus Francis is said to have preached to his sisters the birds.[100] This fellow seems fit to preach to his brother asses and swine. But where did he go off to?

20 **Hilary** To the rest of the herd, of course, by whom he was received with loud applause for a job well done, vigorously done; and over their cups a *Te Deum laudamus* was sung for an *Io, triumphe*.[101]

Levinus This Merdardus fully deserved to have a rope about his neck instead of about his loins. But what curse should we call down on this crass
25 herd that breeds such cattle?

Hilary You could hardly find anything worse to invoke than what they bring down upon themselves, since they are utterly disgraced by these methods and incur the hatred of all good men more effectively than any enemy could contrive. But to wish anyone ill is unbecoming to a Christian.
30 Rather is it devoutly to be wished that the most merciful creator and restorer of things, who turned Nebuchadnezzar the man into an ox and again of an ox made him a man,[102] and who gave Balaam's ass a human tongue,[103] would transform all who are like Merdardus into something better and grant them both speech and understanding befitting men of the gospel.

NOTES

1 These are former servant-pupils of Erasmus. Hilarius Bertholf lived in his household from 1522 until 1524 and kept in touch with him for a longer period. For an informal, confidential letter to Bertholf see Allen Ep 2581; it was written soon after this colloquy was published. He appears as a speaker in three other

colloquies; see 'Inns' n1. Lieven Algoet was in Erasmus' service from 1519 until 1526. He too is in several colloquies; see 'Patterns' n33.

2 Franciscans were known as the seraphic order, as will be evident in this and another dialogue, 'The Seraphic Funeral.' Seraphim, each with six wings, are the highest order of angels; see Isa 6:2–7 and Dante *Paradiso* 8:25–7; 9:76–8; 28:97–102. In September 1224, shortly before Francis discovered, on his hands, feet, and side, wounds – the stigmata – such as those Christ suffered on the cross, he saw a winged seraph, like a heavenly flame, flying towards him; this was Christ indeed *sub specie seraph*, St Bonaventure says (*Legenda maior* 13.3). On the stigmata see further 'The Seraphic Funeral' nn15–16.

3 Cf *Adagia* IV i 38, IV x 98.

4 *evomam* 'vomit'; perhaps recalled from Terence *Adelphi* 510 or *Hecyra* 515

5 *e concione sacra*; but as Hilary immediately indicates, 'sacred' when applied to *this* sermon means 'accursed,' as in Virgil *Aeneid* 3.57. *Contio* (*concio*) usually denoted 'assembly' or 'speech to a political assembly' in classical Latin; in ecclesiastical Latin *concio* was the kind of discourse called 'sermon' and *contionator* or *concionator* 'preacher,' terms that became more common in the sixteenth century. See these words in Alexander Souter *A Glossary of Later Latin to 600 A.D.* (Oxford 1949) and *Revised Medieval Latin Word-List from British and Irish Sources* prepared by R.E. Latham (Oxford 1965; repr 1980, 1983). Hence the subtitle of *Ecclesiastes*, Erasmus' treatise on preaching, is *De ratione concionandi* (Allen Ep 3036:4; and cf line 144 of the same letter). He insists on the urgency of understanding the differences between secular and religious *concio* or *concionator*, the differences between concern with *verbum hominis* and *verbum Dei* (*De concordia* LB V 477D). *Ecclesiastes* is a long book and was the last one published in Erasmus' lifetime. It has not received the attention it deserves, but see the article by John W. O'Malley, 'Erasmus and the History of Sacred Rhetoric' in ERSY 5 (1985) 1–29. *Ecclesiastes* is everything we would expect of Erasmus at the height of his powers: eloquent, learned, instructive, sincere. But, impressive and valuable though it is, it does not have the power of Augustine's *De doctrina christiana*.

6 In Augsburg. See 941:34–8.

7 Cf 'The Abbot and the Learned Lady' 505:5–6.

8 This title was sometimes used of founders of religious orders.

9 One of the favourite legends in the anonymous *Fioretti* or *Little Flowers of St Francis*, a fourteenth-century collection of stories and traditions about the saint and his followers.

10 Luke 1:46–55

11 The Franciscans were strong proponents of the doctrine of the Immaculate Conception of Mary; Dominicans opposed it. We hear of this dispute in 'The Seraphic Funeral; see 1007:10–15 and n51.

12 A dig at their reputed eagerness to collect fees for their ministrations. See 'The Godly Feast' n288; 'The Funeral' 769:9–11.

13 Erasmus' invention. Cf ἀριστοτελικώτατος (applied to St Thomas Aquinas) in *Moriae encomium* LB IV 469B / ASD IV-3 156:498.

14 *Gaudentes* is Erasmus' term for Conventual Franciscans. He refers to St Francis' admonition (Rule of 1221 chapter 7) that his followers 'should let it be seen

that they are happy in God, cheerful and courteous, as is expected of them, and be careful not to appear gloomy or depressed like hypocrites' (*The Writings of St. Francis of Assisi* trans Benen Fahy, with introduction and notes by Placid Hermann OFM [Chicago 1964] 38; *St. Francis of Assisi, Writings and Early Biographies: English Omnibus of the Sources for the Life of St Francis* ed Marion A. Habig [Chicago 1973] 38). Conventuals were originally so called simply to distinguish their churches from parish or collegiate ones, but the name also identified Franciscans who rejected the stricter views of Observants on corporate poverty. Note however Erasmus' comment that 'the most select set ... rejoice [*gaudent*] in the name of Observants.'

Although Conventuals wore black habits (and still do), and others grey or brown, grey became the official colour in the fourteenth century; whence the common English name of 'Grey Friars' for the order. In modern times the standard colour is brown for Friars Minor, black for Friars Minor Conventual. The earliest Franciscans doubtless went barefoot, as Francis did; later ones commonly wore sandals (*calceis fenestratis*). See 'A Fish Diet' n211. For Franciscans to wear whole shoes (*calceis integris*) was thought a 'crime' (*piaculum*), Erasmus remarks (*Lingua* LB IV 713E / ASD IV-1A 118:31–2 / CWE 29 350), though exceptions were allowed if necessary (see 'The Seraphic Funeral' n76). Franciscans wore a distinctive flax or hempen cord around the waist; hence they were called 'Cordeliers' in France.

15 On the interpretation of the vow of poverty, which caused dissension within the Franciscan order, see 'The Seraphic Funeral' n70 and the 'Note on Franciscan Poverty' 1026–32; on touching money, ibidem 1009:36–1011:11, with the notes.

16 Brother of Charles V and his successor as emperor (1556). When this colloquy was printed he was archduke of Austria and king of Hungary and Bohemia. See 'The New Mother' n9.

17 A waste of time; *Adagia* I iv 62 LB II 172B

18 Proverbial; *Adagia* III vii 58

19 The usual position in depictions of Christ on the cross, but see 'The Seraphic Funeral' n2. Mention of this detail here suggests that the words are ironic, since the preacher fancies himself a defender of orthodoxy.

20 A reference to the diet, summoned by Charles V, that met in Augsburg in June–September 1530 to try to settle differences between Catholics and Lutherans. This it failed to do, but it was memorable in the history of Lutheranism, because the statement of faith known as the Augsburg Confession, drawn up by Melanchthon and approved by Luther, was first presented there (25 June 1530). It was rejected by the emperor and the majority of delegates, and attempts at compromise were finally abandoned. The Augsburg Confession nevertheless became authoritative as an exposition of Lutheran faith. For texts see Kidd *Documents* 256–300 nos 112–23. Friends of Erasmus hoped he would serve as a mediator at the diet (Allen Epp 2333:42–4, 2335:19–22), but the emperor did not invite him to attend (Allen Ep 2371:21–2); nor was he eager to go (Allen Epp 2341, 2343:1–4, 2344:19–20, 2347).

21 In the first edition, September 1531, the title, running heads, and every mention of the preacher's name in the text have 'Merdardus.' In the March 1533 edition,

running heads have 'Medardus,' but in the text the name is 'Merdardus' everywhere except in the last sentence, where 'Medardus' occurs. The *Opera omnia* 1540 also prints 'Medardus' in the title and the final sentence; elsewhere 'Merdardus.' LB corrects to 'Merdardus' throughout. 'Merdardus' has to be correct, for Erasmus' denunciation of his critic would lose much of its force if the demeaning name 'Merdardus' were changed to something more polite. Erasmus considered that he had no reason to treat Medardus with anything but contempt.

22 *doctor asinus*. Erasmus was accustomed to this and similar disparaging labels such as 'Erasinus' and its synonym 'Herr Ass' (Allen Ep 2408:11) and 'Balaam' (Allen Ep 2134:168); 'Errasmus' from *errando* 'erring'; 'Arasmus' from *arando* 'ploughing,' or from *arare littus* 'to plough the seashore,' meaning 'to waste time in useless labours' (Allen Ep 2468:92–3; *Adagia* I iv 51).

23 Arcadians had a reputation for being invincibly stupid; *Adagia* III iii 27.

24 In the *Metamorphoses* or *Golden Ass*

25 This charge, often accompanied by abuse for his substitution of *sermo* for *verbum* in translating John's Gospel 1:1, had been made against Erasmus since his note on Luke 1:48 in the 1516 New Testament. For a few examples see Allen Epp 948:94–117, 1062:84–5, 1196:382–403 / CWE Epp 948:99–121, 1062:93–4, 1196:413–35, Allen Epp 1805:40–4, 1891:197–204, 1967:139–51, 2045:42–53, 2807:67–73. Elsewhere Erasmus says he heard a learned doctor, unnamed, declare in a sermon that those who presume to correct the Magnificat sin against the Holy Spirit (*Apologia adversus monachos* LB IX 1018E).

26 Erasmus quotes the Greek, ἀδελφικήν 'brotherly.' Here the word is used ironically of friars, but it can also be taken as 'undelphic,' that is, false or unreliable. See *Adagia* IV x 7, then Allen Epp 1792:16–17, 2956:38–40. I owe the reference to ASD.

27 Medardus accuses Erasmus of having written *vilitatem*, but Erasmus had not done so; he kept the Vulgate *humilitatem* but took it to mean 'low estate,' not 'meanness' as a moral defect (*vilitatem*) as Medardus implies. This misunderstanding is cleared up at 945:10–16.

28 Luther translates by 'Niedrigkeit' and 'Nichtigkeit.' See n59 below.

29 Luke 17:10

30 1 Cor 15:9; see n43 below.

31 Proverbial; *Adagia* I i 6

32 Medardus and others of his kind

33 Luke 1:48 'For he hath regarded the low estate of his handmaiden.' When Hilary states that the preposition (*ad*) added by Erasmus 'is not lacking in Luke,' he refers to ἐπὶ in Luke's Greek text. The Latin preposition is not found in the Vulgate (*respexit humilitatem*) but is needed, he thinks, to make the meaning of Luke's Greek more clear. He insists in the next half dozen paragraphs on the importance, if Luke's language is to be understood properly, of the difference between 'looking upon' in the sense of 'having regard for' and merely 'seeing' or 'having sight of.' Therefore the Vulgate *respexit* needs *ad* before *humilitatem* to make the distinction as evident in Latin as it is in Greek. This is the reason for the annotation in LB VI 225F–227C. The exposition of this point here is typical of many of Erasmus' elucidations of Scripture,

designed to emphasize his conviction that accurate exegesis depends first of all on grammar. When theology deals with the Word as words, it needs the aid of philology.

34 *Phormio* 740
35 *Eunuchus* 84
36 *Eunuchus* 342
37 Juvenal 10.275
38 *Phormio* 434
39 Which has the force of 'looked away from all others to give steadfast attention to one'
40 For an elaborate comparison of humility and modesty see John Henry Newman *The Idea of a University* (1873) part 1, near the end of discourse 7: 'Liberal Knowledge Viewed in Relation to Religion.'
41 *ancillae* (Luke 1:48), and see *Expositio concionalis in psalmum* LXXXV LB V 548B–C.
42 *Adagia* II iii 61
43 Erasmus makes the same point, citing 1 Cor 15:9 (used earlier at 943:20–2 above), in criticizing Origen's interpretation of Luke 1:48 (*Ecclesiastes* LB V 1028A–C).
44 1 Cor 15:10; Gal 2:6
45 2 Cor 11:30, 12:5, 9, 10; 2 Cor 12:11
46 Col 2:18. 'Voluntary humility' is the Authorized Version's rendering of ἐν ταπεινοφροσύνῃ (*in humilitate* Vulg). See *Annotationes in Novum Testamentum* LB VI 891E–F and the paraphrase in LB VII 1011C.
47 Col 2:22–3; 'in will worship' is the Authorized Version's rendering of ἐν ἐθελοθρησκίᾳ (*superstitione* Vulg). Cf *Annotationes* LB VI 893D–E.
48 1 Pet 5:5. See *Annotationes* LB VI 1055E and the paraphrase in LB VII 1099C–D.
49 Phil 2:3. See *Annotationes* LB VI 867C–D and the paraphrase in LB VII 995F–996A.
50 James 1:9–10; 'in that he is made low' is ἐν τῇ ταπεινώσει αὐτοῦ. Erasmus glosses it as *in humiliatione sive deiectione* in *Annotationes* LB VI 1027D; cf the paraphrase in LB VII 1120A–B.
51 Phil 3:21. The Greek of the phrase quoted here is literally 'the body of our vileness.' The Vulgate has *corpus humilitatis nostrae*; Erasmus' translation *corpus nostrum humile* (*Annotationes* LB VI 876A).
52 Ps 9:13 Vulg, 9:14 in English version; Greek from the Septuagint
53 Ps 118:50 Vulg, 119:50 in English versions; Greek from the Septuagint
54 Genesis 29:32. For the key word in this and the next note Erasmus uses the Septuagint.
55 Deut 26:7
56 Another example of Erasmus' conviction that 'there is no discipline which is more dependent on languages than theology' (*Apologia contra Latomi dialogum* LB IX 85E). Cf *Ecclesiastes* LB V 1026A and, in the *Colloquies*, 'The Abbot and the Learned Lady' n4; 'The Epithalamium' n19. He was equally convinced that scholastic philosophy was no help, and deprecated the temerity of those who set out to interpret Holy Scripture 'untaught and unpractised in Greek, Latin, and Hebrew ... equipped with a few frosty syllogisms and some childish sophistries.' It is possible to come to a right conclusion unaided by the laws of dialectic or Aristotelian principles, but not without knowledge of the biblical

languages. See *Adagia* I ix 55 LB II 354E–355B / CWE 32 212. 'It is better to pay no attention to some of Aristotle's pronouncements than to be ignorant of Christ's decrees' (*Ratio verae theologiae* LB V 137B / Holborn 162:4–5 (*Methodus*), 304:12–14).

57 Accommodating a standard or rule to whim or custom rather than vice versa. The phrase is common and proverbial; *Adagia* I v 93. As for distorting Scripture by employing this 'rule,' see *Ratio verae theologiae* LB V 89F / Holborn 204:23–33; *Enarratio in psalmum XXII* LB V 323C.

58 In commenting briefly on Luke 1:48, Bede contrasts Mary's humility with the pride (*superbia*) of Eve, which brought woe upon mankind (*In Lucae evangelium expositio* 1 PL 92 321D). Erasmus, who cites Bede a few times in his *Annotationes*, considered him learned for the times in which he lived, but his style rather dull (*Antibarbari* LB X 1736F, 1738F / CWE 23 105:29, 109:36).

59 In his *Enarrationes* on the Gospels he emphasizes that Mary attributed everything to the divine mercy, nothing to herself or to whatever virtue she had. Erasmus quotes the passage in his note on Luke 1:48 (*Annotationes* LB VI 226E–F). On his respect for Theophylact see 'The Godly Feast' n181. The *Enarrationes* were translated into Latin by Oecolampadius (Basel 1525).
Gerson (on whom see 'The Shipwreck' n43) wrote in 1427–8 a vast *Collectorium super Magnificat* (*Oeuvres* VIII 163–534 no 418). This is divided into many parts, including a series of dialogues between master and pupil. Erasmus was acquainted with some of Gerson's writings, but whether he read this one is uncertain. In its denseness, complexity, and totally scholastic formality it is a composition at the opposite extreme from the manner in which Erasmus addressed such subjects.
Luther too wrote a commentary on the Magnificat (1521), which Erasmus may have read, since it was printed in Latin translation (1525, 1526), but there is no evidence that he did so. Luther's commentary (WA 7 544–604) is worth notice, however, because his interpretation of Luke 1:48 and Erasmus' are essentially in agreement. See WA 7 559–60 / LW 21 312–13, where Luther, like Erasmus, rejects the notion that *humilitatem* 'low estate' in Luke 1:48 means 'humility,' as though Mary boasts of this virtue. 'That is very wide of the mark, for no man can boast of any good thing in the sight of God without sin and perdition. In his sight we ought to boast only of his pure grace and goodness, which he bestows on us unworthy ones' (LW 21 313). Luther translates *humilitatem* by 'Niedrigkeit' in his 1522 New Testament (WA *Deutsche Bibel* 6 212) and by 'Nichtigkeit' in his commentary (WA 7 559). He too agrees that the emphasis lies on *respexit*, not *humilitatem* (WA 7 562–4 / LW 21 314–18).

60 colophon; *Adagia* II iii 45 (see introductory note CWE 33 392), III x 82

61 Luke 1:46

62 Luke 1:48

63 *Satires* 1.6.45–64

64 Hilary] In the September 1531 edition, the edition of March 1533, and *Opera omnia* 1540, the lines from here to 950:5 ('Because he was accepted ... no mention of merits') are assigned to Levinus, whose name is then repeated at line 950:6 before 'But ... modesty'; thus he is identified twice as the speaker of lines 949:25–950:7. This awkwardness can be avoided, as in LB, by assigning lines 949:28–950:5 ('What follows ... no mention of merits') to Hilary and the

brief comment in lines 950:6–7 to Levinus. I believe this change is correct and consistent with the roles of the two interlocutors: Hilary the expositor and Levinus the inquirer.

65 Luke 1:49
66 2 Cor 12:9
67 Luke 1:52
68 Luke 1:53
69 Luke 1:54
70 Luke 1:55

71 Erasmus had good reason for this remark, for more than once he had to defend his own declamations – among them *De contemptu mundi*, *Encomium matrimonii*, *Moriae encomium*, and *De pueris instituendis* – from critics who ignored or denied the elementary but essential distinction between intentional fiction and, on the other hand, expressions of an author's personal judgments or opinions. Classical declamation, as Erasmus expected his readers to know, is a rhetorical exercise and should be treated as such. The real difficulty lies with works of art, of imagination, containing dialogue by created characters: are those words the author's own sentiments or simply words appropriate to particular characters and circumstances in the fiction? *Moriae encomium*, for example, is both a work of imagination and in form a declamation. Accordingly it was a pleasure for some readers and a problem for others in Erasmus' time, and even today. See his *Apologia pro declamatione matrimonii* LB IX 105E–112A and his statement on Clichtove LB IX 811F–814D.

72 Ie many; see 'The Funeral' n76.

73 On the meaning of virginity, chastity, and celibacy see 'Courtship' n53 and 'The Girl with No Interest in Marriage' introduction 279–81; on concubinage, 'The Well-to-do Beggars' n6.

74 St Francis was no scholar and did not pretend or aspire to be one, as we are reminded elsewhere (*Ecclesiastes* LB V 912C; *Supputatio* LB IX 553D). See, for example, 2 Celano sections 102, 189, 194, 195 (Habig [n14 above] 446, 513, 517–19); *The Mirror of Perfection* sections 4, 69, 72 (Habig 1129–31, 1197–98, 1202–4). He knew some Latin, but not enough to satisfy Erasmus. Nor did he strive to promote learning in his order. Yet within a generation after his death (1226), as a historian of the order points out, the Franciscans 'had become one of the most learned institutions in the world' (Moorman 123). The Christian philosophy of Bonaventure added a new dimension to the ecstatic spirituality of Francis. On this theme see A.C. Pegis 'St Bonaventure, St Francis and Philosophy' *Mediaeval Studies* 15 (1953) 1–13.

75 *Capero* was a hood worn by friars and most monks; often confused with a cowl (*cuculla*). *Galerus* or *galerum* was a hat or cap with a broad brim; cf classical *petasus* or *pileus*. A *galerum purpureum* was the 'red hat' distinguishing cardinals (as in Allen Ep 3048:91–2; *De bello Turcico* LB V 365F). When St Francis appeared to Erasmus in a dream he wore no peaked cowl but a hood (*capero*) attached to the back of his robe or cloak, to be used as a rain-hat or in hot or cold weather (Allen Ep 2700:44–5).

76 The point is that, according to Erasmus, Francis mistakenly treated *vestimenta* (second declension, therefore *vestimentis* in the dative and ablative plural) like *vestes* (third declension; dative and ablative plural *vestibus*). I have not found

vestimentibus in the published writings of St Francis. At the end of section 13 of chapter 2 (*De receptione et vestimentis fratrum*) in the first extant Rule (1221), Francis quotes *mollibus vestiuntur* from Matt 11:8 (*mollibus vestitum* occurs in the same verse) and may have had in mind also *mollibus vestimentis indutum* from Luke 7:25. Did Erasmus misremember this passage in the Rule when ascribing to Francis the solecism *vestimentibus*? Francis uses *vestimentum* and *vestis* more or less synonymously, as the Vulgate New Testament does.

77 Francis was not a priest, but he was commanded by Pope Honorius to preach (1221) and with his earliest followers received the tonsure (Bonaventure *Legenda maior* 3). Of the dozen earliest Franciscans, none was a priest, but it was not long before priests began to join the order. Erasmus is correct as to Benedict of Nursia (d 550), founder of monasticism in the West and author of the Benedictine Rule, the most influential of all monastic codes of discipline. He is probably wrong as to Dominic; the question is not definitely settled.

78 The papacy

79 See 943:34–5, 945:10–16 above.

80 In addition to poverty, chastity, and obedience

81 With this catalogue of contemporary ills compare 'The New Mother' 592:17–35. 'The ancient example of the giants' refers to the rebellion of the sons of Ge (Earth) who attacked the gods but were defeated by them. Erasmus compares that primeval struggle with the Peasants' Revolt and the more recent Anabaptist disturbances in Germany.

82 Levinus alludes mainly to the power and presumption of the monks, mendicant friars, and other religious clerics whom Erasmus accused of stirring up trouble in church and state. See *Adagia* II viii 65; 'Charon' n17, and references in Thompson *Inquisitio de fide* 10, 12, 46 for examples. He is very severe on their support and incitement of princes who wage wars of conquest, and on what he regards as their share of responsibility for the Lutheran troubles.

83 *Adagia* I ii 9 and 10

84 Proverbial; *Adagia* II viii 78. Erasmus quotes the Greek. Cf Paul on the Cretans in Titus 1:12.

85 *Adagia* II iv 93; often found in Erasmus

86 A fool who passes for a wise man amongst those even more stupid than he is (*Adagia* I vii 12). Another adage relates how the ignorant people of Cumae were deceived by a donkey that donned the hide of a dead lion (I iii 66). The story is in Lucian *Piscator* 32. Cumae, near Naples, was the oldest Greek colony in Italy.

87 See Allen Ep 1196:382–423 / CWE Ep 1196:413–56 on the impatience of those who have to put up with over-aggressive preachers. On theatrical antics in the pulpit see *Ecclesiastes* LB V 986E–987F and 'A Fish Diet' n219.

88 This is what people ought to do: teach such brawlers manners by leaving them without hearers (Allen Epp 1188:8–19, 1196:382–403 / CWE Epp 1188:11–23, 1196:413–35).

89 So Erasmus was informed by Adriaan Wiele, who was present when the offensive sermon was preached (Allen Ep 2408:15–16). Nowadays, Erasmus wrote in 1527, listeners to sermons behave better in church than they did in earlier times, even if the preacher says something absurd; the more regrettable, then, is the scarcity of good preachers. 'If people today, as used to be the

case, hissed and stamped their feet if they disliked what they heard, I am afraid they would not only hiss but stone the preacher' (Allen Epp 1800:221–8, 1891:288–91). On preaching and preachers see also 'The Well-to-do Beggars' nn46, 48.

90 Cicero *De oratore* 3.1.3–4; Quintilian 8.3.89. The man who protested the consul's refusal to recognize him as senator was L. Licinius Crassus (d 91 BC); the consul, L. Marcius Philippus.

91 'If anyone, by the instigation of the devil' are the opening words of a momentous passage in the canon law decreeing excommunication for any person or persons who 'laid violent hands' on a cleric or monk or other religious; for the text of this decree and the comment on it see Gratian *Decretum* part 2 C 17 q 4 c 29 (Friedberg I 822–3). Whoever committed this sacrilege could be absolved only by the apostolic see. The decree, known as *Si quis suadente*, was first enunciated by Innocent II at the synod of Rheims in 1131, then repeated at the Second Lateran Council in 1139 (canon 15; Tanner I 200). It was a potent manifestation of papal prerogative, important because of its emphasis on the status of clerics as against laity. It concerned everyone, therefore, and became everyday knowledge – as Hilary's remark implies: 'you know the law.' Excommunication was a far from simple penalty, however; the legislation was complex and acquired many interpretations, conditions, and nuances in the analyses of canonists. On these subjects see, besides the older works, the valuable study by Elisabeth Vodola, *Excommunication in the Middle Ages* (Berkeley 1986).

92 Proverbial; *Adagia* I i 60

93 The pope's comment is reported in Allen Ep 694:28–31 / CWE Ep 694:29–33; then in these lines of the present colloquy and in 'The Seraphic Funeral' 1012:24–5. Burton quotes it in *The Anatomy of Melancholy*, 'Democritus Junior to the Reader' (I 35). Erasmus may have heard it in his Parisian or Italian years. At any rate it fits, for Alexander had some exasperating troubles with the Dominican Savonarola, whom he excommunicated, and, like other popes, with Franciscans (Moorman 535–6). As is true of tyrants, Erasmus remarks, the mendicant friars would rather be feared than loved, even by kings; popes are afraid of them (Allen Epp 1870:18–21, 1875:150).

94 See n20 above.

95 Mary of Austria, sister of Ferdinand and Charles V, became queen of Hungary through marriage to Louis II. When he died in 1526, she served as regent for Ferdinand during his first year as king. From 1531 to 1556 she was regent of the Netherlands. She admired Erasmus, who dedicated to her his *De vidua christiana* (1529). See CEBR.

96 Bernhard von Cles (d 1539), bishop of Trent and cardinal since March 1530, a trusted administrator and advisor in the service of Ferdinand, was a firm friend and frequent correspondent of Erasmus. In the affair of the sermon by Medardus, however, Erasmus apparently exaggerates Bernhard's reaction. Writing to Erasmus a year after the incident, the cardinal says that he personally heard no abuse by Medardus and that he would not have borne any abuse patiently had he heard it. He promises, though, to make inquiry into the report of Medardus' invective and to let Erasmus know what he learns (Allen Ep 2504:25–34); but if he did so the letter has not survived.

97 Balthasar Merklin (d 1531), a successful careerist in the service of the Hapsburgs and the church. He became bishop of Constance in 1530.

98 Johannes Fabri of Leutkirch, who became bishop of Vienna in 1530, was another important ecclesiastic whose friendship with Erasmus was mutually beneficial. In the Medardus affair his response was no doubt more pleasing to Erasmus than Bernhard's, since he strongly rebuked Medardus for his impudence (Allen Ep 2503:1–5). On these bishops see CEBR.

Erasmus alludes in August 1532 to a letter sent by Medardus to a person or person at Ferdinand's court, complaining about Erasmus (Allen Ep 2700:26–37). Nothing more is known of the letter.

99 Cf 'The Apotheosis of Reuchlin' 249:6–9. The devils are *cacodaemones*; see 'The Repentant Girl' n7.

100 See n9 above.

101 Horace *Odes* 4.2.49–50, as at 'Cyclops' 869:21–2. The addition of 'over their cups' sets off neatly the ironical juxtaposition of the *Te Deum* of Christian praise and the exclamation of pagan pride.

102 Dan 4:30–7

103 Num 22:21–31

THE LOVER OF GLORY

Philodoxus

First printed in the September 1531 edition.

Desire and glory and pursuit of fame may be, as Montaigne tells us, the most universal of illusions (*Essays* 1.41 'Of Glory'; Frame 187), but he reminds us of Cicero's remark that even philosophers who write exhortations to scorn ambition take care to inscribe their names on the title-page (*Pro Archia* 11.26; *Tusculan Disputations* 1.15.32–5). The idea of imperishable human glory was almost obsessive in some of the ancient Greek and Roman heroes, statesmen, and poets. Much the same might be said of comparable figures in the late medieval and Renaissance societies in which Erasmus lived. In Dante, then in Petrarch and many others, we find recurrent concern in their poetry and eloquence with glory and fame. Whether this longing for immortality was prompted by heroic deeds or artistic achievements, it took many forms of expression. At its best, noble ambition could inspire the famous lines (70–84) in Milton's *Lycidas* beginning 'Fame is the spur that the clear spirit doth raise.' At the other extreme, ambition can be, as it is for Philodoxus in this colloquy, an incurable itch for recognition in one who is 'sick and tired of obscurity.'

Admiration and study of antiquity had much to do with the prevalence or popularity of this theme, as had social and political conventions and perhaps facets of personality now only partially perceived or understood. Jacob Burckhardt gave passing attention to the subject in his *Civilization of the Renaissance in Italy* trans S.G.C. Middlemore (Vienna c 1937) 75–80, but for extensive historical and critical treatment see Alberto Tenenti *Il senso della morte e l'amore della vita nel Rinascimento* (Rome 1957); O.B. Hardison Jr *The Enduring Monument: The Idea of Praise in Renaissance Literary Theory and Practice* (Chapel Hill 1962); Françoise Joukovsky *La gloire dans la poésie française et néolatine du xvie siècle* (Geneva 1969).

In some of his dialogues and moral essays Erasmus examines the thirst for fame or, on a somewhat lower plane, the winning of deserved esteem. His wisdom on such subjects is both typical and practical, usually a restatement of classical or Christian ethics or both as occasion serves. In 'The Lover of Glory' – an exception in this respect – all names and allusions and examples or anecdotes are classical, save for a short reference to behaviour in church and at the end to Christ. Moralistic observations are often enlivened, as in *Moriae encomium* and letters and colloquies, by amusing or satirical sketches of men and manners. 'The Lover of Glory' has sound and interesting comment on social customs, but because it is more homiletic than dramatic it does not equal the more familiar dialogues. In some respects it is the counterpart of 'The Knight without a Horse,' where an unprincipled and untalented pretender receives ironic advice about how to get on in the world. Here an honest but rather naïve inquirer is shown the nature of true glory. He needs, and hears from Symbulus, the Socratic counsel, that the best and only way to any fame worth having is to strive to be what one wishes to be thought. For princes and others in far more exalted stations than that of Philodoxus, fame may seem easier to attain, yet has its own risks. Rulers are exposed to flattery by everyone almost from birth, and consequently are liable to pride, overconfidence, and disaster. See *Institutio principis christiani* LB IV 561A–616F / ASD IV-1 136–219 / Born / CWE 27 205–88.

For Erasmus' testimony about his own attitude towards fame and glory we may compare a few words in a letter of July 1514 with a long passage in one written nearly a year later. In the earlier letter he tells Servatius Rogerus, the prior at Steyn, 'I haven't the slightest passion for fame' (Allen Ep 296:52–3 / CWE Ep 296:54). In the 1515 letter, defending himself against Maarten van Dorp's criticism of *Moriae encomium*, he protests that he has no interest in fame or reputation won by injuring others. His sole desire is that his books be useful (Allen Ep 337:26–35 / CWE Ep 337:29–38). He is confident that they serve the cause of learning and piety. He defended them when doing so seemed necessary, but although sensitive to attacks, he was not vain or boastful.

PHILODOXUS, SYMBULUS[1]

Philodoxus Symbulus, I interpret this running into you as a lucky omen.
Symbulus I only wish there were some way I could bring you luck,
5 Philodoxus.
Philodoxus What's more auspicious than for god and man to meet?
Symbulus Nothing, I'm sure, even if six hundred[2] owls[3] flew about. But what god do you mean?
Philodoxus I mean you, Symbulus.
10 **Symbulus** Me?
Philodoxus Yes, you.
Symbulus I never thought gods who went to stool were worth anything.[4]
Philodoxus If the proverb 'Whoever helps a man is a god'[5] doesn't lie, you can be a god to me.
15 **Symbulus** Let others see to the trustworthiness of the proverb; for my part, I'm certainly eager to do a friend a favour if I can.

LB I 857E / ASD I-3 667

Philodoxus You've nothing to fear, Symbulus – I won't touch you for a loan. Counsel is a holy thing;[6] just help me with that.

Symbulus But this *is* asking for a loan, since between friends service of this kind ought to be mutual, just as everything else should.[7] But what's the
5 subject on which you want my advice?

Philodoxus I'm sick and tired of obscurity; I want to be famous. Show me how.

Symbulus Look, here's a quick, easy way for you: imitate Erostratus, who set fire to the temple of Diana;[8] or one very much like him, Zoilus, who
10 railed at Homer;[9] or think up some other memorable crime, and you'll be renowned[10] along with the Cecropes[11] and Neros.

Philodoxus Others may win a reputation by wickedness; I covet an honourable name.

Symbulus Then show yourself the sort of person you wish to be thought.[12]
15 **Philodoxus** But many persons of exceptional virtue are unknown to fame.

Symbulus Whether that's true I don't know; but even if it should be as you say, virtue is its own lavish reward.[13]

Philodoxus You're right, and you put it quite philosophically. Still, as this world goes, I think glory is the special ornament of virtue,[14] which delights
20 in recognition, just as the sun loves to shine, and for the same reason: to benefit as many people as possible and to allure as many as possible to imitate it. Finally, I don't see how parents could leave to their children a more splendid inheritance than the immortal memory of a glorious name.[15]

Symbulus As I see it, you want the glory that comes from virtue.
25 **Philodoxus** Of course.

Symbulus Then take as models those who are celebrated in everyone's writings: Aristides, Phocion, Socrates, Epaminondas, Scipio Africanus, the two Catos (Cato the Elder and Cato of Utica), Marcus Brutus, and other such men, who strove in peace and war to serve the commonwealth as well as
30 they could. For here is glory's most fertile field.[16]

Philodoxus But of those famous men, Aristides was ostracized, Phocion and Socrates drank hemlock, there was a demand for Epaminondas' head, as for Scipio's too, Cato the Elder was forty times a defendant, Cato of Utica took his own life, and so did Brutus. I'd want a glory unstained by envy.
35 **Symbulus** But Jove did not grant that even to his son Hercules, for after conquering so many monsters by his valour Hercules had his greatest and most desperate struggle with the serpent.

Philodoxus I'll never envy Hercules his glorious labours. I simply count those men fortunate who acquire a reputation unstained by envy.[17]
40 **Symbulus** You want to live pleasantly, I see; for that reason you fear envy. You're not mistaken about that, for it's the worst wild beast of all.

Philodoxus Yes.

Symbulus Therefore 'Spend your life keeping out of sight.'[18]

Philodoxus But that's to be dead, not alive.

Symbulus I understand what you're after: you love to walk in the brightest
5   sunlight without any shadow.

Philodoxus Impossible.

Symbulus Equally impossible to attain glory that is unstained by envy.
Glory follows of its own accord upon good deeds; envy accompanies glory.[19]

Philodoxus But the old comic poet teaches us that glory can come without
10   envy: 'so that you may very easily gain a reputation without incurring
jealousy and win friends.'[20]

Symbulus If you're content with the praise that young Pamphilus[21] won
by complaisance and courtesy, you can look to the same source whence
you plucked that sentiment for the means of getting what you seek. In
15   everything remember: 'Nothing too much,'[22] but moderation in all things.[23]
Be good-natured about putting up with other people's ways; wink at their
lighter faults; don't be inflexible and over-insistent on your own opinion
but accommodate yourself to others' inclinations; insult nobody, but show
yourself agreeable to all.[24]

20   **Philodoxus** Most persons are partial to youth, and it's not too hard to win
this praise when you're young; but I long for some glorious fame that will
echo throughout the whole world, grow even brighter with age, and shine
still more brilliantly after my death.

Symbulus Truly I commend this noble nature of yours, Philodoxus. But if
25   you want the glory that comes of virtue, the principal virtue is to give no
thought to glory; and the highest praise is not to court praise, which is more
likely to follow the man who shuns it. Beware, then, lest the more eagerly
you aim at it the more you miss it.

Philodoxus I'm not a dispassionate Stoic;[25] I'm subject to human feelings.

30   **Symbulus** If you claim to be a man and would not reject what goes with the
human lot, why seek what even a god cannot have? For you know that saying
of Theocritus, one as true as it is witty, that 'Jove can't please everyone either
by rain or by fair weather.'[26]

Philodoxus Where there's smoke there's fire,[27] perhaps; yet there *are*
35   smokeless fires.[28] If human glory cannot be won without being darkened
by some shadow of envy, still there are ways, I suppose, of keeping the
proportion of envy to a minimum.

Symbulus Then you'd like these to be pointed out to you?

Philodoxus Very much.

40   **Symbulus** Be modest about displaying your virtue and you'll be the less
troubled by spite.

Philodoxus But glory isn't glory unless it's conspicuous.

Symbulus Look, here's an infallible way for you: perform some splendid deed and die; you'll be renowned without envy, along with the Codri, Menoecii, Iphigenias, Curtii, and Decii.[29] 'Envy feeds on the living, but after
5 death it sleeps.'[30]

Philodoxus Well, to be perfectly frank, I wish to leave my children and grandchildren the inheritance of a good name, but I should like to enjoy the fruit of it for a while in my lifetime.

Symbulus Come, I won't keep you in suspense any longer. The surest path
10 to celebrity is to deserve well:[31] of individuals in your private life and of all men in your public life. This is partly a matter of services, partly of liberality. Liberality must be so tempered that you aren't compelled to take from some what you bestow on others, for grants of this kind receive more disapproval from good men than approval from bad. And praise from bad men is more
15 truly infamy than glory. Furthermore, the stream of benefaction is dried up by dispensing gifts. Kindness that consists of services has no bottom; rather, the more generously it is used up, the more abundantly it flows. There are many mitigations of envy and enhancement of fame that nobody can achieve for himself; they come by the free grace of God. 'More pleasing valour when
20 with beauty joined,'[32] but physical beauty is within no one's gift. High birth carries much dignity with it, but this too is the gift of Fortune. The same view must be taken of wealth which, well got, has descended to us from grandparents and remote ancestors; not even this can be achieved by oneself. The same with cleverness, pleasing speech, gentleness, and affability; they
25 are inborn, not acquired. Finally, there is a certain mysterious propriety, nay felicity, whose effect we see every day in many persons.[33] No one can explain it. Don't we often observe that when the same things are said or done by various people, one who spoke or acted worse wins much favour while one who performed better is hissed instead of applauded? The ancients
30 attributed this quality to one's 'genius,'[34] for they used to say everyone is lucky in the particular thing he was born for; on the other hand, what one attempted 'contrary to Minerva's wishes,'[35] and those of his presiding genius would come to little.

Philodoxus There's no room here for advice, then?

35 **Symbulus** Scarcely any. But those who are capable judges discern in young men certain signs by which it may be divined which pursuits or callings or careers they are suited for.[36] Similarly we have a certain hidden instinct that prompts us to avoid some things for no apparent reason and to be irresistibly attracted by others.[37] This is why one man succeeds in the
40 military profession, another in public affairs; another, you would say, was born to be a scholar. Yet there is also a wonderful diversity within each of

these professions – as great as among the professions themselves. Nature bore one man to command; another to be a brave soldier; to one whom she richly endowed she granted that, in Homer's words, he should be equally distinguished as spearman and general.[38] In civil affairs, likewise, one excels

5 in counsel, another in pleading cases, another likes to go on embassies and does the work successfully. What need is there to mention the diversity of interests? Some men are so captivated by a monastic rule – not by just any rule whatever but by a particular one – that they think life bitter unless they attain their heart's desire.[39] On the other hand, some have such an

10 extreme distaste for it that they would rather die than become monks – not from perversity or for a definite reason but because of some inexplicable, instinctive feeling.

Philodoxus What you say is true of a good many persons. I've encountered it more than once and I've often wondered at it.

15 **Symbulus** If, therefore, pride and display are absent, those goods freely bestowed on us by the bounty of nature will occasion much less envy. Beauty or rank or wealth or eloquence is more amiable in those who seem unaware of their superiority in these endowments. Courtesy and modesty do not diminish these advantages at all but add a grace, just as they dispel envy.

20 Moreover, this courtesy and gentleness should be constant in all the actions of life, unless Minerva flatly opposes;[40] for it was useless, I imagine, for Xenocrates to try what worked so well for Socrates and Diogenes, useless for Cato the Censor to try what made Laelius popular.[41] Yet Terence's Demea showed plainly enough by his sudden change how important it is

25 to humour everyone's inclinations and feelings for the purpose of gaining good will.[42]

But whenever the right is compromised, true glory degenerates to transient popularity. Enduring glory is the kind that is rooted in virtue and served by the judgment of reason. Feelings hold sway for a time, but as soon

30 as they fade we begin to detest what pleased us so strongly before, and accordingly applause changes to hissing, praise to blame. An innate tendency can't simply be reversed, true, but it can be to some degree corrected.

Philodoxus I'm waiting for what you may add.

Symbulus A man who is naturally congenial can take care not to stray

35 from honour while trying to be agreeable with everyone,[43] and not to be untrue to himself while, like the cuttlefish,[44] accommodating himself to every circumstance.

Philodoxus I've known many such slippery fellows, and so false they ought to be ashamed.

40 **Symbulus** Again, those who are naturally stern should try to unbend, but in such a way that their behaviour does not appear insincere or that they

don't from time to time revert to their former nature; for instead of praise
this would bring a double disgrace upon them: for behaving too strictly at
times and for being inconsistent. So powerful is consistency that persons
who have developed a bad streak are nevertheless tolerated more readily
5   because they're 'always themselves'! But deceit, even when well-intentioned,
causes dislike the instant it's found out. Furthermore, pretence can't escape
detection forever; some day it must come to light, and once it does – all that
fine glory vanishes into thin air and becomes a byword.

Philodoxus Then (as I see it) you advise me to depart very little from nature
10   and least of all from honour.

Symbulus That's right. You know, too, that whatever comes suddenly into
the limelight is exposed to jealousy. Hence the pejorative term νεόπλουτοι
with the Greeks,[45] 'new men' with the Romans, 'upstarts' and 'people fallen
from the sky' with both.[46] But fame that grows gradually is the hardiest, just
15   as it is the least subject to envy, as Horace, the shrewdest of poets, declares:
'Through course of time, by silent growth, / Marcellus' glory thrives.'[47] If,
then, you seek glory which is genuine, lasting, exposed as little as possible to
envy, listen to Socrates, who said it often happens that those who start too
fast finish out of the running.[48]

20   **Philodoxus** But man's life is short.

Symbulus Therefore strive to do good, not to win glory, which comes of its
own volition. It's not long life you're after, I suppose, for that's the gift of
the Fates who spin the thread and cut it when they deem best.

Philodoxus Would that you could help me in this too!

25   **Symbulus** Never, Philodoxus, have the gods been so generous as to bestow
all gifts on one man. What they take away in years they requite by a glorious
name. Some men, but very few, they favour so lavishly that these while yet
alive – surviving themselves, as it were – enjoy their posthumous fame.
But those 'whom a kind Jove loved' are few and far between. Some, 'the
30   offspring of gods,'[49] have perhaps attained to this state, but that blessedness
isn't relevant to this discussion.

Philodoxus Often I fall to wondering at the spitefulness of Nature or
of Fortune, which grants mortals nothing entirely advantageous without
offsetting it by some disadvantage.

35   **Symbulus** Then what's the conclusion, my friend, except that since we're
born mortal men, we must bear with equanimity the mortal lot? Now
you can alleviate envy to no small degree if you keep firmly in mind the
characteristics of nations, classes, and individuals you've observed[50] – if,
in fact, you imitate those who undertake to keep and train wild animals,
40   since their main concern is to mark what enrages or calms the beast. I don't
mean merely the difference between bird and quadruped, snake and fish, or

between eagle and vulture, elephant and horse, dolphin and seal, viper and
asp, but the endless variety existing in every genus of animal.[51]

Philodoxus What comes next? I'm waiting.

Symbulus Dogs are all included in one species, but this species is divided
5   into so many types that you'd say they were identified by genera, not
species. Now in the very same species, how various are the tempers and
characteristics of dogs?

Philodoxus There's an enormous variation.

Symbulus Suppose what's been said of dogs to apply to every kind of
10   animal. In none does more difference show up than in horses.

Philodoxus True, but what of it?

Symbulus Reflect that whatever variation there is in kinds or classes of
animals, or in individual ones, all this exists in mankind. There you'll find
different sorts of wolves, dogs of indescribable variation, elephants, camels,
15   asses, lions, sheep, vipers, apes, serpents, eagles, vultures, swallows, and
what not else?

Philodoxus What of it?

Symbulus No animal is so wild that it can't be tamed for some use or at
least rendered harmless.

20   **Philodoxus** I don't yet see what you're driving at.

Symbulus Isn't there a difference between Spaniard, Italian, German,
Frenchman, and Englishman?[52]

Philodoxus Surely.

Symbulus What's more, each individual in any one group has some
25   particular characteristic.

Philodoxus Granted.

Symbulus If you observe this variation shrewdly and allow for individuals'
traits, you'll succeed easily in making friends of them all, or at any rate you
won't make enemies.

30   **Philodoxus** If you bid me turn into a cuttlefish,[53] where's right and honour?

Symbulus In everyday affairs there's a conformity that by no means
violates honour. In Italy, for example, men greet men with a kiss; if you
did the same in Germany it would seem ridiculous – instead of a kiss they
give you the right hand. Again, in England men kiss women by way of
35   greeting, even in church; if that happened in Italy it would be considered
an outrage.[54] Likewise, in England good manners call for offering your cup
to someone who arrives when you're dining; in France this is an insult.[55] In
this and in other such matters it's perfectly proper to do as everybody else
does.

40   **Philodoxus** But it's so hard to understand national customs and individual
traits.

Symbulus All the same, Philodoxus, if you seek surpassing glory, glory derived from virtue, you must also practice uncommon virtue. You know that 'virtue dwells with hardships,' as Hesiod taught[56] before the Peripatetic.[57] So if you want honey, you must put up with bees.

5 **Philodoxus** I know and I remember. But we're looking for a means of alleviating envy.

Symbulus Then see that in war you prefer to be a general rather than a private, and that the fighting in that war be against a hated enemy rather than fellow citizens or allies. In political life it's very important to hold

10 offices that win friends and good will; for example, it's more conducive to popularity to defend than to prosecute, to confer honours than to punish. But if – as is bound to happen – you can't dodge duties that by their very nature cause resentment, you can nonetheless temper them with courtesy.[58]

Philodoxus How?

15 **Symbulus** If you act as judge or arbitrator, one side has to lose; but you should so conduct the case that (if this be possible) even the loser may have cause to thank you.

Philodoxus How so?

Symbulus Suppose there's a charge of theft or sacrilege. If possible, change

20 the indictment and make it a case of disputed claim; by doing so you help the defendant without injuring the plaintiff. Furthermore, tone down the whole charge so as to be fair to the defendant without loss to the plaintiff. Last of all, lighten the convicted man's punishment somewhat. Avoid a forbidding look or sharp speech or peevishness, which cause some persons to be less

25 grateful for a favour received than others are when one is refused. At times a friend must be reproved, but if there's no hope of reforming him it's better to keep quiet. If the matter's fairly serious and there *is* hope of improvement, the kind of rebuke used makes a lot of difference. Often one who rebukes clumsily or unseasonably only makes matters worse and turns a friend into

30 an enemy.

Tact is even more important if you're dealing with a prince, for there are times when their whims must be resisted.[59] But if this is done cleverly and adroitly, those who resisted will shortly get more thanks than those who complied. What satisfies desire is transitory; what is done with right reason

35 is approved forever.

For the most part, bad feeling is the result of reckless speech.[60] How much hatred is sometimes aroused by a single word rashly uttered! How often has an ill-timed witticism or joke had fatal consequences! Praise, therefore, but praise those who deserve it, and do this sparingly; but censure

40 more sparingly still. However, if somebody must be blamed at all, don't be long-winded, since it's very hard to talk long and well at the same time.

Philodoxus I agree with all of this, but I think writing books is an excellent way to become famous.

Symbulus True enough, unless a mob of scribblers blocks your path. But if this method attracts you, take care to write precisely rather than profusely.

5 Be especially careful to choose a topic that isn't trite or hackneyed; also one that's as inoffensive as possible. Bring to it whatever choice material you've collected from long years of reading, and by your treatment produce something that combines pleasure and instruction.

Philodoxus You'll have given me sound and agreeable advice indeed,

10 Symbulus, if you'll add one thing: how glory can be gained in a hurry. I see many men who are scarcely known to fame by the time they die, and some – as the saying goes – are noticed only after they're buried.

Symbulus On this subject I've no better advice than the piper's to his partner: 'Be on good terms with those whose reputation is already high

15 and who are free of envy. Win the friendship of those whose approval will readily bring you popularity.'[61]

Philodoxus But what remedy have you to offer if envy does appear after a while?

Symbulus Act like people who boil pitch: if it bursts into flames they pour

20 water on it. And the fire rages and roars all the more if you don't do so often and regularly.

Philodoxus What riddle is this?

Symbulus Stamp out incipient envy by kindnesses instead of revenge. Hercules accomplished nothing by cutting off the Lernaean hydra's heads;[62]

25 he overcame the fatal monster with Greek fire.

Philodoxus But what do you call Greek fire?

Symbulus What blazes even in water.[63] Whoever is injured by evildoers but does not cease to deserve well of everyone uses this fire.[64]

Philodoxus What's this I hear? So kindness is fire at one moment, water the

30 next?

Symbulus Why not? Since allegorically Christ is now sun, now fire, now a jewel.[65] I've spoken in earnest. If you find something better, follow that and disregard my advice.

NOTES

1 'Lover of glory' and 'counsellor'
2 Innumerable; see 'The Funeral' n76.
3 Night-owls (*noctuae*), sacred to Minerva (the Greek Athena) and therefore a favourable omen; *Adagia* I i 76
4 *nunquam feci pili*, literally 'I never cared a hair about'; *Adagia* I viii 4

5 *Adagia* I i 69, one of the best in the first part of the collection

6 *Adagia* II i 47

7 For 'friends have all things in common' (*Adagia* I i 1 and 2)

8 Or Herostratus. His mad ambition to win immortal fame led him to set fire to the famous temple of Diana in Ephesus. By general agreement his name was never mentioned thereafter. See Valerius Maximus 8.14 ext 5; Gellius 2.6.18; Erasmus *Parabolae* CWE 23 224:26–30, from Pliny *Naturalis historia* 36.95; Allen Ep 1053:204–5 / CWE Ep 1053:220–1, Allen Ep 1967:52–3.

9 Zoilus was notorious for the asperity of his criticism; *Adagia* II v 8.

10 Greek in the original: ἀοίδιμος, which means 'famed' in song and story, whether in a good or bad sense. Here the association with Cecropes and Neros makes the meaning clear.

11 Monsters, since their ancestor Cecrops, legendary first king of Athens, had a body terminating in serpents (Ovid *Metamorphoses* 14.86–100)

12 *Apophthegmata* LB IV 156C (from Xenophon *Cyropaedia* 1.66.22 and *Memorabilia* 2.6.39, quoted in Cicero *De officiis* 2.12.43) and *Modus orandi Deum* LB V 1117A.

13 Cf 'The Sober Feast' 928:20–5 and n20.

14 Cf *Adagia* IV viii 68 and 71, v i 83.

15 See 'The Apotheosis of Reuchlin' n10.

16 On Aristides see *De copia* CWE 24:391:4n and 'The Sober Feast' n8; on Phocion, CWE 24 391:3n and 'The Sober Feast' n6; on Socrates 'The Godly Feast' 194:1–6, 23–34 and 'The Sober Feast' nn10 and 20. Epaminondas (420–362 BC) was a famous Theban general; see Plutarch's life of him. On Scipio Africanus Major (226–183 BC), victor over the Carthaginians in Spain, see 'The Profane Feast' n139; on Scipio Africanus Minor, who besieged and destroyed Carthage in 146 BC, see 'Copiousness' n17. Cato the Elder, the Censor (234–149 BC), soldier, statesman, and author, is the principal speaker in Cicero's *De senectute*, which is quoted and discussed in 'The Godly Feast' 192:28–194:20. His great-grandson, Cato the Younger 'of Utica' (95–46 BC), political opponent of Julius Caesar, killed himself when Caesar's forces won the civil war. His integrity and courage brought Cato of Utica imperishable fame. Marcus Brutus (c 78–42 BC) took his life when defeated by Antony and Octavian in the battle of Philippi in 42 BC.

As stock examples for writers and orators, these venerated names were nearly as common in Erasmus' era as in Roman times. In a long catalogue of comparative adjectives in *De copia*, we meet such phrases as 'more saintly than Socrates,' 'more incorruptible than Aristides,' 'more intransigent than Cato (the Elder),' 'more just than Phocion' (CWE 24 391:3–5, 392:1).

17 In one of Erasmus' longer adages, 'The labours of Hercules' (III i 1), he alludes to the struggle with the Lernaean hydra as the greatest and most difficult (LB II 707E–708F / CWE 34 168–9), quoting Horace *Epistles* 2.1.10–11, who takes the hydra to be envy, the most dangerous monster of all. 'Who can avoid ill-will that follows like a shadow,' Erasmus asks, 'unless he equally avoids the light that is cast by excellence? The two things have a close mutual connection, and that which is the best of all things has the worst of all things as its inseparable companion.'

18 The proverb quoted in *Adagia* II x 50 is more concise: λάθε βιώσας 'Live secretly,' though Erasmus' Latin translation of Plutarch's essay on this aphorism (*Moralia*

1128A–1130E *An recte dictum sit latenter esse vivendum*) has 'So live that no one may know you have lived' (LB IV 51A / ASD IV-2 241). Plutarch finds fault with it, first because it is insincere, for if one wishes to be entirely unknown, why does he proclaim the fact? He fails to follow his own advice. Secondly, the advice is bad because if one is virtuous his virtues may do good to others by being known. Moreover to know and to wish to be known is natural to man. On this aphorism and variations of it see M. van Rhijn in *Nederlands Archief voor Kerksgeschiedenis* new series 38 (1952) 164–78.

19 See 'The Old Men's Chat' n25.

20 Terence *Andria* 65–6. Cf 'The Poetic Feast' 395:3–27.

21 Leading character in *Andria*

22 *Ne quid nimis*, from Terence *Andria* 61; often quoted by Erasmus. See *Adagia* I vi 96.

23 The 'golden mean' of Horace *Odes* 2.10.5. For 'a middle state is sage,' as Glycion says in 'The Old Men's Chat' when relating the secrets of his happy and successful life. The entire passage there (451:25–452:16) is an elaboration of the counsel summarized here. See *Adagia* I vi 95.

24 Terence *Adelphi* 864

25 Horatian (*Odes* 3.3.1–8). 'Dispassionate' here is Greek ἀπαθής. With the purport of the line compare 'A Fish Diet' 697:30–2.

26 *Idylls* 4.43, which Erasmus quotes in *Adagia* I viii 65; and see *Adagia* II vii 55. He remembers too Lucian *Icaromenippus* 25–6, which he had translated (1512; published 1514).

27 Proverbial in English; not classical in this form, but 'out of the smoke and into the fire' (rather like our 'out of the frying pan into the fire') was a Greek and Latin phrase; see *Adagia* I v 5.

28 Sacrifices without smoke; *Adagia* I x 11

29 Codrus, an early king of Athens, sacrificed himself to save his country from invasion by the Spartans; see *De ratione studii* CWE 24 676:25. Menoeceus, a legendary Theban hero, fulfilled a prophecy by killing himself to save Thebes; see Euripides *Phoenissae* 905–1018. Iphigenia, daughter of Agamemnon and Clytemnestra, is the heroine of Euripides' *Iphigenia in Taurus* and *Iphigenia in Aulide*. The second was translated into Latin verse by Erasmus and printed with his version of Euripides' *Hecuba* in 1506 (Paris: Josse Bade). Marcus Curtius on horseback leaped into a chasm in the Roman forum when soothsayers announced that Rome's chief strength (arms and valour) must be sacrificed before the chasm would close (Livy 7.6.5); see *De copia* CWE 24 613:18. The Decii, father (fourth century BC), son, and by some accounts a grandson, sacrificed themselves to save the Roman republic (Cicero *De officiis* 1.18.61; *De divinitate* 1.24.51); see Erasmus' *De copia* CWE 24 613:18, 631:13–14. Marcus Curtius, the Decii, Codrus, and Menoeceus are all named as examples of courage in *De taedio Iesu* LB V 1273A–B.

30 Ovid *Amores* 1.15.39, quoted in *Adagia* II vii 11, which comments on the convention of withholding deserved praise from the living and overpraising the dead

31 Cf *Ecclesiastes* LB V 939D–F.

32 Virgil *Aeneid* 5:344

33 Cf Pope's 'grace beyond the reach of art' (*Essay on Criticism* 1.155).

34 Or attendant spirit, whether friendly or malevolent. See *Adagia* I i 72 and 'Rash Vows' n22. Cf *Adagia* II iv 74.

35 *Adagia* I i 42, and cf I i 37–8. Without the aid of Minerva (Athena to the Greeks) and one's genius, wisdom and the arts cannot flourish.

36 In the *Colloquies* as in other writings touching education, Erasmus discusses the variety and choice of careers. See 'Youth' 98:20–99:7 and n76.

37 In the case of Erasmus himself, his hatred of lies and liars ('Sympathy' 1045:33–1046:7); and by contrast his innate attraction to literature 'by a kind of secret natural force' (Allen I 2:30 / CWE Ep 1341A 42–3, Allen Ep 1110:1–11 / CWE Ep 1110:3–14 / CWE 23 16:1–13)

38 *Iliad* 3:179

39 Erasmus' memories of his own unhappy experiences as a religious (perhaps exaggerated; see Ep 447, the letter to 'Grunnius'), and the observations of his mature years, are evident in his numerous warnings against committing oneself or one's children to a religious life without due thought. One should be twenty-eight years old before making an irrevocable decision. See 'Youth' n76.

40 See n35 above.

41 Xenocrates was a follower of Plato and later (339–314 BC) head of the Academy where Plato had taught. *Adagia* III v 33 tells of his 'wondrous frugality.' He was respected but austere; Plato told him to 'sacrifice to the Graces.' Anecdotes about Xenocrates are preserved in Diogenes Laertius 4.2.6–16. The point of Symbulus' remark in the colloquy is that in temperament and manner of discourse Xenocrates differed from Socrates and the Cynic Diogenes. Similarly, the severity and obstinacy of Cato were a contrast with the wit and charm of Gaius Laelius, statesman, orator, soldier, and intimate friend of Scipio Africanus Minor. Laelius is an interlocutor in Cicero's *De amicitia* and *De senectute*.

42 Events in *Adelphi* change him from a harsh, unkind person to a genial one. See *De copia* CWE 24 584:10–13.

43 So 966:14–19 above

44 Which changes colour according to environment and circumstances. See *Adagia* I i 93, II iii 91. When human beings behave like cuttlefish, their purposes may be either good, or bad, or simply prudential. Thus Erasmus advises his servant-pupil Nicolaas Kan, who is about to go to England, 'You'll get along easily if you imitate a cuttlefish. Uncover your head, shake hands, give place, smile, but without trying to confide in anyone you don't know. Above all, don't criticize or scoff at anything in the neighbourhood' (Allen Ep 1832:55–9).

45 The Greek term Erasmus uses for the newly rich is found in two of his favourite authors, Lucian (*Quomodo historia conscribenda sit* 20) and Aristotle (*Rhetoric* 2.9 1387a19).

46 *terrae filiorum* and *e coelo delapsorum*. On *parvenus* of this sort see *Adagia* I viii 86. Erasmus describes one in 'The Knight without a Horse.'

47 *Odes* 1.12.45–6

48 See *Adagia* III v 60, which quotes Plato *Politicus* 264A–B, *Republic* 3.394E, and other texts on the futility of undertaking the study of philosophy, or engaging in other important enterprises, too quickly and without thorough, patient preparation. *Adagia* II i 1: *Festina lente* is a more familiar Erasmian treatment of this theme.

49 The quotations are from Virgil *Aeneid* 6.129–31.

50 To Erasmus this sort of knowledge was always attractive and useful; it was a clue to understanding human behaviour and therefore an effective aid in discourse. On large political or cultural questions he was, by preference and principle, a cosmopolitan, unusual by his avoidance of national or provincial arrogance, whether in matters of scholarship or politics. He never forgot he was Dutch, yet he was at home wherever he lived. He could think of England as a second home. He speaks sometimes of 'our France' and 'my Germany'; on one occasion he says he is uncertain whether he is French or German (Allen Ep 928:40–42 / CWE Ep 928:47–9); but what difference does it make? As an observant traveller, at various times resident in England, France, the Netherlands, Italy, Germany, and Switzerland, and with friends in many parts of Europe, he noticed or heard of many varieties of manners and customs, places, sights, and sounds. He seems never to have forgotten them, since he often alludes in his writings – no matter what the subject – to regional or national or individual characteristics. In the *Colloquies*, 'Inns,' 'A Fish Diet,' 'Charon,' 'The Profane Feast,' and (as he would say) in 'six hundred' other places in his texts, illustrations come to mind. He likes to generalize about the French, English, Italians, and Germans among whom he lived. For to observe and report what one has learned of other peoples enforces practical wisdom. On comparison of Erasmus' cosmopolitan and patriotic sides, see Johan Huizinga 'Erasmus über Vaterland und Nationen' in *Gedenkschrift* 34–49; Craig R. Thompson 'Erasmus as Internationalist and Cosmopolitan' ARG 46 (1955) 167–96; on his 'Dutchness' Cornelis Reedijk 'What is Typically Dutch in Erasmus?' *Delta* (Amsterdam) 12 (1969) 73–80. J.-C. Margolin has assembled and analysed much of the evidence on these topics in 'Erasme et la psychologie des peuples' *Ethnopsychologie* 25 (1970) 373–424.

51 See especially 'Sympathy.'

52 *Adagia* IV iii 24. Spaniards boast of their military exploits. Italians claim primacy in literature and believe that they alone are not barbarians. Romans compare themselves to the ancient Romans. Venetians and Scots are vain of their nobility. The English think they are the handsomest and their food the best. Germans take pride in their stature and their knowledge of magic and, like the English, Danes, and Poles, are fond of eating. The French congratulate themselves on their elegant manners; Parisians think they are the best theologians (*Moriae encomium* LB IV 448B–E / ASD IV-3 128:59–129:75 / CWE 27 117). For other notices of national characteristics or customs see *Ecclesiastes* LB V 845A; *De civilitate* LB I 1034A and 1035E (on Spaniards), 1035C (on Germans), 1036D and 1041F (on Italians), 1036D–E (on English), 1036E (on French) / CWE 25 274, 276, 278, 287. In the *Colloquies* see for example 'Inns' nn8, 19, 28, 32; 'The Profane Feast' 139:39 and n46; 'The Well-to-do Beggars' 479:18–480:2; 'A Fish Diet' n247; 'Penny-Pinching' 988:28–34, 990:27–8.

53 See n44 above.

54 In a much-quoted passage in a letter of 1499, Erasmus praises the beauty of Englishwomen and tells with amused appreciation of their freedom in kissing visitors and guests. Wherever one turns, there's kissing (Allen Ep 103:15–24 / CWE Ep 103:17–29). That this report was sent to Fausto Andrelini helps to explain its jollity, for Erasmus was not likely to understate the matter to him.

(See their correspondence in Allen and CWE, and on Fausto consult CEBR). Other travellers also refer to the English custom of kissing. Leo of Rozmital, the young Bohemian nobleman who visited England in 1466, found the women there not only free with kissing but excessively so. Like Erasmus later, he noticed that with the English, 'to offer to kiss is the same as to hold out the right hand, for they do not shake hands.' In France he was surprised that the queen embraced him and kissed him on the mouth, but the king told her to do so (*Travels* 54, 69). Another German traveller's impressions of the English custom (1484) were similar to Leo of Rozmital's (W.D. Robson-Scott *German Travellers in England 1400–1800* [Oxford 1953] 14–15). Still another example, involving Henry VIII's sister Mary and Cardinal Wolsey, is furnished by George Cavendish *The Life and Death of Cardinal Wolsey* (EETS 243 [London 1959] 56:24–6 and the note, 216–17). Enea Silvio Piccolomini (later Pope Pius II) who visited Scotland in 1435, says the women there thought less of a kiss than Italian ones did of a shake of the hand (*Memoirs of a Renaissance Pope: The Commentaries of Pius II* trans Florence A. Gragg, ed Leona C. Gabel [New York 1959; repr 1962] 33). Erasmus' report differs little from what a Milanese ambassador wrote a few years later about the Swiss (J.M. Vincent *Switzerland at the Beginning of the Sixteenth Century* Johns Hopkins University Studies in History and Political Science 22 no 5 [Baltimore 1904] 18). In 'A Marriage in Name Only' 854:3–6, Erasmus writes less amiably, though for sound reasons, on kissing.

55 On the common drinking cup, see 'A Marriage in Name Only' n58.

56 *Works and Days* 285–90

57 Aristotle, who taught that men are made virtuous by habituation. They must practise what is good; 'moral virtue is the result of habit.' See *Nicomachean Ethics* 2.1 1103a14–1103b2, 10.9 1179b20–1180a9.

58 Such is the conduct of Glycion in 'The Old Men's Chat,' who has held public office. See n23 above.

59 Eusebius in 'The Godly Feast,' commenting on Proverbs 21:1–3, has a different opinion: 'Whenever princes have their minds set on anything they should be left to their whims.' See 184:4–185:25 and notes to those pages.

60 'The tongue can no man tame; it is an unruly evil, full of deadly poison' (James 3:8); see *Adagia* II ii 39, where Erasmus refers to the passage and to 'Death and life are in the power of the tongue' (Proverbs 18:21). The power of words for good, and just as often for evil, is a recurrent topic in Erasmus, who lamented that much of his time was consumed by having to deal with detraction and controversy. See his *Lingua* (1525) on the use and abuse of the tongue (LB IV 657–754 / ASD IV-1A / CWE 29 249–412). Despite some unevenness of structure *Lingua* is a readable and illuminating essay. For pertinent criticism see Marcel Bataillon 'La situation présente du message érasmien' in *Colloquium Erasmianum* (Mons 1968) 3–16; M.M. Phillips 'Erasmus on the Tongue' ERSY 1 (1981) 113–25; Chomarat *Grammaire et rhétorique* II 118–55; Laurel Carrington 'Erasmus' *Lingua*: The Double-Edged Tongue' ERSY 9 (1989) 109–18; and R.J. Schoeck *Erasmus of Europe: The Prince of Humanists 1501–1536* (Edinburgh 1993) 310–19.

61 Perhaps proverbial of something that failed or is no longer suitable in changed circumstances, as in *Romeo and Juliet*, when the musician, after hearing of Juliet's death, says 'Faith, we may put up our pipes and be gone' (4.5.96–7). Not in *Adagia*, but see Lucian *Harmonides* 2, where a piper who longs to become

famous is told to play his pipe in the theatre but not to pay attention to the crowd. Erasmus was familiar with this dialogue (see *De copia* CWE 24 574–5).

62 See n17 above.

63 'Probably a mixture of quicklime, naphtha, and pitch from petroleum and sulphur,' used as an incendiary explosive in war as early as the seventh century (A.B. Crombie *Medieval and Early Modern Science* 2 vols, rev ed [Garden City, NY 1959] I 218). 'The secret additive that caused ignition on contact with water was certainly calcium phosphide, probably manufactured by heating a mixture of lime and bones with urine' (Colin McEvedy *Penguin Atlas of Medieval History* [Harmondsworth, Middlesex 1961] 90n). Consult John R. Partington's treatise *A History of Greek Fire and Gunpowder* (Cambridge 1960) on the long history of uncertainties about the exact composition and manufacture of this explosive. What is not uncertain is that it was a terrifying weapon when first used. How much Erasmus had read or heard about Greek fire we do not know. His statement here seems to be his only allusion to it. For later readers Gibbon's account provided references to Byzantine sources (*The Decline and Fall of the Roman Empire* chapter 52).

64 Possibly a recollection of Rom 12:20 'Therefore if thine enemy hunger, feed him; if he thirst, give him drink; for in so doing thou shalt heap coals of fire on his head.'

65 Christ as sun or light: Mal 4:2 as interpreted by early Christians, Luke 1:78–9, John 8:12, Rev 21:23; as fire: 2 Thess 1:8, Heb 1:7, and cf 'The Sermon' n2 on the seraph that conferred the stigmata on St Francis; as a stone or jewel (*lapis*): Matt 13:46 and 21:42, 1 Cor 10:4, Eph 2:20, 1 Pet 2:6

PENNY-PINCHING

Opulentia sordida

First printed in the September 1531 edition.

As a diverting sketch of daily life in a notable Venetian household, when Erasmus the Dutchman came to dinner and stayed for eight months, this dialogue seems fairly uncomplicated. Like some other colloquies, however, it is a by-product of the literary history of his early work on the *Adagia* and of a much later reaction to the hostility of certain critics, some of them Italians. As a reader familiar with Erasmus' personal history will recognize, this colloquy has echoes of a notoriously acrimonious and prolonged quarrel over his *Ciceronianus* (March 1528, with *De recta pronuntiatione*; the first issue of the second edition of *Ciceronianus* was appended to the March 1529 edition of the *Colloquies*).

The first edition of the *Adagia*, a small volume called *Adagiorum collectanea*, containing 818 classical proverbs with brief explanations or comments, appeared in the summer of 1500 (Paris: Johannes Philippi); the second edition, slightly enlarged, in 1506 (Paris: Josse Bade). Erasmus expanded it more than once. The final edition (1536) contained 4,151 adages, with many of the comments enriched until some had become fully developed essays. In its enlarged form this was an enormously useful and popular book: a repository of classical learning, a ready resource book for writers and speakers, instructive and entertaining. The best introduction to it is Margaret Mann Phillips' *The 'Adages' of Erasmus: A Study with Translations* (Cambridge 1964). A complete English translation is being published in CWE 30–6.

In the late summer of 1506, Erasmus departed for Italy, where he remained until midsummer 1509. He was in Bologna, Florence, then in Bologna again in November 1506. A year later (October 1507) he was once again in Bologna. From there he wrote to Aldo Manuzio, the famed printer and founder of the 'New Academy' in Venice, to sound him out on reprinting his translations of two tragedies by Euripides, *Hecuba* and *Iphigenia in Aulide* (previously printed in 1506 in Paris by Josse Bade). Aldo Manuzio agreed and issued them promptly in December 1507. This connection with Manuzio led to Erasmus' going to Venice in order to continue or resume work on a new and enlarged edition of the *Adagia*. This edition, henceforth called *Adagiorum chiliades*, contained 3,260 proverbs. Erasmus says he stayed in Venice 'eight or nine months more or less' (*Adagia* II i 1 LB II 405C); 'nearly eight months' (*Apologia adversus rhapsodias Alberti Pii* LB IX 1137B). Since he seems to have remained for several months (until December) after finishing work on the *Adagia* (Allen I 13:4 / CWE Ep 1341A:440–1, Allen I 61:156), his arrival in Venice may be dated c March or April 1508. When he came there, he was invited by Aldo Manuzio to join the household Aldo's family shared with his father-in-law, Andrea Torresani, the senior partner in the printing firm. Although Erasmus and Aldo became close friends, Erasmus was in a formal sense the guest of Torresani, who owned the house. 'Penny-Pinching' is mainly about Torresani; Aldo is a secondary figure.

Torresani had detractors in Venice, some of whom probably envied his prosperity, others who resented his selfishness (as they saw it) and his niggardliness. To what degree he deserved his reputation is an interesting question, though for readers of this colloquy a minor one. It is true that Erasmus' account of him seems a rude return for hospitality. Still, Torresani could not have been harmed by it, since the dialogue was not printed until several years after his death (1528). Erasmus' description of him as head of the household is unflattering, to say the least, and was intended to be so, but Erasmus might have retorted, 'Well, that's what the old miser was like.' The art of satire requires that its object be true to life and deserving of the treatment he receives. The satirist must please the reader while censuring the vices or eccentricities of his targeted victim.

Several years before 'Penny-Pinching' was published, Erasmus had caused a stir with another dialogue, *Ciceronianus*. In this he examined the claims and excesses of authors, past and present and of various nationalities, who carried adulation and imitation of Ciceronian style to an extreme. He himself upheld a doctrine of imitation chosen in accordance with one's informed standards of taste and – as he took pains to emphasize – one's own *genius* or *ingenium*, not a slavish attempt to imitate another writer. His candid yet tempered judgments of various authors from these standpoints were resented by some, as he may have expected. He went further by denouncing the paganism, open or latent, of certain modern writers and speaks darkly of a group in Rome who 'have more literature than religion' (LB I 1017B / ASD I-2 694:22 / CWE 28 432).

An unanticipated protest against Erasmus' treatment of Cicero and Ciceronians may have supplied the immediate occasion for 'Penny-Pinching.' In March 1529, Julius Caesar Scaliger, a hitherto obscure Italian admirer of Cicero, fired with a desire for fame and with indignation at *Ciceronianus*, wrote an *Oratio pro M. Tullio Cicerone contra Des. Erasmum Roterodamum* (published in September 1531), in which he charged among other things that Erasmus had been given to drunkenness in his Venetian days. Scaliger later wrote a second 'oration' against Erasmus, but that came out in 1537, after Erasmus' death, and does not concern us here. (On Scaliger see a life by Vernon Hall in *Transactions of the American Philosophical Society* new series 40 no 2

[1950] 86–170, especially 94–114, where the two orations are summarized; see also the bibliography in CEBR.) Before he had even read the *Oratio* of 1531, Erasmus insisted that it was not the work of Scaliger but of Girolamo Aleandro, who had been papal legate to Germany but was well known to Erasmus as a promising young scholar in Venice, where they were good friends and lived together (Allen Epp 2565:24–7, 2575:6–7, 2577, 2579:35–8, 2581:1–13, 2587:9–12, 2736:1–7). The oftener he repeated this conviction about Aleandro's authorship, the more strongly Erasmus believed it. Aleandro swore that he had never heard of Scaliger's attack until Erasmus accused him of writing it (Allen Ep 2638:15–23 and Ep 2639). Erasmus did not willingly change his mind. However much Aleandro protested, and whether or not the published *Oratio* purported to come from the pen of Scaliger, Erasmus believed Aleandro was at the bottom of this intolerable slander. 'I recognize Aleandro's language there as well as I know his face' (Allen Ep 2565:24–6). So he wrote in November 1531. A year later he concedes that he has not read the *Oratio* thoroughly, but 'I know the author as surely as I know I'm alive' (Allen Ep 2736:5). On Aleandro see further n25 below.

'Penny-Pinching,' then, is both a Lucianic entertainment about Andrea Torresani, Mr Moneybags, and, indirectly, the expression of a mood of irritation at some of Erasmus' recent critics. Alberto Pio had accused him of going to Venice to improve his Greek and Latin with Aldo's help. Erasmus replies scornfully, 'I knew Greek and Latin better when I went to Italy than I do now' (*Apologia adversus rhapsodias Alberti Pii* LB IX 1137A–C; on this work see the introduction to 'The Seraphic Funeral' 996–7). As for drunkenness, he shows in 'Penny-Pinching' how far from debauchery life in the Torresani household was; the food and drink were so bad that he has felt the effects ever since, for he blames his recurrent attacks of kidney stone on those months in Venice (see n13 below). The notion that he worked for the press he rebuts by pointing out that he did not work for Aldo Manuzio but for himself, spending all his time on the *Adagia* and passing the sheets, as he finished them, to compositors to set in type.

The earliest printed translation of this colloquy into Italian appears to be the version by Pietro Lauro (Venice 1545, 1549). A modern one is included in Manlio Dazzi's monograph *Aldo Manuzio e il dialogo veneziano di Erasmo* (Vicenza 1969). On Venetian humanism see Deno J. Geanakoplos *Greek Scholars in Venice* (Cambridge, Mass 1962) and Margaret L. King *Venetian Humanism in an Age of Patrician Dominance* (Princeton 1986). On the Aldine press the most important of older works is A. Renouard, *Annales de l'imprimerie des Alde* 3 vols (Paris 1825; 3rd ed 1934; repr 1953); of modern ones, and indispensable, is Martin Lowry *The World of Aldus Manutius* (Oxford and Ithaca 1979); on other aspects of printing in Venice consult Paul Grendler

The Roman Inquisition and the Venetian Press (Princeton 1977); on Erasmus in Italy, A. Renaudet *Erasme et l'Italie* (Geneva 1954), which supersedes P. de Nolhac's briefer *Erasme et l'Italie* (Paris 1898). John F. D'Amico *Renaissance Humanism in Papal Rome* (Baltimore 1983) has relevant material on Erasmus. On Erasmus' reputation in Italy see Myron P. Gilmore's articles; three of these are mentioned in the introduction to 'The Seraphic Funeral' 999 below; a fourth is 'Anti-Erasmianism in Italy: The Dialogue of Ortensio Lando on Erasmus' Funeral' *Journal of Medieval and Renaissance Studies* 4 (1974) 2–14. For other studies of the survival of Erasmus' books and ideas in Italy by Silvana Seidel Menchi see Margolin 'Travaux érasmiens (1970–1985)' 616–17. A census of Erasmus holdings in Vatican, Roman, and other Italian libraries is provided by Marcella and Paul Grendler 'The Survival of Erasmus in Italy' *Erasmus in English* 8 (1976) 2–22 and 'The Erasmus Holdings of Roman and Vatican Libraries' *Erasmus in English* 13 (1984) 2–29.

The frequent allusions to Italian people and places and to his experiences in Italy testify to the significance of that chapter of Erasmus' biography. Many other studies besides those listed here are recorded in Margolin's bibliographies and Lowry's book.

JAMES, GILBERT[1]

James Where have you been? You're so dried up you might have been feeding on dew[2] with the cicadas. So far as I can see, you're a mere shell[3] of
5 a man.
Gilbert Shades in hell are filled with mallow and leek,[4] but I've lived for ten months where not even that comes your way.
James Where, if you please? Not carried off to a galley, were you?
Gilbert Oh, no – at Synodium.[5]
10 **James** You were in danger of starvation in so prosperous a city?[6]
Gilbert Most certainly I was.
James How come? Were you broke?
Gilbert No lack of money or friends.
James What was the trouble, then?
15 **Gilbert** The trouble had to do with my host, Antronius.[7]
James Mr Moneybags?
Gilbert Yes, but a real skinflint.
James That sounds odd.
Gilbert Not at all. That's the way it is with people who go from rags to
20 riches.
James Then why were you willing to stay so many months with such a host?

Gilbert I had a reason, so at the time I simply decided to stay.

James But do tell me exactly what his style of living was like.

Gilbert I'll tell you, since remembrance of trials past is generally pleasant.[8]

James It will be so to me, surely.

5 **Gilbert** The weather[9] added to the discomfort. While I was there the north wind blew for three whole months, except that for some reason or other it never persisted more than eight days at a time.

James Then how did it blow for three whole months?

Gilbert About the eighth day it swerved from its course, so to speak, but

10 after eight hours moved back to its earlier place.

James A person of slight physique would need a glowing fire there.

Gilbert With enough wood we'd have had enough fire, but our friend Antronius refused to go to this expense. From little farms out on the islands he dug up – usually at night – roots of trees overlooked by others. With

15 these, damp as they were, a fire was made. It had plenty of smoke but no flame;[10] it gave off no heat but did enable him to deny the charge that there was no fire at all. So slowly did it burn that this one fire lasted all day.

James A hard place to winter in!

Gilbert But much harder to summer in.

20 **James** How so?

Gilbert Because the house was so full of fleas and bedbugs you had neither peace by day nor sleep by night.

James What miserly riches!

Gilbert Especially in that sort of herd.

25 **James** The women there must be lazy.

Gilbert They keep to themselves; they don't move among the men. As a result, the women there are – just women; men don't get the services usually provided by that sex.

James But didn't this treatment annoy Antronius?

30 **Gilbert** Since he was brought up in such niggardliness, the only thing he cared about was money. He'd live anywhere rather than at home, and he had a finger in every pie. You know that city, above all others, is a centre of trade.[11] There was once a famous painter who thought the day wasted if he had not painted a stroke.[12] Antronius mourned far more if a day went by

35 without a profit. When this did happen, he'd go try his luck at home.

James What would he do?

Gilbert He had a cistern in the house, as is customary in that city. From this he drew some buckets of water that he poured into wine jugs. This was sure gain.

James Maybe the wine was too strong.

40 **Gilbert** No, on the contrary it was worse than flat, since he bought only spoiled wine, which he could get at a lower price. To avoid wasting any, he'd

often mix ten years' dregs with it (he hadn't allowed any of the dregs to be wasted!), stirring all together to make it seem like new wine.

James But if the medical men are to be believed, such wine causes kidney stones.

5 **Gilbert** The medics aren't mistaken, for that household didn't get through a year without one or two deaths from the stone.[13] *He* wasn't afraid of a house of mourning.

James No?

Gilbert He made money even from the dead;[14] didn't scorn even the
10 slightest advantage.

James Theft, you mean.

Gilbert Business men call it profit.

James But what would Antronius himself drink?

Gilbert Usually the same nectar.

15 **James** Without ill effect?

Gilbert He was so tough he could eat hay;[15] and, as I've said, he was brought up on such delicacies from tender youth. – He thought nothing was more certain than this gain.

James Why so?

20 **Gilbert** If you count wife, sons, daughter, son-in-law,[16] workmen, and servants, he supported nearly thirty people in the household.[17] Now the more the wine was diluted, the more sparingly they drank and the more slowly it was drained. Just figure what a bucket of water added each day amounts to in a year – no mean sum.

25 **James** The stinginess of it!

Gilbert But he made no less saving on bread.

James How?

Gilbert He bought spoiled wheat nobody else would take. Here was an immediate gain, because he bought for less. But he was expert enough to
30 remedy what was spoiled.

James How, exactly?

Gilbert There's a kind of white clay,[18] something like grain, that horses are evidently fond of; they gnaw at walls having this clay and drink more readily from ponds muddied by it. The bread he made was one-third clay.

35 **James** Is this what you mean by 'remedying'?

Gilbert Anyway the badness of the wheat was less noticeable. And do you imagine this profit was to be sneezed at? Here's another clever dodge: he kneaded the bread at home, not oftener than twice a month, even in summer.

James That's serving stones, not bread.[19]

40 **Gilbert** Or something harder than stones, if it's possible. But for this difficulty too he had a ready remedy.

James What?

Gilbert He soaked hunks of bread in cups of wine.

James That was in character.[20] But did the workers stand for such treatment?

Gilbert I'll describe first the fare prescribed for the heads of the family, to
5   let you guess more easily how the workers might be treated.

James I want to hear about it.

Gilbert Breakfast wasn't mentioned there. Lunch was usually put off until
one o'clock.[21]

James Why?

10   **Gilbert** They were waiting for the master, Antronius. Dinner was sometimes
served towards ten in the evening.

James Yet you used to fret when hungry.

Gilbert For that reason I'd often protest to Orthrogonus,[22] Antronius'
son-in-law, since we used to meet in the same dining room. 'See here,
15   Orthrogonus, don't Synodians eat today?' 'Antronius will soon be here,'
was the cheerful reply. When I saw no signs of food and my stomach was
barking, I said, 'Look, Orthrogonus, must I starve today?' He apologized
for the hour, or something of the sort. When I could no longer stand the
barking in my stomach, I interrupted him once more. 'What's it to be?' I said.
20   'Must I die of hunger?' When Orthrogonus had evaded the issue as long
as he could, he went to the servants and told them to set the table. At last,
when Antronius did not return and nothing was prepared, Orthrogonus,
overcome by my loud reproaches, went down to his wife, mother-in-law,
and children, bawling to them to get dinner ready.

25   **James** Now, at least, I expect dinner.

Gilbert Don't be in a hurry. Finally a lame servant assigned to this job – a
fellow reminding you of Vulcan – came in and laid the tablecloth. This was
the first prospect of dinner. At last, after much clamour, glass bowls of clear
water are brought in.

30   **James** Another sign of dinner.

Gilbert Don't be in a hurry, I say. Again a frightful din, then a jar filled
with that foul nectar[23] is fetched.

James Bravo!

Gilbert But without bread. Not that there was the slightest risk; nobody,
35   even if starving, would willingly drink such wine. More shouting until
they're hoarse;[24] then, at long last, the bread – which a bear could hardly
break with his teeth – is served.

James Surely they've now decided to save your life.

Gilbert Towards midnight Antronius finally arrived, generally with a most
40   ominous prologue; he'd complain of a stomach-ache.

James Why was this a bad omen?

Gilbert Because then there was nothing to eat – for what would you expect of a host who felt ill?

James Was he really sick?

Gilbert So sick he'd have devoured three capons by himself if someone had
5   made him a present of them.

James I'm waiting for the feast.

Gilbert First he was served a dish of bean meal, the sort of sops commonly sold there to the poor. He said he used this as a cure for every kind of ailment.

10 **James** How many of you guests were there?

Gilbert At times eight or nine, among whom was the learned Verpius[25] (not unknown to you, I believe) and the elder son of the household.

James What were they served?

Gilbert Isn't the fare Melchisedek offered to Abraham,[26] victor over five
15   kings, good enough for ordinary mortals?

James Nothing by way of sops, then?

Gilbert Something.

James What?

Gilbert We numbered nine guests at table,[27] I remember, though in the dish I
20   counted only seven tiny lettuce leaves swimming in vinegar, but without oil.

James So he ate his beans by himself?

Gilbert He had bought scarcely halfpennyworth, yet he didn't object if someone sitting by him wanted to taste them. But it seemed impolite to take the poor fellow's food away from him.

25 **James** Were the lettuce leaves chopped up, as the adage says of cumin?[28]

Gilbert No, but after the lettuce was eaten by the first comers, the other diners dipped their bread in vinegar.

James What followed the seven lettuce leaves?

Gilbert Why, a cheese, of course: the finale of feasts.

30 **James** Was this always the fare?

Gilbert Nearly always, except that once in a while, if he'd been lucky in business that day, it was a little more elaborate.

James What had you then?

Gilbert He'd order three bunches of fresh grapes for a copper, an event that
35   would overwhelm the entire family with joy.

James Why not?

Gilbert This was done only when grapes were cheapest there.

James Then except in autumn he squandered nothing?

Gilbert Yes, he 'squandered.' The boatmen there dig up a tiny sort of
40   shellfish (especially from latrines) and hawk their wares. From time to time

he bought a farthing's worth (what they call a *bagattino*) from them. Then truly you'd have said there was a wedding feast in that household, since a fire was needed (although the shellfish are very quickly cooked). These were served after the cheese as dessert.[29]

5   **James** A distinguished dessert, by Hercules! But you never got meat or fish?
Gilbert In the end, when overcome by my complaints, he began to be extravagant. Whenever he wished to pose as a Lucullus[30] the courses were usually these –
James I can hardly wait to hear this, you may be sure.

10   **Gilbert** – first a soup was served, called – I don't know why – *minèstra*.[31]
James Rich, I dare say.
Gilbert Seasoned with spices, as follows. A pot of water, with some pieces of buffalo cheese[32] tossed in, was put on the fire – the cheese so aged it was hard as a rock; you'd need a good sharp ax to break it. When these pieces

15   start to melt in the hot water they discolour it; no longer can it be called mere water. This broth is their appetizer.
James Fit for hogs.
Gilbert Next on the menu is a piece of old tripe, boiled a fortnight earlier.
James Rotten, then.

20   **Gilbert** Of course, but there's a remedy for that.
James What?
Gilbert I'll tell you, but I'm afraid you'll copy it.
James Certainly I will.
Gilbert They beat an egg in warm water and soak the meat in this broth,

25   so your eyes are fooled more than your nose, for the stench gets through everything. If it's a fish day, they sometimes serve three giltheads – not big ones, though, despite seven or eight diners.
James Nothing else?
Gilbert Nothing except that rocklike cheese.

30   **James** You tell me of a new kind of Lucullus. But could such slender fare be enough for so many diners, especially when they had tasted no breakfast?
Gilbert What's more – I don't want you to miss this point – mother-in-law, daughter-in-law, younger son, maidservant, and several youngsters were fed on the leftovers from this feast.

35   **James** Well, you've aroused my wonder but not dispelled it.
Gilbert I can scarcely describe the scene to you unless I first sketch the arrangement of the feast.
James Sketch it, then.
Gilbert Antronius was at the head, though I sat at his right as if I were the

40   guest of honour; opposite Antronius, Orthrogonus, with Verpius beside him;

Strategus the Greek[33] beside Verpius. On Antronius' left sat his elder son;[34] if some dinner guest arrived, the place was yielded to him out of respect.

To begin with, there was very little danger of running out of broth and little difference in the servings, except that pieces of the buffalo cheese
5   floated in the dishes of the principal diners. But a sort of barricade was made of the water and wine jars, usually four in number, to prevent anyone – except the three before whom the bowl was set – from touching what was served. Anyone else who touched it would have been treated as absolutely brazen and as a trespasser.[35] After a short stay this bowl was carried off, in
10   order that something might be left for the family.

James What did the rest eat, then?

Gilbert They feasted sumptuously, as a rule.

James How?

Gilbert They soaked that chalky bread in the very mustiest wine.
15   **James** A feast like that must have been decidedly brief.

Gilbert Often it lasted over an hour.

James How could it?

Gilbert After removal, as I said, of what was in danger of being eaten, cheese was served. No danger of anyone's being able to slice any of it with a
20   knife! That choice musty wine and everybody's sop of bread remained on the table, and over this dessert stories went safely round. Meanwhile the distaff side were having their meal.

James What of the workers all this while?

Gilbert They had no connection with us. They lunched and supped at their
25   own hours but spent scarcely half an hour a day on meals.

James What sort of fare had they?

Gilbert That's for you to guess.

James But the Germans can hardly get through breakfast in an hour. They need the same amount of time for a snack, an hour and a half for lunch, two
30   hours for dinner;[36] and unless they're well filled with choice wine, good meat, and fish, they quit their master and run off to war.[37]

Gilbert Every nation has its own customs.[38] The Italians spend very little on food or drink;[39] they prefer money to pleasure[40] and are sober by nature as well as habit.
35   **James** Well, I'm no longer surprised you came back to us so thin, but I'm amazed that you came back alive at all, especially since you'd been used to capons, partridges, doves, and pheasants.

Gilbert Undoubtedly I'd have died had not a remedy been found.

James It's a bad business that needs so many remedies.
40   **Gilbert** Since I was now wasting away, I arranged to have a quarter of a boiled chicken at each meal.

James Now you'll begin to live!

Gilbert Not quite. To save money, they bought a thin little chicken; half a dozen of that kind wouldn't have made a breakfast for one Polander with a good appetite. And they wouldn't feed it after they bought it – too expensive! So they cooked a wing or leg of the half-starved bird; the liver they gave to Orthrogonus' young boy,[41] but the broth, with more water constantly added to it, was drunk again and again by the women. And so a joint drier than pumice, and more tasteless than a rotten stick, came to me. The broth was nothing but water.

James Yet I hear that poultry there is very plentiful, choice, and cheap.

Gilbert True, but they love money more.[42]

James You were punished enough even if you'd killed the pope or desecrated St Peter's tomb.[43]

Gilbert But hear the story out. You know we eat meat five days a week.

James Of course.

Gilbert Therefore they bought only two chickens. On Thursday they'd pretend they forgot to buy them, to avoid serving a whole chicken on that day and having anything left over.

James Well, this Antronius beats Plautus' Euclio.[44] But how did you contrive to save your life on fish days?

Gilbert I had arranged for a friend to buy me three eggs every day at my cost, two for lunch and one for dinner. But – once more – the women substituted half-rotten ones for the expensive fresh ones, so that I counted myself very lucky if one out of three was edible. And finally, I'd bought with my own money a skin of better wine, but the women broke into my room and drank it up within a few days – not that Antronius minded.

James So nobody there felt sorry for you?

Gilbert Sorry? Far from it. To them I seemed a glutton and a gormandizer to consume so much food by myself. Consequently Orthrogonus often warned me to follow the custom of the country and to take thought for my health, and he called to mind some of our acquaintances whose gluttony had brought them to death or a terrible disease. When he saw me bolstering my feeble body with certain dainties (made of pine nuts[45] or pumpkin and melon seeds and sold by pharmacists there), a body broken by incessant labour, undernourishment, and now even disease, he'd secretly prevail upon my good friend the doctor to advise me to eat more lightly.[46] And the man earnestly did so. I soon sensed that he'd been put up to it, but I said nothing. When he became more insistent on the subject and wouldn't stop admonishing me, I said, 'Tell me, my good friend,[47] do you mean this or are you joking?' 'I'm serious,' he replied. 'Then what are you trying to get me to do?' 'Give up dinner entirely and make your wine at least half water.' At this advice I laughed and said, 'If you want to kill me off, it would be fatal for this poor, lean, excessively delicate body to miss a single dinner. I've learned this so often by experience that I daren't try it again. What do you suppose will happen if, after the sort of lunch I eat, I abstain from dinner? And you

5 bid me add water to the sort of wine I drink? As if it wouldn't be better to drink pure water than bad wine! I've no doubt Orthrogonus ordered you to tell me this.' The doctor smiled and toned down his advice. 'I don't tell you these things, most learned Gilbert, to make you cut out dinners entirely. You may eat an egg and take one drink; that's how *I* live. For dinner I have an egg

10 boiled; then I take half the yolk and give the rest to my son. Next I drink off half a cup of wine – and I study until late at night.'

James The doctor wasn't telling the truth, was he?

Gilbert The absolute truth. Once I happened to be walking down the street on my way home from church and a companion remarked that the doctor lived

15 nearby. I was curious to see his domain. Now this was on a Sunday. I knocked at the door; it was opened; I entered and encountered the doctor eating lunch with his son and the servant. The fare was two eggs – nothing else.

James They must have been bloodless men.

Gilbert On the contrary, they were well built, with good colour, rosy cheeks,

20 and sparkling eyes.

James It's hardly credible.

Gilbert But I'm telling you exactly what I found. And he's not the only man who lives like that; many others, of distinguished family and fortune, do the same. Heavy eating and drinking, believe me, are matters of habit, not of

25 nature. If one worked up to it by stages, one could, in the end, match Milo's feat of consuming a whole ox in a single day.[48]

James Good Lord! If you can preserve your health on such a slim diet, how much money the Germans, English, Danes, and Poles must waste.

Gilbert A lot, unquestionably, and not without serious injury to both mental

30 and physical health.

James But why wasn't that diet good enough for you?

Gilbert Because I was accustomed to different ones, and it was too late to change my habit. The scarcity of the food, however, did not bother me so much as the badness of it. Two eggs would have sufficed had they been

35 fresh; one cup of wine was enough had not musty dregs been served up for wine; half a loaf of bread would have sustained me had not chalk been served instead of bread.

James Is Antronius so stingy when he's so rich?

Gilbert His fortune amounted to not less than eighty thousand ducats,[49] I

40 believe, and there wasn't a single year in which he failed to increase it by a thousand ducats at least.

James But the young men for whom he made all this money weren't so stingy, were they?

Gilbert Yes, but only at home. Away from home they lived high, whored, gambled, and while the father grumbled at spending a farthing on the most honourable guests, the young fellows sometimes lost sixty ducats a night at dice.[50]

James That's how riches scraped together by miserliness generally disappear. But after safely surviving such great dangers where are you off to now?

Gilbert To the delightful company of the French,[51] to make up for lost time.

NOTES

1 James and Gilbert cannot be identified confidently, but it is reasonable to think the name Gilbert is borrowed from Gilbert Cousin (Gilbertus Cognatus), who was at this time one of Erasmus' secretaries; on him see the introduction to 'The Master's Bidding.'

2 *Adagia* IV iv 16

3 *syphar*, a Greek word Gilbert Cousin uses of Erasmus in a Greek epigram (see Preserved Smith *Erasmus: A Study of His Life, Ideals and Place in History* [New York and London 1923; repr New York 1962] 407). On this proverbial term see *Adagia* I i 26 and I iii 56.

4 Cf 'Courtship' 258:27–31 and 'Charon' 822:31–2.

5 This name, here denoting Venice, is a variant of *synodus*, a meeting-place, whether for ecclesiastics or scholars (as above in 'The Philological Society') or of traders. Here it has both meanings, for Venice was a major commercial centre and prominent in the printing and publishing of scholarly and literary works, as Erasmus often reminds us. A description of the city in the last decade of the fifteenth century, about the time Aldo Manuzio arrived there, can be found in Arnold von Harff's journal of his pilgrimage to Jerusalem; on this see 'Rash Vows' n3. Erasmus is not concerned in this dialogue with Venice as a city renowned for its art, wealth, and political importance; his interest here lies in the attractions and resources of Venice for classical scholars like himself. On these and related topics a good place to begin is D.J. Geanakoplos *Greek Scholars in Venice*; Martin Lowry's copious bibliography in his *The World of Aldus Manutius* can be consulted for other studies (on these see also the introduction 981–2 above).

6 See 983:32–3 below.

7 Also the name of the blustering abbot in 'The Abbot and the Learned Lady.' 'Antronius' is synonymous with 'ass,' but in the proverb (*Adagia* II v 68) where it is discussed, the name implies corpulence as well as asininity. Andrea Torresani di Asola (1451–1528) in the present colloquy is far from stupid and is not gross in the sense that the well-fed abbot in the earlier dialogue is. Rather, he is an 'Antronius' because of his stubbornness and stinginess or, to give it a

better name, his single-mindedness. For despite all his unamiable traits, he is shrewd and conspicuously successful (as was Andrea Torresani).

Torresani, often called Asulano or Asulanus, was printing in Venice, as early as the 1470s, Latin books on law, philosophy, and literature. Although many details of his association with Aldo Manuzio remain obscure, the two men appear to have become partners in 1495, a decade earlier than was formerly assumed (Lowry [introduction 981–2 above] 82–6, 103 n50). There was a third partner too: Pierfrancesco Barbarigo, son of a Venetian doge. He took no part in printing operations, but his capital and influence in the company were clearly essential. Torresani had more technical and commercial experience than Aldo Manuzio, but to Erasmus and the literary humanists of his age, as to ours, the Aldine press meant Aldo Manuzio, not Torresani, who had little classical or literary knowledge. None the less the two printers were closely associated – Aldo married a daughter of Torresani in 1505 – and the combination of their individual talents brought them success. By the time of Aldo Manuzio's death in 1515, Torresani had been converted, so to speak, to the significance of Aldo's interests, particularly Greek, and endeavoured to preserve them in his publishing, as he informs Erasmus (see Ep 589). After Aldo's death, Torresani brought out Pausanias, a Greek New Testament, the *editio princeps* of Aeschylus, and Galen, all of which, as editorial projects, were probably begun in Aldo's lifetime.

8 A classical commonplace. See *Adagia* II iii 43 and 'The Shipwreck' n2.
9 Greek in the original
10 Cf *Adagia* I x 11: *Sacrum sine fumo* 'A smokeless sacrifice,' said of a dinner that has no cooked food – a thin meal, short commons.
11 *Mercurialem*, dedicated to or under the patronage of Mercury, god of commerce and thievery. See *Adagia* IV vii 2, 4
12 Apelles, according to Pliny *Naturalis historia* 35.84; see *Adagia* I iv 12 and *Parabolae* LB I 601C / CWE 23 228:11–12.
13 Erasmus in 1523 and 1526 dated his first attacks of kidney stone to his Venetian days. See Allen and CWE Ep 1349:2–4 and *Adagia* II i i LB II 405C.
14 By fair means or foul; see *Adagia* I ix 12.
15 *Adagia* III i 91; Allen Ep 2899:44
16 Orthrogonus. See n22 below.
17 Excluding guests, members of the family, and servants leaves about fifteen persons who were workmen in the printing shop.
18 Potter's earth
19 Self-explanatory, but possibly a memory also of Matt 4:3 or Luke 4:3
20 *Adagia* I x 71; see 'Military Affairs' n28.
21 Two or three hours later than the customary time for *prandium*. For another complaint about meals delayed see 'Inns' 371:26–7 and the description that follows. On the usual hours for meals see 'The Godly Feast' n15.
22 Aldo Manuzio. His name in this dialogue is 'compounded of the Greek words for "dawn" or "early morning" and "born," as if Manutius were derived from *mane* and *natus*' (Smith *Key* 53).

Erasmus completed the 1508 edition of the *Adagia* when writing in Aldo's printing shop. *Adagia* II i 1: *Festina lente* 'Make haste slowly' contains a long description of an ancient coin belonging to Aldo that showed a dolphin wound about an anchor – a symbol that became familiar to readers everywhere as the trademark of the Aldine press. Erasmus explains the meanings of this symbol and why it is so appropriate to Aldo Manuzio and his work. These comments are followed by an encomium of Aldo's splendid services to classical learning. In the 1526 edition Erasmus added a long passage in praise of good printing in general and of Aldo in particular, naming Johann Froben as a worthy successor to Aldo and calling attention to Froben's equally familiar symbol or trademark, the serpent and dove.

23 The wine described at 983:39–984:14

24 *Adagia* IV i 70. A Greek idiom, Erasmus says, but the only example cited is Plautus *Aulularia* 336.

25 'Circumcised,' meaning Girolamo Aleandro, whom Erasmus liked to taunt by pretending to believe he was a Jew. Aleandro (1480–1542), a precocious student, once taught Hebrew in Venice, a fact that lent some colour to Erasmus' epithet. An appointment (1503) in the household of Domenico Grimani, bishop and later cardinal, gave Aleandro an early start up the ladder of preferment. Young as he was, he was praised for his learning by Aldo Manuzio, who dedicated to him the Aldine edition of Homer (1504). A few years later he assisted in the preparation of the edition of Plutarch's *Moralia*. In 1508 he shared a room with Erasmus, with whom he was then on cordial terms. Thence on to Paris, where he taught with success (1508–13) and became principal of a college. After that he was secretary to bishops and became Vatican librarian. When his patron, Cardinal Giulio de' Medici, became Pope Clement VII, Aleandro was made archbishop of Brindisi (1524). Finally, in 1536, he became a cardinal.

Like his good friend Alberto Pio, Aleandro in his later years was severely critical of Erasmus' religious writings and opinions and a vigorous enemy of Lutheranism. When papal legate to the Diet of Worms in 1521, he considered Erasmus worse than Luther. Erasmus, he declared, was the source of all the troubles (*fomes malorum*) caused by Luther (*Aleander und Luther, 1521 . . .* ed Th. Brieger [Gotha 1884] I 51–4, 82). He even accused Erasmus of having written Luther's *De captivitate Babylonica ecclesiae* (1520); see Allen Ep 1218:1–21 / CWE Ep 1218:1–24. But when the papal bull *Decet Romanum pontificem* – pronouncing on Luther the sentence of excommunication threatened in *Exsurge Domine* (June 1520) – was signed in Rome in January 1521, Aleandro deliberately withheld publication of it for six months or longer. It seemed to him so drastic, so explosive, that he sent it back to Rome to be toned down. See Thompson *Inquisitio de fide* 5, 22–3, 78–9.

26 Bread and wine; see Gen 14:18–20.

27 On this number see 'The Profane Feast' n102.

28 'A slicer of cumin' was a niggardly fellow, a miser; *Adagia* II i 5.

29 *bellaria*. Also at 988:21 below; Gellius 13.11.6–7.

30 Roman general and statesman noted for wealth and luxury; see 'The Profane Feast' n18.

31 Any of many kinds of soup, but at this meal decidedly meagre fare

32 Mozzarella cheese, made from the milk of water buffalo

33 Probably Caesar Strategus, who was a copier of manuscripts in Florence and Venice. See CEBR.

34 Gianfrancesco Torresani (c 1480–1558), who succeeded his father as head of the printing house in 1528. He quarrelled with Aldo's son and successor, Paolo, for a time, but afterwards they collaborated until 1539, when the firm was dissolved. See CEBR.

35 *Adagia* I x 93

36 On German meals see 'Inns' 371:26–375:4, and cf 'Charon' 824:17–22.

37 If German labourers did so, even though they had plenty to eat, it is not surprising that workers in the Aldine shop sometimes deserted. Aldo was not an easy master. See Lowry 55–6.

38 *Adagia* IV iii 25: *Mores hominum regioni respondent*

39 So *Ecclesiastes* LB V 916C. This is a contrast with the swilling Germans ('Inns' n28).

40 The French also are parsimonious. See 'The Profane Feast' 139:39 and n46.

41 Aldo Manuzio had three sons. The oldest, and the only one Erasmus could have known, was Manuzio (1506–68). He must be the person meant here. He joined his brothers in the family business for a short time and later held a benefice, but seems to have failed at whatever he undertook. The second son, Antonio (1511–59), was an agent for the firm in Bologna, but he too was unsuccessful. The true heir of Aldo Manuzio as a scholar and printer, and the only son who prospered, was his youngest son Paolo (1512–74), who printed in Venice until 1558, when he moved to Rome and carried on the business there until his death. See CEBR.

42 A friend who had visited Venice recently told Erasmus in February 1532 that at the Torresani establishment *opulentia sordida* still prevailed: the place reeked of money (Allen Ep 2594:12–16).

43 *Adagia* II viii 23. Here as in 'A Marriage in Name Only' 845:36 the translation is a euphemism for 'urinated on,' an act of shocking contempt for the person buried there and for the meaning and principles of his life – the supreme insult.

44 The old miser in Plautus' *Aulularia*

45 The edible seeds of various pine trees

46 Typical advice of an Italian physician, according to *Ecclesiastes* LB V 875D. German doctors, on the other hand, like to bleed you or send you to the public baths (on which see 'Inns' n20).

47 Ambrogio Leoni (Ambrosius Leo), a physician who turned to Greek studies. He was physician to Aldo's family when Erasmus was in Venice. Erasmus praises his learning in *Adagia* I ii 63 (LB II 95F) and II iii 50. One letter from him to Erasmus and one from Erasmus to him survive (Epp 854, 868), both of 1518.

48 One of the anecdotes told of Milo of Croton (*Adagia* II iii 10; cf I ii 51). He was a famous athlete (sixth century BC), who is said to have won at six or seven Olympic games and six times at the Pythian games. See *De copia* CWE 24 303:13–17, 392:1, 591:1–2, and *Adagia* II iv (misnumbered in LB II) 43, 44 and III x 85.

49 How Erasmus arrived at this figure it is idle to inquire. He may have heard of it as gossip or may have simply plucked it out of the air. No matter, for the rhetorical effect, which is like that of 'He's a millionaire' in our idiom, fits the impression of Torresani gained from the preceding pages. He hoarded money as skilfully as he made it.

The Venetian gold ducat was an 'international medium of exchange *par excellence*' (CWE 1 314). What its purchasing power today would be is not easily answered, but its comparative value in Erasmus' time gives some inkling of what he is saying when he speaks of eighty thousand ducats. A proofreader in fifteenth-century Venice earned four to six ducats monthly. The printer (Paganinis) of Nicholas of Lyra's commentary on the Bible (1492) claimed to have spent four thousand ducats producing the book. The brothers Giunti, printers in Florence and Venice, had joint assets of between twelve and fifteen thousand ducats in 1505. Rent for Torresani's house and shop appears to have been sixty ducats per year. The five volumes of Aldo Manuzio's Aristotle cost one and a half to three ducats each; Gaza's Greek grammar sold for one ducat. (These figures are from Lowry 13, 116, 156, 94, 115; see also 98–100 on the expenses of the household and printing shop.)

50 For evidence that Torresani's sons were fond of gambling see Curt F. Bühler 'Some Documents concerning the Torresani and the Aldine Press' *The Library* 4th series 25 (1944–5) 118–20.

51 Where he can be sure of a cordial welcome and good food. See 'Inns' 370:1–37 on French hospitality.

THE SERAPHIC FUNERAL

Exequiae seraphicae

First printed in the September 1531 edition.

Like the earlier dialogue on Reuchlin this colloquy is a work of creative imagination but based on historical fact. It is one document of many that would merit attention in a comprehensive study of Erasmus' relations with the Franciscan order and his judgment of their claims. He knew and approved of some Franciscans – Vitrier, for example – and presents two worthy Observant Franciscans in 'The Well-to-do Beggars.' More often, however, they are the objects of his criticism, as in 'The Sermon' and the present colloquy. For in recent years (1528–31) he had been the target of repeated attacks and denigration by Observant theologians. His irritation is noticeable in the correspondence of those years (see for example Allen Epp 1968:37–48, 2037:208–18, 2094:1–5, 2126:160–74, 2205:175–263, 2263:105–14, 2275:1–76, 2299:136–47, 2301:15–26, 2315:256–77, 2466:30–5), and in many pages of his controversial works and in the *Colloquies* he comments sharply, at times resentfully, about attacks by Franciscans on his religious opinions and writings.

A 'seraphic funeral' is one in which the corpse is buried in the Franciscan habit, as contrasted with *pro laico sepultura* (see Allen Ep 2449:92–3, 'The Sermon' n2, and n4 below). The occasion of this colloquy was the dying and burial in Franciscan dress of Alberto Pio (c 1475–1531), hereditary prince of Carpi (near Modena in northern Italy), at Paris in January 1531. The antecedent cause was a long quarrel between Erasmus and Alberto Pio. Alberto was a person of distinction: nephew of Pico della Mirandola; in youth a pupil and later a patron of Aldo Manuzio, who dedicated to him his great edition of Aristotle (1495–8); a man of letters well connected in learned circles; a diplomat in the service of Louis XII of France, then of Maximilian the German emperor, and later of Francis I. He survived the sack of Rome in 1527 but lost his estates and princedom of Carpi in the Italian wars. Erasmus, who enjoyed discovering facetious etymologies, decided that Alberto was called Carpensis *a carpendi libidine* 'from his passion for finding fault' and 'Pio' because of his posture of devoutness in donning Franciscan dress three days before his death (Allen Ep 2466:103–8; cf *Apologia adversus rhapsodias Alberti Pii* LB IX 1125A–B).

In October 1525 Erasmus heard that he had been slandered in Rome by Girolamo Aleandro (on whom see the introduction to 'Penny-Pinching' 980–1) and Alberto Pio. Aleandro's disparagements were circulated in manuscript but apparently not printed (Allen Epp 1744:129–36, 1804:248–54). Whereupon Erasmus wrote to Alberto, complaining of reports that Alberto had accused him of being ignorant of philosophy and theology and – even worse – was charging him with heavy responsibility for some of Luther's teachings (Allen Ep 1634:10–15, 69–74). Charges of this kind were nothing new; they had been made by other critics too, but that fact did not deter Erasmus from taking offence and defending himself vigorously in a pamphlet warfare that lasted as long as he lived. Alberto answered Erasmus' reproach with a *Responsio accurata et paraenetica* ... (May 1526; whether it was printed before the Paris 1529 edition is uncertain, but Erasmus evidently saw a manuscript copy). Alberto credited Erasmus with services to literature but insisted that he had injured orthodox religion.

Erasmus went to work at once on a reply, *Responsio ad epistolam paraeneticam Alberti Pii* (Basel, March 1529; text in LB IX 1095A–1122E). When this publication reached Alberto, he read it with predictable indignation and set about as promptly as illness allowed to prepare a counter-attack intended to devastate Erasmus' claims: *Alberti Pii Carporum ... tres et viginti libri ... in locos lucubrationum variarum D. Erasmi* (Paris 1531). After commenting on Erasmus' *Responsio*, he lists in twenty-three sections what he perceived to be errors by Erasmus on many subjects: monasticism, churches, clergy, marriage, and confession, among others. Alberto died in January 1531, before his book was printed; it came out in March of that year. It was an important contribution to the polemical literature of the Reformation, for, as Professor Gilmore writes, this was 'perhaps the most compete expression of the thesis that Erasmus prepared the Reformation and shared the religious opinions of Luther' ('Erasmus and Alberto Pio, Prince of Carpi' in *Action and Conviction in Early Modern Europe* ed Theodore K. Rabb and J.E. Seigel [Princeton 1969] 313). Alberto, needless to say, had supporters who urged him on; among them, Erasmus says, were the Franciscans of Paris (Allen Ep 2443:336–40).

Even though he knew of Alberto's death, Erasmus wanted to have the last word. He hurriedly composed an *Apologia adversus rhapsodias ... Alberti Pii* (Basel: Froben, June 1531; text reprinted with a different title, probably of Leclerc's devising, in LB IX 1123A–1196D). He answers Alberto's charges seriatim and once more sets forth his own views and why these are valid. The peroration of this apology (LB IX 1196A–D) is unusually harsh for Erasmus, and is intended to be harsh. But he did not have the satisfaction of writing the last word in the controversy after all, for Juan Ginés de Sepúlveda (1491–1572), a friend and client of Alberto, brought out an *Antapologia pro Alberto Pio in Erasmum* (Rome and Paris, March 1532). On Sepúlveda see Allen Ep 2637 introduction and CEBR.

Well before Sepúlveda's defence of Alberto Pio's work appeared, however, a timely coincidence inspired Erasmus to write of his adversary in a different and more effective though characteristic manner. He knew, no later than 6 March 1531, of Alberto's death in January of that year, and also of his burial in Franciscan garb (Allen Ep 2441:64–70). He says on 27 March that he has not yet seen Alberto's posthumous publication against him (Allen Ep 2466:115), but it must have come to hand soon afterwards. In any event he could not have written 'The Seraphic Funeral' before learning the essential fact of Alberto's dying as a Franciscan by intention. Therefore this colloquy was in all probability written between March and September. In the September 1531 edition it was next to last among five new colloquies.

Here then was Erasmus' opportunity not only to strike again at an enemy (whom death had already dispatched) with well-tried weapons of satire and irony, but to raise fundamental questions about Franciscan claims and customs. The purpose of this satire, as he takes pains to make clear, is to correct ignorance and misconduct, to emphasize the difference between the ideals of Francis and the questionable practices of some of his followers. For the claim made by Theotimus, the eulogist and expositor of the benefit of dying in Franciscan dress, is unequivocal: 'A man who makes a profession is instantly enriched by the surpassing merits of the whole order; he is assuredly grafted to the body of a most holy company' (1004:37–9). Friends who shared Erasmus' opinions undoubtedly welcomed such a dialogue. One of them, Johann Koler (Choler, Coler), a canon of Augsburg and frequent correspondent of Erasmus, may have contributed to the shaping of this colloquy when, in a letter of 26 June 1531 expressing impatience to read Erasmus' *Apologia adversus rhapsodias Alberti Pii* (published in that same month), he added that news of the dying Alberto's receiving Franciscan dress reminded him of George in Erasmus' colloquy 'The Funeral,' who did the same (Allen Ep 2505:55–60).

Writing on 5 March 1531 to a bishop and sometime papal secretary, Jacopo Sadoleto, Erasmus reports that Alberto Pio died with his new book against Erasmus unprinted. 'That is surely, as the proverb says, "to throw your javelin and flee"' (or 'to shoot and run'; *Adagia* i i 5, repeated in Allen Epp 2443:346, 2466:102). To another friend he writes of Alberto, 'I hope his soul finds delights among seraphic minds. For his body, three days before his death, was adorned with Franciscan dress and in that finery was carried through the streets of the city on the shoulders of Franciscans, in solemn procession, to a monastery, with none of the rites omitted that are customarily performed for the true sons of Francis' (Allen Ep 2441:69–76). 'I pray God to have mercy on his soul and I hope he will find better defenders in the presence of the supreme Judge than he himself provided for the French against the emperor or for the pope against the emperor's forces, or for himself in protecting his princedom' (Allen Ep 2443:347–50). Again: 'Not without reason was he styled "Pius." Three days before his death he donned the robe of St Francis and in that dress was borne on the shoulders of Franciscans through the streets – face, feet, and hands bare – and buried in a monastery. I don't belittle the man's preference for the religious life (it's common with Italians), but I marvel that those fathers [the friars], although not unaware of what this age is like, provoke ill will towards themselves by such ceremonies (superstitions, rather) when that is already more than sufficiently vehement of itself' (Allen Ep 2466:106–14).

Finally, on 20 August 1531, Erasmus writes to another friend to tell him of the 'big book of Alberto Pio, once prince of Carpi, then exile in France, next a sycophant, finally a Franciscan . . . So much for me, as though I condemned everything the church does or teaches! Nor had the man, a prince aged and long sinking to the grave, a sense of shame. Now at last, conjoined with the seraphic band, he spreads deadly slander by his obvious falsehoods' (Allen Ep 2522:65–72; cf *Apologia adversus rhapsodias Albertii Pii* LB IX 1123A–E). 'The Seraphic Funeral' appeared in print a few weeks after these words were written. The polite voice and ironic tone in that dialogue are wholly appropriate to its purpose, but passages like the one just quoted reveal the bitterness Erasmus still felt towards Alberto Pio.

On Pio consult Allen Ep 1634 introduction, CEBR, and studies by Myron P. Gilmore: 'Erasmus and Alberto Pio, Prince of Carpi' in Rabb and Seigel *Action and Conviction* 299–318; '*De modis disputandi*: The Apologetic Works of Erasmus' in *Florilegium historiale* ed J.G. Rose and W.H. Stockdale (Toronto 1971) 75–82; a later version of this article appears in *Colloquia Erasmiana Turonensia* II 725–32. See also Gilmore's 'Italian Reactions to Erasmian Humanism' in *Itinerarium Italicum* ed H.A. Oberman and Thomas A. Brady Jr (Leiden 1975) 70–84, and '*Apologiae*: Erasmus's Defenses of Folly' in *Essays on the Works of Erasmus* ed Richard L. DeMolen (New Haven and London 1978) 111–23.

An English translation of *Exequiae seraphicae*, printed by John Byddell probably c 1534, was recorded in 1595, but no copy is now known. See Devereux 68 no 4.11.

THEOTIMUS AND PHILECOUS[1]

Philecous Where does our Theotimus come from with his new religious look?

5   **Theotimus** New? How so?

Philecous Because of the stern brow, eyes glued to the ground, head inclined somewhat to the left shoulder,[2] rosary in your hands.[3]

Theotimus If you wish to know what's none of your business, my friend, I come from a show.

Philecous Did you see a rope artist, or a magician, or something of that sort?

5 **Theotimus** Not so very different from that, perhaps.

Philecous Well, I've never before seen anyone back from a show with this sort of countenance.

Theotimus But this show was of such a kind that had you been there, you might have turned up even gloomier than I am.

10 **Philecous** Then tell me, won't you, what's made you so devout?

Theotimus I'm returning from a seraphic funeral.

Philecous What do I hear? So angels die too?

Theotimus No, but their partners do.[4] But – not to keep you in suspense any longer – you're acquainted, I suppose, with that learned and distinguished

15 man Eusebius,[5] here in Pelusium?[6]

Philecous The one who was deprived of his office as ruler and from a private citizen became an exile, from an exile virtually a beggar – I had almost added, toady?[7]

Theotimus A good guess.

20 **Philecous** But what happened to him?

Theotimus He was buried today. I'm on my way home from his funeral.

Philecous Must have been quite a sad affair to send you back to us so sad.

Theotimus I fear I can't hold back the tears in describing for you what I've seen.

25 **Philecous** Yet I fear I can't listen without laughter. But do tell me, please.

Theotimus You're aware that Eusebius had long been in wretched health.

Philecous I know that for some years he had been very feeble.

Theotimus In diseases of this kind, which gradually destroy a man, doctors can usually predict the day of death by means of certain tell-tale signs.

30 **Philecous** Of course.

Theotimus They warned the man that everything medical science could do to help him had been done with the utmost care; that God was more powerful than all the resources of physicians; but that by the best human calculation he wouldn't last over three days.[8]

35 **Philecous** What happened then?

Theotimus Straightway the distinguished Eusebius clothes his poor, weak body in complete Franciscan dress; he receives the tonsure, puts on an ashen cowl, a robe of the same colour, a knotted cord, and sandals.[9]

Philecous He's going to die?

40 **Theotimus** Yes. And what's more, he promises in a voice already that of a dying man to enlist as Christ's soldier according to the Franciscan Rule if –

contrary to doctors' expectations – God should grant him life.[10] Witnesses, men noted for their holiness, are fetched for this profession. In this garb the eminent man dies at the time foretold by the doctors. A good many members of the order come to take part in the funeral procession.

5   **Philecous** I wish I had been present at that spectacle!

Theotimus You'd have wept to see how devotedly the seraphic brethren bathed the corpse, fitted that holy garment on it, crossed his hands, bared the feet and kissed them, and even brightened the face with ointment according to gospel precept.[11]

10   **Philecous** A marvellous humility for seraphic men to act as undertakers and pallbearers!

Theotimus After this they laid him on a bier, and in accordance with Paul's teaching, 'Bear ye one another's burdens,'[12] the brethren bore their brother on their own shoulders through the street to the monastery. There they

15   buried him with solemn dirges. When that holy procession was moving along the street, I observed many persons weeping in spite of themselves at the sight of such a man, whom earlier they had seen clad in purple and fine linen,[13] now in Franciscan clothing, girded with a hempen cord and made to look so devout from head to foot. For the dead man's head was

20   bent towards his shoulder[14] and (as I said) his hands were placed one across the other. Everything else likewise showed an awesome religious feeling. Yes, and the seraphic company itself, with heads bowed, eyes fixed on the ground, and dirges so mournful that I should think the very ghosts of the dead could not howl more dolefully, drew tears and sobs from many

25   people.

Philecous But didn't he have the five wounds of Francis?[15]

Theotimus I couldn't swear to that. Some slightly black-and-blue marks were evident on his hands and feet and his robe had a small hole on the left side.[16] But I didn't dare look too closely, for in such matters, they say,

30   curiosity has been fatal to many.

Philecous But didn't you notice anybody laughing there?

Theotimus I did, but they were heretics, I suspect; the world's full of them these days.

Philecous To be frank with you, my dear Theotimus, I myself could scarcely

35   have refrained from laughter had I seen that sight.

Theotimus God grant you haven't been infected with this same malady!

Philecous No danger of that, my excellent Theotimus. As for me, ever since I was a boy I've always had a sincere, reverent veneration for St Francis, who by worldly standards was neither wise nor learned but was most dear to God

40   by reason of his extreme mortification of worldly desires, and along with him, for all those who, following in his footsteps, endeavour sincerely to live

St Francis receiving the stigmata
Panel painting from the workshop of Giotto
According to St Bonaventure, the stigmata were conferred
by the crucified Christ *sub specie seraph*.
Louvre, Paris

unto Christ, dead to the world.[17] The dress I care nothing about,[18] but I'd be glad to learn from you what good it does a dead man.

Theotimus You know we're commanded by the Lord himself not to cast pearls before swine or give that which is holy unto dogs.[19] If, therefore, you

5   ask for the purpose of ridicule, you'll hear nothing from me. But if you really and truly desire to learn, I'll be glad to tell you what I learned from them.

Philecous I promise to be a good, attentive, and receptive pupil.

Theotimus In the first place, you're aware that some men are so eager for prestige that they're not satisfied with having lived in proud and arrogant

10   fashion unless they can also be buried ostentatiously when they die. Dead, they have no feeling; yet while alive they take a certain pleasure and satisfaction in imagining what their funeral procession will be like. Whatever the worth of renouncing worldly ambitions, you won't, I suppose, deny a certain measure of devotion in it.

15   **Philecous** Granted, if pride in funerals can't be avoided by any other means. In my opinion, however, it's more modest for a prince when dead to be wrapped in ordinary linen, carried by common pallbearers to the public cemetery, and there interred among common corpses. For those who are borne to the grave as Eusebius was appear to have changed their pride rather

20   than to have shunned it.

Theotimus Whatever is done with good intent is pleasing to God. Yet it is his prerogative to judge the heart of man. But what I've told you is trifling. The rest is more important.

Philecous What?

25   **Theotimus** Before death they profess the Rule of Francis.

Philecous To keep it in the Elysian fields, obviously!

Theotimus No – here, if they recover. And it sometimes happens that men condemned by the verdicts of physicians do get well, by God's help, the moment they don the sacred dress.

30   **Philecous** The same thing often happens to those who don't don it.

Theotimus One must walk the way of faith in single-mindedness.[20] If there weren't exceptional profit in this custom, there wouldn't be so many men of distinguished birth and eminent scholarship, especially among the Italians, eager to be buried in the sacred garb. And – that you may not reject the

35   examples of men unknown to you – Rodolphus Agricola,[21] whom you rightly esteem very highly, was buried in this manner. So, recently, was Christopher Longolius.[22]

Philecous What men rave about when they're dying makes no difference to me. I want to learn from you what great good it does a man who is

40   overwhelmed by the terror of death and agitated by despair of the certainty of life to make the profession or put on the garb. Why are vows invalid unless

made with clear and serious intent, after mature deliberation, not under pressure of fear, fraud, or force? To avoid these dangers, such profession is not binding until after a year's probation, when the professed are ordered to wear the cloak with hood; for thus saith that seraphic man.[23] And so if they
5 recover they are not bound, for two reasons: a vow made in overwhelming dread of death or hope of life is no vow, and profession does not bind before the cowl is worn.

Theotimus Whatever the force of the bond, they certainly regard themselves as bound; and the dedication of their whole will cannot but be most pleasing
10 to God, since it is for this reason that the good works of monks – other things being equal – are more pleasing to God than are the good works of other men; because they proceed from the best source.[24]

Philecous I won't, at this time, go into the question of how important it may be for a man to dedicate himself completely to God when the matter is no
15 longer in his power.[25] I myself believe that any Christian dedicates himself completely to God in baptism when he renounces all the pomps and vanities of Satan and enlists as a soldier of Christ, to fight for him thereafter as long as life lasts.[26] And Paul, treating of those who die unto Christ, so that they now live not to themselves but to him who died for them, does not refer
20 especially to monks but to all Christians.[27]

Theotimus Your reminder about baptism is apropos, but in old times the dying were dipped in water or sprinkled.[28] By that means they were given hope of eternal life.

Philecous What bishops promise doesn't matter so much; what God may
25 be pleased to bestow is unknown to us. Had it been certain that by such sprinkling with drops of water men suddenly become citizens of heaven, what greater opportunity could there have been[29] for the worldly to indulge their wicked lusts to their heart's content all their lives and then at the last get a little sprinkling when they no longer had the power to sin?[30] But
30 if this profession corresponds to such a baptism, clearly it is planned for sinners, so they won't perish; in other words, live unto Satan and die unto Christ!

Theotimus Nay – if it is lawful to divulge any seraphic mysteries – their profession is more efficacious than that of baptism.
35 **Philecous** What do I hear?

Theotimus In baptism sins are only washed away; the soul is left pure but destitute. A man who makes a profession is instantly enriched by the surpassing merits of the whole order; he is assuredly grafted to the body of a most holy company.
40 **Philecous** So he who through baptism is grafted to the body of Christ receives nothing, either from head or body?

Theotimus Nothing from the seraphic accumulation unless he deserves it for a kindness or favour.

Philecous What angel revealed this to them?

Theotimus No angel, my good friend, but Christ himself with his own
5   mouth disclosed this and many other things personally to St Francis.

Philecous I beg you, I beseech you, in the name of our friendship, don't hesitate to share those words with me.

Theotimus They are most secret mysteries, nor is it permissible to communicate them to the profane.

10 **Philecous** What do you mean, 'profane,' my friend? I've never wished better to any order than to the seraphic one.

Theotimus But you taunt them rather offensively at times.

Philecous This in itself is proof of affection, Theotimus. Since none do that order more damage than those who live under its shadow unworthily,[31] it is
15 necessary for anyone who wishes the order well to be very angry with its subverters.

Theotimus I'm afraid of incurring Francis' anger if I blab his secrets.

Philecous What harm do you fear from that most harmless man?

Theotimus What? That he may blind me or drive me mad, as he is said to
20 have done to many who spoke against the marks of his five wounds.

Philecous So saints are more vindictive in heaven than they were on earth? Francis, I've heard, had so gentle a nature that when boys along the road put cheese, milk, rubbish, and stones into the rustic cowl hanging down his back, he was not at all offended but went along cheerful and happy.
25 And has he now become irascible and vengeful? On another day, after hearing a companion call him thief, perpetrator of sacrilege, murderer, drunkard, committer of incest, and whatever crimes the worst criminal could be accused of, he thanked the man abjectly, pleading guilty to the charges. When a friend wondered why he talked like this, he said, 'All these things
30 and worse had I done had not God's goodness preserved me.'[32] How is it he has now become vengeful?

Theotimus That's the way it is: saints reigning in heaven won't take insults. What could be more mild than Cornelius,[33] more gentle than Antony,[34] more patient than John the Baptist[35] while they lived? But now what terrible
35 afflictions they send unless they're properly venerated![36]

Philecous I'd have been readier to believe they remove maladies rather than inflict them. But what you tell me you won't be confiding to a profane person; and you may be assured I'll keep my mouth shut.

Theotimus Well, then, taking your word for that, I'll tell you the relevant
40 facts of the matter. (I beseech thee and thy brethren, O Francis, that by thy gracious favour I may lawfully declare what I have heard.) Paul, you know,

possessed a secret wisdom he uttered not in public but privately, among the perfect.[37] So too have the Franciscans certain secrets[38] they don't divulge to just anybody but impart confidentially to holy widows and other devout and chosen persons who are kind to the seraphic flock.

5   **Philecous** I await the thrice-sacred revelation.[39]

Theotimus First of all, God foretold to the seraphic patriarch that the larger the seraphic flock grew, the more abundantly he would nourish it.[40]

Philecous This immediately cancels every complaint of those who insist that the daily increase in men of this sort is a public nuisance.

10   **Theotimus** Next, he revealed that annually, on the feast day of Francis,[41] all souls, not only of the brethren who wear that sacred garb but also of those well disposed towards the order and of those deserving well of the members, would be released from the fire of purgatory.[42]

Philecous Did Christ usually converse with him so informally?

15   **Theotimus** Why not? As with a friend and companion, just as God the Father used to converse with Moses. Moses delivered to the people the law received from God. Christ promulgated the gospel law. Francis handed on to the seraphic brethren his own law, written twice by the hand of an angel.[43]

20   **Philecous** I await the third revelation.

Theotimus That excellent patriarch feared lest the enemy destroy by night the good seed which was sown and thus the wheat be rooted up with the tares. This anxiety the Lord removed, promising him he would see to it that the half-shod and rope-girded tribe should fail not, even unto the final Day

25   of Judgment.[44]

Philecous O the mercy of the Lord! Otherwise God's church had been done for. – But continue.

Theotimus Fourth, he revealed that no one of wicked life could long continue in that order.[45]

30   **Philecous** Hasn't one who lives sinfully fallen away from the order?

Theotimus No, for a wrongdoer hasn't denied Christ straightway; though men whose deeds belie their promises do deny God in some sense.[46] But whoever throws off the sacred garb has fallen away from the order irreparably.

35   **Philecous** What are we to say, then, of so many monasteries of Conventuals who possess money, who drink, dice, fornicate, and openly keep concubines at home, to say no more?

Theotimus Francis never wore habit of that shade – it's too dark! – nor did he use a girdle of white cord.[47] Therefore, when they knock at the door, it

40   shall be said, 'I know you not,' because they have no wedding garment.[48]

Philecous Is there anything more?

Theotimus So far you've heard nothing. In the fifth place, Christ revealed to him that those ill disposed towards the seraphic order – of whom, alas! there are too many – would never complete half their divinely allotted span of life unless they anticipated their end, but all would die a terrible death as
5 swiftly as possible.[49]

Philecous At various times we've seen this sort of thing happen to many others, and recently to Cardinal Matthew of Sion,[50] who used to speak and think very ill of the half-shod. He died before reaching his fiftieth year, I believe.

Theotimus You're right, but he had also attacked the cherubic order. For
10 according to report, it was due mostly to his efforts that the four Dominicans were consigned to the flames at Bern,[51] when otherwise they would have won the pope over with money.

Philecous But those men, it is said, contrived a fiction of shocking wickedness. By faked apparitions and bogus miracles they tried to persuade
15 people that the Virgin Mary had been tainted with original sin; that St Francis had not had the true marks of Christ's wounds; that those of Catherine of Siena[52] were more authentic, but that the most perfect stigmata were promised to a converted layman whom they had secretly bribed to play this role; and for the purpose of this imposture they took liberties with the host
20 and later used even clubs and poisons. In short, this plot was not the work of one monastery, they say, but of the heads of the entire order.[53]

Theotimus However that may be, God did not say without reason, 'Touch not mine anointed.'[54]

Philecous I'm waiting, if there's anything else.

25 **Theotimus** There's the sixth revelation, in which the Lord swore to him that patrons of the seraphic order, no matter how sinfully they lived, would nevertheless obtain the Lord's mercy sooner or later and would close a wicked life with a blessed end.[55]

Philecous Even if they were killed when caught in the act of adultery?[56]

30 **Theotimus** What the Lord hath promised cannot fail of accomplishment.

Philecous But precisely how do they measure patronage and good will, then?

Theotimus Oh, you're uncertain about that? Whoever gives something, provides food or clothing, has long loved the order.

35 **Philecous** Doesn't one who gives instruction and admonition love it?

Theotimus They've plenty of that at home; and such favours they're in the habit of conferring on others, not accepting from others.

Philecous Then the Lord has promised more to the disciples of Francis than to his own. If a kindness is done to any Christian for his sake, he suffers it to
40 be ascribed to him,[57] but he does not promise eternal life to those who live wickedly.

Theotimus Nothing wonderful about that, my friend, for the utmost power of the gospel was reserved to this order. But now listen to the seventh and last revelation.

Philecous I'm here.

5 **Theotimus** The Lord swore to him that no one who died in seraphic garb would come to a bad end.[58]

Philecous But what do you call a bad end?

Theotimus A man comes to a bad end if his soul, after leaving the body, is borne straight to hell, from which there is no redemption.

10 **Philecous** So the garb does not release one from the fire of purgatory?

Theotimus No, unless one dies on the feast day of St Francis.[59] But does protection against hell seem a small matter to you?

Philecous For my part, I think it a very great matter indeed. But what's to be thought of those who are dressed in the sacred garb after they're already

15 dead? They don't *die* in it.

Theotimus If they sought this while alive, the wish is taken for the deed.[60]

Philecous When I was in Antwerp I was present, along with other kin, at the death of a certain matron. A Franciscan was there, a man who commanded great respect. When he noticed the woman was already gasping

20 for breath, he put one of her arms up his sleeve, so that it even touched part of his shoulder. Some people present were undecided whether the whole woman or the part that had been covered would be safe from the gates of hell.[61]

Theotimus The whole woman was safe, just as in baptism part of a person

25 is dipped in water but all of him made Christian.

Philecous It is amazing how devils[62] are terrified of that garment.

Theotimus More terrified than they are of the Lord's cross. When Eusebius was borne to his grave I saw – and not I alone – troops of black devils, in the form of flies, attacking the corpse, yet none of them dared to touch it.

30 **Philecous** But meantime his face, hands, and feet were in danger, since they were exposed.

Theotimus As snakes can't bear the shade of an ash tree, though it extend a considerable distance,[63] so devils feel the bane of that sacred dress even from afar.

35 **Philecous** Consequently, I don't think such bodies decay, else worms would have more courage than devils.

Theotimus Very true.

Philecous How lucky the lice who live forever in so holy a garment![64] But when the garment is brought to the grave, what is it that protects the soul?

40 **Theotimus** The garment takes the shade[65] along with it and keeps it safe; so safe that no member of that order, they insist, comes to the fire of purgatory.

Philecous If what you say is true, I rate this revelation above John's. Indeed this one shows a quick and easy way of escaping eternal death without labour, without trouble, without penance, after a whole lifetime spent agreeably in pleasure.

5 **Theotimus** I agree.

Philecous Accordingly I no longer wonder if many persons attribute a great deal to the seraphic brethren. But I can't get over the fact that there's no lack of people who don't hesitate to deride them.

Theotimus You ought to realize that those people, however many you see,
10 are given over to depraved feeling and blinded by their own malice.[66]

Philecous Hereafter I'll be more careful; and I'll try to die in the holy habit. But some men may be found in our day who teach that man is justified by faith alone, without the aid of works.[67] It would be the greatest boon, therefore, if a garment should confer a blessing without faith.

15 **Theotimus** Not merely without faith; don't be mistaken, Philecous.[68] To believe that what I have told you was promised by Christ to the patriarch Francis is sufficient.

Philecous Will the garment save even a Turk, then?

Theotimus Even Satan himself, if he allowed it to be put on and trusted the
20 revelation.

Philecous You won me over long ago, but I'd like you to rid me of one or two difficulties.

Theotimus Say on.

Philecous I've heard that Francis calls his way of life an evangelical one.

25 **Theotimus** Correct.

Philecous But all Christians profess the rule of the gospel, at least in my opinion. Now if their way of life is an evangelical one, it follows that as many as are Christians are also Franciscans.[69] And among these, Christ, with his apostles and his most blessed Mother, will hold first place.

30 **Theotimus** You would persuade me, surely, were it not that Francis had added some things to Christ's gospel.

Philecous What?

Theotimus The ashen garb, hempen cord, and bare feet.

Philecous By those marks, then, we distinguish the evangelical Christian
35 from the Franciscan?

Theotimus They differ also with regard to their contact with money.[70]

Philecous Yet, as I hear, Francis forbids it to be *received*, not touched. But either the master or procurator or creditor or heir or commissioner receives it.[71] And though protected by gloves when he counts it,[72] he is said to have
40 received it nonetheless. Whence this new interpretation, that not to receive it means not to touch it?

Theotimus Pope Benedict so interpreted.

Philecous But as a Franciscan, not as pope. Apart from that: don't the most observant of Observants, when they travel, receive money in a linen cloth?[73]

Theotimus They do so when necessity compels them.

5 **Philecous** But it's better to die than break the more than evangelical Rule. Secondly, don't they receive money here and there through their agents?

Theotimus Why not, even if they're given some thousands – as happens not infrequently?

Philecous But the Rule says 'neither by themselves nor through others.'

10 **Theotimus** But they don't *touch* it.

Philecous Nonsense. If touch is unholy, still they touch it through others.

Theotimus But they have no dealings with fiscal agents.

Philecous Don't they? Anyone who has a mind to could put that theory to the test!

15 **Theotimus** Christ is said never to have touched money.

Philecous Granted, though probably Christ as a little boy often bought butter, vinegar, and herbs for his parents. But unquestionably Peter and Paul touched it. Praise for holiness of life lies not in avoiding contact with money but in despising it. Contact with wine is much more dangerous than with

20 money. Why aren't they afraid of that danger?

Theotimus Because Francis didn't forbid it.

Philecous Don't they stretch out their hands, soft from a lazy life and beautifully washed,[74] for ladies' greetings, and when perchance some money is offered to their gaze, jump back and defend themselves with the sign of

25 the cross – Lord, how evangelically! Now I'm confident that Francis, though he may have been entirely uneducated,[75] was not such a fool as to forbid any and all contact with money. Yet if he did mean that, to what risk did he expose his flock, whom he commanded to walk in their bare feet,[76] since it can hardly be avoided that, without knowing it, they step on money that's

30 lying on the ground.

Theotimus But they don't touch it with their hands.[77]

Philecous Doesn't the sense of touch apply to the whole body?

Theotimus Yes. And if such a thing does happen they don't say mass unless they've confessed.

35 **Philecous** How scrupulous!

Theotimus But all quibbling aside, I'll tell you how the matter stands. To many persons, money is and will remain a source of the greatest evils.

Philecous Admitted, but to others the same money is the means of many benefits. I read that the love of riches is condemned;[78] that money is

40 condemned I don't read.

Theotimus You're right. But contact with it was thus forbidden that they might be further removed from the vice of avarice, just as in the Gospel we are forbidden to swear lest we fall into perjury.[79]

Philecous Then why isn't looking at it forbidden?

5 **Theotimus** Because restraining the hands is easier than restraining the eyes.

Philecous Yet death has entered through those windows.[80]

Theotimus And therefore those who are truly Franciscans pull their cowls down over their brows and walk with eyes covered and fixed on the ground, lest they see anything except the road; just as we observe that horses drawing

10 loaded wagons wear leather blinders to prevent them from seeing anything except what is in front of them.

Philecous But tell me, now: is it true, as I hear, that the Rule forbids the procuring of an indult from the pope?[81]

Theotimus It is.

15 **Philecous** Yet I hear that no class of men is furnished with more indults – to such an extent that they may kill by poison or bury alive persons condemned by their sentence without the slightest risk of irregularity.[82]

Theotimus That's no mere story you've heard. A certain Pole, a man by no means given to lying, told me he had slept off a bout of drunkenness in

20 the Franciscan church, in that corner where women sit when they confess through metal gratings. Awakened by the night Office, he didn't dare show himself. After the nocturns had been sung as usual, the whole band of brethren descended into the crypt. There a pit, fairly wide and deep, had been dug. Two young men, hands tied behind their backs, were standing by.

25 A sermon was preached in praise of obedience. They were assured that God would pardon all their transgressions. Some hope was even held out that God might incline the minds of the brethren to mercy if they went down into the pit of their own accord and lay down on their backs. They did so; the ladder was pulled up; and instantly everyone heaped earth on them.

30 **Philecous** But did the witness keep quiet while this was going on?

Theotimus Certainly, since he was very much afraid that if he showed himself, a third man would be added to the grave.

Philecous Is even this allowed them?

Theotimus Yes, whenever the honour of the order is at stake. – As soon as

35 he escaped he related far and wide, at every dinner party, what he had seen, arousing the great hatred of the seraphic tribe. Wouldn't it have been better for him to be buried alive?

Philecous Perhaps. But all quibbling aside, how does it happen that though the founding father bade them walk barefoot,[83] nowadays they go about in

40 sandals for the most part?

Theotimus This rule was made more lenient for two reasons: first, that they might not touch money unawares; secondly that cold or thorns or snakes or flinty stones or some such thing wouldn't harm them, since they must walk all over the world. But to avoid violating the integrity of the Rule, the slit in
5 the sandal shows the bare foot – part for the whole.[84]
Philecous They affirm that they're vowed to evangelical perfection, which consists, they say, in the counsels of the gospel. About those, fierce quarrels rage among scholars. There's room for evangelical perfection in every walk of life. But among all the evangelical precepts, which do you think especially
10 perfect?
Theotimus In my opinion, everything Matthew sets forth in the fifth chapter, ending thus: 'Love your enemies . . . do good to them that hate you, and pray for them which despitefully use you and persecute you; that ye may be the children of your Father which is in heaven: for he maketh his
15 sun to rise on the evil and the good, and sendeth rain on the just and the unjust . . . Be ye therefore perfect, even as your Father which is in heaven is perfect.'[85]
Philecous Well answered. But that Father is rich and bounteous to all and does not beg from anyone.
20 **Theotimus** They too are bounteous, but in spiritual treasures, that is, in prayers and good works, whereof they have great store.
Philecous Would that among them were examples of gospel love, which repays slanders with blessings and injury with kindness! What's the meaning of Pope Alexander's famous dictum that it is safer to offend a mighty king
25 than anyone belonging to the Franciscan or Dominican order?[86]
Theotimus An affront to the dignity of the order must be revenged; and a wrong done unto one of the least of these is done to the whole order.[87]
Philecous But why isn't it, rather, that the good done to one be done to the whole order? And why doesn't an affront to one Christian excite the whole
30 Christian world to revenge? Why didn't Paul, so often beaten and stoned,[88] cry for help against the violators of his apostolic dignity? Now if, according to the saying of the Lord, 'It is more blessed to give than to receive,'[89] then assuredly the man who, living and teaching righteously, gives of his substance to the needy is more excellent than the one who merely accepts
35 it. Otherwise Paul boasts in vain that he had preached the gospel without charge.[90] And the special test of that much-praised devotion seems to be this: whether men can restrain their wrath when slandered, whether they can feel charitable towards those who ill deserve it. What merit is there if a man – who's going to live more comfortably at another's expense – gives up
40 some of his money when he nurses a desire for vengeance? Of rope-girded, half-shod men we have everywhere a great plenty.[91] One who would practise

what the Lord calls perfect[92] – what the apostles constantly displayed – is indeed a rare bird[93] among them.

Theotimus I'm not unaware of the gossip some of the godless circulate about them; but for my part, I'm so taken with them that whenever I see that most holy garb I think God's angels are present and that house blessed whose threshold is worn down by their feet.

Philecous And as for me, I think that there are fewer barren women where they are frequent visitors! But may Francis be merciful to me, Theotimus, so mistaken have I been up to now. I used to consider their dress nothing but dress, no better in itself than that of a sailor or cobbler unless enhanced by the holiness of the wearer – as Christ's garment, when touched, healed the woman who had an issue of blood.[94] Otherwise I'd have been uncertain whether the weaver or the keeper of the wardrobe had conferred that power on it.

Theotimus Whoever gives the form gives the power, unquestionably.

Philecous Hereafter I'll live a more carefree life and not torture myself with the fear of hell, the tedium of confession, or the torment of penance.

NOTES

1 Theotimus means 'pious,' 'God-fearing'; Philecous, 'eager to hear.'

2 See 'The Sermon' 941:32, where we are told that Merdardus' head leans towards the right shoulder. The right side was the usual position of honour in Christian art and in heraldic and iconological convention. In some representations of the crucifixion, especially in wood carvings, Christ faces front. In what is said to be the earliest surviving representation of Christ crucified, a wooden panel in the church of Santa Sabina in Rome (c 430), he looks straight ahead (CHB II 536 and plate 5). In a few others his head is bowed; in still others it leans to the left. For examples see Gertrud Schiller *Iconography of Christian Art* trans Janet Seligman, 2 vols (Greenwich, Conn 1971–2) II plates 337, 494, 666. In plate 494 Christ's head is turned left and upward. A drawing of the crucifixion by Michelangelo shows Christ with head upright but turned to the left. (This is thought to be a preliminary drawing for a painting made for Vittoria Colonna c 1545. It is reproduced in *The Complete Paintings of Michelangelo* ed Ettore Camesasca [New York 1966] 106, also in R.H. Bainton *Women of the Reformation in Germany and Italy* [Minneapolis 1971; repr Boston 1974] 215. See Guido Cimino *Il crucifisso di Michelangelo per Vittoria Colonna* [Rome 1967], a reference I owe to Bainton). But the customary posture shows the head leaning to the right.
Why then is Theotimus described as having his head turned to the left? Attentive reading of this colloquy may give a clue. The statement is merely the first of many indications of Theotimus' fallible self-assurance. If the man who believes every legend about St Francis, however far-fetched, makes an elementary blunder of this kind and on this subject, it is not surprising that he is equally forgetful or ignorant about much else in his defence of Francis and Franciscans.

3 The opening lines of a satire of Observants, *Franciscus ad fratres* (1538), by George Buchanan, the Scottish poet, scholar, and historian, resemble these lines and may have been suggested by Erasmus' colloquy.

4 Franciscans were the 'seraphic' order (see 'The Sermon' n2), Dominicans the 'cherubic' order. Seraphim are named only once in the Bible, in Isa 6:2–7, which is the source of their presence in subsequent Christian literature and art. Seraphim and cherubim were the highest of the choirs of angels in the *Celestial Hierarchy* traditionally attributed to Dionysius the Pseudo-Areopagite c 500 AD. See also Dante *Paradiso* canto 28. 'Partners' (*sodales*) refers to mortal men who profess 'seraphic' or Franciscan teachings.

5 Alberto Pio, the 'pious' or 'devout.' 'Eusebius' is the Latin transliteration of the equivalent Greek word.

6 Paris, where Alberto Pio died. *Lutetia*, the Latin name for Paris, recalls *lutum* 'mud,' which is the equivalent of Greek πηλός. Derivation of *Lutetia* from *lutum* is found elsewhere too; see 'The Soldier and the Carthusian' n48. Perhaps 'Pelusium' is additionally appropriate here because of Alberto Pio's 'mud-slinging' habits (Smith *Key* 54).

7 See the introduction 996 above. The allusions refer to Pio's loss of his title and estates, exile in France, and dependence in his last days on the bounty of Francis I. 'Toady' (*sycophantam*) may refer to that dependence or to some shady dealings at an earlier time.

8 Other accounts by Erasmus of Alberto Pio's dying mention the interval of three days. Cf 'The Funeral' 767:3–12, where George's physicians wait until they receive their fees before warning that the patient is near death.

9 The description of Francis' dress in the dream Erasmus describes in one of his letters is slightly different; see n17 below. On variations in the Franciscan habit see 'The Sermon' n14; on sandals vs bare feet, n76 below.

10 In *Apologia adversus rhapsodias Alberti Pii*, Erasmus remarks how much better it would have been for Pio to repeat a psalm describing Christ's passion (LB IX 1125A). That is what the godly Cornelius does in 'The Funeral' 779:4–6.

11 Matt 26:6–13, in which Jesus commends the woman who anointed his head with ointment 'for my burial'

12 Gal 6:2

13 *purpura byssoque*, the phrase used of the rich man in Luke 16:19

14 See n2 above.

15 The wounds or 'marks' (stigmata) in the hands, feet, and side of Francis, corresponding to the five wounds of the crucified Christ. Some narratives tell of their bleeding, others of excrescences or impressions of nails. The stigmata were believed by the faithful to have been received by Francis in an ecstatic experience (September 1224) on the mountain top of Alvernia or La Verna (see 'The Sermon' n2). This event became known almost immediately to a very few of Francis' companions, soon afterwards to others, and before his death (October 1226) to many. It is described in devout language in early lives of the saint, including the two memoirs by his first biographer, Thomas of Celano; these are known as 1 Celano, written as early as 1228, and 2 Celano, completed in 1246–7. See 1 Celano sections 94–5, 2 Celano sections 135–8. Other sources are St Bonaventure's *Legenda maior* chapter 13; *The Legend of the Three Companions* chapter 17; and a very important addition to the *Fioretti* on the

five 'considerations on the holy stigmata' by an unidentified author who may have been a contributor to 1 Celano. In 1260 the general chapter of the order instructed Bonaventure, then the master-general, to prepare a new life, which should supersede all the others. Bonaventure's became a classic but never completely replaced Celano's or the collection of anecdotes in the *Fioretti* or the *Legend of the Three Companions*. Translations of these texts are conveniently available in *St. Francis of Assisi, Writings and Early Biographies: English Omnibus of the Sources for the Life of St. Francis* ed Marion A. Habig (Chicago 1973).

Christians regarded all wounds (stigmata) or physical injuries received in the Lord's service as badges of honour. So Paul writes: 'From henceforth let no man trouble you; for I bear in my body the marks of the Lord Jesus' (Eph 6:17). See for other examples F. Arndt and F. Gingrich *A Greek-English Lexicon of the New Testament* (Chicago and Cambridge 1957) sv στίγμα.

Erasmus always praised Francis' holiness and charity, but his judgment and writing about the saint were tempered by a characteristic scepticism about hagiography. Nor is it at all surprising that the Francis he saw in a dream bore no traces of the stigmata shown by painters and described by panegyrists (Allen Ep 2700:51–2). Collections of stories about saints and miracles were too numerous, and many of the tales too marvellous, to impress him. The true marvel of St Francis was that although dedicated to poverty and a life of utmost simplicity, he drew so many followers by the example of his spirituality. See *Ecclesiastes* LB V 841F and 912C–D.

16 In Christian art Christ's fifth wound, caused when one of the attendant soldiers pierced his side with a lance (John 19:34), is usually on his right side. Similarly in most representations of St Francis the wound or mark is on his right side. Giotto's painting, in the Chiesa di Santa Croce at Florence, of Francis receiving the stigmata is one of many examples. Brother Elias' letter, written very soon after Francis' death, does not say which side was pierced. Testimony in *The Three Companions* chapter 17 specifies the right side, as do 1 Celano section 95, 'The Third Consideration on the Stigmata,' the story about Brother Rufino in 'The Fourth Consideration,' and Bonaventure *Legenda maior* 13.3. Many illustrations in Schiller *Iconography of Christian Art* (n2 above) confirm this report.

Theotimus in the colloquy, however, speaks of the hole in Alberto Pio's Franciscan robe as being on the left side. This need not be taken as an error, or an authorial device to discredit Theotimus, but simply recourse to a different tradition. In ecclesiastical art from northern Italy, Christ's wound is sometimes on his left side, 'and consequently in pictures or reliefs that represent the doubting Thomas approaching his Master, the disciple comes from the spectator's right, advancing to touch the wound in the Saviour's left side' (C.R. Morey *Christian Art* [London, New York, Toronto 1935] 11). Furthermore Schiller directs attention to the connection, in the late Middle Ages, between the tradition of the five wounds and the cult of the Sacred Heart of Jesus (*Iconography of Christian Art* II 194–6). If the mark or wound is on the saint's left side, the artist is clearly responsive to the devotion of the Sacred Heart, as if the lance penetrated to the heart.

17 A paraphrase of various expressions in the New Testament (Col 2:20, 3:3; cf Rom 6:2, Gal 6:14, Phil 1:21). On this phrase see 'The Old Men's Chat' n62. Here

it is meant seriously, but Erasmus sometimes uses it ironically. On carrying virtues in one's heart instead of boasting about them see 'Cyclops' 865:15–31,' 866:26–867:9.

Of particular interest for readers of 'The Seraphic Funeral' is a passage in a letter printed by Erasmus in 1532. The letter was written 9 August in that year to a young friend, Karel Uutenhove (on whom see 'Knucklebones' n1). It tells of a dream 'after midnight' in which St Francis appeared and spoke to Erasmus (Allen Ep 2700:37–53). His opponents, Erasmus says, imagine the saint is angry with him because of what he has written about men who 'promise heaven to those who are buried in Franciscan dress.' These critics are mistaken, for in the dream Francis looked kindly upon him and thanked him warmly for disclosing what needed correction – things Francis himself had always detested – and he then gives assurance that Erasmus is enrolled among friends of the order. Francis 'was not dressed as he is shown in pictures; he did not have a woolen robe of different colours but of dusky wool undyed, "undipped" as the Greeks say, just as it was when clipped from the sheep. He did not have a peaked cowl but a hood attached to the back of his tunic with which he could cover his head in a downpour – the sort of thing we see in the dress of some of the Irish. Nor had he a fancy knotted cord; it was unknotted, plain, like a peasant's. His robe did not reach the ground but was a palm [about eight inches] or more above his ankles. Nor did he wear sandals but was entirely barefoot. I saw no traces whatever of the five wounds [the stigmata] shown in paintings. As he took his leave, he gave me his right hand, saying "Fight the good fight; you will soon be one of mine."' The picture of a credible Francis, as Erasmus liked to think of him. Surprisingly, it omits mention of avoiding money, a question that fills several pages of the colloquy, but perhaps there is a hint of that subject in the phrase about 'what needed correction.'

After telling of his dream of St Francis, Erasmus refers to the six *alae* or 'wings' of the seraph. These are interpreted by St Bonaventure as 'six graded illuminations which begin with creatures and lead us to God whom no one rightly reaches except through the Crucified . . . six steps of contemplation leading from creatures to God' (so A.C. Pegis 'St. Bonaventure, St. Francis and Philosophy' *Mediaeval Studies* 15 [1953] 4). They comprise zeal for justice, compassion, patience, exemplary life, prudent discernment, and devotion to God. For Bonaventure's exposition of them see his *De sex alis seraphim* trans J. de Vinck in *The Works of Bonaventure* III: *Opuscula*, 2nd series (Paterson, NJ 1966) 133–96. Erasmus names the wings as complete obedience, evangelical poverty, spotless chastity, profound humility, peaceful simplicity, and seraphic charity (Allen Ep 2700:55–9). He adds, about the Franciscans, 'Would that they all carried these in their hearts as well as within their robes,' alluding to their custom of carrying a copy of the Rule with them.

Erasmus owned a copy of the Rule and of the *Testamentum* that was dictated by Francis in his last days; the two texts were often printed together (see Husner in *Gedenkschift* 244 no 387). This fact, however, merely confirms what was already known from Erasmus' writings: that he was not only interested but well informed with respect to Franciscan literature, leaders, customs, and legends.

18 To Philecous, religious dress is merely a means of identification, whereas Theotimus likes to think it has real talismanic power. Erasmus often dwells on the variety of superstitions attached to dress; see for example, in the *Colloquies*, 'A Fish Diet' 705:3–32, 'The Soldier and the Carthusian' 329:3–330:4, 'The Well-to-Do Beggars' 480:3–15, 'The Council of Women' 909:22–910:14. Notice that Erasmian opinions on this subject in 'The Well-to-Do Beggars' are expressed by an Observant Franciscan.

That spiritual benefits might be won by retiring from the world and becoming a monk or nun had been the conviction and refuge of many Christians throughout the history of monasticism and before. Similarly, benefits could be gained after death, according to medieval belief, by donning a monk's or friar's costume when near death. After the mendicant orders were founded, the idea of seeking safety in friar's dress soon appeared. Also, by a gift of money to be used on behalf of an order, one could win the privilege, through a 'letter of fraternity,' of receiving the prayers of the brethren and, dressed in the order's habit, be buried in their monastery or cemetery ([On religious and their privileges], Tanner I 647, and see Moorman 514–16). This custom existed in other orders as well as the Franciscan. Poliziano, the Italian humanist scholar greatly admired by Erasmus, was buried in a Dominican habit; so was Giovanni Pico della Mirandola. Desire for such a death and burial could be a sign of true piety or, at the other extreme, credulity or superstition. The contrast between the dressing of George in a friar's robe and the dismissal of all such trumpery by Cornelius in 'The Funeral' is typical of Erasmus, whose other allusions to burial of laymen in a habit are consistently depreciatory or ironical. For a few examples see Allen Ep 447:504–9 / CWE Ep 447:554–60; Allen Epp 1805:312–17, 1886:73–6, 1891:243–59, 2700:73–8, 2899:31–6; *Enchiridion* LB V 31D–E / CWE 66 72; *Ratio verae theologiae* LB V 136C–D; *De praeparatione ad mortem* LB V 1305E; *Lingua* LB IV 716F / ASD IV-1A 123:199–124:200 / CWE 29 355.

19 Matt 7:6

20 Cf the Vulgate *simplicitate cordis* in Acts 2:46; Eph 6:5; Col 3:22.

21 A native of Groningen, Rodolphus Agricola (1444–85) was eminent as one of the early humanists of northern Europe. After studies in Germany, at Louvain, and possibly Paris, he went to Italy, where he learned Greek, made translations from Greek into Latin, and wrote a treatise on logic in rhetoric, *De inventione dialectica*, which was reprinted more than fifty times, and *De formando studio*, a defence of humanistic studies. At one time he was the instructor of Alexander Hegius, Erasmus' teacher in Deventer. To Erasmus he was an exemplar as well as an expositor of 'good letters' and moreover a fellow countryman whom he delighted to praise: 'among the Greeks he was the best Greek of them all, among the Latins the best Latin ... a second Virgil' (*Adagia* I iv 39); 'the glory and ornament of our Germany' (*Ratio* LB V 79A and *Annotationes in Novum Testamentum* LB VI 882C); 'worthy of eternal fame' (*Ecclesiastes* LB V 920F). See CEBR; two studies in *Itinerarium Italicum: The Profile of the Italian Renaissance in the Mirror of its European Transformations* ed Heiko A. Oberman and Thomas A. Brady Jr, Studies in Medieval and Reformation Thought 14 (Leiden 1975): Josef IJsewijn 'The Coming of Humanism in the Low Countries' 193–301 and Lewis W. Spitz 'The Course of German Humanism' 371–436, especially 400–2; and R.J. Schoeck 'Agricola and Erasmus: Erasmus' Inheritance of Northern

Humanism' in *Rodolphus Agricola Phrisius 1444–1485* ed F. Akkerman and A.J. Vanderjagt (Leiden 1988) 181–8.

22 Christophe de Longueil (c 1488–1522), regarded as a brilliant young scholar and man of letters. He studied Greek in Italy, where he made many friends but annoyed other Italians by his excessive praise of the French. In 1519 he wrote in a letter to a friend an interesting and perceptive comparison of Budé and Erasmus as writers, weighing the merits and weaknesses of each. For the text see Ep 914 and for Erasmus' comments Ep 935.

In Longueil's own writings Erasmus detected an over-anxious affectation of Ciceronian diction (Allen Ep 1675:19–20). Consequently some readers have thought the character Nosoponus, a pedantic imitator of Ciceronian style in Erasmus' *Ciceronianus* (1528), was modelled on Longueil. See Allen Ep 914 introduction and CEBR; CWE 28 324–6.

Erasmus says that Longueil died 'recently,' but Longueil died in 1522.

23 Ie Francis, in the Rule of 1221, 2.7; of 1223, 2.12

24 Commenting on Matt 24:23, 'If any man shall say unto you, Lo, here is Christ, or there, believe it not,' Erasmus ridicules the rival claims of regulars and seculars. 'Christ is not divided ... Wherever there are feelings worthy of Christ, he is present' (*Annotationes in Novum Testamentum* LB VI 125D).

25 With this discussion of vows compare 'Rash Vows'; 'A Fish Diet' 693:34–694:22, 697:36–699:1.

26 Cf *Paraclesis* LB V 142F–143A. On the meaning of baptism see 'The Godly Feast' n229; 'The Girl with No Interest in Marriage' nn27 and 57; 'The Soldier and the Carthusian' 332:4–7. For a defence of his writings on this subject see *Declarationes ad censuras Lutetiae vulgatas* LB IX 820A–822E, and for a summary of his opinions John Payne *Erasmus: His Theology of the Sacraments* (Richmond 1970) 155–78.

27 Romans 6 is the key text. See also 2 Cor 5:15; Col 3:3; 2 Tim 2:11.

28 On methods of baptism see 'The Godly Feast' n227.

29 Literally 'what larger window could have been opened'; cf *Adagia* I iv 3.

30 The perilous folly of postponing baptism until near the end of life is condemned in *De praeparatione ad mortem* LB V 1305F and *De concordia* LB V 479D–E. In the early centuries of Christianity such delay was common, as Theotimus observes, but in the sixth century and thereafter infant baptism was the general custom and became universal among the orthodox. Paul alludes to baptism on behalf of the dead (1 Cor 15:29). Erasmus has no comment on this topic in *Annotationes in Novum Testamentum*.

31 Said with specific reference to Franciscans in *Ecclesiastes* LB V 885B, and cf 961B–C; Allen Ep 2700:25–6. See also 'The Well-to-do Beggars' 482:1–4 and cf 'The Usefulness of the *Colloquies*' 1104:35–1105:11, 35–9 (on the friars in 'The Funeral').

32 These lines derive from Erasmus' recollections of various passages in the Franciscan literature he had read: legends met in Giovanni di Ceprano, Thomas of Celano's biographies of Francis, the writings of Brother Leo and his companions, the authorized life by St Bonaventure, the *Fioretti*, and some of the surviving writings of Francis himself. In his *De immensa Dei misericordia* (1524) Erasmus tells a story concerning Socrates (LB V 566A): when a physiognomist, looking him over, told him he was a drunkard, glutton, lecher, and worse,

Socrates replied meekly that he would have been all of these and more, had not philosophy saved him from such vices. This comes from Cicero *Tusculan Disputations* 4.37.80 or *De fato* 5.10; Erasmus uses it again in *Apophthegmata* (1531) LB IV 163D. The anecdote corresponds to lines 25–31 here and Erasmus seems deliberately to have declined an opportunity to compare the virtuous pagan with the Christian saint. In *De immensa misericordia*, however (LB V 566B), Erasmus remarks: 'But what Socrates ascribed to philosophy the excellent Francis more properly attributed to the mercy of God.' Erasmus' veneration of Socrates is sufficiently prominent elsewhere (see 'The Godly Feast' 194:1–7, 23–34).

33 Cornelius the centurion (Acts 10) is not officially a saint, but according to tradition he became a bishop, either of Caesarea or of Scepsis in Mysia (*The Catholic Encyclopedia* IV [New York 1913] sv 'Cornelius'). A more likely candidate here is Pope St Cornelius, who is believed to have been a martyr after two years as pope (251–3). He was strongly supported by St Cyprian in controversies, as Erasmus knew (Allen Ep 1000:188–91 / CWE Ep 1000:195–9).

34 Of Egypt, on whom see 'The Well-to-Do Beggars' n43.

35 Who was imprisoned and finally beheaded

36 Rabelais may have had this passage in mind when he has Grangousier, in *Gargantua* 1.45, denounce the belief that saints inflict diseases (Raymond Lebègue 'Rabelais, the Last of the French Erasmians' *Journal of the Warburg and Courtauld Institutes* 12 [1949] 94). Cf 'A Pilgrimage' 628:3–10 above.

37 1 Cor 2:6–8

38 The 'most secret mysteries' of 1005:8 above. One day when Francis was anxious about the future of his order, an angel revealed to him the seven 'secrets' or privileges God vouchsafed to the Franciscans. These are divulged by Theotimus.

39 Greek in the original, but 'thrice-sacred' is not a New Testament word, as 'revelation' ('apocalypse') is.

40 The first revelation is the divine promise that the seraphic flock will flourish. This assurance is not restricted to a single passage or found in exactly the words spoken by Theotimus, but it can be elicited from passages in the 'Second Consideration on the Stigmata' and the *Speculum perfectionis* (*Mirror of Perfection*) 71, where the Lord tells Francis: 'See that your Order remains in the state in which it was founded, for nothing but this will remain to Me in the whole world ... And when the world loses its faith, no light will remain save that of your Order, because I have set it as a light to the world' (Leo Sherley-Price *St Francis of Assisi: His Life and Writings as Recorded by his Contemporaries* [London 1959] 89–90; repr in Habig [n15 above] 1201–2).

41 4 October

42 The second revelation refers to the Indulgence of the Portiuncula, granted, according to tradition, by Pope Honorius III. It provided that whoever, after due confession of sins, visited the little chapel known as Portiuncula, close to Assisi, would gain the indulgence. The origins of the privilege are disputed; for a good summary see NCE XI 601–2. On claims for the extraordinary indulgence of the Portiuncula see also H.C. Lea *A History of Auricular Confession and Indulgences in the Latin Church* 3 vols (Philadelphia 1896) III 236–53, 341.

On purgatory and indulgences see 'Rash Vows' n20; 'Military Affairs' nn24–6; 'A Pilgrimage' n93. In *Collectio judiciorum de novis erroribus* ... ed C. du Plessis d'Argentré, 3 vols (Paris 1728–36; repr Brussels 1966) I part 2 318–9 under the year 1486 is *Qualificationes errorum fratris Johannes Mercatoris*, a Franciscan condemned for errors or heresies in his public preaching in Besançon. Most of his errors concerned the stigmata, but one was his assertion that Francis went to purgatory and delivered the souls of Franciscans and that persons friendly to the friars (see n55 below) could be buried in Franciscan garb.

43 Francis says in his *Testamentum* that 'the Most High himself' revealed to him that he must live the life of the gospel, and consequently he wrote a Rule for his followers (see *Opuscula S. Francisci et scripta S. Clarae Assisiensium* ed and trans [Italian] Giovanni Boccali and Luciano Canonici [Assisi 1978] 148–50; Habig [n15 above] 68). This means the primitive Rule (1209), no longer extant; 'written twice' refers to the surviving Rules of 1221 and 1223.

44 See Matt 13:24–30 on the wheat and tares. The divine promise is in 'The Second Consideration on the Stigmata.'

45 Also in 'The Second Consideration on the Stigmata'

46 On this theme as it applies to religious, cf *Ecclesiastes* LB V 1021B–1025F, which in eloquence and severity is equal to the earlier criticism in Allen Ep 447:410–742 / CWE Ep 447:448–819.

47 On the habit described see 'The Sermon' n14; here it is 'too dark' figuratively as well as literally. Francis' cord of hemp was coarse and a darker colour.

48 The biblical allusions are to parables of Christ's coming; see Matt 25:11–13 and Luke 13:22–7; Matt 22:1–14.

49 Fifth revelation, in 'The Second Consideration on the Stigmata.' Another entry in the *Qualificationes* cited in n42 above deals with the assumption that Francis had a divine promise that friars who did not keep the Rule could not remain long in the order or in this world; also that if anyone spoke evil of the friars he would be punished severely in this world and the next. In his lifetime Francis revealed this only to Brother Leo, his closest friend and confessor.
In exceptional circumstances Francis was reputed to be a stern disciplinarian. A learned friar founded a house of studies in Bologna. To Francis this was shockingly subversive, contrary to the holy purposes of the order, whose members were to spend their time in prayer and preaching, not study. Believing that the friar's thoughts were destructive in intent, Francis cursed him, and afterwards that friar died a horrible death. See *The Little Flowers of St. Francis* Additional chapters 12 (Habig [n15 above] 1492–3).

50 Matthäus Schiner (1470–1522), bishop of Sion (Sitten) in south-western Switzerland (1499) and later of Novara, west of Milan, and cardinal from 1511, was active as a diplomat in the service of the emperor and sometimes of the pope. Erasmus dedicated his Paraphrases on the Epistles of James and John to him (1520, 1521). Schiner was a member of two commissions that investigated the Dominican case at Bern, described in the next note. Whether Theotimus is correct in saying that condemnation of those Dominicans was due principally to the cardinal's efforts is uncertain but could be true.

51 A sensational event at Bern in May 1509, long remembered in western Europe. In a grotesque climax to a series of pious frauds intended to gain an advantage over the Franciscans in the prolonged dispute over the Immaculate Conception

Uon den fier ketzeren Prediger ordēs der obseruantz zü Bern im Schweytzer land verbrant / in dē jar noch Christi geburt .M.CCCC.ix. vff dē nechstē donderstag noch Pfingsten.

Mit vil schöne figürlin vū lieblichen reymsprüchen neüwlich geteütscht

 Wer sich des nimpt in iibels an
Dz ich die sach beschriben han
Der schaff dz solichs nym geschee
So schweig ich das añ anders mc.

The burning of the four Dominicans near Bern, 31 May 1509
From the title-page of Thomas Murner's *De quattuor heresiarchis ordinis Praedicatorum de Observantia nuncupatorum apud Suitenses in civitate Bernensi combustis Anno Christi MDIX* (Strasbourg 1509)
Special Collections, Van Pelt Library, University of Pennsylvania

of the Virgin Mary, and secondly to win prestige for their own order and monastery, four Dominican friars, including the prior, were seized, tried, tortured, and after confessing guilt were handed over to the secular power and burned. Erasmus has a very brief but significant allusion to this affair in a letter of October 1519 addressed to a leading prelate, Albert of Brandenburg, cardinal-archbishop of Mainz: significant because it cites the fate of the friars in Bern and of Savonarola, another Dominican who was burned (at Florence in 1488), as evidence of the villainy the order was capable of (Allen Ep 1033:247–52 / cwe Ep 1033:271–6). Another brief allusion occurs in 'The Usefulness of the *Colloquies*' 1103:24.

The Immaculate Conception of Mary is the doctrine that from the instant of her conception Mary, by divine grace and in consideration of the merits of Christ, was free from all stain of original sin. Support for this belief, its advocates argued, could be found in patristic theology or deduced therefrom. The doctrine did not command much public attention until the Middle Ages, when the cult of Mary became popular. From the thirteenth century on, the Immaculate Conception was a topic of theological inquiry and controversy. Men as eminent as Bernard of Clairvaux, Bonaventure, Peter Lombard, and Thomas Aquinas rejected the doctrine, but Franciscans (except Bonaventure) zealously defended it. Their greatest philosopher, Duns Scotus, argued for it. In the end, Franciscan arguments and propaganda triumphed. Dominicans opposed the doctrine as long as they dared, but gradually popes and councils came to accept it, although official promulgation of it as a dogma binding upon all the faithful was never issued until 1854 (*Ineffabilis Deus*; text in Denzinger-Schönmetzer *Enchiridion* 561 nos 2803–4).

On Erasmus' attitude towards the Immaculate Conception of Mary consult J.-P. Massaut 'La question de l'Immaculée Conception' in *Critique et tradition à la veille de la Réforme en France* (Paris 1974) 37–45 and L.-E. Halkin 'La Mariologie d'Erasme' ARG 68 (1977) 39–43. Although recognizing fully the difficulties of the question, and impressed as he was by Thomas Aquinas' arguments against it, Erasmus inclined to favour it; he thought it 'more likely to be right' (Allen Ep 1196:58–9 / cwe Ep 1196:66–7 and *Apologia adversus rhapsodias Alberti Pii* LB IX 1163E). But he was cautious, exercising his right to go no further in a matter not yet enunciated authoritatively by the church. 'It is irreverent to take away praises from the Virgin, who is never sufficiently praised; but it is most dangerous by far to make any creature equal to Christ' (*Supputatio* LB IX 570B). For arguments that the four friars were innocent see N. Paulus *Ein Justizmord an vier Dominikaner begangen* (Frankfurt 1897); R. Steck *Der Berner Jetzerprozess (1507–1509) in neuer Beleuchtung* in *Schweizerischer Theologischer Zeitschrift* (1901) and separately (Bern 1902); Georg Schuhmann *Die Berner Jetzertragödie im Lichte der neuern Forschung und Kritik* (Freiburg im Breisgau 1912). For a judicious appraisal of essential questions see R. Reuss 'Le procès des Dominicains de Berne en 1507–1509' *Revue de l'histoire des religions* 52 (1905) 237–59. Kurt Guggisberg *Bernische Kirchengeschichte* (Bern 1958) 35–40 has a brief review of the case.

52 A popular and energetic writer and worker for the peace of the church during the 'Babylonian Captivity,' appropriately named here because she was a tertiary (member of the Third Order of Dominicans). On her canonization in 1461 see 'The Apotheosis of Reuchlin' n43.

53 Not of the entire order but probably the provincials of southern Germany and Switzerland

54 Ps 105:15 (104:15 Vulg), a favourite clerical quotation

55 These and other persons 'well disposed' (1006:12 above) would certainly include those who left legacies to the order. Critics of mendicants often accused them of pestering or beguiling the well-to-do to leave money to them. See Allen Ep 2700:73–92 and 'The Funeral' 771:28–772:25, with the notes.
This assurance given in 'The Second Consideration on the Stigmata' helps to explain the custom of burial in a friar's garb.

56 As an example of the perversity of human judgments, Erasmus writes in 1524, a Franciscan who exchanges his grey robe for a black one would fear that a devil would seize him and carry him off to hell, yet might not be afraid to commit adultery or some worse sin. Such people think that violating human ordinances is worse than breaking God's commandments (Allen Ep 1469:185–92 / CWE Ep 1469:195–201). This is a major theme in 'A Fish Diet'; see, on clerical dress, 705:3– . 32. See also *Lingua* LB IV 716B–717B / ASD IV-1A 122:165–124:217 / CWE 29 354–6.

57 Matt 25:36–46

58 Carmelites are said to have had a comparable tradition. The Virgin Mary appeared in a vision to St Simon Stock, head of the order (1147–65), and told him that whoever died in the Carmelite habit would not suffer hell-fire (Lea *Confession and Indulgences* [n42 above] 263, 266–70).

59 'The Third Consideration on the Stigmata' says that annually on the anniversary of Francis' death (evening of 3 October) the saint 'may go to Purgatory and by virtue of your Stigmata you may take from there and lead to Paradise all the souls of your Three Orders, that is, the Friars Minor, the Sisters, and the Continent, and also others who have been very devoted to you, whom you may find there.' 'The Fifth Consideration' says the same thing but does not mention 'others who have been very devoted to you.' See *The Little Flowers of St. Francis* trans Raphael Brown (Garden City, NY 1958) 192, and cf 211; repr Habig (n15 above) 1450, and cf 1469.

60 Cf Allen Ep 447:508–9 / CWE Ep 447:559–60. Intention indicates 'devotion' and therefore suffices.

61 The phrase 'gates of hell' is an echo of Matt 16:18.

62 *cacodaemones*; see 'The Repentant Girl' n7. The 'troops of black devils' attacking Eusebius' corpse are *agmina nigrorum daemonum*.

63 Pliny *Naturalis historia* 16.64; see 'Sympathy' n76.

64 This *reductio ad absurdum* recalls a passage in Erasmus' *Modus orandi Deum* (1524) where an example of vulgar adoption of religious idiom in non-religious context is 'bringing in St Francis' tunic' to try to rid a house of lice and fleas (LB V 1120E). The origin of such illustrations as this must be sought in early legends about Francis. He was almost fanatical in his love not only of birds but of all creatures great and small, including insects, and in his zeal for protecting them (see 1 Celano sections 80–2). 'I am a worm and no man,' he would say (Ps 22:6 [21:7 Vulg]), and would pick up worms and put them in a safe place lest they be trampled. Lice and fleas were all too familiar domestic companions of kings and commoners alike in the Europe of Francis and of Erasmus. See the stories about Louis XI of France in 'The Fabulous Feast' 580:10–27 and the remark in 'The Fish Diet' 715:21–3. In Caesarius of Heisterbach's *Dialogus*

miraculorum (c 1223) 4.48 we read of a knight who wanted to become a monk but recoiled at the lice-infested robes. Finally he steeled himself to enter the order and rejoiced ever afterwards, despite the lice.

65 *umbram,* the 'ghost' or 'spirit'; but 'soul' in the preceding line is *animam.*

66 Rom 1:28

67 Referring to Luther's emphasis on *sola fide,* a doctrine that to Erasmus was one of Luther's 'paradoxes' that he did not understand (Allen Ep 1384:5–14 / CWE Ep 1384:6–16, to Zwingli). He himself believed that although good works do not 'justify,' they are certainly essential and are characteristic of the true Christian. They are not sources but evidence, not causes but consequences of one's faith. But too often what are treated as 'works' are merely 'ceremonies' and outward forms ('The Godly Feast' 196:3–39). On these topics see Erasmus' commentary on Romans and Galatians in *Annotationes in Novum Testamentum* (LB VI) and Paraphrases (LB VII and CWE 42). John B. Payne 'Erasmus: Interpreter of Romans' in *Sixteenth Century Essays and Studies* ed Carl S. Meyer (St Louis 1971) 2–35 is a good guide.

68 Philecous] The first edition, September 1531, prints 'Philecoe' (ASD I-3 691:313). Several other early editions, including Froben's of March 1533 and the *Opera omnia* of 1540, have 'Philaetie' ('fault-finder'). LB has 'Philecoe.'

69 Erasmus is insistent on this point. Cf *Responsio adversus febricitantis libellum* (1529) LB X 1675A–B.

70 Such things as the habit, cord, and going barefoot soon became identified with Franciscans (on bare feet see n76 below), but made little difference to public or ecclesiastical opinion of the friars. Interpretation of their vow of poverty, on the other hand, did make a difference. What poverty meant to Francis was clear enough. What it ought to signify for others in his order was a troublesome legacy for many generations. See the 'Note on Franciscan Poverty' following n94, 1026–32 below.

71 Cornelius Agrippa says some 'haue a Iudas to carrie theire purses, and giue them an accompt, in the meene while they presume to say, as Peter and Iohn did, we have no golde and siluer with vs' (*De vanitate* chapter 65 trans Sanford [1569] 106v / *Of the Vanitie and Vncertaintie of Artes and Sciences* ed Catherine M. Dunn [Northridge, CA 1974] 227). For Peter and John see Acts 3:4–6.

72 In *Moriae encomium* Folly mentions a friar who boasted that for sixty years he had never touched money without wearing two pairs of gloves (LB IV 473C / ASD IV-3 162:563–5 / CWE 27 132; Allen Ep 2700:70–2). Compare a long story in *Adagia* II v 98 (LB II 580F–583C / Phillips '*Adages*' 361–8 / CWE 33 286–90). Conradus Pellicanus, a Franciscan for thirty-three years, says that he knew nothing about money, and had never touched it, until he left the order in 1526 (*Chronikon* ed B. Riggenbach [Basel 1877]). On Pellicanus see introductions to 'The Apotheosis of Reuchlin' and 'The Well-to-Do Beggars'; H. Meylan 'Erasme et Pellican' *Colloquium Erasmianum* (Mons 1968) 245–54.

73 Handkerchief or neckerchief, as in Allen Ep 2700:70–2

74 See 'The Funeral' 768:30–4, where mendicants are denounced by a secular priest for haunting rich men's houses and avoiding a laborious, austere life. But Erasmus allows that some religious are exceptionally devout and deserve as much praise as the others deserve blame. See for example *Ecclesiastes* 816C–817E.

75 *omnis literaturae rudens.* See 'The Sermon' n74.

76 The Rule of 1221 says nothing about footwear. The 1223 Rule says (chapter 2): 'Those who are forced by necessity may wear shoes [*calceamenta*]' (*Opuscula* ed Boccali and Canonici [n43 above] 124; Habig [n15 above] 59). The same passage paraphrases Matt 10:9–10 (cf Luke 5:4), which commands those who would follow Christ to 'provide neither gold nor silver nor brass in your purses, nor scrip for your journey, neither two coats, neither shoes, nor yet staves; for the workman is worthy of his meat.' On shoes and sandals see Erasmus' note on Mark 6:9, where we are told that whether Christ wore shoes or sandals or went barefoot at times is unimportant. Nor should his injunctions about such matters be taken too literally. He did not come into the world to teach us how to be shod or how to dress (*Annotationes in Novum Testamentum* LB VI 172E–173D). Francis wore sandals in the first year or two of his life as a hermit, but then, inspired to take the scriptural injunction (Matt 10:9–10) literally, he joyfully cast away staff, sandals, and purse, and dressed as he lived, with utmost simplicity (*Legend of the Three Companions* chapter 8). In paintings Francis is usually barefoot, as are some of his early followers. Later Franciscans commonly wore sandals. Erasmus is careful to record that in his dream of Francis the saint was barefoot (Allen Ep 2700:47–51; see n16 above).
See also 'A Fish Diet' n211.

77 'You carry teeth but no money with you,' the innkeeper tells the two Observant Franciscans who ask for shelter 'The Well-to-do Beggars' 471:33. 'Francis ... hated money above all else. He always urged his brethren both by word and example to avoid it as they would the devil' (*Speculum perfectionis* section 14 trans Sherley-Price in *St Francis of Assisi* [n40 above] 28; repr in Habig [n15 above] 1140).

78 1 Tim 6:10

79 Matt 5:34. On this theme see 'A Fish Diet' nn131, 132.

80 Cf Jer 9:21.

81 A licence from the pope to do something that ordinarily is not permitted by canon law, an exception (not to be confused with an indulgence). Francis required that his followers be humble, obedient, and seek no privileges. These precepts are both implicit and explicit in the Rule. In his final *Testament* he warns again that the friars are not to look for privileges (text in *Opuscula* ed Boccali and Canonici [n43 above] 146–56; translation in Habig [n15 above] 67–70). Nevertheless the use and abuse of privileges played a prominent role in the order's later history, as Philecous notes. Erasmus remarks elsewhere that the Franciscans ascribe higher authority to the pope than to Christ when their requests are granted; when they are denied, they reject the pope's authority (Allen Ep 447:545–52 / CWE Ep 447:600–9, Allen Ep 1875:150–4).

82 Philecous' scandalous gossip, dependent on hearsay, is made to seem the more credible by the assurances of the order's defender, Theotimus. The tale of the execution of two Franciscans by friars of the order was mentioned briefly by Erasmus also in a letter of 1516 to Lambertus Grunnius, not printed until 1529. The letter was part of a campaign, planned in London with Ammonio, to support his appeal to the papacy to be released from his earlier commitments as an Augustinian canon. In that letter, the present report was attributed to Matthäus Schiner of Mühlebach, cardinal-bishop of Sion, who had been

involved in the investigation into the case of the Dominican friars in Bern (see
n50 above); see Allen Ep 447:600–2 / CWE Ep 447:664–6. In the same passage
(Allen lines 596–600 / CWE lines 660–4) Schiner related how some Dominicans
had buried a young man alive because his father was demanding the return of
a son, taken by stealth.

The present story seems to be traceable to an episode told in much detail
in the life of Blessed Thomas of Scarlino, also known as Thomas of Florence
and Thomas Bellaci. He was a Franciscan lay brother (c 1370–1447) who, after
a profligate youth, entered the Franciscans of the Observance at Fiesole c
1392. Although only a lay brother, he became master of novices, renowned
for his piety and exemplary life, and he was an important personality to the
Observant tradition where it was reported, *inter alia*, that after his death, John
of Capistrano had to summon him to stop him working miracles, lest the
canonization of Bernardine of Siena should be impaired.

The main source for Thomas' life is *La Franceschina: testo volgare Umbro del secolo
xv scritto dal P. Giacomo Oddi di Perugia* ed P. Nicola Cavanna OFM (Florence
1931) I 215–49. In that account, there appears (234–6) the report of a pretended
funeral held for two young novices as a test of their humility and obedience.
It was also intended, however, to induce a spirit of remorse and renewed
austerity amongst the brethren of the convent who witnessed the trial, and
who in begging for mercy for the love of God for the novices, promised on
their behalf to purify themselves entirely and lead a better and more spiritual
life than in the past. What version of the story Erasmus heard cannot of course
be confirmed. Both in this text and in the letter, Erasmus implies that such an
act was approved by the pope, and in the letter to Grunnius such tolerance
is contrasted with the ostracism suffered by a man seeking to give up his
religious habit, as Erasmus sought to do.

The editor wishes to acknowledge the important assistance of Servus Gieben
OFM Cap of the Istituto Storico dei Cappuccini, Rome, in tracing the history of
this episode.

83 See n76 above.
84 'By synecdoche,' as Theotimus puts it. See *De copia* 23 CWE 24 341:1–24.
85 Matt 5:44–5, 48
86 See 'The Sermon' n93.
87 This echo of Matt 25:40 ('Inasmuch as ye have done it unto one of the least of
  these my brethren, ye have done it unto me') testifies to Theotimus' naïve but
  insuperable confusion of mendicant and evangelical charity.
88 Acts 14:19; 17:22–3; 2 Cor 11:25
89 Quoted by Paul in Acts 20:35
90 2 Cor 11:7
91 See Allen Ep 2700:109–14.
92 Ie the virtues proclaimed in the sermon on the Mount; see 1012:11–17 above
93 *Adagia* II i 21
94 Matt 9:20–2; Mark 5:25–34; Luke 8:43–8

NOTE ON FRANCISCAN POVERTY

Francis meant exactly what he said in the Rule about poverty and avoiding
money and property, but how to reconcile his uncompromising requirements
with the conditions of life, the growth of the order, and its governance taxed

the ingenuity of his sympathizers, successors, and their critics. The Rule of
1221 stipulated that friars must not receive (*recipiant*) money or cause it to be
received through an intermediary (chapters 2 and 8; the Rule of 1223 says the
same, but more briefly, in chapter 4). But is *recipere* ('to receive') the same as
attingere, contingere, tangere ('to touch'), verbs that also occur in the discussion
of poverty in this colloquy? 'Whence this new interpretation, that not to
receive it means not to touch it?' Philecous asks (1009:40–1). 'Pope Benedict so
interpreted,' he is told. The rejoinder to this answer, 'But as a Franciscan, not as
pope,' is puzzling. It may be a slip on Erasmus' part or perhaps simply a way
of showing that Theotimus, the credulous admirer of the order, is not so well
informed as he imagines. Neither Benedict XI (1303–4), Benedict XII (1334–42),
nor Benedict XIII (1394–1417, one of the 'Clementine' antipopes at Avignon
during the Great Schism of 1378–1417), was a Franciscan. All of these popes
were involved in matters that affected Franciscan privileges, but none of them
made important rulings in the controversies over the doctrine of poverty. The
person meant here is far more likely to be Bonaventure, minister-general of the
Franciscan order (1257–74) and author of the classic treatise *Apologia pauperum*
(1269) on the question of the absolute poverty of Christ and the apostles and of
Franciscans.

Debates on poverty, which divided Franciscans into factions and called forth
many writings over many generations, demanded the attention of popes and
councils. They continued so long, and were so difficult a sequel to Francis'
simple and devout efforts to give up everything to follow the injunctions
of Christ, as he understood these, that a brief review of decisive events
should be helpful. The number of documents, histories, and studies of this
and related topics is daunting, but the subject was so important and so long
argued that some titles must be cited. The best single-volume history of the
Franciscan order in English is John Moorman's (Oxford 1968), with excellent
bibliographies. On the controversies over poverty consult also M.D. Lambert
Franciscan Poverty (London 1961); Gordon Leff *Heresy in the Later Middle Ages*
2 vols (Manchester and New York 1967) I 51–166 and passim; Lydia von Auw
Angelo Clareno et les spirituels italiens Uomini e dottrine 25 (Rome 1979); David
Burr *Olivi and Franciscan Poverty: The Origins of the 'usus pauper' Controversy*
(Philadelphia 1989); Decima Douie *The Nature and the Effect of the Heresy of the
Fraticelli* (Manchester 1932).

Francis' words on money and poverty in the two Rules were intended not as
mere exhortations but as injunctions. 'We who left everything behind must take
care not to lose the kingdom of heaven for a trifle' (Rule of 1221 chapter 8). His
own example and sense of urgency about rejecting money and property could
persuade his earliest followers to practise what he preached. But the rapid
growth of the order, after Pope Honorius III confirmed the 1223 Rule, soon
began to show that the hard rules on poverty and rejection of money were less
practicable than they had been for the first brethren. (The Rules of 1221 and
1223 are translated in Leo Sherley-Price *St Francis of Assisi* [n40 above] 205–26,
228–34; also in Habig [n15 above] 31–53, 54–64.) Even holy friars could not
depend solely on alms when their numbers equalled, and then exceeded, the
five thousand who, as the Gospels relate, had been fed miraculously with five
loaves and two fish (Matt 14:15–21; Mark 6:31–42; Luke 9:12–17; John 6:3–13).
As early as 1221, Francis perceived clearly but helplessly that he was losing

control of his order. His successors, John Parenti and then Brother Elias, had
to deal with problems that Francis himself neither could nor would address.
Poverty was only one of these. Another was whether the order should support
learning and provide university training for priests, a question tentatively
settled during the lifetime of St Francis and definitively by 1230. A third
difficulty was relations between regulars and secular clergy. Some bishops and
monks wanted to suppress all mendicant orders at the Second Council of Lyon
(1274), but the pope would not allow such a radical move and specifically
exempted the Friars Minor and the Dominicans (the Friars Preachers) from
discussion of the future of the mendicants.

For many reasons the question of Franciscan poverty took longer to resolve. In
the Rule of 1223, still today the governing constitution of the Order of Friars
Minor, in the interim version of 1221, and in his *Testament* (1226), the founder's
intentions were, he believed, clear and emphatic as regards the doctrine of
absolute poverty and adherence to the Rule. Nevertheless constitutions seeking
to bind the future to the past may require interpretation, or reinterpretation,
if they are not to become dead letters. Provisions of the Rule concerning
poverty were watered down or amended from time to time both by Franciscan
and papal decisions, for the greater good and welfare of the order, as the
proponents of change argued.

Francis died in 1226. Even before that date differences arose between friars
who believed in strict poverty, manual work, and begging for food, and those
who, in spite of Francis' directions and example, wanted a more conventional
religious life. Pope Gregory IX, a personal friend of Francis, at the request
of general chapter decided that some definitive rulings must be made on
how the Rule's strictures on poverty were to be understood and followed.
Gregory's bull *Quo elongati* (1230) was the first in a series of papal decisions
and influential writings analysing, interpreting, and adjudicating the Rule
and its pronouncements on poverty. *Quo elongati* examined the concept of the
use of things (*usus rerum*), whether money or other goods, without *possession*
or ownership of them. The pope, or a cardinal designated by him, Gregory
suggested, could be the legal owner. Such distinction between use and
possession was presented as a rational solution, a sensible method of furnishing
food, shelter, clothing, and other necessities to the friars without their violating
the Rule by actually possessing money. The bull held that Francis' *Testament*
did not bind his successors; only the Rule was binding. But even that could not
bind unless popes, not Francis, had authority, as Gregory showed by using
his bull to interpret the Rule (text of *Quo elongati* in Luke Wadding *Annales
minorum* 8 vols [Lyon 1625–54; 3rd edition, 28 vols Quaracchi 1931–41] II 275–8).
See Moorman 89–91.

Bonaventure, minister-general from 1257 until 1274, is sometimes called the
second founder of the Franciscan order. His *Apologia pauperum* (1269) upheld
the doctrine of Christ's absolute poverty and stressed its spiritual value for
devout Christians who sought to emulate Christ. On that point, he argues,
the Rule is entirely correct. True, an aspiration to emulate Christ perfectly
with respect to poverty is impossible, since doing so would demand perfect
charity, and Christ alone had perfect charity. Yet striving to do as much as
possible towards that end is laudable and, for the sincere friar, necessary. As

for the compatibility of the doctrine of absolute poverty with the use of things, Bonaventure accepted the distinctions between use and possession made in *Quo elongati* but emphasized strict use, not mere use, for he insists on austerity. (On Bonaventure consult Leff I 83–100, where the Latin texts of Bonaventure's definitions are added; and Lambert 126–48.)

Bonaventure's *Apologia pauperum* supplied the foundation of the bull by Nicholas III, *Exiit qui seminat* (1279), which stressed the ideal of evangelical poverty in the Rule, especially its prescriptions on poverty as the authentic teaching of Christ. This bull was mainly a reworking of *Quo elongati* but with important refinements from *Apologia pauperum*. Its importance was that it confirmed Franciscan poverty by papal ruling. In addition it forbade any reopening henceforth of the question of the absolute poverty of Christ (see text in Leff I 97 n3). *Exiit* did, however, make distinctions between 'use of right' (*usus iuris*) and 'use in fact' (*usus facti*). The Rule permitted 'use in fact' but not 'use of right.' But even 'use in fact' must be interpreted as requiring strict austerity. For *Exiit qui seminat* see *Bullarium Franciscanum* ed J.H. Sbaralea 7 vols (Rome 1759–1904; facs repr 1983–   ) III 404–16; Moorman 179–81; and the analysis by Lambert 141–8.

Meanwhile small groups of dissident Franciscans in Italy and Provence, dedicated to rigorous observance of the founder's precepts, were protesting what they perceived as betrayal of the Franciscan ideals. These dissidents were the Zelanti or Spirituals. Opposed to them were friars who were willing to accept change, believing strongly in keeping the order together and promoting the gospel by teaching, learning, and foreign missions as well as by a holy life. These were the predecessors of the Conventuals, a term first used in a papal document of 1432. For them obedience was the test of piety in the order. To the order the Spirituals were schismatics, some even heretics, for by denying the now official distinction between use and ownership they were, in effect, denying the authority of the pope – and that meant courting trouble. The Spirituals had able spokesmen, and their adherents were willing to risk persecution for a cause they considered sacred. They won sympathy from some popes, reluctant but firm opposition from others, since the papacy could not permit dissidence to become outright contumacy. At a general chapter of the Franciscan order in 1292, Peter Olivi, a learned theologian and leader of the Spirituals, made no objection to the distinction between use and possession but demanded personal dedication and the practice of austerity (*usus pauper*). Like Bonaventure, Olivi made austerity the *sine qua non*, the integral test of a friar's faithfulness to his vows to follow the path of evangelical perfection (see Lambert 149–61). Olivi and other Spirituals criticized the papacy severely for what they regarded as interference with the pure doctrine of poverty. The orthodoxy of some of Olivi's theological writings was called into question, but he survived and was a hero to fellow Spirituals (Leff I 100–39). In 1294 Pope Celestine V, who sympathized with the Spirituals, allowed some of them to leave the Order of Friars Minor and form a new order, the Poor Hermits of Pope Celestine. But this pope reigned only a few months. His successor, Boniface VIII, was a formidable pontiff with stern views on the need for strict discipline and for obedience to papal decrees. He got rid of the minister-general, Raymond

Gaufridi, and appointed one who had no sympathy with the Spirituals. Olivi died in 1298, but other Spirituals continued his teachings. At last continued agitation by Spirituals and persecution of them compelled Pope Clement v to make an elaborate official inquiry (1309) into the differences between Spirituals and the order, but this action did little to improve matters.

The Council of Vienne (1311–12), also in the pontificate of Clement v, clarified existing rules about friars' privileges and relations with secular clergy. From this council came a long constitution *Exivi de paradiso* (1312) on the Franciscan Rule (text in Wadding *Annales minorum* VI 227–37; text and translation in Tanner I 392–401). The document is difficult because it labours to placate both Spirituals and the community by finding good things to say about both, but in the main it supports the community more than the Spirituals were prepared to accept. It agrees with *Quo elongati* on the authority of the Rule: 'Wishing, then, to give peace to the friars' consciences and to put an end to these disputes, we declare that the Friars Minor in professing their rule are obliged specially to the strict and restrained use expressed in the rule. To say, however, as some are said to assert, that it is heretical to hold that a restricted use of things is or is not included in the vow of evangelical poverty, this we judge to be presumptuous and rash' (Tanner I 400). That is, while Franciscans are bound by vow to poverty, as to obedience and chastity, they are not bound to more than is expressed in the Rule. This even-handedness in the decree did not satisfy the Spirituals, who remained unreconciled.

After John XXII (1316–34) became pope, both he and the minister-general tried to settle the long-standing quarrel by forcing the order to abandon relaxations of the Rule and the Spirituals their obstinate independence. Accordingly the pope issued a series of bulls. In *Quorumdam exigit* (1317), he accepted the fact that Franciscans now kept large stores of goods (such as oil and bread) and were no longer forced to beg for their day-to-day sustenance. At the same time John exalted the virtue of obedience (Wadding *Annales minorum* VI 308–13). A few friars resisted the bull; four who held out were declared heretical for defying the authority of the church, refused to recant, were handed over to the secular power, and burned (Marseilles 1318). Another bull, *Sancta Romana* (also 1317), denounced a group of Franciscan rebels, the Fraticelli, who refused to obey papal commands (Moorman 311–12). Some left the order; a few joined other orders; but worse was to come.

Spirituals believed and taught that by living without possessions, Christ set the pattern for all who would preach the gospel. Nicholas III had endorsed this interpretation in the preamble to *Exiit qui seminat* (1279), as the Spirituals often reminded their critics. They unwisely challenged the pope on the issue by declaring in their chapter that it was not heretical but Catholic teaching to say that Christ and the apostles did not own anything. John XXII was not a man to defy. He collected opinions from theologians on the question; respondents differed as to the Spirituals but upheld the absolute poverty of Christ. The time for decisive action had come. In *Quia nonnunquam* (1322) John asserted the legality of a pope's changing the decrees of his predecessors (Wadding *Annales minorum* VI 446–7; Moorman 315–16). In *Ad conditorem canonum* (1322) he rejected 'use' without possession; who owns the piece of cheese a friar eats? They are owners of what they have, in spite of their notions about the absolute poverty of Christ (Moorman 316–17; Lambert 230–5). Moreover the pope ruled that things (except church buildings) given to friars were no longer the property of the church as legal 'owner' (as provided in *Quo elongati*). Thus with this bull John xxii 'effectively destroyed Franciscan poverty' (Leff i 165) and made the Friars Minor like any other religious order.

Then came John's *Cum inter nonnullos* (1323), a bull very brief but devastating to Spirituals, for it declared the doctrine of the absolute poverty of Christ and his apostles 'erroneous and heretical' (text in Wadding *Annales minorum* vii 3 and Denzinger-Schönmetzer 228–9 nos 930–1; translation in Lambert 235–6). Christ and his apostles, the bull affirms, although they may have had few possessions, had some. John dismisses the legalistic arguments (as found in *Exiit qui seminat*) based on distinction between *usus iuris* and *usus facti*. To assert or imply that Christ and his apostles did not have a right to use things that Scripture says they possessed contradicts Scripture and Catholic doctrine. This bull, in which one pope (John xxii) dismissed as heretical what another (Nicholas iii) had declared true, came as a shock to the Spirituals, for it gave an immediate and alarming signal to those who might presume to preach a doctrine of Christ's absolute poverty. A sequel to this brief bull was a longer one, *Quia vir reprobus* (1329) in which John xxii returns to the topic of poverty in order to prove from Scripture at greater length that Christ and his apostles did have some property. Again the pope affirms that to maintain the contrary is heretical (Moorman 322; Lambert 242–3). For papal bulls on Franciscan topics consult Moorman's note (601) on the *Bullarium Franciscanum*. Titles, incipits, and dates of papal bulls important for Franciscan history, in Wadding and other collections, are listed in Moorman's index 619–20.

The authority of *Cum inter nonnullos* settled the question of Franciscan poverty, though echoes of the debate were heard for many years (see 'A Fish Diet' 690:3–7). John xxii made many enemies in this quarrel, among whom the philosopher William of Ockham was one of the most vigorous and prolific. Differences between Spirituals and the larger community were leading to worrisome questions whether the Order of Friars Minor could put its affairs in order or would divide into two orders. Bands of dissidents had existed in Italy since the second decade of the century if not earlier. One of the smallest groups, living in the harshest austerity, included a devout man called Paul de' Trinci. He and his companions kept strict observance of the Rule, attracted others to their ways, and won papal support from Gregory xi (1373), who permitted them to live separately from the rest of the Friars Minor while continuing under the authority of the minister-general. Once again the majority of friars were critical, but adherents of the new movement grew in numbers and influence. They were known henceforth as Observants. By 1415 they even had possession of the Portiuncula in Assisi, the sacred place of Franciscans, and they gradually won favour with popes and kings – not always, to be sure, and not without the risks and complexities of ecclesiastical and secular politics (Moorman 368–83). By the last decade of the fifteenth century Observants and Conventuals appear to have been nearly equal in numbers, though in different countries or regions one might have preponderance: Observants in Spain, for example, whereas in England, in the era of Erasmus, most Franciscans were

Conventuals. Like the monastic orders, the mendicants had the usual tensions with secular clergy.

The two branches of Franciscans lived in fraternal rivalry for nearly a century and a half. On this period of their history see Moorman chapters 35 and 37; and with particular reference to South Germany, P.L. Nyhus 'The Franciscans in South Germany, 1400–1590: Reform and Revolution' *Transactions of the American Philosophical Society* new series 65 no 8 (1975) 1–47. A lingering hope that, even though separated, they might have a single general who would exercise ultimate administrative authority, under the pope, came to nothing. At long last Pope Leo x in 1517 divided all Franciscans into two orders: Observants and the various communities of reformed friars (*reformati*) would constitute one order, the Friars Minor; all Conventuals would constitute a separate order, the Friars Minor Conventual. Each order would elect its own head, the Friars Minor a minister-general, the Conventuals a master-general. In all processions and ceremonies Observants would have precedence over Conventuals. Thereafter the Observants gradually became the dominant order of Franciscans. A few years before 'The Sermon' and 'The Seraphic Funeral' were printed, another group of Observants wrote a set of constitutions, received papal sanction, and soon became a large and active component of the Franciscan family. These were the Capuchins, the third independent group (Friars Minor Capuchin), but they were too new to receive attention from Erasmus. In his writings we read, as in these two colloquies, of Observants and Conventuals. The name 'Observants' was finally abrogated by papal decree in 1897.

The editor would like to thank Maurie Sheehan OFM Cap of Cromwell, Connecticut for his generous assistance in the revision of this historical note.

SYMPATHY

Amicitia

First printed in the September 1531 edition.

   This is the first of two dialogues on nature in the September 1531 edition. 'Sympathy' deals with natural history, 'A Problem' with what used to be called natural philosophy. Many pages in the *Colloquies* and many passages in other writings by Erasmus testify to his lifelong interest in such topics, an interest reflecting literary and rhetorical inclinations as much as 'scientific' curiosity. His knowledge of nature came both from books and from observation, but mainly from books. Erwin Panofsky was correct in noting that 'Erasmus' response to art, like that of all Northern humanists, was literary rather than visual' ('"Nebulae in pariete": Notes on Erasmus' Eulogy on Dürer' *Journal of the Warburg and Courtauld Institutes* 14 [1951] 37), and it is equally true that his response to nature was often literary rather than visual. A fundamental postulate of his conception of history, whether of nature or any other subject, was that to understand it one should go first, and repeatedly, to ancient authors. Almost everything worth knowing, he wrote in 1514, has been set forth in Greek and Latin (*De ratione studii* LB I 521B, 522A / ASD I-2 114:2–4, 116:12–14 / CWE 23 667:2–4, 669:25–6). In assessing Erasmus' life work, achievements, and fame we must accept these convictions as fundamental. To affirm that nearly everything worth knowing has been said in Greek and Latin would have been a reckless utterance at the end of the century, but in 1514 the claim was defensible. Moreover, in the context of education, where the claim is made, it was accepted as sound long after the sixteenth century. Still, not everything in 'Sympathy' comes from books. Erasmus does not allow the dialogue to become a mere lecture. Instead he enlivens it by anecdotes from his experiences in Italy and England. Such tactics were elementary rhetorical practice, but effective in this as in most Erasmian dialogues.

   Throughout the world of nature and its wondrous variety of flora, fauna, insects, birds, and fish, patterns of what the Greeks term sympathy and antipathy – connatural affinities and hostilities – are discernible to observers. They were well known to ancient naturalists and treated as worthy of notice, mysterious though they were. Aristotle, Theophrastus (his successor as head of the Lyceum), the Elder Pliny, and Dioscorides mention many examples, as do other authors. They offer some ingenious explanations of sympathies and antipathies, usually on anthropocentric assumptions, or simply resort to metaphors. For a few examples see Pliny *Naturalis historia*

10.203–8, 19.156, 20.21–2, 24.1–2, 32.1–4, 37.59; Aristotle *Historia animalium* 9:1; Cicero *De natura deorum* 2.47–52. Some of this lore was proverbial, some preserved in poetry or legend. Aristotle and Theophrastus in Greek and Latin were available in printed books before the end of the fifteenth century; Pliny as early as 1469.

Erasmus in his colloquy borrows also from Plutarch *Moralia*, Aelian *De natura animalium*, and Oppian *Halieutica*. Of all the writers named, Aristotle and Theophrastus were in a class by themselves. They were skilled investigators and classifiers, not merely compilers. (Linnaeus and Cuvier were 'schoolboys to old Aristotle,' Charles Darwin wrote after reading one of Aristotle's zoological works in his old age; see *Life and Letters* ed Francis Darwin [New York 1887] 427.) The *Materia medica* of Dioscorides (first century AD) was for centuries invaluable as an illustrated herbal and guide to pharmacology, on which medieval medicine was based. Pliny was a historian of sorts, a compiler of everything he could learn, in a lifetime of incessant labour, about the natural world and its creatures. Like Dioscorides, he produced a work that, despite errors, quaintness, and other faults, was none the less found useful by posterity. In the Middle Ages Dioscorides and Pliny were classics, authorities. Their books contain both fact and fancy, fables and folklore, but for many readers this simply made them more attractive. Erasmus had comparatively little to do with Dioscorides, except now and then in the *Adagia*, but was very familiar with Aristotle and Pliny, whom he read with pleasure and respect. Christian theology and teleology, with their moralizing of nature and fondness for allegorizing, expressed and emphasized wonder. The spectacle of nature taught Augustine, Aquinas, Erasmus, and all thoughtful, devout Christians, when they contemplated nature, to turn their thoughts to the author of nature. 'Sermons in stones' was a meaningful trope; the book of nature a bounteous resource for the expositor of Sacred Scripture (see *Ecclesiastes* LB V 866A–867B).

The description of Eusebius' house and garden at the beginning of 'The Godly Feast,' typical of its author and of sixteenth-century taste, demonstrates how natural history could be used for artistic embellishment and moral instruction. Later colloquies furnish additional examples of the application of science to literary and moral ends. That much of the science was derived from literary sources would not have diminished seriously its credibility or utility for Erasmus and his readers, for most of the accessible sources of information about the world of nature were discursive or descriptive ones. To painters, preachers, poets, and orators, natural history offered a treasury of materials for the purposes of pictorial and literary art. This is why so many of the parallels in *Parabolae* are bits of natural history from Aristotle and Pliny, accompanied by moral applications by Erasmus (see CWE 23 134, 219–77). It is why we have a brilliant exhibition of what Erasmus' imagination, supported by his erudition, could do with a few lines of Pliny in the essay on the beetle and the eagle in *Adagia* III vii 1 (LB II 869A–883E). And it is why, in a lesson on *copia*, Erasmus tells the aspirant that he must memorize the qualities of a great many things found in natural science in order to make comparisons of them ('A Short Rule for Copiousness' 169:1–3; cf *De copia* LB I 79B / CWE 24 581). Unless a preacher or theologian is familiar with the properties of plants, animals, and gems, he will miss the deeper meanings of similes and allegories in the Bible, as Augustine warned long ago (*De doctrina christiana* 2.16.24 PL 34 47). Or what good are syllogisms in a disputation on the crocodile if you don't know what kind of tree or animal a crocodile is (*Ratio verae theologiae* LB V 80A–B / Holborn 186:3–5)? Finally, if Erasmus is right, knowledge of our own instinctive preferences and aversions, for instance hatred of lies and liars (1045:33–1046:7 below), should be taken into account in the choice of career or companions.

The genesis of 'Sympathy,' as of some other colloquies (among them 'The Apotheosis of Reuchlin,' 'An Examination concerning the Faith,' 'A Pilgrimage for Religion's Sake,' 'Charon,' 'The Sermon,' 'The Seraphic Funeral') can be established without difficulty. In 1525, Erasmus wrote a preface to a new edition of Pliny's *Naturalis historia* (Basel: Johann Froben). He praises it as 'a treasure house, a veritable encyclopaedia of all that is worth knowing' (Allen Ep 1544:32–3 / CWE Ep 1544:34–5). Like Plutarch, Pliny is an author every educated person ought to have read; he is at the head of the list of the best authors in *De ratione studii* (see LB I 523B / ASD I-2 120 / CWE 24 673:1–2; on Erasmus' estimate of the ancients see CWE 23 xlviii–xlix). In 'Sympathy' the main speaker, Ephorinus, tells his friend John many curious facts about sympathy and antipathy in nature. Anselmus Ephorinus, a young scholar educated at Cracow, an admirer of Erasmus who had himself made an edition of Pliny (1530), visited Erasmus in Freiburg for five months, April–September 1531, bringing with him a youth named Jan Boner, whom he was tutoring, and another youth. It was a long but cordial visit. No doubt Pliny and his book were discussed during that summer. What is certain is that one of the new colloquies ready for the September 1531 edition, 'Sympathy,' had Ephorinus and Boner as interlocutors. On Ephorinus and Boner see CEBR and Allen Epp 2539, 2533.

On the history of natural history consult Thorndike *Magic and Experimental Science* and A.C. Crombie *Medieval and Early Modern Science* 2 vols, rev ed (Garden City, NY 1959). *The Development of Natural History in Tudor England* by F.D. and J.F.M. Hoeniger (Folger Shakespeare Library 1969) is recommended as a supplementary study, and C.S. Lewis *The Discarded Image* (Cambridge 1964) as an essay on the medieval world-view. J.-C. Margolin's helpful essay on 'L'idée de nature dans la pensée d'Erasme' is in his *Recherches*

érasmiennes 9–44. See Chomarat *Grammaire et rhétorique* I 42–50 on Erasmus
and the language of nature, and for some additional material on Pliny, 'A
Pilgrimage for Religion's Sake' n109. Filippo Picinelli's vast *Mundus symbolicus* shows how complex and detailed the lore of nature was when interpreted
by the evidences of classical, literary, emblematic, religious, and 'scientific'
experience.

EPHORINUS, JOHN

Ephorinus Often I fall to wondering what deity Nature consulted when she
mingled certain mysterious sympathies and antipathies in everything under
5   the sun – improbable ones by any known causes, except that apparently she
enjoyed this spectacle,[1] just as we find entertainment by setting cocks among
quail.[2]
John I'm not yet clear about your meaning.
Ephorinus Then if you want it put more plainly,[3] I'll tell you. You know
10   snakes are a species hostile to man.
John I know that between them and us there is ancient, irreconcilable enmity
– and will be as long as we remember that ill-omened apple.[4]
Ephorinus You know the lizard.
John Of course.
15   **Ephorinus** Italy has big green ones.[5] This animal is by nature both friendly
to man and unfriendly to snakes.
John What's the evidence?
Ephorinus Wherever a man looks, there are lizards gathered, heads tilted,
gazing intently at him. If you spit, they lick up the spittle dropped from
20   your mouth;[6] I've seen them drink boys' urine, too.[7] Yes, and boys handle
and even hurt them without harm to themselves; and when held up to your
mouth they're fond of licking the saliva. But if set against one another when
captured, it's wonderful how fiercely they fight among themselves, ignoring
the person who set them to fighting. If someone in the fields walks by a
25   hollow, they get his attention by their rustling in the bramble bushes here
and there. A person unfamiliar with this custom would suspect a snake;
when you look closely, there are the lizards, gazing at you with heads cocked
until you stand still; if you walk on, they follow. Also they bring themselves
to a man's attention when he's busy with something else. You'd say they're
30   having fun and are extremely delighted by the sight of a man.[8]
John A marvellous tale!
Ephorinus One day I saw a quite large and brilliantly green lizard fighting
with a snake in the mouth of a cave. At first we wondered what was the

matter, for the snake was not easily visible.[9] An Italian warned us that the enemy was in the cave. Soon afterwards the lizard came up to us, as though displaying his wounds and appealing for aid. He would almost allow himself to be touched, but whenever we stood still he too stood still,

5   watching us. The snake had gnawed almost all of one side, making the green one red.[10]

John Had I been there, I'd have wanted to avenge the lizard.

Ephorinus But the enemy[11] had already withdrawn to the inner part of the cave. Some days later, however, we feasted our eyes with revenge.

10 **John** Glad you did. But how?

Ephorinus We happened to be walking by the same place. The snake had drunk at a spring nearby, as the heat was intense – so much so that we too were desperate with thirst. At that very moment a boy from the fields came by, a lad of thirteen, son of the household in which we were staying (because

15 of the plague scare in Bologna).[12] He was carrying a rake, the kind farmers gather hay with, and as soon as he saw the snake he let out a yell.

John From fear, perhaps.

Ephorinus Not at all – from joy, as if exulting over a captured foe. He hits the snake with the rake; it coils; the boy keeps on hitting until the snake,

20 head crushed, stretches his length. Now this they don't do unless they're dying. Hence the fable you've often heard about the crab who kills his lodger the snake: when he sees the snake stretched out full length, he says, 'That's how you should have gone when alive.'[13]

John Well done! What next?

25 **Ephorinus** The boy picked up the snake with his rake and hung it from a bush above the cave. Several days later we saw the branches there stained with gore.

Countrymen in those parts told us for a fact something else that was astonishing. Farmers sometimes take a nap in the field when they're tired,

30 and they keep by them a jug of milk they use both for food and drink. Snakes are extremely fond of milk. So it happens not infrequently that they glide into the jug. For this mischief the farmers have a ready remedy.

John What, if you please?

Ephorinus They smear the rim of the jug with garlic, the smell of which

35 frightens the snakes away.

John Then what did Horace mean when he wrote that garlic was a poison more harmful than hemlock,[14] since (as you say) it's a remedy against poisons?[15]

Ephorinus But listen to what's harder to believe: sometimes they creep slyly

40 into the open mouth of the sleeper and worm their way into his stomach.[16]

John Doesn't a man with such a lodger die presently?

Ephorinus No, he lives – most miserably, without any relief for his pain unless they feed the guest milk and other food a snake likes.

John Is there no remedy against such a misfortune?

Ephorinus Eating plenty of garlic.

5 **John** No wonder, then, if reapers love garlic.

Ephorinus And there's another remedy sometimes available to those exhausted by work and heat. In this danger it's not unusual for a lizard, tiny as he is, to save a man.

John How can he?

10 **Ephorinus** When he sees a snake lying in wait, he scampers over the man's face and neck and keeps doing this until he's awakened him by scratching and scraping his claws.[17] Then the man who wakes up, when he sees the lizard nearby, soon realizes that an enemy lurks thereabouts, and he searches until he finds it.

15 **John** The marvellous power of nature!

Ephorinus Now no animal is more hostile to man than the crocodile, which often swallows men whole and resorts to cunning to further his malice. With the water he's drunk he makes slippery the paths down to the Nile; when men go down to draw water, he gobbles them up as they tumble in.[18] And

20 you're aware that the dolphin,[19] though born in a different element, is a lover of mankind.[20]

John I've heard the famous story of the beloved boy,[21] but a more famous one about Arion.[22]

Ephorinus Yes, and fishermen hunting mullets use dolphins as their

25 'hounds.' After receiving a small share of the prey, the dolphins take their leave – indeed[23] they even submit to punishment if they've been remiss in their hunting. Often they appear to sailors at sea, leaping for joy and sporting on the crest of the waves, sometimes swimming up to the ship, sometimes leaping across the swelling sails.[24] So delighted is the dolphin by

30 the company of man. But as it is fond of man, likewise is it a mortal foe of the crocodile. The dolphin comes out of the sea and dares to ascend the Nile, the crocodile's kingdom, to engage a monster armed with teeth and claws and with scales more impenetrable even than iron. He himself is not so well equipped for biting, as he has a mouth bent towards his breast. But he charges

35 the enemy and, when close to him, suddenly dives under and with dorsal fins erect pierces the soft underbelly of the otherwise invulnerable crocodile.[25]

John It's astonishing that an animal should instantly recognize his enemy, even if he's never seen it before, and know why it should be attacked and where it's vulnerable or can protect itself, since this knowledge is denied to

40 man, who wouldn't even shrink from a basilisk[26] unless warned or taught by bitter experience.

IOANNES FROBENIVS LECTORI S. D.

EN DAMVS

C. PLINII SECVNDI DI

VINVM OPVS CVI TITVLVS, HISTORIA MVNDI,
multo quàm antehac unquam prodijt emaculatius: idǫ primum ex annota
tionibus eruditorum hominum, præsertim Hermolai Barbari: deinde
ex collatione exemplariorum, quæ hactenus opera doctorum no
bis quàm fieri potuit emendatissime sunt excusa: postremo ex
fide uetustissimorum codicum, ex quibus non pauca restitui
mus, quæ alioqui nemo, quamlibet eruditus, uel depre
hendit, uel deprehendere poterat. Absit inuidia di
cto. Vicimus superiores omneis. Si quis hanc pal
mam nobis eripuerit, non illi quidē inuide
bimus, sed studijs publicis gratulabi,
mur. Bene uale lector, & fruere
Ἀγαϑῆ τύχη.
Additus est index, in quo nihil desideres.

Basileæ apud Io. Frobenium, Mense
Martio. An. ‾M‾.‾D‾.‾X‾X‾V‾.

Pliny *Naturalis historia* title-page
Basel: Froben 1525
Reproduced by courtesy of the Centre for Reformation and Renaissance Studies,
Victoria University, Toronto

Ephorinus The horse,[27] as you know, is an animal naturally obedient to man. Between it and the bear, a creature harmful to man, there is deadly enmity. It recognizes the enemy sight unseen and instantly prepares for battle.

John What weapons does it fight with?

5 **Ephorinus** Cunning rather than strength. It jumps over the bear and in its leap kicks his head with its rear hoofs. Meantime the bear slashes the horse's belly with his claws.

Against the asp, whose poison is fatal to man,[28] the ichneumon wages war.[29] This same creature is a deadly foe of the crocodile.[30] Elephants are 10 similarly disposed towards man, for they'll kindly escort a traveller back to the road when he's far astray; and they recognize and love their trainer.[31] Stories are told too of their devotion to certain persons; for instance, in Egypt one fell in love with a girl who sold garlands, the sweetheart of Aristophanes the grammarian.[32] Another was so infatuated with Menander, a Syracusan 15 youth, that it refused to eat if its beloved was out of sight.[33] But, to proceed no further with examples – which abound – when King Bocchus determined to behave cruelly towards thirty men, he had them tied to stakes and thrown before as many elephants. When men were sent to rush among the elephants and incite them, they could never make them act as executioners of the 20 royal cruelty.[34] And there is deadly warfare between this animal, a lover of man,[35] and Indian snakes (said to be the largest kind), often ending in mutual destruction in battle.[36] The snake, moreover, is hostile to man, even when unprovoked. Between the eagle and lesser snakes a comparable enmity exists,[37] though the eagle is harmless to man; more than that, it is even 25 said to feel amorous passion for certain girls.[38] There is murderous warfare between this bird and the cymindis[39] or night-hawk. An elephant detests a mouse, a creature bothersome to man also, and abhors fodder in which it has seen a mouse. Why this hatred exists is unknown. They do have good reason to dread a leech, because if they swallow one while drinking they 30 suffer grievous torture.[40]

Scarcely any animal is more friendly to man than a dog, none less so than a wolf, the very sight of which strikes a man dumb.[41] Between these is the bitterest enmity, as the wolf is the greatest bane to sheep, a species totally dependent on the surveillance of men, whose special care it is to 35 protect an animal harmless and naturally serviceable to the human race.[42] Against the wolf, in truth, as against a public enemy, all men go armed, with dogs as their main allies; a fact that gave rise to a proverb, 'We'll show no more mercy than we do to wolves.'[43] The sea hare is incurable poison if a man rashly tastes it, yet the touch of man is death to the hare.[44] A panther is 40 savage towards man and yet so terrified of a hyena that it refuses even to come near it. Hence the saying that if a man carries a piece of hyena hide with him he's safe from attack by a panther. So acute is natural instinct. And they add that if you hang up the skins of both beasts back to back, the hair of the panther's comes off.[45]

5   The spider is a domestic creature, so far as man is concerned, but so deadly to a snake that if he chances to spy one sunning itself under a tree, he lowers himself carefully on a thread and stings the snake on top of the head so sharply that it writhes in agony and finally dies.[46] I've been told by those who've witnessed it that there exists a similar feud between spider and toad; but a toad that has been stung cures itself by eating plantain.

10   Now for a British story.[47] Floors there, you know, are covered with green rushes.[48] A certain monk had carried some bundles of rushes to his cell, intending to spread them when he had time. As he was taking a nap after lunch, a large toad crawled over him and blocked his mouth, its four feet fixed on his upper and lower lips.[49] To pull off the toad was certain

15   death;[50] not to remove it was something more cruel than death. Some persons recommended that the monk be carried, face up, to the window, on which a large spider had his web. This was done. Presently the spider, at the sight of his enemy, lowers himself on a thread, plants his sting on the toad, and returns to the web by the thread. The toad swelled up but was not dislodged.

20   Again the spider stung; the toad swelled more but still lived. When stung a third time it withdrew its feet and fell off, dead.[51] This favour the spider did for his host.

John   That's a wonderful tale you tell.

Ephorinus   I'll add something I didn't read but saw with these very eyes.

25   A monkey has an extraordinary dread of a tortoise. In Rome a certain man showed me an example of this fact. He put a tortoise on his boy's head and covered it with a cap. Then he brought him to the monkey. At once the monkey leaped joyfully on the lad's shoulders, ready to hunt lice. When the cap was removed, he discovered the tortoise. It was an astonishing sight, the

30   extreme horror with which the brute jumped down, how terrified he was, how fearfully he looked back to see if the tortoise were coming after him.

Here's another example. We tied a tortoise to the chain by which the monkey was fastened, so he couldn't escape but could nevertheless see the tortoise. His agony was unbelievable; he nearly died of fright, turning his

35   back at times and with his hind feet trying to drive the captive animal away. Finally he evacuated whatever was in his bowels or bladder. The scare gave him a fever, so that we had to release him from the chain and revive him with a mixture of water and wine.

John   But there's no reason for a monkey to dread a tortoise.

40   **Ephorinus**   Perhaps some reason concealed from us but known to nature.[52] Why a finch should hate an ass is obvious: because the ass rubs itself against

the thistles in which the little bird nests, and eats the flowers. The finch is so terrified that whenever she hears an ass bray far off, she pushes the eggs out and her chicks fall from the nest in a fright. Yet she doesn't let her enemy go unpunished.

5 **John** But how does a finch harm an ass?

Ephorinus Pecks the sores it has from beatings and burdens and pricks the tender parts of its nostrils.

Something of the reason for the mutual enmity between foxes and kites can be guessed, too: that the greedy bird traps the other's young. Perhaps

10 foxes do the same thing in return. (This is the reason for the feud between shrewmice and herons.) The same relation generally exists between the merlin, a small bird, and the fox. The merlin breaks raven's eggs; foxes prey on merlins and merlins on foxes, by nipping their cubs. When ravens see this they go to the aid of the foxes, as if against a common foe. But to account for

15 the hatred between swans and eagles, raven and oriole, crow and owl, eagle and wren[53] is almost impossible, unless the eagle is envied because he's called king of birds. Why is the owl at odds with other, smaller birds, weasel with crow, dove with pyralis,[54] ichneumon-wasps with spiders,[55] ducks with gulls,[56] falcons with buzzard-hawks, jackals with lions? Why, moreover, do

20 shrewmice dread a tree full of ants?[57] Whence so irreconcilable[58] a warfare between beetle and eagle, whose very natures provide the basis for a fable?[59] Why is it beetles won't live if brought to a certain district near Olynthus? And among water animals, why the fierce hatred between mullet and wolf-fish, as between eel and moray, which gnaw each other's tails?[60] A lobster has

25 such great horror of a polypus that if it sees one nearby it dies of fear.[61]

So too a certain mysterious bond of affection unites some creatures in an extraordinary way, as peacocks and pigeons, doves and parrots, blackbirds and thrushes, crows and herons (which help each other in turn against foxes), and falcon and kite against the buzzard-hawk, their common

30 enemy.[62] The musculus, a tiny fish, acts as guide to whales by swimming ahead of them;[63] just why it wishes to perform this service is not clear. That the crocodile opens his jaw wide for the plover, a small bird, cannot be termed friendship, since each benefits by it. The crocodile is pleased to have his teeth cleaned and welcomes the pleasure of a scraping; the little bird

35 hunts food, feeding on bits of fish left between the teeth.[64] For a similar reason the raven rides on a sow's back. Between the yellow wagtail[65] and titmouse animosity is so persistent that it is said their blood can't be mixed, just as it is said other birds' feathers are consumed if mingled with those of eagles.[66] A hawk is troublesome to doves, but these are defended by the

40 kestrel, a small bird whose sight and sound the hawk strangely fears. This is not unknown to the doves. Wherever the kestrel is found, there they abide,

confident of their protector.[67] Who could explain why the kestrel is well
disposed towards doves or why the hawk dreads the kestrel?

    And as a very tiny animal is sometimes helpful to a monstrous big one,
so, on the contrary, are the smallest deadly to the largest. There's a little fish
5 resembling a scorpion, the size of a spider fish.[68] Sometimes it stings tunnies
so sharply under the fin – tunnies bigger than a dolphin – that they jump
into ships. It does the same to mullets.[69] Why is the lion, a beast that puts
everyone in a tremble, scared of a cock's crow?[70]

John Lest I fail to contribute my share[71] to this feast, I'll relate what I once
10 saw with my own eyes at the house of the distinguished Englishman,[72]
Thomas More. He kept at home a large monkey, which at that time, as it
happened, was allowed to run loose in order to recover from a wound.
At the end of the garden was a rabbit hutch; and a weasel had designs on
the rabbits.[73] The monkey would watch this from a distance, quietly and
15 idly, as long as he saw the rabbits were in no danger. But after the weasel
had pried the pen loose from the wall and there was now danger that the
rabbits, exposed to attack from the rear, would fall prey to the enemy, the
monkey dashed up and by climbing on a board pulled the pen back to its
former position so skilfully that a man could not have done it better – plain
20 evidence of the fondness monkeys have for rabbits. The rabbits themselves
didn't understand their danger but kissed their enemy through the fence.
The monkey came to the rescue of innocence imperilled.

Ephorinus Monkeys delight in all young animals and love to fondle and
embrace them.[74] But that devoted monkey deserved some reward for his
25 devotion.

John He had it.

Ephorinus What?

John He found there a scrap of bread – thrown by boys, I suppose. He
snatched it and ate it.

30 **Ephorinus** But more wonderful, in my opinion, is the fact that this type
of sympathy and antipathy – for so Greeks call the natural feelings of
friendship and hostility – is found even in things lacking soul or sense.[75]
I say nothing of the ash tree, whose shadow, no matter how far it extends,
snakes won't endure; so that if you surround the spot with a ring of fire,
35 a snake would go into the flame sooner than take refuge at the tree.[76] We
have countless examples of this sort of thing. Caterpillars encased in skin
are transformed into butterflies by the secret operation of nature.[77] They
show every sign of being dead; they don't even move when touched – unless
a spider passes by. They don't feel a man's finger pressing, and yet they
40 sense the delicate tread of the lightest of creatures. Thereupon the caterpillar
comes to life at last.

John An insect yet unborn senses its mortal enemy![78] Not altogether different from this are the stories told about victims of stabbings: if other persons approach, nothing unusual happens; but if the killer comes close, they begin to bleed at once, as though from a fresh wound. And by this sign,
5   it is said, the murderer is often betrayed.[79]

Ephorinus That's no mere fiction you've heard, either. But – to avoid hunting out Democritical stories[80] – don't we find by experiments an antipathy between oak and olive so strong that each dies if put in the other's trench?[81] An oak is at such odds with a walnut tree that it dies if placed
10   nearby,[82] though indeed the walnut is harmful to almost all crops and trees.[83] Again, though a grapevine usually clasps everything with its tendrils, it shuns only cabbage, turning off in a different direction exactly as if it were aware of what it was doing.[84] Who warns the vine that its enemy is near? For cabbage juice is the antithesis of wine and is taken to prevent drunkenness.[85]
15   And the cabbage is not without an enemy of its own, since it dries up if placed against cyclamen and wild marjoram.[86]

A similar feeling exists between hemlock and wine: hemlock is fatal to man, wine to hemlock.[87] What[88] is the mysterious bond between lily and garlic that causes them to take pleasure in each other's company when they
20   grow side by side?[89] For the garlic is stronger and the lily's flowers more fragrant. What need to call to mind, in this connection, the marriage of trees, the females of which are sterile unless male ones are in the vicinity?[90] Oil mixes only with lime, though they have equal hatred of water.[91] Pitch absorbs oil, though each is thick.[92] Everything except gold floats on quicksilver; gold
25   alone it attracts to itself and encloses.[93] What natural affinity causes adamant, resistant to anything however hard, to melt in goat's blood?[94] Nay,[95] you may even see antipathies among poisons themselves. If a scorpion happens to crawl through wolfsbane, it turns pale and becomes numb.[96] The herb named cerastes is so injurious to it that whoever has touched the seed
30   merely with his fingers may handle a scorpion without harm.[97] But study of these matters, which are without number, is the province of the medical profession.

What is that power, whether of sympathy or antipathy, between steel and a magnet that causes a substance heavy by nature[98] to advance towards
35   the magnet, 'cling' to it as if by a kiss, and withdraw without touching it?[99] Though water mixes readily with everything, especially with itself, there are nevertheless bodies of water that avoid mixing, as though from mutual hatred, as for example the stream that is carried on the surface of Lake Fucino, the Adda on Como, Ticino on Maggiore, Mincio on Garda, Oglio on
40   Iseo, Rhône on Geneva. Some of these, in the course of many miles, carry only their own 'visiting' waters and emerge no larger than they entered.

The Tigris flows into Lake Arethusa and is borne through it as if a guest, so that neither colour nor fish nor the essential quality of the waters mingles. Moreover, though other rivers usually hurry on to meet the sea, some hide themselves in the earth before reaching the sea, as though from hatred

5   of it.[100] We observe something comparable in winds, too. The south wind is noisome to man; the north, on the contrary, is healthful. One produces clouds; the other scatters them.[101] If astrologers are to be trusted, there are certain dispositions of sympathy and antipathy in stars also.[102] Some are friendly to man, some dangerous; again, some protect him against the power

10 of evildoers. Thus there is nothing anywhere in nature that does not do man good or harm through these sympathies and antipathies.
    John Perhaps man may discover something beyond the heavens, too, for if we believe the sages every mortal is attended by two spirits, one friendly, the other malevolent.[103]

15 **Ephorinus** Enough for us to have reached as far as the sky, my friend, even if we don't jump beyond the pit.[104] 'Back to beeves and horses.'[105]
    John A big jump indeed!
    Ephorinus More surprising is it that we find traces of love and hatred in the same species of animal, for no apparent reason. So grooms and cowherds

20 try to convince us. In the same pastures or the same stables an ox likes to have a particular ox, a horse a certain horse, next to him, and won't endure a different one. In fact comparable feelings exist in animals of every kind, I believe, quite aside from partiality for sex. But in no species is it more evident than in man, since what Catullus declares about his feeling for

25 Volusius is obvious in many:

        I love you not, Volusius, and can't tell why;
        I can say only this: I love you not.[106]

30 In adults, perhaps, various explanations could be conjectured; in children, who are guided solely by instincts, what is it that draws one to another by so strong an affection and, furthermore, separates him from still another by so strong a dislike?[107] I myself, when a boy about eight, fell in with someone my age, or maybe a year older, who had such inordinate vanity that at every

35 opportunity he would make up monstrous fibs on the spur of the moment. We would meet a woman. 'See her?' he'd say. 'I see her.' 'I've slept with her ten times.' We would go across a little narrow bridge by a mill. When he saw me shuddering at the sight of the water, which revealed its depth by its blackness, he said, 'I fell into this water once.' 'What's that you say?' 'I found

40 the body of a man there, wearing a purse with three rings in it.' Since he never stopped lying, I, a boy, dreaded the fellow more than a viper, while

others were delighted by his lies – there was no particular reason, it was simply a strange instinctive reaction. This was not merely a stage I passed through; even today I have such a natural aversion to boastful liars that I feel a physical repulsion at the sight of them.[108] Homer notes something
5 similar in Achilles, who declares liars are as hateful to him as the gates of hell themselves.[109] Though I was born with this trait, I seem to be fated, contrariwise, to have dealings all my life with liars and cheats.

John But I don't yet see the point of all this talk.

Ephorinus I'll tell you in a few words. Some people seek happiness by
10 magic arts, some from the stars. I believe, for my part, that a person can find no surer road to happiness than by avoiding the kind of life from which he instinctively recoils and by following that to which he is attracted (always excluding what is dishonourable). Furthermore, he should avoid the company of those whose characters he finds incompatible with his own and
15 associate with those to whom he is drawn by natural sympathy.

John In that event he'll have few friends.

Ephorinus Christian charity extends to the whole world; intimate friendship should be restricted to a few. And he who wrongs no man, however wicked, who will rejoice if the sinner repents – he loves all men, I should say, in the
20 proper Christian spirit.[110]

NOTES

1 This prologue, like so much of what follows, is consonant with other remarks in Erasmus' main sources, Aristotle and Pliny; see for example Aristotle *Historia animalium* 9.1–2 608a10–610b19, Pliny *Naturalis historia* 10.203–8. Pliny especially is a frequent and sometimes entertaining moralizer in his encyclopaedic survey of the wonders of the visible world.

2 Perhaps proverbial but not in *Adagia*, though the mutual hostility of cocks and partridges, which are closely related to quail, is attested by an Aesopic fable. See *Babrius and Phaedrus* ed and trans Ben Edwin Perry, Loeb Classical Library (London 1965) Appendix 425 no 23. Pliny has a pleasant account of cocks, the domestic roosters, in *Naturalis historia* 10.46–8.

3 With less learning, *crassiore Minerva*; see *Adagia* I i 37.

4 'Whose mortal tast' by Eve and Adam 'Brought Death into the World, and all our woe' (Milton *Paradise Lost* 1.2–3).

5 One of many recollections of sights seen and stories heard during Erasmus' Italian years, 1506–9. Parts of his description of lizards on pages 1036:13–1038:15 are translated, with acknowledgment to this colloquy, in Edward Topsell's *History of Serpents* (1608; STC 24124) 209–10.

6 Long known or believed to be fatal to snakes. Aristotle *Historia animalium* 8.29 607a29–30; Pliny *Naturalis historia* 7.15; Lucretius 4.638

7 On the medicinal properties of urine see Pliny *Naturalis historia* 28.65–7.

8 For some other reports of their friendliness towards man see B.J. Whiting's review of *Standard Dictionary of Folklore, Mythology, and Legend* ed Maria Leach, 2 vols (New York 1949–50) in *Speculum* 27 (1952) 232–3.

9 for . . . visible] Added in the March 1533 edition

10 *ex viridi rubrum fecerat.* To an English reader, Erasmus' Latin immediately calls to mind the striking closure of a familiar passage in *Macbeth* 2.2.60–2:

> . . . this my hand will rather
> The multitudinous seas incarnadine,
> Making the green one red.

On these lines see Kenneth Muir's note in his edition of *Macbeth* Arden Shakespeare, 7th edition revised (London 1951) and Michael Cameron Andrews 'Erasmus and Macbeth: 'Making the Green One Red' *Erasmus in English* 15 (1987–8) 30–1. *Macbeth* is believed to have been written in 1605 or 1606 but was not printed until the first folio of 1623. Topsell comes fairly close to 'making the green one red' ('of green he made him appear red') in *History of Serpents* (n5 above) 210. There is no direct evidence of Shakespeare's having read Topsell, or Erasmus' *Colloquia* either, but a reader may reserve the right to suspend disbelief.
Lizards bitten by snakes heal themselves by eating the herb dittany, as Erasmus says in *De pueris instituendis* (LB I 496B / CWE 26 309). This is from Pliny *Naturalis historia* 8.97.

11 the enemy] Substituted for the ambiguous *ille* (1531) in the March 1533 edition

12 in Bologna] Added in the March 1533 edition.
The plague scare there in 1506 was an experience Erasmus never forgot. See Allen Epp 296:175–204, 447:471–96, 1436:110–11 / CWE Epp 296:185–219, 447:514–45, 1436:120–1; also Beatus Rhenanus in Allen I 59:112–60:146.

13 *Adagia* III vii 38. An Aesopic fable; see *Babrius and Phaedrus* (n2 above) Appendix 458–9 no 196. Cf Pliny *Naturalis historia* 9.99, 32.55.

14 Horace detested garlic, 'more deadly than hemlock' (*Epodes* 3). On the poisonous hemlock see 1044:17–18 and n87 below. For garlic's effect on snakes, see Pliny *Naturalis historia* 20.50.

15 as you say . . . poisons] The first edition had only 'it's a remedy.' Garlic was also said to be a remedy for snakebite; see n89 below.

16 Whether fact or improbable fiction, a well-known peril. Rabelais tells of an example (*Gargantua and Pantagruel* 4.44); for another see Shakespeare *As You Like It* 4.3.105–15 or *2 Henry VI* 3.2.254–63. Sacchetti (fourteenth century) speaks of making a snake come out of a man's stomach by having the man lie face down in a bowl of milk; the snake comes up to drink (D.P. Rotunda *Motif-Index of the Italian Novella in Prose* [Bloomington, Ind] no J1115.2.3).

17 scratching and scraping his claws] *pruritu scalptuque ungium.* The 1531 edition had 'scratching his feet' (*pruritu pedum*).

18 On the malicious cunning of the crocodile see Aelian 12.15 and *Adagia* II iv 60 on 'crocodile tears.'

19 Lord of the fishes (Oppian *Halieutica* 1.643) and, like the elephant, a favourite subject for writers on natural history, for both creatures were admired for their fabled intelligence, strength, and docility. Pliny's account of the dolphin (*Naturalis historia* 9.20–33) is typical but more picturesque and imaginative than that

of Aristotle (*Historia animalium* 9.48 631a8–b4), who is more interested in their structure and habits. Like the elephant, lion, and eagle, the dolphin is prominent in emblematic art and in literature. In *Adagia*, for instance (II i 1 LB II 399E–402B), we hear much about the dolphin because of Aldo Manuzio's famous trademark of dolphin and anchor; on this see 'Penny-Pinching' n22. For an excellent compendium of fact and tradition about dolphins see D'Arcy W. Thompson *A Glossary of Greek Fishes* (London 1947) 52–6. They appear to delight modern as well as ancient naturalists. Their capacities as hunters and herders were reported long ago, as Erasmus reminds us, and see Pliny *Naturalis historia* 9.29–32.

20 Greek in the original

21 A dolphin carried him across a bay to school and back every day. Pliny (*Naturalis historia* 9.25–7) says he would hesitate to tell such a story were it not that others too have written about it (cf Gellius 6.8 and Pliny the Younger *Letters* 9.33).

22 A musician whom sailors intended to kill for his money. But when he persuaded them to allow him first to play on his harp, the music attracted a shoal of dolphins (who are fond of music). Then the harper jumped overboard and a dolphin carried him to shore. The story is often told, but versions differ (Herodotus 1.24; Pliny *Naturalis historia* 9.28; Aelian *De natura animalium* 2.6, 6.15; Gellius 16.19; Plutarch *Moralia* 160E–162B *Septem sapientium convivium*).

23 indeed ... their hunting] Added in the March 1533 edition

24 Aristotle says that, swimming under water, they hold in their breath like divers; the compressed air, when released, propels the dolphin over the ship (*Historia animalium* 9.48 631a22–33).

25 See Pliny *Naturalis historia* 8.91–2.

26 An imaginary serpent believed to frighten all other creatures by its hiss, kill vegetation by its touch, and man by looking at him; Pliny *Naturalis historia* 8.78, 29.66. Cf Erasmus *Parabolae* CWE 23 250:5–7; *Lingua* LB IV 694C–D / ASD IV-1A 86:15–87:24 / CWE 29 320; and see 'The Godly Feast' 181:18–19 and n66.

27 The horse ... his claws.] Added in the March 1533 edition. Pliny says that the bear has a weak head (*Naturalis historia* 8.130).

28 'Asps kill those they strike by torpor and coma, inflicting of all serpents the most incurable bites' (Pliny *Naturalis historia* 29.65; see also 8.86–7). Cf Aristotle *Historia animalium* 8.29 607a22; *Adagia* IV v 43; *Lingua* LB IV 694B / ASD IV-1A 86:7–8 / CWE 29 320.

29 Aristotle *Historia animalium* 9.6 612a17–20; Pliny *Naturalis historia* 8.87–8; Aelian 3.22. This ichneumon was the Egyptian rat, now identified with the mongoose. In spite of his smallness, the ichneumon overcame enemies; hence Luther thought it a 'type' of Christ (WA *Tischreden* 3 and Clemen 8 no 3851).

30 So Pliny *Naturalis historia* 8.90; *Adagia* III vii 1 LB II 874F

31 Pliny gives a long account of elephants (*Naturalis historia* 8:1–37). They were almost unknown to the Greeks before the wars of Alexander the Great and the writing of Aristotle's *Historia animalium* in the fourth century BC. Hannibal introduced them to Europe when he crossed the Alps to invade Italy in 218 BC, bringing thirty-seven elephants with him. At first the Roman soldiers were terrified of them, but quickly recovered (Appian *Roman History* 7.7). All the elephants perished in the Italian campaign. Romans did not, either then or afterwards, employ elephants in war but at a later period in their history

used them in fights in the Roman Circus, where these beasts were a popular attraction (Pliny *Naturalis historia* 8.19–22).

No elephants are known to have been brought into Europe between the ninth and thirteenth centuries, but in the later Middle Ages they were known by pictures, and a few captive elephants existed in western Europe. Fifteenth- and sixteenth-century readers found them as fascinating as Aristotle, Pliny, and their successors had, not only because of size and strength but of their reputed intelligence, gentleness, sensitiveness (see Aristotle *Historia animalium* 9.46 630b19–30), and their sense of fairness and justice, of which Pliny and his literary descendants tell many wondrous tales. By the time Erasmus wrote of them, elephants had a special place in human opinions of undomesticated animals; they had even become moral and emblematic symbols or allegories, as Renaissance and Baroque art can show. This significance is treated definitively by W.S. Heckscher in 'Bernini's Elephant and Obelisk' *Art Bulletin* 29 part 3 (1947) 155–82, a study of the marble elephant supporting an Egyptian obelisk in Rome. This work (1667) was commissioned by Pope Alexander VII.

For elephants helping travellers, see Pliny *Naturalis historia* 8.9; ibidem 8.6 on an elephant, a slow learner apparently, that was seen rehearsing by himself at night the lessons he had failed to learn satisfactorily that day. This story is in Plutarch *Moralia* 968C–D *Terrestriane an aquatilia animalia sint callidiora*.

32 *Adagia* III vii 1 LB II 875D; Pliny *Naturalis historia* 8.13; Aelian 7.43. Aristophanes of Byzantium was head of the Alexandrian library c 195.

33 This Menander was a soldier (Pliny *Naturalis historia* 8.15).

34 Pliny *Naturalis historia* 8.15

35 Greek in the original, as at 1038:20–1 above

36 Pliny *Naturalis historia* 8.32–4. Struggle between elephant and serpent became an established topos in medieval and post-medieval art. See Heckscher (n31 above) 159. Cf *De pueris instituendis* LB I 510D–E / CWE 26 337 on teaching children about snakes and elephants.

37 On the enmity between eagles and snakes see Pliny *Naturalis historia* 10.17; Aristotle *Historia animalium* 9.1 609a4.

38 *amatorios ignes sentire erga certas puellas* (and cf *De copia* CWE 24 616:2). Pliny is less dramatic; he tells of an eagle that had been reared by a girl and showed its gratitude by bringing birds and other game to her (*Naturalis historia* 10.18).

39 Or cybindis. Pliny says this night-hawk wages war to the death with the eagle (*Naturalis historia* 10.24).

40 Pliny *Naturalis historia* 8.29

41 Proverbial, as in Plato *Republic* 336C–D; Virgil *Eclogues* 9.53–4; Pliny *Naturalis historia* 8.80; Erasmus in Allen Ep 2191:71–2; *Adagia* I vii 86. See also 'The Fabulous Feast' n60.

42 Cf 'A Pilgrimage' 649:1–3.

43 *Adagia* II ii 27

44 The *lepus marinus*. Thompson *Greek Fishes* (n19 above) 142–3; Pliny *Naturalis historia* 9.155 and 32.8 describes its poison as exceptionally strong. Cf *Adagia* II i 15 and 'A Fish Diet' 680:11.

45 'Panther' and 'leopard' are usually synonymous in the writings of early naturalists. Its animosity towards hyenas is often mentioned (as by Aelian 6.22). Aristotle and Pliny supply miscellaneous information on panthers, leopards,

and hyenas; see *Historia animalium* 9.6 612a7, 6.32 579b15–29 and *Naturalis historia* 8.62, 105–6. The 'saying' is in Pliny 28.93.

46 Pliny *Naturalis historia* 10.206; cf Artistotle *Historia animalium* 9.39 623a33–623b3.

47 Presumably a story Erasmus heard during one of his visits to England, but nothing more is known. In Christian art the toad became a symbol of evil and of a devil; so in *Paradise Lost* the good angels find the devil 'Squat like a Toad, close at the eare of Eve' (4.800). See 'A Pilgrimage' n117.

48 An Italian visitor to England (1497) comments on the custom of keeping fresh rushes on floors of houses because of the constant amount of mud from the streets (*Two Italian Accounts of Tudor England* ed and trans C.V. Malfatti [Barcelona 1953] 34). In a letter of 1532, addressed to an English physician and friend, Erasmus expresses strong disapproval of this custom because the rushes, which have in them all kinds of filth, are not changed often enough. Fresh rushes are merely laid on top of old ones: a danger to health as well as a malodorous nuisance (Allen Ep 1532:12–16 / CWE Ep 1532:15–21).

49 For a striking but slightly different example (four toads, covering the face) see T.S.R. Boase *Death in the Middle Ages* (London 1972), illustration 33 on page 45.

50 The toad's venomous breath would kill the man on whose mouth it rested or anyone who attempted to remove it. See the seventh story of the fourth day in Boccaccio's *Decameron* on the pervasive power of the poison. Aelian says that the toad's breath produces a pallor that lasts several days (17.12); he also says the toad can kill with a belch a person who touches it (9.11).

51 On the thread see Pliny *Naturalis historia* 10.206, and for accounts of how spiders weave their webs Pliny *Naturalis historia* 11.80–4 (11.84 describes how they hunt young frogs and lizards) and Aristotle *Historia animalium* 9.39 622b28–623b1. In his *History of Serpents* (n5 above) 192–3, Topsell includes this anecdote 'related by Erasmus in his book on friendship.' Sir Thomas Browne in *Pseudodoxia epidemica* (1646) says that when by way of experiment he put seven spiders in a glass with a toad, the toad ate them (3.27.6).

52 Many of the antagonisms and sympathies mentioned by Ephorinus are noted (although not in the same order) in Pliny *Naturalis historia* 10.203–7 and Aristotle *Historia animalium* 9.1–2 608b19–610b20; a few are listed in Aelian 5.48. Some of the examples appear also in *Adagia* III vii 1 LB II 874E–875B. Only additional or different references will be noted here.

53 On crow and owl see also Aelian 5.48 and 3.9. 'Wren' is a common translation of *trochilus*, a Latin transliteration of a Greek word also taken to mean 'sandpiper'; see Aristotle *Historia animalium* 8.3 593b12 in *The Works of Aristotle* ed W.D. Ross IV trans and ann D'Arcy W. Thompson (Oxford 1910). On warfare between eagle and wren, see Aristotle *Historia animalium* 9.1 609b13, 9.12 615a16–19.

54 A fly or moth believed to live in fire; Aristotle *Historia animalium* 9.1 609a19; Pliny *Naturalis historia* 10.204, 11.119

55 Venomous spiders, *phalangia*. The ichneumon meant here is not the Egyptian rat of 1040:8 above but a species of wasp (Aristotle *Historia animalium* 9.1 609a5 and n4 in the Oxford *Works* [n53 above]; Pliny *Naturalis historia* 11.72).

56 Pliny has *brenthos* (*Naturalis historia* 10.204), water-birds of uncertain species; Aristotle is equally vague (*Historia animalium* 9.1 609a23). Erasmus renders by *anatibus* 'ducks.'

57 So Erasmus' text: *sorices formicosam horreant arborem*, but some texts of Pliny
Naturalis historia 10.206 have *formicosam arborem urucae cavant* 'caterpillars
hollow out an ant-infested tree.' Other texts, including the one Erasmus
obviously used, read *cavent* 'are wary of,' 'avoid.'

58 Whence so irreconcilable . . . near Olynthus?] Added in the edition of March
1533.
Olynthus is in Thrace. Pliny reports that the place is fatal to beetles but does
not tell us why (*Naturalis historia* 11.99).

59 'Beetle' is *scarabaeus* or *cantharias*, the dung-beetle. On enmity between beetle
and eagle see *Adagia* III vii 1 and 'Patterns' n78.

60 Pliny *Naturalis historia* 9.185; Aristotle *Historia animalium* 9.2 610b14–18; Aelian
5.48. Aelian does not mention that the fish gnaw each others' tails. On the
mullet or mugil and the pike or *lupus* see Thompson *Greek Fishes* (n19 above)
108–10, 140–2. The moray is the murena, a favourite fish of the Romans; see
'The Profane Feast' 144:6 and 'The Epicurean' 1085:21.

61 This polypus is an octopus. See Thompson *Greek Fishes* (n19 above) 163–4; Pliny
Naturalis historia 9.185; Aelian 6.22.

62 In addition to Pliny *Naturalis historia* 10.207 and Aelian 5.48 see for example
Xenophon *Cyropaedia* 2.1.28 and *Memorabilia* 2.3.4.

63 The sea-mouse; Pliny *Naturalis historia* 9.186

64 The bird that cleans the crocodile's teeth is said by Aristotle (*Historia animalium*
9.6 612a20–4) and Pliny (*Naturalis historia* 8.90) to be a trochilus, which here is
probably the Egyptian plover (see n53 above, and D'Arcy W. Thompson's n2
on Aristotle *Historia animalium* 612a20).

65 yellow wagtail] The first edition of the colloquy had *florum*, changed to *anthum*
in the edition of March 1533.

66 On the wagtail and titmouse see Pliny and Aristotle as cited in n52 above;
on the incompatibility of the eagle's feathers with those of other birds, Pliny
Naturalis historia 10.15.

67 Pliny *Naturalis historia* 10.109

68 A weever or viper-fish or spider-fish, which has a sharp sting. See Thompson
Greek Fishes (n19 above) 56–7.

69 Pliny *Naturalis historia* 9.55

70 Pliny *Naturalis historia* 10.48; a commonplace. Erasmus' comment is typical: 'In
the same way great princes are sometimes made to fear the hostile attacks of
humble folk' (*Parabolae* CWE 23 249:22–4).

71 *asymbolus*. See 'Faith' n124.

72 distinguished Englishman] In the first edition (September 1531) More was
identified accurately as 'now chancellor of the realm; that is, the highest judge.'
He had been appointed to this office in October 1529. He resigned as chancellor
on 16 May 1532, and accordingly Erasmus changed the text here to bring it up
to date.
All of More's biographers speak of his fondness for birds and animals,
particularly his pleasure in watching their behaviour. He kept many different
kinds of birds as well as a fox, ferret, weasel, rabbits, and monkey. These
creatures, as Erasmus was the first to record from personal recollection in his
1519 account of More and his family (Ep 999), were of interest to the author
of the *Colloquies* too. He shared More's dislike of hunting animals; see the

introduction to 'Hunting' 109 and the description of a bullfight witnessed in Rome (Allen Ep 3032:417–33). In Holbein's pen-and-ink sketch of the More family (1527) the monkey is shown at lower right. Holbein gave this drawing to Erasmus; after Erasmus' death it was owned by Bonifacius Amerbach and later was sold to the city of Basel, where it remains. A copy by Rowland Locky (d 1616) of Holbein's painting of the More family added a dog at More's feet.

73 One of More's Latin poems concerns a rabbit that escaped a weasel only to be caught in a hunting net (*Latin Epigrams* 27 and 149 no 19).

74 As Pliny had noted (*Naturalis historia* 8.216) and probably Erasmus had observed for himself. Consult H.W. Janson *Apes and Ape Lore in the Middle Ages and Renaissance* Studies of the Warburg Institute 20 (London 1952).

75 But they have a 'vegetative' soul, as Eutrapelus explains to Fabulla in 'The New Mother.' See particularly 603:1–605:2.

76 Pliny *Naturalis historia* 16.64. Also in *Parabolae* CWE 23 265:30–6 and *Lingua* LB IV 694F–695A / ASD IV-1A 88:43–9 / CWE 29 320–1.

77 See Aristotle *Historia animalium* 5.19 551a13–25 and Pliny *Naturalis historia* 11.75–6.

78 An insect . . . enemy!] 'It senses . . . enemy' in the 1531 edition becomes 'An insect yet unborn . . . enemy!' in the edition of March 1533.

79 Tales of this kind are so numerous that it is impossible to know whether Erasmus was thinking of specific cases or of legends. A slain man can disquiet his killer in many ways (Plato *Laws* 9.865E). Even if the murderer acted upon what he deemed justifiable principles, not mere passion, he may be pursued by the Furies, like Orestes. For examples, from different cultures, of the surprising discovery that murder will out, see Stith Thompson *Motif-Index of Folk-Literature* rev ed (Bloomington, Ind and London 1966) VI, entries on 'Murder' and 'Murderer.'

80 A reference to incredible stories attributed by Pliny in *Naturalis historia* 28.112–19 and 10.137 to Democritus. Gellius (10.12.1–8) relates the tales but maintains that they are not worthy of the name of Democritus.

81 Pliny *Naturalis historia* 24.1

82 Ibidem; cf Erasmus *In Nucem Ovidii* LB I 1197B / ASD I-1 156:24–6 / CWE 29 141.

83 Pliny *Naturalis historia* 17.89, 91

84 Pliny *Naturalis historia* 24:1, and cf *Adagia* I v 38.

85 Pliny *Naturalis historia* 20.84, and see *Adagia* I v 38.

86 Pliny *Naturalis historia* 24:1–2

87 Pliny *Naturalis historia* 14.58, and cf 14.138; cf Erasmus *Lingua* LB IV 688A, 695B / ASD IV-1A 77:677–8, 88:62–3 / CWE 29 309, 321. See also Plutarch *Moralia* 61B–C *Quomodo adulator ab amico internoscatur* (translated by Erasmus LB IV 1A–22E). The moral, Plutarch adds, is that flattery and candor do not mix; a conclusion repeated by Erasmus in *Parabolae* CWE 23 146:12–17 and more extensively in the dedicatory letter to Pieter Gillis (Allen Ep 312:58–69 / CWE Ep 312:63–76 / CWE 23 131–4).

88 What is . . . vicinity?] Added in the March 1533 edition

89 I have not found the source of this assertion, but some inferences or conjectures are permissible. Dioscorides says that both garlic and lily are remedies for the bites of venomous snakes; see *Materia medica* ed Max Wellmann 3 vols (Berlin 1958) 2.152; in John Goodyer's English translation 2.182. Goodyer's translation was made c 1655 but never printed until 1933: *The Greek Herbal of Dioscorides* ed

Robert T. Gunther (Oxford 1933; repr New York 1959). Pliny says the same; see *Naturalis historia* 20.51 (garlic), 21.126 (lily root). A plant named scordion, which smells like garlic, is also efficacious (Pliny ibidem 25.63, 100, 127); see Dioscorides 3.111 (Wellmann) / 3.123 (Gunther). On the lily see Dioscorides 3.102 (Wellman) / 3.116 (Gunther). 'Scordion' is a Greek word borrowed by Latin and used in ancient medical texts; it is recorded in Henry George Liddell and Robert Scott *Greek-English Lexicon* rev ed (Oxford 1968) and *Harper's Latin Dictionary* rev Charlton D. Lewis and Charles Short (New York 1879). 'Lily' is a notably inclusive name in ancient usage, for instance in the Bible, for various plants. Erasmus calls attention to the differences between lily and garlic, but they are not totally dissimilar. Botanically garlic belongs to the lily family. Nor is the lily always fragrant, at least in folklore. 'Lilies are fair in show but foul in smell' (Thomas Lodge *Rosalind* [1590], first poem). Cf Shakespeare: 'Lilies that fester smell far worse than weeds' (Sonnet 94:14). But Erasmus is at liberty to fancy that they like to live in the same neighbourhood.

90 Cf Theophrastus *Historia plantarum* 3.8.1 and Erasmus *De conscribendis epistolis* LB I 417E–F / ASD I-2 4102–5 / CWE 25 134.

91 Pliny *Naturalis historia* 24.3

92 Ibidem

93 Pliny *Naturalis historia* 33.99–100

94 Cf Pliny *Naturalis historia* 20.2; Erasmus *Parabolae* CWE 23 221:26–9 (where Pliny 37.59, which is about the hardness of adamant but does not mention goat's blood, is cited).

95 Nay … without harm.] Like the passage above on lily and garlic, these lines were added in the edition of March 1533.

96 Pliny *Naturalis historia* 27.6

97 In the sentence about 'the herb named cerastes,' 'injurious to it' means to a scorpion; 'seed' means seed 'of the herb named cerastes.' That Erasmus wrote 'cerastes' there must be accepted, unless we prefer to suspect a copyist's or printer's error. The entire sentence survived unchanged in the *Opera omnia* of 1540 and in LB. But there is a difficulty, because 'cerastes' is not the name of a herb or plant but commonly of a snake, the venomous 'horned' viper of northern Africa (Pliny *Naturalis historia* 8.85; Aristotle *Historia animalium* 2.1 500a4, and see note 4 in the Oxford *Works* IV [n53 above]; Nicander *Theriaca* 258). Pliny names many kinds of plants that are remedies for, or protection against, a scorpion's sting (examples in *Naturalis historia* book 20 subsections 25, 41, 46, 50, 62, 117, 121, 125, 129, 145, 157, 162, 164, 171, 175, 182, 185, 209, 223, 232, 236, 245, 252, 256), but we may search in vain for mention of cerastes among them. Both 'cerastes' and 'scorpion' had more than one meaning in ancient texts. 'Cerastes' usually meant the horned viper, but the name also denoted an insect harmful to fig trees (Theophrastus *Historia plantarum* 4.14.5, 5.4.5; Pliny *Naturalis historia* 17.221). 'Scorpion' had a variety of meanings. It denoted 1/ the poisonous arachnid often described by naturalists and other writers (see for example Pliny *Naturalis historia* 11.86–91 on 'this curse of Africa'). 'Scorpion (or 'scorpaena') meant also 2/ a small sea fish with sharp spines (see Aristotle *Historia animalium* 5.9 543a7 and n4 in the Oxford *Works*; Pliny *Naturalis historia* 20.150, 32.102; Thompson *Greek Fishes* [n19 above] 245–6). It was 3/ the name of a plant having seed that resembles the tail of a scorpion (Pliny *Naturalis historia* 13.116, 22.39); this was also called *tragos* 'goat,' 'goat-plant' (Pliny *Naturalis*

historia 27.142). Additionally 'scorpion' referred to 4/ a spiny, leafless plant (mentioned by Theophrastus *Historia plantarum* 6.1.3, 6.4.1–2; Pliny *Naturalis historia* 21.91). Furthermore 'scorpion' sometimes referred to 5/ wolfsbane, which 'has a root like a scorpion' (Theophrastus *Historia plantarum* 9.18.2).

Two passages in Pliny invite particular attention. In 20.25 he writes: 'Radishes [*raphani*] are also useful for poisons, counteracting the sting of the cerastes and of the scorpion. With hands rubbed with radish or its seed you may handle these creatures without fear, and a radish placed on scorpions kills them' (*Naturalis historia* Loeb Classical Library, 10 vols [London and Cambridge, Mass 1949–62] VI trans W.H.S. Jones [1951] 17; Dioscorides 2.112 [Wellmann] / 2.137 [Gunther] says radish seed is an antidote to the bite of a viper but omits the scorpion). In 22.39 Pliny repeats that the seed of the scorpion plant will overpower scorpions. The assertion in the colloquy that whoever has touched the seed of the plant 'may handle a scorpion without harm' surely comes from these lines. The presence together of 'cerastes' and 'scorpion' in the first sentence above from Pliny *Naturalis historia* 20.25 suggests that when Erasmus wrote 'the herb cerastes' he may have forgotten momentarily which word, 'viper' or 'scorpion,' denoted a plant as well as an arachnid.

98 On 'light' and 'heavy,' see the next colloquy, 'A Problem.'

99 *Adagia* I vii 56, citing Pliny *Naturalis historia* 36.126–30

100 These examples are taken from Pliny *Naturalis historia* 2.224–5; cf 9.75. 'Arethusa' is misleading. The Arethusa most widely known was a spring near Syracuse in Sicily (see Ovid *Metamorphoses* 5.573–640). Another Arethusa was a town on the Orontes in Syria. But the Arethusa flowing in the Tigris is Aretissa (*Naturalis historia* 2.226), later called Arsissa and today Van. On this lake consult *Enciclopedia Italiana* 34 962 sv 'Van' or Jean Beaujeu's notes in his edition of Pliny *Naturalis historia* book 2 (Paris 1950) 257–8.

101 Pliny *Naturalis historia* 2.126–7

102 For Erasmus' opinions on astrology and astrologers see 'The Soldier and the Carthusian' n14.

103 See *Adagia* I i 76 and 'Rash Vows' n22.

104 Proverbial for not only doing well but succeeding beyond all expectations. The reference is to an ancient Greek athlete who in addition to leaping over a fifty-foot pit landed five feet beyond it. *Adagia* I x 93 cites Lucian *Somnium* 6 and many other texts.

105 That is, back to what concerns us most; a memory of Homer *Iliad* 1.154. See *Adagia* II vii 97. I owe the reference to Erika Rummel.

106 Catullus 36 and 95 express his contempt for Volusius, an obscure scribbler, but the lines quoted here are from Martial 1.32 (and cf 3.17), and are addressed to one Sabidius, otherwise unknown. An English imitation by Tom Brown (d 1704) about the Oxford dignitary John Fell is well known:

> I do not love thee, Doctor Fell,
> The reason why I cannot tell;
> But this alone I know full well:
> I do not love thee, Doctor Fell.

The Latin verses, again with the name Volusius, are quoted by Erasmus in *Institutio christiani matrimonii* when contrasting the mysterious agreements or differences in temperament that cause us to like or reject someone (*Institutio christiani matrimonii* LB V 671A–C).

107 These lines remind one of what Erasmus had written of his own irresistible attraction to literature 'by a kind of secret natural force.' See CWE 23 xxii n6.

108 This recollection of a boastful liar he knew when a boy may or may not be authentic autobiography, but Erasmus' deep-rooted aversion to liars and charlatans was sincere and unmistakable. It is found many times in his letters and other writings, for instance in the *Compendium vitae* (Allen I 51:137–9 / CWE 4 409:154–7). *Moriae encomium* and the *Colloquies* (for example 'The Liar and the Man of Honour' and 'Things and Names') include many illustrations of his detestation of lies and liars; see Margolin 'Erasme et la vérité in *Recherches érasmiennes* 45–69. He could say with the psalmist: 'Facientes praevaricationes odivi' (100:3 Vulg). If his writings have few single passages on truth and falsehood as memorable and quotable as some in Montaigne's 'Of Presumption' (*Essays* 2.17) or Bacon's 'Of Truth,' they have a forceful eloquence of their own that emphasizes Erasmus' commitment to 'truth in the inward parts.'

109 *Iliad* 9.312–13

110 And he . . . Christian spirit] Added in the March 1533 edition

A PROBLEM

Problema

First printed in the March 1533 edition.

In this brief dialogue Erasmus attempts to clarify the meaning of a topic in Aristotelian physics, as in an earlier colloquy, 'The New Mother,' he included a lesson on the soul from Aristotle's psychology in *De anima*. Aristotle's philosophy of nature, set forth in the *Physics, De caelo*, and *De generatione et corruptione*, opposed the doctrines of the Pythagoreans and presocratic philosophers on many fundamental questions and differed also in important ways from those of Plato's *Timaeus*. Most of the topics discussed in 'A Problem' are treated in *De caelo*, especially book 4, which is obviously the main source of Erasmus' dialogue. The Greek text of *De caelo*, with translation and notes by W.K.C. Guthrie (1960) is easily available in the Loeb Classical Library series. Translations of *Physics, De caelo*, and *De generatione et corruptione* are printed together in *The Works of Aristotle* ed W.D. Ross II (Oxford 1930), which is the source of quotations in this introduction and in the notes; the translation of *De caelo* was made by J.L. Stocks. There are many valuable commentaries, old and modern.

The questions posed by the two speakers take for granted the structure of the Aristotelian cosmos. What puzzles Curio is the centre of the earth and the meaning of 'heavy' and 'light.' Since these are subdivisions or corollaries of previous and major topics in *De caelo*, the reader may find useful a brief but characteristic statement of Aristotle's conception of the universe, a conception on which nearly everything said about 'heavy' and 'light' is based: 'The heaven as a whole neither came into being nor admits of destruction, as some assert, but is one and eternal, with no end or beginning of its total duration, containing and embracing in itself the infinity of time' (*De caelo* 2.1 283b26–9). The heaven (a word usually singular in Greek and Latin but plural in English when denoting the firmament or vault of the sky) is a vast system of revolving spheres whose movement, being divine, is therefore eternal. At its centre is a stationary, spherical earth (2.3 286a10–21). (On its position, its immobility, and spherical shape see 2.13–14 293a15–298a20.) About this fixed sphere the celestial spheres revolve and the natural movements of 'simple' terrestrial bodies such as fire and earth take place (1.2 268b20–269b13). Fire is always light and moves upward, while earth and all earthy things move downwards or towards the centre ... Now, that which produces upward and downward movement is that which produces weight and lightness, and that which is moved is that

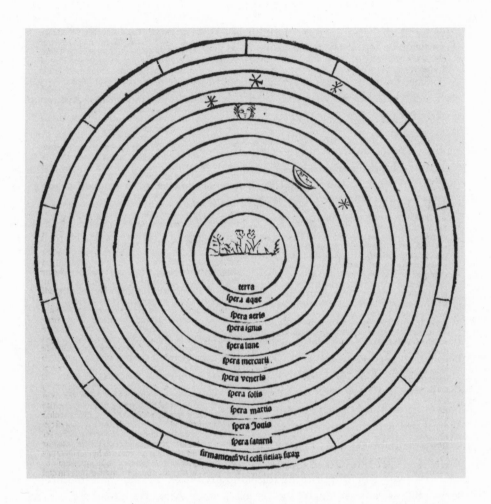

terra
ſpera aque
ſpera aeris
ſpera ignis
ſpera lune
ſpera mercurii
ſpera veneris
ſpera ſolis
ſpera martis
ſpera Jouis
ſpera ſaturni
firmamentū vel celū ſtellaꝝ fixaꝝ

The geocentric universe according to Aristotle, showing the round earth,
its four concentric spheres, one for each of the four elements, and, surrounding
these, the seven planetary spheres. The outermost sphere is identified as
'firmament or heaven of fixed stars,' and its twelve segments signify the zodiac.
Aristotle *Libri de celo et mundo*, Huntington Library 89094 fol 44, 1495
Reproduced by permission of the Huntington Library, San Marino, California

which is potentially heavy or light, and the movement of each body to its own place is motion towards its own form' (4.2 308b13–15, 4.3 310a31–310b1).

The dominance of Aristotelian thought in many fields of study during the medieval epoch in western history is an oft-told tale. Aristotle's influence lasted through Erasmus' century and for some subjects still continues. With regard to physics, however – to cosmology, dynamics, theories of motion, space, and gravity – critics in the later Middle Ages produced significant modifications and objections or refutations. For example, Jean Buridan (d c 1358), emphasized the power of *impetus* or 'accidental gravity' (see the quotations in A.C. Crombie *Medieval and Early Modern Science* 2 vols, rev ed [Garden City, NY 1959] II 67–73). Another Frenchman, Nicole Oresme (d 1382), a bishop and like Buridan rector of the University of Paris, found fault with Aristotle in his *Traité de la sphère* and *Livre du ciel et du monde*, a commentary on *De caelo*. He argued for the possibility of other worlds and opposed Aristotle's theory that the heavenly spheres moved around a stationary earth. His *Livre du ciel et du monde* denied that the universe has a fixed centre; he thought the earth moves with a daily motion but the heavens do not, a conclusion which foreshadows those of Copernicus and Galileo. Nevertheless at the end of his book 2 he concedes that since Scripture states plainly that the earth cannot be moved (Psalm 93:1; Vulg 92:1 and the Septuagint have 'will not' instead of 'cannot'), it is best to believe the heaven moves and the earth stands still (in the edition and translation by A.D. Menut and A.J. Denomy [Madison, Wis 1968] 537–9; this edition appeared in *Mediaeval Studies* 3 [1941] 185–280, 4 [1942] 159–297, and 5 [1943] 167–33, and then separately [New York 1943]).

Two years before printing this colloquy, Erasmus had written a prefatory letter to an edition of the Greek text of Aristotle edited by Simon Grynaeus. This letter, addressed to John More (1508–47), the youngest child and only son of Thomas More, praises Aristotle as supreme philosopher and urges John to emulate his distinguished father (Ep 2432). Erasmus wrote also a preface to the Ptolemy (Ep 2760) issued by the Froben press in 1533; this was the first Greek edition to be printed.

A few works, mainly in English, may be recommended to those who are not already acquainted with the history of science. One of the best surveys is Crombie's *Medieval and Early Modern Science*, with essential bibliographies. Others are C.S. Lewis' *The Discarded Image* (Cambridge 1964); S.K. Heninger's *The Cosmological Glass: Renaissance Diagrams of the Universe* (Huntington Library, San Marino California 1977), which has many illustrations; and J.-C. Margolin's essay on Erasmus and nature (see the bibliographical note at the

end of the introduction to 'Sympathy,' 1035–6 above). Selected writings of An-
neliese Maier on late medieval natural philosophy are translated and edited
in Steven D. Sargent's *On the Threshold of Exact Science* (Philadelphia 1982).

Erasmus' colloquy adds nothing to Aristotelian scholarship, nor was it
intended to do so, but as exposition in dialogue on a specific Aristotelian
topic – heavy and light – it needs no apologies. It is designed to do something
all useful instruction aims at, namely, to stimulate curiosity and encourage
further inquiry besides imparting information.

CURIO, ALPHIUS[1]

Curio There's something I'd be glad to learn from you, an expert on many
subjects, if it would be no trouble to you.

5   **Alphius** Go ahead, Curio, ask whatever you please, so you won't fail to live
up to your name.
Curio Well, I don't mind being called Curio, provided you don't add that
monosyllabic name of an animal hateful to Venus and Minerva alike.[2]
Alphius Tell me what you want, then.

10   **Curio** I want to know what we mean by heavy and light.
Alphius You might just as well ask what hot and cold are. Problems of this
sort you put to porters rather than to me; or, if you prefer, to asses, who
show the weight of their burden by drooping ears.[3]
Curio But I'm looking for a philosophical answer, not an asinine one,

15   especially from Alphius.
Alphius 'Heavy' is that which by its own nature is borne downward; 'light,'
that which is borne upward.
Curio Then why don't the antipodes, who are below us, fall into the sky
beneath them?[4]

20   **Alphius** People there wonder in like manner why you don't fall into the sky
that hangs over and not beneath you. For the sky is above everything that
is included within. The antipodes aren't below you any more than you're
above them; they can be opposite but not below us. Otherwise you'd do
better to wonder when rocks on the surface of the antipodes don't fall and

25   break the sky.
Curio What, then, is the natural resting place of heavy things and, on the
other hand, of light ones?
Alphius All heavy things are borne earthward by their natural motion; all
light ones skyward.[5] We're not speaking now of forcible or animate motion.[6]

30   **Curio** So there's some motion called 'animate'?

Alphius Yes.

Curio What is it?

Alphius Movement according to the four positions of the body: forward, backward, to the right and left, and in a circle.[7] In the beginning and end it is
5   swifter, in the middle slower. In the beginning, energy increases the speed; towards the end, hope of reaching the creature's destination.

Curio What happens to other creatures I don't know, but I have a maidservant who's tired before she starts work and worn out before she finishes.[8] – But go on with what you began.

10   **Alphius** It's by their natural motion, I say, that heavy things are borne downward. And the heavier anything is, the faster the motion with which it is borne to earth; the lighter it is, the faster the motion with which it is carried aloft.[9] In forcible motion, on the contrary, what is more rapid at the start gradually slows down; in natural motion the opposite would happen:
15   as for instance an arrow shot into the sky and a stone falling from a height.[10]

Curio But I used to think, for my part, that men run over the globe like tiny ants over a huge ball; they stick to it everywhere and not one falls off.

Alphius The reasons are: some unevenness of the surface of the globe; next, a certain roughness on the feet of the ants as well – nearly all insects have it;
20   finally, the lightness of minute bodies. If you don't believe this, try a glass sphere quite smooth and bare. You'll see that the only ants that don't fall off are those which walk on the top.

Curio If some god bored straight through the middle of the earth – through the centre perpendicularly to the antipodes, as cosmographers are wont to
25   do when representing the position of the whole earth with wooden globes – then, if you threw a stone into the hole, how far would it be carried?

Alphius To the centre of the earth, the resting place of all heavy bodies.[11]

Curio And what if the antipodes sent a stone from the opposite side?

Alphius Then stone would meet stone near the centre and each would rest
30   there.

Curio Come, now: were your statement true – that natural motion is speeded more and more if nothing intervenes – a stone or lead thrown into the hole would go past the centre, because of the force of the motion; and once the centre is passed, the motion will resume its force.

35   **Alphius** Lead would never reach the centre without being melted, but if a stone should go past the centre by forcible motion, it would first slow down and would return to the centre in just the same way that a stone thrown high by force returns to earth.[12]

Curio But returning by natural motion, it is again carried past the centre by
40   the impetus produced; so the result will be that the stone never does come to rest.

Alphius In the end it will rest – going back and forth until an equilibrium is reached.

Curio But if there's no vacuum in nature, that hole must be full of air.

Alphius Granted.

5 **Curio** Therefore a body naturally heavy will hang in air.

Alphius Of course, just as steel hangs in air when magnets are in equilibrium.[13] But what cause for wonder is it if one stone should hang in mid-air when the whole earth, loaded down by so many rocks, hangs in the same manner?

10 **Curio** But where is the centre of the earth?

Alphius Where is the centre of a circle?

Curio Well, it's an indivisible point. If the centre of the earth is so infinitesimal, whoever bores through the middle of the earth will destroy the centre, and heavy objects will have no place to which they can be carried.

15 **Alphius** You're trying to be funny.

Curio Don't be annoyed, please; whatever I say springs from a desire to learn. If a person bored through the earth, not through the exact centre but to the side, missing the centre by a dozen miles, say, where then will a stone thrown in be carried to?

20 **Alphius** It won't be carried straight through the hole; rather, it *will* go straight, but to the centre, and thus before reaching the middle will lie at rest in the earth on the left, if the centre's on the left.

Curio But what is it that makes a body heavy or light?

Alphius To this question let God answer why he made fire the lightest,
25 thing of all, air the next lightest; earth the heaviest, water the next heaviest.[14]

Curio Why then do clouds of water hang in the upper air?

Alphius Because, by attraction of the sun, they assume a fiery nature, as smoke is expelled from damp wood by extreme heat.

Curio Then why do they fall with so much weight that they sometimes level
30 mountains?

Alphius Condensation[15] and density add weight. Otherwise they might seem supported by the air below, as a thin sheet of iron is supported in the surface of the water.

Curio And so you think that whatever has the most fiery nature is lightest
35 and whatever has the most terrestrial one is heaviest?

Alphius You're not far from the mark.[16]

Curio But not every kind of air is equally light, nor is every kind of earth equally heavy. The same goes for water, perhaps.

Alphius No wonder, since those you've named are not pure elements but
40 mingled with various others. Thus it is probable that the lightest earth is that which has the most fire or air mixed with it; the heaviest water that

containing the heavier earth – such as ocean and salt water, I believe.[17] Likewise the air nearest to water or earth is heavier, or certainly less light, than that which is far from the earth.

Curio Which has more of a terrestrial nature, a stone or lead?

5   **Alphius** A stone.

Curio And yet lead is heavier than stone, proportionately.

Alphius Because of density: for a stone is more rarefied and therefore has more air than lead has. That's why we see a certain kind of dry earth does not sink but floats if thrown into water. For the same reason we see whole

10   fields floating,[18] held up by the hollow roots of reeds and other marshy plants interwoven.

Curio Hence perhaps the lightness of pumice-stones, too.

Alphius Because they're full of cavities. Besides, they're dried out by intense heat, for they're produced in burning places.

15   **Curio** Why is cork light?

Alphius The reason has been stated already: rarefaction.

Curio Which is heavier, lead or gold?

Alphius Gold, in my opinion.

Curio Yet gold seems to have more of a fiery nature.

20   **Alphius** Because it shines by night like fire, as Pindar says?[19]

Curio Of course.

Alphius But the density is greater in gold.

Curio How do we know that?

Alphius Goldsmiths will tell you that neither silver nor lead nor copper nor

25   any similar kind of metal is hammered more thin than gold. By the same reasoning philosophers discovered that nothing is more fluid than honey and oil, because if you spread these by smearing them, the liquid is diffused very widely and dries more slowly.

Curio But which is heavier, oil or water?

30   **Alphius** If you mean linseed oil, I think oil is heavier.

Curio Then why does oil float on water?

Alphius Not because of its lightness but because of the fiery nature of oil, as well as a peculiar resistance to water that all fats have[20] – the same that is found in what is called 'unsinkable'[21] grass.

35   **Curio** Then why doesn't white-hot iron float?

Alphius Because heat isn't natural to it and therefore the iron penetrates the water more quickly, since the intense heat dispels the resistant moisture. Thus an iron wedge goes to the bottom more quickly than a thin sheet.

Curio Which is harder to handle, white-hot or cold iron?

40   **Alphius** White-hot.

Curio Then it's heavier.

Alphius Yes – if it's easier to carry burning straw than cold flint in your hand!

Curio Why is one piece of wood lighter or heavier than another?

Alphius Density and rarefaction.

5 **Curio** Yet a certain member of the British royal household,[22] with whom I was personally acquainted, showed us at dinner a piece of what he said was aloe wood. It was so solid it could be taken for stone, so light when you balanced it in your hands that it seemed like a reed – and lighter, if there's anything lighter than a dry reed. Placed in wine (a means of expelling poisons, he

10 thought), it sank to the bottom at once, almost more quickly than lead.[23]

Alphius This is not always due to density or rarefaction but to a special and mysterious affinity in things that causes attraction or repulsion, as a magnet attracts steel,[24] and a vine avoids cabbage,[25] and fire leaps even from a distance towards naphtha in a lower place;[26] though naphtha is heavy by

15 nature, fire light.

Curio Every kind of brass floats on quicksilver; gold alone sinks and is covered over, though quicksilver is an extremely light substance.[27]

Alphius I've no explanation except a special affinity in nature, for quicksilver is so constituted that it refines gold.

20 **Curio** Why does the river Arethusa cross the Sicilian Sea underneath and not flow on the surface instead – since you said earlier that sea water is heavier than river water?[28]

Alphius Some natural yet mysterious discord is the reason.

Curio Why do swans float when men entering the same water go to the

25 bottom?

Alphius The reason is not only the hollowness and lightness of their wings but the dryness, too, which water shuns. That's why water or wine forms a ball if put on extremely dry linen but spreads quickly on damp cloth. Likewise, if you fill a dry cup or a grease-lined one with liquid, and pour in

30 a little more than the cup holds, the liquid in the middle collects into a round before it spills over the edge.

Curio Why do ships carry lighter cargoes in rivers than in the sea?

Alphius Because river water is more rarefied. For the same reason birds balance themselves more easily in heavier than in extremely rarefied air.

35 **Curio** Why don't 'floaters'[29] sink?

Alphius Because their skin is dried out by the sun and is made both lighter and more resistant to moisture.

Curio Why does iron hammered into a wide sheet float when the same iron sinks if a solid mass?

40 **Alphius** The reason is partly dryness, partly air gathered between water and sheet.

Curio Which is heavier, water or wine?

Alphius Wine won't yield to water, in my judgment.

Curio Why then do people who buy wine from wineshops find water instead of wine at the bottom of the jug?

5 **Alphius** Because wine has a certain oil-like fattiness that resists water. A ready proof is that the better the wine, the harder it is to mix with water, and the more strongly it burns if ignited.

Curio Why does no living body sink in the Dead Sea?[30]

Alphius It's not up to me to account for all of nature's miracles. It has certain
10 secrets we're to marvel at, not comprehend.

Curio How can a thin man be heavier than a stout one if they're alike in other respects?

Alphius Because bones are thicker than flesh and therefore heavier.

Curio Why is the same man heavier when hungry than after lunch, when he
15 has added weight to his body?

Alphius Spirits are enlarged by meat and drink and add lightness to the body. Hence too a merry man is lighter than a sad one and a dead one much heavier than a live one.[31]

Curio But how come the same man may make himself heavier or lighter
20 when he pleases?

Alphius When he holds his breath he makes himself lighter; when he exhales, heavier. So a bladder, inflated and tied shut, floats; punctured, it sinks. – But when will Curio stop harping on 'why'?

Curio I'll stop if you'll answer just a few more questions. Is the sky heavy
25 or light?

Alphius Whether it's light, I don't know. Certainly it can't be heavy, since it has a fiery nature.

Curio Then what's the meaning of the old proverb 'What if the sky should fall?'[32]

30 **Alphius** The simple ancients, relying on Homer, believed the sky was made of iron. But Homer called it 'iron' because of its resemblance in colour, not weight;[33] as we call something 'ashen' if it has the shade of ash.

Curio Is the sky coloured then?

Alphius Not really, but it seems so to us on account of the air and the
35 moisture in mid-air; just as the sun now seems to redden, now gleams yellow, now is dazzling white, though in fact it undergoes no such changes. Likewise the image of the rainbow is not in the sky but in the moist air.

Curio But – to come to an end – you admit there's nothing higher than the sky, however it covers the earth?

40 **Alphius** Admitted.

Curio And nothing deeper than the centre of the earth?

Alphius Quite right.

Curio Of all species of things, what's the heaviest?

Alphius Gold, I suppose.

Curio On this matter I disagree with you emphatically.

5   **Alphius** Do you know anything heavier than gold?

Curio Yes, a great deal heavier.

Alphius Well, then, *you* take a turn at teaching *me*, since you know what I confess I don't know.

Curio Isn't what forced those fiery spirits from the height of heaven down

10 to the depths of hell – for this is thought to be the centre of the earth – necessarily the heaviest thing of all?

Alphius Granted – but what was that?

Curio Sin,[34] which also sank human souls, called by Virgil 'the radiance of ethereal air,'[35] to the same depth.

15 **Alphius** If you like to go in for that sort of reasoning, I admit both gold and lead are of feathery lightness when compared with sin.

Curio How then will it be possible for those weighed down by this burden to fly up to heaven?

Alphius Indeed I don't see how.

20 **Curio** But men getting ready to race or jump don't only rid themselves of any burden but even make themselves a bit lighter by holding their breath; and yet for *this* race and leap, by which we're carried to heaven, we neglect to throw off what is heavier than all stone and lead.

Alphius We'd get rid of it if we had a grain of common sense.

NOTES

1 Curio suggests *cura* 'care,' for he is both thoughtful and inquisitive; in the best sense of the word, 'curious.' This name had been used in the original edition of the *Formulae* (November 1518) 23. 'Alphius,' if adapted from ἀλφεῖν, means here 'busy,' 'energetic' about getting knowledge. Cf *Odyssey* 6.8; 13.261.

2 Addition of the 'monosyllabic name' *sus* (pig) gives *curiosus*. See *Adagia* I i 40: *Sus Minervam* 'The sow (teaches) Minerva' on the presumptuous folly of an ignoramus trying to compete with a wise person or (as Erasmus adds) to rival Venus in beauty.

3 *Adagia* IV vi 99. See Horace *Satires* 1.9.20–1.

4 Depending on the context, 'antipodes' in this colloquy signifies either ₍ne region or the supposed inhabitants. On early controversies about the existence of the antipodes and the question of life there see Andrew D. White *History of the Warfare between Science and Theology* 2 vols (New York 1899) I 102–8. Augustine did not deny that there is a side of the globe diametrically opposite ours, but did deny that it is inhabited by creatures who 'walk with their feet opposite ours.' For such an absurd conjecture violates the evidence of

Scripture (*De civitate Dei* 16.9 PL 41 487–8). When a spokesman for Tyndale cited Lactantius *Divinae institutiones* 3.24 (PL 6 425–8) on the folly of believing in the existence of the antipodes, More reminded him of the voyages of Magellan and his company, who had circumnavigated the globe (1519–22), proving that they did exist (*Dialogue Concerning Heresies* [1529] Yale CWM 6 part 1 66, part 2 618).

5 'All movement is either natural or unnatural, and . . . the movement which is unnatural to one body is natural to another – as, for instance, is the case with the upward and downward movements, which are natural and unnatural to fire and earth respectively. It necessarily follows that circular movement, being unnatural to these bodies, is the natural movement of some other' (*De caelo* 1.2 269a32–269b2).

6 *motu violento aut animali.* 'Forcible' means caused by something external to it. Latin *animalis* in this context has its original meaning of 'animate,' 'living.' Animate bodies contain a principle of movement within themselves. The point of Alphius' next remarks is that heavy things fall and light ones rise because of their intrinsic nature. 'Everything that is in motion must be moved by something' is an Aristotelian axiom (*Physics* 7.1 241b24). In animate bodies, which can move themselves, this 'something' is an intrinsic principle; in non-living things movement is simply a 'natural' or involuntary activity (*De caelo* 2.2 284b25–34).

7 A natural body or element (fire, air, water, earth) can move in three ways: up or down from or to the centre, or in circular motion. These are what Aristotle calls 'simple motions.' Since circular motion is unnatural to the four elements, there must be another element to which it *is* natural because it is continuous and eternal. That body is the so-called 'fifth element,' which is perfect and more divine than the four known in the terrestrial world (*De caelo* 1.2 268b11–269b17).

Heaviness and lightness – in relative and not absolute terms – move naturally down to the centre or upward away from it. The heavy moves downward, the light upward to realize their inherent potentiality. To ask why 'is the same as to ask why the healable, when moved and changed *qua* healable, attains health and not whiteness' (*De caelo* 4.3 310b16–19).

8 Perhaps alluding to Erasmus' formidable housekeeper, Margaret. See introduction to 'The Poetic Feast' 390.

9 *De caelo* 4.2 (308b13–28)

10 For Alphius' explanation here see *De caelo* 1.8 276a22–30: 'A thing moves naturally to a place in which it rests without constraint, and rests naturally in a place to which it moves without constraint. On the other hand, a thing moves by constraint to a place in which it rests by constraint, and rests by constraint in a place to which it moves by constraint. Further, if a given movement is due to constraint, its contrary is natural. If, then, it is by constraint that earth moves from a certain place to the centre here, its movement from here to there will be natural, and if earth from there rests here without constraint, its movement hither will be natural.' With the comparison compare Shakespeare 2 *Henry IV*:

> And as the thing that's heavy in itself
> Upon enforcement flies with greatest speed,
> So did our men, heavy in Hotspur's loss,

Lend to this weight such lightness with their fear
That arrows fled not swifter toward their aim
Than did our soldiers, aiming at their safety,
Fly from the field.   (1.1.119–25)

11 In book 6 of his *Confutation of Tyndale's Answer* (1532–3), More tells a diverting
story of how he tried to explain to his wife that the earth is in the centre of the
world, and the centre of this earth 'the most inward place of the whole world,'
and also why what is heavy falls and what is light rises. Here too we meet the
answer – to reassure doubters – that if a hole were bored through the earth and
a millstone thrown down from above, the stone would finally rest there in the
centre of the earth; and even if the hole went further than the centre, the stone
would not fall through, since that would mean ascending, which is impossible
for the stone. More's explanation was in vain. Dame Alice, dismissing it as
nonsense, counters with a question of her own. Suppose a spindle with a whorl
(flywheel to steady its motion) ten miles thick. If a hole were bored through the
whorl and a millstone thrown into the hole, would the stone stop at the centre?
Not at all, as he would discover if he stood five miles beneath! For the anecdote
see Yale CWM 8 part 2 604–6 and note in 8 part 3 1618–19.
The first three books of the *Confutation* were issued in one volume in 1532, the
remaining five in 1533 (London: William Rastell). As both the volume with
the anecdote and Erasmus' 'A Problem' came out in the early months of 1533,
More could hardly have seen this colloquy, or Erasmus the *Confutation*, before
writing about the earth's centre. More's last extant letter to Erasmus (Ep 2831)
alludes to Tyndale but says nothing about the *Confutation* or the *Colloquies*. The
coincidence of their writing about the earth's centre at the same time proves
only that the subject was nothing novel. The question about boring through the
centre had been asked by others, for example by the medieval encyclopaedist
Vincent of Beauvais (1190?–1264), whose answer was the same as Erasmus'
and More's. Nevertheless images of heavy and light and earth's centre as
resting place, like so many other Aristotelian legacies, survived as powerful
commonplaces in human affairs and as sources of provocative imagery in
literature and art. In the core of hell, where Satan abides, Dante and Virgil, after
descending feet first on his body, can go down no further. Here at the centre
of gravity they turn themselves around, or rather topsy-turvy, and begin to
ascend to the antipodes (*Inferno* 34:76–139). In *Romeo and Juliet*, when Romeo is
first attracted to Juliet, he exclaims:

Can I go forward when my heart is here?
Turn back, dull earth, and find thy center out.   (2.1.1–2)

But earth's centre (Juliet here) can be an image not only of the resting place
of joy (as it is, uniquely, in the verses just quoted) but of mortality and the
'heaviness' of sin that we read of in the concluding lines of this colloquy. Thus
in Donne's *Devotions Upon Emergent Occasions* (1624) 2, Meditation: 'Earth is the
center of my Bodie, Heaven is the center of my Soule; these two are the naturall
places of those two; but those goe not to these two in an equall pace: My
body falls downe without pushing, my Soule does not go up without pulling:
Ascension is my Soules pace and measure, but precipitation my bodies: and

even Angells, whose home is Heaven, and who are winged too, yet had a Ladder to goe to Heaven, by steps.'

12 'Earth in motion, whether in a mass or in fragments, necessarily continues to move until it occupies the centre equally every way, the less being forced to equalize itself by the greater owing to the forward drive of the impulse' (*De caelo* 2.14 297b10–13).

13 Pliny *Naturalis historia* 36.125–30 on magnets does not include this example. Cf n24 below.

14 Fire is hot and dry, air hot and moist ('a sort of aqueous vapour'); water is cold and moist, earth cold and dry (Aristotle *De generatione et corruptione* 2.3 330b3–5). Cf Erasmus *Ratio verae theologiae* LB V 88F.

15 Here *concretio*; *condensatio* is rare and non-classical.

16 *Adagia* I x 30

17 Pliny *Naturalis historia* 2.224 remarks that sea water is heavier than fresh water.

18 So Pliny *Naturalis historia* 2.209

19 *Olympians* 1.1–2

20 Cf Pliny *Naturalis historia* 2.234 and *Parabolae* CWE 23 246:26–8.

21 ἄβαπτος; used again in *Ecclesiastes* LB V 933A. The meaning intended in each passage is clear: 'unsinkable' here and 'unbaptized' in LB V 933A; but ἄβαπτος (of iron 'not tempered') instead of ἀβάπτιστος is uncommon for 'not baptized.'

22 Since the date of this incident is unknown and we are told nothing more about the person who spoke of the aloe wood, it is hard to guess who is meant. Mountjoy perhaps, or Linacre, who as a physician would be entitled to an opinion on poisons.

23 Pliny *Naturalis historia* 27:14–20 has much to say about aloe's medicinal uses but nothing specific about its efficacy in expelling poisons or its solidity or lightness.

24 See *Adagia* I vii 56, where Erasmus quotes some lines from Pliny *Naturalis historia* 36.126–7.

25 Pliny *Naturalis historia* 24.1

26 Pliny *Naturalis historia* 2.235; cf *Parabolae* CWE 23 246:29–31. Thus Erasmus describes his innate attraction to literature (Allen Epp 23:37–42, 1110:1–19 / CWE Epp 23:39–45, 1110:3–23).

27 Pliny *Naturalis historia* 33.99–100. Quicksilver is mercury.

28 See 'Sympathy' n100 and n17 above.

29 *flotae*; more correctly *flutae* as in Varro *Res rusticae* 2.6.2 and Columella 8.17.8. Floaters are identified with morays; see D'Arcy W. Thompson *A Glossary of Greek Fishes* (London 1947) 162, 203.

30 Pliny *Naturalis historia* 2.226 and 5.72

31 In 'The New Mother' the young mother is told that boys who overeat have dull wits and poor memories (n50), but here 'spirits' are said to be enlarged by food and drink. The connection between lightness and merriment, heaviness and sadness, is a conviction of proverbial wisdom. 'A merry heart maketh a cheerful countenance, but by sorrow of the heart the spirit is broken' (Prov 15:13) Rabelais repeats that a man is 'more terrestrial' and heavy when fasting (*Gargantua and Pantagruel* 4.65), adding that some people contend a dead man weighs more than a live one. These vulgar errors are examined in Sir Thomas Browne's *Pseudodoxia epidemica* (1646) 4.7.

32 An ironical proverb about irrational and unnecessary fear (*Adagia* I v 64).
   Aristotle (*Metaphysics* 5.23 1023a19–21) alludes to the myth that the heavens are
   upheld by Atlas (cf Hesiod *Theogony* 517 and Plato *Phaedo* 99C). Suppose Atlas
   tired of bearing the world? A more sophisticated speculation was that of the
   philosopher Anaxagoras who, according to Diogenes Laertius 2.12, predicted
   that if the velocity of the firmament slowed down, the sky would fall. Not to
   worry, Horace advises (*Odes* 3.3.1–8).

33 *Odyssey* 15.329, 17.565 on the iron sky. *Iliad* 17.425 and *Odyssey* 3.2 call it brazen.

34 As a weight or burden, sin is a biblical trope, as in Heb 12:1 'let us lay aside
   every weight' (*pondus* Vulg). In *Dante's Purgatorio* 10–12, the proud are bowed
   down beneath the weight of heavy stones. The gravity of sin, literally and
   figuratively, has ever been a common theme of Christian preaching. For 'no
   weight is heavier than the burden of sin' (Erasmus *Enarratio in psalmum* XXXIII
   LB V 383D).

35 *Aeneid* 6.747

THE EPICUREAN

Epicureus

First printed in the March 1533 edition.

Like many other colloquies, this one begins with a question, which is then clarified, analysed, and answered. The question concerns the 'ends' of goods and evils. Accordingly the inquiry produces a critique of Epicurean ethics and comparison and contrast with Christian teachings and principles: a topic appropriate as a conclusion to the *Colloquies*. For obvious reasons, Erasmus' approach to such a subject lacks the jocularity of some earlier colloquies, but it has the familiar blend of pertinence, amiability, and informality we expect of him. The expositor of Epicureanism, Hedonius, with customary Erasmian conviction and language, tries to persuade Spudaeus, apparently with success, that if hedonism is judged from a Christian perspective and with Christian insights, Christianity will be seen as the superior source and arbiter of pleasure.

Another typically Erasmian procedure is to begin with a text, here Cicero's *De finibus bonorum et malorum*. By using a book on ends at the end of his series of dialogues, Erasmus is not simply playing on the word *finis*. He resorts to an ancient classic by a favourite author because with him that is a common way of introducing ethical or political topics of importance in modern life: looking first at what the great ideas, books, or philosophical systems of classical antiquity thought on these or comparable themes, then examining them critically. Much of his life and work was devoted to expounding classical civilization in this manner.

Brief allusion to Stoic and Peripatetic ethics occurs in 'The Epicurean,' but the central and almost exclusive subject is Epicurean hedonism and in what senses, if any, Christianity is 'Epicurean.' Erasmus has nothing to say on Epicurean physics, the atomic theory borrowed by Epicurus from Democritus, but is interested only in the typical Epicurean ethical doctrine, inherited from Aristippus, that immediate pleasure is the sole good. The dialogue is too brief to allow long dissertations on nuances of philosophical vocabulary, but long enough for Erasmus to present and defend his main proposition, stated by Hedonius at the outset: 'There are no people more Epicurean than godly Christians' (1075:29). This claim, we learn, depends on agreement that 'true' pleasure is virtue, righteousness. No one lives happily unless he lives righteously. The true Christian is the person who lives most righteously. And since the Epicurean criterion of goodness is pleasure, the conclusion must be that the Christian is the true Epicurean.

Spudaeus' initial doubts about such a claim are not surprising when we consider the persistence through the centuries of 'Epicurean' as synonymous with 'libertine,' 'sensualist,' 'godless.' In the fifteenth and sixteenth centuries, however, Epicureanism received more attention from philosophers and other scholars than it had known since antiquity. Intermittent debate on the meaning and merits of the Epicurean doctrine of pleasure began with Lorenzo Valla's dialogue *De voluptate* (1431, but after 1533 called *De vero bono*; some parts revised in 1444–9). He presents arguments for Stoic, Epicurean, and Christian ethics, though the terms 'Stoic' and 'Epicurean' are used more loosely than in ancient writings. The defender of Epicureanism contends, against the Stoics, that what is natural is good and that pleasure is the greatest good. This means physical as well as intellectual pleasures: he denounces celibacy and approves of sexual liberty and even, the text implies, adultery; Plato was right to establish community of wives in his state. In the third book the apologist for Christianity, presumably voicing Valla's own opinions, concurs with the argument that what is natural is good and therefore pleasure is a good, and furthermore that the greatest good and hence the greatest pleasure is virtue. But he does not stop there, for otherwise the essential message of Christianity would be ignored. Epicureanism thinks gods are useless to men. Stoics believe all that need be said of or for virtue is that virtue is its own reward. Christianity believes in future judgment and believes the righteous will have felicity in heaven. Virtue is necessary, but the pleasure it brings in this life is not the final or greatest good; that happiness is to come in another life.

In the judgment of most but not all readers, this conclusion is Valla's own belief. A difficulty for sceptical readers was that his praise of nature and the natural contains paradoxes and that he writes strongly against asceticism, whether pagan or Christian. He prefers Epicureanism to Stoicism, as being closer to Christianity. Erasmus' Hedonius in the colloquy is of the same opinion. Christian doctrine, based on revelation (not philosophy), has its own unique authority. Christ, not nature, is its guide.

Valla's *De voluptate* is a complex, powerful, sometimes audacious work to which justice cannot be done in a few paragraphs. That Erasmus, who knew all of Valla's writings, would have been unaffected by it is most unlikely. He could not have failed to appreciate its rhetorical force and its learning or its concluding pages on the felicities of paradise; pages that should be compared with those at the end of *Moriae encomium* on the mystical joys of Christians.

Valla's *Opera omnia* (Basel 1540) were reprinted (Turin 1962) with a preface by E. Garin. The most useful edition of *De voluptate* now is that of A. Kent Hieatt and Maristella Lorch (New York 1977), which has the Latin text and English translation on facing pages, with an introduction and notes.

On Valla and this dialogue consult also P.O. Kristeller *Eight Philosophers of the Italian Renaissance* (Stanford 1964; repr 1966) 19–36.

The most popular and significant of sixteenth-century writings on the philosophy of pleasure was not a treatise but a work of fiction, book 2 of More's *Utopia* (1516) edited and translated by Edward Surtz in Yale CWM 4. *Utopia* does not contain the words 'Epicurus' or 'Epicurean,' which More evidently and perhaps wisely chose to avoid, yet it describes a society that lives rationally and successfully by following pleasure as the operative principle of life. Utopians are hedonists in More's sense but are not Epicureans whom Epicurus would accept. They believe in the immortality of the soul, divine providence, and future judgment, all of which Epicurus rejected. Nor is their society by any means perfect, if we accept the account by Hythloday, the narrator; but it is far more humane and more secure than the European societies with which we are invited to compare it. Utopians think happiness is man's supreme good, and the best part of happiness is pleasure. They endure hardships in the hope of future happiness. Of earthly pleasures the highest form is the practice of virtue in a life lived in accordance with nature. The end or goal of virtue is eternal felicity after death. Utopians agree with Stoics and Epicureans in preferring higher to lower pleasures, a trait which may account for their addiction to lectures, for they take nothing more seriously than adult education. But as regards religion, providence, and future judgment, they are at the opposite extreme from Epicurus. They are rationalists, but theistic rationalists. They have had a variety of religions, but most agree in belief in one supreme being. Latterly, after hearing from Hythloday and his companions about the miracles and teachings of Christ, many of them have become followers of the gospel, though nobody compelled them to do so; in Utopia there is freedom of choice in such matters. On their daily life and social institutions see further Surtz' *The Praise of Pleasure* (Cambridge, Mass 1957) and *The Praise of Wisdom* (Chicago 1957).

In Erasmus' 'The Epicurean,' Hedonius' argument – that classical and Christian values need not be thought irreconcilable – carries an implied condition that pagan values must be tried and tested by Christian knowledge before their worth can be accepted. At the same time an honest effort to recognize and respect what is good in classical philosophies must be made. An example of such consideration is the passage in 'The Godly Feast' in which speakers whose Erasmian sympathies are unmistakable argue that despite its paganism classical literature should not be rejected (192:5–194:36). A properly educated Christian ought to be able to discriminate between what is harmful and what is profitable for Christian readers. This is a subject Erasmus had to deal with from time to time; for example, in *Antibarbari* and *De ratione studii*. See CWE 23 xxix–xxxii, 55–61; CWE 24 663–4.

Many years before writing 'The Epicurean,' Erasmus had invoked the name of Epicurus in chapter 11 of his *De contemptu mundi* (written, he says, in his twentieth year or c 1486), a tract in the form of a letter written by a monk to his nephew, commending monastic life. 'Our whole way of life is Epicurean,' he says, 'for we are content with little, have no worldly ambitions, and our consciences are clear, as Epicurus advises (LB V 1257A–1258B / CWE 66 165–7).

On other Italian humanists interested in the 'rehabilitation' of Epicurus and his hedonism, among them Poggio Bracciolini, Francesco Filelfo, Giovanni Pico della Mirandola, Cristoforo Landino, and Marsilio Ficino, see the survey by D.C. Allen 'The Rehabilitation of Epicurus and His Theory of Pleasure in the Early Renaissance' *Studies in Philology* 41 (1944) 1–15. For additional studies of Epicureanism in the Renaissance consult Marie Delcourt and Marcelle Derwa 'Trois aspects humanistes de l'épicurisme chrétien' in *Colloquium Erasmianum* (Mons 1968) 119–33 and R. Bultot's excellent article on book 11 of *De contemptu mundi*, with some pages on 'The Epicurean' also, 'Erasme, Epicure et le *De Contemptu Mundi*' in *Scrinium Erasmianum* II 205–38. For other sixteenth-century texts and commentaries on Epicurus and Epicureanism see F. Joukovsky 'Quelques sources épicuriennes au xvie siècle' BHR 31 (1969) 7–25. Two books by Charles Trinkaus, *Adversity's Noblemen* (New York 1940) and particularly *In Our Image and Likeness* 2 vols (Chicago 1970) are valuable comparative studies in Renaissance philosophy.

The first known English translation of Erasmus' *Epicureus*, by Philip Gerrard (London 1545; STC 10460) survives in two copies, one of which has a few textual variants. This translation is carefully edited, along with an anonymous English version of *Funus*, by Robert R. Allen (Chicago 1969). Gerrard was a minor official in the household of Prince Edward, later Edward VI.

HEDONIUS, SPUDAEUS[1]

Hedonius What's my Spudaeus hunting, bent double over his book, mumbling something or other to himself?
Spudaeus True, I'm hunting, Hedonius – but only hunting.
5   **Hedonius** What's the book you have in your lap?
Spudaeus Cicero's dialogue *On the Ends of Goods*.[2]
Hedonius How much better it would be to seek the beginnings of goods rather than their ends![3]

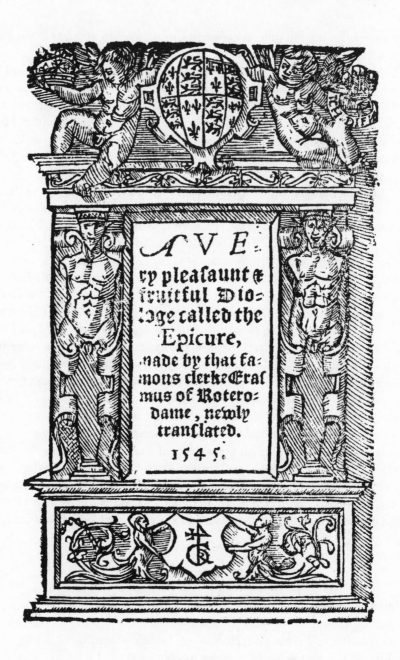

A VE:
ry pleasaunt &
fruitful Dio=
:oge called the
Epicure,
made by that fa:
mous clerke Eras
mus of Rotero=
dame, newly
translated.
1545.

Title-page of the 1545 English translation of *Epicureus*
London: Richard Grafton
By permission of the Folger Shakespeare Library

Spudaeus But Marcus Tullius[4] calls the 'end' of good the 'complete, perfect good,' which, if one attains it, leaves nothing to be desired.

Hedonius That's a work famous for learning and eloquence; but you don't imagine, do you, that in return for your trouble you've discovered
5   truth?

Spudaeus I've profited to this extent, I think: that I'm even more doubtful about ends than I was before.

Hedonius Farmers are the ones to dispute about boundaries or ends.[5]

Spudaeus I can't get over the fact that on so important a subject there was
10   so much conflicting opinion among such eminent men.

Hedonius No wonder, because error is prolific while truth is single.[6] Missing the head and source of the matter, they all rant and rave. But which doctrine strikes you as closer to the mark?[7]

Spudaeus When I hear Marcus Tullius opposing them, every one displeases
15   me. Again, when I hear him defending them, straightway I suspend judgment.[8] However, in my opinion the Stoics come closest to the truth; next, the Peripatetics.

Hedonius But no school attracts me more than the Epicurean.

Spudaeus Yet none is more universally detested.[9]

20   **Hedonius** Let's disregard bad reputations – Epicurus was whatever you please – and consider the matter in itself. Human happiness, he holds, is the product of pleasure, and he deems that life most blessed which has the most pleasure and the least sorrow.

Spudaeus So he does.

25   **Hedonius** What judgment could have been more holy than this?

Spudaeus On the contrary, everybody protests that this is the language of a beast,[10] not a human being.

Hedonius I know, but they're mistaken about the names of things. In plain truth, there are no people more Epicurean than godly Christians.

30   **Spudaeus** Christians are closer to Cynics, because they wear themselves out by fasting and bewailing their sins.[11] Either they're poor or their kindness towards the needy brings them to poverty; they're oppressed by the stronger and scorned by the multitude. If pleasure brings happiness, this sort of life seems as far as possible from pleasure.

35   **Hedonius** Do you accept the authority of Plautus?

Spudaeus If what he says is true.

Hedonius Then attend to the rascally slave's saying, a wiser one than all the paradoxes of the Stoics.[12]

Spudaeus I'm waiting.

40   **Hedonius** 'Nothing is more wretched than a bad conscience.'[13]

Spudaeus A saying I don't reject; but what's your inference?

Hedonius If nothing is more wretched than a bad conscience, it follows that nothing is more blessed than a good one.[14]

Spudaeus The inference is correct, but where in the world will you find this conscience free of wrong?

5 **Hedonius** By 'wrong' I mean whatever destroys amity between God and man.

Spudaeus And from this kind of wrong very few, I think, are free.

Hedonius For my part, I regard those who have been cleansed as free of it. Those who have washed away their stains by the lye of tears and the soap of

10 repentance or the fire of charity are not only unharmed by sins but the sins often pave the way to a greater good.

Spudaeus Soap and lye I'm acquainted with, but that spots are removed by fire I never heard.

Hedonius But if you go to silversmiths' shops you'll see gold refined by

15 fire. There's a kind of flax, too, that doesn't burn when thrown into the fire but glitters more brightly than any liquid could and on that account is known as 'live flax.'[15]

Spudaeus Really, you present us with a paradox topping all the paradoxes of the Stoics.[16] Do those whom Christ called 'blessed' because they mourn[17]

20 live a life of pleasure?

Hedonius To the world they appear to mourn, but in fact they're joyful and live agreeably, 'smeared all over with honey,' as the saying goes;[18] so that compared with these, Sardanapalus, Philoxenus, Apicius,[19] or any other famous voluptuary experiences a sad and miserable life.

25 **Spudaeus** You tell me novelties, but they're hard to believe.

Hedonius Test them and you'll say over and over again that everything I've told you was true. Nevertheless I'll try my best to make it even more convincing.

Spudaeus Go ahead.

30 **Hedonius** I'll do so if you'll concede something first.

Spudaeus Only ask what's fair.

Hedonius I'll pay a profit if you'll put up the capital.

Spudaeus Go on.

Hedonius First of all, you'll grant, I suppose, that there's some difference

35 between body and soul.[20]

Spudaeus As much as between heaven and earth, mortal and immortal.

Hedonius Next, that false goods are not to be reckoned among goods.[21]

Spudaeus No more than shadows are to be considered substances,[22] or magicians' illusions[23] or the mockeries of dreams held for true.

40 **Hedonius** So far I'm pleased with your answers. You'll grant this, too, I suppose: that true pleasure befalls only a sane person.

Spudaeus Of course. A blear-eyed man doesn't enjoy the sun; a feverish man who has lost his taste doesn't care for wine.

Hedonius Unless I'm mistaken, Epicurus himself wouldn't embrace pleasure that entailed agony much greater and more lasting.

5   **Spudaeus** I don't think any sensible person would.

Hedonius And you won't deny that God is the supreme good,[24] than which nothing is more beauteous, more lovely, more dear.

Spudaeus Nobody will deny that unless he's more savage than the Cyclopes.[25] What follows?

10   **Hedonius** You've already granted that none live more enjoyably than those who live righteously,[26] none more wretchedly and miserably than those who live wickedly.

Spudaeus Then I granted more than I thought.

Hedonius But, as Plato says, what's properly given away you can't demand
15   back.[27]

Spudaeus Go on.

Hedonius Doesn't a puppy that's spoiled and overfed, sleeps on a soft bed, and plays and romps incessantly live enjoyably?

Spudaeus It does.

20   **Hedonius** Would you desire such a life?

Spudaeus Perish the thought! Not unless I wished to be a dog instead of a man.

Hedonius Then you admit that the principal pleasures come from the mind, as from a fountain-head?

25   **Spudaeus** Evidently.

Hedonius For so great is the power of mind that frequently it takes away the feeling of physical pain. Sometimes it renders pleasant what is in itself bitter.

Spudaeus This we witness every day in lovers, to whom long vigils and
30   sleeping at the beloved's gates on winter nights are sweet.

Hedonius Now consider: if there's so much power in mortal love, which is something we have in common with bulls and dogs, how much stronger must be that heavenly love proceeding from the spirit of Christ. So great is its power that even death – than which nothing is more dreadful – is made pleasing.[28]

35   **Spudaeus** What others may feel privately I don't know, but unquestionably those who live a strictly religious life miss many pleasures.[29]

Hedonius Which ones?

Spudaeus They don't grow rich, win honours, feast, dance, sing, reek of perfume,[30] laugh, play.

40   **Hedonius** You shouldn't have mentioned riches and honours, which bring not a pleasant life but rather one of care and anxiety. As for the rest, let's

discuss the ones sought most eagerly by those who are bent on enjoying life. Don't you see every day drunkards, fools, and madmen laughing and dancing?

Spudaeus I do.

5 **Hedonius** You don't think they enjoy themselves, do you?

Spudaeus I'd wish that sort of enjoyment to my enemies.

Hedonius Why?

Spudaeus Because it's madness.

Hedonius Then would you prefer to bend over a book, hungry, than enjoy
10 yourself in that way?

Spudaeus Yes. I'd much rather dig ditches.

Hedonius For between a rich man[31] and a drunken man the sole difference is that the one's madness is cured by sleep; the other scarcely recovers even with physicians' care. A natural fool differs from a brute beast only in bodily
15 appearance; but the brutes nature produces are less wretched than those stupefied by monstrous lusts.

Spudaeus I admit that.

Hedonius Well, you don't regard as sober or sane, do you, those who for the sake of shadows and illusions of pleasures neglect the real pleasures of the
20 mind and bring real torments upon themselves?

Spudaeus No, I don't.

Hedonius They're not drunk with wine, to be sure, but with love, anger, avarice, craving for power, and other sinful lusts far more dangerous than drunkenness from wine. Syrus in the comedy, after sleeping off the sup
25 of wine he had drunk, talks sober sense;[32] but how reluctantly a mind drunk with sinful desire recovers! For how many years do love, wrath, hatred, lust, gluttony, and obsessive ambition beset the mind! How many men do we see who from youth to feeble old age never sober up, never recover from the intoxication of desire for power, of greed, lust, and
30 debauchery!

Spudaeus I know too many of that kind.

Hedonius You've granted that false goods are not to be reckoned among goods.

Spudaeus I don't take it back.

35 **Hedonius** Nor is something a true pleasure unless produced by the true.

Spudaeus Admitted.

Hedonius Therefore what the common crowd hunt by fair means or foul[33] aren't true goods.

Spudaeus I don't think they are.

40 **Hedonius** If they were true goods, they would befall only good men and would render happy those whom they befall. Now what is pleasure? What

comes not from true goods but from deceitful shadows of goods doesn't seem to be true pleasure, does it?

Spudaeus Not at all.

Hedonius But pleasure causes us to live enjoyably.

5 **Spudaeus** Of course.

Hedonius Then no one lives enjoyably unless he lives righteously; that is, enjoys true goods. Only righteousness renders a man blessed – only righteousness,[34] which alone reconciles God, the source of the supreme good, to man.

10 **Spudaeus** I'm in entire agreement.

Hedonius Now just see how very far from pleasure are those who openly pursue nothing but pleasures. In the first place, their minds are stained and corrupted by the leaven of lusts, so that if anything sweet does happen to them it turns sour at once, as water from a polluted well necessarily has a

15 bad taste. Secondly, there's no true pleasure except what is comprehended by a sound mind. Nothing is more agreeable to an angry man than vengeance, but this pleasure turns to sorrow as soon as the disease leaves his mind.

Spudaeus No objection.

Hedonius Finally, those pleasures are taken from false goods; whence it

20 follows that they are deceptions also. What would you say, moreover, were you to see a victim of magic eat, drink, dance, laugh, and clap his hands when none of the things he believes he sees was really present?[35]

Spudaeus I'd say he was mad and miserable both.

Hedonius I've witnessed such a sight at times. There was a priest skilled in

25 magic –

Spudaeus He hadn't learned *that* from Holy Scripture!

Hedonius On the contrary, from the most unholy scriptures. Some court ladies used to pester him for an invitation to dinner, reproaching his meanness and stinginess. He gave in and issued an invitation. They came

30 with empty stomachs, in order to dine with the better appetite. They sat down to dinner: no lack of rich dishes, as it seemed. They took their fill and when the feast was over thanked their host and went home. But soon they began to feel hungry. They wondered what this marvel meant – being hungry and thirsty just after a sumptuous meal. At last the truth came out,

35 and the joke was on them.

Spudaeus Served them right, too. They'd have done better to satisfy their hunger with a bit of breakfast at home than to entertain themselves with empty illusions.

Hedonius But far more ridiculous is it, in my opinion, for the common herd

40 to embrace empty shadows of goods for true goods and to delight in these deceptions which end not in a laugh but in eternal grief.

Spudaeus The more I reflect on it, the more sense this seems to make.

Hedonius Come, now, let's grant that sometimes things which are not true goods acquire the name of pleasure. You wouldn't call mead sweet if it contained much more aloes than honey?[36]

5   **Spudaeus** I wouldn't call it sweet if it were one-third aloes.

Hedonius Or would you like a bad case of mange for the sake of the pleasure of scratching?[37]

Spudaeus Not if I were in my right mind.

Hedonius Figure out for yourself, then, how much bitterness is mingled

10 with those pleasures, falsely so called, produced by shameless love, unlawful passion, excessive wining and dining – not to mention the worst of all: torments of conscience, enmity with God, expectation of eternal punishment. I ask you: which sort among these 'pleasures' does not bring in its train also a vast throng of external evils?

15 **Spudaeus** What evils?

Hedonius Again, let's omit avarice, thirst for power, anger, pride, envy, which are sad evils in themselves; let's consider those things especially recommended in the name of enjoyment. When fever, headache, colic, fuzzy-mindedness, disgrace, loss of memory, vomiting, ruined digestion,

20 and palsy follow too much drinking, would even Epicurus think that a pleasure worth seeking?

Spudaeus He'd advise us to shun it.

Hedonius When young men get from whoring the new disease now euphemistically[38] called the 'Neapolitan itch'[39] – and generally they do get it

25 – through which they are so often doomed to a living death, always carrying a living corpse about,[40] don't they seem to 'Epicurize' beautifully?

Spudaeus Not at all; they seem to be looking for a 'cure.'[41]

Hedonius Now weigh the pleasure against the pain: would you want the agony of toothache for as long as the pleasure of drinking or whoring lasted?

30 **Spudaeus** Well, I'd prefer to do without both, for to buy pleasure with pain is not getting but spending. In this respect the state of painlessness[42] Cicero ventured to call 'indolence'[43] is better.

Hedonius Consequently the stimulus of unlawful pleasure, in addition to being far less intense than the torture it causes, lasts but a short time,[44]

35 whereas the pox you get torments you all your life and often kills you before you die.

Spudaeus Epicurus would not acknowledge such disciples.

Hedonius Poverty, a heavy and miserable burden, is the constant companion of gluttony; paralysis, palsy, inflammation of the eyes, blindness, and leprosy

40 – and not only these – of intemperate sexual indulgence. A strange bargain, is it not? And you wouldn't care to exchange a pleasure neither true nor

genuine – and brief besides – for so many more serious and lasting ills, would you?

Spudaeus Even if no torture resulted, one who exchanged jewels for glass[45] would seem to be a very foolish bargainer.

5 **Hedonius** You mean one who sacrifices the true goods of the mind to the deceitful pleasures of the body?

Spudaeus Yes, that's my opinion.

Hedonius Now let's resume our stricter calculation. Neither fever nor poverty always accompanies gluttony; and the new pox or paralysis doesn't

10 always accompany intemperate sexuality. But agony of conscience – and we've agreed there's nothing worse – is always the companion of unlawful pleasure.

Spudaeus What's more, it sometimes runs ahead and pierces the heart in the midst of pleasure. Yet there are people who, you would say, lack this

15 feeling.

Hedonius The worse for them. Who wouldn't prefer to feel pain than have a body numbed and without feeling? But as in some their intemperance in pleasures (drunkenness, for example) or addiction to vices or a certain callousness destroys the sense of evil during youth, when old age arrives

20 and when – besides the innumerable discomforts accumulated by the sins of earlier life – death, which no mortal escapes, stands close at hand to terrify,[46] the more insensible a man has been throughout his life, the more excruciatingly his conscience torments him. For now his mind is alert whether he wishes it to be or not. Though old age is by its very nature

25 unhappy,[47] exposed as it is to many natural discomforts, how much more miserable and even disgraceful is it for one oppressed by a bad conscience! Wining and dining, love affairs, song and dance, and other things delightful to a young man are bitter to an old one. Age has no other prop but the recollection of a virtuous life and the hope of a better life to come.[48] These

30 are the two staffs by which old age is supported. If you take them away and substitute the double burden of remembrance of a life ill spent and despair of future happiness, what beast can be imagined more wretched or afflicted?

Spudaeus I see none, not even an old, worn-out horse.[49]

Hedonius In brief, then, 'The Phrygians are wise too late,'[50] and it is truly

35 said, 'The end of mirth is heaviness,'[51] and 'There is . . . no joy above the joy of the heart,'[52] 'A merry heart maketh a cheerful countenance,'[53] 'A broken spirit drieth the bones';[54] likewise 'All the days of the afflicted are evil,' that is, distressed and wretched, 'but he that is of a merry heart hath a continual feast.'[55]

40 **Spudaeus** Wise are they, therefore, who make their fortune early and gather provision for coming old age.

Hedonius Mystical Scripture[56] does not descend so low as to measure human happiness by the goods of fortune. In the last analysis, one is extraordinarily poor who is destitute of all virtue and owes both body and soul to Death.[57]

5 **Spudaeus** Death's an implacable collector indeed.

Hedonius The truly rich man is one who has God's favour. What should he fear if he has such a defender? Men? The power of all men in the world against God is less than that of a gnat against an Indian elephant. Death? For good men it is the way to eternal bliss. Hell? But the righteous man says

10 confidently to God: 'Though I walk through the valley of the shadow of death, I will fear no evil, for thou art with me.'[58] Why should he fear devils, having in his heart him whom devils dread? For that a righteous man's mind is the temple of God, Scripture, which cannot be contradicted,[59] declares in more than one passage.[60]

15 **Spudaeus** I don't see how these arguments could be refuted, though for the most part they seem far from common sense.

Hedonius How so?

Spudaeus Because according to your reasoning, any Franciscan would lead a more pleasurable life than a man rich in money, honours, and, in short,

20 luxuries of every kind.

Hedonius Add a king's sceptre if you like; add the pontifical crown and make it a hundredfold instead of triple; only take away a good conscience and I'll be bold to say that this Franciscan, barefoot, girded with a knotted cord, poorly and cheaply dressed, worn by fasting, vigils, and labours,

25 without a farthing in the world, lives more delightfully – provided only that he has a good conscience – than six hundred Sardanapaluses rolled into one.[61]

Spudaeus Then why is it we see the poor usually sadder than the rich?

Hedonius Because most are doubly poor. It is true, disease, hunger,

30 watchings, labours, and nakedness weaken one's physical condition, yet not in these states only but even at death itself cheerfulness breaks through. Though the mind is in fact attached to a mortal body, nevertheless, since mind is the stronger, it somehow assimilates the very body, especially if spiritual energy[62] is added to the impetuous force of nature. Hence it is that

35 we often see truly righteous men die with more cheerfulness than others feast.

Spudaeus Yes, I've often wondered at that.

Hedonius But you should not think it wonderful that where God, the fount of all joy, is present, there insuperable happiness exists. What's strange about

40 the mind of a truly righteous man rejoicing continually in a mortal body, since if that same man goes down to the depths of hell he will suffer no

loss of happiness?[63] Wherever is a pure heart, there God is. Wherever God is, there is paradise, heaven, happiness. Where happiness is, there is true gladness and unfeigned cheerfulness.

Spudaeus But they would live more pleasantly if they didn't have certain
5 discomforts; and delights would be available that they disregard or don't attain.

Hedonius Exactly what 'discomforts' do you mean? Those to which we as human beings are liable by universal law – hunger, thirst, disease, weariness, old age, death, thunderbolts, earthquakes, floods, wars?

10 **Spudaeus** Yes, those among others.

Hedonius But we're discussing things subject to human control, not those beyond human control.[64] And yet even in these misfortunes, the lot of the righteous is far more tolerable than that of men who pursue carnal pleasures by hook or by crook.[65]

15 **Spudaeus** How so?

Hedonius In the first place, since their minds are disciplined to temperance and endurance they bear unavoidable ills more steadfastly than others do. Secondly, since they understand that everything is sent by God either to cleanse us of faults or to test our virtue, they receive it not only patiently but
20 gladly, as obedient sons from the hand of a gracious father; and they even give thanks, both for his merciful chastisement and for their inestimable gain.[66]

Spudaeus But many bring ills of the flesh upon themselves.

Hedonius More employ physicians' remedies, however, to safeguard
25 or recover their health. On the other hand, to invite troubles, that is, poverty, bad health, persecution, disgrace, except when Christian charity compels, is not piety but folly. But whenever they are afflicted for Christ's and righteousness' sake, who would dare to call them unfortunate when the Lord himself terms them blessed and bids them rejoice at these
30 things?[67]

Spudaeus All the same, these afflictions cause terrible suffering.

Hedonius They do, but what the fear of hell on the one hand, and hope of eternal blessedness on the other, easily swallow up. Come: were you convinced you would never be ill or feel any bodily discomfort in your
35 whole life if you allowed the surface of your skin to be pricked once by a pinpoint, wouldn't you accept so little pain willingly and gladly?

Spudaeus Of course. More than that, if I knew for certain I'd never have toothache in my whole life, I'd be content to let a needle be inserted quite deeply and even have both ears pierced through by an awl.[68]

40 **Hedonius** But whatever affliction befalls us in this life is lighter and briefer, in comparison with eternal sufferings, than is a tiny, temporary wound

in comparison with man's life, however long, because there is no analogy between finite and infinite.[69]

Spudaeus You're absolutely right.

Hedonius Now if somebody convinced you that you would be free of
5 trouble all your life long if you passed your hand once through a flame (which Pythagoras forbade),[70] wouldn't you be glad to do it?

Spudaeus I'd do it even a hundred times, provided the one who promised didn't deceive me.

Hedonius God cannot deceive. But that sensation of the flame lasts longer,
10 in comparison with a man's whole life, than a whole life compared with heavenly bliss, though you outlived three Nestors;[71] since that thrusting of the hand, however brief, is *some* portion of this life; but the entire life of man is no portion of eternity.

Spudaeus I've nothing to say against that.

15 **Hedonius** Do you believe, then, that those who press on to this eternity with their whole heart and an assured hope will be tormented by the ills of this life, when the passage is so short?

Spudaeus I don't think they will, provided they have a settled conviction and a firm hope of attaining eternity.

20 **Hedonius** I come now to the delights you cited by way of objection. 'They refrain from dances, revels, shows.' They despise them, inasmuch as they enjoy far more agreeable ones and have no less delight, but in a different fashion: 'Eye hath not seen, nor ear heard, neither have entered into the heart of man, the things which God hath prepared for them that love him.'[72] St
25 Paul knew well what songs, dances, exultings, revels the godly have even in this life.

Spudaeus But there are some permissible pleasures they deny themselves.

Hedonius Immoderate use even of permissible pleasures is not permissible. But that apart, those who seem to lead a hard life win on all other counts.
30 What spectacle can be more splendid than the sight of this world? Men dear to God derive far more pleasure from this than others do; for those, whilst they behold this admirable work with curious gaze, are tormented in mind because they fail to comprehend the causes of it all. Some among them even murmur, Momus-like,[73] against the maker, often calling Nature stepmother
35 instead of mother[74] – nominally a slander against Nature but actually an unfavourable reflection upon the creator of Nature,[75] if there is any 'Nature' at all. But the godly man beholds with reverent, innocent eyes, and with surpassing inward delight, the works of his Lord and Father, marvelling at every one, finding fault with none but giving thanks for all, since he
40 considers them all to be created for man's sake. And so in individual things he reveres the creator's omnipotence, wisdom, and goodness, of which he

discerns traces in created objects.[76] Just imagine, now, that there is really some such palace as Apuleius imagines for Psyche,[77] or one more splendid and magnificent if possible. Bring to it two spectators: one a stranger who came only to view it, the other a servant or son of the man who built this
5   building. Which will be more enthusiastic about it, the stranger to whom the building means nothing personally, or the son who to his immense delight beholds in the structure his beloved father's genius, wealth, and splendour, and whose pleasure is enhanced when he reflects that this whole structure was made for his own sake?
10   **Spudaeus** Your question needs no answer. But most men, even the undevout, know that the heavens and what is encompassed by the heavens are created for man.

Hedonius Nearly all of them know it but they don't all remember it. If it does occur to them, however, the one who takes more pleasure in it is he
15   who loves the maker more; just as he who aspires to the heavenly life gazes at the heavens more eagerly.

Spudaeus Very likely.

Hedonius Now the deliciousness of banquets does not consist in choice foods or the seasonings of cooks but in sound health and a good appetite.[78]
20   Beware, then, of thinking any Lucullus dines more enjoyably off the partridges, pheasants, doves, hares, scari,[79] sheat-fish, or morays served to him than does a godly man off black bread, herbs, or legumes, with water or small beer or well-diluted wine for his drink. Think, moreover, that he receives these as gifts from a kind Father; that prayer seasons everything;
25   that grace before meals sanctifies everything; that his companion is Sacred Scripture, refreshing his mind more than food his body; that he finishes his meal with a thanksgiving; that finally he rises from table not stuffed but revived, not surfeited but restored in mind and body alike. Or do you suppose any vulgar gourmand dines more enjoyably?
30   **Spudaeus** But if we believe Aristotle, sexual love offers the greatest pleasure.[80]

Hedonius Here too the godly man wins, no less than in dining. Look at it this way: the stronger his devotion to his wife, the more pleasurable is the marriage-bed. No men love their wives more ardently than those who
35   cherish them as Christ cherished the church,[81] for men who 'love' their wives for the sake of physical pleasure do not even love them. Add to this that sexual intercourse is sweeter for being infrequent, a fact known even to the profane poet who wrote that 'temperance enhances pleasures.'[82] Though the least part of the pleasure is the actual sexual union. Much greater
40   is the pleasure derived from unbroken intimacy, which cannot be more delightful than among those who love each other equally and sincerely

with Christian love. Among other persons love often cools when physical passion wanes. Christian love grows stronger as carnal pleasure fades. Or haven't I convinced you yet that none live more enjoyably than those who live righteously?

5 **Spudaeus** I only wish everyone were as convinced as I am.

Hedonius But if people who live agreeably are Epicureans, none are more truly Epicureans than the righteous and godly. And if it's names that interest us, no one better deserves the name of Epicurean than the revered founder and head of the Christian philosophy, for in Greek ἐπίκουρος means

10 'helper.'[83] He alone, when the law of nature was all but blotted out by sins, when the law of Moses incited to lusts rather than cured them,[84] when Satan ruled in the world unchallenged, brought timely aid to perishing humanity. Completely mistaken, therefore, are those who talk in their foolish fashion about Christ's having been sad and gloomy in character and calling upon us

15 to follow a dismal mode of life. On the contrary, he alone shows the most enjoyable life of all and the one most full of true pleasure;[85] but let the Tantalean rock be far away![86]

Spudaeus What's that riddle?

Hedonius You'll smile at the story, but this is a joke with a serious meaning.

20 **Spudaeus** I'm waiting for the serious joke.

Hedonius Those who in ancient times liked to teach philosophical wisdom under the guise of fables tell us that a certain Tantalus was invited to the table of the gods, which (we are assured) was a sumptuous one. When the hour came for the guests to leave, Jupiter, thinking his bounty required that

25 the guest should not depart without a going-away gift,[87] permitted him to request anything he liked; whatever he asked he would receive. Tantalus, being a dull creature who measured human happiness in terms of throat and belly, expressed a desire to recline at such a table all his life. Jupiter assented; the prayer was granted. Tantalus sits at a table furnished with all sorts of

30 dainties; he has nectar at hand; there is no lack of roses or perfumes such as can delight the nostrils of gods; the cupbearer Ganymede, or someone like Ganymede, is at his side;[88] the Muses stand near, singing sweetly; comic Silenus dances;[89] jesters too are present; in short, whatever can delight any human sense is there. But in the midst of all these he sits sad, depressed, and

35 anxious, neither merry with laughter nor touching anything set before him.

Spudaeus Why?

Hedonius Because above his head, as he reclines at table, a huge stone hangs by a hair and seems about to fall.

Spudaeus I'd get away from such a table!

40 **Hedonius** But what he prayed for has become destiny, since Jupiter is not so lenient as our God, who cancels men's disastrous prayers if only they repent

of them. And besides, that same stone which forbids Tantalus to eat keeps
him from escaping, because he fears that if he makes a move it will fall and
crush him.

Spudaeus An amusing story.

5   **Hedonius** But now hear something you won't think amusing. The common
crowd seek a pleasant life in external things, though that is unattainable
unless the mind is free of anxiety; for those with a bad conscience have a
much heavier stone hanging over them than hangs over Tantalus – indeed,
not hanging over but pushing and pressing their minds. And it is by no

10   empty fear that the heart is afflicted, but every single hour it expects to be
cast into hell. What, I ask you, in human affairs is so sweet that it could really
cheer a mind menaced by such a stone?

Spudaeus Nothing, surely, except madness or unbelief.[90]

Hedonius If young men who are crazed by pleasures as by Circe's cup[91]

15   and welcome honeyed poison in place of what is truly pleasurable would
ponder these facts, how zealously would they guard against thoughtless
acceptance of what might consume their hearts all their lives! What would
they not do to lay up against approaching old age the provision of a good
conscience and an unstained honour! What is more wretched than that old

20   age which beholds with great horror, whenever it looks back, how comely
are the things it neglected, how sordid the ones it eagerly embraced; again,
when it looks ahead and perceives the last day coming close and, directly
after this, the everlasting torments of hell?

Spudaeus The most fortunate, I think, are those who kept their youth

25   unsoiled and who, always advancing in their pursuits of righteousness, have
reached the goal of old age.

Hedonius The next place is due to those who recover early from youthful
debauchery.

Spudaeus But what counsel have you for that wretched old man?

30   **Hedonius** 'While there's life there's hope.'[92] I urge him to take refuge in
God's mercy.

Spudaeus But the longer he's lived, the larger his mass of sins has grown.
By now it exceeds the sands of the sea.[93]

Hedonius But God's mercies far outnumber those sands. Even if sands

35   cannot be counted by man, still they are finite in number; but the mercy of
the Lord knows neither bound nor limit.

Spudaeus But one who's shortly to die hasn't time.

Hedonius The shorter the time, the more passionately should he cry aloud.
What can reach from earth to heaven is long enough with God: and even a

40   brief prayer gets through to heaven,[94] provided it is uttered with fervent
force of spirit. The woman who was a sinner, in the Gospel, is said to have

done lifelong penance.[95] But with how few words the dying thief won paradise from Christ![96] If he[97] cries with his whole heart, 'Have mercy on me, O God, according to the multitude of thy tender mercies,'[98] the Lord will take away the Tantalean stone, will grant him the hearing of joy and
5   gladness, and his bones broken by contrition shall rejoice for sins forgiven.[99]

NOTES

1 The names mean 'devoted to pleasure' and 'earnest,' 'diligent.' Spudus, a variant of the second name, appears in 'A Feast of Many Courses.'

2 *De finibus bonorum et malorum* (45 BC), an analysis of Stoic, Epicurean, and Academic systems of ethics. In books 1 and 2, Epicurean ethics are explained, then criticized by a Stoic; in books 3 and 4, Stoic ethics are described, then refuted by Cicero as an Academic; book 5, after summarizing Peripatetic ethics, considers whether virtue alone confers happiness. The Old Academy, the school of Plato and Platonism, was succeeded in the fourth and third centuries BC by a New Academy, in which both scepticism and controversies over the certitude of knowledge flourished. Antiochus of Ascalon (first century BC) claimed that he had reconciled the differences in the teachings of his predecessors as heads of the Academy. By the time of Cicero, exclusive doctrines and distinctions among Epicureans, Stoics, and Academics or Peripatetics (new or old) were less precise and less clear, though persons professing one system or another continued to use the old identifying name.

Francis Bacon observed that to the heathen, moral philosophy had the place filled in the modern age (his own) by theology (*New Organon: Aphorisms* 1.79). Of all branches of philosophy, the most important in Erasmus' judgment was not logic or metaphysics but that which is productive of wisdom, *sapientia* (Allen Ep 2533:109–13). For him, therefore, moral philosophy was the most helpful as well as the most congenial of philosophic studies, and a discipline ancillary to theology. He responded to such writings as Cicero's *De officiis*, the *Tusculan Disputations*, *De amicitia*, and *De senectute* with aesthetic and intellectual satisfaction, while dialectic and metaphysics he could read as a duty but with little pleasure or profit. He valued *De finibus* too. That book seems never to have been the favourite the *Tusculans* were, but it had, and still has, importance as an exposition and comparison of influential types of Greek thought on perennial topics dealing with human experience, reason, and values. For many readers in the world of Erasmus, if we may judge by the evidence of printing and publishing history, moral philosophy had a strong literary appeal in addition to its homiletic and other uses.

The complete works of Plato and Aristotle in Greek and Latin were available to scholars and other serious students. Few of Epicurus' texts survived, but we have a collection of his forty-odd 'golden maxims' on the art of living. Later readers could learn of Epicurean doctrines not merely from quotations or fragments but from Lucretius' famous poem *De rerum natura* (unknown in the Middle Ages, though Lucretius was a contemporary of Cicero), which expounds the atomistic theory adopted by Epicurus from Democritus and defends Epicurean ethics. There was a wealth of Stoic texts; for example by the younger Seneca, Cleanthes, Epictetus, and Marcus Aurelius. Cicero's writings, coloured by his strong sympathy with Stoic ethical ideals (as in the final book of the *Tusculan Disputations*) and his scepticism as to epistemology, offered eloquent arguments for the New Academic and Peripatetic positions. To Renaissance readers, the literary form and manner of philosophical discourse, whether in verse or prose, and very often dialogue, was no hindrance to its effectiveness. On the contrary, it was a distinct advantage: it made philosophy attractive by making it readable, and by rhetorical power made it persuasive.

3 Cicero speaks of goods and evils as having 'ends' because, like other thinkers, he inherited Aristotle's emphasis on the aim or ultimate purposes of human acts. Indeed everything in nature, whether human or not, has an end or purpose, some drive towards completion of what it is 'for'; as an acorn's 'end' is an oak tree. Similarly, by the Aristotelian doctrines of potentiality and actualization, development or growth in human behaviour moves towards greater goods or greater evils. What then is the principle or assumption according to which states of goodness can be defined, assessed, and chosen? These are questions discussed and criticized in *De finibus*. The good is 'that which is by nature perfect,' 'that to which all right actions are a means while it is not itself a means to anything else' (*De finibus* 3.10.33, 2.2.5 trans H. Rackham, Loeb Classical Library [London and Cambridge, Mass 1914] 253, 83). The chief good, *summum bonum*, is virtue; nothing more can be desired (4.17.46).

4 Cicero. He was often called Tully by English writers.

5 Cf Terence *Heautontimorumenos* 499

6 *Adagia* I iii 88

7 Cf *Adagia* I x 30.

8 Greek in the original; a technical term in ancient philosophy

9 Stoics stressed that 'appropriate' actions must be preferred; that is, actions in harmony with nature; but the chief good is the rational, willed achievement of virtue, not merely the struggle to attain it. Things done in accordance with nature – good conduct – are necessary steps towards the goal, virtue itself, which is the end to which all else is a means (*De finibus* 3.6.20–1). No matter what his circumstances, the truly virtuous man is happy; even when suffering he is happy. Cf *Tusculan Disputations* 5.28.80–1. Peripatetics considered themselves the legatees of Aristotle in ethical philosophy. Aristotle defined human good as 'activity of soul in accordance with virtue, and if there are more than one virtue, in accordance with the best and most complete' (*Nicomachean Ethics* 1.7 1098a16–17 trans W.D. Ross in *The Works of Aristotle* IX [Oxford 1925]). 'Epicureanism' was used and is still used to mean 'hedonism' or addiction to pleasure and avoidance of pain at all costs. As Spudaeus says in the colloquy, no school was more detested. But pleasure is of many kinds, and both Aristippus (founder of the Cyrenaic school; see 'The Profane Feast' n40) and Epicurus held that moderation and self-control should regulate pleasure. Epicurus thought a quiet, retired life of virtue was the best. Lucretius, whose *De rerum natura* is unsurpassed as a guide to Epicureanism, had lofty conceptions of the good life, but in contrast with Stoicism, Epicureanism was indifferent to gods. Gods exist, but are irrelevant to men. They did not create the world nor do they govern it. Popular religion is merely superstition. There is no immortality.

Death is the annihilation of personality; the atoms of which man is made simply disperse. Stoics taught that because man has reason, he ought to be able, by self-discipline, to resist passions. Peripatetics argued that passions are not altogether avoidable or dangerous or useless; they are natural. Yet nature must be overcome. Therefore the passions are tests, incentives to virtue if rightly understood. Erasmus preferred this judgment to the inhumane rigour of the Stoic view (*Enchiridion* LB V 13E–14F / Holborn 44:18–45:6 / CWE 66 44). Yet he admired the courage and steadfastness of the true Stoic.

All the major systems of pagan ethics had precepts of value for modern as well as ancient peoples, and representatives we can admire. Not only that; they had at least some ethical principles consonant with those held by Christians. Plato, Socrates, Epictetus, Aristotle, even Epicurus were seekers after truth. Even pagan philosophies, at their best, 'concern Christ' in Erasmus' phrase, because, by divine ordinance, they contributed to knowledge and enlargement of mind and thus were part of the preparation for Christ. See the passage in 'The Godly Feast' cited in the introduction to the present colloquy and the notes to those pages; *Paraclesis* LB V 142A–D or VI *4 recto; CWE 23 xxx.

10 Cicero *Paradoxa Stoicorum* 1.14
11 More had said the same thing in his letter to Thomas Ruthall accompanying his translation of Lucian's *Cynicus*. See Yale CWM 3 part 1 3, 5, 138–9.
12 In *De finibus* 4.74–7, Cicero criticizes some of the extravagant claims of the Stoics, their unreasonable assertions or paradoxes that contradict common experience and judgment. He discusses such language briefly in his *Paradoxa Stoicorum*, where he attributes (or pretends to attribute) it to Cato the Censor and amuses himself by feigning to show how acceptable these paradoxes can be, for example 'only what is morally noble is good,' or 'virtue is sufficient for happiness' (1.6, 2.16).
13 Plautus *Mostellaria* 544–5
14 Cf *Enchiridion* LB V 42B–C / Holborn 94:33 / CWE 66 89–90.
15 The mineral asbestos (Pliny *Naturalis historia* 19.19–20)
16 Greek in the original
17 Matt 5:4
18 *Adagia* II x 9
19 Sardanapalus, legendary king of Assyria (ninth century BC) was notorious for luxuriousness and effeminacy; see *Adagia* III vii 27. Philoxenus and Apicius were Greek and Roman gourmands and experts on cookery. They are named together in CWE 23 106:15. On Apicius see 'The Profane Feast' n5.
20 See 'The New Mother' 601:31–605:2.
21 Cf *Ecclesiastes* LB V 914E–F, 969A.
22 Proverbial; *Adagia* III ii 98
23 See 1079:24–35 below.
24 Cf 'Faith' 430:22.
25 The one-eyed giants in Homer *Odyssey* 9; *Adagia* I x 69
26 Not merely 'virtuously' but *pie*, which in this context, as often in Erasmus' writings, has a definitely religious as well as ethical connotation. Cf n34 below.
27 *Adagia* IV vii 98, citing Plato *Philebus* 19E
28 Cf 'The Funeral' 766:7–35 and n6; Cornelius in that colloquy approaches death with joy and hope.

29 See *Enchiridion* LB V 42B–D / Holborn 94:30–95:14 / CWE 66 90.

30 Terence *Adelphi* 117

31 a rich man] The first edition (March 1533), *Opera omnia* 1540, and LB all read *divitem*. Schrevelius (Leiden 1655; repr Amsterdam 1693) and Rabus (Rotterdam 1693) question *divitem* and suggest *dementem* 'mad.' This change makes better sense than *divitem*, but *divitem* makes sufficient sense, and other forms of the same word for 'rich' occur above ('grow rich ... riches'). If rendered 'Dives' after the rich man of Luke 16:19–31, the reading *divitem* is even more appropriate here.

32 Terence *Adelphi* 785–6

33 *per fas nefasque*; Livy 6.14.10 and Horace *Epodes* 5.87. See 'Youth' n33.

34 *pie ... pietas*. See n26 above.

35 The theme of illusory tricks and specifically of magic banquets is as old as Homer (*Odyssey* 11.582–92 on Tantalus) and the Bible (the temptation of Christ by Satan in Matt 4:1–11 and Luke 4:1–13). One of many examples in Renaissance literature is the magic banquet in Shakespeare's *The Tempest* 3.3.18–68. See Jacqueline E.M. Latham 'The Magic Banquet in *The Tempest' Shakespeare Studies* 12 (1979) 215–27 on this and other examples. In *Adagia* II vii 31, Erasmus refers to a story he found in Suidas' *Lexicon* (tenth century) of a magician, Pases, who, like the one in the colloquy, could produce magically a splendid banquet and then just as quickly cause it to vanish. In 'The Epicurean,' as earlier in 'Alchemy,' the magician is a priest. Magicians were suspect, for they used 'curious arts' (Acts 19:19) and might be invoking occult powers (as 'from the most unholy scriptures' here). A priest had better think twice before learning magic and producing illusions, even if these seem harmless. Erasmus in 1501 tells a lurid tale of a sorcerer near Orléans who learned magic from a wicked priest and thus was able to summon the devil for evil purposes (Allen Ep 143:68–185 / CWE Ep 143:74–202). See *Explanatio symboli* LB V 1186F and 'The Usefulness of the *Colloquies*' n49.

36 Proverbial; *Adagia* I viii 66

37 A question asked by Plato in *Gorgias* 494C and *Philebus* 46A, 51D

38 Greek in the original

39 Syphilis; also known as the Italian, French, or Spanish pox. See 'The Soldier and the Carthusian' n45 and 'A Marriage in Name Only' n12.

40 *Adagia* II iv 3

41 'Epicurize' and 'cure' are an attempt to reproduce the pun in two Greek expressions in the original. Literally translated, they mean 'to Epicurize' and 'to rush to the barber's shop.' The point is that barbers were also surgeons. Men who caught the 'Neapolitan itch' went to a barber in search of a cure.

42 Greek in the original

43 *De finibus* 2.4.11

44 Cf *De finibus* 1.11.39

45 A variant of *Adagia* I ix 30 ('The treasure consisted of coals')

46 See 1077:34 above.

47 See Allen Epp 2720:31–44, 2745:22–3, both written in 1532. One of Erasmus' best poems is about old age; see CWE 85–6 12–25, 412–39 no 2 / Reedijk *Poems of Erasmus* 280 no 83. This was written in 1506, when Erasmus was close to forty.

48 Like that of Cornelius in 'The Funeral'

49 Greek in the original; *Adagia* II i 32

50 *Adagia* I i 28. The Phrygians hesitated too long to intervene in the Trojan war, when they might have prevented so much bloodshed. Christians are even more hesitant about ending war among Christians, Erasmus adds.

51 Prov 14:13

52 Ecclus (Sirach) 30:16

53 Prov 15:13

54 Prov 17:22

55 Prov 15:15

56 'Mystical' refers to those biblical texts which either contain truths given by direct revelation or in the mystical experiences of the writer or which, in contrast with what may be understood in a literal or historical sense, convey or emphasize the spiritual, allegorical, or anagogical senses (pertaining to a future life); for instance the Gospel of John 1:1–18, 6:32–58, 8:12–32, 10:14–17; Eph 3:2–11; Col 1:25–9

57 Orcus, the abode of the dead, or Orcus lord of the underworld

58 Ps 23:4 (22:4 Vulg). Erasmus wrote a commentary on this psalm (1530); text in LB V 311C–346B.

59 Greek in the original

60 1 Cor 3:16; 2 Cor 6:16

61 On Sardanapalus see n19 above; on 'six hundred,' 'The Funeral' n76; on a Franciscan as an example here, 'The Seraphic Funeral,' especially the 'Note on Franciscan Poverty' 1026–32.

62 Greek in the original

63 Ps 139 (138 Vulg):8–12

64 For a list of current discomforts, disasters, and calamities see 'The New Mother' 592:17–35.

65 See n33 above.

66 Cf Prov 3:11–12; Heb 12:1–13; Rev 3:19–20.

67 Matt 5:10–12

68 Self-explanatory; yet the words recall something more, for Erasmus' phrase *subula perforari* is the one used in Exod 21:6 Vulg in describing the ceremony by which a man accepts lifelong slavery in return for permission to keep his wife and children, whom he would lose if he chose freedom.

69 Compare More's *Four Last Things* (between 1520 and 1525): 'If virtue were all painful, and vice all pleasant, yet since death shall shortly finish both the pain of the one and the pleasure of the other, great madness were it if we would not rather take a short pain for the winning of everlasting pleasure, than a short pleasure for the winning of everlasting pain. But now, if it be true, as it is indeed, that our sin is painful and our virtue pleasant, how much is it then a more madness to take sinful pain in this world, that shall win us eternal pain in hell, rather than pleasant virtue in this world, that shall win us eternal pleasure in heaven?' (*English Works* 495).

70 Forbidden by Pythagoras because fire is a divinity. Fire was said to occupy the centre of the universe because it was 'more precious' than earth and was called the 'Guard-house of Zeus' (Aristotle *De caelo* 2.13 293a20–293b4).

71 *Adagia* I ii 56

72 1 Cor 2:9

73 Momus was a minor deity who did nothing constructive himself but found fault with what other gods did. Finally they expelled him from Olympus. Folly implies that they might have done better to listen to him sometimes (LB IV 416C–417B / ASD IV-3 88:294–312 / CWE 27 94).

74 On 'stepmother' as synonymous with harshness or cruelty compare 'Marriage' n62. In the adage *Dulce bellum inexpertis*, which denounces war and warmongers, Nature declares man is now so wicked and degenerate that it is no wonder people call her a stepmother instead of mother (*Adagia* IV i 1 LB II 954D–955A / Phillips 'Adages' 316–17).

75 *qui naturam condidit.* 'Creator' (*creator*) is always a standard theological term in Judaic and Christian writings, but as predicate Erasmus sometimes used 'formed' or 'established' (*condiderit*) instead of 'created' or 'made' (*Explanatio symboli* LB V 1147B–D). 'Author' is another word he liked because of its precision, which however is not so evident in English. See 'Faith' nn89, 90 and 'The Usefulness of the *Colloquies*' 1108:31–1109:3.

76 Eusebius in 'The Godly Feast' tells his guests the beauty of blooming nature reminds him that 'God the creator's wisdom is equal to his goodness' (175:27–8), and see *Explanatio symboli* LB V 1092E–F. This has been a persistent and familiar theme in theistic literature since the time of the Hebrew psalmists and Plato (*Timaeus* 28–30 and *Laws* 10), to name no others. In these lines of his colloquy, Erasmus goes further by contrasting reverence for the creation's creator with the stubborn denial of those who 'fail to comprehend' the First Cause.

77 In his *Metamorphoses* or *Golden Ass* 5.1–3

78 Similar truisms on moderation in feasting are repeated in other *convivia* of the *Colloquia*. On Lucullus, see 'The Profane Feast' n18.

79 Or parrot-fish, as in 'The Profane Feast'; see n83.

80 *De generatione animalium* 1.18 723b33–724a3

81 Eph 5:28–9

82 Juvenal 11.208

83 Or 'guardian,' 'guide'

84 See 'The Godly Feast' 187:28–191:37; 'A Fish Diet' 682:39–687:8, 691:2–701:16.

85 For Christ 'makes all men to rejoice' ('The Godly Feast' 183:18 and n98).

86 *Adagia* II vi 14, II ix 7, IV iii 31. In Homer's brief version of the myth, Tantalus, always thirsty, tries to drink from the lake in which he stands, but when he lowers his head the water disappears. Above his head are trees loaded with fruit, but when he reaches to pluck it the wind blows it away (*Odyssey* 11.582–92). Some later ancient versions, cited in *Adagia* II ix 7, tell of the huge stone above Tantalus, seemingly about to fall on him. Erasmus has Tantalus sitting at a table and the stone hanging by a hair. He may have borrowed this episode from the story of Damocles (on which see Cicero *Tusculan Disputations* 5.21.61–2).

87 *xenio*. Cf 'The Godly Feast' n287.

88 Cf the ironical description of the waiter in 'Inns.'

89 See 'A Fish Diet' n237 for evidence that in another context Silenus could be, to Erasmus, very different from a comic figure.

90 In his lectures on Ps 90 (89 Vulg), delivered between October 1534 and the end of May 1535, Luther objected to these lines. Commenting on Ps 90:7, 'Quia defecimus in ira tua, et in furore tuo turbati sumus,' he asks 'How can human

nature bear to think of God's wrath without tears? . . . How can it be indifferent to death, since it knows that it must die because of sin and as a result of God's wrath? Since reason is determined to escape God's wrath, it proposes either the way of disdain or the way of blasphemy.' Then Luther calls attention to the myth of Tantalus in Erasmus' 'The Epicurean,' which he had read in 1533 or 1534. Referring to Erasmus' interpretation here, he says 'What can be, so Erasmus argues, a more effective remedy against this evil' – that is, against condemnation to eternal punishment – 'than unbelief or insanity, which refuses to believe God's threat? That is the way reason argues.' But such thoughts lead to blasphemy. 'Therefore,' he adds, 'Epicurus advises: "Become either insane or incredulous and thus rid yourself of this feeling of wrath and sin when you find yourself in the throes of miseries and death."' Foolish advice, of course, and leading only to hopeless despair in those who disdain or blaspheme (LW 13 107–9 / WA 40 part 3 537:14–540:16).
Luther errs seriously by assuming Spudaeus' comment on 'madness or unbelief' expresses the approval of the author, Erasmus. But Luther takes the passage out of context. This is not surprising, because he had concluded years earlier that Erasmus, like too many other learned men, was an Epicurean, in the most derogatory senses of the epithet; see WA Tischreden 1 nos 352, 432, 466, 468; 3 no 3795 (all five selections are also in Clemen 8); Allen Ep 1670:28–32. He had been corrupted in Venice and Rome, Luther adds; we all know that Epicureanism is rife in Italy.

91 Adagia IV ix 43. Circe was the sea nymph and enchantress who turned Ulysses' companions into swine but was later persuaded to turn them into men again and release them (Homer Odyssey 10).

92 Proverbial; Adagia II iv 12

93 Biblical (Gen 22:17, 32:12; Rev 20:8) as well as classical (Adagia I iv 44, I vii 87)

94 Cf Ecclus (Sirach) 35:20–1 Vulg. When Rabelais paraphrases this verse (Gargantua 1.41), he adds 'and long swilling empties the cups' ('et longa potatio evacuat scyphos'), words taken by his editors as a probably monkish dictum (as in the Oeuvres de François Rabelais ed Abel Lefranc et al 6 vols [Paris 1912–55] II 347 n22). Anyone familiar with medieval satire or Goliardic verse or with the Epistolae obscurorum virorum would be inclined to agree, though I do not recall another instance of this particular example.

95 Luke 7:37–50; that she had done lifelong penance is not stated explicitly.

96 Luke 23:39–43

97 The Latin text does not make clear whether the subject (understood) is the dying thief or any – or every – repentant sinner.

98 Ps 51:1–2 (50:3 Vulg)

99 Ps 51:8 (50:10 Vulg)

THE USEFULNESS OF THE *COLLOQUIES*

De utilitate Colloquiorum

First printed in the June 1526 edition, where it follows the first printing of the anonymous *Scholia*, brief explanatory notes on colloquies published before June 1526. These *Scholia* were reprinted in many early editions of the *Colloquia*. 'The Usefulness of the *Colloquies*' was included at or near the end of most editions of the text thereafter and with some translations as well. As though to prepare readers for its vigour and emphasis, a few excerpts from Erasmus' letters, under the title *Coronis apologetica*, preceded it in the Rabus and Schrevelius editions (1693), LB (1703), and others. Erasmus' correspondence and other contemporary evidence of many kinds – from readers, printers, booksellers, scholars, and dignitaries secular or ecclesiastical in every important nation of Europe – testify to the wide circulation, popularity, and influence of the book. But there was another side to its success. An attentive reader of these dialogues today, even if his knowledge of fifteenth- and sixteenth-century civilization is limited, can hardly avoid an inference that not all contemporary readers could have been pleased by them. Satire and irony, and other combinations of criticism and wit, can sting or anger a proud profession or institution and its representatives. Like Swift or Voltaire, Erasmus was certain that he understood his opponents, in fact understood them only too well. However tiresome their complaints, he often insisted that by exposing their errors and ignorance, impugning their motives, and mocking their pretensions, he was really doing them, and the cause of enlightenment, a service. Naturally his critics did not agree with him. Academic critics (notoriously those in Paris and Louvain but not only those), literati in France and Italy, monks and friars, even prelates, found fault with his editing, translating, and interpreting of Scripture and his opinions on certain ordinances and customs affecting Christians. *Enchiridion, Moriae encomium*, and many of the colloquies were particularly disliked.

That conservative divines, unsympathetic with humanism, should have been offended by passages in the *Colloquies*, on both moral and religious grounds, is understandable. Erasmus' lively pages on friars, monasticism, pilgrimages, fasting, clerical morality, and superstitious practices sometimes troubled even readers he esteemed and who esteemed him. Such readers he tried to mollify. Resentful churchmen, major or minor, who detected traces of heresy in his pages, could not be appeased. The probability that some of them discovered themselves, in thin disguise, in the very colloquies under suspicion did nothing to lessen their desire to make difficulties for Erasmus.

No doubt they were perfectly sincere, most of them, in their conviction that the *Colloquies* was a pernicious book, and they were too sure of themselves to be patient with what they considered equivocations by an irreverent satirist. Not all denunciations came from defenders of the Roman church. Luther spoke vehemently against Erasmus, as many entries in the *Tischreden* confirm. He detested the *Colloquies* and what he fancied was its author's sly subversion of religion in that and other books: verily a Lucian and Epicurus, he says of Erasmus more than once (see the introduction to these volumes xxviii and 'The Epicurean' n90). Although disputes between Luther and Erasmus require a long chapter in their biographies, they play only a slight part in 'The Usefulness of the *Colloquies*,' which is concerned with adversaries in the academic and ecclesiastical establishments.

As early as 1522 Erasmus was defending the purposes, methods, and utility of his *Colloquies* against assaults led by the Carmelite Nicolaas Baechem (Egmondanus) of Louvain (see Allen Epp 1299:4–71, 1300:1–42, 1301 / CWE Epp 1299:6–79, 1300:1–47, 1301; and 'Rash Vows' n14). By May 1526, his enemies in the faculty of theology at Paris, who had been complaining about him for several years, succeeded in carrying a motion of censure against the *Colloquies*. (This is the point of the allusion to 'deputies' at 1106:16 below). Sixty-nine passages in the book were denounced as erroneous or tending to corrupt youthful morals. These censures were not printed until 1531 but were well known to Erasmus, who rebutted them in his *Declarationes ad censuras Lutetiae vulgatas* (1532; LB IX 928D–954E, where the charges as well as the replies are reprinted). A few weeks before the faculty acted, Erasmus chose to defend his *Colloquies* in a letter (Ep 1704, dated 30 April 1526) to the bishop of Lincoln, John Longland, in which he sums up what is said more diffusely in 'The Usefulness of the *Colloquies*.' On criticisms of the *Colloquies* and Erasmus' defence of them see the introduction to these volumes sections 5 and 6.

To the edition of June 1526, Erasmus added most of the apology called 'The Usefulness of the *Colloquies*,' that is, his account of most of the colloquies published before June 1526 (as far as 1105:11 below). This defence is dated 21 May 1526, a date carelessly left unchanged in all later editions. In June 1528, the Parisians again condemned the *Colloquies*. This time the faculty of theology was supported by the faculties of arts, canon law, and medicine. In September of that year Erasmus again defended his *Colloquies* in a letter to Longland (Allen Ep 2037:13–38), especially what he had written on morals, pilgrimages, and confession. In the edition of March 1529 Erasmus added to 'The Usefulness of the *Colloquies*' comments on two colloquies published in 1527 and six published in that March 1529 edition; in September 1529 he inserted further remarks justifying a few of the colloquies he had already defended in June 1526. See n61 and n75 below.

This apology, addressed to the reader, bears obvious marks of hasty composition. It pays much more attention to some dialogues than to others that are of equal or greater importance; it gives several pages, for instance, to 'Rash Vows' but only a few lines to 'A Pilgrimage for Religion's Sake.' It omits mention of 'The Shipwreck' and several other colloquies already in print ('Inns,' 'The Epithalamium of Pieter Gillis,' 'Echo'), perhaps because most of those were not controversial. Not all colloquies mentioned are named in order of printing. Some of the titles vary from the usual ones. Most of the titles Erasmus names are in the ablative case, preceded by *in* (as 'in *Peregrinatione religionis ergo*,' 'in *Funere*,' 'in *Senatulo*'). Elsewhere titles are nominative (*Diversoria* or *Militaria*) or genitive (*Proci et puellae*, *Abbatis et eruditae*) or ablative after *de* (*De rebus ac vocabulis, De . . . Reuchlino*). Whatever the reason, the oddities or irregularities of 'The Usefulness of the *Colloquies*' remained unchanged in successive early editions I have checked.

So far as we know, Erasmus made no further changes in 'The Usefulness of the *Colloquies*' after September 1529. He had answered Spanish critics in *Apologia adversus monachos quosdam Hispanos* (1528; LB IX 1015D–1094A). When occasion invited, he continued to defend his *Colloquies* in letters. That the author's protestations appeased his critics is unlikely, nor does it matter much. In the long run the book speaks for itself.

DESIDERIUS ERASMUS ROTERODAMUS TO THE READER

To such an extent does Slander,[1] with its train of Furies, rage nowadays against everyone and everything throughout the entire world that it is not
5   safe to publish any book except under armed guard. But what could be safe enough against the sting of a backbiter who, like an adder deaf to the spell of the charmer,[2] ignores all explanation, no matter how reasonable? The first part of this work – which was mine and not mine[3] – was issued through someone's rashness. When I saw it was cordially welcomed by students, I
10   took advantage of the public's desire for the improvement of studies. As physicians do not always prescribe the most efficacious remedies for patients but make some allowance for their cravings,[4] so likewise I thought it well to allure the young – who respond more readily to pleasing than to strict or harsh treatment – with this kind of bait. Accordingly I revised what was
15   published, then added what might help to develop manners also; stealing (as it were) into the minds of young folk, who, as Aristotle truly wrote, are unsuitable hearers of moral philosophy,[5] at least of the sort that is taught by formal rules.

Now if someone protests that it is undignified for an old man to play
in this childish fashion, my answer is: 'I don't care how childish, if only it's
useful.' And if greybeard grammar masters are commended for coaxing
youngsters with bits of cake into wanting to learn the rudiments,[6] I don't
5   think I should be reproached for attracting youth with like zeal to refinement
of Latin speech and to good conduct.[7] Add, that to be acquainted with the
foolish caprices and baseless notions of the public is part of good, practical
sense. Young people learn these things better from this little book, I believe,
than from experience, the teacher of fools. To many people the rules of
10   grammar are repulsive. Aristotle's *Ethics* is not suited to boys, the theology
of Scotus still less[8] – it's not of much use even for improving the minds of
grown men! But to implant from the start a taste for excellence in young
minds is urgent. Moreover, I'm not sure anything is learned better than what
is learned as a game.[9] To confer a benefit through a trick is surely deception
15   of the most innocent sort. Doctors who deceive patients in this manner are
praised.[10]

Well, if I had only been joking in this affair, my critics apparently
would have put up with it. But now, since in addition to dealing with
refinement of language I have added here and there some passages to direct
20   the mind towards religion, they slander me; and they probe the syllables
through and through, precisely as if the dogmas of the Christian creed were
solemnly spelled out in these pages! How mischievously they do this will
be plainer when I have demonstrated the uncommon utility of some of the
Colloquies.

25   For – quite aside from so many earnest maxims mingled with
pleasantries, so many stories, so many histories, so many valuable
explanations of things – in the colloquy 'Rash Vows,'[11] the superstitious
and shameful fancy of some folk who think the essence of holiness is to
have visited Jerusalem[12] is curbed.[13] Hither, over such vast stretches of land
30   and sea, hasten venerable bishops,[14] deserting the flocks committed to their
care; hither princes, their household and realm abandoned; hither husbands,
their wives and children – of whose conduct and virtue the husband is
necessarily guardian – left at home; hither young men and women, not
without grave risk to morals and chastity. Some run back and forth again
35   and again, do nothing else all their lives; and meanwhile the name of
religion is used as a cover for superstition, faithlessness, foolishness, and
recklessness. The deserter of his family, a violator of Paul's teaching, wins
praise for his 'sanctity' and thinks of himself as one who has fulfilled
the whole duty of man. Paul declares boldly in 1 Timothy 2, 'But if any
40   provide not for his own, and especially for those of his own house, he
hath denied the faith and is worse than an infidel.'[15] But here Paul seems

to refer to widows who neglect their children and grandchildren (and
that under pretence of religion!) while binding themselves completely to
the church's observances. What is to be said of husbands who set out for
Jerusalem, leaving behind them destitute children and impoverished young
5   wives?

Of many examples I shall cite a single one, not so recent as to provoke
hard feelings or so old but that grandchildren of the man are still alive; their
loss was too great to permit them to forget the event. A certain magnate
determined – from motives of piety, to be sure, but hardly from prudence –
10   to visit Jerusalem before he died. So he put his affairs in order, committing
all his wealth, his wife (whom he left pregnant), towns, and castles to the
care and protection of an archbishop, as to a parent. When rumours reached
him that the man had died on his pilgrimage, the archbishop acted the part
of robber instead of parent. He seized all the dead man's possessions, then
15   stormed and took the fortified castle to which the pregnant wife had fled. In
order that no avenger of this most dreadful deed might survive, the woman
was stabbed, perishing with her unborn child. Would not it have been a
work of piety to dissuade such a husband from a perilous and unnecessary
journey?[16] How many examples of this kind might be found, I leave for
20   others to estimate – to say nothing of the money spent! Even if we grant it
is not completely wasted, no man of common sense will deny it could have
been put to much better uses.

As for religious scruples, St Jerome commends Hilarion because, native
and resident of Palestine though he was, he visited Jerusalem only once;
25   it was close by and he did not want to appear disdainful of holy places.[17]
If Hilarion, a close neighbour, was deservedly praised for keeping clear
of Jerusalem lest he seem to confine God to a narrow place – visiting it
but once, on account of its nearness, so as not to offend people – what are
we to say of men who travel to Jerusalem from England and Scotland at
30   such large expense and through so many dangers, especially when their
dearest relatives, to whom (according to the apostle's teaching) they owe
unremitting care, have been left at home? 'To have been in Jerusalem is not
of great importance, but to have lived righteously *is* important,' St Jerome
proclaims.[18] Yet it is likely that in Jerome's era more visible remains of
35   antiquities were extant than now survive. Argument over vows I leave to
others; the point of the colloquy is simply that one should not swear such
vows rashly. That this is true, my words on page [38:27–9] show: 'especially
when I had at home a wife still young and vigorous, children, and a family
dependent upon me and supported by my daily labour,' etc.[19] Of vows
40   sworn, then, I shall say nothing, except that if I were pope, I would have
little reluctance in releasing those who were bound by them. As for swearing

vows, just as I grant it is possible for someone to gain spiritual benefit from going to Jerusalem, so I would not hesitate to advise many, in the circumstances, to spend their time, money, and labour on other things more conducive to true godliness.

5   These, I believe, are righteous admonitions. Therefore, because of the irresponsibility, ignorance, or superstitiousness of many folk, I thought I should do well to warn youth on this subject, and I don't see who could be offended by this warning, except perhaps those who put profit above righteousness.

10   Nor do I condemn papal indulgences or briefs there;[20] but I do reprove the utterly frivolous man who, without even a thought of amending his life, puts his whole hope in human pardons. If, in this connection, a person but reflected how much men's devotion is impaired, partly by the fault of those who hawk papal indulgences, partly by the error of those who receive
15   pardons otherwise than as they should, he will admit it is worth while for youth to be warned about this matter. 'But in so doing you've given little thought to the commissioners.'[21] I hear you, my good friend! If they are good men, they'll rejoice that the unsophisticated are warned; if they care more for profit than for righteousness – away with them!

20   In the colloquy 'In Pursuit of Benefices,' I reprove those who rush off to Rome to hunt for livings, frequently with serious loss of morals and money both; hence my remark that a priest should entertain himself with good authors instead of a concubine.[22]

In 'Military Affairs,'[23] I condemn the wicked deeds and ungodly
25   confession of soldiers, to deter young men from such behaviour.

In 'A Lesson in Manners,'[24] I teach a boy modesty and manners suitable to his age.

In 'The Whole Duty of Youth'[25] do I not inspire the young mind, by means of godly precepts, with a zeal for righteousness? The carping by some
30   persons at the part on confession was sheer slander, to which I replied long ago. I teach that confession ought to be accepted as though instituted for us by Christ. But whether it *was* so instituted, I have no intention either of asserting or of denying, because I am not altogether convinced of it, nor could I prove it to others.[26] As for my warning about taking your time in
35   deciding on a career and about choice of a priest to whom to commit your secrets[27] – this I thought needed by young people, and I see no reason to apologize for it. 'But then there will be fewer monks and priests.' Maybe there will – but better ones.[28] Any monk worthy of the name will back me on that. Furthermore, the ones who hunt proselytes for the sake of profit, or
40   because of superstition, fully deserve denunciation in everybody's writings to bring them to their senses.

In 'The Profane Feast,' I do not condemn the ordinances of the church concerning fasts and choice of foods, but I expose the superstition of certain persons who attach excessive importance to these matters while neglecting those that contribute more to godliness. Also I condemn the callousness
5   of those who exact such observances of people whom the church does not intend to burden. Likewise the absurd holier-than-thou attitude of those who condemn their neighbour on such grounds. If, now, one will consider what a blight on true godliness this attitude produces among mankind, one will grant that scarcely any other admonition is more urgently needed. But on
10   this topic we shall have more to say at another time.[29]

In 'The Godly Feast,' since I make all my characters laymen and married men, I give ample demonstration of what the feasting of all Christians should be like. If certain priests and monks patterned their own banquets after this model, they would understand how far short they are of that high standard,
15   a standard which should be higher than that of the laity.

In 'The Apotheosis [of Reuchlin],'[30] I show how much honour is owed to distinguished men who, by their assiduous labours, have done service to the liberal arts.

There are foolish persons who think the colloquy 'Courtship' indecent,
20   though nothing more chaste could be imagined. If marriage is an honourable estate, then it is also honourable to be a suitor. And would that all suitors were such as I picture here, and marriages contracted with no other conversations! What can you do with those sour natures who are lacking in every grace, and to whom anything friendly and light-hearted seems immodest? This
25   girl refuses the suitor a kiss when he is about to leave, in order to preserve her virginity intact for him. But what don't girls commonly grant suitors nowadays? Again, critics fail to notice how much thoughtful counsel is mingled with the pleasantries: about not rushing into marriage, about the selection not only of bodies but much more of minds, about the stability of
30   marriage, about not contracting a marriage without parental consent, about keeping marriage pure, about rearing children in a godly way. Finally the girl invokes Christ's blessing upon the marriage. Aren't these matters proper for young people to know? And those who think their children's reading of this is harmful because of its 'indecency' make no objection to their reading
35   of Plautus and the *Jests* of Poggio.[31] Brilliant judgment!

In 'The Girl with No Interest in Marriage,'[32] I denounce those who, despite the opposition of parents, lure boys and girls into a monastery, playing upon their innocence or their superstitiousness, persuading them there is no hope of salvation outside a monastery.[33] If the world is not full of
40   such fishermen; if countless happy natures, which had been chosen vessels of the Lord had they sensibly taken up a career suited to their natural talents,

are not most miserably buried alive by these creatures – then I have been wrong in my warning. But if ever I am compelled to speak my mind plainly on this topic,[34] I will give such a description of those kidnappers, and the magnitude of their mischief, that all will agree I had plenty of reason to utter

5 these warnings. I wrote politely, however, to avoid giving malevolent men an occasion for making trouble.

In the next colloquy[35] I present, not a girl who has abandoned the monastic life after taking vows, but one who has returned to her worthy parents before taking vows.

10 In 'Marriage,'[36] how much wisdom there is about overlooking the failings of husbands, not breaking good will between married persons, making amends for injuries, improving husbands' behaviour, complying with their humors! What else do Plutarch, Aristotle, and Xenophon teach? The only difference is that here the characters add a certain liveliness to the discourse.

15 In the colloquy 'The Soldier and the Carthusian,' I depict at one stroke both the folly of young fellows who run off to war and the life of a holy Carthusian: a life inevitably gloomy and dismal unless accompanied by devotion to studies.

In 'The Liar [and the Man of Honour],' I depict the character of certain

20 people who are born liars. There is no more detestable class of men; would they were scarcer![37]

In the colloquy 'The Young Man and the Harlot,' do I not make even brothels pure? What could be said more effectively, either for the purpose of impressing upon young minds the safeguarding of their chastity or for

25 reclaiming prostitutes from a course of life as wretched as it is shameful? A single word has upset some readers, for the immodest girl, playing up to the young man, calls him her 'cocky.' But this expression is very common among us, even with respectable ladies.[38] Anyone who cannot bear it may write 'my darling' or anything else instead of 'cocky' if he prefers.

30 In 'The Poetic Feast,' I show what sort of feast scholars should have: frugal, but gay and mirthful; seasoned with learned stories; without quarrels, bickering, or slander.

In 'An Examination [concerning the Faith],'[39] I summarize the Catholic creed, and that somewhat more clearly and explicitly than is done by some

35 highly respected theologians, including Gerson (whose name I mention with all due respect nevertheless). And I invent the character of a Lutheran in order to make it easier for those who agree on the main articles of the orthodox creed to resume good relations. The rest of the 'Examination' I omitted,[40] however, because of the bad feeling now prevalent.

40 In 'The Old Men's Chat,'[41] how many things are shown, as though in a mirror, that should be avoided in life or that render life serene! Better

that young people learned these from pleasant chats than from experience. Socrates brought philosophy down from heaven to earth; I have brought it even into games, informal conversations, and drinking parties.[42] For the very amusements of Christians ought to have a philosophical flavour.

5   In 'The Well-to-do Beggars,'[43] how many things are there by which country pastors – crude and unlettered, and anything but shepherds – may amend their lives! How much, in addition, to help get rid of foolish pride in clothes; again, for checking the extravagance of those who condemn the monastic garb, as if the dress in itself were bad. And incidentally a pattern
10   for the conduct of itinerant monks is described. There aren't many of the sort I picture here.

In 'The [Abbot and the] Learned Lady,'[44] at one stroke I revive the ancient example of Paula, Eustochium, and Marcella, who combined devotion to learning with purity of morals, and by the example of the young
15   wife I incite monks and abbots – haters of sacred studies, men given over to gluttony, idleness, hunting, and dicing – to pursuits of a different and, for them, more appropriate kind.

In 'The Spectre,'[45] I expose the tricks of impostors accustomed to play upon the credulous minds of simple folk by feigning apparitions of demons,
20   souls, and heavenly voices. How great a plague, truly, has this charlatanism brought upon Christian devotion! But since a naïve and simple-minded time of life is especially liable to frauds of this kind, I thought it wise to describe the method of the trickery by an amusing example. Pope Celestine was similarly imposed upon;[46] so the youth of Bern, by monks;[47] so are many
25   even today, by faked oracles.

By no means the slightest of human afflictions is alchemy,[48] a disorder so intoxicating, once it strikes a man, that it beguiles even the learned and prudent. Related to it[49] is magic, which goes by the same name but entices us by the additional title of 'natural.' I denounce similar impostures in 'The
30   Cheating Horse-Dealer' and in 'Beggar Talk'[50] and again in 'The Fabulous Feast.' If boys learn nothing else from these but how to talk Latin, how much more praise my labour deserves, for accomplishing this through jokes and entertainment, than is due to men who cram *Mammethrepti*, *Brachylogi*, *Catholicons*,[51] and 'modes of signifying'[52] down the wretched youngsters'
35   throats!

In 'The New Mother,' besides knowledge of matters physical, how many moral precepts are there about mothers' care of children: first of babies, then of older children!

In 'A Pilgrimage for Religion's Sake,' I reproach those who with much
40   ado have thrown all images out of the churches;[53] also those who are mad about pilgrimages undertaken in the name of religion – something clubs,

too, are now organized for. Those who have been to Jerusalem are dubbed knights[54] and address one another as 'brother.' On Palm Sunday they behave ridiculously, dragging an ass by a rope[55] – themselves not very different from the wooden ass they pull. Those who have been to Compostella imitate

5   them. Let these things be conceded, of course, to men's whims, but for these people to arrogate holiness to themselves from all this is intolerable. Attention is called also to those who exhibit doubtful relics for authentic ones, who attribute to them more than is proper, and basely make money by them.

10   In 'A Fish Diet,'[56] I take up the question of human ordinances, which some people, straying far from right reason, reject out of hand. Some put them almost above divine commandments. Others, again, abuse both divine and human ordinances for gain and arbitrary power. And so I try to persuade each group to moderation, asking where the human ordinances came from

15 and by what degrees they have reached their present position; whom they bind and to what extent; what good they do; how much they differ from divine ones; noting, in passing, the ridiculous human judgments the world has long been filled with; noting also what has caused all this present uproar everywhere. These topics I have treated at some length, to provide learned

20 men with an opportunity of writing on them more correctly; for what they have published to date does not satisfy thoughtful readers. To denounce whoring, drunkenness, and adultery would not touch the heart of the matter, since these evils deceive nobody. The danger to true godliness comes rather from evils that are not perceived or that entice in the guise of righteousness.

25 If I am accused of allowing a theological argument to be carried on by lewd fellows of the baser sort,[57] the answer is that such topics are disputed by these men at every dinner party nowadays; and people of this kind need somebody who will discuss the subject informally and bluntly.

       In 'The Funeral,' – since death is usually a test of Christian faith – I

30 have portrayed in two laymen[58] a contrast in modes of dying, placing before your eyes, as though in an actual picture, the different departures from life of those who put their trust in vanities and those who have fixed their hope of salvation in the mercy of the Lord. Incidentally, I reproach the supremely silly ostentatiousness of the rich who extend their pomp and pride, which

35 death at least should have removed, beyond the grave. At the same time I attack the wickedness of those who for their own profit take advantage of rich men's foolishness; which they ought rather to have been particularly diligent to correct.[59] For who will dare to warn the rich and powerful freely if monks, who claim to be dead to the world, whitewash those men's sins?

40 If there are none such as I have described, still an example of what is to be avoided is shown. If, on the other hand, things far more reprehensible than

those I have presented are commonly reported, fair-minded persons should acknowledge my modesty and amend their own faults; and if blameless themselves, they should curb and correct others who do wrong. I have attacked no order,[60] unless perchance one who has uttered a warning against corrupt Christian morals impugns all Christianity! Men so sensitive about the honour of an order should be among the first to restrain those who openly disgrace the order by their deeds. Now, when they acknowledge them as blood-brothers, support and protect them, what effrontery to complain that the order's good name is harmed by a timely reproof! And what logic enjoins that you should have such regard for this or that organization that you neglect the general welfare of Christians?

In 'Things and Names,'[61] I rebuke the preposterous opinions of some persons.

In 'A Feast of Many Courses,'[62] I teach a lesson in manners.

In 'Charon,' I denounce war among Christians.

In 'A Meeting of the Philological Society,' I make fun of the zeal of a certain Carthusian – most erudite in his own conceit – who, though he usually raves against Greek studies in a most idiotic way, now attaches a Greek title to his own book, but in an absurd fashion; calling *anticomaritans* those whom he might have called *antimarians* or *antidicomarians*.[63]

In 'Cyclops,' I rebuke certain persons who always have the gospel in their mouth though in their manner of life there is nothing evangelical at all.

In 'A Marriage in Name Only,'[64] I demonstrate the folly of those numerous people who, in betrothals, count up only the dowry and take no account of the groom's pox – something worse than leprosy. And this is so commonplace nowadays that nobody wonders, despite the fact that nothing could be more cruel for children.

In 'The Knight without a Horse,'[65] I depict a class of men who think they can get away with anything under the semblance of nobility; they are a special plague to Germany.

In 'The Council of Women,' I was going to treat of some feminine failings – politely, however, so that no one would expect the sort of thing found in Juvenal! But while I was doing this, up popped the knight without a horse, like the wolf in the proverb.[66]

The rest of the colloquies were intended to give pleasure, yet no vulgar pleasure. This is not defaming the religious orders but instructing them. Hence it would be better for all orders, both privately and publicly, if (the rage for slander laid aside) we all sincerely esteemed whatever is honestly proffered for the public good. There is diversity of gifts and tastes; men are drawn to godliness by a thousand means. Juvencus is praised for his zeal in putting the gospel story into verse.[67] Nor is Arator without his due

praise for doing the same with the Acts of the Apostles.[68] Hilary thunders
against heretics,[69] Augustine disputes,[70] Jerome contends in dialogues,[71]
Prudentius wars in various forms of verse,[72] Thomas and Scotus fight with
the help of dialectic and philosophy.[73] All have the same purpose, but each
5   uses a different method. Variety is not condemned so long as the same goal
is sought. Peter of Spain[74] is taught to boys to prepare them the more readily
for proceeding to Aristotle. One who instils a liking for something does
much. And this little book, if taught to ingenuous youth, will lead them to
many more useful studies: to poetry, rhetoric, physics, ethics, and finally
10   to matters of Christian piety. I have played the part of a fool in making
myself eulogist of my own writings, but I was forced to it, partly because of
the villainy of slanderers, partly because of service to Christian youth, for
whom we must do all we can.

Though this is how matters stand,[75] and though they are perfectly clear
15   to everyone who has learned his ABCs, there is nonetheless a strangely dense
class of men, called 'deputies'[76] by the French – I suppose because they are in
ill repute or at least have more than sufficient reputation – who declare my
Colloquies ought to be shunned, especially by monks (whom they style 'the
religious')[77] and young people, on the ground that fasts and abstinences of
20   the church are belittled; that intercession of the Blessed Virgin and the saints
is held up to ridicule; that virginity, if compared with marriage, is regarded
as of little or no importance; that everyone is dissuaded from entering
religion; that in this book hard and troublesome questions of theology are
propounded to beginners,[78] in violation of the oath sworn by masters of arts.
25   You recognize, dear reader, the Attic eloquence!

To answer the last charge first, what masters of arts propound to
beginners I do not know. In the Colloquies, what is said on Creed, mass, fasts,
vows, confession has no theological difficulty but is the sort of thing no one
should be ignorant of. And if Paul's Epistles are taught to boys, what is so
30   bad about their getting a taste of theological controversy? Besides, since
my critics are not unaware that boys who are novices at sophistry[79] are,
from the start, given extremely puzzling questions – not to say hair-splitting
questions – concerning the divine Persons, why are they unwilling for boys
to learn what concerns common life? If they think it makes no difference
35   which character says what, they realize, I suppose, how many passages are
met in the Gospels and apostolic writings that – according to this rule –
contain obvious blasphemy!

In many places I approve of fasting; nowhere do I condemn it. Whoever
maintains the contrary I shall denounce as an impudent liar. 'But,' they say,
40   'in "The Whole Duty of Youth"[80] the text reads: "With fasting I have nothing
to do."' Imagine these words said in the person of a soldier or a drunkard;

does that make Erasmus a condemner of fasts? I think not! As they now
stand, they are spoken by a youngster not yet grown up, of an age not
required by law to fast. Nevertheless this youngster is preparing himself for
suitable fasts, for he adds: 'If, however, I feel the need, I lunch and dine more
5 frugally, in order to be the keener for devotions throughout a holy day.'[81]

In fact, how I 'condemn' abstinences these words in 'The Profane
Feast' make clear: 'In many matters it's not the fact but the intention that
distinguishes us from the Jews. They used to refrain from certain foods as if
from unclean things that would defile the mind. We, though we know that
10 to the pure all things are pure, nevertheless deny nourishment to the lustful
flesh as if to an unruly steed, so as to render it more obedient to the spirit.
Sometimes we discipline our excessive use of delicacies by the vexation of
abstinence.'[82] Shortly after this the speaker explains why the church has
forbidden the eating of certain foods: everyone will benefit, he says, 'for the
15 poor may eat snails or frogs, or gnaw an onion or leek; the middle class will
reduce somewhat its daily fare; but if the rich use this occasion to indulge
themselves, they should blame their own gluttony and not find fault with
the church's ordinance.'[83] A little later I say things similar to these. Again,
somewhat further on: 'I'm aware that a fish diet is emphatically condemned
20 by physicians, but our forefathers, whom we are bound to obey, thought
differently.'[84] Therein do I teach directly that in this matter even the slightest
offence to the weak should be avoided.

Equally false is it that in the *Colloquies* intercession of the Virgin Mary
and other saints is mocked.[85] But I do mock those who seek from saints
25 what they would not dare to ask of a respectable man, or seek from certain
saints in the belief that this or that one would grant something or other more
readily, or be able to perform it more readily, than would Christ himself. On
the contrary the lad in 'The Whole Duty of Youth'[86] speaks thus: 'I gave some
greetings.' 'To whom?' 'To Christ and to several saints.' And a little later:
30 'Again I salute Jesus and all the saints briefly, but particularly the Virgin
Mother and my patron saints.' And further on he mentions by name which
saints he daily greets.

It is surprising indeed that a suitor, a man in love, praises marriage
and says that a chaste marriage is not far short of virginity in worth, when
35 Augustine prefers the polygamy of the patriarchs to our celibacy![87]

How patently absurd their criticism of entering the religious life is,
my words in 'The Girl with No Interest in Marriage' make evident.[88] The
young woman asks: 'Do you condemn the whole monastic life, then?' 'By no
means,' the young man replies. 'But just as I wouldn't want to argue that a
40 girl who entered this kind of life should try to get out of it, so I wouldn't
hesitate to warn all girls, particularly the talented ones, against throwing

themselves rashly into something there's no escape from afterwards.' This is
the conclusion of that colloquy, however much the questions are disputed.
I ask you, is this dissuading everyone from entering the religious life? Not
entrance but headlong recklessness is condemned. – These passages, then,
5   they twist maliciously for the purpose of slander.

Yet they fail to consider how many of the things beginners learn
there oppose the pronouncements of the Lutherans. In 'The Whole Duty of
Youth,'[89] the method of hearing mass properly and profitably is described.
The method of confessing properly and effectively is taught; the boy is
10 warned to purge his soul by confession before he takes communion. In
the same place beginners are taught certain Christian customs which, even
though not found in Sacred Scripture, ought to be so kept that we may
not be a stumbling-block to anyone. In 'The Profane Feast' they are taught
to comply with pontifical ordinances rather than the advice of physicians;
15 only they are warned that in a case of necessity a human ordinance and
legislator's intention lose their force.[90] In the same place a character endorses
a benefaction to monasteries, provided it is given for use, not for soft living,
and especially if given to those who scrupulously observe the discipline of
the religious life.[91]

20 As for human ordinances, these words are spoken in 'The Fish Diet':[92]
'Let those who want to fight do so. I myself believe the laws of our forefathers
ought to be reverently received and dutifully obeyed, as though they came
from God. It is neither safe nor right to conceive or sow harmful suspicion
concerning public authority. And if there is some tyranny, but not enough
25 to force us to wrongdoing, better to endure it than to oppose it seditiously.'
Many things of this sort beginners learn from my *Colloquies*, about which
these fellows mutter so. 'But for a theologian to crack jokes is unseemly.' At
least they should grant me the right to do with boys what they, grown men,
permit themselves publicly during 'Vespers' – insipid name for an insipid
30 thing.[93]

I have shown that the foolish slanders invented by some in Spain are
mere fancies of men who are neither sober nor acquainted with Latin.[94] No
less uninformed is one man's assertion that the statement in 'An Examination
concerning the Faith' that the Father is called 'absolutely the author of all that
35 are' is heretical. Taken in by his ignorance of Latin idiom, he thinks 'author'
means nothing else than 'creator' or 'maker.'[95] But if he consults expert
Latinists,[96] if he turns the pages of Hilary and other ancient writers, he
will find *auctoritas* used for what the schoolmen call 'the supremely perfect
Reason of the Beginning'; and on that account they attribute it especially to
40 the Father, often designating the Father by the name of 'author' when they
compare the Persons. Whether the Father is correctly called 'cause' of the Son

does not concern me, since I have never used this word. It is true, however,
that we cannot speak of God except by inadequate terms; and 'fount' or
'beginning' or 'origin' is no more adequate than 'cause.'

5   Now consider from this, reader, what sort of people they are who
sometimes drag men to the flames by their condemnations. Nothing is
more base than to censure what you do not understand. But this mania for
slandering anything and everything – what does it produce but bitterness
and dissension? Instead, let us interpret fairly judgments that differ from
our own, neither desiring ours to be accepted instantly as oracles nor taking
10   as oracles the judgments of those who do not understand what they read.
Wherever bad feeling prevails in debate, there you find blind judgment.
May the peacemaker among all men, the Holy Spirit, who employs his
instruments in divers ways, make us all united and of one accord in sound
doctrine and godly living, that we may all alike come into the fellowship of
15   the heavenly Jerusalem, which knows no strife. Amen.

    Basel, 21 May 1526[97]

NOTES

1 Greek in the original
2 The 'deaf adder that stoppeth her ear' of Ps 58:4–5 (57:5–6 Vulg). Cf *Adagia* III i
   85.
3 The Froben edition of November 1518; 'mine and not mine' because although
   Erasmus' work, it was brought out without his knowledge, he says, and
   therefore had some inaccuracies. When he speaks a few lines below of having
   'revised what was published, then added' he refers to the March 1519 edition
   (Louvain: Martens), for which he made some corrections, and to two 1522
   (March and July–August) and subsequent editions. But reprints of the original
   (Froben 1518) text and of those containing minor variations appeared in
   many places between 1518 and 1522. For details see BE 2nd series *Colloquia* I.
   Authorized and fully acknowledged editions begin with the March 1522 book.
4 Cf n10 below.
5 *Nicomachean Ethics* 1.3 1094b28–1095a11; cf Shakespeare's *Troilus and Cressida*
   (1609): 'Unlike young men, whom Aristotle thought / Unfit to hear moral
   philosophy' (2.2.167–8). Shakespeare's immediate source is unknown. He may
   have borrowed from this colloquy or from a Latin translation of Aristotle. The
   same passage in Latin is quoted in Bacon's *De augmentis scientiarum* 3.7 (1623).
   Erasmus and Bacon were correct, of course, in translating Aristotle's πολιτικῆς
   as *ethicae* (Erasmus) or *moralis* (Bacon) instead of 'political.' For Aristotle
   considered ethics and politics as two parts of one discipline. That discipline
   studies human happiness, described as activity in accordance with virtue, first
   in the individual, then in its necessary setting, the state or community. Ethics is
   the study of human character (ethos), politics of man in society. Inquiry into
   politics can be pursued fruitfully only after character is understood. But young

men lack sufficient experience of life for this study; hence they are not ready for 'political science' either. Cf Plato *Republic* 6.498A–C.

6 Horace *Satires* 1.1.24–6

7 The twofold purpose of the *Colloquies* as enunciated on the title-page of the book since March 1522

8 See *Convivium religiosum* 'The Godly Feast' n190.

9 Highly recommended by Erasmus in *De pueris instituendis* LB I 511B–F / ASD I-2 70:10–20 / CWE 26 339

10 Lucretius 1.935–42. So Erasmus: Allen Ep 337:104–6 / CWE Ep 337:111–13

11 *De visendo loca sacra*, alternative title for *De votis temere susceptis*

12 'Is it any great feat to visit Jerusalem bodily when within you there is Sodom, Egypt, and Babylon?' (*Enchiridion* LB V 38A / Holborn 87:2–3 / CWE 66 82).

13 The dubious wisdom of going on pilgrimage – so often undertaken, Erasmus complains, for the wrong reasons – is the theme of a short colloquy, 'Rash Vows' and a long one, 'A Pilgrimage.' For Erasmus to give more attention to the short one than to the long one here, in fact more attention than he bestows on any other colloquy in this apology, is surprising. One reason for dismissing 'A Pilgrimage' in a dozen lines is that that dialogue was published in February 1526, only a few months before 'The Usefulness of the *Colloquies*.' The longer dialogue has much description of Walsingham and Canterbury. 'Rash Vows' says little about Jerusalem (which was a disappointing place to the pilgrim) but much about the foolishness and futility of going there, as Erasmus now emphasizes again. In 'A Pilgrimage' the reader will make the proper inferences for himself.

14 The duty of a bishop was to stay in his diocese, administer its affairs, and preach. See 'A Fish Diet' 711:30–4. The *Consilium de emendanda ecclesia*, a report to Pope Paul III by a special papal commission on reform of the church (1537), denounces clerical and particularly episcopal absenteeism as an evil that above all others must be corrected (Kidd *Documents* 313 no 126; Hubert Jedin *A History of the Council of Trent* trans Dom Ernest Graf OSB [Edinburgh and London 1957] I 424–33).

15 Actually 1 Tim 5:8. A hard saying, but true; Erasmus agrees with St Paul (and with Aquinas; see *Annotationes in Novum Testamentum* LB VI 940D–E on the interpretation of this verse). A man who for ostensibly pious reasons deserts his family and sets out for Jerusalem is a modern example of 'worse than an infidel.' Erasmus often alludes to the disastrous effects of pilgrimages on families.

16 This anecdote is repeated, with attribution to Erasmus, in Foxe's *Acts and Monuments* (VIII 653). One of the speakers in Γεροντολογία 'The Old Men's Chat' tells of accompanying an elderly nobleman to Jerusalem: another miscalculation (458:30–8 above).

17 Jerome Ep 58.3 to Paulinus of Nola, written to dissuade Paulinus from making a pilgrimage to the Holy Land. St Hilarion (d 371), a devout hermit dwelling in the Palestinian wilderness, saw Jerusalem only once, for a single day. That brief visit, says Jerome, was enough to prove that Hilarion did not neglect holy places and showed that he wanted to avoid any appearance of confining God to one place. Mesopotamia, Egypt, and Armenia are full of monks who have never seen Jerusalem. A true Christian can reach heaven just as easily from any other land. For Jerome's life of Hilarion see PL 23 (1883) 29–54; translation in NPNF 2nd series VI 303–15.

18 Jerome Ep 58.2. The quotation is not quite complete, for Jerome repeats 'in Jerusalem' after 'lived righteously.' This dictum is a memory of Cicero *Pro Murena*: 'Non Asiam numquam vidisse, sed in Asia continenter vixisse, laudandum est' (5.12). A papal official, Alvarus Pelagius (d 1352), condemning students who waste their parents' money in idleness, neglect studies, and return home ignorant, resorts to this same aphorism. ' "It is praiseworthy, not to have seen Jerusalem, but to have lived well." So, not to have studied at Paris or Bologna, but to have done so diligently merits praise' (Thorndike *University Records* 174).

19 Folly claims as one of her own the man who abandons his family to go off to Compostella or Jerusalem (*Moriae encomium* LB IV 456B / ASD IV-3 138:250–1 / CWE 27 122). Throughout Christan history, pilgrimage and the figure of the pilgrim have been primal metaphors both in devotional and in secular literature and art. 'Strangers and pilgrims on the earth,' these *viatores* sought an actual or symbolic Jerusalem. The pilgrim's progress was a manifestation of effort to perform acts of penance or to venerate shrines and images of saints, or simply to enjoy a tour, however laborious, to a famous holy place. Given the mixed motives and varieties of religious and worldly types among the travellers, the misfortunes and abuses to which Erasmus calls attention were bound to occur. To a critical mind and a sceptical, satirical temperament, pilgrimages seemed inexcusable expeditions of little value and much peril to most of the people who took part in them.

20 In 'Rash Vows' 39:11–23; see also 'Military Affairs' 58:24–34 and 'A Pilgrimage' 635:25–636:13, with the notes.

21 Agents or officials who were in charge of selling indulgences (as at 'Military Affairs' 58:28–9)

22 A paraphrase of 'Benefices' 48:2–13

23 *Militis confessio*, alternative title for *Militaria*

24 *Monita paedagogica*, the title in some editions

25 *Pietas puerilis*, the alternative title of *Confabulatio pia* in some editions

26 See 'Youth' 96:31–97:24 with the notes.

27 On choosing a career, 98:39–99:7; on choosing a confessor, 97:25–35

28 A desideratum often mentioned by Erasmus; for example Allen Epp 1747:105, 1891:214–18, 2037:179–80, 2700:109–11; *De concordia* LB V 498D; *Institutio christiani matrimonii* LB V 647E; *De esu carnium* LB IX 1201A–B; see introduction to 'The Girl with No Interest in Marriage' 279–85; 'The Funeral' n26. More was of the same opinion; see *Utopia* Yale CWM 4 130–31.

29 On the subjects mentioned, see 'The Profane Feast' 143:15–146:7. Cf Erasmus' later comments on this colloquy at 1107:6–22.

30 Here called simply *Apotheosis*

31 Although named together here, they are irreconcilable as authors for youth in school; Erasmus accepts Plautus but rejects Poggio Bracciolini. The comedies of Plautus – those that were 'free from impropriety' – are well suited to young readers (*De ratione studii* CWE 24 669:10–12). The *Facetiae* of Poggio (d 1459), a brilliant scholar with a taste for writing irreverent and indecent anticlerical tales (*impia* and *spurca*, as Erasmus says in Allen Ep 337:335–6) would not be acceptable in any Erasmian curriculum intended for grammar-school boys. Plautus was a pagan; Poggio might be assumed to have been a nominal Christian. Pagan literature, Greek and Latin, played a major part in Renaissance

curricula, but some educators (Colet was one), while accepting the fact, were uneasy about how to justify it. Erasmus dealt with this problem more than once. His defence of the classical curriculum, partisan but rational, was typical of the arguments repeated by humanists over many generations: ancient literature was uniquely appropriate as the foundation of liberal education, but the texts taught must be suitable to the age of the pupils, and the master must know what to omit in Lucian or Terence or the lyric poets and how to treat a text with tact (*Apologia contra Latomi dialogum* LB IX 92D–E). *Antibarbari* and *De ratione studii* are good examples, historically and pedagogically, of humanist and specifically Erasmian arguments for classical education. See also CWE 23 introduction xxvi–xxxii, xliii–xlvi. *De ratione studii* provides practical advice to teachers on how to approach a Terentian comedy and Virgil's second eclogue (CWE 24 682–90).

32 *Virgo misogamos*. Here and at 1102:10, 1103:5, 1103:30, 1104:10, 1107:37, Erasmus transliterates Greek titles.

33 A parody of the familiar phrase *nulla salus extra ecclesiam*; see 'Faith' n108 and 'A Fish Diet' n74.

34 On this and related subjects he did so many times. See the references in the introduction and notes to 'The Girl with No Interest in Marriage.'

35 'The Repentant Girl'

36 *Mempsigamos*, transliteration of the Greek title ('complaining of marriage') used as an alternative title for *Coniugium*

37 would they were scarcer!] Added in March 1529. The colloquy is here called simply *Pseudochei*.

38 The word in question was appropriate in its context (382:9). Sexual language or allusion in serious contexts (including Scripture) is another matter, on which Erasmus writes interestingly in *Purgatorio adversus epistolam Lutheri* LB X 1548C–1550C.

39 Here called simply *Inquisitio*

40 On this statement see my edition of *Inquisitio de fide* 35–8.

41 *Senile colloquium*, alternative name for Γεροντολογία

42 A proverb about our inability to penetrate the secrets of the heavens, 'What is above us does not concern us,' was quoted by Socrates, according to Lactantius (*Divinae institutiones* 3.20 PL 6 416; see *Adagia* I vi 69 and Allen Ep 1334:177–98 / CWE Ep 1334:189–212). Lactantius adds that if Socrates meant that therefore we may ignore the creator of heaven and earth, he made a deplorable mistake. Erasmus repeats the proverb in Allen Ep 1572:65, but there credits Plutarch with bringing moral philosophy into households. Recalling that remark of April 1525 about Plutarch, Erasmus now, in May 1526, says he himself, through his *Colloquies*, has brought philosophy into 'games, informal conversations, and drinking parties.' 'Our daily conversations show us as we are' (*Paraclesis* LB V 140C or VI *3 verso / Holborn 142:24–5).

43 *Ptochoplusii*, a transliteration of the Greek title

44 Here called *Erudita puella*. On Paula and Eustochium, aristocratic Roman ladies who became Christians and followed Jerome to Palestine, see n28. Marcella, whose Roman background was like theirs, remained in Rome. Most of what is known of these women, all of whom are saints, is learned from Jerome's correspondence; see especially his Epp 22, 108, 127.

45 'Exorcism,' here given its alternative title, *Spectrum*

46 This pope was tricked twice, but which experience Erasmus has in mind is uncertain. Celestine had been, and hoped to continue to be, a hermit monk. In July 1294, however, at the age of eighty-five, he was elected pope through the efforts of a group of cardinals and wholly against his own wishes. As pope, Celestine was totally incompetent and quickly became eager to abdicate. For papal abdication no precedents were known, but he was persuaded that such precedents did exist. Celestine then resigned (December 1294). His successor was cardinal Benedetto Gaetani, who became Boniface VIII. The new pope put Celestine in confinement, where he spent the rest of his life. He died in 1296 and was canonized in 1313. Dante places him in the anteroom of hell, presumably because of his 'great refusal,' which enabled Dante's enemy Boniface VIII to reign as pope (*Inferno* 3.58–61). Boniface is, or will be, in worse straits (*Inferno* 19.40–60).

47 Probably an allusion to Johann Jetzer, who was twenty-three when he joined the Dominicans of Bern as a lay brother in 1506 and was the central figure in the scandal concerning the Dominicans there. See 'The Seraphic Funeral' n51.

48 *Alcumistica*, capitalized in the first and other editions of this apology; apparently intended to identify both the title of the colloquy ('Alchemy') and the 'disorder' described in it

49 Related to it ... 'natural.'] In the first edition (June 1526) this sentence precedes 'By no means ... prudent,' but it belongs here, as in the edition of March 1533, *Opera omnia* 1540, and LB. Natural magic is 'white magic,' which does not invoke the devil or other evil spirits, as witchcraft or 'black magic' does. On magic in the sixteenth century see notes and references in 'Alchemy'; chapter 3 of Wayne Shumaker's *The Occult Sciences in the Renaissance* 108–59 discusses white magic.

50 *Ptochologia*, a transliteration of the Greek title

51 On these medieval lexicons and grammars, which Erasmus enjoys mocking, see 'The Philological Society' nn7 and 10.

52 Erasmus refers to authors and teachers of what he finds desperately dreary treatises on speculative grammar, for example Michael Modista and Peter of Spain, who are concerned to explain and justify by logic the differences between parts of speech. (On Peter of Spain see n74 below.) Erasmus, as one would expect, was more interested in using traditional grammar correctly for accurate reading and writing than in overwhelming it (and the youthful students) with logic and dialectic. See *Antibarbari* CWE 23 34:2n. Chomarat's summary of Michael Modista and modes of signifying in *Grammaire et rhétorique* I 215–24 is the most useful exposition for readers of Erasmus.

53 See 'A Pilgrimage' n25 on Zwinglian hostility to images.

54 *equites aurati*; see 'The Funeral' n72. Doubtless an allusion to a confraternity, but which one is unknown.

55 The procession with the ass commemorates the entry of Christ into Jerusalem (Matt 21:1–9; John 12:12–15). On a scandalous, profane procession on Palm Sunday see 'A Fish Diet' 707:25–708:11.

56 *Ichthyophagia*, a transliteration of the Greek title. This exceptionally important dialogue was first printed in the February 1526 edition.

57 This familiar phrase (Acts 17:5 AV) matches the tenor of Erasmus' *personis sordidis*, referring to the butcher and salt fish seller in 'A Fish Diet.' For theirs are vulgar trades (Cicero *De officiis* 1.42.150; Terence *Eunuchus* 257).

58 *idiotis*. Sometimes *idiotae* has this meaning, depending on context. So *Supputatio* LB IX 636C–D.

59 A biographer writes of the description of George's dying in 'The Funeral': 'It is hardly conceivable that any such scene was ever enacted at any bedside in any Christian land' (J.J. Mangan *Life, Character and Influence of Desiderius Erasmus* 2 vols [New York 1927] II 142). Objections of this kind are nothing new; they were made in Erasmus' lifetime. They ignore what he says here: that he has pictured the kinds of dying described in the dialogue *ut imagine viva* 'as though in an actual picture.' The colloquy is fiction, not reported fact; yet it is truthful representation according to Erasmus' purpose and belief. To censure it as literally untrue is like dismissing the laws and customs of the Utopians because Utopia does not exist. If no such friars as he depicts really exist, Erasmus says, he has at any rate shown what should be avoided; and if any do exist, then good friars ought to thank him for exposing the bad ones.

60 Not untrue but less than the whole truth. He never attacks an order as such, but the words and behaviour of some of the friars and monks in his dialogues do nothing to dispel unfavourable inferences about their societies. Some of his sixteenth-century readers rejected such inferences outright; others found that the characters and characterizations in question confirmed their own opinions or surmises.

61 In 'Things and Names' . . . instructing them.] Added in the March 1529 edition. The colloquies named in these lines appeared in the 1527 and March 1529 editions; see the introductions to them. 'Charon,' however, had been first printed in 1523 but not in the *Colloquies*. See the introduction to it 818–19. 'Things and Names' is here called *Differentia verborum ac rerum*.

62 Here called *Convivium varium*

63 See 'The Philological Society' n3

64 Here called *Coniugium impar*, its alternative title

65 Here called *Ementita nobilitas*, its alternative title

66 *Adagia* IV v 50, perhaps implying that he interrupted the writing of 'The Council of Women' to write 'The Knight without a Horse' or wrote it immediately afterwards. In the order of printing the latter comes first.

67 Juvencus was a Christian Latin poet (early fourth century). He versified the four Gospels (first printed at Deventer c 1490 and often reissued). Erasmus approved of the work, and Colet wanted such authors read in St Paul's School (see CWE 23 xxx–xxxi).

68 Arator was an Italian Christian Latin writer (sixth century). His *De actis apostolorum* (text in PL 68 63–250) narrates the deeds of Peter and Paul. It was popular in the Middle Ages.

69 Especially in his *De Trinitate*, opposing the Arians. See Ep 1334, Erasmus' introduction to his edition of Hilary (Basel 1523). Like his editions of Augustine and Jerome, it was published by the Froben house.

70 In his controversies with the Manichaeans, Donatists, and Pelagians

71 For instance, against the Pelagians, Vigilantius, Helvidius, Jovinianus, and others

72 Prudentius was a contemporary (348–c 410) of Augustine and Jerome, best
known as a writer of hymns, some of which are still used, and of *Psychomachia*,
an allegory of the spiritual life. Erasmus, who considered Prudentius the most
fluent of Christian poets (*De ratione studii* LB I 523E / CWE 24 675:5–6) and 'our
Pindar' (LB V 1340A / CWE 29 176), wrote commentaries on two of his poems
(LB V 1337C–1358C / CWE 29 125–218).

73 Thomas Aquinas is seldom named in the *Colloquies*, but Erasmus refers to him
many times in his *Annotationes in Novum Testamentum*, usually with respect,
though he laments Thomas' weakness in Greek, a handicap that diminished
his value as an exegete. But he is certainly better than Lyra and other biblical
commentators of his times. See *Capita argumentorum contra morosos quosdam ac
indoctos* LB VI ***1 verso and 'The Godly Feast' n190. On Scotus see the same
note.

74 Medieval scholar and prelate (d 1277). He taught medicine in Siena, then rose
in the church to become cardinal bishop of Tusculum; he was elected pope as
John XXI (xx) in 1276. His *Parva logicalia* or *Summulae logicales* was used as a
textbook for four centuries (*Petri Hispani Summulae logicales* ed I.M. Bocheński
OP [Turin 1947] and, more recently, *Peter of Spain [Petrus Hispanus Portugalensis]:
Tractatus, called afterwards Summule logicales* ed L.M. De Rijk [Assen 1972]). Its
subtleties and aridity invited the disparagement of later humanists, including
Erasmus (Allen Ep 447:97–9 / CWE Ep 447:103–5) and More (*Correspondence*
38–42). See Clarence Miller's note in his edition of *Moriae encomium* ASD IV-3
156:501n (page 157).

75 Though this is how matters stand … judgment.] The passage from here to
1109:11 was added in the September 1529 edition.

76 Representatives of the faculty of theology who reported in the presence of
the masters their judgments on the *Colloquies* and other writings of Erasmus
in May 1526. For the official statement to which Erasmus refers here, see
Declarationes ad censuras Lutetiae vulgatas LB IX 928E–929B; cf *Collectio judiciorum
de novis erroribus* … ed C. du Plessis d'Argentré, 3 vols (Paris 1728–36; repr
Brussels 1966) II part 1 53–77, and for the 1526 condemnation, ibidem 47–52.

77 Idiomatic for members of religious orders. Erasmus discusses the term in
Ecclesiastes LB V 1022D–1023A; *Supputatio* LB IX 615D–E, 714B–C.

78 *grammaticuli*, as a few lines below and at 1108:6, 1108:11, 1108:26

79 *sophistices candidatis*. The same phrase is used in *De copia* CWE 24 304:6 for
aspirants to *copia*. Compare Quintilian's *candidatus eloquentiae* (12.2.27). In
academic parlance 'sophistry' was the study of sophistic logic, the 'sophistical
elenchi' in Aristotle's treatise of that name. For some examples see 'The Poetic
Feast' 400:32–404:9. Erasmus thought boys should learn the elements of logic,
which was the third part of the trivium, but warns against too much of this or
other branches of formal philosophy for young people (1097:16–18, 1098:10–11
above). See More's critique of dialectic in his letter to Maarten van Dorp
(1515) defending Erasmus' *Moriae encomium* (Yale CWM 15 14/15–38/9). The
humanists generally shared this conviction about the dangerous prevalence of
excessive cultivation of formal logic in youth. A master at Magdalen School,
Oxford, wrote (c 1500): 'It is an hevy case that Childernn in their best age and
metist to lurne grammer shall be take from yt and be sett to sophistre … Ther
be many nowadays goth to sophistre the which can scant speke thre wordys in

latyn' (*A Fifteenth Century School Book* ed William Nelson [Oxford 1956] 19 nos
75–6).

80 Here called *Pietas puerilis*. See 'Youth' 96:14.

81 'Youth' 96:16–18

82 'The Profane Feast' 143:32–7. Cf 1101:1–10 above.

83 'The Profane Feast' 144:15–18

84 'The Profane Feast' 145:9–11

85 Critics cited 'The Shipwreck' (see n19) and 'A Pilgrimage.'

86 *Puerilis pietas*; see 'Youth' 91:6–8, 92:20–1, 93:4–5.

87 This ironical comparison between Pamphilus' praise of marriage in 'Courtship'
(265:20–267:15) and Augustine's comments on polygamy is less than fair to
Augustine, since it ignores the differences in purpose and manner between
the colloquy, a work of imagination and wit, and Augustine's totally serious
passage on polygamy. Erasmus may be thinking of Augustine's short treatise
De bono coniugali 26.34–5, where chastity and continence are exalted (PL 40
395–6). The good of marriage, we are told there, is its fruitfulness, never
the sensuality or lust which, since the sin of Adam and Eve, has infected
the human race. Another commendation of polygamy can be found in *De
doctrina christiana* (3.12.20 PL 34 73–4), where Augustine emphasizes, as other
theologians did, that polygamy was permitted in early Hebrew society because
of the divine injunction to 'be fruitful and multiply' (Gen 1:28; 35:11). In those
times, when the world was young, fecundity was necessary, and polygamy
practised accordingly – by men only, for women could have only one living
husband. But had devout men of old lived at the time the gospel of Christ was
proclaimed, they would have made themselves eunuchs for the kingdom of
heaven's sake (*De doctrina christiana* 3.18.27 PL 34 76).
Jerome had some difficulties with Solomon's seven hundred wives (1 Kings
[3 Kings Vulg] 11:3), but here too the key to interpretation is the distinction
between Law and gospel. It is one thing to live under the law, another to live
under the gospel (*Adversus Jovinianum* 1.24 PL 23 [1883] 254–5). This world
will not long endure; 'the time is short ... they that have wives be as though
they had none' (1 Cor 7:29). Polygamy was acceptable for the patriarchs, for
David and Solomon and some others, but no longer. The Christian church
sanctified monogamous marriage, yet from patristic times prized virginity
as a superior state. Erasmus' friend Colet agreed; see 'Courtship' nn53,
59. Erasmus did not. He could even argue that the holiest (*sanctissimum*)
kind of life was chaste and pure marriage (*De conscribendis epistolis* LB I
419D / CWE 25 137; *De vidua christiana* LB V 734C–735D / CWE 201–3). For his
opinions on such topics see the 'Courtship,' 'The Girl with No Interest in
Marriage,' 'Marriage,' 'The Young Man and the Harlot,' 'The New Mother,'
'A Marriage in Name Only,' and 'The Well-to-Do Beggars' (n6 on sacerdotal
celibacy).

88 *Virgo misogamo*; see 'The Girl with No Interest in Marriage' 293:9–13.

89 *Puerilis pietas*; see 'Youth' 95:3–96:12 (on hearing mass), 96:31–97:35 (on
confession).

90 See 'The Profane Feast' 144:38–145:11, 145:31–2.

91 Not in 'The Profane Feast' but 'The Godly Feast' 199:33–6

92 The title is given in Greek. See 'A Fish Diet' 702:17–22.

93 Not the canonical Hour (Evensong) but an important academic occasion for disputations and related ceremonies for those qualifying for admission as doctors of theology (at Oxford and Paris) or masters of arts (Oxford). It brought with it access to the privileges of professional status (see Farge *Orthodoxy and Reform* 27–8). *Vesperia* were prolonged, difficult, and sometimes captious, even frivolous – hence Erasmus' dismissal of them as insipid. He had little patience with what he regarded as the tiresome pretentiousness of academic pomp. See Hastings A. Rashdall *The Universities of Europe in the Middle Ages* (Oxford 1895), new ed F.M. Powicke and A.B. Emden, 3 vols (Oxford 1936) I 460–2 (on Paris), III 70 (on Oxford).

94 This paragraph alludes to 'Faith' (which is here called *Symbolum*) 428:30–40.

95 The reference is to an unnamed theologian of Paris (Allen Ep 2466:195–202).

96 Such as Valla, who says *auctor* does mean 'maker' (*factor*) but shows that it has additional though related meanings as well (*Paraphrasis in Elegantias Vallae* ASD I-4 226:504–11). Cf 'The Epicurean' n75.

97 Unfortunately this date was not changed in later editions to make allowance for additions to this apology. See nn61 and 75 above.

ERASMUS AND ERASMIUS

THE RETURN TO BASEL

EDITIONS OF THE *COLLOQUIES*

ALPHABETICAL LIST OF THE COLLOQUIES

WORKS FREQUENTLY CITED

SHORT-TITLE FORMS
FOR ERASMUS' WORKS

INDEX OF BIBLICAL AND APOCRYPHAL
REFERENCES

INDEX OF CLASSICAL REFERENCES

INDEX OF PATRISTIC, MEDIEVAL,
AND RENAISSANCE REFERENCES

GENERAL INDEX

On Erasmus' godson, Johannes Erasmius Froben, to whom the *Colloquia* was dedicated in 1522 and again in 1524 (Epp 1262 and 1476), see 'Sport' n37. 'Erasmius' is a character in three early dialogues and a later one: first in the section of 'Sport' (1522) called 'The game of sending a ball through an iron ring'; then in 'The Whole Duty of Youth' (1522), 'The Profane Feast' (1522), and 'The Art of Learning' (1529). In 'Sport' and 'The Art of Learning' the name is correct and appropriate. In 'The Whole Duty of Youth' it is erroneous, I believe, and was corrected in a later edition. In 'The Profane Feast' it must be accepted, since there is no evidence that it was unintended, and it was never changed; but its appropriateness there can be challenged.

In the earliest printed text of 'The Whole Duty of Youth,' which appeared in March 1522, and the later edition of July or August 1522, the name of Gaspar's questioner is Erasmius. Those readers of the dedicatory preface who were acquainted with Erasmus or the senior Froben, like many readers afterwards, apparently assumed that the Erasmius in this colloquy was named for the printer's son. This inference was natural but involved difficulties, for Gaspar's inquisitor asks pointed questions, and he comments favourably on the youth's conduct and piety, in the manner of a mature person, older than Gaspar. In the exchange between 'Erasmius' and Gaspar in 'Sport,' some pages earlier, both speakers are unmistakably schoolboys. Gaspar in 'The Whole Duty of Youth' is sixteen years old. The other and older speaker, who has informed opinions (based on personal experience) about confession, keeps up with theological disputes, and knows John Colet 'as well as I know you,' cannot be a schoolboy. He is Erasmus Roterodamus.

The reading 'Erasmius' in 'The Whole Duty of Youth' rests on a single occurrence of that name in each of the 1522 editions. The name is spelled out only in the line below the title; thereafter the speakers are identified only as 'E' and 'G.' 'Erasmius' was retained until the final edition issued in Erasmus' lifetime (March 1533), where it was sensibly changed to 'Erasmus' in the line below the title. The 1540 *Opera omnia* and LB texts print 'Erasmus' and abbreviate by 'Er.' Preserved Smith argued that the change of 'Erasmius' to 'Erasmus' spoiled the appropriateness of the questions and answers (*Key* 6n). I believe it makes the dialogue more convincing. True, the questioner says at the end of the conversation that he will try to imitate the edifying practices Gaspar has described. These words, however, are not the moral resolutions of an emulous companion but the polite if slightly patronizing approval of a sympathetic adult.

In 'The Profane Feast' the names have a different history: the earliest printed text (1518) had 'Erasmus,' but this was changed in 1522 to 'Erasmius.' When names so similar in spelling do not seem to fit the context, it may be tempting to suspect that one occurrence of the word or words in question may have been a compositor's error which, once made, was repeated by the same compositor's faithful copying of his own mistake or by other compositors' repetition of the same error. In dealing with early printed texts such suspicion is sometimes justified, sometimes not, or must be judged 'not proven.' 'The Profane Feast' provides an instructive example at pages 139:22, 140:6, 147:9, 15, 20 of this translation, where the vocative case is used. In the 1518 text Erasmus himself takes part and is addressed in the required vocative, 'Erasme.' Bierlaire called attention to the fact that in the five places where the 1518 text prints 'Erasme,' the first completely authentic editions of the *Colloquia*, March and July–August 1522, print 'Erasmi,' vocative of second-declension proper names ending in *-ius;* in this instance of 'Erasmius.'[1] Elsewhere these editions identify the name as 'Er,' 'E,' or 'Eras.' Accordingly and properly, the ASD editors expand these abbreviations to 'Erasmius' wherever they occur in the colloquy (though in the dedication of the March 1522 edition to Erasmius, his name is misspelled 'Eramio,' an apt reminder of compositorial frailty).

'Erasmius' then is the established reading in 'The Profane Feast.' If the change from 'Erasmus' and 'Erasme' to 'Erasmius' and 'Erasmi' was made by Erasmus, as we must assume, it should be accepted as authoritative. Since his dedicatory preface of 1522, addressed to Erasmius Froben, refers to schooling his pen and sentiments 'to suit your tender years' (Ep 1262), it is clear that he wished to honour his godson and to guide him towards grammar and godliness. What is not so clear is why he thought Erasmius would be a suitable member of the company in 'The Profane Feast.' We are asked to regard Erasmius, who was a mere lad in 'Sport,' an older boy but still a youth in 'The Whole Duty of Youth,' as a well-read, witty speaker who in 'The Profane Feast' banters on equal terms with the other guests. This may or may not be credible; but that Thomas More, who arrived unexpectedly, would wish to see Erasmius, not Erasmus, strains verisimilitude. If such an incongruous incident is not an oversight, it must be an example of the author's plan of having 'elegant young gentlemen' (*pueros aut bellos homunculos*) as speakers in his 1522 dialogues (Allen Ep 1301:17–19 / CWE Ep 1301:39). Whatever the explanation, the name of the speaker is Erasmius. The words are his; the substance is pure Erasmus. The voice is Jacob's voice, but the hands are the hands of Esau.[2]

NOTES

1 F. Bierlaire 'La première édition reconnue des *Colloques* d'Erasme' *Les études classiques* 37 (1969) 47 and *Erasme et ses Colloques* 46–7. The five places are: in the March 1522 edition h2 verso, h3 recto, h7 verso, h8 recto; in the July–August 1522 edition g6 verso, g7 recto, h4 verso, h5 recto; in ASD I-3 202:2505, 203:2530, 209:2739, 2744, 2749.

2 At one time Erasmus preferred the name 'Erasmius' for himself. In 1495 he used 'Herasmus Roterdam' in addressing a letter (Allen Ep 45), but 'Erasmus' was the usual form. At times he wished he had used the form 'Erasmius.' So we are told by Beatus Rhenanus; see Allen I 70:545–79, and Marjorie O'Rourke Boyle 'The Eponyms of Desiderius Erasmus' *Renaissance Quarterly* 30 (1977) 12–23. He is called Erasmius (in Greek) by Henricus Glareanus in September 1516 (Allen Ep 463:70) and signs himself Erasmius (in Greek) in February 1517 (Allen Ep 539:11). In March 1517 he is Erasmon (in Greek) in a letter to Andrea Ammonio (Allen Ep 551:16). In his first few years the boy Erasmius Froben was called Erasmus, not Erasmius, but by 1522 his name had been changed to Erasmius (Allen Ep 635:20n).

In Erasmus' colloquy 'The Funeral,' the conduct and discourse of Cornelius as he calmly awaits death testify to his steadfastness and religious faith; they delineate the Erasmian conception of how a pious Christian life should close. Cornelius is representative of a type of layman – the Christian gentleman – whom we have met earlier in 'The Godly Feast.' That Cornelius' judgments are Erasmus' own, not merely those of a character created by him, is confirmed by comparing what is said and done in the pages on Cornelius' death with the expositions or arguments in Erasmus' writings on the New Testament, the Psalms, and many other texts: *Enchiridion*, *Ratio verae theologiae*, *Paraclesis*, *Exomologesis*, *De concordia*, *Ecclesiastes*, *Modus orandi Deum*, *Explanatio symboli*, *De praeparatione ad mortem*, besides an early and minor *Declamatio de morte*. *De praeparatione ad mortem* is a perfect example of the popular genre known as *ars moriendi*, which the early printers and booksellers could readily provide. But many treatments of dying and death can be found in the equally popular though less formal pages of the *Colloquies*, *Adagia*, and letters. 'The Funeral' has pages of satirical comedy exposing the absurd and even vicious efforts of a dying man, George Balearicus, who tries to bribe his way into heaven. He dies with a Franciscan robe laid upon him, hoping thus to share in the mercies shown to the devout. (Burial in a monk's or friar's dress is one of the main topics in 'The Seraphic Funeral.') The contrast between such scenes and the edifying death of Cornelius is unmistakable, as the author intended it should be. See his paragraph on that colloquy in 'The Usefulness of the *Colloquies*' 1104:29–1105:11..

This appendix is directed to those who may have wondered what Erasmus' own end was like and how it fits the pattern of his life. What is known of his last days? Enough to satisfy curiosity about his mature religious convictions and his moral character. 'The Funeral' is only one of many pieces of evidence, and fiction at that, but if we take the affirmations of Cornelius as true to certain fundamental beliefs of Erasmus, they make it easy and instructive to compare a death in fiction with a death in fact. When reading contemporary accounts of Erasmus' own death, we are perforce aware of the differences between an imagined death and the hard and painful end of one who, though he had good friends in Basel, was dying in what he now thought was the wrong place.

Despite its modest size (population said to be about 10,000 in 1501, the year when Basel joined the Swiss Confederation), Basel was an ancient city founded by Romans, an important centre of trade, and a place of many proud traditions. It was an episcopal see as early as the seventh century, the site of the Council of Basel (1431–49), of a university (1460), of a beautiful cathedral (the original structure was consecrated in 1019). Hans Holbein the Younger lived there for some years. An important advantage for Erasmus was the flourishing printing and publishing industry there. Basel had more than seventy print shops. Some of its leading printers are still well known to everyone concerned with the history of books in the Renaissance. Johann Amerbach settled in Basel in 1478 and soon became a leading printer of works of scholarship. Johann Froben, Erasmus' friend and favourite publisher, arrived later but in time won a comparable reputation as an enterprising printer and bookseller. These two men produced many editions, texts, translations, commentaries, and studies of classical and patristic authors, theologians, and the like: books of and for *studia humanitatis*, *bonae literae* – the humanities or liberal-arts subjects. When Johann Froben died (1527), his son Hieronymus carried on the business. Johannes Petri and his nephew Adam were also great printers. Adam was one of the main printers of Luther's writings, including his German Bible. Froben's specialty was Greek and Latin books, Petri's was vernacular texts.

Erasmus lived in Basel longer than in any other city. It was his chosen home from November 1521 to April 1529 and again from June 1535 to July 1536. Basel was a civilized place, but it was not Utopia. Like other Swiss cities, notably Zürich, Basel in the 1520s experienced social, economic, and religious disputes, disorders that shocked the community. Winds of doctrine from Wittenberg and Zürich fanned by Luther, Zwingli, and their adherents soon reached Basel. When Johann Froben brought out a collection of writings by Luther (1518, 1519), Erasmus urged him not to do so again, and Froben reluctantly took this advice. By 1520-1 the formal and assumed unity of Christendom began to seem to Erasmus and to others who shared his anxieties to be in danger of fracture. He was equally anxious about public disorders. He often alludes to these difficulties in his correspondence of the 1520s. One friend and sometime colleague (he had assisted Erasmus' edition of the Greek New Testament by checking the Hebrew in the notes and by reading proofs), Johannes Oecolampadius, returned to Basel in 1522. He became the acknowledged leader of the reformers and was appointed professor of theology in the university (along with Conradus Pellicanus).

Tensions and disruptions of civic and religious life in Basel during that decade came to a climax at the end of 1528 and in the early weeks of 1529. On 8 February 1529, 800 guildsmen meeting in the Franciscan church elected a committee to submit proposals to the city government for both ecclesiastical and economic reforms. They wanted a more democratic government. They demanded, successfully, the resignation or dismissal of the twelve Catholic members of the Little Council. Next day they marched to the churches, including the cathedral, and smashed or burned or removed images and church treasures.[1] Temporarily all the churches were closed and whitewashed. The mass was abolished in all homes and churches, but Protestant services were held in the city and in villages. A new church order was prepared and approved. Oecolampadius was the first Protestant preacher in the minster, the first head preacher (*antistes*) of the Basel Reformed church.

The consequence of this brief revolution was that Basel, by the popular will (or so it seemed), became a predominantly Protestant city. Erasmus had been asked for advice. Predictably, he argued for peace and toleration. He deplored the violence. He sympathized with the intentions of moderate reformers but pleaded, as he always did in disputes, for *concordia*. He realized, however, that in the prevailing circumstances Basel was no longer a place where he could work comfortably. He accepted invitations to move to Freiburg im Breisgau, settled there in April 1529, and resumed his 'Herculean labours' (see Adagia III i 1), producing *De concordia* in 1533, *De praeparatione ad mortem* in 1534, and his great treatise on preaching, *Ecclesiastes*, in 1535. He continued his work on Origen, which was issued by the Froben firm in September 1536 after Erasmus' death. For the reader of 'The Funeral,' *De praeparatione ad mortem* has the special interest of recording Erasmus' last meditations on this most solemn of subjects.

By the spring of 1535, Basel having recovered from its civil disturbances, Erasmus, now tired of Freiburg, was ready to return. He had thought of going back to Brabant or to Burgundy (Besançon), but finally decided on Basel, where he had old friends and was highly esteemed. He moved back there in late May or early June

1535 to Hieronymus Froben's house 'zum Luft' on Bäumleingasse, not far from the minster. This was to be his home for what remained of his life. His earliest surviving letter after his return is dated 18 June 1535 (Allen Ep 3025:18n and see Ep 3028:17–20). He was too ill to wish to go anywhere else, though he was troubled, as he wrote in his last extant letter, by the prospect of dying in a reformed (Protestant) city: 'Because of dissensions over doctrines I would prefer to end my life somewhere else' (Allen Ep 3130:26–8; cf Ep 3049:75–113). On 12 February 1536 he signed his third and final will (printed in Allen XI 363–5 Appendix 25).[2]

The first will (22 January 1527; Allen VI 503–6 Appendix 19) contemplated publication of his collected writings and included twenty names of institutions and individuals that were to receive complimentary copies. After expenses were paid and gifts distributed, the remainder of the estate would go to charity. The second will (November 1533) is lost. The third will made no provision for an edition of his works, apparently because Erasmus was discouraged by the successes of Lutherans, Zwinglians, and other disturbers of the peace of the church, and by the failure of all his own efforts to persuade extremists to end the schism. Towards the end of his life, however, he was changing his mind about an edition of his *opera omnia*. After his death his heir and confidant Bonifacius Amerbach, executor of his will, with the assistance of Hieronymus Froben and Nicolaus Episcopius (co-executors of the will and partners in the Froben printing and publishing firm) revived plans for issuing the collected works.[3] Beatus Rhenanus also was named as a co-executor in the first will but not again in the final will. He was however a very important colleague in the planning of the *Opera omnia* of 1538–41 and is believed to have supervised the preparation of that edition. He had an unrivalled knowledge of Erasmus as an author and of his connections with the Froben press.

As Erasmus notes in his first will, he had sold his library in December 1525 to Jan Łaski, a Polish friend. By mutual agreement Erasmus had use of the books as long as he lived. They were sent off to Łaski in December 1536. The third will leaves gifts, mostly monetary, to a dozen friends. It stipulates, as the first did, that what was left over should be used to aid old or infirm persons, young men of good promise, and respectable young women who needed work.[4]

Erasmus died distinctly wealthy, with a net worth of 5,000 florins (Rhenish?), a total estate of 8,000 florins including property in Brabant, jewellery, and other possessions (Allen XI 362–3 Appendix 25). Most of this wealth, thanks largely to Bonifacius Amerbach's prudent management, became a trust for the support of worthy students at the University of Basel, and for many generations this fund helped needy students. At various times Erasmus had deposited sums of money, totalling 1,960 gold florins, with his friend Conradus Goclenius of Louvain. Whether this money was intended as an outright gift or a deed of trust to be used in Brabant as Erasmus apparently desired – for charitable purposes – is uncertain. When Goclenius died intestate in 1539, his relatives, the University of Louvain, and the treasury of Brabant all laid claim to the money. Amerbach, as the main executor of Erasmus' estate, advised the university to use the money for assisting the poor, and evidently some, perhaps most of it, was used to that end, though the Goclenius family tried for a long time to get control of it (see Allen X 406–24 Appendix 23).[5]

Of the various accounts of Erasmus' last days, the most reliable is that in Bonifacius Amerbach's preface, dated 1 February 1537 (Allen Ep 3141 / LB I *** * 4 recto–verso), to the *Catalogi duo* of Erasmus' writings, an 'official' listing of the authentic works:[6] Amerbach was Erasmus' closest friend. In his first will Erasmus named him his legal heir and Basilius Amerbach (d 1535), Beatus Rhenanus, and Hieronymus Froben executors (Allen VI 503:5–7 Appendix 19). In Basel, where he was a confidential advisor to the city government and (from 1525) professor of law at the university, Bonifacius was a highly respected and influential citizen. Devout, erudite, and tolerant, he was a superior specimen of the Erasmian humanist. In religion he was conservative enough to withhold approval and support from the more radical reformers, yet sympathetic with some of their purposes. After long deliberation he joined the Reformed church (1534 or 1535), submitting to the town council in 1534 a carefully composed *confessio fidei*, which the council accepted as sufficiently orthodox on the Eucharist (a crucial question) and left Amerbach with enough independence on other questions to keep his opinions to himself or to revise them in the light of further knowledge or judgment; the text of this *confessio fidei* (printed in AK IV 477–9) is well worth study. In the preface to the *Catalogi duo*, Amerbach, after eloquent eulogy of Erasmus, describes how gout, in addition to his old troubles with kidney stone, confined him to bed for much of the time. In this extremely painful condition he nevertheless wrote *De puritate tabernaculi sive ecclesiae christianae* (LB V 293A–328), an exposition of Ps 15 (14 Vulg), published by Froben in the spring of 1536. He continued to work at Origen until he was exhausted – for dysentery added still another affliction – and now he simply awaited death. He spoke of the many tokens of divine mercy, 'with his feelings so fixed on Christ that he uttered nothing but the sweet name of Jesus,' repeatedly imploring mercy, begging that the end might come. 'With such holy words, shortly before midnight on 11 July he gave up his soul to the Saviour invoked so often from the depths of his heart' (Allen Ep 3141:72–105).

How many persons were actually present when Erasmus died, and who these were, is not known beyond the shadow of a doubt, but there is every reason to believe that Bonifacius Amerbach, Hieronymus Froben, and Nicolaus Episcopius were there (Allen I 54:41–61); possibly Johann Herwagen too. Luther heard that Simon Grynaeus, a much commended classical scholar and reformer, well acquainted with Erasmus, was at the deathbed. This report came from Wolfgang Faber Capito, writing from Strasbourg on 20 July 1536. He informed Luther that Erasmus had died on the eleventh 'post mediam noctis praesente Grynaeo . . . inter Lutheranos haereticos.' Martin Bucer, who wrote to Luther on 22 July, gave the same news about Erasmus' death and Grynaeus' presence (WA *Briefwechsel* 7 Epp 3048:46–50, 3050:28–32). Reedijk rejects this report as most unlikely because Grynaeus, as one of the most conspicuous Protestant leaders, would not have been an acceptable visitor, nor was he a member of Erasmus' inner circle.[7]

A note from Hieronymus Froben to Bonifacius Amerbach, written from the Froben house probably in the afternoon or early evening of 11 July 1536, brings us close to the scene: 'I have just gone to see our master but without his being aware of it. He seems to me much worse, for his tongue cleaves to his palate, so that you can scarcely understand what he says. His breathing is so deep and rapid that I wonder whether he will live through the night. He has eaten nothing today but chicken broth. I've summoned Sebastian [Sinckeler, the physician]; if he comes I'll see that he is brought into the bedroom without the master's knowledge, to enable him to take in what I've learned. I wanted you to know this, so that you could come earlier' (AK Ep 2036).

Ego nunc mensi Dm, Sed eo nescio. Videtur mihi plurimum
desinere. Na lingua adherem palato, ut loquitur vix intelligas.
Spiritu tam alta et exterius trahit, ut mirari rogat, nui
superating sit instatem north. praeter ius Caponis Zachie adhue
nihil sumpsu. Voraui Sebastianus, si venerit, suuabo ut
et ipsa actio in nescio, in subuule rig introducae, quo
pripme possu na: q et ego audiui. Hor idro Te sine
nolui, ut tempestiuig adsis.
              T. frob.

Hieronymus Froben's note to Bonifacius Amerbach on Erasmus' condition
Universitätsbibliothek Basel, Handschriften-Abteilung, MS KI.AR.7 fol 1 verso

Erasmus died just before midnight on 11 July 1536. Next day his corpse was carried by students to the minster and buried in what had been a small chapel of the Virgin. A brief sermon commending him was preached by Oswald Myconius (a cleric disliked by Erasmus), who was now *antistes* there and professor of theology at the university. Herwagen, writing to Beatus Rhenanus on 17 July, says Erasmus' death occurred 'II Iulii, sub horam duodecimam' (Allen Ep 3135:12–13) but what is printed in Allen as 'II' was an error for '11.'[8] Date and hour are certified by Amerbach as 'v. Id. Iul, sub mediam noctem' (Allen Ep 3141:103; similarly in a letter to Łaski, AK Ep 2065:8–9). The date 'v. Id. Iul.' must mean 11 July, but the preposition *sub* introduces an uncertainty. When referring to time it can mean either 'just before' or 'just after,' and we find that some persons in Erasmus' day and also in our own have assumed that Erasmus died on the twelfth.

In his Book of Hours, which Amerbach used for years after Erasmus' death, he underscores 'Quinto idus Iul,' which means 11 July in Roman reckoning; but in a memorandum added at the top of the same page he writes 'hora prima noctis mortuus est D. Erasmus Roterodamus vir mihi omnium amicissimus ... 1536.' By 'the first hour of the night' he means the hour between midnight and 1 AM, taking *sub* to mean just *after* midnight (that is, 12 July) instead of just *prior* to midnight on the eleventh. This apparent contradiction is explained by a peculiar local custom by which the clocks in the countryside were set one hour ahead of the minster clock in Basel.[9] Owners of those clocks would have heard them strike twelve midnight on 11 July 1536 as Erasmus expired; as a sixteenth-century antiquarian wrote, 'wann es zu mittag anderswo XII schlecht, ists zu Basel eins unnd also fortan.'[10] Another lingering custom was that of counting the first hour of the morning as part of the preceding day, 'secundum horologium Basiliense' as Bonifacius Amerbach and others termed it. (Thus Amerbach recorded the time of his children's births.) For public purposes, so to speak, Erasmus' death occurred on the eleventh, but for reasons of his own Bonifacius Amerbach liked to recall that by dying 'secundum horologium Basiliense' on the twelfth, Erasmus survived longer in Basel than he could have done anywhere else. Amerbach, who had most to do with the three gravestones honouring Erasmus, acted in accordance with his own principles and preferences. The first gravestone (1536) bore only the name. The second (March 1537) recorded the date but not the hour of the death: 'Quarto Eidus Iulias,' that is, 12 July (changed from 'Quinto' 'fifth' by Amerbach's decision). The third, with the epitaph (1538) seen in the minster today, has 'IIII Eid Iul ... MDXXXVI.'[11] Affection for Erasmus, pride in Basel, and a desire to honour both were clearly compelling reasons for Amerbach's care in recording for posterity the twelfth of July as the anniversary of Erasmus' passing. By his own preferred reckoning, 'secundum horologium Basiliense,' he acted correctly.

On the second gravestone the head of Terminus, Roman god of boundaries and for Erasmus a symbol of mortality and the finality of death, the 'ending end,' was added above the epitaph (on Terminus see further 'A Fish Diet' n118). Even this inscription was unsatisfactory, since it had misspelled words and other mistakes. In the final epitaph, the work of Hans Menzinger of Basel (1538), the figure of Terminus crowns the text.[11]

Readers who have met Erasmus in biographies or histories are familiar with paintings or drawings by the younger Holbein, Dürer, and Metsys. Undoubtedly the best known is Holbein's 1523 portrait now in the Louvre. The last of the distinguished portraits is the roundel in the Kunstsmuseum in Basel, painted by Holbein c 1532

hora prima noctis mortuus est d. Erasmus Roterodamus vir... ...anis
Iulius habet dies 31. Lu...

Iouis na 30.

19	g	1	Calendis	Iulii
8	A	2	Sexto nonas	Iulii
	b	3	Quito no.	Iulii
16	c	4	Quarto no	Iulii
5	d	5	Tertio no	Iulii
	e	6	Pridie no	Iulii
13	f	7	Nonis	Iulii
2	g	8	Octauo idus	Iul.
	A	9	Septimo idus	Iul.
10	b	10	Sexto idus	Iul.
	c	11	Quito idus	Iul.
18	d	12	quarto idus	Iul.
7	e	13	Tertio idus	Iul.

B iiii

Mors matris charissime

Anno 1534.

A page from Bonifacius Amerbach's Book of Hours, noting the death of Erasmus
Universitätsbibliothek Basel, Handschriften-Abteilung, MS AN.VI.36

and after Erasmus' death owned by Amerbach. It shows an Erasmus who is plainly ageing, but even though he does not have the serenity seen in the Louvre portrait of 1523, when he was at the height of his powers, he was still working effectively as a productive scholar.

Two final drawings were made at the bedside during that watch on 11 July 1536. One, chalk on reddish-brown paper labelled 'Erasmi mortui effigies,' may be the drawing mentioned in a 1587 inventory of Amerbach property. Nothing is known of the artist, who may have been commissioned by Amerbach. Whoever he was, he gives us a sympathetic picture of a man dying in peace. The other picture, in silver-point, is more stark, a more uncompromising rendering of the arrival of death. In the first drawing the closed lips seem almost to express a slight smile, but they must signify, if anything, resignation. The parted lips in the second picture suggest only suffering. In both drawings the eyes are not yet fully closed. The inscription 'ERASMVS ROTERODAMVS MOR [TVVS?] DES[C]RIPTVS EST on the silver-point drawing may have been added by someone else.

Although Beatus Rhenanus was not in Basel at the time of the death, his account (dated 15 August 1536), in a sketch of Erasmus' life included in the preface to the posthumous volume of his Latin Origen, is known as well as any: 'At last, his strength gradually failing – for he suffered from dysentery for about a month – when he sensed his life's end was near, he displayed as always clear signs of Christian patience and a devout mind in affirming that his whole hope was fixed upon Christ, exclaiming earnestly, "O Jesus, mercy; Lord, set me free; Lord, make an end; Lord, have mercy upon me"; and in the German tongue "Liever Got" (that is, "Dear God") … No other words did he utter. He was fully conscious up to the last moment' (Allen I 53:29–54:37). Some variations of this account occur in the longer memoir composed by Beatus Rhenanus as a preface to the *Opera omnia* on its completion in 1540 and addressed to the emperor Charles V (Allen I 56–71; see especially 70:508–16). Beatus Rhenanus had left Basel in 1526 to live in Sélestat but continued his scholarly work and published it through the Froben press. Very likely he had other sources of information about Erasmus' death besides what he was told by Herwagen. Latin prayers murmured by Erasmus differ slightly in different reports. One example may be cited. A letter believed to have been written from Basel in or near July 1536 by Heinrich Stromer of Leipzig, physician and professor, who seems to have been in the neighbourhood of Basel at this time, gives them as 'O Jesus, Son of God, have mercy on me. I will sing of the mercy and judgment of the Lord' (Ps 101:1; 100:1 Vulg). 'At that point,' Stromer adds, 'death took him' (Allen Ep 3134:20–4). Readers will have noticed that Beatus Rhenanus says Erasmus' last words were in Dutch (or German, as Beatus Rhenanus terms it). Whether this report is correct, and if so how Beatus Rhenanus obtained it, is not known. Did Erasmus, who wrote so voluminously in Latin, revert to the vernacular when departing from this world? Another 'perhaps' is all we can say, despite learned discussions of this topic, which is of minor interest.

On 21 July 1536 a letter about Erasmus' death was written to Bonifacius Amerbach by Ludwig Baer, a canon of Basel cathedral and professor in the university until the triumph of the reformers in 1529, when he too migrated to Freiburg. He was a trusted friend whom Erasmus frequently consulted on theological questions.[12] Baer tells Amerbach of his pleasure in the assurance received from an informant that Erasmus had not only died a Catholic but without wanting to see or hear any 'preachers of the new gospel' (Protestants), and that nobody was at his deathbed

Erasmi mortui effigies
One of two drawings made on 11 or 12 July 1536 at Erasmus' deathbed
Museum Teyler, Haarlem

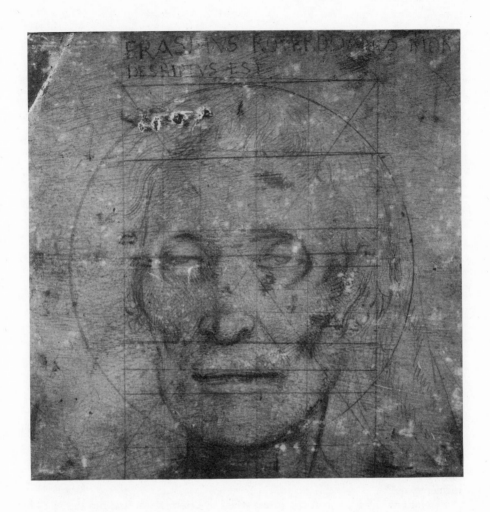

A drawing of Erasmus on his deathbed ascribed to Hans Baldung Grien
Amerbachkabinett, Öffentliche Kunstsammlung Basel, Kupferstichkabinett

except Amerbach and a friend or servant (*familiarem* – apparently Lambert Coomans, of whom more will be said). Baer asks Amerbach to confirm this information (AK Ep 2041:25–33). No reply from Amerbach is known. But Baer's report was seriously inaccurate.

Erasmus declared more than once that he would never leave the Catholic church (Allen Epp 1167:416–26, 1195:28–30, 1386:44 / CWE Epp 1167:467–78, 1195:34–5, 1386:50–1; other references in Allen Ep 2123:14n). Nor did he. Yet his lot was to die in a city now mostly Protestant and to be buried in a cathedral now Protestant. He was, as Reedijk says, 'a Catholic *sui generis*, who had kept the world guessing by returning in the last year of his life to a Protestant city and dying there.'[13] Conflicting claims and arguments about his orthodoxy and his influence, for better for worse, in disputes over religion, did not disappear with his death – on the contrary. Even the circumstances of his dying presented opportunities for admirers and detractors to air their judgments of him.

Three centuries after his death a claim was made by P.F.X. de Ram, on the basis of two seventeenth-century reports, that Erasmus had died in the arms of a priest, Lambert Coomans, murmuring 'O mater Dei, memento mei.'[14] Coomans was a *famulus*, a domestic servant or maybe a servant-pupil, in Erasmus' household for about ten months (September 1535–July 1536). Erasmus liked him and in his will left him 200 florins 'if he is present at my death' (Allen XI 364:19–20 Appendix 25). In the context, however, this language, 'si mihi morienti adfuerit,' means no more than 'if he is still in my service at the time of my death' (language used of another servant in his first will; Allen VI 506:124–5 Appendix 19). That Coomans was present when Erasmus died is credible. No one connected with Erasmus' business affairs objected to the payment of the 200 florins, which Coomans received as promised.[15] According to the article by de Ram, summarized and for the most part accepted by de Vocht in his history of the *Collegium Trilingue*, a catalogue of the deans of St Peter's Church, Turnhout, by Charles Gevaert (1639) was the source of the story about Coomans' role at Erasmus' deathbed. Gevaert (who himself became dean in 1632) records that an elderly colleague, acquainted with Coomans in the 1570s, told him of Coomans' relating how Erasmus had died in his arms, praying 'O mater Dei, memento mei.'

Not only was Coomans no priest when in Erasmus' service, but the tale of Erasmus' calling on the Mother of God is suspect *per se*. *Mater Dei* as a title standing alone is hard to find in Erasmian usage, though the synonym *Genetrix Dei* occurs in the *Liturgia Virginis Matris* (LB V 1331B). It is highly improbable that he uttered 'O Mater Dei' when dying, first because the only evidence that he did so comes from second- and third-hand seventeenth-century sources; secondly because he avoided such phrases, common though they were, since they are not found in Scripture. 'In Christo fixa est nostrae salutis sacra ancora, non in Virgine.'[16]

Coomans did become a priest some years after Erasmus' death, but as he was not in orders in 1536, the picture of Erasmus dying in the arms of a priest vanishes into thin air.[17] So far as we know Erasmus died without priestly ministrations. Reedijk argues, correctly in my opinion, that popular and official sentiment in Basel at this time (June–July 1536) were such that to bring a priest to Erasmus' bedside, in Hieronymus Froben's house, to attend the dying man and perform the old rites, would have been extremely awkward at best and in practice unmanageable, and it is doubtful that Amerbach would have permitted it even if it could have been arranged.

A passage in Erasmus' *De praeparatione ad mortem* provides important evidence of his thoughts in his last two years about the sacraments and ceremonies customary near the time of death. The passage is important not only for what it says but because it was written in late 1533 and printed in 1534, when Erasmus, now advanced in years and in failing health, could not have written on this subject without deliberation and sincerity (on *De praeparatione ad mortem* see the introduction to 'The Funeral' 763).

In this tract Erasmus warns that one who is gravely ill should make confession if possible, through concern for his soul's health rather than his body's. The sacraments, through divine grace, are efficacious, and a Christian must hope he will not lack them. 'But if perchance the services of a priest are not available, then he must not (as the superstitious do) tremble for his soul and despair, but confess with his whole heart his own unrighteousness directly to God, who in his mercy will accept the will for the deed.' All the sacraments are signs of divine grace, but they are also efficacious without external ceremonies when the salvation of the faithful and humble requires. Sacraments are a solace, but it is more Christian to pray for faith and charity, without which sacraments are vain. 'Surely, as I think, many who are unabsolved by a priest, who are without the Eucharist, unaneled, buried without due rites, go to eternal rest, while others, with all ceremonies solemnly performed and even burial in church beside the high altar, are carried off to hell' (LB V 1310F–1311B; ASD V-1 376:899–378:935).[18]

'Sanctissime vixit, sanctissime mortuus est,' wrote Bonifacius Amerbach in his memoir (Allen Ep 3141:108). Many agreed (see the encomia in LB I (9)–(24), *** **** 1 recto – *** *** *** * 1 verso), but some dissented. In 1540, only four years after Erasmus' death, a dialogue entitled *Erasmi funus*, which included strong criticism of him, was published (without a publisher's name) in Basel, of all places. It was the work of Ortensio Lando (c 1505–c 1555), a busy young man of letters who is remembered for, among other things, the first Italian translation of More's *Utopia*. His *Erasmi funus* appeared under the pseudonym 'Philalethes Utopiensis.' In 1534 he had annoyed Erasmus and others by attacking Cicero, and Erasmus' *Ciceronianus*, in his *Cicero relegatus et revocatus*.

In *Erasmi funus* the two speakers are Arnoldus, a German who seems deeply affected by the news of Erasmus' death, and an Italian, Anianus, who takes a more complacent view of that event. Arnoldus praises Erasmus extravagantly – even has him preaching with Bible in hand as he lay dying – but is distressed by word that wicked monks have hailed the death with joy and have even desecrated the tomb in the cathedral. Anianus, on the other hand, deprecates Erasmus' supposed virtues and achievements. Arnoldus has heard that a saintly man had a vision of Erasmus in heaven (Lando may have read the colloquy 'The Apotheosis of Reuchlin'), but Anianus insists there is more to be blamed than praised in Erasmus. All Germany is mourning, Arnoldus protests. No, not all Germany by any means, Anianus retorts; and anyway, Germany has had many learned men besides Erasmus. He himself knows nothing about those wicked monks Arnoldus heard of, but Anianus does think there is much to be said for monasticism. He has known many good monks in Italy.

More than Erasmus' posthumous reputation is involved here. Paul F. Grendler considers the dialogue a satirical rebuke of Swiss reformers for failure to follow Erasmus' progressive principles, and at the same time an endorsement of those principles.[19] Myron P. Gilmore interprets the work as mainly a parody, the extreme grief of Arnoldus as ironic, 'parodies of the usual encomia on Erasmus,' and the dialogue as filled with echoes and criticism of Erasmus by Italian Ciceronians who belittled his Latinity, denounced him for anti-Italian sentiments, and hinted that he was a heretic or at least a man who gave aid and comfort to Luther.[20] Like most successful parody or irony, this dialogue can be read in more than one way. What is certain is that it provoked indignation among the good citizens of Basel. The city fathers appointed Joannes Herold, rector of the university, to reply to it. He did so in a very long oration, *Philopseudes* ('the lover of lies'; text in LB VIII 597–652, filling fifty-four folio columns).

This is an academic performance which no doubt gave satisfaction to a patient audience. It is loaded with classical quotations and allusions and a rich assortment of rhetorical flourishes: the kind of discourse a sixteenth-century audience would expect on such an occasion and would enjoy, for Herold's subject is relevant and of local interest. He has a partisan audience, since he is defending Basel's most famous citizen and the city itself against the mockery of an insolent foreigner. The orator devotes much of his speech to a biography of Erasmus, making use of the *Adagia, Colloquia,* letters, and much else, yet he ignores the controversial writings on the church and religion – not even Erasmus' work on the New Testament is mentioned. But the oration serves its purpose of praising Erasmus and pleasing the citizens. Though printed in LB, it was almost completely ignored even by Erasmian scholars until M.M. Phillips wrote a brief article on it.[21]

As for Luther, we may note that if the evidence in the *Tischreden* is reliable, he judged Erasmus no less harshly when Erasmus was dead than when he was alive: 'He lived and died as Epicurus, without minister [to perform the last rites] and consolation. He went to hell' (WA *Tischreden* 4 no 3963).[22]

NOTES

1 For contemporary accounts of this iconoclasm see a letter of 13 February 1529 by Oecolampadius to Wolfgang Capito (text in Kidd *Documents* 464–6 no 219) and one by Erasmus dated 9 May 1529 to Willibald Pirckheimer (Allen Ep 2158:1–90).

2 For a corrected page of the third will see illustration facing page 48 of Cornelis Reedkijk 'Das Lebensende des Erasmus' *Basler Zeitschrift für Geschichte und Altertumskunde* 57 (1958) 23–66. See also n18 below.

3 In common usage the dates of two of the three great editions of Erasmus' collected works are not quite accurate. The first (Basel), commonly cited as *Opera omnia* 1538–40, was completed in 1541 if we consider that tome III (1538) was revised in 1541. The Leiden (LB), edited by Jean Leclerc (Clericus), was issued in 1703–7, not 1703–6. The Amsterdam (ASD, 1969–   ) proceeds steadily; *festina lente* (*Adagia* II i 1) is the watchword. The history of these noble enterprises is told authoritatively by Dr Reedijk; see 'Erasmus' Final Modesty' in *Actes du congrès Erasme, Rotterdam 27–29 octobre 1969* (Amsterdam and London 1971) 174–92; *Tandem bona causa triumphat* Vorträge der Aeneas-Silvius-Stiftung an der Universität Basel 16 (Basel and Stuttgart 1980); 'The Leiden Edition of Erasmus' *Opera omnia* in a European Context' in *Erasmus und Europa* Wolfenbütteler Abhandlungen zur Renaissanceforschung 7 (1988) 163–82; ASD I-1 vii–xxi (on that edition).

4 For a history of this library and an inventory of its contents see Husner. On the third will see P.P.J.L. van Peteghem 'Erasmus' Last Will, the Holy Roman Empire, and the Low Countires' in *Erasmus of Rotterdam: The Man and the Scholar, Proceedings of the Symposium, Rotterdam 1986* (Leiden 1988) 88–97.

5 See Carl Roth 'Das Legatum Erasmianum' in *Gedenkschrift* 282–98.

6 See Allen I 1–46 / CWE Ep 1341A for the 1523–4 catalogue and Allen Ep 2283 for that of 1530; the division of the works into volumes or series in both catalogues is printed also in CWE 24 697–702.

7 'Das Lebensende des Erasmus' (n2 above) 63. For a different but dubious opinion see the review by E. Droz in BHR 21 (1959) 563–8.

8 See Alfred Hartmann 'Beatus Rhenanus: Leben und Werke des Erasmus' in *Gedenkschrift* 12 n1.

9 See Hartmann ibidem 12–14.

10 Ibidem 13

11 See the illustrations and descriptions in Emil Major 'Die Grabstätte des Erasmus' in *Gedenkschrift* 299–315.

12 On Baer see CEBR and Farge *Paris Doctors* 23–6 no 22.

13 'Erasmus' Final Modesty' (n3 above) 177

14 *Bulletin de l'Académie royale des sciences et belles-lettres de Bruxelles* 9 no 2 (1842) 437–46; other references in Reedijk 'Das Lebensende des Erasmus' (n2 above) 27 n18

15 H. de Vocht *History of the Foundation and Rise of the Collegium Trilingue Lovaniense 1517–1550* Humanistica Lovaniensia 10–13, 4 vols (Louvain 1951–5) III 394–400

16 *Apologia adversus monachos* LB IX 1087B. See also *Declarationes ad censuras Lutetiae vulgatas* LB IX 942C–F; *Supputatio* LB IX 570B; *Apologia adversus rhapsodias Alberti Pii* LB IX 1163A– 1167A.

17 See further Reedijk 'Das Lebensende des Erasmus' 27–33 (n2 above) and V. de Caprariis 'Qualche precisazione sulla morte di Erasmo' *Rivista storica italiana* 63 (1951) 100–8.

18 Reedijk's 'Das Lebensende des Erasmus' is the most valuable study of Erasmus' last days. It is supplemented by N. van der Blom 'Die letzten Worte des Erasmus' in the same periodical, 65 (1965) 195–214, which reviews Roman Catholic and Protestant reactions to the death of Erasmus, examines the 'Liever Got' incident, and considers various discrepancies in the accounts of the dying. *Hermeneus* (Zwolle) 37 (1965–6) 134–7 has an additional note ('Erasmus' laatste woorden') by van der Blom; summary in Margolin *Bibliographie érasmienne (1962–1970)* 119 no 297. See also J. Trapman 'Erasmus' Precationes' in *Actus Conventus Neo-Latini Torontonensis* (Binghamton, NY 1991) 778. Another recent and detailed examination of evidence is that by 'Beat Rudolf Jenny, 'Tod, Begräbnis und Grabmal des Erasmus von Rotterdam' *Basler Zeitschrift für Geschichte und Altertunskunde* 86 no 2 (1986) 61–73, with three appendices 74–104. See also Jenny's 'Rückkehr nach Basel, Lebensende, Grab und Testament' in *Erasmus von Rotterdam, Vorkämpfer für Frieden und Toleranz* Ausstellung zum 450. Todestag des Erasmus von Rotterdam veranstaltet vom Historischen Museum Basel (Basel 26. April bis 7. September 1986) 63–5. Jenny's account includes information not available to Reedijk in 1958. In 1928 Erasmus' conjectural grave had been opened in connection with repairs to the cathedral, and the grave and its skeleton (the skull of which revealed evidence

of syphilis) is referred to in Reedijk's article 'Das Lebensende des Erasmus.' In
1974 a Metsys medal, found in another grave, led to the discovery of the real
skeleton of Erasmus; see Bruno Kaufmann, 'Das Grab des Erasmus im Basler
Münster' in *Erasmus von Rotterdam, Vorkämpfer für Frieden und Toleranz.* Myron
P. Gilmore *Humanists and Jurists* (Cambridge, Mass 1963) has a good chapter on
Erasmus' last years and another on Bonifacius Amerbach. R. Garcia Villoslada
'La muerte de Erasmo' in *Miscellanea Giovanni Mercati* 4 (1946) 381–406 and
W.E. Campbell *Erasmus, Tyndale and More* (London 1949) 274–9 discuss the
dying but accept uncritically the tale of Coomans' being a priest when with
Erasmus; they have no independent value.
The standard work on Basel is Rudolf Wackernagel's *Geschichte der Stadt Basel*
3 vols (1907–24). For additional bibliography see Hans R. Guggisberg *Basel in
the Sixteenth Century* (St Louis 1982) 75–8. This is the best short history. See also
P.S. Allen's essay on Erasmus' relations with his printers in *Lectures* 109–37.
Bainton *Erasmus of Christendom* 215–23 should be read on the tensions in Basel
early in 1529.

19 Grendler reviews Lando's career in his *Critics of the Italian World, 1530–1630*
   (Madison 1969) 21–48, 113–17.
20 'Anti-Erasmianism in Italy: The Dialogue of Ortensio Lando on Erasmus'
   Funeral' *Journal of Medieval and Renaissance Studies* 4 (1974) 1–14
21 'Une vie d'Erasme' BHR 34 (1972) 229–37
22 'Ist gefaren *in bus correptam*' is glossed by editors as a semi-proverbial
   expression in Germany; on this see WA 30 part 2 714. On Luther's own dying
   (18 February 1546) see texts in *The Reformation in Its Own Words* ed and trans
   Hans J. Hillerbrand (London 1964) 404–9. Since that book was published, more
   evidence has come to light. On the back of the last page of a 1545 edition of
   Luther's *An Kurfürsten zu Sachsen, und Landgraven zu Hessen* now in the John
   Hay Library at Brown University is a manuscript account, written on the
   very day of his death, of Luther's last prayer. Whether the anonymous writer
   who was eager to record these words heard them himself or was told them,
   we cannot say. For text and translation see Carolyn R.S. Lenz 'A Recently
   Discovered Manuscript Account of Luther's Last Prayer' ARG 66 (1975) 79–92.

EDITIONS OF THE *COLLOQUIES*

The editions of the *Colloquies* are listed in chronological order. Individual colloquies are named in the first edition in which they appeared. On the contents of the editions before March 1522 see the introduction to these volumes xxiv–xxvi.

November 1518   *Familiarium colloquiorum formulae* (Basel: Johann Froben)

February 1519   *Familiarium colloquiorum formulae* (Basel: Johann Froben)

March 1519   *Familiarium colloquiorum formulae* (Louvain: Dirk Martens)

May 1519   *Familiarium colloquiorum formulae* (Basel: Johann Froben)

October–December 1519   *Familiarium colloquiorum formulae* (Louvain: Dirk Martens)

March 1522   *Familiarium colloquiorum formulae* (Basel: Johann Froben): *Familiaria colloquia* now includes *Alia in congressu* (= *De votis temere susceptis*, its running title from August–September 1524 on), *Alia* (= *De captandis sacerdotiis*, its running title from August–September 1524 on), *Alia militaria, Herilia, Monitoria, De lusu, Confabulatio pia, Venatio, Euntes in ludum,* [Additional *formulae*], which includes *Convivium profanum* (its running title from August–September 1524 on); *Brevis de copia praeceptio; Convivium religiosum* (the beginning, as far as 176:22)

July–August 1522   *Familiarium colloquiorum formulae* (Basel: Johann Froben): *Convivium religiosum* (complete); *De incomparabili heroe Ioanne Reuchlino in divorum numerum relato*

August 1523   *Familiarium colloquiorum formulae* (Basel: Johann Froben): *Proci et puellae; Eubuli et Catarinae* (= *Virgo μισόγαμος*, its title from March 1529); *Eubuli, Catarinae* (= *Virgo poenitens*, its running title from August–September 1524 on); *Coniugium; Militis et cartusiani; Pseudochei et Philetymi; Naufragium; Diversoria; Adolescentis et scorti; Convivium poeticum*

March 1524   *Familiarium colloquiorum formulae* (Basel: Johann Froben): *Inquisitio; Γεροντολογία, sive Ὄχημα; Πτωχοπλούσιοι; Antronius, Magdalia* (= *Abbatis et eruditae*, its running title)

August–September 1524   *Familiarium colloquiorum formulae* (Basel: Johann Froben): *Epithalamium Petri Aegidii; Exorcismus, sive Spectrum; Alcumistica; Hippoplanus; Πτωχολογία; Convivium fabulosum*

February 1526   *Familiarium colloquiorum opus* (Basel: Johann Froben):
                 Puerpera; Peregrinatio religionis ergo; Ἰχθυοφαγία; *Funus*

June 1526   *Familiarium colloquiorum opus* (Basel: Johann Froben): *Echo;*
                 De utilitate Colloquiorum

1527   *Familiarium colloquiorum opus* (Basel: Johann Froben):
                 Πολυδαιτία, *Dispar convivium; De rebus ac vocabulis*

March 1529   *Familiarium colloquiorum opus* (Basel: Hieronymus Froben
                 and Johann Herwagen): *Charon; Synodus grammaticorum;*
                 Ἄγαμος γάμος, *sive Coniugium impar; Impostura; Cyclops,*
                 sive Evangeliophorus; Ἀπροσδιόνυσα, *sive Absurda;* Ἱππεὺς
                 ἄνιππος, *sive Ementita nobilitas;* Ἀστραγαλισμός, *sive Talorum*
                 lusus; Senatulus, sive Γυναικοσυνέδριον; addition to *De*
                 utilitate Colloquiorum

September 1529   *Familiarium colloquiorum opus* (Basel: Hieronymus Froben,
                 Johann Herwagen, and Nicolaus Episcopius): *Diluculum;*
                 Νηφάλιον συμπόσιον; *Ars notoria;* addition to *De utilitate*
                 Colloquiorum

September 1531   *Familiarium colloquiorum opus* (Basel: Hieronymus Froben
                 and Nicolaus Episcopius): *Concio, sive Merdardus;*
                 Philodoxus; Opulentia sordida; Exequiae seraphicae; Amicitia

March 1533   *Familiarium colloquiorum opus* (Basel: Hieronymus Froben
                 and Nicolaus Episcopius): *Problema; Epicureus*

ALPHABETICAL LIST OF THE COLLOQUIES

ENGLISH

LATIN AND GREEK

Charon / 818
Concio, sive Merdardus / 938
Confabulatio pia / 88
Coniugium / 306
Coniugium impar. *See* Ἄγαμος γάμος
Convivium fabulosum / 571
Convivium poeticum / 390
Convivium profanum / 132
Convivium religiosum / 171
Cyclops, sive Evangeliophorus / 863
De captandis sacerdotiis / 44
De incomparabili heroe Ioanne Reuchlino in divorum numerum relato / 244
De lusu / 74
De rebus ac vocabulis / 809
De utilitate Colloquiorum / 1095
De votis temere susceptis / 35
Diluculum / 916
Diversoria / 368
Echo / 796
Ementita nobilitas. *See* Ἱππεὺς ἄνιππος
Epicureus / 1070
Epithalamium Petri Aegidii / 520
Euntes in ludum literarium / 113
Evangeliophorus. *See* Cyclops
Exequiae seraphicae / 996
Exorcismus, sive Spectrum / 531
Familiarium colloquiorum formulae / 5
Funus / 763
Γεροντολογία, sive Ὄχημα / 448
Γυναικοσυνέδριον. *See* Senatulus
Herilia / 64
Hippoplanus / 558
Impostura / 860
Inquisitio de fide / 419
Ἱππεὺς ἄνιππος, sive Ementita nobilitas / 880
Ἰχθυοφαγία / 675
Merdardus. *See* Concio
Militaria / 53
Militis et Cartusiani / 328
Monitoria paedagogica / 70
Naufragium / 352
Νηφάλιον συμπόσιον / 925
Opulentia sordida / 979
Ὄχημα. *See* Γεροντολογία
Peregrinatio religionis ergo / 619
Philodoxus / 963
Πολυδαιτία / 802
Problema / 1056

WORKS FREQUENTLY CITED

This list provides bibliographical information for works referred to in short-title form in volumes 39 and 40. For Erasmus' writings see the short-title list following.

AK	*Die Amerbachkorrespondenz* ed Alfred Hartmann and B.R. Jenny (Basel 1942–)
Allen	*Opus epistolarum Des. Erasmi Roterodami* ed P.S. Allen, H.M. Allen, and H.W. Garrod (Oxford 1906–58) 11 vols and index
Allen *Age of Erasmus*	P.S. Allen *The Age of Erasmus* (Oxford 1914)
Allen *Lectures*	P.S. Allen *Erasmus: Lectures and Wayfaring Sketches* (Oxford 1934)
ARG	*Archiv für Reformationsgeschichte*
ASD	*Opera omnia Desiderii Erasmi Roterdami* (Amsterdam 1969–)
Bainton *Erasmus of Christendom*	R.H. Bainton *Erasmus of Christendom* (London 1970)
Bataillon 'Erasme conteur'	Marcel Bataillon 'Erasme conteur: folklore et invention narrative' in *Mélanges de langue et de littérature médiévales offerts à Pierre Le Gentil* (Paris 1973) 85–104
Bataillon *Erasme et l'Espagne*	Marcel Bataillon *Erasme et l'Espagne* (Paris 1937)
Bataillon *Erasmo y España*	Marcel Bataillon *Erasmo y España* (Mexico City and Buenos Aires 1950; 2nd ed 1966)
Bataillon *Erasmo y España* (1991)	Marcel Bataillon *Erasmo y España* ed Daniel Devoto and Charles Amiel, 3 vols (Geneva 1991)
BE 2nd series	*Bibliotheca Erasmiana* 2nd series *Colloquia* ed F. Vander Haeghen (Ghent 1903–7) 3 vols (part of *Bibliotheca Erasmiana: bibliographie des oeuvres d'Erasme* [Ghent 1897–1950] 12 vols extrait de la *Bibliotheca Belgica*, fondée par Ferdinand Vander Haeghen)
de Beatis *Travel Journal*	*The Travel Journal of Antonio de Beatis: Germany, Switzerland, the Low Countries, France, and Italy 1517–1518* ed J.R. Hale, trans J.R. Hale and J.M.A. Lindon, Hakluyt Society 2nd series 150 (London 1979)
BHR	*Bibliothèque d'humanisme et Renaissance*

Bierlaire *Erasme et ses Colloques*	Franz Bierlaire *Erasme et ses Colloques: le livre d'une vie* (Geneva 1977)
Bierlaire *Les Colloques d'Erasme*	Franz Bierlaire *Les Colloques d'Erasme: réforme des études, réforme des moeurs et réforme de l'Eglise au xvie siècle* (Paris 1978)
Born	*The Education of a Christian Prince by Desiderius Erasmus* ed and trans Lester K. Born (New York 1936; reissued in paperback in the series Records of Civilization 1968)
BRE	*Briefwechsel des Beatus Rhenanus* ed A. Horawitz and K. Hartfelder (Leipzig 1886; repr Hildesheim 1966)
Burton *Anatomy of Melancholy*	Robert Burton *Anatomy of Melancholy* ed Holbrook Jackson, Everyman's Library (London and New York 1932; repr 1961) 3 vols
Calvin ICR	*Calvin: Institutes of the Christian Religion* trans T. McNeill, The Library of Christian Classics 20–1 (London 1960) 2 vols
CCL	Corpus christianorum, series Latina (Turnhout 1954–)
CEBR	*Contemporaries of Erasmus: A Biographical Register of the Renaissance and Reformation* ed Peter G. Bietenholz and Thomas B. Deutscher (Toronto 1985–7) 3 vols
Chaucer	*The Complete Works of Geoffrey Chaucer* ed F.N. Robinson (Boston 1933; 2nd ed 1957)
CHB	*Cambridge History of the Bible*: I *From the Beginnings to Jerome* ed P.R. Ackroyd and C.F. Evans (Cambridge 1970); II *The West from the Fathers to the Reformation* ed G.W.H. Lampe (Cambridge 1969); III *The West from the Reformation to the Present Day* ed S.L. Greenslade (Cambridge 1963)
Chomarat *Grammaire et rhétorique*	Jacques Chomarat *Grammaire et rhétorique chez Erasme* (Paris 1981) 2 vols
Clemen	*Luthers Werke in Auswahl* ed Otto Clemen et al (Berlin 1912-33; numerous reprints) 8 vols
Colet *Opera*	John Colet *Opera* ed and trans J.H. Lupton (London 1867-76; repr Ridgewood, NJ 1965–6) 4 vols
Colloquia Erasmiana Turonensia	*Colloquia Erasmiana Turonensia: Douzième stage international d'études humanistes, Tours 1969* ed J.-C. Margolin (Paris and Toronto 1972) 2 vols

Colloquium Erasmi-
anum

Colloquium Erasmianum: Actes du colloque international réuni
à Mons du 26 au 29 octobre 1967 à l'occasion du cinquième
centenaire de la naissance d'Erasme (Mons 1968)

Coryat Crudities

Thomas Coryat Coryat's Crudities: hastily gobled up in five
moneths travells in France, Savoy, Italy, Rhetia commonly called
the Grisons country ... (1611; facsimile repr Glasgow 1905)
2 vols

CSEL

Corpus scriptorum ecclesiasticorum Latinorum (Vienna and
Leipzig 1866–   )

CWE

Collected Works of Erasmus (Toronto 1974–   )

Denzinger-
Schönmetzer
Enchiridion

H. Denzinger and A. Schönmetzer Enchiridion symbolorum
definitionum et declarationum de rebus fidei et morum
36th ed (Freiburg im Breisgau, Barcelona, and Rome
1976)

Devereux

Edward James Devereux Renaissance English Translations of
Erasmus: A Bibliography to 1700 Erasmus Studies 6 (Toronto,
Buffalo, and London 1983)

Dickinson

J.C. Dickinson The Shrine of Our Lady of Walsingham
(Cambridge 1956)

EETS

Early English Text Society

Epistolae obscurorum
virorum

Epistolae obscurorum virorum ed and trans Griffin Stokes
(London 1909; repr 1925)

ERSY

Erasmus of Rotterdam Society Yearbook

Farge Orthodoxy and
Reform

James K. Farge Orthodoxy and Reform in Early Reformation
France (Leiden 1985)

Ferguson Erasmi
opuscula

Erasmi opuscula: A Supplement to the Opera Omnia ed W.K.
Ferguson (The Hague 1933)

Foxe Acts and
Monuments

John Foxe Acts and Monuments, with a life of the martyrologist,
and vindication of the work, by George Townsend (London
1843–9; repr New York 1965) 8 vols

Frame

The Complete Works of Montaigne trans Donald M. Frame
(Stanford 1958)

Friedberg

Corpus iuris canonici ed E. Friedberg (Leipzig 1879–81; repr
1959) 2 vols

Gardiner *Letters* *Letters of Stephen Gardiner* ed J.A. Muller (New York and Cambridge 1933)

Gedenkschrift *Gedenkschrift zum 400. Todestage des Erasmus von Rotterdam* ed Historische und Antiquarische Gesellschaft zu Basel (Basel 1936)

Gerson *Oeuvres* Jean Gerson *Oeuvres complètes* ed P.G. Glorieux (Paris 1960–75) 10 vols

Holborn *Desiderius Erasmus Roterdamus: Ausgewählte Werke* ed Hajo Holborn and Annemarie Holborn (Munich 1933; repr 1964)

Husner Fritz Husner 'Die Bibliothek des Erasmus' in *Gedenkschrift* 228–59

Hutten *Opera* *Ulrichi Hutteni equitis Germani opera quae reperiri potuerunt omnia* ed E Böcking (Leipzig 1859–61; repr 1963) 5 vols

Kelly *Early Christian Creeds* J.N.D. Kelly *Early Christian Creeds* (London and New York 1950; 2nd ed New York 1964; 3rd ed 1972)

Kelly *Early Christian Doctrines* J.N.D. Kelly *Early Christian Doctrines* (London 1958; 5th rev ed London 1977)

Kelly *Rufinus* *Rufinus: A Commentary on the Apostle's Creed* trans J.N.D. Kelly, Ancient Christian Writers 20 (Westminster, Md and London 1955)

Kidd *Documents* B.J. Kidd *Documents Illustrative of the Continental Reformation* (Oxford 1911)

Knowles ROE David Knowles *The Religious Orders in England* (Cambridge 1948–59) 3 vols

Latimer *Selected Sermons* *Selected Sermons of Hugh Latimer* ed Allan G. Chester (Charlottesville 1968)

LB *Desiderii Erasmi Roterodami opera omnia* ed J. Leclerc (Leiden 1703–6; repr 1961–2) 10 vols

Leo of Rozmital *Travels* *The Travels of Leo of Rozmital through Germany, Flanders, England, France, Spain, Portugal and Italy* ed and trans Malcolm Letts, Hakluyt Society 2nd series 108 (Cambridge 1957)

LP *Letters and Papers, Foreign and Domestic, of the Reign of Henry VIII* ed J.S. Brewer and J. Gairdner (London 1862–1910) 21 vols in 33, and Addenda vol 1 parts 1–2

Lupton *Life of Colet*	J.H. Lupton *A Life of John Colet* (London 1887; 2nd ed 1909; repr Hamden, Conn 1961)
LW	Martin Luther *Works* ed J. Pelikan et al (St Louis 1955–86) 55 vols
Margolin *Bibliographie érasmienne (1936–1949)*	Jean-Claude Margolin *Quatorze années de bibliographie érasmienne (1936–1949)* (Paris 1969)
Margolin *Bibliographie érasmienne (1950–1961)*	Jean-Claude Margolin *Douze années de bibliographie érasmienne (1950–1961)* (Paris 1963)
Margolin *Bibliographie érasmienne (1962–1970)*	Jean-Claude Margolin *Neuf années de bibliographie érasmienne (1962–1970)* (Paris, Toronto, and Buffalo 1977)
Margolin *Recherches érasmiennes*	Jean-Claude Margolin *Recherches érasmiennes* (Geneva 1969)
Margolin 'Travaux érasmiens (1970–1985)'	Jean-Claude Margolin 'Quinze années de travaux érasmiens (1970–1985)' BHR 48 (1986) 585–619
Moorman	John Moorman *A History of the Franciscan Order ... to 1517* (Oxford 1968)
More *Complete Works*	See Yale CWM
More *Correspondence*	*The Correspondence of Sir Thomas More* ed Elizabeth Frances Rogers (Princeton 1947)
More *English Works*	*The English Works of Sir Thomas More* facsimile of Rastell's edition of 1557, ed with a modern version by W.E. Campbell, with introduction and notes by A.W. Reed, R.W. Chambers, and W.A.G. Doyle Davidson (London and New York 1931); page references are to Campbell's version.
More *Latin Epigrams*	*The Latin Epigrams of Thomas More* ed and trans Leicester Bradner and Charles Arthur Lynch (Chicago 1953)
More *Selected Letters*	*St Thomas More: Selected Letters* ed Elizabeth Rogers (New Haven and London 1961)
NCE	*New Catholic Encyclopedia* prepared by an editorial staff at the Catholic University of America (New York 1967–79) 17 vols

Nichols *Pilgrimages*   *Pilgrimages to Saint Mary of Walsingham and Saint Thomas of Canterbury. By Desiderius Erasmus* trans J.G. Nichols (London 1849; 2nd ed 1875)

NPNF   *A Select Library of the Nicene and Post-Nicene Fathers of the Christian Church* (New York 1886–1900)

PG   *Patrologiae cursus completus ... series Graeca* ed J.P. Migne (Paris 1857–1912) 162 vols

Phillips *'Adages'*   *The 'Adages' of Erasmus: A Study with Translations* ed and trans Margaret Mann Phillips (Cambridge 1964)

Picinelli *Mundus symbolicus*   Filippo Picinelli *Mundus symbolicus* ed R.D. August Erath (Cologne 1687); repr Hildesheim and New York 1979).

PL   *Patrologiae cursus completus ... series Latina* ed J.P. Migne (Paris 1844–1902) 221 vols

PS   Parker Society

Reedijk *Poems of Erasmus*   *The Poems of Desiderius Erasmus* ed Cornelis Reedijk (Leiden 1956)

A Relation of England   *A Relation ... of the Island of England ... about the year 1500* ed and trans C.A. Sneyd, Camden Society 1st series 37 (London 1847)

Renaudet *Préréforme et humanisme*   Augustin Renaudet *Préréforme et humanisme à Paris pendant les premières guerres d'Italie (1494–1517)* 2nd ed (Paris 1953)

Roper *Life of More*   William Roper *Life of Sir Thomas More* in *Two Early Tudor Lives: The Life and Death of Cardinal Wolsey by George Cavendish and The Life of Sir Thomas More by William Roper* ed Richard S. Sylvester and Davis P. Harding (New Haven and London 1962; repr 1969) 195-260

Scrinium Erasmianum   *Scrinium Erasmianum: Mélanges historiques publiés ... à l'occasion du cinquième centenaire de la naissance d'Erasme* ed J. Coppens (Leiden 1969) 2 vols

Smith *Key*   Preserved Smith *A Key to the Colloquies of Erasmus* Harvard Theological Studies 13 (Cambridge, Mass 1927)

Spurgeon   *Tudor Translations of the Colloquies of Erasmus (1536–1584)* facsimile reproductions ed Dickie A. Spurgeon, Scholars' Facsimiles and Reprints (Delmar, NY 1972)

STC   *Short-Title Catalogue of Books Printed in England, Scotland, and
                          Ireland and of English Books Printed Abroad* ed A.W. Pollard
                          and G.R. Redgrave (London 1926); 2nd ed rev W.A. Jackson
                          et al (London 1976–91) 3 vols

Strauss *Manifestations* Gerald Strauss *Manifestations of Discontent in Germany on the
of Discontent*   Eve of the Reformation* (Bloomington and London 1971)

Strype *Ecclesiastical*   John Strype *Ecclesiastical Memorials Relating Chiefly to Religion
Memorials*   and the Reformation of It* (Oxford 1812–28) 6 vols

Surtz *Praise of*   Edward Surtz *The Praise of Wisdom: Philosophy, Education, and
Wisdom*   Communism in More's Utopia* (Chicago 1957)

Tanner   *Decrees of the Ecumenical Councils* ed Norman P. Tanner,
                          (London and Washington, DC 1990) 2 vols

Telle *Erasme et le*   E.V. Telle *Erasme de Rotterdam et le septième sacrement* (Geneva
septième sacrement*   1954)

Thompson *Inquisitio*   *Inquisitio de fide* ed Craig R. Thompson (New Haven 1950;
de fide*   2nd ed, with supplementary bibliography, Hamden, Conn
                          1975)

Thorndike *Magic*   Lynn Thorndike *A History of Magic and Experimental Science*
and Experimental*   (New York 1923–58) 8 vols
Science*

Thorndike *University*   Lynn Thorndike *University Records and Life in the Middle Ages*
Records*   (New York 1944; repr 1949, 1975)

Tilley   M.P. Tilley *A Dictionary of the Proverbs in England in the
                          Sixteenth and Seventeenth Centuries* (Ann Arbor, Mich 1950)

Tyndale *Works*   William Tyndale *Works* ed Henry Walter, PS 42-4 (Cambridge
                          1848–50) 3 vols

Vives *Opera*   Juan Luis Vives *Opera omnia* ed G. Majansius (Valencia
                          1782–90; repr London 1964) 8 vols

De Vocht *Earliest*   Henry de Vocht *Earliest English Translations of Erasmus'
English Translations*   Colloquia* (Louvain 1928)

WA   *D. Martin Luthers Werke, Kritische Gesamtausgabe* (Weimar
                          1883–)

WA *Briefwechsel*   *D. Martin Luthers Werke, Briefwechsel* (Weimar 1930–78)
                          15 vols

WA *Deutsche Bibel*   *D. Martin Luthers Deutsche Bibel* (Weimar 1906–61) 12 vols

WA *Tischreden*   *D. Martin Luthers Werke, Tischreden* (Weimar 1912–21) 6 vols

Yale CWM   *The Yale Edition of the Complete Works of St. Thomas More* (New Haven and London 1961–   )

Yates *Memory*   Frances Yates *The Art of Memory* (Chicago 1966; repr 1972)

SHORT-TITLE FORMS FOR ERASMUS' WORKS

Titles following colons are longer versions of the same, or are alternative titles. Items entirely enclosed in square brackets are of doubtful authorship. For abbreviations, see Works Frequently Cited.

Acta: Academiae Lovaniensis contra Lutherum *Opuscula* / CWE 71
Adagia: Adagiorum chiliades 1508, etc (Adagiorum collectanea for the primitive form, when required) LB II / ASD II-1, 4, 5, 6 / CWE 30–6
Admonitio adversus mendacium: Admonitio adversus mendacium et obtrectationem LB X
Annotationes in Novum Testamentum LB VI / CWE 51–60
Antibarbari LB X / ASD I-1 / CWE 23
Apologia ad Caranzam: Apologia ad Sanctium Caranzam, or Apologia de tribus locis, or Responsio ad annotationem Stunicae . . . a Sanctio Caranza defensam LB IX
Apologia ad Fabrum: Apologia ad Iacobum Fabrum Stapulensem LB IX
Apologia adversus monachos: Apologia adversus monachos quosdam hispanos LB IX
Apologia adversus Petrum Sutorem: Apologia adversus debacchationes Petri Sutoris LB IX
Apologia adversus rhapsodias Alberti Pii: Apologia ad viginti et quattuor libros A. Pii LB IX
Apologia contra Latomi dialogum: Apologia contra Iacobi Latomi dialogum de tribus linguis LB IX / CWE 71
Apologiae contra Stunicam: Apologiae contra Lopidem Stunicam LB IX / ASD IX-2
Apologia de 'In principio erat sermo' LB IX
Apologia de laude matrimonii: Apologia pro declamatione de laude matrimonii LB IX / CWE 71
Apologia de loco 'Omnes quidem': Apologia de loco 'Omnes quidem resurgemus' LB IX
Apologia qua respondet invectivis Lei: Apologia qua respondet duabus invectivis Eduardi Lei *Opuscula*
Apophthegmata LB IV
Appendix respondens ad Sutorem LB IX
Argumenta: Argumenta in omnes epistolas apostolicas nova (with Paraphrases)
Axiomata pro causa Lutheri: Axiomata pro causa Martini Lutheri *Opuscula* / CWE 71

Carmina: poems in LB I, IV, V, VIII / ASD I-7 / CWE 85–6
Catalogus lucubrationum LB I
Ciceronianus: Dialogus Ciceronianus LB I / ASD I-2 / CWE 28
Colloquia LB I / ASD I-3 / CWE 39–40
Compendium vitae Allen I / CWE 4
Conflictus: Conflictus Thaliae et Barbariei LB I
[Consilium: Consilium cuiusdam ex animo cupientis esse consultum] *Opuscula* / CWE 71

De bello Turcico: Consultatio de bello Turcico (in Psalmi)
De civitate: De civitate morum puerilium LB I / CWE 25
Declamatio de morte LB IV

Declamatiuncula LB IV

Declarationes ad censuras Lutetiae vulgatas: Declarationes ad censuras Lutetiae vulgatas sub nomine facultatis theologiae Parisiensis LB IX

De concordia: De sarcienda ecclesiae concordia, or De amabili ecclesiae concordia (in Psalmi)

De conscribendis epistolis LB I / ASD I-2 / CWE 25

De constructione: De constructione octo partium orationis, or Syntaxis LB I / ASD I-4

De contemptu mundi: Epistola de contemptu mundi LB V / ASD V-1 / CWE 66

De copia: De duplici copia verborum ac rerum LB I / ASD I-6 / CWE 24

De esu carnium: Epistola apologetica ad Christophorum episcopum Basiliensem de interdicto esu carnium LB IX / ASD IX-1

De immensa Dei misericordia: Concio de immensa Dei misericordia LB V

De libero arbitrio: De libero arbitrio diatribe LB IX

De praeparatione: De praeparatione ad mortem LB V / ASD V-1

De pueris instituendis: De pueris statim ac liberaliter instituendis LB I / ASD I-2 / CWE 26

De puero Iesu: Concio de puero Iesu LB V / CWE 29

De puritate tabernaculi: De puritate tabernaculi sive ecclesiae christianae (in Psalmi)

De ratione studii LB I / ASD I-2 / CWE 24

De recta pronuntiatione: De recta latini graecique sermonis pronuntiatione LB I / ASD I-4 / CWE 26

Detectio praestigiarum: Detectio praestigiarum cuiusdam libelli germanice scripti LB X / ASD IX-1

De taedio Iesu: Disputatiuncula de taedio, pavore, tristicia Iesu LB V

De vidua christiana LB V / CWE 66

De virtute amplectenda: Oratio de virtute amplectenda LB V / CWE 29

[Dialogus bilinguium ac trilinguium: Chonradi Nastadiensis dialogus bilinguium ac trilinguium] Opuscula / CWE 7

Dilutio: Dilutio eorum quae Iodocus Clithoveus scripsit adversus declamationem suasoriam matrimonii

Divinationes ad notata Bedae LB IX

Ecclesiastes: Ecclesiastes sive de ratione concionandi LB V / ASD V-4, 5

Elenchus in N. Bedae censuras LB IX

Enchiridion: Enchiridion militis christiani LB V / CWE 66

Encomium matrimonii (in De conscribendis epistolis)

Encomium medicinae: Declamatio in laudem artis medicae LB I / ASD I-4 / CWE 29

Epistola ad Dorpium LB IX / CWE 3 / CWE 71

Epistola ad fratres Inferioris Germaniae: Responsio ad fratres Germaniae Inferioris ad epistolam apologeticam incerto autore proditam LB X / ASD IX-1

Epistola ad graculos: Epistola ad quosdam imprudentissimos graculos LB X

Epistola apologetica de Termino LB X

Epistola consolatoria: Epistola consolatoria virginibus sacris LB V

Epistola contra pseudevangelicos: Epistola contra quosdam qui se falso iactant evangelicos LB X / ASD IX-1

Euripidis Hecuba LB I / ASD I-1

Euripidis Iphigenia in Aulide LB I / ASD I-1

Exomologesis: Exomologesis sive modus confitendi LB V
Explanatio symboli: Explanatio symboli apostolorum sive catechismus LB V /
    ASD V-1
Ex Plutarcho versa LB IV / ASD IV-2
Expositio concionalis (in Psalmi)

Formula: Conficiendarum epistolarum formula (see De conscribendis epistolis)

Hyperaspistes LB X

In Nucem Ovidii commentarius LB I / ASD I-1 / CWE 29
In Prudentium: Commentarius in duos hymnos Prudentii LB V / CWE 29
Institutio christiani matrimonii LB V
Institutio principis christiani LB IV / ASD IV-1 / CWE 27

[Julius exclusus: Dialogus Julius exclusus e coelis] *Opuscula* / CWE 27

Lingua LB IV / ASD IV-1A / CWE 29
Liturgia Virginis Matris: Virginis Matris apud Lauretum cultae liturgia LB V /
    ASD V-1
Luciani dialogi LB I / ASD I-1

Manifesta mendacia CWE 71
Methodus (see Ratio)
Modus orandi Deum LB V / ASD V-1
Moria: Moriae encomium LB IV / ASD IV-3 / CWE 27

Novum Testamentum: Novum Testamentum 1519 and later (Novum instrumentum
    for the first edition, 1516, when required) LB VI

Obsecratio ad Virginem Mariam: Obsecratio sive oratio ad Virginem Mariam in rebus
    adversis LB V
Oratio de pace: Oratio de pace et discordia LB VIII
Oratio funebris: Oratio funebris in funere Bertae de Heyen LB VIII / CWE 29

Paean Virgini Matri: Paean Virgini Matri dicendus LB V
Panegyricus: Panegyricus ad Philippum Austriae ducem LB IV / ASD IV-1 /
    CWE 27
Parabolae: Parabolae sive similia LB I / ASD I-5 / CWE 23
Paraclesis LB V, VI
Paraphrasis in Elegantias Vallae: Paraphrasis in Elegantias Laurentii Vallae LB I /
    ASD I-4
Paraphrasis in Matthaeum, etc (in Paraphrasis in Novum Testamentum)
Paraphrasis in Novum Testamentum LB VII / CWE 42–50
Peregrinatio apostolorum: Peregrinatio apostolorum Petri et Pauli LB VI, VII
Precatio ad Virginis filium Iesum LB V
Precatio dominica LB V
Precationes LB V

Precatio pro pace ecclesiae: Precatio ad Iesum pro pace ecclesiae LB IV, V

Psalmi: Psalmi, or Enarrationes sive commentarii in psalmos LB V / ASD V-2, 3

Purgatio adversus epistolam Lutheri: Purgatio adversus epistolam non sobriam Lutheri LB X / ASD IX-1

Querela pacis LB IV / ASD IV-2 / CWE 27

Ratio: Ratio seu Methodus compendio perveniendi ad veram theologiam (Methodus for the shorter version originally published in the Novum instrumentum of 1516) LB V, VI

Responsio ad annotationes Lei: Liber quo respondet annotationibus Lei LB IX

Responsio ad collationes: Responsio ad collationes cuiusdam iuvenis gerontodidascali LB IX

Responsio ad disputationem de divortio: Responsio ad disputationem cuiusdam Phimostomi de divortio LB IX

Responsio ad epistolam Pii: Responsio ad epistolam paraeneticam Albert Pii, or Responsio ad exhortationem Pii LB IX

Responsio ad notulas Bedaicas LB X

Responsio ad Petri Cursii defensionem: Epistola de apologia Cursii LB X / Allen Ep 3032

Responsio adversus febricitantis libellum: Apologia monasticae religionis LB X

Spongia: Spongia adversus aspergines Hutteni LB X / ASD IX-1

Supputatio: Supputatio calumniarum Natalis Bedae LB IX

Tyrannicida: Tyrannicida, declamatio Lucianicae respondens LB I / ASD I-1 / CWE 29

Virginis et martyris comparatio LB V

Vita Hieronymi: Vita divi Hieronymi Stridonensis *Opuscula* / CWE 61

Index of
Biblical and Apocryphal References

This index includes references both in Erasmus' text and in the annotator's commentary. For references to Erasmus' Paraphrases and Annotations, see also the General Index under Erasmus, original works: *Annotationes in Novum Testamentum*; *Paraphrasis in Novum Testamentum*. For references to Erasmus' commentaries on the Psalms, see also the General Index under Erasmus, original works: *Commentarius in psalmum secundum*; *De bello Turcico*; *De concordia*; *De puritate tabernaculi*; *Enarratio in psalmum XXII*; *Enarratio in psalmum XXXIII*; *Enarratio in psalmum XXXVIII*; *Expositio concionalis in psalmum LXXXV*; *In psalmum quartum concio*; Psalms, commentaries on the. Unless otherwise noted, the psalm numbers and verses given are those of the Authorized Version. For other commentaries on Scripture see under the names of individual authors in the Index of Patristic, Medieval, and Renaissance References and in the General Index.

Index of Classical References

This index includes references to classical authors, works, persons, and mythological figures. In accordance with CWE practice, the more familiar Greek and Latin works are cited by their English titles. For references to Erasmus' editions and translations of classical authors see the General Index under Erasmus.

Index of
Patristic, Medieval, and Renaissance
References

This index includes references to specific works cited in the commentary. For more general references, and for authors whose works are not cited here, consult the General Index.

General Index

References to the works of authors cited in the commentary may be found in the Index of Classical References and the Index of Patristic, Medieval, and Renaissance References.

n22, 439 n69, 468, 471, 481, 482, 483 n2,
483–4 n4, 486 n36, 487 n39, 490–1 n48,
493 n62, 494 n77, 494 n78, 497 n102,
499, 537, 564, 567, 568 n4, 660 n81, 705,
720, 743 n207, 743 n211, 744 n219, 762
n334, 764, 765, 767, 768, 770, 771, 773,
774, 775, 781 n14, 782 n17, 782 n18, 783
n29, 784 n37, 785 n43, 785 n45, 786 n58,
789–90 n79, 790 n84, 791 n88, 792 n96,
821 n17, 866, 868, 873 n25, 874 n41, 926,
941, 945, 954 n2, 954–5 n14, 959 n74, 960
n77, 961 n93, 996–9, 1000, 1001, 1006,
1008–12, 1013 n2, 1014 n4, 1014 n9,
1016 n17, 1017 n18, 1018 n31, 1019 n38,
1020–2 n51, 1024 n70, 1025 n76, 1025
n77, 1025 n81, 1025 n82, 1026–32, 1082,
1092 n61, 1122, 1123; and Erasmus
253 n12, 282, 388 n22, 469, 483 n1, 483
n4, 486 n35, 494 n77, 782 n18, 996–9,
1006, 1018 n32, 1023 n56, 1026–32; and
preaching 388 n7, 490–1 n48, 601, 784
n30, 1020 n42; Observant(s) 471, 483
n4, 486 n14, 486 n15, 941, 955 n14,
996, 1010, 1014 n4, 1017 n18, 1025
n77, 1026 n82, 1031–2; Conventual(s)
(Gaudentes) 486 n14, 941, 954–5 n14,
1006, 1029–32; Spirituals (Zelanti)
732 n95, 1029–30; and the doctrine
of the Immaculate Conception 954
n11, 1020–2 n51; and the vow of
poverty 954–5 n14, 955 n15, 1026–32;
Fraticelli 1030. See also Alexander v;
Bacon, Roger; Bernardine of Siena, St;
Bonaventure, St; Caracciolo, Roberto;
Ceprano, Giovanni di; Francis, St;
Gaufridi, Raymond; Gregory ix;
Kolde, Dietrich; Medardus von
der Kirchen; Menot, Michel; Mercator,
Johannes; Müller (Molitor), Alexander;
Nicholas iv; Olivi, Peter; Pellicanus,
Conradus; Pio, Alberto; Scotus, John
Duns; Sixtus iv; Standish, Henry;
Titelmans, Frans, Vitrier, Jean; Index of
Patristic, Medieval, and Renaissance
References: Francis, St; Salimbene
Frederick i, king of Denmark 826 n8
Frederick, duke of Saxony. See Saxony,
Frederick ('the Wise') duke of

Frith 661 n93
Froben, Hieronymus xxvi, 5, 27 n30,
172, 818, 1122–3, 1124; and Erasmus'
death 1125–32
Froben, Johann xxii, xxv, xlv n13, 10,
27 n30, 172, 207 n1, 377 n9, 814 n1,
993 n22, 1120–1; Erasmus' Hebrew
epitaph for 209 n27; publishes works
of Luther 1123
Froben, Johannes Erasmius 3 n1, 10, 27
n30, 74, 79, 81, 85–6 n37, 936 n13; and
the Colloquia xl, 2, 3, 85–6 n37, 88,
132, 161 n105, 655 n41, 935 n1, 1120–1;
Erasmus' letters to 2, 3
Froben family 27 n30, 172, 506 n4
Froben press 27 n14, 86 n37, 1122–4;
trademark 993 n22
Fuller, Thomas 448, 653 n18

Gaetani, Benedetto. See Boniface viii
Galileo 1058
Gardiner, Stephen, bishop of Winchester:
and Erasmus 69 n11, 214 n104, 492
n51; and Cranmer 102 n40; obsequies
of 790 n79
Garland, John of 362 n19
Gaufridi, Raymond, Franciscan minister-
general 1029–30
Gaza, Theodorus 891–2, 897, 898, 902
n40, 903 n47; price of his Greek
grammar 995 n44
Gelenius, Sigismundus, and scholia on
the Colloquia xxvi, xliv n13
Geneviève, St: church of, in Paris 635,
660 n89; shrine of 660 n89; Erasmus
prays to 760 n325
George, St 62 n22, 363 n26, 627, 628, 655
n39, 719, 760 n327, 761 n329
George, duke of Saxony. See Saxony,
George, duke of
Gerard, Cornelis, of Gouda xlvi n27, 35,
170 n18, 929 n1
Gerrard, Philip, English translator of
Epicureus 1073
Gerson, Jean: and Erasmus 228–9 n190,
357, 366 n43, 366 n44, 712, 750 n255,
751 n258, 1102; sermons of 489 n46;
on infant baptism 726 n62; Luther's

This book

was designed by

ANTJE LINGNER

based on the series design by

ALLAN FLEMING

and was printed by

University

of Toronto

Press